The Free Press Texts
in Christian Philosophy

GENERAL EDITOR: D. A. DRENNEN

A Modern Introduction to

METAPHYSICS

A Modern Introduction to

METAPHYSICS

Readings from Classical and Contemporary Sources

Edited by **D. A. DRENNEN**

The Free Press, New York
Collier-Macmillan Limited, London

110
D815m

Collier-Macmillan Canada, Ltd., Toronto, Ontario

Library of Congress Catalog Card Number: 62–15360

Seventh Printing December 1968

"And now gentlemen
A word I give to remain in your memories and minds,
As base, and final too, for all metaphysics . . ."
—WALT WHITMAN

"No philosopher is satisfied with the concurrence
of sensible people, whether they be his colleagues
and even his own previous self. He is always
assaulting the boundaries of finitude."
—ALFRED NORTH WHITEHEAD

24300

James M. Somerville, S.J.

Chairman, Department of Philosophy
Fordham University

FOREWORD

POSSIBLY a good half of those who list themselves as philosophers in American educational directories feel uneasy when the word "metaphysics" is mentioned. A not too inconsiderable portion of these would have no objection to being classed as antimetaphysicians; some would insist on it. But the observation of the late Maurice Blondel is still relevant today: If it were necessary to do away with metaphysics, one would have to use metaphysics to do it. For to say "is" or "is not" already implies a metaphysics.

The contemporary picture, however, is not so distressing as it might first appear. Catholics are certainly not alone in maintaining that the human mind is capable of penetrating somewhat into the ultimate nature of reality. Dr. Drennen's book marshals an imposing number of modern philosophers of every stripe whose vision of reality is not circumscribed by the sectarian methodologies that reduce the Great Enterprise to words about words or to an unrelieved positivistic dogmatism. Wisely, he has included typical samples of the latter kind of thinking among his selections so that the student may know what is at stake. It is impossible to grasp the real issues without some acquaintance with the views of those who disagree. Philosophy cannot evolve in a vacuum; and if Christians are to ransom the present age from the slough of metaphysical despond, they must know not only the traditional theses but also the *antitheses*. On this condition alone can a newer synthesis emerge.

A Modern Introduction to Metaphysics is a book of readings that brings forth treasures, old and new. If the task of the Christian philosopher is to penetrate into and interpret the winds of doctrine in each succeeding age without losing a sense of the organic continuity of his own tradition, the present volume offers a program that the alert teacher cannot fail to welcome. The scavenger hunt among badly printed paperbacks for disparate supplementary reading for the textbook course can come to an end. The work has been done. Few teachers have read as widely as Dr. Drennen, or as well. Out of the store of texts that have deepened his own philosophical experience, he has chosen those that admirably portray the central problem of philosophy, the classical resolutions, and the contemporary mood. There is nothing haphazard in this selection. Each text, together with the introduction, opens up another facet of the problem. If, after reading this volume, the student does not experience the full impact of the mystery, if he does not acquire an abiding insight into the importance of metaphysics, there is little that can be done for him.

This book needs a good teacher; but it can also make a more effective teacher out of any teacher. May teachers, good and less good, use it and grow in wisdom and understanding along with the minds that are meant to unfold under their charge.

This text exposes the student to certain key instances of metaphysical experience in a way that he can perhaps best understand them—that is, by making him a party to them. The book departs from the usual text in that it puts into the student's hands as many problematical statements from the West's vast metaphysical literature—both classical and contemporary—as can judiciously be handled within the confines of one course. These materials are designed to raise, and to help the student understand, a single, but nonetheless complicated, question: "What is metaphysics, and what is it *about?*"

Although emphasis has been placed on comparative readings to indicate something about the contemporary scene, this is not a book about contemporary metaphysics, but a book on metaphysics with a present-day orientation. This volume shows the reader a good deal about what "other people" think; however, the emphasis is on a constructive view of the universe, capable of adjusting the demands of unreason to reason, of reason to intuition, and of possibility to actuality.

Like a dialogue of Plato, these materials may be found to pose more questions than they attempt, or even dare, to answer. But this is only because this is a book of problems, intended to help the student grow in metaphysical age, awareness, and wisdom, rather than a set of ready answers that would leave little room for investigation or discussion. As every teacher knows, nothing is more vital to the philosophic habit than the spirit of inquiry and discovery. And the best philosophic instruction tends to develop, rather than to discourage, this spirit. For this reason, the book's themes are designed to fit together, to implicate and amplify one another by suggesting new points of view for common issues. The themes are purposely repetitious only because philosophy bears repeating.

The volume is divided into four main parts. Part One indicates attitudes and motivations that have marked Western man's pursuit of metaphysics; Part Two covers procedure and methodology; Part Three sets out the chief dialectical viewpoints that, both now and in the past, characterize metaphysical practice; finally, Part Four brings together the major themes and central issues of metaphysics. Each of the four parts, as well as each selection, is prefaced by editorial introductions designed to prepare the student for reading, study, and discussion.

Every anthology must have a suitable editorial yardstick by which to measure the materials it includes and to excuse the materials it omits. This poses an especially delicate task for any book that intends to give a fair representation of a literature that has been accumulated over twenty-five centuries of philosophic differences. In the present case, the test was based upon (*a*) the relevance a selection carried to contemporary interests and practice, (*b*) the "story-line" it helped to create, and (*c*) its bearing on the future of Christian philosophy. Each selection has been edited to bring out one or more central points; in the process, excessive footnoting has been snipped away. Cognate citations and other reference devices, however, have been retained in the form of the Study Aids and Bibliographies.

The teacher will find the Study Aids helpful in several ways. These sections are designed as integral parts of the text and are intended to strengthen—by means of review, discussion, and research—the points made in the selections. Review Questions are meant to test the student's mastery of each reading; Discussion Topics provide material for colloquia—or what used to be called "defenses"; Research Themes indicate lines of inquiry for term papers or longer projects. The Bibliographies may be used in conjunction with the Study Aids or for individual assignments.

Naturally, the instructor will want to vary the use of individual selections. Some he may wish to use as background material for discussion; others, for outside assignment. A few, he may feel, require detailed classroom criticism or illumination. Moreover, the instructor should feel free to experiment with the actual presentation of materials so as to fit them into the requirements of the course. For example, he may wish to omit Part Two altogether (or have students read it on their own) and begin with the question of "the object of metaphysics" (Part One, Selections 4, 5, 7, and Part Three, Selections 7, 8, 9), followed by the classic themes on "being" in Part Four, and conclude with the "rival" theories in Part Three. On the other hand, he may, from the beginning, prefer to work critically with materials in Part Three and contrast "traditional" assertions with their counterparts. Or he may decide to follow the pattern already established in the book. But, whatever his preference, it is well for him to understand that the book has been shaped to allow the kind of free choice that philosophers customarily espouse.

I wish to record here a debt of gratitude to all those who have helped make this book possible: to the Rev. James M. Somerville, S.J., Chairman of Fordham University's Department of Philosophy, who graciously consented to write the Foreword; to the Rev. Gustave Weigel, S.J., who took time from his busy schedule to discuss the manuscript; to Dr. Kenneth T. Gallagher, also of Fordham, who suggested certain revisions in Part Four and was otherwise conscientiously helpful; to the Rev. Anselm Burke, O.Carm., Chairman of the Marymount Philosophy Department, who encouraged use of a pilot edition of the text and aided in the selection of bibliographical material; to the

Marymount students who willingly cut their teeth on many of the following selections; to all who have kindly granted copyright permissions; and to my wife, M. Eileen Connolly Drennen, a college teacher herself, who has helped in more than just "many ways" in the preparation of this book.

D. A. D.

CONTENTS

Three METAPHYSICAL PERSPECTIVES

UNIVERSES OF DISCOURSE

REPRESENTATIVE SCHOOLS

Thomist

Existentialist

Metaphoric

Four METAPHYSICAL ISSUES

Freedom

God

INTRODUCTION

METAPHYSICAL THOUGHT, like philosophical inquiry in general, has lately undergone radical revision. Functions, purposes, and mannerisms have been perceptibly redesigned. One result of this alteration, William A. Christian recently has noted, "may be a new way of understanding metaphysical statements."

Without losing sight of the challenge underlying this assertion, we should not be unmindful of the complementary fact that this is not the first time metaphysics has had its face lifted. We should not forget, for example, that, in the eyes of thirteenth-century Parisian doctors, St. Thomas was hardly more than a revolutionary whose ideas, methods, and language threatened to remold Christian philosophy into the image of "pagan" Aristotle. It is impossible to determine whether our own contemporary thought-forms are any more revolutionary than those "barbarous" ideas of an Arabic Aristotle, which caused such embarrassment to most medieval doctors. We do know, however, that, just as in the thirteenth century, our modern innovations have broken with much in traditional thought and have completely disrupted, in the words of Jean École, "the categories that depend on traditional forms."

Like other philosophic enterprises, metaphysics has shifted its way of speaking and seeing. This shift is so much in evidence today that many of the "experts" are not sure that metaphysics has one, and only one, job to do. So we are forced to ask what, beneath all the complications of our present-day "metaphysics," is truly metaphysical and what is its nature? This is a problem of identification, and it constitutes one of the chief complications to current metaphysics.

There is another element, however, that complicates the contemporary metaphysical scene. It might be called the element of competition, and it exists both inside and outside the confines of metaphysics. As in the past, metaphysics has had to face up to what Jacques Maritain once called "competing wisdoms." Where philosophy once wrestled the rhetoric of Gorgias, the sophistry of Protagoras, or the *aperçus* of Isocrates, contemporary metaphysics is threatened by psychology, anthropology, linguistics, and social dynamics— all of which are scrambling toward the seat of wisdom.

These competitors in wisdom simply make the metaphysician's task all the more difficult. He cannot ignore their presence, lest he be trampled over. On the other hand, he must mind his manners, lest he be considered unworthy of occupying the lofty position he claims. He must recognize that his is one type of knowledge among other types, all being pursued by other inquirers. And, while it would be foolish to assume that his knowledge can be reduced to, derived from, or explained away by, theirs, it would be just as foolish to think that his knowledge cannot withstand their competing criticism. Criticism has never destroyed metaphysics. More often, it has renewed, enlarged, and perhaps ennobled it.

Yet the spirit of competition not only camps outside the walls of metaphysics but also takes a place within these walls, and even eats from the best plate at table. It stirs up professional rivalries and pounds the dinnerware in dispute. Wherever one looks, there is a metaphysics claiming to be the only genuine metaphysics. Little wonder, then, that the patience and digestion of metaphysicians are unsettled. When Aristotle said that one should "sit down to the table of inquiry," he certainly could not have had in mind the kind of table found in beer halls; and he certainly could not have meant a table in the Tower of Babel.

Discussion feeds on differences, but where there is only the contempt or raillery of one camp for another, there can be no discussion. Differences that stifle discussion, obscure common goals, or minimize common experiences cannot advance the cause of metaphysics. Students who have befriended, or who are about to befriend, metaphysics can little afford to dissipate their power in such unmetaphysical practice. Good manners at the table of inquiry are just as important for Thomists as they are for logical positivists.

Still, there is this matter of competition to be dealt with. It shows up unmistakably in the classrooms of our colleges and universities, where all kinds of viewpoints are taught, deservingly or not, under the title of metaphysics. Each class simply assumes that its kind of metaphysics is the only kind and that there are no others. The question is hardly solved by the Catholic college class that denies a hearing to any but Thomistic metaphysics.

No matter what view of metaphysics a student studies, he rightfully asks that it do something for him and to him—that it give evidence of some connection with the ways in which Western man has pondered over and shaped the overwhelming details of his experience of life and love and death. The student may, of course, be told that metaphysics stands at the center of his own culture, but he will have to cut through a forest of technical language before he can see how this is so. The student may also wonder why one system of metaphysics is singled out for praise and another for condemnation. And this fact only adds further to the burdens the study of any metaphysics places upon his back. Did Kant write metaphysics? If so, the student may ask, why are we not told about it? If not, why do other people say he did? If St. Thomas was a great metaphysician, why do other people deny it? That students too often come to belittle metaphysics—or worse, think it irrelevant—because of such difficulties is known only too plainly to teachers.

How then can the teacher bring the student to realize that metaphysics is not simply a set of competing doctrines? And where can the teacher draw the line between genuine metaphysics and nonsense disguised as metaphysics? The fact is that the student who is fed only on "doctrines" and "rival theses" will never learn what metaphysics is or what it is about but only what this or that doctrine says. Furthermore, he will never really be brought to an understanding of any doctrine—even of Thomism—unless he also sees its connection with metaphysics. He cannot penetrate into metaphysical issues without first being trained in what metaphysics does.

The student must come to realize that though there are, and always have been, crucial differences between kinds of metaphysics, there are also crucial similarities. To understand these similarities without at the same time losing touch with important differences; to profit from dialectical interchange between viewpoints; to argue through one's own position under the threat of live criticism; to know how far to follow, where to amend, and where to reject a specific metaphysical scheme—all of this, and more, is needed if today's philosophy curriculum is to meet its responsibility to the critical training of students as well as to the critical development of tradition itself. This returns us to the relation between tradition and the contemporary scene.

Students should understand that tradition is an endowment of the present moment by the past. It is not what has occurred but what does occur. It is perennial or it is nothing. Tradition, in all its equivocality and richness, allows the heritage of past experience to develop into present experience. This is as true in metaphysics as it is in art and literature. And often what at first sight appear to be "breaks" in the line of tradition are actually new developments of capacities already inherent in the past.

Now the primary aim of a metaphysics, naturally, is not that it be unequivocally stated, but that it be true. Yet truth in metaphysics has comparative as well as absolute values; that is, the avowal of a value in one kind of metaphysics does not necessarily imply rejection of a value in another. The degree to which a student can deal with metaphysical truths in comparative terms will determine his capacity not merely to point out the shortcomings of a "competing" metaphysical system but also to appreciate the supreme and everlasting relevance of true metaphysics. If he learns to distinguish between statements that are truly metaphysical and statements that are metaphysically true, there is no reason to believe that he will therefore value truth any less. He will then soon see that truth in metaphysics emerges out of healthy conflict and dedicated dialogue not only between two opposing views but also between any two aspects of the same viewpoint. If St. Thomas shows this fact in action —he argued with Augustine against Aristotle at least as often as he argued with Aristotle against Augustine—it is only because he was a true practitioner of metaphysics.

One other problem resulting from the contemporary shift in perspective and its effect on the classroom remains to be pointed out. It concerns today's student. The modern student of metaphysics, by all appearances at least, does not enter upon philosophic studies in precisely the same way as did his father or grandfather. Classroom instruction is forced to take account of this fact. For one thing, the student is required to relate his studies to many new kinds of knowledge in the physical and social sciences that, as little as twenty or thirty years ago, hardly had a place in the college curriculum. Consequently, he is likely to be somewhat more perceptive—or, perhaps, just less naive—than his predecessors and generally less willing to memorize "theses" unless he feels he can relate them to himself and his understanding of the history of mankind. Contemporary students often begin metaphysics with a great many "formula" and historical questions, which teachers years ago rarely bothered to develop or simply assumed could be handled along the way or in cognate courses in the history of philosophy. These questions often indicate heightened interest and motivation that cannot be satisfied through employment of the "Prussian drill tactics," so popular at the turn of the century and—though mistakenly—often identified with "scholasticism."

These threshold questions, as we may call them, may at first sight appear irrelevant or merely peripheral. The student, for example, will want to know how metaphysics got its name, why men have been drawn to its pursuit, and if there is a specifically metaphysical language and methodology or a specifically metaphysical problem. Such questions are healthy and should be encouraged because eventually they will become more detailed and provide the basis for asking metaphysical questions. This is to say, once the student has been introduced into the "metaphysical maze," he will have to learn to distinguish between factual or historical questions, which for the most part can be readily answered, and metaphysical questions, which are not simply answered but are brought to a greater degree of penetration. He will have to learn, as Gabriel Marcel has put it, to distinguish between a problem, which can be solved, and a mystery, which must be illuminated.

The student will also have to develop a sense of the kind of complication that we habitually pack into our everyday words—such as *is, exists, related to, subjecitve*—and a suspicion of labels. If he asks, "Is metaphysics an art?" then he must be ready to deal with other questions, such as "What is art?" "What do we mean when we call something an art?" or "In what 'sense' can metaphysics be called an art?" If he asks, "Do metaphysicians write 'literature' or 'science'?" an answer, he may soon see, must take into account Plato as well as Aristotle and Kant. He will see that St. Thomas considered metaphysics a science, yet A. J. Ayer feels it is hardly scientific at all. "Do both men then mean the same thing by the term 'science'?" "And what," the student may ask, "is the metaphysician's proper study? Is it 'being'? Then how is that 'innocent' term to be understood?" The student will have to be prepared to see that being is one thing to Aristotle and another to Hegel. If he asks, "Is metaphysical procedure a search for 'ultimate reasons'?" then he will have to understand that Whitehead's "ultimate reasons" are not the same as Aristotle's.

We have suggested that, in some respects, today's student is somewhat better prepared to undertake philosophic studies—without, however, losing sight of the fact that he will have to brace himself for the shock of actual metaphysical discipline. We have also suggested that the shifting philosophic scene creates new hindrances for philosophic study. These two propositions, while apparently contrary, are not inimical. They simply demonstrate that philosophical instruction is challenged by the need for new techniques to deal with the problem.

A Modern Introduction to

METAPHYSICS

One

THE SPIRIT OF
METAPHYSICAL INQUIRY

ALFRED NORTH WHITEHEAD ONCE OBSERVED THAT PHILOSOPHY, MORE
than any other science, is dominated by its past literature. Sometimes this can
be a hindrance. For example, the Arabian commentator Avicenna estimated
that he had read Aristotle's *Metaphysics* forty times without understanding it.
(It is hard to guess whether his comment is aimed against Aristotle or against
metaphysics.) On the other hand, its past literature can be a help, for it may
suggest to the philosopher matters for speculation he might not otherwise have
considered. Martin Heidegger, the German existentialist, tells us that the philosopher's most important intuitions consist precisely in "what his sayings leave
unsaid." Experience seems to indicate, however, that for every new truth about
what has been left unsaid, there are two or three old truths that have been
stated often enough to gain for them the title "perennial." The more often they
are meditated on, the greater depth they gain.

This section suggests some of these "old truths" in order to shed light on
three questions found at the threshold of metaphysics. These questions are:

(1) Out of what human experience is metaphysics developed?

(2) What reasons can be given by metaphysics itself to explain its
existence? and

(3) What credentials does metaphysics possess to substantiate its
claims?

In blunter language, these questions about metaphysics come to this: (1)
Why begin it? (2) Why bother with it? (3) Why believe it?

I

We ask a blunt question, such as "What is metaphysics?" and we are told
by the metaphysician with startling precision, "That depends." It depends,
we are told, on whether we mean metaphysics as an attitude and way of life
or whether we mean the nature of metaphysical knowledge, its "proper object,"
or how it goes about its job; that is, a reply must be framed from some viewpoint. It depends, furthermore, we are told, on what second viewpoint one
takes toward the first viewpoint. For instance, if we decide to ask the question

"What is metaphysics?" from the viewpoint of attitude, then we must ask from what viewpoint we take the term "attitude"—the attitude *of* metaphysics or an attitude *toward* metaphysics. To complicate the problem further we will eventually be told that there are additional viewpoints on the second viewpoint originally framed about the first viewpoint—that is, that there are more than two attitudes toward metaphysics.

Philosophers of all kinds have a way of hesitating before they answer our "simplest" questions. It seems to be a form of professional scruple. The philosopher means that this third viewpoint on the question "What is metaphysics?" is concerned with the reactions other philosophers have on the subject of attitudes toward metaphysics. This third class of viewpoint can be divided into two subclasses—general and particular. For example, in general terms, metaphysics has been called by Herbert Schneider "both elusive and attractive," by Morris Lazerowitz "remarkable and mystifying," and by Martin D'Arcy, S.J., "tantalizing." F. H. Bradley once called it "the finding of bad reasons for what one believes on instinct," while Whitehead characterized it as "an attitude of mind toward doctrines ignorantly entertained." These remarks do not specify, but only generalize formulas. Still speaking generally, we learn that Aristotle referred to metaphysics as "the science that we are seeking." If we followed this general characterization to its particular details, we would perceive more concretely what attitude Aristotle had "in the third place" to the question "What is metaphysics?"

Leaving aside Aristotle's particular viewpoint on metaphysics—to which we will return at the conclusion of this Introduction—let us notice first that Aristotle indicates something more about his attitude than what he actually puts into that general phrase. In the first place, he says that metaphysics is a science, hence, not an art. Second, it is something he is looking for, rather than something he has found. Thirdly, it is a science that searches, he later says, for the ultimate explanations behind things. And last, he implies, it is something that requires of its practitioner a unique kind of discernment and penetration, because it is a searching science.

Let us concentrate for the moment, then, on the character of this term "search" in order to see some of its implications, not only from the viewpoint of Aristotle, but also from the viewpoint of other kinds of metaphysics. How, we shall ask, is this search initiated, and where does it begin?

Both Aristotle and Plato believed that metaphysical search begins in man's natural capacity and desire to wonder about himself and the world he lives in. Plato remarks in the dialogue *Theaetetus* (155d) that wonder (*tò thaumázein*) "is the feeling of a philosopher, and philosophy begins in wonder," because (he goes on to say) Iris, the messenger of heavenly wisdom, is called the child of Thaumas, or wonder. Aristotle observes in the *Meta-*

physics (982b12) that "it is owing to their wonder that men both now begin and at first began to philosophize."

But what is this wonder that makes us ask questions? It is a common enough term in our daily language. Consider the way it is used in the following sentences: (*a*) "I wonder if I'll pass this course." (*b*) "I wonder what's for supper tonight." (*c*) "I wonder just who told the Dean I wrote that poison-pen letter." (*d*) "He's wondering if she'll go to the prom with him."

If we analyze these statements, we notice they do not express genuine questions—although there is an interrogative note implied in each; that is, the original form of (*a*) is "Will I pass this course?" whereas the original form of (*d*) must have been "Will she go to the prom with me?" The use of the term "wonder," however, creates a theme that adds to the interrogation, thereby expressing something new. In the first case, doubt is expressed; in the second, expectation; in the third, resentment; and in the fourth, hope. The themes of doubt and hope, and expectation and resentment have an important place in metaphysics. The work of Descartes, Marcel, Dewey, and Nietzsche would illustrate this (although in their work these themes are not identical with wonder but are its accompaniment). On reflection, our examples would hardly be called instances of metaphysical wonder. Instead, they express emotional states in an "inquisitive situation"—inquisitive hope, inquisitive resentment, and so forth. Their "inquisitiveness" might even be called "idle curiosity." Apparently then, the kind of question implied by these statements is not the type Aristotle and Plato were talking about. To understand what they meant we will have to return to the question of attitude.

What Plato and Aristotle meant by philosophic wonder could be called an intellectual attention, or a spiritual posture, that encourages what Aimé Forest has called the "unveiling" of the secrets of reality. What they were talking about was not a passing fancy but the *shape* of the mind and a way of looking at and living through life. Plato gave a good deal of thought to this kind of attitude—his dialogues abound in instances of it—and he concluded that it was no easy thing to come by. Like gold extracted from alloy, he tells us in one of his letters, it requires great effort, constant work, and constant attendance.

We can learn a great deal about wonder from Plato, because he is an ideal example of the activity of philosophic wonder. The way he lived has profoundly influenced what we think (he "has been the source of all that is best and of most importance in our civilization," said Greek scholar John Burnet); what we see (he has "clapped copyright" on the world, Emerson observed); and what we say (Western thought is a series of "footnotes to Plato," Whitehead asserts).

It was Plato, more than the Pythagoreans, who gave currency to the life of wonder (the *bíos theorétikos*) by showing that action and contemplation are two ends of the same fact. When Plato speaks of the ideal representative of such a life (the *Republic's philósophos* or *searcher-after-wisdom*), he draws a self-portrait. The *philósophos,* he says, is a man of great intellectual power and quick apprehension, eager to learn the truths of the world-process. He is engaged in the unrelaxed training of mind and spirit. He avoids easy generalizations and partisan conclusions. Where ordinary men are complacent, he is honest; where proud, he is realistic; where pigheaded, he is dissatisfied— (which reminds us that J. S. Mill once confessed that he "would rather be a dissatisfied Socrates than a satisfied pig").

Like his *philósophos,* Plato was involved in the practical issues and affairs of life. He was an administrator and teacher, scientist and research director; practicing politician, statesman, and diplomat. He was also a playwright and a poet and a man personally dedicated to the highest ideals and the life of wonder, which, we have said, is basic to the *metaphysical attitude.*

In *Epistle VII,* a portion of which introduces the selections that follow, Plato gives a straightforward account of certain basic truths about metaphysics. Outwardly, the letter—written to political adherents of his deceased friend Dion—records some of the circumstances surrounding the last of Plato's three visits to Sicily about 361 B.C. These visits were prompted by the tyrant Dionysius the Younger. Dionysius, though somewhat of a philosophic "boob," had a native shrewdness. Like all tyrants, he was basically dishonest (he had apparently published one of Plato's works under his own name). But Plato soon saw through the perfidy, and his account of the matter throws light upon the kind of spiritual integrity he himself considered basic to the practice of metaphysics.

It is insufficient, he observes, merely to have intelligence and a good memory. Both are equally useless as substitutes for philosophizing, which requires, in addition, a nobility of soul and an inner reverence for reality. There are certain moral requirements, therefore, Plato goes on to say, that the metaphysician must have: dedication, steadfastness, loyalty, sincerity—these are the genuine philosophy. Without them, philosophy becomes mere cleverness. One cannot play falsely with truth; one cannot pretend to have said the final word on it.

True to his own faith, Plato confessed, after a life of teaching, writing, and thinking, that he had written nothing about "the really important things." What was attributed to him, he modestly asserts, is the work of an apprentice, "of a Socrates grown beautiful and young." Seventeen centuries later, St. Thomas expressed similar thoughts. On his deathbed, the story goes, he admitted that the actual world had eluded his best attempts to fathom it: "I cannot write any further," he told his confidant Raynalde, "because everything I have written now seems to me so much straw." Both Plato and St. Thomas seem to imply that the mystery to which they had devoted their lives was not really dissipated.

Two elements, consequently, seem to emerge from the as yet indistinct portrait of metaphysics. In the first place, there is wonder; and in the second mystery. Wonder engenders metaphysics, while mystery engenders wonder Mystery is the world's "unfinished business." So long as it remains, there will be wonder; and because of wonder, there is metaphysics. Hence, metaphysics is partnered with mystery. In the absence of mystery, metaphysics disappears. Or, as F. H. Bradley once put it: "When, in short, twilight has no charm—then metaphysics will be worthless."

There is doubtless good cause for Plato's attitude *toward* metaphysics, which, he also says, is an attitude *of* metaphysics—namely, reverence and humility. If mystery still inhabits our deepest intuitions into reality—in which we and every *each-thing* are soaked—then the metaphysical search is never really completed; because, as Joseph Moeller points out, it can "never wholly contain or fully possess its object."

It would follow, then, that any metaphysician who claims that he has discovered everything about the world has simply given up the search. Like the man who refuses to eat food because he had dinner several months ago, such a "metaphysician" lacks all nourishment; he has nothing to feed on. Either he will continue to accumulate and assimilate, or he will spiritually decompose. His metaphysical death impends, and is only a matter of time.

The fact that there are "moral requirements" that go to make up metaphysical attitudes can cut two ways, however, The sense of reverence, provisionality, of "being on the way" (as Aristotle put it)—all of which find their place in the recognition of mystery—have been considered both assets and liabilities for the metaphysician. Some observers see this sense of "unfinality" as a healthy indication of life. Others consider it a sign of indecision, irresoluteness, and procrastination; the metaphysician, this charge has it, is a cross between Hamlet and Colonel Blimp, who seems uncertain of what he sees, whether he sees anything at all, or whether what he sees is really there. Perhaps we can appreciate some of the sting to this charge when we recall that the imaginary philosopher whom we asked to define metaphysics for us replied: "That depends." We shall have a chance further on to investigate these charges in more detail.

But it should be clearly understood here that most metaphysicians do not suffer merely from indigestion, bad logic, or both, when they contend that what they are searching for is quite inscrutable. It is undeniable that metaphysics has had its "failures" (although we could not consider its failures unless we first knew something of its successes). Presumably we would prefer the metaphysician to tell us, once and for all, that things are this way or that way, and have done with it. Perhaps he, too, would prefer it. But this is not possible. The metaphysician usually realizes that he has not, so to speak, paid the piper; so he cannot very well call the tune. Since he did not invent reality, he cannot pretend to know all about it.

II

At this point it seems logical to ask for motivations; in short, to ask why metaphysicians ask why. We want to account for the final reasons metaphysics is pursued and to find out what really explains the metaphysical search. Saying that it is "wonder" simply leaves us with another question: "Why wonder?" We may be told that man wonders because he is an *animal metaphysicum*. But is he an *animal metaphysicum* because he speaks metaphysics, or does speaking metaphysics make him an *animal metaphysicum?* Is it natural for man to wonder? It must be, replies Jesuit philosopher Frederick Copleston, otherwise nobody would practice metaphysics. Or is it deceptive for man to wonder? It must be, says S. N. Hampshire, because we are "tempted hopelessly" toward it.

Perhaps we can enlighten this problem by putting our questions to four modern thinkers: Immanuel Kant, Arthur Schopenhauer, Martin Heidegger, and Regis Jolivet, all of whom felt, or feel, that wonderment is to be explained by something prior, something that stands at the vestibule of wonder.

Kant believed that the wonder that prompted the desire for metaphysics could be accounted for by the way the mind is constructed. The human mind, he said, is impelled to "categorize" experience. Hence, given the nature of the mind, metaphysics is inevitable, even when it is bad metaphysics. "That the mind will ever give up metaphysical researches," he wrote at the end of the *Prolegomena to Any Future Metaphysics,* "is as little to be expected as that we, to avoid inhaling impure air, should prefer to give up breathing altogether. There will . . . always be a metaphysics in the world . . . ; to forego it entirely is impossible." It is perfectly natural for man, therefore, to "spout metaphysics"; it is the unavoidable result of his having a mind in the first place. Metaphysics is born not out of some abstract wonder but out of "the natural and unavoidable dialectic of pure reason," which superimposes metaphysical categories on experience. At the expense of a seeming detour, let us see what he has meant by this.

Kant framed his conclusion about metaphysics after he had investigated the nature of the kinds of statements we make. Sometimes we make statements that repeat in the predicate another form of the subject we began with. We say, for example, "A triangle is a three-sided plane figure." But we could just as easily have turned it around and said, "A three-sided plane figure is a triangle." This kind of statement Kant called an *analytic a priori,* because it analyzes a subject-term in order to get a predicate-term and does not use sense experience to do it. Since the predicate-term is simply a synonym for the subject-term, we have not gone any farther ahead in the statement than the place we started from. On the other hand, when he say "Hottentots are a disappearing people," we notice that a new situation is present—that is, the predicate-term is not an analysis of the subject-term but a completely new term that adds to the subject. The statement, therefore, synthesizes, or brings together, two elements and bases that synthesis on experience. Kant called this type of statement a *synthetic a posteriori*. In the first case, I know that before I look at any triangle, it will have three sides; hence my knowledge precedes, or is prior to, any experience of triangles. In the second case, it is only after my experience of Hottentots that I can say anything about them.

Consider, however, a third type of statement, such as, "Every change has a cause," or "All bodies have weight," or "A straight line is the shortest distance between two points." In no way can I analyze the subject-terms (change, bodies, and straight line) and obtain the indicated predicates. Hence, these are synthetic, not analytic, statements. But I also know that before I consider any change, lift any body, or draw any straight line, it will be this way. Hence these are not a posteriori, or experiential, statements but a priori statements that experience presupposes. For this reason, Kant called them *synthetic a priori*. But how could he account for them?

Kant's British predecessor, David Hume, had pointed out that experience and analysis cannot account for such notions as "causality." One cannot find the notion of cause in experience; and it cannot be analyzed from any other notion that the mind possesses. Hence, Hume asserted that such notions as cause, relation, substance were not really genuine notions but simply mental trappings that we put on by habit, convenience, and "instinct."

Kant answered Hume's difficulty by asserting that "cause" is one of the mind's categories, built into the mind to permit it to deal intelligibly with events. Thus, he said, man has a natural inclination to make metaphysics, not because of social habit (Hume), but because metaphysical categories are constitutive of the mind. This does not mean, however, Kant added, that man should be duped into believing that what he says metaphysically about the universe can portray the secrets of "reality." Metaphysics does not talk about transcendent reality, and can hardly be called a science. What it is concerned with is simply a way of knowing understanding itself. Man may believe that in metaphysics he is discovering the mysteries of the universe; but, in fact, he is only uncovering the mysteries of his own mind. If metaphysics could "scientifically" achieve knowledge of *inner reality*—the *thing-in-itself*—it would be a *transcendent* science. That is, it would scientifically transcend, or surpass, empirical experience, and arrive at supraempirical knowledge. Whereas, actually, it is a *transcendental* knowledge because it can know only the categories of reason. That metaphysics should claim to know the essence of things—what Kant called *noumena*—was, by definition, incomprehensible to him. Metaphysics knows only its own categories; and these, in turn, are applied to phenomenal experience in order to make the world intelligible. Metaphysics is occupied only with Reason, not with Reality. The "root and peculiarity of metaphysics," he points out, is "the occupation of reason merely with itself, and the supposed knowledge of objects arising immediately from this brooding over its own concepts, without requiring or indeed being able to reach that knowledge through experience."

Let us go a step further by seeing the way in which Schopenhauer may help to answer our question. Schopenhauer was influenced a good deal by Kant's work, in the sense that he reacted to it. Perhaps he tried to find out what Kant had "left unsaid." In any case, he capitalized on the fact that metaphysics is peculiar to the human situation. Leaving Kant's categories aside, Schopenhauer observed that, as man confronts the world of experience, he is overwhelmed by a unique kind of wonder, which is the knowledge of his own contingency. He finds sadness, suffering, and death, and cannot lay aside his sense of the *lacrimae rerum*—the pitifulness of everything. He is haunted by imaginative and meditative melancholy, which pushes him beyond mere appearances, or phenomena, and into the dark halls of hidden, or noumenal, reality. Metaphysics, he concluded, is not an abstractive play around the structure of knowledge—or what Bradley was later to call "a ballet of bloodless categories." It is, rather, an attempt to solve reality's cryptographic code. Metaphysics begins in man and in his situation, because man *is* metaphysics. He himself is a noumenal reality.

One step away from the thought of Schopenhauer, we reach Martin Heidegger, whose insight into the problem may prove valuable. Metaphysics, says Heidegger, is engendered by a unique kind of self-knowledge, which culminates in the recognition of insufficiency. Without this sense of insufficiency, man can have no contact with metaphysics. A penetration into the human situation of being-in-the-world, of *Dasein,* is the presupposition of the disclosure of being. *Dasein* exposes human life with a brutal immediacy and shows that it is shrouded in the experiences of dread and insecurity. Man is then drawn to a recognition of self-being, which is frightening. He asks metaphysical questions, therefore, because he finds himself questionable, because he finds himself unable to explain his own existence.

One further step is required if we are to satisfy our question about metaphysical motivation. The final element we seek has been supplied by Regis Jolivet, Dean of the Faculty of Philosophy at the Catholic University of Lyon. Man's attraction toward wonder, and its formulation in metaphysics, says Jolivet, do indeed result from the human condition—from man's sense of insufficiency, contingency, and perhaps fright. But these experiences are simply another way of showing man's natural desire for infinity and the absolute. In the act of wonder man becomes painfully aware of his inability to satisfy his intellectual and "existential" desires. He is pushed forward to a "why?" that will answer all other "whys?" And these are not just interrogative "whys?" so to speak, but ontological "whys?" He asks whether this need for an ultimate "why?" is illusory and answers that, if so, it is at least a very real illusion.

On the basis of what our four philosophers have said, how then shall we answer our question and account for metaphysical motivation? A moment's reflection will show that certain perspectives appear to agree.

Without committing ourselves to Kant's general explanation, we can nevertheless reasonably be sure of one point that he makes: metaphysics is something peculiar to man, something indigenous to the human mind, and to the way it sees things. Secondly, we can say, with Schopenhauer, that metaphysics begins in man and in the human situation. Thirdly, we can say, with Heidegger, that it begins in man's recognition of his inability to explain himself. And finally, with Jolivet, we can say that it begins in man's recognition of the fact that he is a creature—which is the hidden underside to man's sense of insufficiency and contingency.

At this point we must also realize that we have come full circle to the view of Plato where we began this discussion of metaphysical wonder. Man, Plato has told us, is drawn by natural desire to wonder about things. He is a thing of desire, because *Eros,* the god of desire, causes man to seek the higher values in experience. *Eros* is, therefore, the spirit of philosophy, as Plato pointed out in the *Symposium.*

St. Augustine saw this point particularly well; but he advanced further by joining together the two ends of man's desire and man's creaturehood and fitting them together perfectly. Augustine could, consequently, understand that man is drawn toward metaphysics because he has a creaturely thirst for being, which is to say, for God. "Thou has made us creatures directed toward Thee," he wrote in the *Confessions,* "and our hearts are uneasy until they repose in Thee." Augustine's thought here travels a straight line: Man philosophizes, he says, because he seeks Wisdom; in Wisdom he finds true happiness and the answer to his desire. But true Wisdom is God. If then the philosopher is a lover of Wisdom, he is, by that fact, a lover of God. God is therefore both the *reason* that men search for Wisdom and the *reward* of that search.

St. Augustine, then, would seem to carry Plato's intuitions to a higher level, by giving them the substance of Christian insight; as Father Copleston has put it, "He supplements and completes the wisdom of philosophy with the wisdom of the scriptures." In doing this Augustine was no less what we would call a metaphysician. He simply amplified the experience of things by the experience of belief; or, more correctly, he understood that Scripture, too, is part of Christian experience.

III

We have, finally, to turn our attention to one remaining question: "Why does man believe in the metaphysical search?"

The answer to this question is handled in greater detail in some of the following selections. However, we could say that metaphysics is believable because it is self-justifying and carries its own credentials. We will point this out in these concluding remarks through the observations of Aristotle, St. Thomas, F. H. Bradley, and Gilson, who bring forward philosophical, logical, and historical arguments to substantiate their claims.

Let us consider first the way in which Aristotle and St. Thomas conceived metaphysics. In doing so, we shall at the same time be indicating the particular viewpoint that Aristotle and St. Thomas had toward metaphysics, which has been called the "third class." We shall call this the philosophical warrant for metaphysics.

Metaphysics is a science, Aristotle believed—the highest science, because it governs all other sciences. Where particular sciences treat of the various parts of *what is,* metaphysics treats of the *what is* in itself—insofar as it is the *what is.* For example, "physics" treats of what is in the form of material bodies under the aspect of motion, or *qua mobile;* "mathematics" treats of what is in terms of quantity; but "metaphysics" treats of what is according to being—it treats *ens in quantum ens.* Metaphysics proceeds by searching for the ultimate limiting notions, or causes, of being as being. Metaphysics, therefore, addresses itself to an explanation of all inferior sciences and, in so doing, indicates its proper right to do so.

St. Thomas substantially accepted Aristotle's analysis of knowledge as a hierarchic structure. Though he placed Scriptural Theology above metaphysics—since it deals with revealed truths—he asserted that metaphysics is the highest form of knowledge attainable by the light of the scripturally un-aided reason. The certainty of a science, he goes on to say, is to be judged in terms of the certainty of its first principles. The more basic (and, hence, more abstract) a science, the more applicable its principles will be to other sciences. The science that can account not only for the principles of other sciences but for its own as well will be the highest science. It will be both self-justifying and regulative of all others. It will be the *scientia rectrix,* which, by its intelligibility, crowns all other types of knowledge. As the most intelligible it cannot call upon any other knowledge to justify it because such knowledge would have to be more intelligible; and by definition, no other knowledge is more intelligible, and no other principles are higher than its own. Hence, metaphysics is to be believed because it accounts for its own existence by its own intelligibility.

There is, secondly, the warrant of logic. Logic, says F. H. Bradley, indicates that any attempt to disbelieve metaphysics turns itself into a metaphysical belief. If anyone denies that there is such a thing as metaphysics, he must naturally frame his denial in a proposition that claims to pronounce upon the character of knowledge. But this, in turn, requires antecedent knowledge of what knowledge *is;* and this is precisely a metaphysical inquiry. Deny metaphysics, says Bradley, and you must turn into a "brother metaphysician" with a metaphysics of your own and a rival theory of how it is obtained. Metaphysics, then, is to be believed because it is logically contradictory to disbelieve in it without at the same time practicing a form of metaphysics.

Thirdly, there is the warrant of historical experience. The history of philosophy, Etienne Gilson says, shows that there are perceptible periods of belief and disbelief regarding metaphysics. Because, however, disbelief is always followed by belief, metaphysics gains more from denials against it than it loses. Perhaps, like a "shake-out" in the stock market, sceptics are shown up as poor investors. Historically, metaphysics has never suffered mortally from scepticism and disbelief; it has, in fact, been strengthened by it. The simple fact is that metaphysics "buries its undertakers." Thus, Gilson points out, metaphysics is to be believed if it is true that history's lessons are not without their point.

Plato   1. REGIMEN AND
                                    REVERENCE IN
                                    METAPHYSICS

The following selection is a portion of the most important of Plato's thirteen ex-
    tant letters. It is, along with two others, unquestionably genuine. In it Plato
    appears in a confidential, almost off-guard mood, as he writes to the politi-
    cal followers of his deceased friend Dion. He tells them not only of his
    own experience as advisor to kings but—more importantly—he tells them
    something about the spiritual training necessary for one who wishes to
    understand how all things "fit together." It is here we find the genuine, un-
    caricatured Plato. Once we realize, observes Werner Jaeger, that "the man
    who in the seventh letter speaks of his own spiritual development, and
    whose attitude to his own philosophy is determined by his career, is the
    true Plato, we are bound to revise our whole conception of the significance
    of his philosophy."

The plan of philosophic study, says Plato in the following passage, re-
    quires moral preparation: devotion, a spirit of reverence, dedication. Given
    such preparation and the continued desire to pursue reality, "at last, in a
    flash, understanding . . . blazes up, and the mind, as it exerts all its powers
    to the limit of human capacity, is flooded with light."

The student may be more forcibly reminded of these words after reading
    the essay by Jacques Maritain ("The True Subject of Metaphysics") in

These extracts are from Epistle VII, in *Thirteen Epistles of Plato,* ed. L. A. Post (London: Oxford University Press, 1925). Reprinted by permission of the Clarendon Press, Oxford.

Part Three, which describes the intuition into being as "a sight whose content and implications no words . . . can exhaust or adequately express and in which in a moment of decisive emotion . . . of spiritual conflagration, the soul is in contact . . . with a reality which it touches and which takes hold of it."

WHEN I HAD ARRIVED, I thought I ought first to put it to the proof whether Dionysius was really all on fire with philosophy or whether the frequent reports that had come to Athens to that effect amounted to nothing. Now there is an experimental method for determining the truth in such cases that, far from being vulgar, is truly appropriate to despots, especially those stuffed with second-hand opinions, which I perceived, as soon as I arrived, was very much the case with Dionysius. One must point out to such men that the whole plan is possible and explain what preliminary steps and how much hard work it will require; for the hearer, if he is genuinely devoted to philosophy and is a man of God with a natural affinity and fitness for the work, sees in the course marked out a path of enchantment, which he must at once strain every nerve to follow, or die in the attempt. Thereupon he braces himself and his guide to the task and does not relax his efforts until he either crowns them with final accomplishment or acquires the faculty of tracing his own way no longer accompanied by the pathfinder. When this conviction has taken possession of him, such a man passes his life in whatever occupations he may engage in but through it all never ceases to practise philosophy and such habits of daily life as will be most effective in making him an intelligent and retentive student, able to reason soberly by himself. Other practices than these he shuns to the end.

As for those, however, who are not genuine converts to philosophy, but have only a superficial tinge of doctrine—like the coat of tan that people get in the sun—as soon as they see how many subjects there are to study, how hard the work involved, and how indispensable it is for the project to adopt a well-ordered scheme of living, they decide that the plan is difficult, if not impossible, for them; and so they really do not prove capable of practising philosophy. Some of them, too, persuade themselves that they are well enough informed already on the whole subject and have no need of further application. This test then proves to be the surest and safest in dealing with those who are self-indulgent and incapable of continued hard work, since they throw the blame not on their guide but on their own inability to follow out in detail the course of training subsidiary to the project.

The instruction that I gave to Dionysius was accordingly given with this object in view. I certainly did not set forth to him all my doctrines, nor did Dionysius ask me to, for he pretended to know many of the most important points already and to be adequately grounded in them by means of the second-hand interpretations he had got from the others.

I hear, too, that he has since written on the subjects in which I instructed him at that time, as if he were composing a handbook of his own which differed entirely from the instruction he received. Of this I know nothing. I do know, however, that some others have written on these same subjects, but who they are they know not themselves. One statement at any rate I can make in regard to all who have written or who may write with a claim to knowledge of the subjects to which I devote myself—no matter how they pretend to have acquired it, whether from my instruction or from others or by their own dis-covery. Such writers can in my opinion have no real acquaintance with the subject. I certainly have composed no work in regard to it, nor shall I ever do so in future; for there is no way of putting it in words like other subjects. Acquaintance with it must come, rather, after a long period of attendance on instruction in the subject itself and of close companionship, when, suddenly, like a blaze kindled by a leaping spark, it is generated in the soul and at once becomes self-sustaining. . . .

Besides, this at any rate I know, that if there were to be a treatise or a lecture on this subject, I could do it best. I am also sure for that matter that I should be very sorry to see such a treatise poorly written. If I thought it possible to deal adequately with the subject in a treatise or a lecture for the general public, what finer achievement would there have been in my life than to write a work of great benefit to mankind and to bring the nature of things to light for all men? I do not, however, think the attempt to tell mankind of these matters a good thing, except in the case of some few who are capable of discovering the truth for themselves with a little guidance. In the case of the rest, to do so would excite in some an unjustified contempt in a thoroughly offensive fashion, in others certain lofty and vain hopes, as if they had acquired some awesome lore . . .

To sum it all up in one word, natural intelligence and a good memory are equally powerless to aid the man who has not an inborn affinity with the subject. Without such endowments there is of course not the slightest possi-bility. Hence, all who have no natural aptitude for, and affinity with, justice and all the other noble ideals, though in the study of other matters they may be both intelligent and retentive—all those, too, who have affinity but are stupid and unretentive—such will never any of them attain to an understanding of the most complete truth in regard to moral concepts. The study of virtue and vice must be accompanied by an inquiry into what is false and true of existence in general and must be carried on by constant practice throughout a long period, as I said in the beginning. Hardly after practising detailed com-parisons of names and definitions and visual and other sense perceptions, after scrutinizing them in benevolent disputation by the use of question and answer without jealousy, at last, in a flash, understanding of each blazes up, and the mind, as it exerts all its powers to the limit of human capacity, is flooded with light. . . .

Aimé Forest

2. THE INTERIOR LIFE OF METAPHYSICS

The reflexive and reflective character of metaphysical activity, already mentioned by Plato in the previous selection, is brought out in this statement by Professor Forest in a new and *personalist* way. Metaphysical thought, he contends, implies a commitment to being. It discloses the mind in full confrontation with reality. There is no mere passive reception of "being" by the mind. Rather, something like an artistic shaping of a new relationship takes place. The mind becomes conscious that it is not a spectator of reality but an incarnation of it. Metaphysics, therefore, tends to begin in meditation and self-recognition rather than in any unconcerned and clever systematizing.

Where Plato had perceived the moral training necessary for metaphysics, Forest goes further by subjecting the question of metaphysical preparation to metaphysical analysis. Also, what in Plato is a recognition of ethical motives becomes in Forest an intuition into a new kind of spiritual self-possession and interiority. Without such interiority there can be no metaphysical activity.

The student may later want to compare this analysis by Forest with that in Lavelle's essay ("How Being Is Encountered") in Part Three.

METAPHYSICAL THOUGHT is formed in the reflection by which the mind turns back upon itself and seeks to grasp itself in its primal truth. In this new relationship among things seen in their source the mind attains to its own integration, lays hold of itself. It ceases to dissipate itself in the objects whose diversity tempts it. This experience leads us to an interiority which is completely spiritual. It is a reaffirmation of ourselves before truth. This awakening of the spirit is due to the nature of the attention which inclines us towards the data presented to us. We endeavor to grasp what surrounds them and encloses them, and in this reflection we attain to the spiritual sense of being. We affirm it when we discover in ourselves the source of a pure commitment which is something distinct from desire.

This relation, however, is not perceived in an immediate way. Nevertheless, you can be aware of the point at which each determinate notion

---

These extracts are from an essay entitled "Art and Metaphysics," which appeared in the quarterly *Philosophy Today*, edited at Saint Joseph's College, Rensselaer, Indiana. Translated from the French by Rosemary Lauer.

becomes integrated with self-consciousness. Being is given to us as an object at the end of this endeavor to return to the purity of the mind; it is given in a vision which already has of itself a sapiential character. Our experience, once it has become truly spiritual, is an *intention* which performs the function of unveiling. When we contemplate it in an act of reflection, being is seen to be not only what imposes itself on us, what cannot be denied, but that which can be defined only as what is opposed to nothingness. Being is certainly more pregnant with meaning than that. We form our idea of it by envisaging it in its relationship to the mind, by considering it as that in which the mind is. The act by which we affirm being is an acknowledgment of it, a commitment to it.

Metaphysical thought is less transcendence, or a passing beyond every object, than the recognition of this affinity between being and the mind. Thus it is in itself the expression of the spiritual meaning of being. It is a passage from the consideration of the fact of being to that of the value of being. The spiritual *intention* is itself the light in which truth becomes evident. It is true that being is given initially in the adversity of the determinations which divide our attention; it appears then much more veiled than evident. But we can raise ourselves to a new representation of being when we know how to attain it and how to be deserving of it. The commitment to being reveals to us finally the universality of the value to which all the forms of being are ordered in their diversity. This commitment actualizes the *intention* of metaphysics, which is to pass beyond the appearances, beyond the vision of things in which interiority is lacking. It is the negation of the value which creates the purely phenomenal representation. Things regain at the same time their value and their interiority when they correspond to the movement of the mind which affirms them. They lay hold of the meaning of a *presence* in the axiological sense of that term. Metaphysics is this passage from appearance to value. It is a taking possession both of ourselves and of the value of being. The truth which it affirms allows us to possess ourselves interiorly instead of being dissipated outside ourselves, and reflection is itself the experience by which we find meanings beyond what is given. Truth is grasped in the agreement of a twofold revelation, the one interior, the other exterior. So you can say that metaphysical thought, even before the final justification which a science of being gives us, is much more an orientation toward a spiritual realism than it is a noetic.

Expression in Metaphysics

Metaphysical expression corresponds to the truth it is meant to interpret. It is constructed about the value metaphysics envisages, that of a primal relationship, of an interior correspondence, between the soul and the idea. In order to be completely faithful to its own demands, metaphysics tends to become a work of art. Metaphysical understanding, in the relationship to interiority which it presupposes, can never be an accomplished fact. It must always be a thing of the present, created unceasingly, if it is to be possessed. Metaphysics intends the formation, or rather the revelation, of the idea. It does not look only to interpret it in a notional manner but to enrich it, or better, to constitute it in a reflexive manner by bringing it into relationship with the act by which it is formed. Metaphysics attempts to express community between the idea and the act by which it is formed and, by so doing, brings us, that we might better grasp the truth, an awareness of the experience which is the source of that community. Metaphysics looks to the awakening of ideas. Its task is to bring us to a state of self-awareness, not only as a prerequisite condition, but also as a state which is truly constitutive of the thought content of metaphysics. The advance which metaphysics attempts to create in an ever new way is at one and the same time an undertaking of discernment and of docility. It aims at an ever better interpretation of a common experience and at an understanding arrived at in a sort of continuing self-renewal. . . .

Characteristics Common to Art and Metaphysics

Metaphysics is always mindful of Malebranche's rule: "Nothing is clearer than light." It agrees with Pascal's: "There must be both the pleasant and the real, but it is necessary that what is pleasant be itself caught up in what is true." Metaphysical expression is thus made up of simplicity, ingenuity, and effortlessness. It is by reason of its rapport with the life of the soul that the idea becomes always more simple. Metaphysical truth is not something you arrive at in a construction ever more complex; rather it is something which brings with it its own order, is of itself simple, and corresponds to the purity of interior vision. The metaphysician attempts to parallel the pure and effortless progress of consciousness on its way toward truth. But sometimes, unknowingly, he comes to express what is most intimate to him, the primal form by means of which he submits to universal truth. Metaphysical thought is, in effect, the liberation from what would otherwise be too immediate in our feeling; but metaphysics maintains the values of what is immediate and transforms them by finding at the very source of our conscious life an openness to truth.

It is possible to discover the characteristics of metaphysics so understood in the masterworks of thought today. Bergson desires to lead us to an interior vision of things. This vision is due to the intuition which is prior to all the attention which the mind turns on itself. It is at the same time the discovery of the truth granted to the movement of thought at the term of this taking interior possession of oneself. We know how, then, to think in terms of *duration* and attain to what is at the source of being itself, its inescapable novelty. We are led to truth through the disinterestedness which raises us above the plan for action and leads us to true interiority. Bergson wants to interpret the relationship between the most faithful progress toward interior exigency and the understanding which is formed by it: "It is by reason of ideality alone that we recover contact with reality."

Blondel wants to avail himself of a bond of the same kind. All his work leads us to consider the relationship between act and idea, between life and thought and its elaborated expression. Truth is attained only in the choice, not between two objective visions already established, but between two paths of the soul, one of which is equal to the soul's *élan*. It is in this relationship to the ground of choice that the meaning of being is finally made evident. We recognize it as something which is offered for our choice; thus we form, beyond what is immediately given, a metaphysical certitude. "It is in what it is possible to accept or reject that one must see the true reality of the objects which are imposed upon our consciousness." But if thought is an act undertaken with all the dynamism of the spirit, it is grasped itself only in its relationship to the light which directs it. Blondel always attempts to interpret this relationship faithfully. Truths are recognized in their correspondence to the very movement of the soul. They are to us in their recognition and become at once the light and the goal of intelligence.

Lavelle's aim is to go beyond the duality of the act and what is given, while in a sense retaining that same duality. Thus we form in ourselves a spiritual universe. We recognize meanings that are not only superadded to things but are constitutive of their very being. These meanings become manifest when we know how to exercise a pure and docile activity and thereby enter into wisdom. Lavelle wants to construct a philosophy of the act. He makes himself clear to us on the question of being by making known to us the meaning of what is unceasingly proposed to us as object. Thus we recognize the truth of participation and of "spiritual presence." These truths are possessed in meditation, "as if light were in us always as an effect of earnestness." . . .

The Task of Intellect

The task of intellect, then, is to interpret spiritual progress at the same time as it interprets the truth which corresponds to the progress. It is the linking of these two values that constitutes the thought proper to metaphysics. These values can be grasped in their reciprocity. The objectivity of the real is, properly speaking, the meaning which impregnates it in order to constitute it interiorly and give to the real the character of universality.

Integrity of spirit is itself put to the test when truth becomes a part of this

program and can be made known in this interior sense. Thus truth, when it is
reflected in the soul and takes the form which our receiving the truth gives to
it, takes on, in a certain way, a value which is higher than that which it has
in itself. Truth awakens the spirit to itself, allows it to possess itself interiorly,
to pass from an existence which is a mere fact to an existence which is justified,
to attain to a dignity necessary to raise it above the level of a thing. Metaphysics seeks to interpret spiritual truth understood in this way.

You might say that metaphysics becomes the greatest of the works of
art, that it becomes a work in which spirit recognizes itself and takes itself,
in some sense, as its own proper object when it sees in this work that truth is
related to spirit. The history of philosophy shows us the characteristic traits
of a teaching which seeks such an expression. It is a philosophy of meditation
more than of system, of the essay more than of the treatise. It does not betray
any unfaithfulness to spiritual realism; rather, it expresses the interior exigency
of such a realism. Metaphysical works are, at one and the same time, in an
association which is doubtlessly their special privilege, construction of both
art and thought. . . .

Arthur Schopenhauer   3. MAN'S NEED FOR
                                                    METAPHYSICS

To Arthur Schopenhauer, often dismissed as a mere pessimist, metaphysical knowl-
    edge aims at penetration into the hidden parts of life. It begins not in
    conceptualization (he chastised his predecessor Kant for holding such a
    view) but in the inner recognition of life's suffering, misery, and harrow-
    ing companion, death.

    This inward experience differs, however, from that discussed by Aimé
    Forest in the previous selection. Forest stressed a devotional inwardness,
    or self-possession. Schopenhauer's inwardness, in contrast, is brought about
    by the actual conditions of painful human life and by the recognition of
    man's ontological insecurity. This manifests itself in what he terms "won-
    der."

    Metaphysical wonder, he says, is directed to a knowledge of what is behind
    experience. Experience is to be read like a cryptogram for a hidden mes-
    sage. But it is the whole of experience, not any restricted part of it, such as

From *The World as Will and Representation* by Arthur Schopenhauer, translated and
edited by E. F. J. Payne. Reprinted with kind permission of the translator and The Falcon's
Wing Press, Indian Hills, Colorado.

physics or mathematics, that calls for interpretation. Inner and outer experience are not different but are one; and each thing is connected to all else.

Kant was therefore right, he asserts, in distinguishing between the thing-in-itself (*ding-an-sich*) and the forms of knowledge—that is, between actual hidden reality and the forms through which it is phenomenologically known. But Kant failed to see that each person is himself a hidden reality, enviserated in the world's appearances. The metaphysician's task, Schopenhauer concludes, is to locate and unravel this hidden meaning of reality within phenomena.

The student may want to return to Schopenhauer's ideas on this point after having read the selection by Joseph Moeller ("The Ground of Being") and Nikolai Berdyaev ("Differentiations of the Person") in Part Four.

PHILOSOPHICAL WONDER is conditioned in the individual by higher development of intelligence, though generally not by this alone; but undoubtedly it is the knowledge of death, and therewith the consideration of the suffering and misery of life, that give the strongest impulse to philosophical reflection and metaphysical explanations of the world. If our life were without end and free from pain, it would possibly not occur to anyone to ask why the world exists, and why it does so in precisely this way, but everything would be taken purely as a matter of course. In keeping with this, we find that the interest inspired by philosophical and also religious systems has its strongest and essential point absolutely in the dogma of some future existence after death. . . .

Temples and churches, pagodas and mosques, in all countries and ages, in their splendour and spaciousness, testify to man's need for metaphysics, a need strong and ineradicable, which follows close on the physical. The man of a satirical frame of mind could of course add that this need for metaphysics is a modest fellow content with meagre fare. Sometimes it lets itself be satisfied with clumsy fables and absurd fairy-tales. If only they are imprinted early enough, they are for man adequate explanations of his existence and supports for his morality. . . .

We will now, however, subject to a general consideration the different ways of satisfying this need for metaphysics that is so strong.

By *metaphysics* I understand all so-called knowledge that goes beyond the possibility of experience, and so beyond nature or the given phenomenal appearance of things, in order to give information about that by which, in some sense or other, this experience or nature is conditioned, or in popular language, about that which is hidden behind nature and renders nature possible. But the great original difference in the powers of understanding, and also their cultivation, which requires much leisure, cause so great a variety among men that, as soon as a nation has extricated itself from the uncultured state, no *one* metaphysical system can suffice for all. Therefore in the case of civilized nations we generally come across two different kinds of metaphysics, distinguished by the fact that the one has its verification and credentials *in itself,* the other *outside itself.* As the metaphysical systems of the first kind require reflection, culture, leisure, and judgment for the recognition of their credentials, they can be accessible only to an extremely small number of persons; moreover, they can arise and maintain themselves only in the case of an advanced civilization. The systems of the second kind, on the other hand, are exclusively for the great majority of people who are not capable of thinking but only of believing, and are susceptible not to arguments but only to authority. These systems may therefore be described as popular metaphysics, on the analogy of popular poetry and popular wisdom, by which is understood proverbs. . . .

I turn to a general consideration of the other kind of metaphysics, that which has its authentication in itself, and is called *philosophy.* I remind the reader of its previously mentioned origin from a *wonder or astonishment* about the world and our own existence, since these obtrude themselves on the intellect as a riddle, whose solution then occupies mankind without intermission. Here I would first of all draw attention to the fact that this could not be the case if, in Spinoza's sense, so often put forth again in our own day under modern forms and descriptions as pantheism, the world were an *"absolute substance,"* and consequently a *positively necessary mode of existence.* For this implies that it exists with a necessity so great, that beside it every other necessity conceivable as such to our understanding must look like an accident or contingency. Thus it would then be something that embraced not only every actual, but also any possible, existence in such a way that, as indeed Spinoza states, its possibility and its actuality would be absolutely one. Therefore its non-being would be impossibility itself, and so it would be something whose non-being, or other-being, would inevitably be wholly inconceivable, and could in consequence be just as little thought away as can, for instance, time or space. Further, since *we ourselves* would be parts, modes, attributes, or accidents of such an absolute substance, which would be the only thing capable in any sense of existing at any time and in any place, our existence and its, together with its properties, would necessarily be very far from presenting themselves to us as surprising, remarkable, problematical, in fact as the unfathomable and ever-disquieting riddle; on the contrary, they would of necessity be even more self-evident and a matter of course than the fact that two and two make four. For we should necessarily be quite incapable of thinking anything else than that the world is, and is as it is; consequently, we should inevitably be just as little conscious of its existence *as such,* that is to say, as a problem for reflection, as we are of our planet's incredibly rapid motion.

Now all this is by no means the case. Only to the animal lacking thoughts or ideas do the world and existence appear to be a matter of course. To man, on the contrary, they are a problem, of which even the most uncultured and narrow-minded person is at certain more lucid moments vividly aware, but which enters the more distinctly and permanently into everyone's consciousness, the brighter and more reflective that consciousness is, and the more material for thinking he has acquired through culture. Finally, in minds adapted to philosophizing, all this is raised to Plato's *wonder* or *astonishment* which comprehends in all its magnitude the problem that incessantly occupies the nobler portion of mankind in every age and in every country, and allows it no rest. In fact, the balance wheel which maintains in motion the watch of metaphysics that never runs down, is the clear knowledge that this world's non-existence is just as possible as is its existence. Therefore, Spinoza's view of the world as an absolutely necessary mode of existence, in other words, as something that positively and in every sense ought to and must be, is a false one. Even simple theism in its cosmological proof tacitly starts from the fact that it infers the world's previous non-existence from its existence; thus, it assumes in advance that the world is something contingent. What is more, in fact, we very soon look upon the world as something whose non-existence is not only conceivable, but even preferable to its existence. Therefore our astonishment at it easily passes into a brooding over that *fatality* which could nevertheless bring about its existence, and by virtue of which such an immense force as is demanded for the production and maintenance of such a world could be directed so much against its own interest and advantage. Accordingly, philosophical astonishment is at bottom one that is dismayed and distressed; philosophy, like the overture to *Don Juan,* starts with a minor chord. . . .

We also find *physics,* in the widest sense of the word, concerned with the explanation of phenomena in the world; but it lies already in the nature of the explanations themselves that they cannot be sufficient. *Physics* is unable to stand on its own feet, but needs a *metaphysics* on which to support itself, whatever fine airs it may assume towards the latter. For it explains phenomena by something still more unknown than are they, namely by laws of nature resting on forces of nature, one of which is also the vital force. Certainly the whole present condition of all things in the world or in nature must necessarily be capable of explanation from purely physical causes. But such an explanation —supposing one actually succeeded so far as to be able to give it—must always just as necessarily be burdened with two essential imperfections (as it were with two sore points, or like Achilles with the vulnerable heel, or the devil with the cloven foot). On account of these imperfections, everything so explained would still really remain unexplained. The first imperfection is that the *beginning* of the chain of causes and effects that explains everything, in other words, of the connected and continuous changes, can positively *never* be reached, but, just like the limits of the world in space and time, recedes incessantly and *in infinitum*. The second imperfection is that all the efficient causes from which everything is explained always rest on something wholly inexplicable, that is, on the original *qualities* of things and the *natural forces* that make their appearance in them. By virtue of such forces they produce a definite effect, e.g., weight, hardness, impact, elasticity, heat, electricity, chemical forces, and so on, and such forces remain in every given explanation like an unknown quantity, not to be eliminated at all, in an otherwise perfectly solved algebraical equation. Accordingly there is not a fragment of clay, however little its value, that is not entirely composed of inexplicable qualities. Therefore these two inevitable defects in every purely physical, i.e., causal, explanation indicate that such an explanation can be only *relatively* true, and that its whole method and nature cannot be the only, the ultimate and hence sufficient one, in other words, cannot be the method that will ever be able to lead to the satisfactory solution of the difficult riddle of things, and to the true understanding of the world and of existence; but that the *physical* explanation, in general and as such, still requires one that is *metaphysical,* which would furnish the key to all its assumptions, but for that very reason would have to follow quite a different path. . . .

. . . From Leucippus, Democritus, and Epicurus down to the *Systéme de la nature,* and then to Lamarck, Cabanis, and the materialism cooked up again in the last few years, we can follow the unceasing attempt to set up a *system of physics without metaphysics,* in other words, a doctrine that would make the phenomenon into the thing-in-itself. But all their explanations try to conceal from the explainers themselves and from others that they assume the principal thing without more ado. They endeavour to show that all phenomena are physical, even those of the mind; and rightly so, only they do not see that everything physical is, on the other hand, metaphysical also. Without Kant, however, this is difficult to see, for it presupposes the distinction of the phenomenon from the thing-in-itself. . . .

Accordingly, naturalism, or the purely physical way of considering things, will never be sufficient; it is like a sum in arithmetic that never comes out. Beginningless and endless causal series, inscrutable fundamental forces, endless space, beginningless time, infinite divisibility of matter, and all this further conditioned by a knowing brain, in which alone it exists just like a dream and without which it vanishes—all these things constitute the labyrinth in which naturalism leads us incessantly round and round. The height to which the natural sciences have risen in our time puts all the previous centuries entirely in the shade in this respect, and is a summit reached by mankind for the first time. But however great the advances which *physics* (understood in the wide sense of the ancients) may make, not the smallest step towards *metaphysics* will be made in this way, just as a surface never attains cubical contents however far its extension is carried. For such advances will always supplement only knowledge of the *phenomenon,* whereas *metaphysics* strives to pass beyond the phenomenal appearance to that which appears; and even if we had in addition an entire and complete experience, matters would not be advanced in this way as regards the main point. In fact, even if a man wandered through all the planets of all the fixed stars, he would still not have made one step in *metaphysics*. On the contrary, the greatest advances in *physics* will only make the need for a system of *metaphysics* felt more and more, since the corrected, extended, and more thorough knowledge of nature is the very knowledge that always undermines and finally overthrows the metaphysical assumptions that till then have prevailed. On the other hand, such knowledge presents the problem of metaphysics itself more distinctly, correctly, and completely, and separates it more clearly from all that is merely physical. In addition, the more perfectly and accurately known intrinsic essence of individual things demands more pressingly the explanation of the whole and the universal, and this whole only presents itself as the more puzzling and mysterious, the more accurately, thoroughly, and completely it is known empirically. Of course, the individual simple investigator of nature in a separate branch of physics is not clearly aware of all this at once. On the contrary, he sleeps comfortably with his chosen maid in the house of Odysseus, banishing all thoughts of Penelope. . . . Therefore at the present day we see the *husk of nature* most accurately and exhaustively investigated, the intestines of intestinal worms and the vermin of vermin known to a nicety. But if anyone, such as myself for instance, comes along and speaks of the *kernel of nature,* they do not listen; they just think that this has nothing to do with the matter, and go on sifting their husks. One feels tempted to apply to these excessively microscopical and micrological investigators of nature the name of nature's meddlers. But those who imagine crucibles and retorts to be the true and only source of all wisdom are in their way just as wrong-headed as their antipodes the scholastics were previously. Thus, just as the scholastics, captivated entirely by their concepts, used these as their weapons, neither knowing nor investigating anything besides them, so the investigators of nature, captivated entirely by their empiricism, accept nothing but what their eyes see. With this they imagine they arrive at the ultimate ground of things, not suspecting that between the phenomenon and that which manifests itself therein, namely the thing-in-itself, there is a deep gulf, a radical difference. This difference can be cleared up only by the knowledge and accurate delimitation of the subjective element of the phenomenon, and by the insight that the ultimate and most important information about the inner nature of things can be drawn only from self-consciousness. Without all this, we cannot go one step beyond what is given immediately to the senses, and thus do no more than arrive at the problem. On the other hand, it must be noted that the most complete knowledge of nature possible is the corrected *statement of the problem* of metaphysics. No one, therefore, should venture on this without having previously acquired a knowledge of all the branches of natural science which, though only general, is yet thorough, clear, and connected. For the problem must come before the solution; but then the investigator must turn his glance inwards, for intellectual and ethical phenomena are more important than physical, to the same extent that animal magnetism, for example, is an incomparably more important phenomenon than mineral magnetism. Man carries the ultimate fundamental secrets within himself, and this fact is accessible to him in the most immediate way. Here only, therefore, can he hope to find the key to the ridde of the world, and obtain a clue to the inner nature of all things. Thus, the very special province of *metaphysics* certainly lies in what has been called mental philosophy.

> The ranks of living creatures thou dost lead
> Before me, teaching me to know my brothers
> In air and water and the silent wood: . . .
> Then to the cave secure thou leadest me,
> Then show'st me mine own self, and in my breast
> The deep, mysterious miracles unfold.

Finally, as regards the *source* or *fount* of metaphysical knowledge, I have already declared myself opposed to the assumption, repeated even by Kant, that it must lie in *mere concepts*. In no knowledge can concepts be the first thing, for they are always drawn from some perception. But what led to that assumption was probably the example of mathematics. Leaving perception entirely, as happens in algebra, trigonometry, and analysis, mathematics can operate with pure abstract concepts, indeed with concepts represented only by signs instead of words, and yet arrive at a perfectly certain result which is still so remote that no one continuing on the firm ground of perception could have reached it. But the possibility of this depends, as Kant has sufficiently shown, on the fact that the concepts of mathematics are drawn from the most certain and definite of all perceptions, the *a priori,* yet intuitively known, relations of quantity. Therefore the concepts of mathematics can always be once more realized and controlled by these relations of quantity, either arithmetically, by performing the calculations that those signs merely indicate, or geometrically, by means of what Kant calls the construction of concepts. On the other hand, this advantage is not possessed by the concepts from which it had been imagined that metaphysics could be built up, such as, for example, essence, being, substance, perfection, necessity, reality, finite, infinite, absolute, reason, ground, and so on. For concepts of this kind are by no means original, as though fallen from heaven, or even innate; but they also, like all concepts, are drawn from perceptions; and as they do not, like mathematical concepts, contain the merely formal part of perception, but something more, empirical perceptions lie at their foundation. Therefore nothing can be drawn from them which empirical perception did not also contain, in other words, which was not a matter of experience, and which, since these concepts are very wide abstractions, would be obtained from experience with much greater certainty and at first hand. For from concepts nothing more can ever be drawn than is contained in the perceptions from which they are drawn. If we want *pure* concepts, in other words concepts having no empirical origin, then only those can be produced which concern space and time, i.e., the merely formal part of perception, consequently only the mathematical concepts, or at most also the concept of causality. This concept, it is true, has not sprung from experience, but yet it comes into consciousness only by means of experience (first in sense-perception). Therefore experience is indeed possible only through the concept of causality, but this concept is also valid only in the realm of experience. For this reason Kant has shown that it merely serves to give sequence and continuity to experience, but not to soar beyond it; that it therefore admits merely of physical, not of metaphysical application. Of course, only its *a priori* origin can give to any knowledge apodictic certainty; but this very origin limits it to what is merely *formal* of experience in general, since it shows that experience is conditioned by the subjective nature of the intellect. Therefore such knowledge, far from leading us beyond experience, gives only a *part* of this experience itself, namely the *formal* part that belongs to it throughout and is thus universal, consequently mere form without content. Now since metaphysics can least of all be limited to this, it too must have *empirical* sources of knowledge; consequently, the preconceived idea of a system of metaphysics to be found purely *a priori* is necessarily vain and fruitless. It is actually a *petitio principii* of Kant, which he expresses most clearly in § 1 of the *Prolegomena,* that metaphysics may not draw its fundamental concepts and principles from experience. Here it is assumed in advance that only what we know *prior* to all experience can extend beyond possible experience. Supported by this, Kant then comes and shows that all such knowledge is nothing more than the form of the intellect for the purpose of experience, and that in consequence it cannot lead beyond experience, and from this he then rightly infers the impossibility of all metaphysics. But does it not rather seem positively wrong-headed that, in order to solve the riddle of experience, in other words, of the world which alone lies before us, we should close our eyes to it, ignore its contents, and take and use for our material merely the empty forms of which we are *a priori* conscious? Is it not rather in keeping with the matter that the *science of experience in general* and as such should draw also from experience? Its problem is itself given to it empirically; why should not its solution also call in the assistance of experience? Is it not inconsistent and absurd that he who speaks of the nature of things should not look at the things themselves, but stick only to certain abstract concepts? It is true that the task of metaphysics is not the observation of particular experiences; but yet it is the correct explanation of experience as a whole. Its foundation, therefore, must certainly be of an empirical nature. Indeed even the *a priori nature* of a part of human knowledge is apprehended by it as a given *fact,* from which it infers the subjective origin of that part. Only in so far as the consciousness of its *a priori* nature accompanies it is it called by Kant *transcendental,* as distinguished from *transcendent,* which signifies "passing beyond all possibility of experience," and has as its opposite *immanent,* which means remaining within the bounds of that possibility. I like to recall the original meaning of these expressions introduced by Kant, with which, as also with that of *category* and many others, the apes of philosophy carry on their game at the present day. In addition to this, the source of the knowledge of metaphysics is not only *outer* experience, but also *inner*. In fact, its most peculiar characteristic, whereby the decisive step alone capable of solving the great question becomes possible for it, consists in its combining at the right place outer experience with inner, and making the latter the key to the former. This I have explained thoroughly and fully in the essay *On the Will in Nature* under the heading "Physical Astronomy."

The origin of metaphysics from empirical sources of knowledge, which is here discussed and which cannot honestly be denied, does of course, deprive it of the kind of apodictic certainty that is possible only through knowledge *a priori*. This remains the property of logic and mathematics, but these sciences really teach only what everyone knows already as a matter of course, though not distinctly. At most the primary elements of natural science can be derived from knowledge *a priori*. By this admission, metaphysics gives up only an old claim, which, as appears from what has been said above, rested on misunderstanding, and against which the great diversity and changeable nature of metaphysical systems, and also the constantly accompanying scepticism, have at all times testified. However, this changeable nature cannot be asserted against the possibility of metaphysics in general, for it affects just as much all branches of natural science, chemistry, physics, geology, zoology, and so on; and even history has not remained exempt from it. But when once a correct system of metaphysics has been found, in so far as the limits of the human intellect allow it, then the unchangeable nature of an *a priori* known science will indeed belong to it, since its foundation can be only *experience in general,* not the particular individual experiences. Through these, on the other hand, the natural sciences are always being modified, and new material is constantly being provided for history. For experience, in general and as a whole, will never change its character for a new one.

The next question is how a science drawn from experience can lead beyond it, and thus merit the name of *metaphysics*. It cannot perhaps do so in the way in which we find from three proportional numbers the fourth, or a triangle from two sides and an angle. This was the way of pre-Kantian dogmatics, which, according to certain laws known to us *a priori,* tried to infer the not-given from the given, the ground from the consequent, and thus that which could not possibly be given in any experience from experience. Kant proved the impossibility of a system of metaphysics on this path by showing that, although those laws were not drawn from experience, they had validity only for experience. Therefore he rightly teaches that we cannot soar in such a way beyond the possibility of all experience; but there are still other paths to metaphysics. The whole of experience is like a cryptograph, and philosophy is like the deciphering of it, and the correctness of this is confirmed by the continuity and connexion that appear everywhere. If only this whole is grasped in sufficient depth, and inner experience is connected to outer, it must be capable of being *interpreted, explained* from itself. After Kant has irrefutably proved to us that experience in general arises from two elements, the forms of knowledge and the being-in-itself of things, and that these two can be distinguished from each other in experience, namely what we are conscious of *a priori* and what has been added *a posteriori,* it can be stated, at any rate in general, what in the given experience (primarily mere *phenomenon*) belongs to this phenomenon's *form* conditioned by the intellect, and what remains over for the *thing-in-itself* after the withdrawals of the intellect. And although no one can recognize the thing-in-itself through the veil of the forms of perception, on the other hand everyone carries this within himself, in fact he himself is it; hence in self-consciousness it must be in some way accessible to him, although still only conditionally. Thus the bridge on which metaphysics passes beyond experience is nothing but just that analysis of experience into phenomenon and thing-in-itself in which I have placed Kant's greatest merit. For it contains the proof of a kernel of the phenomenon different from the phenomenon itself. It is true that this kernel can never be entirely separated from the phenomenon, and be regarded by itself as an *ens extramundanum;* but it is known always only in its relations and references to the phenomenon itself. The interpretation and explanation of the phenomenon, however, in relation to its inner kernel can give us information about it which does not otherwise come into consciousness. Therefore in this sense metaphysics goes beyond the phenomenon, i.e., nature, to what is concealed in or behind it . . . yet always regarding it only as that which appears in the phenomenon, not independently of all phenomenon. Metaphysics thus remains immanent, and does not become transcendent; for it never tears itself entirely from experience, but remains the mere interpretation and explanation thereof, as it never speaks of the thing-in-itself otherwise than in its relation to the phenomenon. This, at any rate, is the sense in which I have attempted to solve the problem of metaphysics, taking into general consideration the limits of human knowledge which have been demonstrated by Kant. Therefore I approve and accept his *Prolegomena* to every metaphysical system as valid for mine also. Accordingly, this never really goes beyond experience, but discloses only the true understanding of the world lying before it in experience. According to the definition of metaphysics repeated also by Kant, it is neither a science of mere concepts nor a system of inferences and deductions from *a priori* principles, the uselessness of which for the purpose of metaphysics Kant has demonstrated. On the contrary, it is a rational knowledge (*Wissen*) drawn from perception of the external actual world and from the information about this furnished by the most intimate fact of self-consciousness, deposited in distinct concepts. Accordingly, it is the science of experience; but the universal and the whole of all experience are its subject and its source. I admit entirely Kant's doctrine that the world of experience is mere phenomenon, and that knowledge *a priori* is valid only in reference thereto; but I add that, precisely as phenomenal appearance, it is the manifestation of that which appears, and with him I call that which appears the thing-in-itself. Therefore, this thing-in-itself must express its inner nature and character in the world of experience; consequently it must be possible to interpret these from it, and indeed from the material, not from the mere form, of experience. Accordingly, philosophy is nothing but the correct and universal understanding of experience itself, the true interpretation of its meaning and content. This is the metaphysical, in other words, that which is merely clothed in the phenomenon and veiled in its forms, that which is related to the phenomenon as the thought or idea is to the words.

Such a deciphering of the world with reference to what appears in it must receive its confirmation from itself through the agreement in which it places the many different phenomena of the world with one another, and which we do not perceive without it. If we find a document the script of which is unknown, we continue trying to interpret it until we hit upon a hypothesis as to the meaning of the letters by which they form intelligible words and connected sentences. Then there remains no doubt as to the correctness of the deciphering, since it is not possible for the agreement and consistency, in which all the signs of that writing are placed by this explanation, to be merely accidental; nor is it possible for us, by giving the letters an entirely different value, to recognize words and sentences in this new arrangement of them. Similarly, the deciphering of the world must be completely confirmed from itself. It must spread a uniform light over all the phenomena of the world, and bring even the most heterogeneous into agreement, so that the contradiction may be removed even between those that contrast most. This confirmation from itself is the characteristic stamp of its genuineness; for every false deciphering, even though it suits some phenomena, will all the more glaringly contradict the remainder. Thus, for example, the optimism of Leibniz conflicts with the obvious misery of existence; Spinoza's doctrine that the world is the only possible and absolutely necessary substance is incompatible with our wonder and astonishment at its existence and essential nature; Wolff's doctrine that man has his *existentia* and *essentia* from a will foreign to him runs counter to our moral responsibility for actions resulting with strict necessity from these in conflict with the motives. The oft-repeated doctrine of a progressive development of mankind to an ever higher perfection, or generally of any kind of becoming by means of the world-process, is opposed to the *a priori* view that, up to any given point of time, an infinite time has already elapsed, and consequently that all that is supposed to come with time is bound to have existed already. In this way, an interminable list of the contradictions of dogmatic assumptions with the given reality of things could be compiled. But I must deny that any doctrine of my philosophy could honestly be added to such a list, just because each one has been thought out in the presence of perceived reality, and none has its root in abstract concepts alone. However, as there is in it a fundamental idea that is applied to all the phenomena of the world as their key, this idea proves to be the correct alphabet, and by its application all words and sentences have sense and significance. The discovered answer to a riddle shows itself as the right one by the fact that all the statements of the riddle are consistent with it. Thus my teaching enables us to perceive agreement and consistency in the contrasting confusion of the phenomena of this world, and solves the innumerable contradictions which, seen from every other point of view, are presented by it. Therefore it is, to this extent, like an arithmetical sum that comes out, although by no means in the sense that it leaves no problem still to be solved, no possible question unanswered. To assert anything of the kind would be a presumptuous denial of the limits of human knowledge in general. Whatever torch we kindle, and whatever space it may illuminate, our horizon will always remain encircled by the depth of night. For the ultimate solution of the riddle of the world would necessarily have to speak merely of things-in-themselves, no longer of phenomena. All our forms of knowledge, however, are intended precisely for phenomena alone; hence we must comprehend everything through coexistence, succession, and relations of causality. But these forms have sense and significance merely with reference to the phenomenon; the things-in-themselves and their possible relations cannot be grasped through them. Therefore the actual, positive solution to the riddle of the world must be something that the human intellect is wholly incapable of grasping and conceiving; so that if a being of a higher order came and took all the trouble to impart it to us, we should be quite unable to understand any part of his disclosures. Accordingly, those who profess to know the ultimate, i.e., the first grounds of things, thus a primordial being, an Absolute, or whatever else they choose to call it, together with the process, the reasons, grounds, motives, or anything else, in consequence of which the world results from them, or emanates, or falls, or is produced, set in existence, "discharged" and ushered out, are playing the fool, are vain boasters, if indeed they are not charlatans.

Aristotle

4. THE STUDY OF METAPHYSICS

Though he assuredly practiced metaphysics, Aristotle never used or heard the term. The term, which is also the title of one of Aristotle's central works,

This selection consists of the Appendix to the first book of the *Metaphysics,* translated and edited by John Warrington (Everyman's Library), reprinted by permission of E. P. Dutton & Co., Inc., and J. M. Dent & Sons Ltd.; and the first two chapters of the same book from *The Works of Aristotle Translated into English,* edited by J. A. Smith and W. D. Ross, reprinted by permission of The Clarendon Press, Oxford.

was "accidentally" devised by his literary executors to indicate a collection of problematic treatises. These seemed to be a sequel to his work on what we today would call theoretic physics. The new work was thus *metà tà physicá*—literally, *after* or *beyond* the books on physics. The ambiguity of the term *metà* has come to suggest not only an editorial decision but the character of the work—that is, that it goes beyond or transcends physical questions.

Exactly who first coined the title is still unclear, although today it is generally attributed to the first century (B.C.) Andronicus of Rhodes. But whoever else might have been responsible for it could not have lived before the early fourth century nor after the first century B.C. It is also generally recognized that the *Metaphysics*—divided by its ancient editor into fourteen books, as against the six divisions suggested by Sir David Ross—is not a finished work but, rather, a collection of disparate treatises composed as lectures either for the Platonic circle at Assos or for Aristotle's own school, the Lyceum. This school was named after its location in the grove of Apollo Lyceius, just north of Athens. The editors of the work (presumably philosophers themselves) tried to reconstruct Aristotle's "first philosophy," but doubtless realized that they had done a makeshift job.

The selection that follows is prefaced by a portion of the so-called *álpha élatton,* or "little alpha," which is probably a remnant of lectures recorded in the Lyceum by either Pasicles of Rhodes or Ammonius. Ancient editors used it as an appendix to Book *Alpha,* although originally it may have been a preface to the study of physics. Some critics (for example, John Warrington) feel it is out of place in the *Metaphysics,* but tradition has sanctified its inclusion.

Book *Alpha* actually begins at the fifth paragraph below with the words, "All men by nature desire to know." The sentence is indicated as "980a," which refers to Bekker's nineteenth-century edition of Aristotle's work, published by Berlin's Prussian Academy.

Men, says Aristotle, naturally want to know about the world they live in. The object of their wonder is truth, an object both difficult and easy to achieve; that is, truth is never completely achieved, nor is it completely outside the possibility of attainment. The truth that will satisfy man's search is wisdom, which sees the reasons behind all things. The "wise man" understands the meaning of all things because he understands the principles of reality itself.

The student may want to return to this selection after reading the essay in Part Three by Woodbridge ("The Scope of Metaphysics"). It should also be read in conjunction with the selection by St. Thomas, which follows immediately.

THE SEARCH FOR truth is in one sense difficult, but in another it is easy. This is shown by the fact that while no one can obtain an adequate grasp of it, no one fails entirely. Every thinker has something true to say about the nature of the universe; and if individually they contribute little or nothing to the inquiry, taken together their conjectures amount to a good deal. In so far, then, as truth is like the proverbial door, which no one can miss, its study presents no difficulty; but the fact that we cannot, although having some grasp of the whole, grasp a particular part shows it on the other hand to be far from easy.

Difficulty, however, may be accounted for in two ways; its cause may reside in the object of study or in ourselves. For just as the eyes of bats are dazzled by sunlight, so it is with human intelligence when face to face with what is by nature most obvious.

Justice requires our gratitude not only to those whose opinions we inherit, but also to those earlier thinkers whose superficial views gave the mind its necessary practice in thinking. If there had been no Timotheus we should lack much of our lyric poetry, but if there had been no Phrynis, there would have been no Timotheus. It is the same with those who have speculated about the nature of reality: we have derived certain views from the greatest among them, while these in turn have been indebted to others.

Moreover, philosophy is rightly called the knowledge of the truth. For the end of theoretical knowledge is truth, while that of practical knowledge is action; if the latter studies the truth, it is not eternal truth but that which is of the moment and relative to an object. Now we cannot know the truth without the cause; that which imparts to other things a certain character itself has that character in the highest degree, so that what makes other things true is itself most true. Hence the principles of eternal things must be true above all things; for they are not merely sometimes true, nor is there any cause of the existence of other things, so that as each thing is in respect of being, so it is in respect of truth. . . .

All men by nature desire to know. An indication of this is the delight we take in our senses, for even apart from their usefulness they are loved for themselves, and above all others the sense of sight. For not only with a view to action, but even when we are not going to do anything, we prefer seeing (one might say) to everything else. The reason is that this, most of all the senses, makes us know and brings to light many differences between things.

By nature animals are born with the faculty of sensation, and from sensation memory is produced in some of them, though not in others. And therefore the former are more intelligent and apt at learning than those which cannot remember; those which are incapable of hearing sounds are intelligent though they cannot be taught, e.g., the bee, and any other race of animals that may be like it; and those which besides memory have this sense of hearing can be taught.

The animals other than man live by appearances and memories, and have but little of connected experience; but the human race lives also by art and reasonings. Now from memory experience is produced in men, for the several memories of the same thing produce finally the capacity for a single experience.

And experience seems pretty much like science and art, but really science and art come to men through experience; for "experience made art," as Polus says, but inexperience luck. Now art arises when from many notions gained by experience one univeral judgment about a class of objects is produced. For to have a judgment that when Callias was ill of this disease this did him good, and similarly in the case of Socrates and in many individual cases, is a matter of experience; but to judge that it has done good to all persons of a certain constitution, marked off in one class, when they were ill of this disease, e.g. to phlegmatic or bilious people when burning with fever—this is a matter of art.

With a view to action, experience seems in no respect inferior to art, and men of experience succeed even better than those who have theory without experience. The reason is that experience is knowledge of individuals, art of universals, and actions and productions are all concerned with the individual; for the physician does not cure man, except in an incidental way, but Callias or Socrates or some other called by some individual name, who happens to be a man. If, then, a man has the theory without the experience, and recognizes the universal but does not know the individual included in this, he will often fail to cure; for it is the individual that is to be cured. But yet we think that knowledge and understanding belong to art rather than to experience, and we suppose artists to be wiser than men of experience (which implies that Wisdom depends in all cases rather on knowledge); and this because the former know the cause, but the latter do not. For men of experience know that the thing is so, but do not know why, while the others know the "why" and the cause. Hence we think also that the master-workers in each craft are more honourable and know in a truer sense and are wiser than the manual workers because they know the causes of the things that are done (we think the manual workers are like certain lifeless things which act indeed, but act without knowing what they do, as fire burns—but while the lifeless things perform each of their functions by a natural tendency, the labourers perform them through habit); thus we view them as being wiser not in virtue of being able to act, but of having the theory for themselves and knowing the causes. And in general it is a sign of the man who knows and of the man who does not know that the former can teach, and therefore we think art more truly knowledge than experience, for artists can teach, and men of mere experience cannot.

Again we do not regard any of the senses as Wisdom; yet surely these give the most authoritative knowledge of particulars. But they do not tell us the "why" of anything—e.g. why fire is hot; they only say that it is hot.

At first he who invented any art whatever that went beyond the common perceptions of man was naturally admired by men, not only because there was something useful in the invention but because he was thought wise and superior to the rest. But as more arts were invented and some were directed to the necessities of life, others to recreation, the inventors of the latter were naturally always regarded as wiser than the inventors of the former, because their branches of knowledge did not aim at utility. Hence when all such inventions were already established, the sciences which do not aim at giving pleasure or at the necessities of life were discovered, and first in the places where men first began to have leisure. This is why mathematical arts were founded in Egypt; for there the priestly caste was allowed to be at leisure.

We have said in the *Ethics* what the difference is between art and science and the other kindred faculties; but the point of our present discussion is this, that all men suppose what is called Wisdom to deal with the first causes and the principles of things; so that, as has been said, the man of experience is thought to be wiser than the possessors of any sense-perception whatever, the artist wiser than the men of experience, the master-worker than the mechanic, and the theoretical kinds of knowledge to be more of the nature of Wisdom than the productive. Clearly then, Wisdom is knowledge about certain principles and causes.

Since we are seeking this knowledge, we must inquire of what kind are the causes and the principles, the knowledge of which is Wisdom. If one were to take the notions we have about the wise man, this might perhaps make the answer more evident. We suppose first, then, that the wise man knows all things, as far as possible, although he has not knowledge of each of them in detail; secondly, that he who can learn things that are difficult, and not easy for man to know, is wise (sense-perception is common to all, and therefore easy and no mark of Wisdom); again, that he who is more exact and more capable of teaching the causes is wiser, in every branch of knowledge; and that of the sciences, also, that which is desirable on its own account and for the sake of knowing it is more of the nature of Wisdom than that which is desirable on account of its results, and the superior science is more of the nature of Wisdom than the ancillary; for the wise man must not be ordered but must order, and he must not obey another but the less wise must obey him.

Such and so many are the notions, then, which we have about Wisdom and the wise. Now of these characteristics that of knowing all things must belong to him who has in the highest degree universal knowledge; for he knows in a sense all the instances that fall under the universal. And these things, the most universal, are on the whole the hardest for men to know, for they are farthest from the senses. And the most exact of the sciences are those which deal most with the first principles; for those which involve fewer principles are more exact than those which involve additional principles, e.g. arithmetic than geometry. But the science which investigates causes is also instructive, in a higher degree, for the people who instruct us are those who tell the causes of each thing. And understanding and knowledge pursued for their own sake are found most in the knowledge of that which is most knowable (for he who chooses to know for the sake of knowing will choose most readily that which is most truly knowledge, and such is the knowledge of that which is most knowable); and the first principles and the causes are most knowable; for by reason of these, and from these, all other things come to be known, and not these by means of the things subordinate to them. And the science which knows to what end each thing must be done is the most authoritative of the sciences, and more authoritative than any ancillary science; and this end is the good of that thing and in general the supreme good in the whole of nature. Judged by all the tests we have mentioned, then, the name in question falls to the same science; this must be a science that investigates the first principles and causes; for the good, i.e. the end, is one of the causes.

That it is not a science of production is clear even from the history of the earliest philosophers. For it is owing to their wonder that men both now begin and at first began to philosophize; they wondered originally at the obvious difficulties, then advanced little by little and stated difficulties about the greater matters, e.g. about the phenomena of the moon and those of the sun and of the stars, and about the genesis of the universe. And a man who is puzzled and wonders thinks himself ignorant (whence even the lover of myth is in a sense a lover of Wisdom, for the myth is composed of wonders); therefore since they philosophized in order to escape from ignorance, evidently they were pursuing science in order to know and not for any utilitarian end. And this is confirmed by the facts; for it was when almost all the necessities of life and the things that make for comfort and recreation had been secured that such knowledge began to be sought. Evidently then we do not seek it for the sake of any other advantage but as the man is free, we say, who exists for his own sake and not for another's, so we pursue this as the only free science, for it alone exists for its own sake.

Hence also the possession of it might be justly regarded as beyond human power; for in many ways human nature is in bondage, so that according to Simonides "God alone can have this privilege," and it is unfitting that man should not be content to seek the knowledge that is suited to him. If then there is something in what the poets say, and jealousy is natural to the divine power, it would probably occur in this case above all, and all who excelled in this knowledge would be unfortunate. But the divine power cannot be jealous (nay, according to the proverb, "Bards tell many a lie"), nor should any other science be thought more honourable than one of this sort. For the most divine science is also most honourable; and this science alone must be, in two ways, most divine. For the science which it would be most meet for God to have is a divine science, and so is any science that deals with divine objects; and this science alone has both these qualities; for (1) God is thought to be among the causes of all things and to be a first principle, and (2) such a science either God alone can have, or God above all others. All the sciences, indeed, are more necessary than this, but none is better.

Yet the acquisition of it must in a sense end in something which is the opposite of our original inquiries. For all men begin, as we said, by wondering that things are as they are, as they do about self-moving marionettes, or about the solstices or the incommensurability of the diagonal of a square with the side; for it seems wonderful to all who have not yet seen the reason, that there is a thing which cannot be measured even by the smallest unit. But we must end in the contrary and, according to the proverb, the better state, as is the case in these instances too when men learn the cause; for there is nothing which would surprise a geometer so much as if the diagonal turned out to be commensurable.

We have stated, then, what is the nature of the science we are searching for and what is the mark which our search and our whole investigation must reach.

Thomas Aquinas

5. THE NATURE AND EXCELLENCE OF METAPHYSICS

Aristotle—"the Philosopher," as St. Thomas refers to him—had pointed out that several elements joined together in a single purpose share a special kind of relationship. He called this relationship hierarchic.

Man enjoys several kinds of knowledge, St. Thomas maintains, which, though differing in their objects and levels of certitude, share in the common purpose of knowledge: the perfection of man. This perfection is beatitude, or spiritual fulfillment in God. Consequently, there must exist among the various kinds of knowledge a hierarchic relationship, whereby each level of knowledge is governed by a higher, and where each higher knowledge explains and justifies a lower. This being so, there must be a single knowledge that rules all others and, at the same time, is its own justification. Aristotle had called this *Wisdom*.

Because this highest kind of knowledge is the most intelligible, universal, and comprehensive, it is the model against which all other knowledges are to be judged. It is the mistress and ruler of all others—the *scientia rectrix*. Furthermore, says St. Thomas, this knowledge will take different names— natural theology, metaphysics, first philosophy—according to the aspect under which it is considered.

This selection by St. Thomas may later be compared with those in Part Three by Maritain ("The True Subject of Metaphysics") and R. Garrigou-

Lagrange ("The Derivation of First Principles"), and may be reread after studying Dr. Martin's essay ("Kinds of Knowledge") in Part Four.

As THE Philosopher teaches in the *Politics,* when a number of things are ordered to a single thing, one of that number must be regulative or directive, and the others regulated or directed. This indeed is evident in the case of the union of the soul and the body, for the soul naturally commands and the body obeys. So too, within the powers of the soul, the irascible and the concupiscible, by a natural ordering, are governed by the reason. Indeed, all sciences and arts are ordained to one thing, namely, the perfection of man, which is his beatitude. Hence, among them that one must be the mistress of all the others which rightly lays claim to the title of wisdom. For it is the office of the wise to order others.

What this science is and what it treats of can be ascertained if one carefully considers how a person is qualified to rule. Now, as the Philosopher says in the work alluded to, just as men powerful in intellect are naturally the rulers and masters of others—whereas men physically robust yet deficient in intellect are naturally servile—so, that science is by right naturally mistress of the others which is in the highest degree intellectual. This science, however, is the one that treats of the most intelligible things.

The latter we can regard in three ways: firstly, from the standpoint of the order of knowing, for those things that are the source of the intellect's attainment of certitude seem to be the more intelligible ones. Thus, since it is from causes that the intellect achieves the certitude of science, the cognition of causes apparently is in the highest degree intellectual. Consequently that science which considers first causes evidently is regulative of the other sciences.

Secondly, the supremely intelligible objects can be considered from the point of view of the intellect's relation to sense knowledge. For, although the latter is the cognition of particulars, intellect seems to differ from it in this, that intellect comprehends universals. Thus, the science which is maximally intellectual is the one which treats of principles supremely universal. Now, these are being, and those things [or principles] that follow upon being, as one and many, potency and act. Such principles, however, ought not to remain completely indeterminate, since without them full cognition of things proper to a given genus or species cannot be had. Moreover, since each genus of beings needs these principles for the very knowledge of itself, they would with equal justification be treated in any particular science at all. It follows that principles of this kind are not to be dealt with in any one *particular* science. Therefore the task of dealing with such principles devolves upon that single common science which, being in the highest degree intellectual, is regulative of the other sciences.

Thirdly, the supremely intelligible objects of which we speak can be con-

sidered from the standpoint of the intellect's own cognition. Thus, since every
thing has intellective power in consequence of its freedom from matter, those
things must be pre-eminently intelligible which exist in complete separation
from matter. The intelligible object and the intellect must be proportioned to
each other, and must be of one genus, since the intellect and the intelligible are
in act one. Now, those things are in the highest degree separated from matter
which abstract not only from signate matter, "as do natural forms taken universally, of which natural science treats," but which abstract altogether from
sensible matter—and not only according to reason, as mathematical objects
do, but also in respect to actual existence, as with God and the intelligences.
Evidently, therefore, the science that considers these things is supremely intellectual and the chief or mistress of the others.

Now the foregoing threefold consideration belongs by right not to diverse
sciences but to one science. For the separated substances referred to above are
the universal and the first causes of actual being. But it pertains to one and
the same science to consider the proper causes of a genus and the genus itself.
So it is, for instance, that the natural philosopher studies the principles of the
natural body. Of necessity, then, it is the task of the selfsame science to consider not only separated substances but also common being, which is the genus
of which these substances are the common and universal causes.

From what has been said it is apparent that, although this science considers
the three things just mentioned, it does not take this one or that, indifferently,
as its subject, but only common being. The subject of a science is precisely that
whose causes and passions we seek to know, not the causes themselves of any
genus that is inquired into. It is the knowledge of the causes of a genus which
is the end of scientific thought. Although the subject of this science is common
being, the latter is predicated of entities that are wholly separated from matter,
existentially as well as logically. For among things said to be separated existentially and logically are found not only those that never can exist in matter, as
God and intellectual substances, but also those that can be without matter, as
common being. This however would not be the case if they depended upon
matter in their being.

Therefore, in accordance with the aforesaid three things from which the
perfection of this science is derived, it receives three names: "divine science"
or "theology" inasmuch as it considers the substances in question; "metaphysics" inasmuch as it considers being and the things that follow upon it—
for these transphysical principles are discovered in the process of resolution as
the more common after the less common; and "first philosophy" inasmuch as
it considers the first causes of things. It is evident, then, what the subject of this
science is, and how it is related to other sciences, and how it is named.

F. H. Bradley

6. A DEFENCE OF METAPHYSICS

The "peace of spirit," which Bradley mentions in the first paragraph of this selection, affirms once again—but in a new way—the connection between metaphysics and its moral-emotional requirements.

> Spiritual peace, Bradley observes, is necessary for anyone who wants "to comprehend the universe not simply piecemeal or by fragments, but somehow as a whole." But before the metaphysical practitioner can entertain the large view of things in an open and sweeping vision, he must be willing and able to establish the fact that metaphysics has a right to speak in serious discussion. He must also be ready to defend that right.
>
> In the first place, says Bradley, anyone who brands as impossible such knowledge as metaphysics asserts a *de facto* metaphysical proposition. As a "brother metaphysician," he makes a universal claim to genuine knowledge and must thus have universal—which is to say metaphysical—criteria for such a judgment. Consequently, says Bradley, though he denies it, he is on an errand of metaphysical business. He simply refuses to accord status to one kind of universal proposition, while making another that frames this refusal. He must therefore have employed previous analysis, and this analysis—while wrong—is unquestionably "metaphysical."

THE WRITER ON metaphysics has a great deal against him. Engaged on a subject which more than others demands peace of spirit, even before he enters on the controversies of his own field, he finds himself involved in a sort of warfare. He is confronted by prejudices hostile to his study, and he is tempted to lean upon those prejudices, within him and around him, which seem contrary to the first. It is on the preconceptions adverse to metaphysics in general that I am going to make some remarks by way of introduction. We may agree, perhaps, to understand by metaphysics an attempt to know reality as against mere appearance, or the study of first principles or ultimate truths, or again the effort to comprehend the universe, not simply piecemeal or by fragments, but somehow as a whole. Any such pursuit will encounter a number of objections. It will have to hear that the knowledge which it desires to obtain is impossible altogether; or, if possible in some degree, is yet practically useless; or

---

The selection reprinted here is from the Introduction to Bradley's *Appearance and Reality* (New York: The Macmillan Co., 1908), and is used with the kind permission of The Clarendon Press, Oxford.

that, at all events, we can want nothing beyond the old philosophies. And I will say a few words on these arguments in their order.

(*a*) The man who is ready to prove that metaphysical knowledge is wholly impossible has no right here to any answer. He must be referred for conviction to the body of this treatise. And he can hardly refuse to go there, since he himself has, perhaps unknowingly, entered the arena. He is a brother metaphysician with a rival theory of first principles. And this is so plain that I must excuse myself from dwelling on the point. To say that reality is such that our knowledge cannot reach it, is a claim to know reality; to urge that our knowledge is of a kind which must fail to transcend appearance, itself implies that transcendence. For, if we had no idea of a beyond, we should assuredly not know how to talk about failure or success. And the test, by which we distinguish them, must obviously be some acquaintance with the nature of the goal. Nay, the would-be sceptic, who presses on us the contradictions of our thoughts, himself asserts dogmatically. For these contradictions might be ultimate and absolute truth, if the nature of the reality were not known to be otherwise. But this introduction is not the place to discuss a class of objections which are themselves, however unwillingly, metaphysical views, and which a little acquaintance with the subject commonly serves to dispel. So far as is necessary, they will be dealt with in their proper place; and I will therefore pass to the second main argument against metaphysics.

(*b*) It would be idle to deny that this possesses great force. "Metaphysical Knowledge," it insists, "may be possible theoretically, and even actual, if you please, to a certain degree; but, for all that, it is practically no knowledge worth the name." And this objection may be rested on various grounds. I will state some of these, and will make the answers which appear to me to be sufficient.

The first reason for refusing to enter on our field is an appeal to the confusion and barrenness which prevails there. "The same problems," we hear it often, "the same disputes, the same sheer failure. Why not abandon it and come out? Is there nothing else more worth your labour?" To this I shall reply more fully soon, but will at present deny entirely that the problems have not altered. The assertion is about as true and about as false as would be a statement that human nature has not changed. And it seems indefensible when we consider that in history metaphysics has not only been acted on by the general development, but has also reacted. But, apart from historical questions, which are here not in place, I am inclined to take my stand on the admitted possibility. If the object is not impossible, and the adventure suits us—what then? Others far better than ourselves have wholly failed—so you say. But the man who succeeds is not apparently always the man of most merit, and even in philosophy's cold world perhaps some fortunes go by favour. One never knows until one tries.

But to the question, if seriously I expect to succeed, I must, of course, answer, No. I do not suppose, that is, that satisfactory knowledge is possible. How much we can ascertain about reality will be discussed in this book; but I may say at once that I expect a very partial satisfaction. I am so bold as to believe that we have a knowledge of the Absolute, certain and real, though I am sure that our comprehension is miserably incomplete. (But I dissent emphatically from the conclusion that, because imperfect, it is worthless.) And I must suggest to the objector that he should open his eyes and should consider human nature. Is it possible to abstain from thought about the universe? I do not mean merely that to everyone the whole body of things must come in the gross, whether consciously or unconsciously, in a certain way. I mean that, by various causes, even the average man is compelled to wonder and to reflect. To him the world, and his share in it, is a natural object of thought, and seems likely to remain one. And so, when poetry, art, and religion have ceased wholly to interest, or when they show no longer any tendency to struggle with ultimate problems and to come to an understanding with them; when the sense of mystery and enchantment no longer draws the mind to wander aimlessly and to love it knows not what; when, in short, twilight has no charm—then metaphysics will be worthless. For the question (as things are now) is not whether we are to reflect and ponder on ultimate truth—for perhaps most of us do that, and are not likely to cease. The question is merely as to the way in which this should be done. And the claim of metaphysics is surely not unreasonable. Metaphysics takes its stand on this side of human nature, this desire to think about and comprehend reality. And it merely asserts that, if the attempt is to be made, it should be done as thoroughly as our nature permits. There is no claim on its part to supersede other functions of the human mind; but it protests that, if we are to think, we should sometimes try to think properly. And the opponent of metaphysics, it appears to me, is driven to a dilemma. He must either condemn all reflection on the essence of things— and, if so, he breaks, or, rather, tries to break, with part of the highest side of human nature—or else he allows us to think, but not to think strictly. He permits, that is to say, the exercise of thought so long as it is entangled with other functions of our being; but as soon as it attempts a pure development of its own, guided by the principles of its own distinctive working, he prohibits it forthwith. And this appears to be a paradox, since it seems equivalent to saying, You may satisfy your instinctive longing to reflect, so long as you do it in a way which is unsatisfactory. If your character is such that in you thought is satisfied by what does not, and cannot, pretend to be thought proper, that is quite legitimate. But if you are constituted otherwise, and if in you a more strict thinking is a want of your nature, that is by all means to be crushed out. And, speaking for myself, I must regard this as at once dogmatic and absurd.

But the reader, perhaps, may press me with a different objection. Admitting, he may say, that thought about reality is lawful, I still do not understand why, the results being what they are, you should judge it to be desirable. And I will try to answer this frankly. I certainly do not suppose that it would be good for every one to study metaphysics, and I cannot express any opinion as to the number of persons who should do so. But I think it quite necessary, even on the view that this study can produce no positive results, that it should still be pursued. There is, so far as I can see, no other certain way of protecting ourselves against dogmatic superstition. Our orthodox theology on the one side, and our common-place materialism on the other (it is natural to take these as prominent instances), vanish like ghosts before the daylight of free sceptical enquiry. I do not mean, of course, to condemn wholly either of these beliefs; but I am sure that either, when taken seriously, is the mutilation of our nature. Neither, as experience has amply shown, can now survive in the mind which has thought sincerely on first principles; and it seems desirable that there should be such a refuge for the man who burns to think consistently, and yet is too good to become a slave either to stupid fanaticism or dishonest sophistry. That is one reason why I think that metaphysics, even if it end in total scepticism, should be studied by a certain number of persons.

And there is a further reason which, with myself perhaps, has even more weight. All of us, I presume, more or less, are led beyond the region of ordinary facts. Some in one way and some in others, we seem to touch and have communion with what is beyond the visible world. In various manners we find something higher, which both supports and humbles, both chastens and transports us. And, with certain persons, the intellectual effort to understand the universe is a principal way of thus experiencing the Deity. No one, probably, who has not felt this, however differently he might describe it, has ever cared much for metaphysics. And, wherever it has been felt strongly, it has been its own justification. The man whose nature is such that by one path alone his chief desire will reach consummation, will try to find it on that path, whatever it may be, and whatever the world thinks of it; and, if he does not, he is contemptible. Self-sacrifice is too often the "great sacrifice" of trade, the giving cheap what is worth nothing. To know what one wants, and to scruple at no means that will get it, may be a harder self-surrender. And this appears to be another reason for some persons pursuing the study of ultimate truth.

(c)   And that is why, lastly, existing philosophies cannot answer the purpose. For whether there is progress or not, at all events there is change; and the changed minds of each generation will require a difference in what has to satisfy their intellect. Hence there seems as much reason for new philosophy as there is for new poetry. In each case the fresh production is usually much inferior to something already in existence; and yet it answers a purpose if it appeals more personally to the reader. What is really worse may serve better to promote, in certain respects and in a certain generation, the exercise of our best functions. And that is why, so long as we alter, we shall always want, and shall always have, new metaphysics.

I will end this introduction with a word of warning. I have been obliged to speak of philosophy as a satisfaction of what may be called the mystical side of our nature—a satisfaction which, by certain persons, cannot be as well procured otherwise. And I may have given the impression that I take the metaphysician to be initiated into something far higher than what the common herd possesses. Such a doctrine would rest on a most deplorable error, the superstition that the mere intellect is the highest side of our nature, and the false idea that in the intellectual world work done on higher subjects is for that reason higher work. Certainly the life of one man, in comparison with that of another, may be fuller of the Divine, or, again, may realize it with an intenser consciousness; but there is no calling or pursuit which is a private road to the Deity. And assuredly the way through speculation upon ultimate truths, though distinct and legitimate, is not superior to others. (There is no sin, however prone to it the philosopher may be, which philosophy can justify so little as spiritual pride.)

Etienne Gilson

7. LAWS OF METAPHYSICAL EXPERIENCE

In this selection, Etienne Gilson goes a step further than Bradley has already gone. He says that metaphysics is a knowledge that "looks behind and beyond experience for an ultimate ground of all real and possible experience," and calls not only on reason but on twenty-five centuries of historical experience to warrant its activities.

Such experience tells us that man is a metaphysical animal who seeks ultimate explanations through the science of metaphysics. No inferior knowledge can competently judge it. This highest form of knowledge is concerned with "being," which is the first principle of metaphysics only because it is antecedently the first principle of all human knowledge.

Earlier in the chapter from which this selection is taken, Gilson states his first "law" of philosophical experience. It is that "philosophy always buries

This selection from Gilson's *The Unity of Philosophical Experience*, copyright 1937, is reprinted with the kind permission of Charles Scribner's Sons.

its undertakers." This law implies that there is a measurable rise and fall in the history of metaphysical thought. Every sceptical crisis, he says, is followed by the revival of speculation. "Plato's idealism comes first," he asserts. "Aristotle warns everybody that Platonism is heading for scepticism; then Greek scepticism arises. . . . St. Thomas Aquinas restores philosophical knowledge, but Ockham cuts its very root, and ushers in the late medieval and Renaissance scepticism. . . . Then come Descartes and Locke, but their philosophies disintegrate into Berkeley and Hume."

Iт is an observable character of all metaphysical doctrines that, widely divergent as they may be, they agree on the necessity of finding out the first cause of all that is. Call it matter with Democritos, the Good with Plato, the self-thinking Thought with Aristotle, the One with Plotinus, Being with all Christian philosophers, Moral Law with Kant, the Will with Schopenhauer, or let it be the absolute Idea of Hegel, the Creative Duration of Bergson, and whatever else you may cite, in all cases the metaphysician is a man who looks behind and beyond experience for an ultimate ground of all real and possible experience. Even restricting our field of observation to the history of Western civilization, it is an objective fact that men have been aiming at such knowledge for more than twenty-five centuries and that, after proving that it should not be sought, and swearing that they would not seek it any more, men have always found themselves seeking it again. A law of the human mind that rests on an experience of twenty-five centuries is at least as safely guaranteed as any empirically established law. Of course, nature itself may change, but we are dealing with nature as it now is; and observation teaches us that though the pattern and even the content of ideas may change, the nature of the human intellect has remained substantially the same, even after crises from which it should have emerged completely transformed. Let this, therefore, be our second law: *by his very nature, man is a metaphysical animal.*

The law does more than state a fact, it points to its cause. Since man is essentially rational, the constant recurrence of metaphysics in the history of human knowledge must have its explanation in the very structure of reason itself. In other words, the reason why man is a metaphysical animal must lie somewhere in the nature of rationality. Many centuries before Kant, philosophers had stressed the fact that there is more in rational knowledge than we find in sensible experience. The typical attributes of scientific knowledge, that is universality and necessity, are not to be found in sensible reality, and one of the most generally received explanations is that they come to us from our very power of knowing. As Leibniz says, there is nothing in the intellect that has not first been in sense, except the intellect itself. As Kant was the first both to distrust metaphysics and to hold it to be unavoidable, so was he also the first to give a name to human reason's remarkable power to overstep all sensible experience. He called it the *transcendent* use of reason and denounced it as the permanent source of our metaphysical illusions. Let us retain the term suggested by Kant; it will then follow that whether such knowledge be illusory or not, there is, in human reason, a natural aptness, and consequently a natural urge, to transcend the limits of experience and to form transcendental notions by which the unity of knowledge may be completed. These are metaphysical notions, and the highest of them all is that of the cause of all causes, or first cause, whose discovery has been for centuries the ambition of the metaphysicians. Let us, therefore, state as our third law, that *metaphysics is the knowledge gathered by a naturally transcendent reason in its search for the first principles, or first causes, of what is given in sensible experience.*

This is, in fact, what metaphysics is, but what about its validity? The Kantian conclusion that metaphysical knowledge is illusory by its own nature was not a spontaneous offspring of human reason. If metaphysical speculation is a shooting at the moon, philosophers have always begun by shooting at it; only after missing it have they said that there was no moon, and that it was a waste of time to shoot at it. Scepticism is defeatism in philosophy, and all defeatisms are born of previous defeats. When one has repeatedly failed in a certain undertaking, one naturally concludes that it was an impossible undertaking. I say naturally, but not logically, for a repeated failure in dealing with a given problem may point to a repeated error in discussing the problem rather than to its intrinsic insolubility.

The question then arises: should the repeated failures of metaphysics be ascribed to metaphysics itself, or to metaphysicians? It is a legitimate question, and one that can be answered in the light of philosophical experience. For indeed that experience itself exhibits a remarkable unity. If our previous analyses are correct, they all point to the same conclusion, that metaphysical adventures are doomed to fail when their authors substitute the fundamental concepts of any particular science for those of metaphysics. Theology, logic, physics, biology, psychology, sociology, economics, are fully competent to solve their own problems by their own methods; on the other hand, however, and this must be our fourth conclusion: *as metaphysics aims at transcending all particular knowledge, no particular science is competent either to solve metaphysical problems, or to judge their metaphysical solutions.*

Of course Kant would object that, so far, his own condemnation of metaphysics still holds good, for he never said that metaphysical problems could be solved in that way; he merely said that they could not be solved at all. True, but it is also true that his condemnation of metaphysics was not the consequence of any personal attempt to reach the foundations of metaphysical knowledge. Kant busied himself with questions about metaphysics, but he had no metaphysical interests of his own. Even during the first part of his career there was always some book between this professor and reality. To him, nature was in the books of Newton, and metaphysics in the books of Wolff. Anybody could read it there; Kant himself had read it, and it boiled down to this, that there are three metaphysical principles, or transcendental ideas of pure reason: an immortal soul to unify psychology; freedom to unify the laws of cosmology; and God to unify natural theology. Such, to Kant, was metaphysics; a second-hand knowledge, for which he was no more personally responsible than for the physics of Newton. Before allowing Kant to frighten us away from metaphysics, we should remember that what he knew about it was mere hearsay.

In fact, what Kant considered as the three principles of metaphysics were not principles, but conclusions. The real principles of metaphysics are the first notions through which all the subsequent metaphysical knowledge has to be gathered. What these first notions are cannot be known unless we begin by bringing forth some metaphysical knowledge; then we can see how it is made and, lastly, we can form an estimate of its value. Now our analysis of the concrete working of various metaphysical minds clearly suggests that the principles of metaphysics are very different from the three transcendental ideas of Kant. The average metaphysician usually overlooks them because, though he aims at the discovery of the ultimate ground of reality as a whole, he attempts to explain the whole by one of its parts, or to reduce his knowledge of the whole to his knowledge of one of its parts. Then he fails and he ascribes his failure to metaphysics, little aware of the fact that now is the proper time for him to metaphysicize, for the most superficial reflection on his failure would take him to the very root of metaphysics.

When Thales said, six centuries before Christ, that everything is water, though he certainly did not prove his thesis, he at least made it clear that reason is naturally able to conceive all that is as being basically one and the same thing, and that such a unification of reality cannot be achieved by reducing the whole to one of its parts. Instead of drawing that conclusion, the successors of Thales inferred from his failure that he had singled out the wrong part. Thus Anaximenes said that it was not water, but air. It still did not work. Then Heraclitus said it was fire, and as there were always objections, the Hegel of the time appeared, who said that the common stuff of all things was the *indeterminate,* that is, the initial fusion of all the contraries from which all the rest had been evolved. Anaximander thus completed the first philosophical cycle recorded by the history of Western culture. The description of the later cycles could not take us further, for it is already clear, from a mere inspection of the first, that the human mind must be possessed of a natural aptitude to conceive all things as the same, but always fails in its endeavour to conceive all things as being the same as one of them. In short, *the failures of the metaphysicians flow from their unguarded use of a principle of unity present in the human mind.*

This new conclusion brings us face to face with the last and truly crucial problem: what is it which the mind is bound to conceive both as belonging to all things and as not belonging to any two things in the same way? Such is the riddle which every man is asked to read on the threshold of metaphysics. It is an easy one, as, after all, was that of the Sphinx; yet many a good man has failed to say the word, and the path to the metaphysical Sphinx is strewn with the corpses of philosophers. The word is—Being. Our mind is so made that it cannot formulate a single proposition without relating it to some being. Absolute nothingness is strictly unthinkable, for we cannot even deny an existence unless we first posit it in the mind as something to be denied. "If any man," says J. Edwards, "thinks that he can conceive well enough how there should be nothing, I will engage, that what he means by nothing, is as much something, as anything that he ever thought of in his life." This, I think, is true. But if it is true that human thought is always about being; that each and every aspect of reality, or even of unreality, is necessarily conceived as being, or defined in reference to being, it follows that the understanding of being is the first to be attained, the last into which all knowledge is ultimately resolved, and the only one to be included in all our apprehensions. What is first, last and always in human knowledge is its first principle, and its constant point of reference. Now if metaphysics is knowledge dealing with the first principles and the first causes themselves, we can safely conclude that *since being is the first principle of all human knowledge, it is a fortiori the first principle of metaphysics.*

The classical objection to this statement is that, from such a vague idea as that of being, no distinct knowledge can be deduced. This is true, but it is not an objection. To describe being as the "principle of knowledge," does not mean that all subsequent knowledge can be analytically deduced from it, but rather that being is the first knowledge, through which all subsequent knowledge can be progressively acquired. As soon as it comes into touch with sensible experience, the human intellect elicits the immediate intuition of being: X is, or exists; but from the intuition *that* something is, the knowledge of *what* it is, beyond the fact it is something, cannot possibly be deduced, nor is it the task of the intellect to deduce it. The intellect does not deduce, it intuits, it sees, and, in the light of intellectual intuition, the discursive power of reason slowly builds up from experience a determinate knowledge of concrete reality. Thus, in the light of immediate evidence, the intellect sees that something is, or exists; that what exists is that which it is; that that which is, or exists, cannot be and not be at one and the same time; that a thing either is, or it is not, and no third supposition is conceivable; last, but not least, that being only comes from being, which is the very root of the notion of causality. Reason has not to prove any one of these principles, otherwise they would not be principles, but conclusions; but it is by them that reason proves all the rest. Patiently weaving the threads of concrete knowledge, reason adds to the intellectual evidence of being and of its properties the science of *what* it is. The first principle brings with it, therefore, both the certitude that metaphysics is the science of being as being, and the abstract laws according to which that science has to be constructed. Yet the principle of a certain knowledge is not that knowledge; and the first principle of human knowledge does not bring us a ready-made science of metaphysics, but its principle and its object.

The twofold character of the intellectual intuition of being, to be given in any sensible experience, and yet to transcend all particular experience, is both the origin of metaphysics and the permanent occasion of its failures. If being is included in all my representations, no analysis of reality will ever be complete unless it culminates in a science of being, that is, in metaphysics. On the other hand, the same transcendency which makes the first principle applicable to all experience entails at least the possibility of overstepping the limits by which concrete and particular existences are distinguished. This indeed is more than an abstract possibility, it is a temptation, precisely because it is true that the notion of Being applies to all real or possible experience. Yet, if it is also true that everything is what it is, and nothing else, existence belongs to each and every thing in a truly unique manner, as its own existence, which can be shared in by nothing else. Such is the first principle, both universally applicable, and never applicable twice in the same way. When philosophers fail to perceive either its presence or its true nature, their initial error will pervade the whole science of being, and bring about the ruin of philosophy.

When, owing to some fundamental scientific discovery, a metaphysically minded man first grasps the true nature of a whole order of reality, what he is thus grasping for the first time is but a particular determination of being at large. Yet the intuition of being is always there, and if our philosopher fails to discern its meaning, he will fall a victim to its contagious influence. That which is but a particular determination of being, or *a* being, will be invested with the universality of being itself. In other words, a particular essence will be credited with the universality of being, and allowed to exclude all the other aspects of reality. This is precisely what happened to Abailard, to Ockham, to Descartes, to Kant and to Comte. They were truly labouring under a transcendental delusion; Kant himself knew it, but he was wrong in thinking that such an illusion was unavoidable, for it can be avoided; and he was still more wrong in viewing that illusion as the source of metaphysics, for it is not its source but the cause of its destruction; and not only of the destruction of metaphysics, but, for the same reason and at the same time, of the ruin of the very science which has thus been unduly generalized. If every order of reality is defined by its own essence, and every individual is possessed of its own existence, to encompass the universality of being within the essence of this or that being is to destroy the very object of metaphysics; but to ascribe to the essence of this or that being the universality of being itself, is to stretch a particular science beyond its natural limits and to make it a caricature of metaphysics. In short, and this will be our last conclusion: *all the failures of metaphysics should be traced to the fact that the first principle of human knowledge has been either overlooked or misused by the metaphysicians.*

STUDY AIDS FOR PART ONE

Review Questions

1. What personal characteristics, according to Plato, are required for the study of metaphysics?

2. Does Plato discourage any and all attempts to set down metaphysics "in writing"? Explain.

3. What analogy does Plato use to describe the birth of metaphysical understanding in the mind?

4. What connection does Plato make between a spirit of reverence and the study of metaphysics? Is *true understanding* possible, according to Plato, without such a spirit? Give a reason.

5. What inner relation exists among the mental habits that Plato considers necessary for true understanding? Does one habit necessarily imply all or any others?

6. Why does Aristotle contend that the search for truth is both difficult and easy? What reasons does he give for each assertion?

7. In Aristotle's opinion, what does Wisdom "deal with"?

8. What characteristics does Aristotle attribute to the "wise man"? Enumerate them.

9. What evidence does Aristotle present to support his contention that "all men by nature desire to know"?

10. What does Forest mean by saying that metaphysics is "a taking possession both of ourselves and of the value of being"?

11. In what ways does Forest suggest that "metaphysics tends to become a work of art"?

12. What two kinds of metaphysics does Schopenhauer distinguish between?

13. What relation does Schopenhauer perceive between wonder and the feeling of contingency?

14. What reasons does Schopenhauer give for saying that "every physics" depends for its support on "a metaphysics"? What imperfections does he believe "merely physical explanations" suffer from? Why does he say that "naturalistic" explanations will never be sufficient?

15. What "threefold consideration" leads St. Thomas to say there is one science which is "mistress" of all others?

16. What accounts for the three names that St. Thomas applies to the knowledge of "first causes"?

17. Why does Bradley say that the sceptic is a "brother metaphysician"?

18. What three main objections against metaphysics does Bradley criticize?

19. Enumerate Gilson's "laws" of metaphysics.

20. According to Gilson, are the failures of metaphysics to be blamed on metaphysics, or on metaphysicians? Does he see any relation between the origin of metaphysics and the permanent occasion of its failures? Explain your answer.

21. Does Gilson believe that the mind "intuits" or "deduces" metaphysical truths?

Discussion Topics

1. Does Plato's explanation of the birth of metaphysical views have anything in common with the parable of the seeds in the Gospel of Matthew (13:4)? Can you think of any other scriptural parables suggested by Plato's metaphor?

2. Plato asserts that he has composed no other work in regard to metaphysics. How then can you explain the existence of the *Dialogues,* in which he apparently did write about this subject—and, by general acclaim, wrote about it very well?

3. What relation can you establish between Aristotle's conception of the wise man and Plato's conception of the philosopher in Book VI (esp. 484a–490d) of the *Republic?* Would they be the same or different men?

4. Aristotle claims that metaphysics is a "free science." Do you think there is any connection between this view and the socio-political situation of fourth-century (B.C.) Athenian democracy?

5. Compare Aristotle's treatment of the four "causes" in Book *Delta* (ii) of the *Metaphysics* with his treatment in the second book of the *Physics* (II.7). Can you think of some other word to substitute for his term "cause"? Are the causes he speaks of exhaustive categories, or are other terms possible? When Aristotle describes the term, he uses the analogy of a sculptor working on marble: the material cause is the marble being sculptured; the efficient cause is the artist; the formal cause is the specific statue being carved out; and the final cause—the purpose or end—is the "completed" statue as it existed in the mind of the artist before he began his work. Could his point be made just as well if the analogy were altered from that of sculptor to that of musical composer? What would the comparative terms be? What would they be for an oil painter, a lawgiver, and a dispensing chemist?

6. Aristotle indicates (*Posterior Analytics,* I, 17) that it is the office of only one science to demonstrate its own principles; and St. Thomas believes (*In Boethium De Trinitate,* II, q5, a3, ad6) that the more abstract a science, the more applicable are its principles to other sciences. In the light of these remarks is it a logical conclusion or a restatement of Aristotle and St. Thomas to say with Fulton J. Sheen (*The Philosophy of Science* [Milwaukee, Bruce Publishing Co., 1934], p. 57) that "sciences assume their own proximate first principles, which are proved by other superior sciences"? Do the remarks of Aristotle and St. Thomas imply that there is a hierarchy of sciences? Would they apply if there were no demonstrable hierarchy of sciences? Why? C. H. von Weizächer (*History of Nature* [Chicago, University of Chicago Press, 1949], p. 1) suggests that most scientists today are aware of the dangers of specialization, and "are longing for synthesis, searching for the point of vantage from which to gain perspective." Do you think he means a "metaphysical synthesis" or a "mathematical synthesis"? Canon Fernand Van Steenberghen (*Epistemology* [New York, J. F. Wagner, Inc., 1949], p. 293) anticipates that "the ideal of a unified knowledge might one day

be realized." On what basis do you suspect that he makes this statement? (Consult the sources of these quotations if you feel you need more evidence in order to judge.)

7. What relation can you draw between Kant's belief that the human mind will never give up metaphysical researches and Aristotle's contention that all men by nature desire to know? Are they saying the same thing? On what can you base your answer?

8. What relationship does Aristotle establish between theoretical and practical knowledge? How would this distinction account for the traditional view that logic, ethics, and aesthetics are considered "practical" instances of philosophy?

9. In the foregoing selections, Aristotle and St. Thomas seem both to agree and disagree that metaphysics is the highest form of knowledge attainable by man. In what way do they agree? Where do they disagree? Where do Gilson's sympathies lie—with Aristotle, with St. Thomas, or with both? With what qualifications? Do Schopenhauer and Bradley generally subscribe to Aristotle's usage of the term "metaphysics"? To St. Thomas's? Try to bring together the ways in which all five men understand the term "metaphysics."

10. If, as Forest says, the metaphysical task is to bring man to a state of self-awareness, how does this compare with Schopenhauer's "self-awareness"? What special differences can you discover in Schopenhauer's usage of the term "self-awareness" that set it apart from everyday usage?

11. What does Bradley mean by saying that metaphysics looks for "ultimate truths" and "first principles"? Would Aristotle and St. Thomas agree with this? In what way? Bradley denies that "speculation upon ultimate truths" is the highest calling of man. What do you suppose Aristotle would say to this? Would St. Thomas agree? Would St. Thomas, do you think, make a distinction between man's moral and his intellectual calling?

12. Gilson says that man is a metaphysical animal. So does Schopenhauer. Do they both mean the same thing by this term? In either case, give examples.

13. "It is the very nature of objections against philosophy," Gilson wrote in *The Unity of Philosophical Experience,* "to be unphilosophical." Bradley, on the other hand, says that objections to metaphysics are metaphysically relevant and assume the character of a rival metaphysics. Do these assertions automatically exclude one another, or are they equivalent statements? Explain.

14. Is "wonder" the same term for Schopenhauer and Aristotle? In what way does each thinker believe that metaphysics searches for the reasons "behind" things?

15. What common denominator can you discover in the following statements? What do these statements indicate about the metaphysical positions of their authors? Which statements seem to fit best with which other statements, or are they all saying the same thing?

§ ". . . the mental temperament . . . best suited to a philosophical training is . . . neither the impatient and high-flying, nor the unambitious and grovelling, but that which is in the mean between the two."—John of Salisbury, *Polycraticus.*

§ "Moral preparation is necessary for a man to be . . . upright and perfect. . . . For this reason alone one should not teach this subject [metaphysics] to the young. In any case they would not be able to acquire it because of their seething nature and the preoccupation of

their minds . . . in the burning flame of adolescence."—Moses Maimonides, *Guide to the Perplexed.*

§ "The intention of those sayings is to tell you that human intelligence has
a limit at which it stops."—Moses Maimonides, *op. cit.*

§ ". . . philosophic truth implies an initial act of submission and humility,
an admission by the reason that it cannot achieve its own end unaided
. . . ."—E. Gilson, *The Philosophy of St. Bonaventure.*

§ "There is no sin, however prone to it the philosopher may be, which
philosophy can justify so little as spiritual pride."—F. H. Bradley,
Appearance and Reality.

§ "In philosophy we must not seek for an absolute satisfaction. Philosophy
at its best is but an understanding of its object, and it is not an experience in which that object is contained wholly and possessed."—
F. H. Bradley, *Essays on Truth and Reality.*

§ "There is no one aspect deep enough to exhaust the contents of a real
idea, no one term or proposition which will serve to define it; though
of course one representation of it is more just and exact than another
. . . ."—J. H. Newman, *Essay on the Development of Christian Doctrine.*

§ "The invariable mark of wisdom is to see the miraculous in the common."—R. W. Emerson, *Nature.*

16. In *Theaetetus* (155d) and in *Metaphysics* (982), Plato and Aristotle
contend that wonder (*thaumázein*) is both the philosophical emotion and the
cause of philosophizing. Can it be both? In what way? J. V. Langmead Casserly
(*The Christian in Philosophy* [New York, Charles Scribner's Sons, 1951], p. 97)
suggests, "The experience which stings and goads the mind of man on to metaphysics has never yet been captured in a metaphysical definition, and perhaps never
will be." By the phrase, "The experience which stings and goads the mind of man
on to metaphysics," does he mean "wonder"? What makes you think so? With
how many of the statements in the preceding question (No. 15) would you link
this quote from Casserly? Which ones?

17. Metaphysics, says Jacques Maritain (*The Degrees of Knowledge* [New
York, Charles Scribner's Sons, 1938], p. 4), produces no experimental results, no
discoveries, no inventions; it is "useless." But, he points out, "one does not do
manual work in heaven." What does he mean by this? Which of the authors in
this section would agree with him? Why?

Research Themes

1. Read Plato's account of Socrates' speech in the *Symposium* (198a–212b),
and St. Thomas's discussion in *Summa Contra Gentiles* (III: 2–3, 17, 25, 37).
Compare the reasons they give for man's attraction to the study of metaphysical
realities. Read the "myth of the cave" at the beginning of Plato's *Republic*,
Book VII, to see if it casts any light on the passage 210b–211b of the *Symposium.*

THE SPIRIT OF METAPHYSICAL INQUIRY   52

Do you find that Plato's *Eros* appears in another form in St. Thomas's *Contra Gentiles?* Compare these two views with those expressed by Kant at the end of his *Prolegomena to Any Future Metaphysics* ("How is Metaphysics Possible as Science?") in which he states that metaphysical inquiry is inevitable. What relation does his statement have to the first sentence of Aristotle's *Metaphysics Alpha?* Is there any room for *Eros* in Kant's explanation? Summarize your findings in a 1,000-word essay.

2. Reconstruct the general viewpoints and arguments given by W. D. Ross (*Aristotle* [New York, Meridian Books, Inc., 1959], chapter 6) and Werner Jaeger (*Aristotle: Fundamentals of the History of His Development* [Oxford, Clarendon Press, 1950], Chapters VII and VIII), on the dates of composition of the *Metaphysics*. Establish the main lines of agreement and disagreement between them. Work out a 500-word argument to explain what concrete difference to the meaning of *Metaphysics* would be made if it were the product of Aristotle's later career in the Lyceum rather than of his earlier career in the Academy.

3. Analyze the selection "A Defense of Metaphysics" by F. H. Bradley, and compare it, theme for theme, with Chapter One of William James's *Some Problems of Philosophy* (New York, Longmans, Green & Co., 1911). Do you find evidence of common ground between the idealist Bradley and the pragmatist James? Can you find further evidence for, or against, your views in James's initial chapter ("The Present Dilemma in Philosophy") of his *Pragmatism* (New York: Longmans, Green & Co., 1907)?

4. Analyze the arguments set forth by Antonio Gomez Robledo in his article "The Concept of Wisdom in Aristotle" (*Philosophy Today,* II [1958], 189–195). What are the characteristics of Aristotle's notion of wisdom? How much mystery, according to Robledo, did Aristotle invest wisdom with? Was wisdom for him *fully* attainable? Summarize your analyses in a 750-word précis.

5. Read the short account of Sartre's terms *l'en-soi* (being-in-itself) and *le pour soi* (being-for-oneself) in Father I. M. Bochenski's *Contemporary European Philosophy* (Berkeley, 1956), pp. 173–181. Determine the relationship between these terms and Schopenhauer's distinction between the "thing-in-itself" and the "phenomenon," as expressed in the essay reprinted in this section. Set out your conclusions in a 300-word paper.

6. Write a 1,500- to 2,000-word essay on the background and meaning of Plato's *Seventh Epistle,* using the following sources: A. E. Taylor, *Plato, the Man and His Work* (6th ed.; New York, Meridian Books, Inc., 1957), Chapter I; L. A. Post, *Thirteen Epistles of Plato* (Oxford, Clarendon Press, 1925), pp. 56–61; G. C. Field, *Plato and His Contemporaries* (New York, Methuen, 1930), pp. 197 ff; Werner Jaeger, *Paideia* (New York: Oxford University Press, 1942) Vol. II, 82 ff., and Vol. III, pp. 212 ff. Reginald Hackforth, *The Authorship of the Platonic Epistles* (Manchester, Manchester University Press, 1913) may also prove helpful. What eminent conflicts do you find among these critics? Which one of them seems to make the strongest case for his views?

7. Werner Jaeger, in his book *Aristotle* (Oxford, Clarendon Press, 1950), says that the *Metaphysics* cannot be treated as a unity and that any attempt to treat it as such should be rejected. Eduard Zeller (*Outlines of the History of Greek Philosophy* [13th rev. ed.; New York, Meridian Books, Inc., 1957]) flatly denies the work's uniformity because he says it treats the same problems in different forms. The *Metaphysics* is not the expression of a dogmatic system, says Sir David Ross in his Introduction to Warrington's translation (New York, E. P. Dutton &

Co., 1956), but the adventurous record of a mind in search of truth. On the basis of your own investigation into these sources, draw up a paper of 1,000–1,500 words, spelling out the agreements between these citations. Indicate along what general lines they disagree. What divisions of the *Metaphysics* does Ross suggest? Which does Jaeger suggest? Which does Zeller suggest?

8. In the dialogue *Theaetetus* (155d) Socrates contends that "wonder" is *the* philosophical emotion, and implies that it initiates philosophical inquiry. Contrast this assertion with the account in the dialogue *Meno* (84c) that *aporía* (helplessness) initiates inquiry. Does Socrates' *aporía* have anything in common with Schopenhauer's "pain of life," as indicated by the selection in this section? Try to establish a relationship between Schopenhauer's "itching point of metaphysics," Sören Kierkegaard's *Angst,* and Jean-Paul Sartre's *Nausée.* Consult the account given by Frederick Copleston, S.J., in his book *Contemporary Philosophy* [Westminster, Md., Newman, 1956], pp. 125–227). You may also check accounts of Kierkegaard and Sartre in H. J. Blackham's *Six Existentialists* (New York, Harper & Bros., 1952), Chapters I and VI; or in F. J. Heinemann's *Existence and the Modern Predicament* (New York, Harper & Bros., 1959), Chapters III and VII. Determine from the same sources what Martin Heidegger means by the term *Dasein.* Is this term related to any, or all, of the above terms? Consult his essay "What is Metaphysics?" in *Existence and Being* (trans. Hull and Crick [Chicago, Henry Regnery Co., 1949], pp. 336 ff.). Read Blaise Pascal's *Pensées,* Numbers 205 and 206; do you find yet another connection? Make a catalogue of all the terms compared, explaining each in 50–100 words, and write a cover-report comparing all the terms.

9. Based on the conceptions of the philosophers reprinted in this section:

(A) Make a complete tabular list, in side-by-side columns, of the reasons given by each of the philosophers to explain man's attraction to metaphysics. Label this *Exhibit A.*

(B) With the information contained in *Exhibit A,* write a 1,500-word essay describing both differences and similarities in the views of these thinkers. Label this *Exhibit B.*

(C) Use the information in *Exhibit A* as the basis of a five- to ten-minute classroom defense of any thesis that you believe to be demonstrable from the citations at hand. For example, "Metaphysical opinions are the result of man's spiritual insecurity," or "Metaphysics is spiritually, emotionally, rationally, historically, and metaphysically defensible."

(D) Using *Exhibit A* as a group assignment for several students, prepare for a thirty-minute class discussion. Appoint someone to record any disagreements in interpretations that might arise during discussion. On the basis of such information try to establish how disagreements of this nature can arise.

(E) Have two or three students read their essays (*Exhibit B*), and allow members of the class to cross-examine the essayists on their interpretations.

10. When Aristotle says that "all men by nature desire to know," what does he mean by "nature"? Establish the meanings of this term on the basis of interpretations found in the following citations: W. D. Ross, *Aristotle* (New York, Meridian Books, Inc., 1959); Werner Jaeger, *Aristotle: Fundamentals of the History of His Development* (Oxford, Clarendon Press, 1950); A. E. Taylor, *Aristotle* (London, Nelson, 1945); Eduard Zeller, *Aristotle and the Earlier Peripatetics* (London, Longmans, 1897). Analyze the meanings given by Aristotle in *Metaphysics Delta.* Check these against R. G. Collingwood's treatment in *The Idea of*

Nature (New York, Oxford University Press, 1960), Part I, Chap. III, sect. 1. What difference can be found in Heidegger's observation on the term in his essay in Part Three of this volume? Present your conclusions in a 1,000- to 1,500-word essay.

SELECTED BIBLIOGRAPHY
FOR PART ONE

1. Buckley, G. M. *The Nature and Unity of Metaphysics.* Washington, D.C.: Catholic University of America, 1946.
2. Casey, J. T. *The Primacy of Metaphysics.* Washington, D.C.: Catholic University of America, 1935.
3. Church, A. "Ontological Commitment," *Journal of Philosophy,* 55 (1958), 1008–14.
4. Collins, J. "For Self-Examination of Neoscholastics," *Modern Schoolman,* 21 (1944), 225–34.
5. ————. "Metaphysics Under Fire," *America,* 98 (1957), 157–59.
6. Copleston, F. C., S.J. "Man and Metaphysics," *Heythrop Journal,* 1 (1960), 3–17.
7. Cunningham, G. W. "Must We All Be Thomists?" *Philosophical Review,* 57 (1948), 493–504.
8. Dingle, R. J. "Return to Metaphysics," *Nineteenth Century,* 138 (1945), 212–14.
9. Gilson, E. "Historical Research and the Future of Scholasticism," *Modern Schoolman,* 29 (1951), 1–10.
10. Gotshalk, D. W. "The Metaphysical Situation," *Philosophical Review,* 46 (1937), 513–22.
11. Hagen, O. "The Fear of Metaphysics," *Personalist,* 29 (1948), 369–76.
12. Harvanek, R. F., S.J. "The Unity of Metaphysics," *Thought,* 28 (1953), 375–412.
13. Heinemann, F. H. "The West in Search of Metaphysics," *Hibbert Journal,* 47 (1949), 132–37.
14. Hoernlé, R. F. A. *Studies in Contemporary Metaphysics.* New York: Harcourt, Brace & Co., 1920.
15. Holmes, F. O. "The Relevance of Metaphysics," *Hibbert Journal,* 57 (1958), 9–19.
16. Kane, W. H., O.P. "Introduction to Metaphysics," *Thomist,* 20 (1957), 121–42.
17. Kanz, Heinrich. "Humility Before Being," *Philosophy Today,* 1 (1957), 246–50.
18. Klubertanz, G. P., S.J. "The Teaching of Metaphysics," *Gregorianum,* 35 (1954), 3–17, 187–205.
19. Owens, Joseph, C.Ss.R. *St. Thomas and the Future of Metaphysics,* Milwaukee: Marquette University Press, 1957

20. Peirce, C. S. "The Approach to Metaphysics," in *Philosophical Writings of C. S. Peirce,* (ed. Justus Buckler). New York: Dover, 1955, pp. 310–14.
21. Simon, Yves. "Progress in Metaphysics," *Commonweal,* 42 (1945), 5–6.
22. Stace, W. T., Blake, R. M., and Murphy, A. E. "Can Speculative Philosophy Be Defended?" *Philosophical Review,* 52 (1943), 116–43.
23. Stallknecht, N. P. "In Defense of Ontology," *Journal of Philosophy,* 36 (1939), 40–48.
24. Weigel, Gustave, S.J. "Humani Generis: Existentialism and Catholic Doctrine," *Commonweal,* 54 (1951), 525.

Two　　　METAPHYSICAL METHOD

T
HIS SECTION IS CONCERNED WITH THE LEADING TYPES OF PROCEDURE
employed by different kinds of metaphysicians. In our introductory remarks
we shall propose four questions requiring some sort of answer:

1. What does the metaphysician generally expect from a methodology?
2. What usually determines the specific methodology he employs?
3. Is there any "simple" classification of methodologies?
4. What would a "realistic" methodology be?

I

Until perhaps the time of Descartes, Hume, and Kant, the question of
methodology was not so much *assumed,* as *presumed*—not questioned, but
accepted. Ancient and medieval thinkers, of course, had their own way of
doing things. In many cases, they had rather effective ways. But they were
not oriented to the sort of critical and "retro-analytic" techniques that have
characterized metaphysics since Descartes.

For one thing, with Descartes and Kant and their successors, a new and
self-conscious spirit took hold, which was marked by a critical distrust in the
adequacy of language to translate perceptions into propositions and in the
method of "introspection," with its "strained attention," as the basis of rational
theory. Where, previously, noncritical practitioners had only attempted to
expose the "facts" of human experience, critical technicians began to ask,
"What *are* facts?" and "Are there any facts that are *the* facts?"

One of the obvious bases for such questions has been the realization of
how few "facts" can be agreed upon universally. It becomes evident that
facts are never given innocently, but require a system of interpretation, in
which they are understood to *be* facts. And it became recognized that there
are no "brute self-contained matters of fact," as Bradley once put it. There
are no blank checks signed by experience because, in order for experience to
be recognized *as* experience, some prior interpretation must be present. "If
we desire a record of uninterpreted experience," Whitehead points out, "we

must ask a stone to record its autobiography." Hence, certain facts, it seemed clear, are always seen in relation to other facts. No fact stands alone; it leans on other facts, which support and develop it.

The paradox in all this is that such critical technique, however genuine, may be a *cul-de-sac*. Criticism is itself a canon of judgment, and must therefore decide between facts that are meaningful—to it—and facts that are not. Like the "brute fact" it so cavalierly brushes aside, critical technique already implies analysis, which, in turn, implies speculation and speculative doctrine. If the brute fact, as Bradley suggested, is "an ideal scheme of terms and relation . . . in brief, your own half-thought-out theory," so too is the critical device. The conclusion is therefore obvious. Method—even critical method—is hoisted by its own logic. It is not something that precedes metaphysical inquiry but something that follows upon it—or at least arises simultaneously with it.

In saying this, we are not pretending to deny everything that critical technique says about all unadorned facts. We are simply asserting that what it says can be applied to its own procedure. Preoccupation with method, therefore, indicates certain antecedent conditions. Metaphysics does not settle upon one method and then set down to work. On the contrary. Rather than initiating inquiry, method is dependent on an implicit metaphysical judgment, and indicates that metaphysical practice is already in evidence. Far from being a point of origin, method is the first station on a journey already begun. Although the work of method is control of data, it is contingent on a prior decision to determine what kind of control is necessary and what kinds of data are to be employed. Once the subject of metaphysical procedure is introduced, one's metaphysics has evidently shown the direction it is willing to take as a consequence, and has therefore already been, in one or another form, in operation.

As Father Lonergan and Whitehead note below, method is dictated by theory, not the other way around. In other words, one looks for what one expects eventually to find.

II

Thus, deeper than the question of method is the question of *expectation*. If the question of methodology is equivalent to asking of a metaphysician, "What kinds of facts do you think you should be concerned with?" then the prior question is, "What basic attitudes do you bring to your search for metaphysical facts?" For instance, it would be hard to imagine the geometric and God-intoxicated Spinoza publicizing some low form of hedonism. It would be equally difficult to imagine pleasure-loving Aristippus leading the restricted life of a lens-grinder.

Fundamental attitudes, we can say then, precondition—perhaps even determine—the decision to look for some facts and to ignore others. Historicist Wilhelm Dilthey may have gone too far in suggesting that the pre-

requisite of sound philosophical work is the ability to discover one's fundamental attitude to the world, and the assumptions involved in such an attitude.
But, on the other hand, he was not too far wrong.

Of all the attitudes toward procedure, two have had special influence. For
the sake of a name they might be called "scientific" and "rational" procedures.

Perhaps the modern world's chief methodological bias is the "scientific
attitude." Empirical science has doubtless become the model of serious discourse, and its influence on metaphysical methodology, as we shall later see,
has been crucial.

From many quarters come enthusiastic claims for the "truth-values" that
scientific control makes possible. Often the metaphysician stands by helplessly
while the scientist expatiates on the virtues of his technique. "Results," the
metaphysician will be told, "have borne out our claims, have they not?" Not
altogether, the metaphysician might point out—if he could add a word. The
scientist may, of course, maintain that his method is only describing the facts.
But in reality it is selecting the facts that he describes. And, as we have already pointed out, selection of any kind depends upon a theory of selection.
Moreover, once the scientist begins to make universal statements about a
universal methodology, he moves into the arena of metaphysics.

Another basic attitude that colors methodological questions is that of the
deductive system. Though held in disrepute by some, the classic deductive
systems of Descartes, Spinoza, and Hegel are still admired, and have exerted—
for good or evil—considerable influence to this day. The central contention
of rational systematizers is that the human mind, following its own deductive
procedure, can reconstruct the whole of reality from certain crucial axioms.
They assume that nature is orderly and uniform, and is constructed along the
same logical lines as those of the human mind. Once the rationalist metaphysician exposes the leading axiomatic threads—or central truths—of reality,
therefore, he need simply unravel their necessary consequences. He creates an
understanding of the world by creating a logical model of it. "Reality," he
says, "*must* be this way since this is what follows from our premises."

Rational procedure, however, has had to withstand a double attack. It
has been assaulted, in the first place, on grounds that logic is *not* the prime
metaphysical tool. Furthermore, the modern world has developed too many
kinds of logic, each of which has its own presuppositions; hence, one must ask,
"Which logic shall be used?" In the second place, it has been criticized for its
contention that basic propositions are neither universally accessible nor
necessarily attainable. Some of its critics have even gone so far as to point out
that rationalism is only a myth that "rational" men live by. The question of
what deserves the title rational is, they argue, not at all plain. What does
rational really mean?

If by rational A means, "What A can understand," it is evident there is no
guarantee that what A understands, B also can understand; and conversely.

If A means, "What everybody can understand," he touches the very heart of the problem, and would have to count noses to substantiate his claim. Clearly, not all men understand alike. Indeed, were it otherwise, there would never be disagreement among philosophers. But since there are such disagreements, in some form or other, one must question the premise that contains the original assertion. One cannot dismiss the whole affair by saying, "Be sensible. Do it my way" because "my way" may not also be "your way." Furthermore, the assertion that *only* deductive methodologies lead to metaphysical truth can hardly be maintained in the face of these difficulties of consensus.

But we should make clear the fact that the label "rational" is neither to be condemned without distinction nor to be confused with methods that are essentially reasonable. A more realistic form of rational method is suggested by Jacques Maritain when he says that it is that by which "the mind lays hold of substantial essences, not in themselves, but by their rightful accidentals, and only advances deductively by a constant revitalization by experience." The mind, which Maritain considers to be an instrument cut out to conquer reality, thus approaches reality, in this form of rationalism, in an open-handed fashion and begins to read the inner character of reality—*intima rei intus legere* (St. Thomas); it does this through a metaphysical intuition that is amplified by direct experience and deductive control. According to this use of the term, the mind is directed to the penetration of things, and not confined to the task of "finding its own face." "In the mind," A. D. Sertillanges has said, "we have the means of seeing, not the object of sight."

III

Is there, nevertheless, some general way of grouping metaphysical procedures? Loosely speaking, there is, if we agree to distinguish those methods that qualify the "facts" of inner life from those that look to "facts" external to the inquiring self. The former way may be termed "introspective method" because it begins from the point of view of the knower as such, and works outward. Rationalist, intuitivist, existentialist, emotivist, and personalist methodologies would fall under this class. The latter may be called "extraspective method" because it is rooted in "existents" outside and independent of the knower. Experimentalist, realist, empiricist, and objectivist methodologies are of this type. The first type generally looks for facts about and of the knower; the second, for facts external to the knower. Each will use techniques precisely adjusted to the demands of its respective assumptions—for example, that internal data are more important than external data, or conversely. So far, no thinker, including Husserl, has tried to use introspective techniques to control empirical data or extraspective analysis to determine personal states.

Of course, in one sense the division is essentially unfair—or at least as unfair as the classical distinction between subjectivist and objectivist. The object-centered methodology, oriented to the nonself, cannot escape the task of internalizing its object in the knowing self. The self, however, is not an object, over against and opposed to other objects. It can "enflesh" instances of the world-at-large in a special way, by intellectually *becoming* them (St. Thomas) or *having* them (St. Augustine). In knowledge—if not in other types of experience—an intimate connection exists between self and nonself. A realistic methodology would make this intimacy unquestionable and would make use of both object-orientation and subject-orientation.

IV

We may conclude, therefore, by observing that an authentic methodology must not be of one kind but of several kinds. It would be engineered to consider many different kinds of facts that make up reality. It would maintain relations with the best characteristics of each of several procedures.

What would a "realistic" methodology then be? We would suggest that it meet the following paradoxical requisites.

It should be open to the invitation of empirical observation without turning into a catalogue. It should fit the demands of common sense, as well as those of uncommon sense, and take due account of the forms of doubt, as well as of the illusions of deduction. It should be logical, but not simply formalistic, and work between description and interpretation—fitting its elements to their logical foundations and its logic to the nature of things. It should enter spiritually into the presence of each individual reality, while at the same time retaining a sense of the utter objectivity of its ontological relations to every reality. It should retain a feeling for process and development, as well as for durability and achievement, and should unfold the mystery of being—not as one unfolds a newspaper but as one develops the inner knowledge of a person. It should be neither too cautious nor too headlong, neither judge nor advocate, but, instead, arbitrator of the rights of sweeping vision and detailed distinction. It should not remain outside the object, nor separate its own dialectic from the real ground of thought. For it is dialectic, as Hegel puts it, "that moves it on." The same logic that resides in the thing resides in the person, and an authentic methodology should give reverent ear to the claims of both the interpreted and the interpreter.

Dietrich von Hildebrand   1. METHODOLOGICAL
                                      PITFALLS

The problems presented by metaphysics, Professor von Hildebrand points out in
the following essay, do not suffer the easy categorization attainable in
empirical sciences. To follow the path laid out by such sciences would be
to subject philosophical analysis to nonphilosophical criteria.

For one thing, he says, the empirical scientist automatically falls into the
habit of looking for "linear causes," assuming that what is known is only
causally related to what is unknown. For another, the scientist assumes
that all theoretical relations are governed by the inferential norms that
enable him to deduce the unknown from the known. Further, he expects
that each element of his analysis can be fully defined so that it may be
assigned an unmistakable and unalterable position in the deductive edifice.
It is the *system,* therefore, that becomes the *sine qua non* of his activity.

Yet in fact, von Hildebrand contends, such an approach—which has its
own proper place in the natural sciences—cannot but have harmful consequences in metaphysics. Metaphysical problems must take account of
the plenitude of real, rather than artificial, beings. The metaphysician who
feels he cannot reconcile certain fundamental facts has no right to follow
the example of the natural scientist and fling away contradictions. Hence
the cults of *deduction, premature systematization,* or *reconciliation* cannot
but work against metaphysical procedure. Metaphysical method demands
"the constant readiness to revise, modify, or give up any hypothesis" that
cannot face up to ontological standards. And rather than cripple reality,
metaphysics must stand ready to follow its lead without expecting to exhaust, by mere logic, its full possibilities.

THE ATTITUDE TOWARD a philosopher and his theses is often prejudiced by
a tendency to classify prematurely. Sometimes such classification has a historical character, as when one automatically approaches every philosophical
work with the disposition of characterizing the author as a Thomist, an
Augustinian, a Kantian, a Spinozist, a Hegelian, and so forth. Instead of
giving the author credit for some originality, one assumes quite arbitrarily
that, after all, he must be a commentator or at least a formal disciple of some
other well-known philosopher. From the start one looks at his ideas and

theses from this point of view, under this uncalled-for expectation, and consequently bars oneself from a real understanding of his ideas.

This tendency becomes especially grotesque when the main reason for such a classification is a merely terminological similarity. For example, there are some who appear to believe they have sufficient evidence for calling an author strictly a Kantian, simply because they have found in his work the terms "categorical" obligation or *a priori*. . . .

There are philosophers who take it for granted that everything which is accessible to our immediate experience is doubtful, subjective, or at best only a secondary aspect of reality which cannot demand or win our full attention and interest. Some of these philosophers will announce as their proud discovery that there is a total discrepancy between reality and the data given in our prephilosophical experience. They will tell us that in reality a color is nothing but a vibration, beauty nothing but a contraction of the viscera, love nothing but a mere sexual instinct, and so forth.

These men will identify the object either with something related to it by causality, or with something which is in some other way connected with it. Such identification simply confuses the philosophical approach with the approach proper to natural science. Physics, chemistry, or biology not only may discover beings of which we had not the slightest idea in our prescientific knowledge, for instance, certain glands or microbes or cosmic rays, but may also show us that certain things which seem to be quite distinct in our naive experience are in reality the same.

Legitimate as this method of reduction is for the natural sciences with their own special objects and their own purposes of knowledge, it is impossible concerning the objects of philosophy and of no avail toward the end of philosophical knowledge. Philosophy will never discover anything which is absolutely alien to our prephilosophical knowledge. It cannot possibly discover that two different things, such as knowledge and will, are in reality one and the same thing, or that justice in reality is nothing but a fruit of bitter grievance of the weak and mediocre (i.e., what, to be more accurate, we call *ressentiment*). It is quite reasonable to state that a man who pretends to be just is in reality only moved by *ressentiment,* but it is absurd to say that justice is in reality a *ressentiment* of the weak. Granted that it could be maintained that real justice cannot be found anywhere in this world, it is still absurd to say that justice as such is only an invention of the weak in order to overcome the strong. The first thesis can be true or false; the second is simply nonsensical. . . .

Certain authors consider a work as philosophical only when the topic is brought into a system. We grant that it surely belongs to philosophy to treat its topics in a systematic way. We grant, moreover, that it is not enough to discover several important facts without discussing the reaction existing between them, without connecting them with more general facts. In the systematic analysis of a thing it is indispensable that we proceed step by step. But between systematic analyses and the building up of a system there is a great difference. Certainly an ideal fulfillment of an adequate knowledge of the universe would require a system which completely corresponded to the architecture of the universe. But this could obviously be attained only at the end of all philosophical investigation. Granted that certain fundamental general features of being are the first to disclose themselves to us, and that every further step of investigation of a special topic goes hand in hand with some new general differentiations, we must yet be aware of the great danger of a premature systematization.

In the first place, as soon as we believe that from certain general principles we can deduce the rest of the universe, we are bound to build up a system which is not in conformity with reality. . . .

Thus the first danger of premature systematization lies in the temptation to deduce as much as possible from certain general principles. This leads to overlooking all those realities which necessarily require an original intuition in order to be grasped. And this means a crippling of reality in its most general and basic features from the start. . . .

A definition can never exhaust the plenitude of a necessary, intelligible essence; it can only circumscribe it by mentioning some essential features which suffice to distinguish this essence from another. The definition helps also to give a concept of a univocal precision. Only artificial beings which are deprived of an ontological plenitude, only technical objects and mere instruments, can be exhausted by definition. But as soon as we are no longer confronted with artificial beings, we are faced more and more with the mysteries of being; and then our definition should not pretend to exhaust the nature of this being, but only the modest aspiration to fix it univocally by concept. As soon as we believe we have definitely conquered a being intellectually because we have a correct definition of it, we deceive ourselves. Certainly the highest form of philosophical penetration implies the insight into all those necessary facts rooted in the essence, all the essential marks of this being. However, these insights precisely presuppose an intellectual intuition of the object, a full grasping of its nature; they cannot possibly be discovered by approaching the object as if it were readily accessible to our minds by a deduction from other more general notions of being. The anxiety to attain a definition as quickly as possible may well exclude us forever from any genuine insight into the object. . . .

Another danger lurks in a premature systematization: the tendency we have to be caught up by the immanent logic of a system, and to become more anxious to preserve the consistency of this system than to do justice to the nature of a being. The interpretation of a new datum is then determined more and more by the frames built up in the system than by the nature of the object. Even if a philosopher avoids the error of attempting to deduce this datum from general principles, he will nevertheless be blinded to the understanding of the nature of this new datum if he is more preoccupied by fitting it into a system than by the adequate study of the datum itself.

I am not thinking of evident alternatives and general principles which are constantly at the basis of all knowledge, for instance, the alternative of existence or nonexistence: the principle of contradiction. Such general principles must be continuously presupposed in approaching any being; without them everything would become nonsensical. I am thinking of a system which naturally is not composed exclusively of self-evident principles, but which to a large extent consists in explanations, interpretations of the immediately given by means of theories which, whether plausible or not, in any case, have only the character of hypotheses, and not the character of absolutely certain insights into an intrinsically necessary fact.

But obviously the ideal way of proceeding would be the constant readiness to revise, modify, or give up any hypothesis which a new datum renders impossible. Instead of adapting, like Procrustes, the people to the bed, we should always be ready to adapt the bed to the people. . . .

Instead of escaping from these problems by means of violating or denying the true nature of a being, the problems which arise should inspire a new effort to dig deeper, a readiness to accept the difficulties and tiresome task of grappling further with them. We should understand that and wholeheartedly acknowledge this invitation to seek the solution to a problem in a deeper stratum.

This brings us to a third, most important principle: We are not allowed to give up something which has disclosed itself to us unequivocally because we are unable to answer many problems which arise with the admission of this fact. Cardinal Newman stresses this fundamental truth with respect to the content of our faith, in his famous words: "Ten thousand difficulties do not make a single doubt."

Sometimes the reconciliation of fundamental facts is impossible to attain on a level of our natural knowledge. We cannot understand, for example, how freedom and predestination can coexist, nor even how human freedom can be reconciled with efficacious grace. But this should not shake our absolute certitude that both exist. Again, the existence of evil in a world created by an absolutely wise, absolutely powerful, and infinitely good God will always remain an inscrutable mystery. Should we therefore deny the existence of evil in order to escape from this dilemma? Or should we deny the existence of God, because of this indubitable existence of evil? No, we must have the courage to say: I see something with absolute certitude, and I also see something else with absolute certitude. I shall adhere to both even if I know not how they can be reconciled.

Everett W. Hall   # 2. IS THERE A STRICTLY
                             METAPHYSICAL METHOD?

Metaphysics, says Professor Hall, deals with general statements about all kinds of
reality, or with "whatever can be asserted of anything whatever." It tries
to get at "universal constants," as in Berkeley's "*esse est percipi,*" Schelling's "the world is subject-object," or Whitehead's "events are prehensions." Metaphysics does not follow the hypothesis-deduction-verification
technique of the empirical sciences. One cannot claim to give significant
positive verification to metaphysical hypothesis. Metaphysical hypotheses
cannot be translated into predictions, or become the basis for prediction,
as can their scientific counterparts. Verificatory methods are unreliable in
metaphysics.

Metaphysics, however, may use illustrative, rather than verificatory, instances of hypothesis. These can both clarify the meaning of hypotheses
and stimulate the imaginative insight into—or "sizing up" of—large portions of experience in order to locate *dis*verificatory instances. Because
decisive disverification is possible for metaphysics, says Hall, it should be
employed more often and more knowingly. For example, when a materialist
says that every existent has spatio-temporal location, the metaphysician
may attempt to find an existent that does *not* have spatio-temporal location and to disverify such a contention.

Thus, the metaphysician cannot simply ape scientific methodology, for he
would then apply scientific norms to nonscientific subject matter. To do so
would be "a mark of immaturity, of childish imitativeness that seeks the
semblance without the substance of adulthood." The metaphysician "must
rely on total insight," not on mechanical procedures, which can be handled
by clerks.

. . . IT IS A wide-spread (metaphysical) assumption of our age that the
scientific method is the only admissible cognitive method. It has become quite
popular for scientists to argue that ethics is a legitimate field of inquiry, therefore it must become a science, since only scientific method yields knowledge.
So, supposing it comes to be admitted that metaphysics is a permissible field of
inquiry, it might be urged that it should become a science. My reaction can
be anticipated. Metaphysics is concerned with more general problems than

This selection is extracted from a chapter that originally appeared in *Twentieth Century
Philosophy*, edited by Dagobert D. Runes and published by the Philosophical Library, Inc.
(New York, 1948). It is used with the kind permission of the publisher.

are the sciences, and these by their very generality require appropriate methods not utilized in the sciences. Scientific method (if we may speak of anything so manifold as *a* method) is the best method there is, in the sense that it gives us the most reliable evidence *for the sort of beliefs it properly examines.* But it does not follow that it is the best in the sense of the most appropriate to *every* belief. Even within science it is important to distinguish between the problems, "What method is most reliable absolutely?" and "What method is most reliable for a given subject matter?" Many biologists and social scientists argue: "Physics has developed the most reliable procedures, therefore we should adopt its methods in our field." They fail to see that, *when applied to biological or sociological phenomena,* the physicist's methods may be less reliable, since less relevant, than distinctively biological or sociological methods. So, although it is true that scientific methods are more reliable in science than metaphysical methods are in metaphysics, still, I contend, metaphysics should develop its own relevant procedures and not try to force scientific methods to function in its field.

The propositions to which scientific method is appropriate are general, but never completely general, they are of the form, "Every so-and-so is such-and-such" not "Everything whatever or everything observable or experienceable is such-and-such." Clearly pure induction could not go very far towards establishing a completely general belief. For the wider the generalization beyond particular instances observed the weaker the evidential value of these instances. In any case, pure induction plays a minor role in science. Of far greater significance in science and of greater reliability in establishing wide generalizations is the hypothesis-deduction-verification method. This method makes a rather sudden leap (usually mediated by accepted theories) from a set of phenomena to be explained (usually disverificatory of an already accepted theory) to a hypothetical explanation (set in a context of rival, incompatible hypothetical explanations). Then deductions from this hypothesis are made, giving conclusions that can be checked against direct observations. The acceptability of an hypothesis is partly "absolute," i.e., a matter of the number and spread of the verificatory observations, and partly "relative," i.e., a matter of the ratio of its absolute acceptability to that of each rival hypothesis.

It is necessary to examine a little further this matter of verification. An admissible scientific hypothesis is one which is capable of significant, positive verification. This means that it asserts that the phenomenon to be explained is really a variable function of certain variable conditions or factors. When the conditions vary in certain ways, the phenomenon will vary in a certain way (simplest case being, the phenomenon occurs under certain conditions, does not under others). Suppose the phenomenon to be the pressure of a constant quantity of gas. The hypothesis might then be that this is a function of temperature and volume. Positive verification becomes significant because we do not merely add similar confirming observations (this would reduce the process to simple induction instituted by a guess as to its outcome), but because we can increase relevantly dissimilar confirming observations. We find by varying the conditions of volume and temperature that the pressure varies as the hypothesis asserts. This analysis likewise holds of disverificatory observations. Now this sort of thing obtains only if we are dealing with a variable phenomenon under variable conditions. But in metaphysics we are attempting to get at certain "universal constants," what the scholastics called "transcendentals" (not because they transcended all experience, but because they were a constant factor in every experience). A universal constant is whatever can be asserted of anything whatever (or of everything, where "everything" is taken distributively). Here, "can be asserted" means that the assertion must be such that it can be expressed by a meaningful sentence. The only meaningless sentences are those which confuse different semantic levels. I am supposing that a set of words must obey the grammatical rules of the language or it isn't a sentence at all. Again, "anything whatever" does have a restriction; it refers only to that which can be referred to in what the logical positivists call "the object language." That is, it excludes symbolic expressions in their referential aspect (though not as facts, e.g., as marks or vocal emissions).

With this definition of "universal constant" we are in a position to essay a definition of "metaphysics."

Metaphysics is the investigation of the meaning and the evidence for the following types of propositions:

(1) Propositions whose subjects are universal constants, or approximations thereto (such as existence, value, knowledge).

(2) Propositions whose subjects are the main classes or kinds of things of which universal constants can be predicted (such as minds, bodies).

(3) Propositions whose subjects are universal constants as qualified by the defining properties of the classes referred to in (2) (such as mental existence, physical existence).

There are strictly three universal constants: existence, knowledge, and value. (Thus three main subdivisions of metaphysics: ontology, epistemology, and axiology.) But of these existence is peculiar, for knowledge and value are universal constants only potentially and relatively; existence is a universal constant actually and per se. Not everything is a case of knowledge, nor an object of knowledge. Knowledge can be predicated of anything one chooses only in that the thing is knowable, that is, *can be* known *by* a knower under suitable conditions. Likewise for value. Not everything is a case of value (positive or negative). Value can be predicated of anything one chooses only in that that thing is capable of value, that is, *can be* valued *by* a valuer under suitable conditions. But existence is not thus relative to a possible process on the part of some entity other than that exhibiting it.

A metaphysical hypothesis about the general nature of existence or knowledge asserts something equally of all possible observations: the observation is a knowledge of some existent (or existents). And it is not a matter of degree; any actual observation is equally cognitive and existential. You may have more knowledge and more existence in the sense of more instances, but not in the sense that the nature of either is capable of degree. It is thus not possible to give a significant positive verification of a metaphysical hypothesis, i.e., to observe whether existence varies in an asserted fashion with some variation in the conditions of existence. In fact, "the conditions of existence" is itself a misleading phrase. *Any* conditions, if they actually obtain, are existent. We cannot put various conditions together and *then* get something existent, as though we could have conditions before we had anything existent. So Berkeley's "*esse est percipi,*" Hobbes's "the universe is the aggregate of all bodies," Schelling's "the world is subject-object," Whitehead's "events are prehensions," are all assertions of universal constants; any *actual* instance of any general term, these propositions assert, is an instance of the constants involved.

This view that metaphysics is more general than the special sciences, should not be confused with two other views. On the one hand, it should not be confused with the doctrine that metaphysics simply puts together, into one total picture, items furnished it by the sciences. Metaphysical hypotheses are more general than scientific hypotheses not simply in that they are more inclusive in scope, i.e., cover more instances, but in that they are more inclusive *by being more abstract.* The sciences do make assertions about existents; but they are concerned with what *sorts of thing* exist, and the causal dependences in their existence; but metaphysics is concerned with what their *existence* is, what it is to come into existence or cease to be. On the other hand, the view here advocated must be distinguished from the doctrine that philosophy is simply a study of the sciences themselves. I have already criticized the attempt to restrict philosophy to a study of the language of science. I would also oppose the restriction of philosophy to a study of the methodology of science. Any significant methodology is relevant to its proper subject matter. A thorough investigation of methodology considers this factor, and therefore concerns itself with subject matter. Philosophy is as concerned with *what* is known by science as with *how* it is known by science. Furthermore, the sciences are as concerned with their methods as they are with what these methods tell them of the world. The distinction of philosophy from science is not that science investigates the world, and philosophy investigates this investigation. The distinction is one of level of abstractness. In the old terminology, philosophy is concerned with "categorial" analysis.

Furthermore, the fact that the basic concepts of metaphysics are universal constants ("transcendentals," or "categories") indicates why metaphysical propositions are not, in general, translatable into predictions or made the premises from which (with the aid of data stating initial conditions of systems) predictions can be derived. Some scientific concepts are strictly universal or universal throughout an existential realm, as for example, energy. Every physical existent has an energy-characteristic. But this varies for different existents. Thus, it has predictive significance. Existence, on the other hand, is not only universal. It is constant. It is the same in amount everywhere. Thus, it has only "analytic," not predictive, significance.

Clearly then the most reliable method of establishing general beliefs in science, the verificatory, is not available in metaphysics, at least as the basic or distinctive metaphysical method. What are we to do, supposing we still persist in seeking a fitting method of metaphysical investigation? We may, in the first place, play up the difference of metaphysics from science. We may suppose that the factor in metaphysical method differentiating it from scientific is some new, positive factor wholly different from accredited scientific procedure. Let me give two instances. First, there is what I shall call "temperamentalism." It claims that the metaphysician, when making broader generalizations than the scientist, is simply expressing his own, individual temperament. The metaphysician goes beyond scientific findings only by relying on his emotions, his will to live, his faith, on tendencies in his nature other than the critical, empirical-mindedness embodied in science. This point of view is, supposedly, corroborated by the controversies in metaphysics; such controversies spring solely from differences of temperament.

Temperamentalism can, of course, be decidedly baneful to metaphysics. Since what is distinctively metaphysical is based on mere temperament, it may be supposed it has no adequate foundation in objective fact and is, therefore, only of psychological significance. But this supposition remains a sheer supposition unless some evidence for it is forthcoming. And this evidence would have to be of the form "metaphysical beliefs are found (1) to be functions of temperaments of their proponents (2) *and of nothing else.*" There may be some evidence of type (1), though it is not very impressive. For a major portion of the evidence as to what a metaphysician's temperament is is usually precisely his metaphysical beliefs, a very obvious vicious circle. And evidence of type (2) is almost wholly lacking. That is, it is not shown that some determination of metaphysical beliefs by temperament may not also be determination by, e.g., the very object of those beliefs. It may well be that *some* metaphysicians are temperamentally better metaphysicians than others, their beliefs are determined by a temperament more in accord with, better suited to discover, the features of the world constituting their objects. And that this is not the case can hardly be made out by the psychologist; for it requires a knowledge of precisely those aspects of things about which the metaphysician makes assertions—i.e., it would itself be a case of metaphysics, and so fall under its own condemnation.

To make this more pointed, consider a certain type of materialism. It says that all metaphysical beliefs, as contrasted with scientific, are simply expressions of temperament, and that temperament, in turn, is wholly a function of physiological processes, such as secretion of endocrine glands, rate of basic metabolism, etc. There are, it would say, no spiritual forces or insights, only various physical processes. Such a position, however, obviously displays the fallacy I shall call "assumption of special privilege." It supposes that its own materialistic metaphysical beliefs are not merely functions of its adherents' physiological processes, but are determined by their objects, e.g., the physiological processes of other metaphysicians.

But now let it be admitted that temperamentalism is itself metaphysical, and hence cannot be used to destroy all metaphysics. It follows that at least some determination of metaphysical beliefs by temperament is taken to be legitimate. We are now told that science alone is not enough, that life is more than scientific intelligence, that man is incurably metaphysical and instead of being ashamed of the fact he should openly avow it. Temperament may give truths forever closed to mere science. This deferential appeal to temperament may take two forms. First there is the aristocratic form, which supposes some temperaments are better, in this function of giving us metaphysical *aperçus,* than others. James's "tough-minded" temperament is illustrative. But when we ask for a standard on which we may rank temperaments, difficulties arise. For it would seem that, apart from the human but unwarrantable tendency to elevate one's own type of temperament to first place in any comparison, the only standard forthcoming would be one which takes account of objective fact, which says, "That temperament is metaphysically more reliable which is more in accord with, i.e., can give us a less warped account of, the general nature of existence and knowledge." But this is unmistakably an abandonment of temperamentalism.

The other deferential form of temperamentalism is democratic. It asks us to be tolerant, to remember that we are all metaphysicians at heart, that no one can legitimately set up his temperamental reaction to the universe as better than another's. F. C. S. Schiller's relativistic temperamentalism is illustrative. This of course requires a relativistic theory of truth, at least as far as metaphysical issues are concerned. If the tender-mindedness of an idealist is equally good, as a determinant of metaphysical beliefs, as is the tough-mindedness of a materialist, then "The world is my idea" is equally as well established as "The world is bodies in motion." Each is true for its advocate, false for its opponent, and there is an end to the matter. But is this temperamentalism as democratic and tolerant as it would make out? Suppose it faces an aristocratic temperamentalist or a nontemperamentalist. Then it blandly asserts its own tolerance by saying, "Of course my democratic temperamentalism is simply true for me; it is not true for you, *your* view is true for you." Isn't this the very acme of tolerance? No. It is one of the most despicable (since dishonest) forms of intolerance. For such a statement (in quotes above) presupposes the universal truth of nonrelative temperamental relativism and the falsity of any opposing view. To be really tolerant it would have to say not merely "Your denial of temperamental relativism is true *for you*" (for that would be entirely compatible with the truth of temperamental relativism, and is not at all what an opponent claims), but also "and it may be true *in an absolute sense,* quite independent of the temperament of its advocate." But if the temperamental relativist thus really becomes tolerant, he has fallen into self-contradiction: he has admitted a nonrelative truth. However, he need not blame his excessive tolerance. He supposed from the beginning that temperamental relativism was true in a nonrelative sense, was true for every temperament, even those to which it was not temperamentally attractive. Thus his position essentially requires the fallacy of the assumption of special privilege. And this, I think, is the case with all forms of temperamentalism. Each supposes *it* has the "low-down" on all types of temperament and their relation to metaphysical beliefs, that the temperament of *its* advocates can be disregarded, that it is determined by objective fact, all *other views* by the temperament of their advocates.

Besides temperamentalism let us consider what I shall call "definitionism" as an example of a view of metaphysical method stressing its basic difference from scientific method. Science, on this view, is basically concerned with ascertaining the truth or falsity of propositions, metaphysics simply with the laying down and analytical elaboration of definitions of its characteristic terms, such as "existence" or "knowledge." It is supposed that definitions are not judgments, involve no elements of assertion, thus cannot be true or false, though they may be more or less "convenient." Rather, definitions are simply expressions of arbitrary volition as to how the author intends to use the term defined.

Now let us inquire as to definitionism itself. Is *its* position simply a matter of definition—does it simply say, "I define 'metaphysics' and 'definition' so that it follows that metaphysics is not concerned with questions of truth and falsity"? If so, then definitionism is merely an expression of the arbitrary volition of the definitionist, is neither true nor false, and cannot oppose other views as to the difference of metaphysical from scientific method. If it be definitional in basis, it cannot say, "There is no other way of reliably ascertaining truth than the scientific," for this would be passing judgment; nor again can it say, "No metaphysician, so-called, has ever in the past, or will in the future, do anything but lay down and elaborate definitions," for this again would be passing a judgment. This surely is not a very formidable foe to any other view of metaphysical method.

On the contrary, let us suppose definitionism to be nondefinitional in basis, to be assertive of fact. Then it is claiming that the enterprise commonly referred to as "metaphysics" is simply a process of defining, and that the process commonly referred to as "defining" is merely a matter of expressing one's arbitrary intention as to the use of the terms defined. If definitionism be thus assertive, it is definitely false. For most metaphysicians, so-called, e.g., Plato,

Aristotle, Thomas Aquinas, Spinoza, have not simply laid down and elaborated intentions as to their use of words; they have made claims, passed judgments, about the nature of knowledge and about what exists and what it is to exist. If it be said that they really didn't present any empirical evidence for the truth of their assertions, that what they thought was evidence was simply an elaboration of definitions previously laid down, one could retort that this is not so, that some of them, at least, present some empirical evidence. But supposing it were so, still definitionism would not be true. For definitionism claims that metaphysicians simply lay down and elaborate definitions which make no claims, whereas, on the supposition, the truth would be that metaphysicians make claims but offer no evidence, what they take to be evidence being simply an elaboration of definitions. Surely one can distinguish between making claims without supporting evidence and not making any claims at all. If our supposition above about the actual method of metaphysicians were correct, then that method was definitely bad and confused (purporting to give evidence when it didn't); whereas the method of metaphysics as portrayed by definitionism would be, so the definitionist supposes, quite above reproach, logically.

Finally, the definitionist may mean to assert that, since metaphysicians in the past have presented no evidence for their assertions other than elaboration of their definitions, consequently, in the future they ought to make no assertions but restrict themselves to defining their terms. I am not satisfied that the definitionist has or can establish the antecedent here, but even if he had, the consequent would not follow. The actual use of a bad, confused, irrelevant method to establish a claim is not proof that no acceptable method of establishing the claim can be found and that therefore the claim should be relinquished. The definitionist can prove the above consequent only on the assumptions that no method of establishing metaphysical claims can be found, and that no claims should be made for which no method of verification can be found. But at least the first of these assumptions is highly unacceptable: it would presuppose a general view as to the nature of knowledge which, as completely general, would itself be metaphysical.

The objection to the tendency illustrated in temperamentalism and definitionism is that it tries to find in metaphysical method some single, positive factor marking it off *toto caelo* from scientific method. The greater generality of the subject matter of metaphysics does mark it off from the sciences, still it does not make metaphysics wholly different from or independent of the sciences. The sciences generalize, and their generalizations are the best established of any with which the metaphysician of today is acquainted. Therefore it behooves him to use scientific generalizations, as far as possible, as the basis of his own wider generalizations. This means negatively that his theories should agree with scientifically respectable doctrines, they should not require the truth of scientific views which no reputable scientist in the science involved holds. Thus a metaphysical system requiring the fixity of species, a clear break between lower forms of life and man, a beginning to temporal processes not antedating the first appearance of consciousness (say with the anthropoids on our planet), a "fifth essence," i.e., the composition of heavenly bodies out of a substance not found on our planet—such a metaphysical system in so far as involving on of these scientifically objectionable doctrines is itself objectionable. Now since what is scientifically respectable changes with the progress of science, it follows that metaphysics is subject to change. It does not follow that the aim of metaphysics is to change (it is not the aim of science to change). But though the aim of the metaphysician be to attain a perennial philosophy, he should humbly accept it as his lot, under present circumstances, dependent as he is upon changing scientific theories, to achieve only a set of beliefs subject, to an unascertainable degree, to modification in the light of future scientific findings.

Positively, this utilization of science by metaphysics means that metaphysics need not attempt to build from the ground up, to make its broad generalizations wholly and directly from particular instances. It can generalize from scientific generalizations. Such a process is in part sheer induction. But an induction based on highly general propositions themselves established by the hypothesis-deduction-verification method is more reliable than one attempting to establish an equally wide generalization directly from particular instances. The generalization that every physical thing has more properties than have ever been directly experienced by the unaided senses would be very feebly established by sheer induction, but induction superposed on scientific theories (of atoms, micro-organisms, etc.), themselves established by the hypothesis-deduction-verification method, may give it a pretty firm footing.

This does not mean that the function of metaphysics is simply to accumulate and perhaps systematize the theories of the sciences, to give us an "encyclopedia of the sciences." Such a collection simply gives us some (albeit the most general) propositions as found in the sciences. The task of metaphysics is to generalize further on the basis of scientifically established propositions; i.e., to establish, by induction from scientific propositions, propositions that do not occur, at least explicitly, in the sciences at all. The materialist, in seeking to establish his proposition that all existents are physical, usually appeals ultimately to scientific theories, but his proposition is not a scientific theory. and any relevant evidence for it from the sciences involves a process of further abstraction and generalization not present in its scientific bases. This does not mean that encyclopedias of science are valueless; in fact, they are almost a necessity for the modern metaphysician in this day of specialization in science. But they are not metaphysics.

Metaphysics, in utilizing science, must go beyond induction. For, in the various sciences themselves, there are recognized contradictions, viz., rival respectable theories, e.g., discrete and continuous theories of radiation in physics, Gestalt and behavioristic theories of learning in psychology. Further, the process of comparison and abstraction involved in metaphysics brings to light contradictions not recognized in the individual sciences themselves, e.g., certain physiological and sociological accounts of sense perception. Now if it be supposed, as probably every one is willing to suppose, that an acceptable metaphysical system must be free from contradictions, then metaphysics must do something about these contradictions found in science, it cannot build on them by sheer induction. In the first place, it can seek to "generalize beyond them," to ignore them by finding some common features, sufficient for its purpose, in both or all of the conflicting theories. The metaphysician can ignore the conflict between various rival theories of amoeboid motion or of specific genetic function of certain chromosomal segments, since the controversy here is not over sufficiently general matters. In some instances, however, the metaphysician must take sides in scientific conflicts, he must decide which of the contradictory views he will accept and which reject. I think this is the case in the psychological controversy between extreme behaviorism, denying the fact of consciousness, and other theories asserting it, in various forms. This issue has an important bearing both upon the nature of existence and the nature of knowledge. We may perhaps lay it down that the metaphysician must take sides in any conflict of scientific theories where the conflict is over very general issues, issues obviously highly significant for any metaphysical positions.

. . . . The distinction here between a scientific and a metaphysical hypothesis is important. A scientific hypothesis can have significant positive verification in particular instances, since it states a relation between variables. If particular instances are chosen giving values dispersed through the range of these variables, then their verificatory significance is high, even though their number be few relative to the total number of instances that would fall under the hypothesis. But metaphysical hypotheses concern universal constants or transcendentals (or approximations thereto). Now a set of particular positive instances does so little to establish such an hypothesis that they had best not be called "verifications" at all. Yet they do have a role in metaphysics. I shall speak of it as "illustrative" and the instances as "illustrations." The function of an illustration is twofold. First it clarifies, by giving a concrete application of the hypothesis. This it may do by means of a highly typical case, a case where the hypothesis is manifestly exemplified, or by a highly atypical case, by attempting to show that the hypothesis really fits a supposedly disverificatory instance. Secondly, an illustration stimulates imaginative insight. By "imaginative insight" I mean a cursory, memorial-imaginative survey of a large section of direct experience for the purpose of sizing it up, of seeing whether it squares with the proposed hypothesis. Here particular items are not dealt with individually unless one runs across an item that might seem to be disverificatory, when it is thereupon singled out for individual consideration. It is analogous to the perceptual process of sizing up a whole perceptual field, as a good motorist sizes up his whole visual and auditory experience only attending specifically to items of more immediate danger. This process is important in metaphysical method, since it aids in locating possible disverificatory instances, or aspects of a large number of instances which (aspects) are incompatible with a proposed hypothesis. Disverificatory instances are just as decisive against a metaphysical as against a scientific hypothesis. Thus relative to verificatory instances they are far more important in metaphysical procedure than in scientific. Yet unquestionable disverifications in metaphysics seem to be rather rare, certainly far rarer than in science. This is partly due to the way metaphysicians use language. When supposedly caught by a disverificatory instance they reinterpret their hypothesis so that the words are made to harmonize with the supposedly disverificatory case. This disingenuous use of words is highly deplorable. It is to be hoped that the increasing interest in linguistics in philosophy will help to abate this evil. It should come to be recognized that to propound a plausible metaphysical hypothesis which yet can be definitely disverified, and perhaps itself clearly states what sorts of instances would be disverificatory, is far more respectable than to propound one so loosely and ambiguously conceived and stated that no decisive disverification is possible. But we must not suppose that the disingenuousness of metaphysicians is the sole cause of the relative infrequency of decisive disverifications in metaphysics. A metaphysical hypothesis attempts to be completely general (or to approximate thereto). There are relatively few words in current usage that are completely general. If ordinary language is to be used, the metaphysician is almost forced to swell the extension (to impoverish the intension) of the words he uses. This, of course, is an excellent argument for the development of a technical terminology. But this way is not so easy as it might seem, for a technical terminology, to be significant (to be "interpreted" and not merely formal), must, in its undefined elements, be translated either into ordinary language or into nonlinguistic symbolic behavior (such as pointing), and the latter translation is extremely difficult, perhaps impossible, in the case of universal constants. Furthermore, quite apart from the symbolic expression of them, the metaphysician's hypotheses are themselves of such a nature as to make decisive disverifications less frequent than in science. The typical phenomenon the metaphysical hypothesis seeks to describe is a universal constant. There are no instances of anything not instances of it. Thus wherever there is a case satisfying the description, the phenomenon must be present. This rules out a whole type of disverificatory instance as found in science, i.e., where the conditions are satisfied but the phenomenon is not present, or not present to the degree required by the hypothesis. The only sort of disverificatory instance for a metaphysical hypothesis is where the phenomenon is present but the generalized description does not fit. For example, the materialist might say, "To be an existent is to have spatio-temporal location." We could not hope to disverify this by trying to find something with spatio-temporal location which does not exist, though we might significantly try to find an existent which does not have spatio-temporal location. Verification in science requires negative but verificatory instances (negative in that the phenomenon is absent, verificatory in that the hypothesis requires it to be absent under the given conditions), and this immediately gives definite meaning to the possibility of negative disverificatory instances. But metaphysical hypotheses (at least in the extreme) recognize no negative instances.

Metaphysicians should strive to overcome this handicap as far as possible. Since decisive disverification is possible in metaphysics, it should become a methodological desideratum, not merely in the sense of a dialectical weapon to use against rivals, but in the more fruitful sense of a control in the formulation of one's own hypothesis. A metaphysical hypothesis is better (other things disregarded) if it indicates more clearly what sorts of instances from direct experience would constitute decisive disverifications of it.

We must not suppose, however, that the only evidential role of direct experience relative to a metaphysical hypothesis is as a field of possible disverificatory instances. Important as is the role of imaginative survey of direct experience for the purpose of hitting upon disverificatory instances, this process also can serve the purpose of positive corroboration. Single instances, however numerous, go only a very little way in verifying a metaphysical hypothesis. But we are not to suppose that we can get at direct experience only *seriatim,* in a larger or smaller number of particular bits. Such a view is a hang-over from associationistic psychology. Direct experience has its aspects of continuity and persistence as well as of discreteness and variation. We are just as close to it, just as true to it, when we imaginatively survey large sections of it, in terms of pervasive aspects of it, as when we try to remember particular bits, as different from all other bits. Such an imaginative survey may result in a positive imaginative insight of real evidential weight for a metaphysical hypothesis. And especially is this true if we add "imaginative experiment" to this survey. I do not mean an "imagined" experiment. An actual experiment is an actual modification of particular existents in order to test some hypothesis. I suppose an imagined experiment would simply be an imagined modification of this sort. The imaginative experiment I have in mind is one which could not be carried out actually, for it involves a modification not of this or that particular but of all of direct experience in some respect. What would our color-world be without any actual experience of green? Would we have any notion of spatial relations if we had no visual or tactile experience? Here the appeal is to an imaginative survey-type experiment.

All this may sound pretty indefinite and subject to all sorts of subjective vagaries when compared with rigorous scientific verifications. This must, I fear, be granted. The metaphysician has not and, if I am right, never will achieve a method as rigorous as the scientific. Yet he must do the best he can with his own method; to attempt to use a strictly scientific procedure in his nonscientific subject matter is a mark of immaturity, of childish imitativeness that seeks the semblance without the substance of adulthood. And there may be some recompense for this lack of rigor. The very fact that a metaphysician must rely on a total insight, that he has no mechanical procedures, formulae that may be used without appreciation of their derivations or presuppositions, which can be handed over to clerks, gives him a sense of creative discovery which, though the source of many dangers, is also the cause of enduring satisfaction. And it must not be supposed that scientists are free from this reliance on imaginative survey and insight. It is present in their own procedure when they jump to their hypotheses, before the application of rigorous procedures of verification; and to some extent it is involved in scientific verification itself, viz., in deciding what lines of deduction will probably yield conclusions that can be checked against direct observations. Again, every scientist as soon as he steps out of his own special investigations and philosophizes relies on this procedure. For example, Eddington's contention that the objects of scientific knowledge are, ultimately, pointer readings, or Bridgman's assertion that scientific concepts are reducible to operations—these are not established by any rigorous scientific procedure of experiment, of hypothesis-deduction-verification. Instances are used illustratively, to instigate an imaginative survey. The final appeal is to insight. And (though I do not agree with their results) their method here has been appropriate, not as reliable as scientific method but more relevant to the sort of hypothesis involved.

But if metaphysical method is, though the best available for metaphysics, yet highly unreliable, it behooves us to use it with great caution. Let me lay down specifically certain admonitions. We must always remember that since the most rigorous scientific method cannot attain certainty, metaphysical propositions should be put forward even more tentatively. We must remember that disverificatory instances are far more significant in deciding between the claims of rival metaphysical hypotheses than are verificatory, thus we should construct our hypotheses with this in mind, and constantly be alert in weighing them and in advocating them for disverification. We must ever be watchful that we appeal to imaginative survey and insight with complete honesty, as methods of critical inquiry, not of "rationalization" or "wishful thinking." This means not so much that we attempt to get at any "pure" experience, but rather that we be scrupulously honest with rival theories, that we try earnestly to survey experience from the standpoint of each of them, not allowing our satisfaction with any one to keep us from a sincere attempt to see how tolerant experience is of others.

These admonitions lead to a final consideration. Though controversy between rival hypotheses is important in science (without it, hypothesis-deduction-verification would reduce to a form of sheer induction), it is in metaphysics that controversy has its greatest methodological significance. It is high time that metaphysicians cease being apologetic on this score. The aim of metaphysics, as a science, is knowledge, not agreement. And whether or not agreement will actually result after knowledge has been attained, in the process of trying to attain knowledge controversy is highly valuable, whereas premature agreement is disastrous. When the issues are extremely general, when positive verification largely rests on wide imaginative survey, when there is great danger of ambiguity, and decisive disverificatory instances are relatively few, then theoretical controversy becomes extremely important. Every human mind tends to be dogmatic, to favor an already accepted and familiar hypothesis, especially if popularly identified with that individual, to short-circuit the tedious process of revision of old hypotheses and testing of new rivals. These normal human tendencies are quite effectively countered in science by its more rigorous procedures of verification and disverification. In metaphysics they must be more directly and crudely checked by the putting of advocate against advocate. And though this opposition easily degenerates into emotionalism, when it can be kept on an intellectual plane, when it can occur imaginatively in each of the opposing advocates (and not merely actually, between them), then it is of the highest value in the metaphysical enterprise.

Alfred North Whitehead   **3. METHOD AND THEORY**

As Whitehead points out, method is a way of dealing with *evidence*. But there is no evidence that is not also antecedently conditioned by *method*. The only evidence that Method-A can deal with is Evidence-A; it cannot deal with Evidence-B, because it cannot recognize the relevance of Evidence-B. Method is therefore dictated by theory and is a technical extension of that theory. As Whitehead puts it, "You cannot prove a theory by evidence which that theory dismisses as irrelevant." Hume, for instance, has no method for dealing with the interconnectedness of things, since for him sensations are the sole data, and one sensation can reveal nothing of another sensation.

The customary distinction between the method of the ancients and that of the moderns, says Whitehead, indicates a presupposition of method. The ancients asked, "What *do* we experience?" while the moderns ask, "What *can* we experience?" In the substitution of *can* for *do,* there is a presupposition that we place ourselves in an introspective attitude of attention "so as to determine the *given* components of experience. . . ."

But the question is, what is *given?* To Hume, the given is disparate and discrete sensations. To Whitehead, it is the correlatedness of things. In short, Hume's experience, which is to be methodologically processed, is essentially different from Whitehead's. Their theories are different to begin with, so their methods will likewise be different.

Experience, says Whitehead, is never abstract, but concrete. It is enfolded in language, social institutions, and action. Experience—which Whitehead calls "the storehouse of that crude evidence on which philosophy should base its discussion"—must consequently be broadened, rather than restricted, by the practice of metaphysics because no type of experience can be omitted from its activity. This being true, then, Whitehead concludes that the main method of dealing with evidence will be *descriptive generalization,* which seizes upon the many characteristics of facts in all their concrete amplitude.

So FAR AS concerns methodology . . . theory dictates method, and . . . any particular method is only applicable to theories of one correlate species. An analogous conclusion holds for the technical terms. This close relation of theory to method partly arises from the fact that the relevance of evidence depends on the theory which is dominating the discussion. This fact is the reason why dominant theories are also termed "working hypotheses."

An example is afforded when we interrogate experience for direct evidence of the interconnectedness of things. If we hold with Hume that the sole data originating reflective experience are impressions of sensation, and also if we also admit with him the obvious fact that no one such impression by its own individual nature discloses any information as to another such impression then on that hypothesis the direct evidence for interconnectedness vanishes. Again, if we hold the Cartesian doctrine of substantial souls with many adventures of experience, and of substantial material bodies, then on that hypothesis the relations between two occasions of experience qualifying one soul are no evidence as to the connectedness of two such occasions respectively qualifying two different souls, and are no evidence as to the connectedness of a soul and a material body, and are no evidence as to the connectedness of two occasions of agitation of one material body, or of two such occasions respectively belonging to different material bodies. But if we hold, as for example in *Process and Reality,* that all final individual actualities have the metaphysical character of occasions of experience, then on that hypothesis the direct evidence as to the connectedness of one's immediate present occasion of experience with one's immediate past occasions can be validly used to suggest categories applying to the connectedness of all occasions in nature. A great deal of confused philosophical thought has its origin in obliviousness to the fact that the relevance of evidence is dictated by theory. For you cannot prove a theory by evidence which that theory dismisses as irrelevant. This is also the reason that in any science which has failed to produce any theory with a sufficient scope of application, progress is necessarily very slow. It is impossible to know what to look for, and how to connect the sporadic observations. Philosophical discussion in the absence of a theory has no criterion of the validity of evidence. For example, Hume assumes that his doctrine of association holds for all types of impressions of sensation and of ideas of them indiscriminately. This assumption is part of his theory. In divorce from the theory, a separate appeal to experience is required for each type of impression, for example, tastes, sounds, sights, etc., and likewise, not only for the association of tastes *inter se* and of sounds *inter se,* but for the association of tastes with sounds, and so on for every possible type, and for every possible conjunction of types.

To sum up this preface, every method is a happy simplification. But only truths of a congenial type can be investigated by any one method, or stated in the terms dictated by the method. For every simplification is an oversimplification. Thus the criticism of a theory does not start from the question, True or false? It consists in noting its scope of useful application and its failure beyond that scope. It is an unguarded statement of a partial truth. Some of its terms embody a general notion with a mistaken specialization, and others of its terms are too general and require discrimination of their possibilities of specialization.

. . . Philosophy is a difficult subject, from the days of Plato to the present time haunted by subtle perplexities. The existence of such perplexities arising from the common obviousness of speech is the reason why the topic exists. Thus the very purpose of philosophy is to delve below the apparent clarity of common speech. In this connection, it is only necessary to refer to Socrates. Another illustration is to be found in the *Sophist,* where Plato states that "not-being" is a form of "being." This statement is at once an extreme instance of the breakdown of language, and the enunciation of a profound metaphysical truth which lies at the foundation of this discussion. . . .

. . . A method is a way of dealing with data, with evidence. What are the evidences to which philosophy appeals?

It is customary to contrast the objective approach of the ancient Greeks with the subjective approach of the moderns, initiated by Descartes, and further emphasized by Locke and Hume.

But, whether we be ancient or modern, we can only deal with things, in some sense, experienced. The Greeks dealt with things that they thought they experienced, and Hume merely asked, What do we experience? This is exactly the question which Plato and Aristotle thought that they were answering.

To speak of anything is to speak of something which, by reason of that very speech, is in some way a component in that act of experience. In some sense or other, it is thereby known to exist. This is what Plato pointed out when he wrote, Not-being is itself a sort of being.

Speech consists of noises, or visible shapes, which elicit an experience of things other than themselves. In so far as vocables fail to elicit a stable coordination of sound-character, or shape-character, to meaning, those vocables fail to function as speech. And in so far as some meaning is not in some sense directly experienced, there is no meaning conveyed. To point at nothing is not to point.

To speak of the same thing twice is to demonstrate that the being of that thing is independent of either singular act of speech, unless we believe that the two acts presuppose each other or are both presupposed by the thing spoken of. If we cannot speak of the same thing twice, knowledge vanishes taking philosophy with it. Thus, since speech can be repeated, things spoken of have a determined being in abstraction from the occasion of experience which includes that act of speech.

The difference between ancients and moderns is that the ancients asked what have we experienced, and the moderns asked what can we experience. But in both cases, they asked about things transcending the act of experience which is the occasion of asking.

. . . The translation of Hume's question from "What *do* we experience" to "What *can* we experience" makes all the difference, though in his *Treatise* Hume makes the transition, time and again., without explicit comment. For modern epistemology the latter form of the question—with its substitution of can for do—is accompanied by the implicit presupposition of a method, namely that of placing ourselves in an introspective attitude of attention so as to determine the *given* components of experience in abstraction from our private way of subjective reaction, by reflexion, conjecture, emotion, and purpose.

In this attitude of strained attention, there can be no doubt as to the answer. The data are the patterns of sensa provided by the sense organs. This is the sensationalist doctrine of Locke and Hume. Later, Kant has interpreted the patterns as forms introduced by the mode of reception provided by the recipient. Here Kant introduces the Leibnizian notion of the self-development of the experiencing subject. Thus for Kant the data are somewhat narrower than for Hume: They are the *sensa* devoid of their patterns. Hume's general analysis of the consequences of this doctrine stands unshaken. So also does his final reflection that the philosophic doctrine fails to justify the practice of daily life. The justification of this procedure of modern epistemology is twofold, and both of its branches are based upon mistakes. The mistakes go back to the Greek philosophers. What is modern, is the exclusive reliance upon them.

. . . The first error is the assumption of a few definite avenues of communication with the external world, the five sense organs. This leads to the presupposition that the search for the data is to be narrowed to the question, What data are directly provided by the activity of the sense organs—preferably the eyes. This doctrine of sense organs has a vague, general truth, very important for practical affairs. In particular all exact scientific observation is derived from such data. The scientific categories of thought are obtained elsewhere.

But the living organ of experience is the living body as a whole. Every instability of any part of it—be it chemical, physical, or molar—imposes an activity of readjustment throughout the whole organism. In the course of such physical activities human experience has its origin. The plausible interpretation of such experience is that it is one of the natural activities involved in the functioning of such a high-grade organism. The actualities of nature must be so interpreted as to be explanatory of this fact. This is one desideratum to be aimed at in a philosophic scheme.

Such experience seems to be more particularly related to the activities of the brain. But how far an exact doctrine can be based upon this presumption lies beyond our powers of observation. We cannot determine with what molecules the brain begins and the rest of the body ends. Further, we cannot tell with what molecules the body ends and the external world begins. The truth is that the brain is continuous with the body, and the body is continuous with the rest of the natural world. Human experience is an act of self-origination including the whole of nature, limited to the perspective of a focal region, located within the body, but not necessarily persisting in any fixed coordination with a definite part of the brain.

. . . The second error is the presupposition that the sole way of examining experience is by acts of conscious introspective analysis. Such a doctrine of the exclusive primacy of introspection is already discredited in psychology. Each occasion of experience has its own individual pattern. Each occasion lifts some components into primacy and retreats others into a background enriching the total enjoyment. The attitude of introspection shares this characteristic with all other experiential occasions. It lifts the clear-cut data of sensation into primacy, and cloaks the vague compulsions and derivations which form the main stuff of experience. In particular it rules out that intimate sense of derivation from the body, which is the reason for our instinctive identification of our bodies with ourselves.

In order to discover some of the major categories under which we can classify the infinitely various components of experience, we must appeal to evidence relating to every variety of occasion. Nothing can be omitted, experience drunk and experience sober, experience sleeping and experience waking, experience drowsy and experience wide-awake, experience self-conscious and experience self-forgetful, experience intellectual and experience physical, experience religious and experience sceptical, experience anxious and experience care-free, experience anticipatory and experience retrospective, experience happy and experience grieving, experience dominated by emotion and experience under self-restraint, experience in the light and experience in the dark, experience normal and experience abnormal.

. . . We have now reached the heart of our topic. What is the storehouse of that crude evidence on which philosophy should base its discussion, and in what terms should its discussion be expressed?

The main sources of evidence respecting this width of human experience are language, social institutions, and action, including thereby the fusion of the three which is language interpreting action and social institutions.

Language delivers its evidence in three chapters, one on the meanings of words, another on the meanings enshrined in grammatical forms, and the third on meanings beyond individual words and beyond grammatical forms, meanings miraculously revealed in great literature.

Language is incomplete and fragmentary, and merely registers a stage in the average advance beyond ape mentality. But all men enjoy flashes of insight beyond meanings already stabilized in etymology and grammar. Hence the role of literature, the role of the special sciences, and the role of philosophy —in their various ways engaged in finding linguistic expressions for meanings as yet unexpressed.

As a special example, consider the line and a half of poetry in which Euripides compresses the main philosophical problems which have tortured European thought from this day to the present:—"Zeus, whether thou art Compulsion of Nature or Intelligence of Mankind, to thee I prayed." Consider the ideas involved, "Zeus," "necessity [compulsion] of nature" "intelligence of mankind," "prayer." These lines have survived the ages with a modern appeal vivid as when first they thrilled an Athenian audience. The biographer of a modern statesman cites them to express the solemnity of the spectacle of life passing into religious emotion.

Yet Hume would be able to find no "impression of sensation" from which to derive "Zeus" or "compulsion" or "intelligence" or the would-be "persuasiveness" which we term "prayer." John Morley himself selected the quotation in spite of his own positivistic bias which should trivialize these meanings. Also, perhaps even for their original author, the lines represent a triumph of dramatic intuition over temperamental scepticism.

The common practice, interpreted by the common language of mankind, tells the same tale. A statesman, or a president of a business corporation, assumes the "compulsion of recent events" . . . as laying down inexorable conditions for the future. He frames a "policy" upon this assumption and advises that it be "acted on," thereby also assuming that the imposed conditions leave room for the effectiveness of "choice" and "intelligence." He assumes alternatives in contrast to the immediate fact. He conceives an ideal, to be attained or to be missed. He conceives such ideals as effective in proportion as they are entertained. He praises and he blames by reason of this belief.

In the world, there are elements of order and disorder, which thereby presuppose an essential interconnectedness of things. For disorder shares with order the common characteristic that they imply many things interconnected.

Each experient enjoys a perspective apprehension of the world, and

equally is an element in the world by reason of this very prehension, which anchors him to a world transcending his own experience. For it belongs to the nature of this perspective derivation that the world thus disclosed proclaims its own transcendence of that disclosure. To every shield, there is another side, hidden.

Thus an appeal to literature, to common language, to common practice, at once carries us away from the narrow basis for epistemology provided by the sense-data disclosed in direct introspection. The world within experience is identical with the world beyond experience, the occasion of experience is within the world and the world is within the occason. The categories have to elucidate this paradox of the connectedness of things—the many things, the one world without and within.

. . . European philosophy is founded upon Plato's dialogues, which in their methods are mainly an endeavour to elicit philosophic categories from a dialectic discussion of the meanings of language taken in combination with shrewd observation of the actions of man and of the forces of nature.

But in one dialogue, the *Sophist,* Plato explicitly considers the methods of philosophy. One of his conclusions is to point out the limitations of common speech. Mere dialectic, uncriticized, is a fallacious instrument, the mark of the *Sophist.* For example, Plato insists that not-being is itself a form of being. Thus in philosophy linguistic discussion is a tool, but should never be a master. Language is imperfect both in its words and in its forms. Thus we discover two main errors to which philosophic method is liable, one is the uncritical trust in the adequacy of language, and the other is the uncritical trust in the strained attitude of introspection as the basis for epistemology.

But since the life-time of Plato nearly two and a half thousand years have intervened, including the continuous activity of European philosophic thought, pagan, Christian, secular. It is widely held that a stable, well-known philosophic vocabulary has been elaborated, and that in philosophic discussion any straying beyond its limits introduces neologisms, unnecessary and therefore to be regretted.

This alleged fact requires examination. In the first place, if the allegation be true, it is very remarkable. It decisively places philosophy apart from the more special sciences. Modern mathematics, most secure and authoritative of sciences, is largely written in verbal and symbolic phrases which would have been unintelligible eighty years ago. In modern physics the old words, where they are still used, convey different meanings, and the new words are abundant. But it is futile to make a catalogue of the sciences accompanied by this refrain. The conclusion is obvious to the most cursory inspection.

. . . Undoubtedly, philosophy is dominated by its past literature to a greater extent than any other science. And rightly so. But the claim that it has acquired a set of technical terms sufficient for its purposes, and exhaustive of its meanings, is entirely unfounded. Indeed its literature is so vast, and the variations of its schools of thought so large, that there is abundant evidence of most excusable ignorance respecting verbal usages. . . .

. . . The main method of philosophy in dealing with its evidence is that of descriptive generalization. Social institutions exemplify a welter of characteristics. No fact is merely such-and-such. It exemplifies many characters at once, all rooted in the specialities of its epoch. Philosophic generalization seizes on those characters of abiding importance, dismissing the trivial and the evanescent. There is an ascent from a particular fact, or from a species, to the genus exemplified.

It is to be noted that the converse procedure is impossible. There can be no descent from a mere genus to particular fact, or to a species. For facts and species are the product of the mingling of genera. No genus in its own essence indicates the other genera with which it is compatible. For example, the notion of a backbone does not indicate the notions of suckling the young or of swimming in water. Thus no contemplation of the genus vertebrate, taken by itself, can suggest mammals or fishes, even as abstract possibilities. Neither the species nor the instance are to be discovered by the genus alone, since both include forms not "given" by the genus. A species is a potential mingling of genera, and an individual instance involves, among other things, an actual mingling of many species. A syllogism is a scheme for demonstration of ways of mingling.

Thus the business of Logic is not the analysis of generalities but their mingling. Philosophy is the ascent to the generalities with the view of understanding their possibilities of combination. The discovery of new generalities thus adds to the fruitfulness of those already known. It lifts into view new possibilities of combination.

. . . Even the dim apprehension of some great principle is apt to clothe itself with tremendous emotional force. The welter of particular actions arising out of such complex feelings with their core of deep intuition are in primitive times often brutish and nasty. Finally civilized language provides a whole group of words, each embodying the general idea under its own specialization. If we desire to reach the generality common to these various specializations, we must gather together the whole group of words with the hope of discerning their common element. This is a necessary procedure for the purpose of philosophical generalization. The premature use of one familiar word inevitably limits the required generalization by importing the familiar special connotation of that word.

For example, let the working hypotheses be that the ultimate realities are the events in their process of origination. Then each event, viewed in its separate individuality, is a passage between two ideal termini, namely its components in their ideal disjunctive diversity passing into these same components in their concrete togetherness. There are two current doctrines as to this process. One is that of the external Creator, eliciting this final togetherness out of nothing. The other doctrine is that it is a metaphysical principle belonging to the nature of things, that there is nothing in the Universe other than instances of this passage and components of these instances. Let this latter doctrine be adopted. Then the word Creativity expresses the notion that each event is a process issuing in novelty. Also if guarded in the phrases Immanent Creativity, or Self-Creativity, it avoids the implication of a transcendent Creator. But the mere word Creativity suggests Creator, so that the whole doctrine acquires an air of paradox, or of pantheism. Still it does convey the origination of novelty. The word Concrescence is a derivative from the familiar Latin verb, meaning "growing together." It also has the advantage that the participle "concrete" is familiarly used for the notion of complete physical reality. Thus Concrescence is useful to convey the notion of many things acquiring complete complex unity. But it fails to suggest the creative novelty involved. For example, it omits the notion of the individual character arising in the concrescence of the aboriginal data. The event is not suggested as "emotionalized," that is, as with its "subjective form."

Again the term "together" is one of the most misused terms in philosophy. It is a generic term illustrated by an endless variety of species. Thus its use as though it conveyed one definite meaning in diverse illustrations is entirely sophistical. Every meaning of "together" is to be found in various stages of analysis of occasions of experience. No things are "together" except in experience; and no things *are,* in any sense of "are," except as components in experience or as immediacies of process which are occasions in self-creation.

. . . Thus to arrive at the philosophic generalization which is the notion of a final actuality conceived in the guise of a generalization of an act of experience, an apparent redundancy of terms is required. The words correct each other. We require "together," "creativity," "concrescence," "prehension," "feeling," "subjective form," "data," "actuality," "becoming," "process."

At this stage of the generalization a new train of thought arises. Events become and perish. In their becoming they are immediate and then vanish into the past. They are gone; they have perished; they are no more and have passed into not-being. Plato terms them things that are "always becoming and never really are." But before he wrote this phrase, Plato had made his great metaphysical generalization, a discovery which forms the basis of the present discussion. He wrote in the *Sophist,* not-being is itself a form of being. He only applied this doctrine to his eternal forms. He should have applied the same doctrine to the things that perish. He would then have illustrated another aspect of the method of philosophic generalization. When a general idea has been obtained, it should not be arbitrarily limited to the topic of its origination.

In framing a philosophic scheme, each metaphysical notion should be given the widest extension of which it seems capable. It is only in this way that the true adjustment of ideas can be explored. More important even than Occam's doctrine of parsimony—if it be not another aspect of the same— is this doctrine that the scope of a metaphysical principle should not be limited otherwise than by the necessity of its meaning.

Bernard J. F. Lonergan, S.J.   **4. DEDUCTION, DOUBT, EMPIRICISM, AND COMMON SENSE**

Father Lonergan states that any choice of a "method" is a form of begging the question. This is because method clearly anticipates the goal of its inquiry, and settling upon a method implies that the goal itself has been settled upon. But in methodological questions it is precisely the goal that is in dispute. Method and theory, he asserts, are reciprocally related, and must be distinguished between (*a*) axiomatic and (*b*) "guiding" methods. Axiomatic methods are essentially deductive; guiding methods are either sceptical, empirical, "common sensible," or eclectic. Deductive methods are such as can be "handed over to clerks," while guiding methods rest "on the conviction that the [knowing] subject cannot be ignored."

Deductive systems, says Lonergan, begin with certain primitive premises of universal and necessary validity, from which universal and necessary conclusions can be drawn. In order to have any relevance, however, such conclusions must be concrete and existential, not merely abstract and possible. Deductive forms must therefore imply something over and above a mere methodology—namely, a judgment that the mind begins with primitive premises (*synthetic a priori*). The mind is therefore not a "mirror" but "a sort of factory" in which data are "processed into appropriate syntheses." Hence, deduction is not merely a method but a point of view.

Moreover, all forms of universal doubt ("doubt everything that can be doubted") harbor inner contradictions—for example, that analytic statements are indubitable, but analytic principles are not. Still, more importantly, one must ask: "Is the criterion of indubitability itself indubitable?" Lonergan answers, "It is not." As a method, it is a leap in the dark, because it accepts a criterion without being able to determine the

Extracts appearing in this selection were originally published in *Insight* (New York, 1956), and are here reprinted with the kind permisson of the publisher, Philosophical Library, Inc.

precise implications of that criterion. Similarly, empiricism ("observe the significant facts") is a "bundle of blunders." It has no empirical means of determining its essential ingredient—*significance*. Whereas an object is an observable datum, significance accrues to data as a result of an intuition into meanings, rather than as a perception by *sensa*. Knowing, consequently, is not just "taking a look." It is a dynamic pattern of experiencing and reflecting. Empiricism mistakes "what is obvious in knowing" for "what knowing obviously is." Finally, common-sense eclecticism is the least reliable of methodologies. At its very beginning, there is difficulty in deciding between kinds of "common sense." One man's common sense may not be another's.

All four methods, Lonergan concludes, leave much to be desired. Abstract deduction and universal doubt head for emptiness, while concrete deduction is hung up on the question of whether or not it is possible. Empiricism is concrete enough, but in mistaken ways; while common-sense eclecticism "leaves philosophy obtuse, superficial, and divided."

A METHOD CAN DIRECT activity to a goal only by anticipating the general nature of the goal. But the only question to be settled in metaphysics is the general nature of the goal of knowledge, for all questions of detail have to be met by the sciences and by common sense. Accordingly, it would seem that every method in metaphysics must be involved in the fallacy of begging the question. By the mere fact of settling upon a method, one presupposes as settled the very issue that metaphysics proposes to resolve.

This difficulty reveals the significance of the distinction we have drawn between latent and explicit metaphysics. For latent metaphysics is an anticipation of the goal of knowledge that is present and operative independently of any metaphysical inquiry. Inasmuch as metaphysical inquiry aims at making latent metaphysics explicit, it proceeds not from arbitrary assumptions about the goal of knowledge, which would involve it in the fallacy of begging the question, but from matters of fact that any inquirer can verify in his own empirical, intelligent, and rational consciousness.

There is, however, a further aspect to the matter. Because the results obtained in the empirical sciences commonly are far less general than the methods they employ, scientists are not troubled to any notable extent by a predetermination of their results by their choice of method. In metaphysics, however, methods and results are of equal generality and tend to be coincident. It follows that difference in metaphysical positions can be studied expeditiously and compendiously by examining differences in method. Moreover, such a study is not confined to tabulating the correlations that hold between different methods and different metaphysical systems. For there is only one method that is not arbitrary, and it grounds its explicit anticipations on the anticipations that, though latent, are present and operative in consiousness. Finally, besides the correlations between methods and systems, besides the criticism of methods based on the latent metaphysics of the human mind, there is the dialectical unfolding of positions inviting development and counter-positions inviting reversal. It is to this dialectic of metaphysical methods that attention now is to be directed, not of course in the full expansion that would be possible only in a survey of the whole history of philosophy, but in the articulation of its basic alternatives and with the modest purpose of indicating the outlines of a heuristic scheme for historical investigations.

Deductive Methods

Any metaphysical system eventually assumes the form of a set of propositions. The propositions can be divided into primitive and derived, and a logical technique can establish that if the primitive propositions are accepted, then the derived must also be accepted. The problem, then, of a deductive method is to select correctly the primitive propositions.

A first alternative is to assert that one's primitive propositions are universal and necessary truths. Since they are not deduced, they commonly will be claimed to be self-evident. However, a dialectic of method need not scrutinize this claim, for the properties of universal and necessary truths turn out to be sufficiently significant.

If the primitive propositions are universal, then they are abstract. They may refer to existing objects, but they do not assert the existence of any object, unless the universal is supposed to exist. This conclusion is confirmed by such keen logicians as Duns Scotus and William of Ockham, both of whom felt compelled to complement their abstract systems with the affirmation of an intuition of the existing and present as existing and present.

Further, if the primitive propositions are necessary, then they hold not merely for this universe but also for any possible world. It follows that the metaphysical system has no particular reference to this universe, for it holds equally for any universe. Again, it follows that the metaphysical system does aim at integrating the empirical sciences and common sense; for both the empirical sciences and common sense are content to ascertain what in fact is so; but the deductive system in question has no interest in any contingent truth not matter how general or how comprehensive it may be.

Let us now inquire which truths can be regarded as universal and necessary. Clearly, all analytic propositions meet the above requirements. For they suppose nothing but the definitions of their terms and the rules of syntax that govern the coalescence of the terms into propositions. Provided that one does not affirm either the existence of the terms or the existence of operations in accord with the syntactical rules, one can have at one's disposal an indefinitely large group of truths that are universal and necessary, that affirm no existent, and that are equally valid in every possible world. On the other hand, the metaphysical system in question cannnot be based on analytic principles, for the transition from the analytic proposition to the analytic principle is through concrete judgment of fact affirming that the terms, as defined, occur in a concrete existing universe.

It follows that the abstract metaphysics of all possible worlds is empty. Historically, however, this emptiness was discovered by a different route. For the medieval theologians that explored this type of system acknowledged the existence and the omnipotence of God; the only possible restriction upon divine omnipotence and so the only restriction on the range of possible worlds lay in the principle of contradiction. Their metaphysics dealt with all possible worlds and so it dealt simultaneously with every possible instance of the non-contradictory. Not only did this object prove extremely tenuous and elusive, but it soon became apparent that the one operative principle in their thought was the principle of contradiction. Moreover, this principle ran counter to their affirmation of an intuition of the existing and present as existing and present. For it would be contradictory to affirm and deny some occurrence of the intuition; it would be contradictory to affirm and deny the existence of some object; but there is no apparent contradiction in affirming the occurrence of the intuition and denying the existence of its object. If no contradiction is involved, then in some possible world there would occur intuitions of the existence of what did not exist; and as Nicholas of Autrecourt perceived, neither analytic propositions nor intuitions can assure one that the possibility of illusory intuitions is not realized in this world.

The alternative to the abstract deduction that turns out to be empty is, of course, a concrete deduction. The existent does not lie outside the deductive system, but, from the start, is included within it. Instead of operating vainly with analytic propositions, one proposes to operate fruitfully with analytic principles whose terms, in their defined sense, refer to what exists.

Now it is characteristic of a deduction that conclusions follow necessarily from the premises. It follows that a concrete deduction is possible only if an objective necessity binds the existent that is concluded to the existent referred to in the premises. For without this objective necessity logically impeccable inferences would arrive at possibly false conclusions.

Now there are many metaphysical systems that reveal how this objective necessity might be conceived. Thus, a monist would affirm the existence of a single reality with a set of necessary attributes and modes; and clearly enough his chain of syllogisms could be applied validly to a universe conceived in this fashion. Again, emanationist doctrines begin from a necessary being from which proceed necessarily all other beings; the application of a syllogistic chain would be more difficult in this case but there is no point in haggling over the matter. In the third place, one might suppose that God exists necessarily but is bound morally to create the best of all possible worlds; and so in a fashion one would secure a universe for concrete deductivist thought.

However, it is one thing to conceive a variety of universes; it is another to know whether any one of them exists. If one affirms this universe to be monist, because that is the conclusion of one's concrete deduction, it will be pointed out that one's choice of method amounted to begging the question; for the choice of concrete deduction makes it inevitable that one conclude to a monism or an emanationism or an optimism or a mechanist determinism; and so one's argument could be relevant only to discovering which of this limited range of alternatives was the most satisfactory. Clearly, the real issue is to determine, not what follows once the method of concrete deduction is assumed, but whether or not that method is to be employed.

Accordingly, if abstract deduction is empty, concrete deduction sets a prior question. Moreover, since the metaphysical question is the general nature or structure of the universe, the prior question, it seems, must regard the mind that is to know the universe. In this fashion one is led to ask what kind of mind would be needed if the universe is to be known by concrete deduction. Or, to give the issue its more concrete form, what are the constitutive conditions of such a concrete deduction as Newton's *Mathematical Principles of Natural Philosophy?*

Since the deducing can be performed satisfactorily by an electronic computer, the problem may be limited to the origin of the requisite premises. These premises, it would seem, must be both synthetic and a priori. They must be synthetic. For analytic propositions lack both relevance and significance; for they are obtained by studying the rules of syntax and the meanings of words, and clearly that procedure does not yield an understanding of this universe. Again, the required premises must be a priori. They are not to be known merely by taking a look at what is there to be seen; for what is there to be seen is particular; and no amount of mere looking endows it with the significance that explains the existing universe. The possibility, then, of a concrete deduction, such as Newton's, coincides with the possibility of synthetic a priori premises. But this possibility implies that the mind must be, not a mirror that simply reflects reality, but a sort of factory in which the materials supplied by outer and inner sense are processed into appropriate syntheses. Finally, if the mind is a factory of this type, it is capable of performing concrete deductions of the scientific type but it does not seem at all capable of performing concrete deductions of the metaphysical type.

Various objections have been raised against such a deduction of the possibility of concrete deduction, but the most fundamental seems to be that the problem is not envisaged in its full generality. It is not enough to account for Newton's deduction alone or for Einstein's deduction alone. What has to be accounted for is a series of concrete deductions, none of which is certain and each of which is the best available scientific opinion of its time. The mind is not just a factory with a set of fixed processes; rather it is a universal machine tool that erects all kinds of factories, keeps adjusting and improving them, and eventually scraps them in favour of radically new designs. In other words, there is not some fixed set of a priori syntheses. Every insight is an a priori; insight follows on insight to complement and correct its predecessor; earlier accumulations form viewpoints, there is the activity of critical reflection with its demand for the virtually unconditioned and its capacity to estimate approximations to its rigorous requirement.

Universal Doubt

In its simplest form the method of universal doubt is the precept: Doubt everything that can be doubted. Let us begin by attempting to determine the consequences of following out this precept by applying rigorously its criterion of indubitability.

First, all concrete judgments of fact are to be excluded. For while they rest on invulnerable insights, still the invulnerability amounts to no more than the fact that further relevant questions do not arise. A criterion of indubitability is more exigent. It demands the impossibility of further relevant questions, and in concrete judgments of fact such impossibility neither exists nor is apprehended.

Secondly, both empirical science and common sense are excluded. For both aim at ascertaining what in fact is so, and neither succeeds in reaching the indubitable. No doubt, it would be silly to suppose that there are further relevant questions that would lead to the correction of the insights grounding bare statements of fact or elementary measurements. But that is beside the point, for the question is not what certainly is true or false but what indubitably is true or false; and indubitability requires not the fact but the impossibility of further relevant questions.

Thirdly, the meaning of all judgments becomes obscure and unsettled. For the meaning of a judgment can be clear and precise only if one can assign a clear and precise meaning to such terms as reality, knowledge, objectivity. A clear and precise meaning can be assigned to such terms only if one succeeds in clarifying the polymorphic consciousness of man. Such a clarification can be effected by a lengthy, difficult, and delicate inquiry into the facts of human cognitional activity. But if one excludes all concrete judgments of fact, one excludes the clarification and so one is bound to regard the meaning of every judgment as obscure and unsettled.

Fourthly, all mere suppositions satisfy the criterion of indubitability. For the mere supposition excludes the question for reflection, and doubt becomes possible only after the question for reflection arises. Thus, if you suppose that A is B, and I ask whether A really is B, you are entitled to point out that you are merely supposing A to be B, and that my question tries to put an end to mere supposing. On the other hand, there is no possibility of doubting whether or not A is B until that question arises, and so all mere suppositions are indubitable. It follows that all analytic propositions are indubitable, inasmuch as they rest on rules of syntax and on definitions of terms, and all such rules and definitions are regarded as mere suppositions. On the other hand, analytic principles are not indubitable, for they require concrete judgments of fact in which occur the defined terms in their defined sense; and, as has been seen, all concrete judgments of fact are excluded by the criterion of indubitability.

Fifthly, the existential subject survives, for the existential subject is the subject prior to the question, Am I? The criterion of indubitability does not eliminate the experienced centre of experiencing, the intelligent centre of inquiry, insight, and formulations, the rational centre of critical reflection, scrutiny, hesitation, doubt, and frustration. Indeed, the method of universal doubt presupposes the existence of this centre and imposes frustration upon it. One can argue that before I can doubt, I must exist, but what does the conclusion mean? What is the "I"? What is existing? What is the meaning of affirming? All these questions can be given answers that are correct in fact. But as long as the criterion of indubitability remains in force, they cannot be given any clear or precise answer, for that would suppose a clarification of the polymorphism of human consciousness.

Sixthly, not even the criterion of indubitability is indubitable. It is clear enough that one makes no mistake in accepting the indubitable. It is not at all clear that one makes no mistake in rejecting everything that in fact is true. But the criterion of indubitability excludes all concrete judgments of fact, no matter how true and certain they may be. Therefore, the criterion of indubitability is not itself indubitable. It follows that the frustrated existential subject practising universal doubt cannot console himself with the thought that there is anything rational about his doubting.

Seventhly, every assignable reason for practising universal doubt is eliminated by a coherent exercise of the doubt. Thus, one might adopt the method of universal doubt in the hope of being left with premises for a deduction of the universe; but the exercise of the doubt removes all premises and leaves only mere suppositions; moreover, even if it left some premises, it would question the validity of the project of deducing the universe, for it is not indubitable that the universe can be deduced. Again, one might adopt the method of universal doubt, because one felt the disagreement of philosophers to reveal their incompetence and to justify the use of a violent remedy; but the exercise of the doubt leaves nothing for philosophers to disagree about and, as well, it leaves open to suspicion the assumption that their disagreement stems from their incompetence; for it is conceivable that philosophic process is dialectical with positions inviting development and counter-positions inviting reversal.

Eighthly, the method of universal doubt is a leap in the dark. If we have been able to determine a list of precise consequences of universal doubt, we also have presupposed our account of the structure of human knowledge and of the polymorphism that besets it. But that account is not indubitable. At most, it is true as a matter of fact. Accordingly, to accept the criterion of indubitability is to deprive oneself of the means of ascertaining what precisely that criterion implies; and to accept a criterion without being able to determine its precise implications is to make a leap in the dark.

Ninthly, while the consequences of universal doubt will come to light in the long run, the proximate results of the method will be arbitrary and illusory. Proximate results will be arbitrary, for the exact implications of the method are unknown. Moreover, proximate results will be illusory. For doubting affects not the underlying texture and fabric of the mind but only the explicit judgments that issue from it. One can profess in all sincerity to doubt all that can be doubted, but one cannot abolish at a stroke the past development of one's mentality, one's accumulation of insights, one's prepossessions and prejudices, one's habitual orientation in life. So one will have little difficulty in seeing that the views of others are very far from being indubitable; at the same time, because the doubt is applied arbitrarily, one's own rooted convictions not merely will survive but also will be illuminated with the illusory splendour of having passed unscathed through an ordeal that the views of others could not stand. Accordingly, it will be only in the long run that the full implications of universal doubt will come to light, when the method has been applied by many persons with quite different initial convictions.

However, if I believe that universal doubt was practised more successfully by Hume than by Descartes and, perhaps, more successfully by the existentialists and some of the logical positivists than by Hume, I must also recall that my topic has been, not the concrete proposal entertained by Descartes, but the consequences of interpreting literally and applying rigorously the precept: Doubt everything that can be doubted. Clearly enough, the implications of that precept fail to reveal the profound originality and enduring significance of Descartes, for whom universal doubt was not a school of scepticism but a philosophic programme that aimed to embrace the universe, to assign a clear and precise reason for everything, to exclude the influence of unacknowledged presuppositions. For that programme we have only praise, but we also believe that it should be disassociated from the method of universal doubt whether that method is interpreted rigorously or mitigated in a fashion that cannot avoid being arbitrary.

Finally, it should be noted that a rejection of universal doubts implies a rejection of the excessive commitment with which it burdens the philosophic enterprise. The only method to reach the conclusions of science is the method of science. The only method reach the conclusions of common sense is the method of common sense. Universal doubt leads the philosopher to reject what he is not equipped to restore. But philosophers that do not practise universal doubt are not in that predicament, and it is only a mistaken argument from analogy that expects of them a validation of scientific or common-sense views.

Empiricism

. . . A [third] method that offers to guide the subject issues the precept: Observe the significant facts. Unfortunately, what can be observed is merely a datum; significance accrues to data only through the occurrence of insights; correct insights can be reached only at the term of a prolonged investigation that ultimately reaches the point where no further relevant questions arise; and without the combination of data and correct insights that together form a virtually unconditioned, there are no facts. Such, I believe, is the truth of the matter, but it is an extremely paradoxical truth, and the labor of all the pages that precede can be regarded as a sustained effort both to clarify the nature of insight and judgment and to account for the confusion, so natural to man, between extroversion and objectivity. For man observes, understands, and judges, but he fancies that what he knows in judgment is not known in judgment and does not suppose an exercise of understanding but simply is attained by taking a good look at the "real" that is "already out there now." Empiricism, then, is a bundle of blunders, and its history is their successive clarification.

. . . description is not enough. If it claims simply to report data in their purity, one may ask why the arid report should be added to the more lively experience. If it pretends to report the significant data, then it is deceived, for significance is not in data but accrues to them from the occurrence of insight. If it urges that it presents the insights that arise spontaneously, immediately, and inevitably from the data, one must remark that the data alone are never the sole determinants of the insights that arise in any but an infantile mind and that beyond the level of insight there is the level of critical reflection with its criterion of the virtually unconditioned. If it objects that at least one must begin by describing the facts that are accessible to all, one must insist that knowledge of fact rests on a grasp of the unconditioned and that a grasp of the unconditioned is not the starting-point but the end of inquiry. Moreover, if one hopes to reach this end in an inquiry into knowledge, then one had better not begin with the assumption that knowing is "something there to be looked at and described." For knowing is an organically integrated activity: on a flow of sensitive experiences, inquiry intelligently generates a cumulative succession of insights, and the significance of the experiences varies concomitantly with the cumulation of insights; in memory's store of experiences and in the formulation of accumulated insights, reflection grasps approximations towards the virtually unconditioned and attainments of it to issue into probable and certain judgments of fact. To conceive knowing one must understand the dynamic pattern of experiencing, inquiring, reflecting, and such understanding is not to be reached by taking a look. To affirm knowing it is useless to peer inside, for the dynamic pattern is to be found not in this or that act but in the unfolding of mathematics, empirical science, common sense, and philosophy; in that unfolding must be grasped the pattern of knowing and, if one feels inclined to doubt that the pattern really exists, then one can try the experiment of attempting to escape experience, to renounce intelligence in inquiry, to desert reasonableness in critical reflection.

In brief, empiricism as a method rests on an elementary conclusion. What is obvious in knowing is, indeed, looking. Compared to looking, insight is obscure, and grasp of the unconditioned is doubly obscure. But empiricism amounts to the assumption that what is obvious in knowing is what knowing obviously is. That assumption is false, for if one would learn mathematics or science or philosophy or if one sought common-sense advice, then one would go to a man that is intelligent and reasonable rather than to a man that is stupid and silly.

Common-sense Eclecticism

The . . . [fourth] of the methods that would guide the philosopher to his goal is common-sense eclecticism. If it rarely is adopted by original thinkers, it remains the inertial centre of the philosophic process. From every excess and aberration men swing back to common sense, and perhaps no more than a minority of students and professors, of critics and historians, ever wander very far from a set of assumptions that are neither formulated nor scrutinized.

As has been seen, however, common sense is variable. The common sense of one age is not that of another; the common sense of Germans is not that of the Frenchmen; the common sense of Americans is not that of Englishmen and still less that of Russians. Roman Catholics have their common sense, Protestants theirs, Moslems theirs, and agnostics a fourth variety. Clearly such variations preclude hard and fast rules, yet general tendencies are not too difficult to discern. For commonly a distinction is drawn between the activities of theoretical understanding, which not undeservedly are to be distrusted, and the pronouncements of prephilosophic reflection, which ground human sanity and human co-operation and therefore must be retained.

Theoretical understanding, then, seeks to solve problems, to erect syntheses, to embrace the universe in a single view. Neither its existence, nor its value, nor the remote possibility of its success is denied. Still common sense is concerned not with remote but with proximate possibilities. It lauds the great men of the past, ostensibly to stir one to emulation, but really to urge one to modesty. It remarks that, if there are unsolved problems, and, no doubt,

there are, at least men of undoubted genius have failed to solve them. It leaves
to be inferred that, unless one is a still greater genius, then one had best regard such problems as practically insoluble. But emphatically it would not
discourage anyone inclined to philosophy. A recognition of one's limitations
need not prevent one from studying philosophy, from teaching it, from contributing to reviews, from writing books. One can become learned in the
history of philosophy. One can form one's reasoned judgments about the
views of others. By taking care not to lose the common touch, by maintaining
one's sense of reality, by cultivating balance and proportion, one can reach a
philosophic viewpoint that is solidly reliable and, after all, sufficiently enlightened. For opinions are legion; theories rise, glow, fascinate, and vanish;
but sound judgment remains. And what is sound judgment? It is to bow to the
necessary, to accept the certain, merely to entertain the probable, to distrust
the doubtful, to disregard the merely possible, to laugh at the improbable, to
denounce the impossible, and to believe what Science says. Nor are these precepts empty words, for there are truths that one cannot reject in practical
living, there are others which it would be silly to doubt, there are claims to
truth that merit attention and consideration, and each of these has its opposites. List the lot, draw out their implications, and you will find that you
already possess a sound philosophy than can be set down in a series of propositions confirmed by proofs and fortified by answers to objections.

Such, approximately, is the programme of common-sense eclecticism, and
I must begin by clarifying which of its aspects I shall single out for comment
and criticism. The present topic is the method of philosophy. On common-
sense eclecticism as a practical attitude, as a pedagogy, as a style in composing text-books, as a technique in discussing issues, I have no remarks to make.
But I began by pointing out that one's method in philosophy predetermines
what one's philosophy will be, and now I have to examine what is the philosophy or lack of philosophy to which one commits oneself by adopting common sense eclecticism as a method.

In the first place, attention must be drawn to the difference between the
foregoing eclecticism and my own concessions to common sense. In the
method outlined after defining metaphysics, common sense no less than science
was called upon to supply secondary minor premises in the argument; for the
aim was to integrate science and common sense and an integration is not independent of its materials. However, before being invited to play this subsidiary role, both science and common sense were to be subjected to a reorientation which they did not control; in particular, the liability of common
sense to dramatic, egoistic, group, and general bias, had been noted; the
ambiguities of such terms as reality, knowledge, and objectivity had been examined; and only a criticized and chastened common sense was entrusted with
no more than a subsidiary philosophic role. The method of common-sense
eclecticism not only dispenses with such criticism and reorientation but also

allows uncriticized common sense to settle by its practicality the aim of philosophy and to measure naively the resources at the philosopher's disposal. Let us attempt to expand these points briefly.

Secondly, then, common-sense eclecticism brushes aside the aim of philosophy. For that aim is the integrated unfolding of the detached, disinterested, and unrestricted desire to know. That aim can be pursued only by the exercise of theoretical understanding and, indeed, only by the subtle exercise that understands both science and common sense in their differences and in their complementarity. But common-sense eclecticism deprecates the effort to understand. For it, problems are immutable features of the mental landscape, and syntheses are to be effected by somebody else, who, when he has finished his system, will provide a name for merely another viewpoint.

Thirdly, common-sense eclecticism denies the vital growth of philosophy. It restricts significant activity to men of genius, and it takes it for granted that they are very few and very rare. But within the context of the philosophic process, every discovery is a significant contribution to the ultimate aim. If it is formulated as a position, it invites the development of further coherent discovery. If it is formulated as a counter-position, it invites the exploration of its presuppositions and implications and it leads to its own reversal to restore the discovery to the cumulative series of positions and to enlighten man on the polymorphism of his consciousness. This activity of discovery, of developing positions, and of reversing counter-positions, is not restricted to the men of genius of whom common sense happens to have heard. It results from all competent and conscientious work, and, like natural growth, it goes forward without attracting widespread attention. So far from being the product of genius, it produces genius. For the genius is simply the man at the level of his time, when the time is ripe for a new orientation or a sweeping reorganization; and it is not the genius that makes the time ripe, but the competent and conscientious workers that slowly and often unconsciously have been developing positions and heading towards the reversal of counter-positions. But common-sense eclecticism brushes all this aside with a homily on the acknowledgement of one's personal limitations. The exercise of theoretical understanding is to be left to men of genius, and common sense will see to it that no effort is made to prepare their way and no comprehension is available to greet their achievements.

Fourthly, while common-sense eclecticism discourages the effort to understand, it encourages a wide exercise of judgment. But this is to overlook the fact that understanding is a constitutive component in knowledge, that before one can pass judgment on any issue, one has to understand it. Nor is the requisite understanding to be estimated by average attainment, by the convictions of common sense, by the beliefs of a given milieu, but solely by that absence of further relevant questions that leads to reflective grasp of the virtually unconditioned. Unless one endeavours to understand with all one's heart and all one's mind, one will not know what questions are relevant or when their limit is approached. Yet eclecticism, while discouraging understanding, urges one to paw through the display of opinions in the history of philosophy and to discriminate between the necessary and the certain, the probable and the doubtful, the possible, the improbable, and the impossible.

The fallacy of this procedure is, of course, that it fails to grasp the limitations of common sense. The proper domain of common sense is the field of particular matters of fact; it is that field, not as a single whole, but divided up and parcelled out among the men and women familiar with its several parts; it is such a part, not in its basic formulated actuality, but simply in its immediate relevance to human living in the mode and fashion of such living in each region and each age. One can entrust common sense with the task of a juror; one cannot ask it to formulate the laws of a country, to argue cases in its courts, to decide on issues of procedure, and to pass sentence on criminals. One does not have to be a scientist to see the colour of litmus paper or to note the position of a needle on a dial; but one cannot rely on mere common sense to devise experiments or to interpret their results. Similarly, in philosophy, if one presupposes an independently established set of philosophic concepts and positions, then common sense can provide the factual boundary conditions that decide between theoretical alternatives. But it is vain to ask common sense to provide the philosophic concepts, to formulate the coherent range of possible positions, to set the questions that can be answered by an appeal to commonly known facts. By deprecating theoretic understanding and by encouraging a wide exercise of judgment, common-sense eclecticism does what it can to make philosophy obtuse and superficial.

Fifthly, common-sense eclecticism cannot be critical. Not only is common sense a variable but also it is subject to a dramatic, an egoistic, a group, and a general bias. Once the aim of philosophy is brushed aside, once the resources of its natural growth are ignored, once a vain programme of incompetent judgment is established, not only common sense but also its bias are in charge and they are there to stay. Distinct philosophies emerge for the changing tastes and fashions of racial, economic, regional, national, cultural, religious, and anti-religious groups and even sub-groups. Spice and originality are added by the special brands of common sense peculiar to psychoneurotics, assertive egoists, and aspiring romanticists. And if human society tires of muddling through one crisis into another, then there arises the temptation that the only means to attain an effective community of norms and directives is to put the educational system, the press, the stage, the radio, and the churches, under the supervision of a paternal government, to call upon social engineers to channel thought and condition feeling, and to hold in reserve the implements that discipline refractory minds and tongues. For common-sense eclecticism is incapable of criticizing common sense. It is not by discouraging theoretical understanding that the polymorphism of human consciousness can be grasped, and it is not by appealing to what common sense finds obvious that the correct meaning of such terms as reality, knowledge, and objectivity is to be reached.

G. W. F. Hegel   **5. DIALECTIC**

Hegel wrote his *Science of Logic* while headmaster and philosopher-professor of a Nürnberg high school. In it, he contends that the method, object, and content of metaphysical science are not separate, but one. There can be no methodology critically arrived at prior to metaphysics (as in Kant), for method implies a metaphysics. Thus, a theory of knowledge and a methodology are not independent of one another, but are implicative of each other, and both imply a general theory of being.

In language anticipatory of the phenomenological methods of Edmund Husserl, Hegel says that a start is made from empirical and sensuous consciousness by a kind of absorption of data: "We must just absorb that which is presented." He strikes toward immediacy in the form of "pure knowledge" as the starting point. The "beginning," he says, must be an absolute; it must be the "immediate" itself. Hence the beginning must be pure being. This beginning, however, is also the "end," and what is "immediate" involves also the mediated and the relational.

In short, there is for Hegel reciprocity between the initiation of inquiry and the result of inquiry, and between the totality and all of its forms. The totality forms a cycle by which the foundation of thought-and-being stretches out to the result, while the result stretches back to the foundation. As he puts it, "The line of scientific advance becomes a circle," because, as he says elsewhere, "The truth is the totality."

There is thus both unity and multiplicity, which enter into inquiry. But inquiry ends in unity because it starts in unity. There is a difference, however, between the two stages of unity. Pure being, as Hegel says, is the unity into which pure knowledge returns, for it is the content of pure knowledge. In different ways, then, pure being is absolutely immediate and absolutely mediated.

Hegel does not begin with the ego or with consciousness, as he felt his modern predecessors had done. He begins with being and the processive

From the 1816 edition of Hegel's *Logic*, as translated by W. H. Johnston and L. G. Struthers, in *The Philosophy of Hegel*. Reprinted by permission of the publisher, George Allen & Unwin Ltd., London.

consequences of being, which dialectically implicate both the differentiated and the undifferentiated, or the concrete and the abstract, or beings and pure being itself.

IT HAS ONLY RECENTLY been felt that there is a difficulty in finding a beginning in philosophy, and the reason for this difficulty, as well as the possibility of solving it, has been much discussed. The beginning of philosophy must be either mediate or immediate, and it is easy to show that it can be neither the one nor the other: so that either method of beginning is refuted.

It is true that the principle of any philosophy also expresses a beginning, but this beginning is objective and not subjective; it is the beginning of all things. The principle is a content somehow determined—water, the one, *nous,* idea—substance, monad, and so forth; or, where it relates to the nature of cognition and so is designed rather to be a criterion than an objective determination of the content to which interest is directed. On the other hand, the beginning as such, considered as something subjective in the sense of some contingent way of introducing the exposition, remains neglected and indifferent; and so the need of the question, with what we are to begin, still seems unimportant compared with the need of a principle, which alone seems to contain the interest of the matter—the interest as to what is the truth and the absolute basis of all things.

The modern embarrassment about a beginning arises from yet another need with which those are unacquainted who, as dogmatists, seek a demonstration of the principle, or who, as sceptics, seek a subjective criterion with which to meet dogmatic philosophy—a need which, finally, is entirely denied by those who begin with explosive abruptness from their inner revelation, faith, intellectual intuition, and so forth, and desire to dispense with method and logic. If thought at first is abstract and concerns itself merely with the principle regarded as content, but in the progress of its evolution is forced to regard also the other side, the behavior of cognition, then subjective activity is perceived as an essential moment of objective truth, and the need arises of uniting method with content and form with principle. The principle is to be the beginning, and the actual *"prius"* for thought is also to be first in the logical thought-process.

We have here only to consider how the logical beginning appears; the two aspects in which it can be taken, mediately as a result or immediately as a beginning proper, have already been named. The question which seems so important to contemporary Thought, whether knowledge of the truth is immediate and simply begins, whether it is an act of faith, or a mediated knowledge, is not to be discussed here. In so far as such consideration can be undertaken preliminarily, this has been done in another (in my *Encyclopedia of the Philosophical Sciences,* 3rd Edn. *Vorbegriff,* §§ 61 ff.) work. We need only quote here that there is nothing in Heaven, Nature, Spirit, or anywhere else, which does not contain immediacy as well as mediacy, so that these two determinations are seen to be unseparated and inseparable, and the opposition between them null. As regards philosophical discussion, the determinations of mediacy and immediacy, and hence the discussion of their opposition and truth, occur in every logical proposition. With regard to thought, knowledge, and cognition, this opposition receives the more concrete shape of knowledge, mediate or immediate; and the nature of cognition is considered within the science of logic itself, in so far as cognition, in its wider and concrete form, falls within the science of spirit and the phenomenology of spirit. But to ask for clearness about cognition before the beginning of the science is to demand that it shall be discussed outside its precincts; but outside the precincts of Science this cannot be done—at least not in a scientific manner, and such a manner alone is here in question.

The beginning is logical in that it is to be made within the sphere of thought existing freely for itself, in other words, in pure knowledge; its mediacy here arises from the fact that pure knowledge is consciousness in its last and absolute truth. We have remarked in the introduction the "Phenomenology of Spirit" is the science of consciousness, demonstrating that consciousness has for result the concept of Science, that is, pure knowledge. The science of manifested spirit, which involves and demonstrates the necessity, and hence the proof, together with the mediation in general, of that standpoint which is pure knowledge, is thus presupposed by logic. In this science of manifested spirit we start from empirical and sensuous consciousness; this is immediate knowledge proper, and in the work mentioned its validity is discussed. Other kinds of consciousness, such as faith in divine truths, inner experience, knowledge through inner revelations, and so on, are shown on slight reflection to be very inappropriate as instances of immediate knowledge. In the treatise referred to, immediate consciousness is also the first and immediate element in the science, and therefore the presupposition: in the logic, that is, presupposition which appeared as the result of those reflections—namely, the idea as pure knowledge. Logic is pure science, that is, pure knowledge in the whole extent of its development. In its result, this idea has determined itself to be certainty become truth; certainty which in one aspect is no longer over against the object, but has incorporated it with itself and knows it to be itself; and, from another aspect, has given up its conviction that it is opposed to and destructive of the object: it has renounced this subjectivity and is one with this renunciation.

Starting from this determination of pure knowledge, the beginning of the science of knowledge is to remain immanent; and in order to effect this, no more is requisite than that we must contemplate, or rather, putting aside all reflections and opinions otherwise held, we must just absorb, that which is presented.

Pure knowledge, taken as shrunk into this unity, has transcended all reference to an other and to mediation; it is the undifferentiated, and as such ceases to be knowledge; nothing is there but simple immediacy.

Simple immediacy is itself an expression of reflection, and refers to its distinction from the mediated: properly expressed, this simple immediacy is therefore pure being. Just as pure knowledge is to mean nothing except purely abstract knowing as such, so pure being is to mean nothing except being in general; being and nothing else, without any further determination or filling.

Being is here the beginning represented as arising from mediation, a mediation which transcends itself; it being assumed that pure knowledge is the result of finite knowledge of consciousness. If no assumption is to be made, and the beginning is to be taken immediately, it determines itself only this way, that it is to be the beginning of logic, of independent thought. Nothing is there except the decision (which might appear arbitrary) to consider thought as such. The beginning must be an absolute, or, what here is equivalent, an abstract beginning: it must presuppose nothing, must be mediated by nothing, must have no foundation: itself is to be the foundation of the whole science. It must therefore just be something immediate, or rather the immediate itself. As it cannot have any determination relatively to Other, so also it cannot hold in itself any determination or content; for this would be differentiation and mutual relation of distincts, and thus mediation. The beginning therefore is pure being.

To this simple exposition of what is proper to the subject of the perfectly simple, which is the logical beginning, the following further reflections may be added; their function however cannot be to elucidate or confirm this exposition, which is complete in itself, since they are rather the result of ideas and reflections which, though they may come in our way at the outset, must, like every other preliminary prejudice, be disposed of within the science itself; so that really they should be made to await such disposal.

It has already been perceived that the absolutely true must be a result, and that, conversely, a result presupposes some primary truth; which, however, because it is primary, is not necessary, considered objectively, and, from the subjective side, is not known. Consequently the idea has arisen in recent times that the truth with which philosophy begins must be hypothetical or problematical, and that hence philosophy at first must be mere seeking. . . .

If it is considered that progress is a return to the foundation, to that origin and truth on which depends and indeed by which is produced that with which the beginning was made, then it must be admitted that this consideration is of essential importance; and it will be more clearly evident in the logic itself. Thus consciousness is led back on its road from immediacy, with which it begins, to absolute knowledge as its inmost truth; and the first term, which entered the stage as the immediate, arises, precisely, from this last term, the foundation. Still further, we see that absolute spirit, which is found to be the concrete, last, and highest truth of all being at the end of its evolution freely passes beyond itself and lapses into the shape of an immediate being, it resolves itself to the creation of a world which contains everything included in the evolution preceding that result; all of which, by reason of this inverted position, is changed, together with its beginning, into something dependent on the result, for the result is the principle. What is essential for the science is not so much that a pure immediate is the beginning, but that itself in its totality forms a cycle returning upon itself, wherein the first is also last, and the last first.

Hence it equally results on the other hand that we must regard as result that to which the movement returns as into its foundation. From this point of view the first is equally the foundation, and the last derived: it is a result, in so far as we start from the first and reach the last (the foundation) by a series of correct conclusions. And further, the movement away from the beginning is to be considered merely as a further determination of it, so that the beginning remains the foundation of all that follows without disappearing from it. The movement does not consist in the derivation of an other, or in a transition into something veritably other, in so far as such a transition occurs, it cancels itself again. Thus the beginning of philosophy, the basis which is present and preserves itself in all the developments which follow, remains a something immanent throughout its further determinations.

What is one-sided in the beginning, owing to its general determination as something abstract and immediate, is lost in this movement: it becomes mediated, and the line of scientific advance becomes a circle. It also follows that the constituents of the beginning, since at that point they are undeveloped and without content, are not truly understood at the beginning: only the science itself fully developed is an understanding of it, complete, significant, and based on truth.

Now precisely because the result stands out as the absolute foundation, the advance of this knowledge is not something provisional, problematical, or hypothetical; it must be determined by the nature of the subject and the content. This beginning is not arbitrary nor temporarily accepted, nor is it something which, appearing arbitrary and assumed under correction, in the event turns out rightly to have been made the beginning. (The case is not that of the construction we are directed to make in order to prove a theorem in geometry, where it is only the proof which shows that we did right to draw just these lines, and then, in the proof itself, to begin with comparisons of just those lines or angles. For itself, the drawing of such lines and making of such comparisons does not render the proof self-evident.)

In this way the reason why in the pure science we begin from pure being was above indicated immediately in the science itself. This pure being is the unity into which pure knowledge returns, or, if pure knowledge as form is to be kept separate from its unity, then pure being is the content of pure knowledge. It is in this respect that pure being, the absolutely immediate, is also absolutely mediated. But it is equally essential to take it one-sidedly as pure immediacy, just because it is here taken as the beginning. Were it not to be taken as this pure indeterminateness, then, in so far as it were determinate, it would be taken as mediated and as thus already carried a step further; for what is determinate contains an other for a first element. It is therefore in the nature of the beginning to be being and nothing else. For entering into philosophy there is therefore no further need of preparations, nor of other considerations or connection.

We cannot extract any close determination or positive content for the beginning from the fact that it is the beginning of philosophy. For here at the beginning, where there is as yet no philosophy, philosophy is an empty word, or an idea taken at random and not justified. Pure knowledge affords only this negative determination, that the beginning must be the abstract beginning. In so far as pure being is taken as the content of pure knowledge, the latter must draw back from its content and leave it to itself without further determining it. Or again, if pure being is to be regarded as the unity into which knowledge has collapsed at the point where its union with the object is consummated, then knowledge has disappeared into this unity, leaving no distinction from it, and hence no determination for it. Nor is there any other something, nor any content, which could be used to make a more closely determined beginning.

But even the determination of being, which has been accepted so far as beginning, could be omitted, so that the only requirement would be to make a pure beginning. There would then be nothing but the beginning itself, and it would remain to be seen what that is. This position might be used to pacify those who partly will not be satisfied because we begin with being (from whatever considerations), still less with the resulting transition of being into nothing, partly know no better than that in any science a beginning is made by presupposing some idea—such idea being next analyzed, so that it is only the result of this analysis which affords the first definite concept of the science. Were we too to observe this procedure we should have no particular object before us, because the beginning, as being the beginning of thought, must be perfectly abstract and general, pure form quite without content; we should have nothing but the idea of a bare beginning as such. It remains to be seen what we possess in this idea.

So far, there is nothing: something is to become. The beginning is not pure nothing, but a nothing from which something is to proceed; so that being is already contained in the beginning. The beginning thus contains both, being and nothing; it is the unity of being and nothing, or is not-being which is being, and being which is also not-being.

Further, being and nothing are present in the beginning as distinct from one another: for the beginning points forward to something other, it is a not-being related to being as to an other: that which *is-beginning*, as yet *is* not: it is advancing toward being. The beginning therefore contains being as having this characteristic that it flies from and transcends not-being, as its opposite.

And further, that which is-beginning, already is, and equally, as yet, is not. The opposites being and not-being are therefore in immediate union in it: in other words, it is the undifferentiated unity of the two.

The analysis of the beginning thus yields the concept of the unity of being and not-being, or (in a more reflected form) the unity of the state of being differentiated, and of being undifferentiated, or the identity of identity and non-identity. This concept might be considered as the first or purest (that is, most abstract) definition of the absolute, which in fact it would be were we concerned with the forms of definitions and the name of the absolute. In this sense, this abstract concept would be the first definition of the absolute, and all further determinations and developments would be richer and more closely determinate definitions of it. Being may be rejected as a beginning by some because of its transition to nothing and the resulting unity of being and nothing: let these see whether their beginning, which starts with the idea of the beginning, and the analysis of this (which, though doubtless correct, also leads to the unity of being and nothing), will turn out more satisfactory than the method by which being is made the beginning.

But there is yet a further observation to be made on this method. This analysis presupposes as already known the idea of the beginning: it has therefore copied the methods of other sciences. These presuppose their object, and take leave to assume that everyone has the same idea of it, and is likely to discover in it roughly the same determinations that they themselves indicate and extract from the object in various ways by analysis, comparison, and other forms of reasoning. But that which constitutes the absolute beginning must likewise be something otherwise known; now if it is something concrete, and therefore contains a multiplicity of determinations within itself, then this relation, which it is in itself, is assumed as something known: it is asserted to be something immediate, and this it is not; for it is merely a relation of distincts, and therefore contains mediation. Further, in the concrete the contingency and arbitrariness proper to analysis and to varying determination begin to operate. The determinations which are extracted depend on what each individual finds given in his own immediate and contingent idea. The relation contained in a concrete, that is, a synthetic unity, is necessary only in so far as it is not a datum, but is produced by the inherent movement of the moments tending back into this unity—a movement which is the opposite of the analytic method, which is an activity belonging to the object and external to the object.

What has been said implies this further point, that that with which we must begin, cannot be something concrete, something containing a relation within itself. For such presupposes a mediation and a transition within itself from a first to an other, of which process the concrete, now reduced to simplicity, would be the result. But the beginning must not be a first *and* an other: in a thing which in itself is first *and* an other, progress has already advanced a step. That which constitutes the beginning (and that is, the very beginning itself) must therefore be taken, in its simple immediacy without content, as something not admitting analysis, hence as pure vacuity, as Being.

If anyone, impatient of the consideration of the abstract beginning, should demand that we begin, not with the beginning, but directly with the matter itself, the answer is that the matter is just this empty being: it is in the course of the science that we are to discover what the matter is; the science must not therefore presuppose this as known.

If any form is taken for the beginning in preference to empty being, then the beginning suffers from the flaws mentioned. Those who remain dissatisfied with this beginning are asked to set themselves the task of beginning differently in order to avoid these faults.

There is however one novel beginning in philosophy, which recently has become famous and cannot be passed over without mention, namely that which begins with the ego. It arose partly from the reflection that all that follows must be derived from the first truth, partly from the need that the first truth should be something known and, even more, something immediately certain. Such a beginning generally is not a contingent idea which can take a different form in different subjects. For, the ego, this immediate consciousness of self, first manifests itself partly as something immediate, partly as something known in a far higher sense than any other idea; things otherwise known, though they belong to the ego, are a content distinct from it and therefore contingent, whereas the ego is simple certainty of itself. But the ego in general is also something concrete, or rather the most concrete of all things—consciousness of self as of a world infinitely complex. In order to make ego the beginning and basis of philosophy, this concrete element must be removed by an absolute act by which the ego is purged of itself and is presented to its own consciousness as abstract ego. But this pure ego is now no longer immediate, nor is it the known and ordinary ego of our consciousness, to which the science was to be linked immediately and equally for all. Such an act would really be an exaltation to the standpoint of pure knowledge, where the distinction between subjective and objective has disappeared. But as this elevation is demanded immediately, it is a subjective postulate: in order to prove itself a legitimate demand the movement of the concrete ego from immediate consciousness to pure knowledge would have to be proved and demonstrated upon itself from inner necessity. Without this objective movement pure knowledge, even when defined as "intellectual intuition," appears as an arbitrary standpoint, or even as one of the empirical conditions of consciousness, with regard to which all depends on whether one individual finds it within himself or can produce it, and another not. But this pure ego must be pure essential knowledge, and pure knowledge is posited in the individual consciousness only through the absolute act of self-exaltation—it is not present immediately in consciousness; and it is just in this respect that the advantage is lost which is to arise from this beginning of philosophy, namely that it is something thoroughly well known which everyone finds immediately within himself as the starting point of further reflection. Rather, in its abstract essential nature this pure ego is something quite unknown to ordinary consciousness, something which it does not find in itself. And here, on the contrary, there sets in the disadvantage of the illusion that we are speaking of something known, namely the ego of empirical self-consciousness, whereas in fact we are speaking of something remote from this consciousness. The determination of pure knowledge as ego involves a permanent recollection of the subjective ego, the barriers of which are to be forgotten, and preserves the idea that the propositions and relations yielded in the further development of the ego occur or are found in ordinary consciousness, since it is this of which they are asserted. This confusion, instead of immediate illumination, produces so much the more glaring complications and indeed a total loss of direction; among laymen especially it has led to the crudest misunderstandings.

Next, as regards the fact that the ego in general is determined as subjective, it is true that pure knowledge clears the ego of its limited meaning according to which the object presents to it an insuperable opposition. But for this very reason it would at least be superfluous to retain this subjective attitude and the determination of pure essence as ego. Such a determination, however, not only involves this disturbing ambiguity, but, more closely regarded, it still remains a subjective ego. The actual development of the science which starts from the ego shows that the object there persists in having and retaining its determination as *other* relatively to the ego, so that this ego from which we start is not pure knowledge which has veritably overcome the opposition of consciousness, but is still imprisoned in the sphere of appearance.

This further essential observation must here be made: it is true that the ego in itself can be defined as pure knowledge or intellectual intuition, and asserted as a beginning; but in philosophy what matters is not that which is there already in itself, or internally, but the present *in thought* of the internal element and the determinateness in which the latter thus presents itself. Whatever element of intellectual intuition is present at the beginning of the science, it cannot be anything but primary, immediate, and simple determination; or, if the object of such intuition is called the eternal or the divine or the absolute, the same applies to what ever of these elements is present in the beginning. Whatever name be applied of richer content than that expressed by mere being, the only matter for consideration is how such an absolute enters into thinking knowledge and the expression of this. True, intellectual intuition is the forcible rejection of mediation and of demonstrative external reflection.

But if it asserts more than simple immediacy, it asserts something concrete, something containing distinct determinations. But it has already been remarked that to express and represent such a thing is a mediating movement, which begins with one of the determinations and proceeds to the other, even although the latter returns to the former; and further, such a movement must not be arbitrary nor assertory. Hence in such a representation a beginning is not made with the concrete, but with the simple immediate whence the movement starts. Further, if a concrete thing is taken as the beginning, there is lacking the proof which is demanded by the complex of determinations contained in the concrete.

The expression of the absolute, the eternal, or God (and God has the most undisputed right that the beginning should be made with Him), or the contemplation or thought of these, may contain more than pure Being: if that is so, such content has yet to manifest itself to thinking (and not to presentational) knowledge; for, however rich this content, the first determination which emerges into knowledge is something simple, for it is only the simple which does not contain something more than pure beginning: the immediate alone is simple, for there only no transition has taken place from one to another. If these richer forms of presentation, such as the Absolute, or God, express or contain anything beyond being, then this is, in the beginning, but an empty word and mere being; so that this simple vacancy without further meaning is, absolutely, the beginning of philosophy.

Henri Bergson   6. INTUITION

Despite profound differences Bergson's thought has much in common with Hegel's. To Bergson movement is the authentic stamp of reality. This movement emanates from the primordial simplicity of being. Intuition bespeaks our real contact with reality, he says, but we are constrained to translate such contact into the acceptable currency of concepts. Concepts are always inadequate. Hence, in a sort of dialectic, one theory must engender another corrective theory—one correction, another complication; one complication, a further theory; and so on—until at last the true pulse of the intuition has been insulated in abstractions. But though we can never recapture the original concrete intuition into reality, we need not fall into the trap

This selection, originally appearing under the title "Philosophical Intuition," is from Bergson's *The Creative Mind* published by Philosophical Library, Inc. (New York, 1946). It is used with the kind permission of the publisher.

of abstract complexity. Somewhere between the two it is possible to discover the essential central image—in the shadow, as it were, cast forth from the intuition. It is this "receding and vanishing image," Bergson says, "which haunts . . . the mind of the philosopher, which follows him like his shadow through the ins and outs of this thought." And again, "It is in concepts that the system develops; it is into an image that it contracts when it is driven back to the intuition from which it comes."

This central image possesses, in the first place, a negative selective capacity, or the power of rejecting some facts about reality while affirming others. Moreover, the image is itself a unity that focuses reality into a simple optical arrangement. No philosopher can either see, or say, "more than a simple thing; and even then it is something he has tried to say, rather than actually said." Nonetheless this original simplicity of contact is pluralized in a dialectic unfolding, consequent upon contact. It furnishes impulse, not thought. This in turn furnishes a movement of meanings that become visible through the dust of previous associations and memory, which it collects along the way. Thus, "the thought which brings something new into the world is . . . obliged to manifest itself through the ready-made ideas it comes across and draws into its movement." The secret of methodology is, therefore, never to mistake concepts for images, nor images for intuitions.

THERE IS A REMARK that those of us who teach the history of philosophy might make, those who frequently have occasion to come back to the study of the same doctrines and to go ever more deeply into them. A philosophical system seems at first to appear as a complete edifice, expertly designed, where arrangements have been made for the commodious lodging of all problems. In contemplating it in that form we experience an aesthetic joy intensified by a professional satisfaction. Not only, in fact, do we find here order in complexity (and order to which we sometimes like to add our little word as we describe it), but we also have the satisfaction of telling ourselves that we know from whence come the materials and how the building is done. In the problems the philosopher has stated we recognize the questions that were being discussed around him. In the solutions he gives to them we think we recognize, arranged or disarranged, but only slightly modified, the elements of previous or contemporary philosophies. Such a view must have been given to him by this one, another has been suggested by someone else. With what we read, heard and learned we could doubtless reproduce most of what he did. We therefore set to work, we go back to the sources, we weigh the influences, we extract the similitudes, and in the end we distinctly see in the doctrine what we were looking for: a more or less original synthesis of the ideas among which the philosopher lived.

But if we go on constantly renewing contact with the philosopher's thought, we can, by a gradual impregnation, be brought to an entirely different view. I do not say that the work of comparison undertaken at the outset was time lost: without this preliminary effort to recompose a philosophy out of what is other than itself, and to link it up to the conditions which surrounded it, we should perhaps never succeed in grasping what it actually is; for the human mind is so constructed that it cannot begin to understand the new until it has done everything in its power to relate it to the old. But, as we seek to penetrate more fully the philosopher's thought instead of circling around its exterior, his doctrine is transformed for us. In the first place its complication diminishes. Then the various parts fit into one another. Finally the whole is brought together into a single point, which we feel could be ever more closely approached even though there is no hope of reaching it completely.

In this point is something simple, infinitely simple, so extraordinarily simple that the philosopher has never succeeded in saying it. And that is why he went on talking all his life. He could not formulate what he had in mind without feeling himself obliged to correct his formula, then to correct his correction: thus, from theory to theory, correcting when he thought he was completing, what he has accomplished, by a complication which provoked more complication, by developments heaped upon developments, has been to convey with an increasing approximation the simplicity of his original intuition. All the complexity of his doctrine, which would go on ad infinitum, is therefore only the incommensurability between his simple intuition and the means at his disposal for expressing it.

What is this intuition? If the philosopher has not been able to give the formula for it, we certainly are not able to do so. But what we shall manage to recapture and to hold is a certain intermediary image between the simplicity of the concrete intuition and the complexity of the abstractions which translate it, a receding and vanishing image, which haunts, unperceived perhaps, the mind of the philosopher, which follows him like his shadow through the ins and outs of his thought and which, if it is not the intuition itself, approaches it much more closely than the conceptual expression, of necessity symbolical, to which the intuition must have recourse in order to furnish "explanation." Let us look closely at this shadow: by doing so we shall divine the attitude of the body which projects it. And if we try to imitate this attitude, or better still to assume it ourselves, we shall see as far as it is possible what the philosopher saw.

What first of all characterizes this image is the power of negation it possesses. You recall how the demon of Socrates proceeded: it checked the philosopher's will at a given moment and prevented him from acting rather than prescribing what he should do. It seems to me that intuition often behaves in speculative matters like the demon of Socrates in practical life; it is at least in this form that it begins, in this form also that it continues to give the most clear-cut manifestations: it forbids. Faced with currently-accepted ideas, theses which seemed evident, affirmations which had up to that time passed as scientific, it whispers into the philosopher's ear the word: *Impossible!* Impossible, even though the facts and the reasons appeared to invite you to think it possible and real and certain. Impossible, because a certain experience, confused perhaps but decisive, speaks to you through my voice, because it is incompatible with the facts cited and the reasons given, and because hence these facts must have been badly observed, these reasonings false. What a strange force this intuitive power of negation is! How is it that the historians of philosophy have not been more greatly struck by it? Is it not obvious that the first step the philosopher takes, when his thought is still faltering and there is nothing definite in his doctrine, is to reject certain things definitively? Later he will be able to make changes in what he affirms; he will vary only slightly what he denies. And if he varies in his affirmations, it will still be in virtue of the power of negation immanent in intuition or in its image. He will have allowed himself lazily to deduce consequences according to the rules of a rectilinear logic; and then suddenly, in the face of his own affirmation he has the same feeling of impossibility that he had in the first place in considering the affirmation of others. Having in fact left the curve of his thought, to follow straight along a tangent, he has become exterior to himself. He returns to himself when he gets back to intuition. Of these departures toward an affirmation and these returns to the primary intuitions are constituted the zigzaggings of a doctrine which "develops," that is to say which loses itself, finds itself again, and endlessly corrects itself.

Let us get rid of this complication and get back to the simply intuition, or at least to the image which translates it: in so doing we see the doctrine freed of those conditions of time and place upon which it seemed to depend. Doubtless the problems which the philosopher worked upon were the problems which presented themselves in his day; the science he used or criticized was the science of his time; in the theories he expounds one might even find, by looking for them, the ideas of his contemporaries and his predecessors. How could it be otherwise? In order to have the new understood, it must be expressed in terms of the old; and the problems already stated, the solutions provided, the philosophy and science of the times in which he lived, all these have been for each great thinker the material he was obliged to use to give a concrete form to his thought. Not to mention that it has been traditional, from ancient times, to present all philosophy as a complete system, which includes everything one knows. But it would be a strange mistake to take for a constitutive element of doctrine what was the only means of expressing it. Such is the first error to which we are exposed, as I was just saying, when we undertake the study of a system. So many partial resemblances strike us, so many parallels seem to be indicated, so many pressing appeals to our ingenuity and erudition are sent out from all directions, that we are tempted to recompose the philosopher's

thought with fragments of ideas gathered here and there, praising him afterwards, of course, for having been able—as we have just shown ourselves to
be—to execute a pretty piece of mosaic. But the illusion does not last long, for
we soon perceive that in the very places where the philosopher seems to be
repeating things already said, he is thinking them in his own way. We then
abandon the idea of recomposing; but in so doing we tumble more often than
not into another illusion, less serious perhaps but more tenacious than the
first. We are inclined to imagine the doctrine—even though it be that of a
master—as growing out of earlier philosophies and representing "a moment of
an evolution." This time, to be sure, we are not completely wrong, for a
philosophy resembles an organism rather than an assemblage, and it is still
better to speak of evolution in this case than of composition. But this new
comparison, in addition to the fact that it attributes more continuity to the
history of thought than is really in it, has the disadvantage of keeping our attention fixed upon the external complication of the system and upon what its
superficial form allows us to foresee, instead of inviting us to put our finger
on the novelty and simplicity of the inner content. A philosopher worthy of
the name has never said more than a single thing: and even then it is something he has tried to say, rather than actually said. And he has said only one
thing because he has seen only one point: and at that it was not so much a
vision as a contact: this contact has furnished an impulse, this impulse a
movement, and if this movement, which is as it were a kind of swirling of dust
taking a particular form, becomes visible to our eyes only through what it
has collected along its way, it is no less true that other bits of dust might as
well have been raised and that it would still have been the same whirlwind.
Thus a thought which brings something new into the world is of course obliged
to manifest itself through the ready-made ideas it comes across and draws into
its movement; it seems thus, as it were, relative to the epoch in which the
philosopher lived; but that is frequently merely an appearance. The philosopher might have come several centuries earlier; he would have had to deal
with another philosophy and another science; he would have given himself
other problems; he would have expressed himself by other formulas; not one
chapter perhaps of the books he wrote would have been what it is; and
nevertheless he would have said the same thing.

Let me take an example. I have appealed to your professional memories:
with your permission I am going to recall some of my own. As professor in
the Collège de France I devote one of my courses each year to the history of
philosophy. In that way I have been able, during several consecutive years, to
practice at length upon Berkeley and Spinoza the experiment I have just
described. I shall not discuss Spinoza; he would take us too far afield. Nevertheless I know of nothing more instructive than the contrast between the form
and the matter of a book like the *Ethics:* on the one hand those tremendous
things called Substance, Attribute and Mode, and the formidable array of

theorems with the close network of definitions, corollaries and scholia, and that complication of machinery, that power to crush which causes the beginner, in the presence of the *Ethics,* to be struck with admiration and terror as though he were before a battleship of the Dreadnaught class;—on the other hand, something subtle, very light and almost airy, which flees at one's approach, but which one cannot look at, even from afar, without becoming incapable of attaching oneself to any part whatever of the remainder, even to what is considered essential, even to the distinction between Substance and Attribute, even to the duality of Thought and Extension. What we have behind the heavy mass of concepts and Cartesian and Aristotelian parentage, is that intuition which was Spinoza's, an intuition which no formula, no matter how simple, can be simple enough to express. Let us say, to be content with an approximation, that it is the feeling of a coincidence between the act by which our mind knows truth perfectly, and the operation by which God engenders it; the idea that the "conversion" of the Alexandrians, when it becomes complete, is indistinguishable from their "procession," that when man, sprung from divinity, succeeds in returning to it, he perceives that what he had at first taken to be two opposed movements of coming and going are in fact a single movement—moral experience in this case undertaking to resolve a logical contradiction and to fuse, by an abrupt suppression of Time, the movement of coming with that of going. The closer we get to this original intuition the better we understand that if Spinoza had lived before Descartes he would doubtless have written something other than what he wrote, but that given Spinoza living and writing, we were certain to have Spinozism in any case.

I come to Berkeley, and since it is he whom I take as example you will not think it amiss that I analyze him in detail: brevity here could only be at the expense of a strict examination of the subject. A mere glance over the work of Berkeley is enough to see that, as if of itself, it resolves into four fundamental theses. The first, which defines a certain idealism and to which is linked up the new theory of vision (although the philosopher had judged it wise to present the latter as independent), the first, I say, would be formulated thus: "Matter is a cluster of ideas." The second consists in the claim that abstract and general ideas are merely words: that is nominalism. The third thesis affirms the reality of minds and characterizes them by the will: let us say that it is spiritualism and voluntarism. The last, which we might call theism, posits the existence of God, basing itself principally on the consideration of matter. Now, nothing would be easier than to find these four theses, formulated in practically the same terms, among the contemporaries or predecessors of Berkeley. The fourth is found among the theologians. The third was in Duns Scotus; Descartes said somewhat the same thing. The second fed the controversies of the Middle Ages before becoming an integral part of the philosophy of Hobbes. As to the first, it greatly resembles the "occasionalism" of Malebranche, the idea and even the formula of which we should already discover in certain texts of Descartes; nor, for that matter, had Descartes been the first to point out that dreams have every appearance of reality and that there is nothing in any of our perceptions taken separately which guarantees us the existence of a thing outside us. Thus, with the philosophers of already distant times or even, if we do not care to go back too far, with Descartes and Hobbes to whom Locke might be added, we shall have the elements necessary for the external reconstitution of Berkeley's philosophy: we shall at most leave him his theory of vision, which would then constitute his own individual work and whose originality, reflected through the rest, would give to the doctrine as a whole its original aspect. Let us then take these slices of ancient and modern philosophy, put them in the same bowl, add by way of vinegar and oil a certain aggressive impatience with regard to mathematical dogmatism and the desire, natural in a philosopher bishop, to reconcile reason with faith, mix well and turn it over and over conscientiously, and sprinkle over the whole, like so many savoury herbs, a certain number of aphorisms culled from among the Neo-Platonists: we shall have—if I may be pardoned the expression—a salad which, at a distance, will have certain resemblance to what Berkeley accomplished.

Well, anyone who went about it in this way would be incapable of penetrating Berkeley's thought. I am not speaking of the difficulties and impossibilities which he would come up against in explaining the details: a strange sort of "nominalism" that was, which ended by raising a number of general ideas to the dignity of eternal essences, immanent in the divine Intelligence! a strange negation of the reality of bodies that which is expressed by a positive theory of the nature of matter, a fertile theory, as far removed as possible from the sterile idealism which tries to assimilate perception to dreaming! What I mean to say is that it is impossible for us to examine Berkeley's philosophy carefully without seeing the four theses we have discovered in it first approach, then penetrate one another, in such a way that each of them seems to become pregnant with the other three, to take on breadth and depth, and become radically distinguished from the earlier or contemporary theories with which one could superficially identify it. Perhaps this second point of view from which the doctrine appears as an organism and not as a mere assemblage, is still not the definitive point of view. It is at least closer to the truth. I cannot go into all the details; but nevertheless I must indicate, for at least one or two of the four theses, how any of the others could be extracted from them.

Let us take idealism. It does not consist merely in saying that bodies are ideas. What good would that do? We should indeed be obliged to continue to affirm everything about these ideas that experience has led us to affirm about bodies, and we should simply have substituted one word for another; for Berkeley surely does not think that matter will cease to exist when he has stopped living. What Berkeley's idealism signifies is that matter is co-extensive with our representation of it; that it has no interior, no underneath; that it hides nothing, contains nothing; that it possesses neither power nor virtuality of any kind; that it is spread out as mere surface and that it is no more than what it presents to us at any given moment. The word "idea" ordinarily indicates an existence of this kind, I mean to say a completely realized existence, whose being is indistinguishable from its seeming, while the word "thing" makes us think of a reality which would be at the same time a reservoir of possibilities; that is why Berkeley prefers to call bodies ideas rather than things. But if we look upon his "idealism" in that light, we see that it coincides with his "nominalism"; for the more clearly this second thesis takes shape in the philosopher's mind, the more evidently it is restricted to the negation of general abstract ideas,—*abstracted,* that is, *extracted* from matter: it is clear in fact that one cannot extract something from what contains nothing, nor consequently make a perception yield something other than the perception itself. Color being but color, resistance being only resistance, you will never find anything in common between resistance and color, you will never discover in visual data any element shared by the data of touch. If you claim to abstract from the data of either something which will be common to all, you will perceive in examining that something that you are dealing with a word: therein lies the nominalism of Berkeley; but there also, at the same time, is the "new theory of vision." If an extension which would be at once visual and tactile is only a word, it is all the more so with an extension which would involve all the senses at once: there again is nominalism, but there too is the refutation of the Cartesian theory of matter. Let us not even talk any more about extension; let us simply note that in view of the structure of language the two expressions "I have this perception" and "this perception exists" are synonymous, but that the second, introducing the same word "existence" into the description of totally different perceptions, invites us to believe that they have something in common between them and to imagine that their diversity conceals a fundamental unity, the unity of a "substance" which is, in reality, only the word *existence* hypostasized: there you have the whole idealism of Berkeley; and this idealism, as I was saying, is identical with his nominalism. Let us go on now, with your permission, to the theory of God and the theory of minds. If a body is made of "ideas" or, in other words, if it is entirely passive and determinate, having neither power nor virtuality, it cannot act on other bodies; and consequently the movements of bodies must be the effect of an active power, which has produced these bodies themselves and which, because of the order which the universe reveals, can only be an intelligent cause. If we are mistaken when under the name of general ideas we set up as realities the names that we have given to groups of objects or perceptions more or less artificially constituted by us on the plane of matter, such is not the case when we think we discover, behind this plane, the divine intentions: the general idea which exists only on the surface and which links body to body is no doubt only a word, but the general idea which exists in depth, relating bodies to God or rather descending from God to bodies, is a reality; and thus the nominalism of Berkeley quite naturally calls for this development of the doctrine as found in the *Siris,* and which has wrongly been considered a Neo-Platonic fantasy; in other words, the idealism of Berkeley is only one aspect of the theory which places God behind all the manifestations of matter. Finally, if God imprints in each one of us perceptions, or as Berkeley says, "ideas," the being which gathers up these perceptions, or rather which goes to meet them, is quite the reverse of an idea: it is a will, though one which is constantly limited by divine will. The meeting-place of these two wills is precisely what we call matter. If the *percipi* is pure passivity, the *percipere* is pure activity. Human mind, matter, divine mind therefore become terms which we can express only in terms of one another. And the spiritualism of Berkeley is itself found to be only an aspect of any one of the other three theses.

Thus the various parts of the system interpenetrate, as in a living being. But, as I was saying at the beginning, the spectacle of this reciprocal penetration doubtless gives us a more precise idea of the body of the doctrine; it still does not enable us to reach the soul.

We shall get closer to it, if we can reach the mediating *image* referred to above,—an image which is almost matter in that it still allows itself to be seen, and almost mind in that it no longer allows itself to be touched,—a phantom which haunts us while we turn about the doctrine and to which we must go in order to obtain the decisive signal, the indication of the attitude to take and of the point from which to look. Did the mediating image which takes shape in the mind of the interpreter, as he progresses in his study of the work, exist originally in the same form in the master's thought? If it was not that particular one, it was another, which could belong to a different order of perceptions and have no material resemblance whatsoever to it, but which nevertheless would equal it in value as two translations of the same work in different languages equal one another. Perhaps these two images, perhaps even other images, still equivalent, were present all at once, following the philosopher step by step in procession through the evolutions of his thought. Or perhaps he did not perceive any one of them clearly, being content only at rare intervals to make contact directly with that still more subtle thing, intuition itself; but then we are indeed forced, as interpreters, to re-establish the intermediary image, unless we are prepared to speak of the "original intuition" as a vague thought and of the "spirit of the doctrine" as an abstraction, whereas this spirit is as concrete and this intuition as precise as anything in the system.

In Berkeley's case, I think I see two different images and the one which strikes me most is not the one whose complete indication we find in Berkeley himself. It seems to me that Berkeley perceives matter as a *thin transparent film* situated between man and God. It remains transparent as long as the philosophers leave it alone, and in that case God reveals Himself through it. But let the metaphysicians meddle with it, or even common sense in so far as it deals in metaphysics: immediately the film becomes dull, thick and opaque, and forms a screen because such words as Substance, Force, abstract Extension, etc. slip behind it, settle there like a layer of dust, and hinder us from seeing God through the transparency. The image is scarcely indicated by Berkeley himself though he has said in so many words "that we first raise a dust and then complain we cannot see." But there is another comparison, often evoked by the philosopher, which is only the auditory transposition of the visual image I have just described: according to this, matter is a language which God speaks to us. That being so, the metaphysics of matter, thickening each one of the syllables, marking it off, setting it up as an independent entity, turns our attention away from the meaning to the sound and hinders us from following the divine word. But, whether we attach ourselves to the one or to the other, in either case we are dealing with a simple image that we must keep in view, because if it is not the intuition generating the doctrine, it is immediately derived from it, and approximates it more than any of the theses taken individually, more even than the combination of all of them.

Is it possible for us to recapture this intuition itself? We have just two means of expression, concept and image. It is in concepts that the system develops; it is into an image that it contracts when it is driven back to the intuition from which it comes: so that, if one wishes to go beyond the image by rising above it, one necessarily falls back on concepts, and on concepts more vague, even more general than those from which one started in search of the image and the intuition. Reduced to this form, bottled as it were the moment it comes from the spring, the original intuition will then become superlatively insipid and uninteresting: it will be banal in the extreme. If we were to say for example that Berkeley considers the human soul as partially united with God and partly independent, that it is conscious of itself at every moment as of an imperfect activity which would join a higher activity if there were not interposed between the two, something which is absolutely passive, we should be expressing all of the original intuition of Berkeley that can be directly translated into concepts, and still we should have something so abstract as to be almost empty. Let us stick to these formulas since we cannot find better ones, but let us try to put a little life into them. Let us take all that the philosopher has written, let us bring back these scattered ideas to the image from which they had descended; and let us raise them, enclosed now in the image, up to the abstract formula enlarged by its absorption of the image and ideas, let us now attach ourselves to this formula and watch it, simple as it is, grow simpler still, all the more simple for our having pushed into it a greater number of things; finally let us rise with it, go up to the point where everything that was given extended in the doctrine contracts in tension: we shall picture to ourselves this time how from this centre of force, which is moreover inaccessible, there springs the impulse which gives the impetus, that is to say the intuition itself. It is from this that the four theses of Berkeley came, because this movement met on its way the ideas and problems the contemporaries of Berkeley were raising. In other times Berkeley would doubt-less have formulated other theses; but, the movement being the same, these theses would have been situated in the same way with regard to one another; they would have had the same relationship to one another, like new words of a new sentence through which runs the thread of an old meaning; and it would have been the same philosophy.

The relation of a philosophy to earlier and contemporary philosophies is not, then, what a certain conception of the history of systems would lead us to assume. The philosopher does not take pre-existing ideas in order to recast them into a superior synthesis or combine them with a new idea. One might as well believe that in order to speak we go hunting for words that we string together afterwards by means of a thought. The truth is that above the words and above the sentence there is something much more simple than a sentence or even a word: the meaning, which is less a thing thought than a movement of thought, less a movement than a direction. And just as the impulsion given to the embryonic life determines the division of an original cell into cells which in turn divide until the complete organism is formed, so the characteristic movement of each act of thought leads this thought, by an increasing sub-division of itself, to spread out more and more over the successive planes of the mind until it reaches that of speech. Once there it expresses itself by means of a sentence, that is, by a group of pre-existing elements; but it can almost arbitrarily choose the first elements of the group provided that the others are complementary to them; the same thought is translated just as well into diverse sentences composed of entirely different words, provided these words have the same connection between them. Such is the process of speech. And such also is the operation by which philosophy is constituted. The philos-opher does not start with pre-existing ideas; at most one can say that he arrives at them. And when he gets there the idea thus caught up into the movement of his mind, being animated with a new life like the word which receives its meaning from the sentence, is no longer what it was outside the vortex. . . .

. . . in order to reach intuition it is not necessary to transport ourselves out-side the domain of the senses and of consciousness. Kant's error was to believe that it was. After having proved by decisive arguments that no dialectical effort will ever introduce us into the beyond and that an effective metaphysics would necessarily be an intuitive metaphysics, he added that we lack this intuition and that this metaphysics is impossible. It would in fact be so if there were no other time or change than those which Kant perceived and which, more-over, we too must reckon with; for our usual perception cannot get out of time nor grasp anything else than change. But the time in which we are naturally placed, the change we habitually have before us, are a time and change that our senses and our consciousness have reduced to dust in order to facilitate our action upon things. Undo what they have done, bring our perception back to its origins, and we shall have a new kind of knowledge without having been obliged to have recourse to new faculties.

If this knowledge is generalized, speculation will not be the only thing to profit by it. Everyday life can be nourished and illuminated by it. For the world into which our senses and consciousness habitually introduce us is no more than the shadow of itself; and it is as cold as death. Everything in it is arranged for our maximum convenience, but in it, everything is in a present which seems constantly to be starting afresh; and we ourselves, fashioned artificially in the image of a no less artificial universe, see ourselves in the instantaneous, speak of the past as of something done away with, and see in memory a fact strange or in any case foreign to us, an aid given to mind by matter. Let us on the contrary grasp ourselves afresh as we are, in a present which is thick, and furthermore, elastic, which we can stretch indefinitely backward by pushing the screen which masks us from ourselves farther and farther away; let us grasp afresh the external world as it really is, not superficially, in the present, but in depth, with the immediate past crowding upon it and imprinting upon it its impetus; let us in a word become accustomed to see all things *sub specie durationis:* immediately in our galvanized perception what is taut becomes relaxed, what is dormant awakens, what is dead comes to life again. Satisfactions which art will never give save to those favoured by nature and fortune, and only then upon rare occasions, philosophy thus understood will offer to all of us, at all times, by breathing life once again into the phantoms which surround us and by revivifying us. In so doing philosophy will become complementary to science in practice as well as in speculation. With its applications which aim only at the convenience of existence, science gives us the promise of well-being, or at most, of pleasure. But philosophy could already give us joy.

Paul Weiss   7. SYSTEMATIC SYNOPSIS

The theme of Hegel and Bergson—unification—is re-echoed in this essay by Professor Weiss. Specialisms, he says, demand a new search for common principles, categories, and values. The methodological deliverance promised by analytic philosophers has not been realized. Furthermore, analysts overlooked the fact that special kinds of knowledge require a grasp of the

The essay here reprinted is from the Introduction to Paul Weiss's *Modes of Being, 1958,* and appears through the courtesy of the publisher, Southern Illinois University Press.

whole—"incoherent though this may be." Thus, the search for a way into metaphysics, Weiss observes, must become "at once more bold and humble, more catholic and cautious, freer and more disciplined than ever before."

In his early work, *Reality,* Weiss recognized that nature and knowledge are reciprocal. Like Hegel, he saw their circularity. He saw, also, the way in which each being, though independent, points to all others—that each brings to realization in a special way the common objective that "is inseparable from the very nature of individual things."

As a beginning, therefore, Weiss chooses four facts, or *modes of being,* which he terms *Actuality, Ideality, Existence,* and *God.* By Actuality, he means all finite, spatio-temporal beings; by Existence, the energized field in which Actualities act; by Ideality, the Good-as-striven-for; and by God, "a unity" in which all Actualities and the Good can be together, and "in which Existence finds the unitary essence it needs in order to be intelligible." Each, furthermore, presupposes the other. These modes, reminiscent of terms used by Whitehead, are to be analyzed by all methods, he says, including "dialectic," "sympathy," imagination," and "abstraction."

EVERY ONE OF US, in these last decades, has often heard the complaint that the world of knowledge has grown enormously and that it is now too big for anyone to envisage. Too many of us have too quickly said that it is futile to hope that the meaning of the whole, or even of man's place within it, can be grasped by anyone. A man must be content, it has been supposed, to master limited branches of knowledge, to try to learn exactly what is the case here or there; he should give up the attempt to say something more. No one seemed to have a real fear that such self-restraint might turn him into a partial man. Encyclopedias and staff conferences, surveys and texts, it was felt, could bring him and all the rest together in harmony. Co-operation, interchange, and communication would produce well-made parts, and interrelate them, to give a clearer, more lasting, a better articulated account of whatever fraction of the totality of things was available for knowledge. As a consequence, many today are somewhat content to be community thinkers, union men, who know how to work together.

It seems safe to say that the intellectual advances made in recent years over a wide range of disciplines are in good part traceable to the fact that we have specialized together. But it is equally safe to say that these achievements depended in part on our refusal to use our rational powers to the full. A world of experts, each concerned with asserting only what he himself really knows, is a world of men who must accept without cavil what the other experts offer to them as data, method, and outcome—or it is a world of separated items, cut off from all else. Such experts practice what none is willing to preach. On the one side they accept nothing but what they can themselves certify, and on the other they embrace with equal confidence that which they confessedly could not possibly certify.

He who simply accepts whatever others affirm unwarrantedly supposes that those others are right in result, method, and value. He does not really know whether or not their frames are wide enough, their methods sound enough, their values rich enough for the world in which we all live. By putting the actual failure or inadequacy of other disciplines outside the reach of real questioning he denies himself the opportunity of knowing whether or not they are really sound, and whether or not they will ever betray him. To know how reliable other disciplines are, he must know something more than what they report of themselves.

It is fairly safe to say that the successes of our modern ways of thought depend in good part on the chance that the methods and outcomes of our different specialized inquiries happen for the time to fit together. When parts are dealt with in independence of one another, discords almost inevitably arise among them. Even now different disciplines are sometimes found to conflict. The realms of specialized knowledge are not yet integrated. There are methods and results in almost every vigorous science which no one has made cohere with the rest. Nor has anyone ever related the achievements and methods of all the sciences to one another, or brought the natural sciences into harmony with history, law, and anthropology. And what has been discerned by the poets, the mystics, the philosophers is still far from being united with what has been learned elsewhere.

But, it will perhaps be said, this is as it should be. Every living enterprise is incomplete; its problems are its nerve ends, its growth tips. It would be foolhardy to force the different disciplines into harmony now, to try to get rid of the gaps in and between them at once. The critical powers, it can justly be urged, should not be suspended, nor should they be allowed to destroy the tolerance on which co-operative inquiry depends. We should be patient. The occasional breaks and discords in and between the different disciplines will soon and surely must eventually be overcome. Knowledge is accumulative and grows in cohesiveness as it grows in magnitude. Ignorance, and ignorance alone, is what keeps honest inquiring men apart.

There is force in this reply. We have a right to expect, as we progress in our mastery of the world and of ourselves, that what we know will form a more solid block than it now does. Yet, what might at the end of an inquiry have the status of knowledge in that inquiry may not have had that status when outside it or when it is made part of a different inquiry. There are certainties in some disciplines and only probabilities in others; some prefer local truths while others specialize in cosmic ones. Their different claims must be assigned different weights; account must be taken of their different methods and ranges. What we call knowledge in physics is not exactly what we call knowledge in history or philosophy or perhaps even biology. The items in one discipline are obtained along a different route and must meet criteria and be certified in ways not relevant to the items in other disciplines. It makes no difference whether or not we take one of the disciplines as the model for the others, or whether or not we look outside them all for some standard in terms of which we can determine what is and what is not knowledge. In either case we are forced to evaluate and perhaps modify or qualify the claims which each, even at the end of its road, takes to be reliable and true. Some, and perhaps even all, of a given discipline's certified truths might have to be altered if they are to be brought into accord with the certified truths of other inquiries. Unless we can somehow stand outside all disciplines, unless we can somehow use common principles, categories, values, we cannot hope to adjudicate authoritatively the claims which each discipline makes even within its own framework; we can therefore have no surety that its results will ever form part of a single harmonious body of knowledge.

It seemed for a time as if this challenge would be accepted in a most promising way. A group of well-trained, meticulous, energetic "analytic" philosophers seemed willing to take as their task the discovery of criteria and principles by means of which the efforts and outcomes of the different disciplines could be evaluated and organized. Through a fresh union of modern logic, linguistics, and methodology, they produced a new discipline, and used this to promote and clarify other subjects. The gathering of data they left to others; it was not their task, they thought, to try to add more facts to those which the empirical sciences provided. They sought only to occupy themselves with a study of the structures, procedures, implications, grammar that are inevitably exhibited in every sound scientific inquiry; nothing was sensible or legitimate, they claimed, unless it was certifiable by the methods which such inquiries endorsed.

Bold, perhaps even a little arrogant and contemptuous of older ways, these thinkers were nevertheless at once modest and cautious. They said of themselves that they were just inquirers, without set dogmas or pre-established goals. They sought only to be clear, precise, rigorous, and thorough. But very soon, and perhaps inevitably, they turned themselves into another race of specialists, alongside the others, concentrating on the quite restricted task of clarifying the intent, language, usage, or practice of scientific men. They were forced to take for granted the suppositions, methods, claims, tests, and outcomes of fields which, by the very nature of the case, they could not know firsthand or really master. As a consequence, while presenting themselves as at once careful and open-minded, they rather uncritically and dogmatically adopted views which should have been examined, criticized, and perhaps discarded. The irony of history was once more manifest: those who set themselves to be merely critical, sceptical, hesitant, modest, often become great dogmatists.

These analysts have accomplished much. But they could not do all that needs to be done if knowledge is to make—at least in principle—one exhaustive, coherent whole. For that, their specialty would have to become all-encompassing. Not only the methods, assertions, structures, but the values and results of the various disciplines need evaluation. Ends as well as means must be critically examined. We must know not only how sound the various procedures are but what place the different results of the different disciplines can have within a comprehensive account. But then something must be known of the whole. We ought not be content to be solely one among many inquirers; we must also be a one for them, a one over against them, including them and much else besides.

No one of course knows everything. No one even knows one limited field exhaustively. Yet if we did not somehow grasp the nature of all there is, we would not be able to have specialties, nor could we deal adequately with their different claims and contributions. Only if we know what it is to be a man can we engage in co-ordinate investigations into his nature; only if we know what it is to be a man can we estimate the rival contentions of doctors, biologists, psychologists, anthropologists, and the rest. Only if we know what it is to be, to inquire, to understand, can we recognize that we are all dealing with different phases of the same subject, and can know how to bring together the different results that were obtained along different routes of investigation. Before, while, and after we specialize, we have and must have a grasp of the whole, vague, blurred, and even incoherent though this may be. To ignore that whole is to ignore our roots, to misunderstand our aims, to lose our basic tests. It is to forget that we engaged in limited inquiries in order to understand what is real from many independent and, we hoped, convergent sides. It is to adopt the prejudice that only the limited and piecemeal is significant and intelligible, and that without any guidance each bit will inevitably form one seamless unity with all the rest. It is to be so impatient to get down to work that no time is left to ask what it is that is being sought, and why. If we are to engage in limited enterprises, if we are to know what they diversely seek and express, if we are to understand what contribution they can make to the enterprise of life and learning, we must somehow take account of all there is and can be known. Whether we wish it or not, we must, we do think cosmically. Our choice is only to do it uncritically, precipitately moving to the body of some limited enterprise and vainly trying to remain there always, or critically, by taking some thought of where we start and ought to end, and in a sense always are.

No matter how much this last observation be softened, it can, I fear, never be entirely freed from the smell of paradox and dogmatism, presumption and foolhardiness—and of decayed and discarded systems of the past. There is something repugnant in the temper of the grand philosophers, the system builders, the wholesale thinkers. They sound like gods and yet are only men. Even the best of them contradict themselves and one another, omit much that should have been included, and at crucial points are most unclear and unreliable. Their errors are fabulous. But then so is their vision. They leave us with no alternative but to try for ourselves to understand the real world in a way they could not. And this is possible, for they taught us through their achievements and by their failures something of what we ought to say and what we ought to avoid. And we also have at our disposal, as they unfortunately did not, such excellent guides and instruments as the history of later thought, modern science, modern poetry, modern music, modern printing, recent analysis, and symbolic logic.

There are today, I think, signs of a renewed interest in fundamental questions on the part of many thinkers. There is a new spirit just beginning to stir, transforming the world of ideas. Occupied primarily in getting a firm grip on reality, it has so far ignored the question of how to judge and adjudicate the various specialized inquiries. These must eventually look to it, and it to them. But first it must come to clearer and more systematic expression. What now seems likely is that a re-examination of fundamentals will force us to entertain a view of ourselves and of the world which is quite different from that entertained in the past.

We must become at once more bold and humble, more catholic and cautious, freer and more disciplined than before. For too long a time prejudice has been allowed to narrow our perspectives; for too long a time impatience has made us receptive to ideals and values not adequate to our full being and the world. We need a new viable systematic philosophy which is alert to the basic questions raised by the various sciences, by metaphysics and theology, by history and the arts, if we are to remain intellectually abreast of the world in which we live.

One of the objectives of the present work is to outline the nature of this new philosophy. Its main features were unknown to me until after I had struggled through the writing of three books. Reflections on the implications of the first of these drove me on to the second, and this in turn led to the third. The present book in a way continues the progress. An independent venture, it systematizes while it purges, moves beyond while it takes advantage of the previous works.

The first of the books, *Reality*, presented a systematic account of what I took to be the essential features of both knowledge and nature. It maintained that knowledge and nature presupposed one another, making the philosophic enterprise a circle, but one large enough to encompass all forms of thought and reality. Every item of knowledge and being was seen to be incomplete since there was something beyond it, real and obstinate, which it needed and sought. The book made an effort also to work, not as Russell does with a minimum vocabulary, or as others do with a minimum number of presuppositions. It tried in fact to avoid taking for granted anything outside the system, except of course the world which that system portrayed. The world it knew was not philosophy; but philosophy, it also knew, had to omit nothing of the essence of the world.

It is sound, I still think, to hold that philosophy is a circle, that every item in thought and in being is incomplete, and that what a good philosophic account presupposes is not beyond its capacity to encompass conceptually. It is sound too, I think, to maintain as was done in *Reality,* that each thing necessarily points to all the others, as the object of its needs, what it must take account of in order to be complete. The rest of the world must be considered, if we are to understand a thing's nature and why it acts as it does. But the point needs supplementation. Alone it cannot stand, since it fails to do justice to what now seems to me to be a rather obvious truth.

If, as *Reality* maintains, each thing is directed towards and acts in terms of all the rest, no two things would have exactly the same objectives. No two would point in exactly the same direction. Each would act to realize a partly different objective, and thus a different prospective future from that which concerns others. Since the existence of each would be spent in the area defined by its distinct objective, there would be no assurance that any of them, contemporaries at one moment, will be contemporaries at the next. Each would confront the world from an independent standpoint; there would be no necessary connection between the various standpoints. Each being would have its own private time, and this would have its own characteristic rhythm, divisions, pace, not necessarily shared by other times. But then, what reason would there be for supposing that the private time of one would intermesh with the times characteristic of others; how could there be a single time and thus a single cosmos in which all things dwell together?

If each being is occupied with a future proper to it, it will endeavor to make it present in its own way and at its own pace. The different futures would of course share a number of features, making it possible to treat the things as members of various classes. But the things would not act in terms of those common features. The features, because abstractions from, derivatives of a set of disconnected singular objectives, could not possibly keep contemporary beings in temporal accord.

This is a serious difficulty, and not peculiar to the system explored in *Reality.* It faces Aristotle's philosophy, and Whitehead's too. Aristotle's contemporaneous objects move together in time, not on their own account, but because they are confined within a single spatial whole whose rhythms and pace limit the rhythms and pace of the subordinate realities within it. Whitehead's contemporaneous objects keep abreast in time, not because they must intrinsically do so but because the diverse final causes which govern them are under the supervision of an interested God. Whitehead here reminds one of Leibniz with his doctrine of a divinely pre-established harmony which guarantees that the independent adventures of things are in accord with one another. Aristotle here reminds one of Kant and his attempt to treat time as having two sides, the one private or ideal, the other public or actual, which, though quite different in purport and in experienced content, are thought somehow to have the same divisions and rate of passage. Aristotle and Kant overcame the difficulty, of showing how distinct beings can be persistently contemporary, by means of special cosmological assumptions; Whitehead and Leibniz did it by introducing a special theological twist. But these are exteriorly imposed devices. In principle these thinkers allow that things may move in time independently of one another and therefore may, if contemporary today, not be contemporary tomorrow. Yet no matter whether beings are sluggish or quick, asleep or awake, lost in privacies or engaged in public work, all, while living at their own pace, live together in a common time.

There are contemporary beings. Otherwise there would be nothing to interact with us, nothing with which we could be together, nothing which could limit us and thus define us as incomplete. And some beings, contemporary now, are contemporary later. All move into the next moment together, some altering in nature or position, others remaining unchanged or unmoved. One can imagine all of them in the grip of some single cosmic being, some dialectical force, or some all-encompassing power which both drives them forward and keeps them concordant. But this idea compromises the basic fact that it is individuals who act, and act in their own ways and at their own rates. The time through which I live is my own; if there be another time or temporal power keeping me abreast of others, it is more powerful than I and they, and wise beyond belief. There must of course be something common to us all, which limits and even controls us somewhat, so as to enable us, despite our independent existence and adventures in time, to be co-ordinate now and later. But if we suppose it to be something like a cosmic agent running alongside or overhead, keeping us adjusted one to the other, or some all-embracing time or being out of which the individual times are conjointly precipitated, we reverse an obvious state of affairs, since we then overlook the irreducible ultimacy of individuals, and the fact that it is they who spend energy and dictate what the common pattern of the world will be. Things are members of various groups, not because they happen to share some character but because they all have the same objective. Despite their individuality, spatio-temporal beings form a single contemporaneous set of actualities, because each inevitably points towards the very same prospect pointed towards by the rest. A number of them may further specify that common prospect in common ways, and thereby reveal themselves to be members of some more limited group as well. But whether they do this or not, each and every one of them acts as a distinct being, and thus brings the common objective to realization in an individual way.

It is desirable to show that there is and must be one objective, subtending whatever limited objectives individuals or groups of them may be directed towards. And it is important to know the nature of that common objective.

Nature and Man, my next book, was written in part to satisfy these reasonable and therefore imperious demands. The book stresses the fact that the common objective is essential, that it is inseparable from the very being of individual things. Nothing existed, it saw, solely in the present; each being was partly in the future and was governed in part by that common objective in which it essentially terminated. This defined its direction, and, when specialized as a limited objective, defined the range of things the being could do.

The discovery that all beings inevitably point to the same common future objective made it possible to show how they could exist together in time even though they acted independently, and sometimes even came into conflict. And an awareness that the common objective was itself somewhat indeterminate in nature made it possible to understand why it needed realization and could be realized—questions which were unanswerable by Plato and others who, like him, recognize that there is a common objective to which all beings are directed but who mistakenly suppose that it is itself perfect, complete, wholly determinate.

If one avoids the Platonic supposition that the idea of perfection is itself perfect, that the idea of the good is itself the best of beings, one could safely agree with Plato to call the common inescapable objective of all beings by that grandest of titles, The Good. A recognition of the nature and needs of that Good makes it possible to offer new ways of understanding the nature of causation, inference, action—all change in fact. Every occurrence, it could then be shown, is at once limited and free, occurring in the present but within bounds determined by what is still future. The separation of theories of artistic creation and logical deduction, of history and physics, which had ruined so many philosophies, could at last be avoided. Every act and thought, *Nature and Man* saw, was present, concrete, transitory. It recognized that they were unpredictable in their full concreteness, because produced only then and there, and thus were incapable of being known in advance. Every act and thought it also saw was, while still future, indeterminate and fixed but yet predictable because entailed by present actualities. Art and history, logic and physics have both an unpredictable and a predictable side, the first two stressing the one, the second two the other. Although they have different starting points, media, objectives, and go through different processes, they exhibit the same fundamental laws and principles.

Nature and Man affirmed, even more vigorously than did *Reality,* that man was not only an integral part of nature, but also a product of evolution. It tried to show that the advance which began with the inanimate, moved through the animate, and ended with man was the consequence of an occasional successful strategy on the part of frustrated beings. These, to overcome grave obstacles, to avoid defeat and annihilation, changed their directions, pointed to new relevant objectives, thereby becoming transformed in nature and in promise.

The book concluded that man, while distinct in kind and not merely in degree from all other things, alone possessed a persistent self. That self stood out over against the body and the rest of the world because it alone was persistently occupied with the realization of that single, all-inclusive objective, The Good. And because he had a self, it said, man had self-identity, and was capable of self-discipline and self-criticism, privileges which were outside the reach of any other being in nature.

The position explored in *Nature and Man* does not I think have to be changed in any fundamental respect. But it has important implications which it did not pursue. It was one of the tasks of *Man's Freedom* to note these implications and to complete the account. The book stressed the fact that the Good was focused on and striven for by man, for the most part without consciousness but with a freedom peculiar to him. This freedom was exhibited primarily in three more and more effective and inclusive forms, as preference, choice, and will. They were man's primary agencies by which he freely adopted and tried to realize the all-inclusive Good.

Man does and man ought to try to bring the Good to its most complete realization. It is his task to do good, and nothing but good, to every being whatsoever. But he is finite, feeble, ignorant; he must inevitably fail to do what he ought. Man is the guilty animal. But this is paradox. That paradox cannot be overcome by narrowing the range of man's obligations. No area of responsibility is so small as to be within the power of man to fill completely. No one ever does all that ought to be done even to only one other being. No one does or can do all he ought, even to himself. A man has too little knowledge, too little strength, too unstable a constitution to be able to do full justice to the rights of any being. Nor can his knowledge, strength, and constitution be so improved that he will eventually do all he ought. Finite always, he will always fall short of his full obligations.

I find this paradox intolerable. My struggle with it led me to see my previous speculations as part of a much wider four-dimensional whole. Suggestions of the nature of those four dimensions can be found in *Reality* and in other places, but they became clear to me only when I turned to the study of ethics and saw the full force of the paradox that a man had obligations which he could not himself fulfill. As long as I worked with anything less than a four-pronged view I found that the paradox could not be resolved. One had, I became convinced, to distinguish and assume in turn the perspectives of four distinct realities—Actuality, Ideality, Existence, and God. All four, one had to affirm, are final, irreducible modes of being with their own integrity and careers. The universe they together exhaust requires for its understanding a system in which each is recognized to be as basic, as explanatory, and as incomplete as the others.

It is the task of this work to lay bare the nature of these four beings and to grasp something of the way they affect one another. Before engaging in it, it is desirable, I think, to know why it is necessary for any one—not only the author—to consider these four. It may be worth while too to have some preliminary idea of their diverse natures and roles.

Actualities are finite beings in space and time. To complete themselves they strive to realize relevant, essential objectives which, in different ways, they specify out of a single common future Good. Since man is the only Actuality who can focus on the Good in its full universal form, only he can seek to realize that Good in himself and in others. He cannot, as an individual, do full justice to that Good. That can be done only through the conjoint effort of all that there is. A man can hope to do all he ought only if he can accept as his own all the work done, on behalf of the Good, by all the rest. We would, with this observation, reach an end to our system were it not that we had presupposed Existence as an energizing field in which Actualities act. This terminates in the Good, and endows the divine with a temporal dignity. We also presupposed God as a unity in which all Actualities and the Good can be together, and in which Existence finds the unitary essence it needs in order to be intelligible. Both Existence and God are of course also presupposed by the Good; these sustain it in different but necessary ways.

And we ought to make a beginning with Good—or rather with the Ideal, which is the Good when this has been freed from an exclusive reference to realizing Actualities. It has a nature of its own, as is evident from the fact that it is striven for. Indeed it has power enough to attract a man and to make him concerned with its fulfillment. The Good is a correlate of Actualities, a possibility which acts to master Actualities by turning them into types, meanings, representatives of itself. From the standpoint of the Good all that ought to be done is done if whatever there be is idealized, turned into an instance of the Good. This action of the Good on Actualities is the reciprocal of action by those Actualities on it. And, like those Actualities, the Good presupposes material to work upon. Just as Actuality presupposes the Good, the Good presupposes Actuality, and both of them presuppose Existence and God as regions in which they can be together.

The Good is incomplete, indeterminate. It needs completeness, and achieves this only so far as it is fractionated into more determinate and limited forms of itself. It demands not specific activities by Actualities but the provision of opportunities so that it can transform those Actualities from what is external to it into what is subordinate. By offering the Actualities attractive objectives, desirable goals, commanding choices, obligating goods, restraining laws, and finally a luring destiny, it turns the Actualities into purposive, preferring, choosing, willing kinds of beings, into citizens of a state, and finally into beings who could fulfill themselves while enabling all other Actualities to be similarly idealized.

From the perspective of the Good men are required to adopt roles, to become public and representative beings. So far as they achieve this status the

Good becomes determinate, not by virtue of the introduction of alien material, but by the Good's adoption of what for it are nothing more than diverse, fragmentary, and harmonious parts of itself. Man's task from the standpoint of the Good is the making of this fractionization easy, complete, and concordant, just as it is the task of the Good, from the standpoint of man, to be receptive of his efforts to make it concrete. The Good ennobles, universalizes Actualities when and as they sustain it, just as Actualities enrich the Good, make it concrete when and as it lures and guides them.

Actualities and the Ideal, even when made one by mastery or fractionization, have an integrity of their own, continue to enjoy an independent status. An examination of them separately and in relation to one another enables us to encompass much of what is—but not all. God and Existence are also essential realities, inescapable dimensions of the universe, illuminating what is left dark by the joint use of the perspectives of Actuality and Ideality.

God is that being who, among other things, makes a unity of what otherwise would be a detached set of occurrences. He sees to it that the Ideal is realized, and that Actualities are perfected. This means that men should recognize that they inevitably submit themselves and their acts to God, as the being who alone can make them adequate to the demands of the Ideal. Since men, their acts, and their aspirations are part of a realm of Existence, where alone they can be vital and present, no account of God can be complete which forgets that Existence is his counterweight, the locus of the data he supports and interrelates.

Existence is a restless force at once ingredient in and overflowing the borders of Actualities, connecting each with every other and coming to a focus in the Ideal. Actuality and Ideality are consequently subject to a single, cosmic flux. But any study which begins with Existence should be supplemented with accounts where God, the Ideal, and the Actual are recognized to have independent natures and function. Without them there would be no unified world of values, no focused and uniting futures, and no distinct loci of action.

Actuality, the Ideal, Existence, and God are data for one another. Each has a role to play in relation to the others, and requires the others to assume a role for it. In addition, all merge with and qualify one another. They can have these different functions only because each has an irreducible, final being of its own, outside of which and over against which the others are. Each stands out against the rest as possessing a distinctive career and a characteristic way of dealing with the others. Actualities strive to be completely adjusted to all there is; the Ideal strives to encompass everything; Existence is engaged in a perpetual effort to separate itself off from all else; God strives to make unity present everywhere. Each helps and restrains the others, making it possible for them to attain a greater success than they otherwise could, and preventing them from ever achieving perfect success. No one of them can ever advance

beyond the stage where it is but one of a number of beings. Being is diversely and exhaustively exhibited in four interlocked, irreducible modes.

This swift survey through which I have just gone will arouse rather than quiet a number of persistent questions and doubts: Is there a real need to acknowledge as many as four fundamental, irreducible realities? Are just the items here isolated *the* modes of being? Is there not a need to acknowledge five or six or perhaps even a greater number, as basic and as essential as any of these? The work as a whole, and particularly the last chapters offer answers to these questions. But it may help now to remark that no one can avoid acknowledging something Actual, for that is what each one of us is, and what each one of us daily confronts. But Actuality can be made intelligible, we will find, only if account is taken of the other three modes as well. Each of these three in turn demands the acknowledgment of Actuality and two other modes. Each mode requires at least three others. We cannot acknowledge any less than four modes without being confronted with insoluble problems, and without making something in the nature or function of the universe unnecessarily mysterious or unintelligible. But there is no need to acknowledge more than four, until and unless there are difficulties which cannot be resolved except by taking this further step. One ought not to multiply entities beyond necessity.

Each mode stands apart from the rest, and is also a component in them. Each offers evidence regarding the nature and reality of the others. But so long as we remain with any one of them, those others will seem to be nothing more than attenuations of it, imagined or fanciful objects, or the termini of hazardous inferences. One must get over to where those others are. Nothing less than an adequate grasp of the other modes in their own terms will enable us to have the data in terms of which an initially accepted mode can be fully understood. There are many ways in which this result can be achieved. Dialectic is a primary way, but there is also sympathy and imagination, direct encounter and a use of abstractions. All will be acknowledged in their appropriate places.

Each mode of being needs the others to enable it to be itself. The universe is an interlocked whole of four modes of being, no one of which can be unless the others also are effective in it, and effective apart from it. The names that have here been assigned to them may occasionally prove misleading for while the ideas are somewhat new, the language is rather old. Some of the functions of the modes have perhaps even been misconstrued, for not all parts of the cosmos come equally well into the focus of one endeavor. In view of the manner in which the view gradually unfolded, and in the light of our western tradition's emphasis on things and men, and its readiness to look with suspicion at anything which is not directly known, there may be an undue stress here on Actuality. The greatest obstacle in the way of understanding what is here intended is, more likely than not, the author's and perhaps the reader's tendency to minimize the reality or the function of the Ideal, Existence, or God. Completeness and impartiality require that all four modes be dealt with as equally real, equally indispensable.

Irwin C. Lieb   8. UNTWINING
                                                METAPHYSICAL
                                                PROBLEMS

The marriage between theories of reality and theories of knowledge is further tested in this essay by Irwin Lieb. Here, Lieb points out some of the problems involved in giving exclusive primacy to either type of theory.

Each such theory, he says, automatically selects methods consonant with its goals, but, in so doing, it tends to be arbitrary. The so-called critical philosophies, he observes, maintain that the starting point of metaphysics is to be found in a type of knowing that will in turn arbitrate all issues concerning the nature of things. In contrast, so-called realistic philosophies tend to begin with statements about the nature of things, which similarly determine questions concerning the nature of knowledge.

Lieb maintains that since the choice of either theory tends to be arbitrary, suitable methodologies likewise tend to become arbitrary. Theories of knowing frame their methods and presentation according to the "linear ideals" of geometry. Theories of the nature of things follow the fashion of the biological or physical sciences, which also betray linear, or straight cause-effect, relationships.

Neither theory, however, must be given primacy. Each must be primary in its own way, and the claims of each must be pressed against the claims of the other. Progress will then be derived from a sort of dialectic that proceeds not in a straight line but in a spiral fashion.

To PROVIDE A complete metaphysics, some philosophers have held that the problems of knowledge and existence have to be untwined, and that one of them has to be settled before progress can be made upon the other. If we could untwine the problems, with which one would we have first to deal? The an-

---

Portions used in this selection are from *American Philosophy*, edited by R. W. Winn (New York, 1955), and appear here through the courtesy of the publisher, Philosophical Library, Inc.

swers that philosophers give have been divided. Some have held that we must take a way of knowing as *primary,* and that every other method of acquiring knowledge has to be validated by a sort of *derivation* from the primary method. Others have held, however, that some fact about the nature of things must be taken as primary, and that ways of knowing are validated only if they reveal the known nature, or are *derived* from methods by which that nature is apprehended.

It is easy to find examples of these two ways of proceeding. The example of Descartes's philosophy is one of the best. According to Descartes, metaphysics properly begins with a program of doubt. If doubting is relentlessly pressed to its extreme, it would, Descartes thought, be a method of acquiring knowledge. It would, he thought, yield a residue that cannot in principle be further doubted, from which everything knowable could be built up in appropriate ways. For Descartes, a way of knowing was thus taken to be primary. For him the problem of existence became manageable only after the problem of knowledge had its solution.

This same emphasis on ways of knowing is made by those who endorse the methods of the sciences. Unlike Descartes, they don't believe that a method can assure a single result beyond possibility of doubt; yet many of them affirm, as beyond dispute, the general efficiency of the methods of science. Everything that can be known, so runs the claim, can be known through the use of scientific methods—and perhaps can be known best only through those methods. A ready extension to this would be that everything there is can be isolated by the methods of science, and that whatever cannot be so isolated is not real but subjective or illusory.

Again, the same priority to ways of knowing is given by those who begin metaphysics with a *critique.* A critique doesn't summarize what we know. It tries, instead, to sort out the *equipment* we have for knowing things and for expressing our knowledge. Some philosophers have generated their critiques from arguments to show that the senses alone are our instruments for acquiring knowledge; others, from arguments about the separate contributions of sense and mind, or the inseparable contributions of sense and mind. Still others have begun with arguments about what can and cannot be meaningfully expressed— in ordinary or in specialized languages.

All of these attempts are, in general, attempts to make questions about knowing prior to questions about existence. They are attempts to argue that because of the ways in which we can confidently know things, because of the only ways in which we can know or formulate things, questions about the existence of things are subsequent to the necessarily prior questions about the ways in which we can and should know.

There are philosophers, however, who reverse these procedures. They too believe that the problems of knowledge and existence can be satisfactorily untwined. But they think that questions about existence have to be settled before substantial progress can be made in solving the problem of knowledge. Some philosophers have believed, for example, that it is because of the nature of the existent Divinity that anything else is enabled to exist and be known. Others have believed that metaphysics must be founded on the fact that there are real things whose characters are independent of what any man may think of them. Instruments for acquiring knowledge, they think, have to be accommodated to the characters of things; for otherwise they believe we should not be able to explain how it is that we can make mistakes, change our methods, and accept the corrections continual use of our methods may involve.

Both these ways of proceeding to solve the untwined problems of knowledge and existence have their strengths and, it seems to me, their weaknesses. The strengths of these procedures are that they separately give strong and acute accounts of the methods of knowing and the nature of the real. Their general weakness is that their answers to one of the two problems tend to be arbitrary. Philosophers who attack the problem of knowledge before the problem of existence seem prepared to accept as existents whatever issues from the use of their different methods. But they have to face a question about the reasons there are for believing that their favored methods acquaint us with what is real. Why, after all, is just this or that way of knowing right or preferential? Usually the answer to this question involves reference to some fact about the world which the favored methods do not themselves certify. It may be claimed, for example, that the method *works,* or that nothing besides what is known in *just* this way ever in fact presents itself or intrudes upon us. But the methods of science do not themselves guarantee that they will *work*. And that nothing is known besides what is perceived is something to which perception does not itself testify. These and similar answers really refer to the objects of our knowledge and the characters they have. It therefore seems that even those who place primary emphasis upon ways of knowing do not wholly leave aside questions about existence. Perhaps it is simply that they do not attend to them well enough.

The same tendency toward arbitrariness can be found in the works of philosophers who place first emphasis on the problem of existence. For them, what is real has certain distinctive marks, and different ways of knowing are graded according to the security they lend to apprehending what bears those marks. What qualifies a thing as real has, however, to be found out and certified. The marks of distinction are not handed down before all inquiries, like a tablet of judgments. To find out the marks and to certify them, methods of discovery and justification are needed. Because they are, even if we pay first attention to the problem of existence, the problem of knowledge edges to a coordinate place in our inquiry.

The attempts to regard one of the problems of metaphysics as logically prior to the other illustrate the difficulties philosophers have found in untwining the problems and in solving them. I think they also suggest that the problems are not finally logically separable, that the difficulties which come to light have little to do with the problems of metaphysics as such, but that they may be owed to ideals philosophers have held about the way in which a metaphysics should be presented. What I have in mind is this: thinking about questions of metaphysics, like thinking about any sort of question, is not so neat and orderly a thing as classical rhetoricians and copy-book logicians would make us think. Our thoughts chase one another in discontinuous ways, turning now toward one end, now toward another. When the course of our thought is run, we often want and have to reconstruct it. If we wish to present our thought to others, ideals of an impeccable, persuasive organization and presentation come readily to mind. Throughout the history of philosophy, two models for ideal presentations have been especially captivating. One of these is a model of the geometrical system. The other is the model of the physical sciences, especially biology and experimental physics. The feature of all these models which bears on untwining the problems of metaphysics is that the models are *linear* ones. In adapting the case of geometry, for example, the persuasive ideal is that we begin with assured truths and proceed by unimpeachable rules to derive *one after another* the results which constitute metaphysics. The adaptation of physics is similar. Instead of assured truths, we begin with reliable methods, and persist in using them, holding metaphysical results to be provisional upon further uses of those methods. Where the model of biology differs from that of physics, its classification schemes, proceeding stepwise from acknowledged general truths to subordinate ones, are adapted. Few or none of the philosophical adaptations are, of course, perfect. But even if these models function as ideals, as indeed they seem so many times to have done, their use can readily have forced artificial separations between the problems of knowledge and existence. For, as *linear* models, their adaptation organizes the problems of metaphysics one after the other. If the geometrical or biological model is the paradigm for explanation and justification, it seems plainly right to take questions about the existence as primary. If the model of physics is seen to be without flaw, there seems no recourse but to begin with questions about method.

But both models, all ideals of linear development, in fact, have disadvantages if they are taken as models for metaphysics. We've already seen one: metaphysics that are modeled on geometry or physical science make their starting place unexaminable. Another closely related to the first, is obvious. It is that those who take linear development as the model for metaphysics are not able to give an account of the self-referential character essential to metaphysics. Because of these disadvantages, a metaphysics that adopts a linear model tends to be either arbitrary or to be theoretically incomplete. The model we need cannot be so compromising. It cannot bind us so tightly that the peculiarity of the connections between the problems of metaphysics becomes the idiosyncrasy that buries metaphysics. The peculiarity of the connections is granted. But to deal with it, the devices we need are not those modeled on a line or combination of lines. We seem to need something more like a *spiral*. If we were to take something like that as an ideal, we might do best justice to the full content of metaphysics; and we might also deal with the problems of knowledge and existence without denying their mutual connections.

Gabriel Marcel   # 9. UNFOLDING THE
                                ## ONTOLOGICAL MYSTERY

The relation between being and knowledge, knower and known, has already been underscored from several points of view. In this essay, Gabriel Marcel indicates the existential link between knower and known—the concrete person.

In the real situation of the person, he says, there is no question of the knower, over and opposed to the known, and related in the scale of the knower's logical thought. There is rather a question of an incarnation of ontological fact in which the problem of Being encroaches on its own data, and is "studied actually inside the subject who states it."

Marcel points out, however, that Being is not merely a problem to be solved. Problems can be solved serially, after the manner of the sciences. They imply the use of techniques and starting points. Mysteries, on the other hand, transcend techniques, have no starting points, and cannot be isolated in logical forms. Mysteries are, of course, not to be confused with the unknowable.

Being is neither a problem nor an unknowable, but a mystery. The phrase "the problem of being" is therefore grossly inexact. For this reason, concrete approaches to Being—the ontological mystery—cannot be maintained merely at the level of logical thought. Prior questions are always implied, because no "first beginning" in logic can completely exclude the possibility of an antecedent. The ontological order is therefore not recognized in an abstract knowledge of an abstract knower. There is no ontological datum for what Kant would call "consciousness in general" (*Bewusstsein überhaupt*), or for "any consciousness whatsoever," but only for the person in the fullness of concrete personality. The "ontological order can only be recognized personally by the whole of a being involved in a drama which

This selection, part of Gabriel Marcel's "A Metaphysical Diary," appeared in his *Being and Having*, and was published by Dacre Press, A. & C. Black Ltd., London. It is reprinted here with the kind permission of the publisher. *Being and Having* will be published in this country by Harper & Brothers in their Torchbooks Edition.

is his own, though it overflows him infinitely in all directions. . . ." The act
of the person is therefore something more than "thinking" or "doubting."
It is an ontological act, exposing the meaning of Being.

THE TRADITIONAL TERMS in which some people are today still trying to
state the problem of being, commonly arouse a mistrust which is hard to overcome. Its source lies not so much in the adherence, whether explicit or implicit, to Kantian or simply idealist theories, as in the fact that people's minds
are soaked in the results of Bergsonian criticism. One sees this even in those
minds which would not stand by Bergsonianism in its metaphysical aspects.

On the other hand, the complete withdrawal from the problem of being
which characterises so many contemporary philosophical systems is in the
last analysis an attitude which cannot be maintained. It can either be reduced
to a kind of sitting on the fence, hardly defensible and generally due to laziness
or timidity; or else—and this is what generally happens—it really comes down
to a more or less explicit denial of Being, which disguises the refusal of a hearing to the essential needs of our being. Ours is a being whose concrete essence
is to be in every way involved, and therefore to find itself at grips with a fate
which it must not only undergo, but must also make its own by somehow re-
creating it from within. The denial of Being could not really be the empirical
demonstration of an absence or lack. We can only make the denial because
we choose to make it, and we can therefore just as well choose not to make
it.

It is also worth noticing that I who ask questions about Being do not in the
first place know either *if* I am not *a fortiori what* I am. I do not even clearly
know the meaning of the question "What am I?" though I am obsessed by it.
So we see the problem of Being here encroaching upon its own data, and being
studied actually inside the subject who states it. In the process, it is denied
(or transcended) as problem, and becomes metamorphosed to mystery.

In fact, it seems very likely that there is this essential difference between a
problem and a mystery. A problem is something which I meet, which I find
complete before me, but which I can therefore lay siege to and reduce. But a
mystery is something in which I am myself involved, and it can therefore only
be thought of as a sphere where the distinction between what is in me and what
is before me loses its meaning and its initial validity. A genuine problem is
subject to an appropriate technique by the exercise of which it is defined:
whereas a mystery, by definition, transcends every conceivable technique. It
is, no doubt, always possible (logically and psychologically) to degrade a
mystery so as to turn it into a problem. But this is a fundamentally vicious proceeding, whose springs might perhaps be discovered in a kind of corruption
of the intelligence. The problem of evil, as the philosophers have called it,
supplies us with a particularly instructive example of this degradation.

Just because it is of the essence of mystery to be recognised or capable of recognition, it may also be ignored and actively denied. It then becomes reduced to something I have "heard talked about," but which I refuse as only being *for other people;* and that in virtue of an illusion which these "others" are deceived by, but which I myself claim to have detected.

We must carefully avoid all confusion between the mysterious and the unknowable. The unknowable is in fact only the limiting case of the problematic, which cannot be actualized without contradiction. The recognition of mystery, on the contrary, is an essentially positive act of the mind, the supremely positive act in virtue of which all positivity may perhaps be strictly defined. In this sphere everything seems to go on as if I found myself acting on an intuition which I possess without immediately knowing myself to possess it—an intuition which cannot be, strictly speaking, self-conscious and which can grasp itself only through the modes of experience in which its image is reflected, and which it lights up by being thus reflected in them. The essential metaphysical step would then consist in a reflection (in a reflection "squared"). By means of this, thought *stretches out* towards the recovery of an intuition which otherwise loses itself in proportion as it is exercised.

Recollection, the actual possibility of which may be regarded as the most revealing ontological index we possess, is the real place in whose centre this recovery can be made.

The "problem of being," then, will only be the translation into inadequate language of a mystery which cannot be given except to a creature capable of recollection—a creature whose central characteristic is perhaps that he is not simply identical with his own life. We can find the proof or confirmation of this nonidentity in the fact that I more or less explicitly evaluate my life. It is in my power not only to condemn it by an abstract verdict, but to set an effective term to it. If I cannot set an effective term to my life considered in its ultimate depths, which may escape from my grasp, I at least have power over the finite and material expression to which *I am at liberty to believe* that this life is reduced. The fact that suicide is possible is, in this sense, an essential point of reference for all genuine metaphysical thought. And not only suicide: despair *in all its forms,* betrayal *in all its aspects,* in so far as they appear to us as active denials of being, and in so far as the soul which despairs shuts itself up against the central and mysterious assurance in which we believe we have found the principle of all positivity.

It is not enough to say that we live in a world where betrayal is possible *at every moment, in every degree,* and *in every form.* It seems that the very constitution of our world recommends us, if it does not force us, to betrayal. The spectacle of death as exhibited by the world can, from one point of view, be regarded as a perpetual provocation to denial and to absolute desertion. It could also be added that space and time, regarded as paired modes of absence,

tend, by throwing us back upon ourselves, to drive us into the beggarly in-
stantaneity of pleasure. But it seems that at the same time, and correlatively,
it is of the essence of despair, of betrayal, and even of death itself, that they
can be refused and denied. If the word transcendence has a meaning, it means
just this denial; or more exactly, this overpassing. (*Überwindung* rather than
Aufhebung.) For the essence of the world is perhaps betrayal, or, more accurately, there is not a single thing in the world about which we can be certain that its spell could hold against the attacks of a fearless critical reflection.

If this is so, the concrete approaches to the ontological mystery should not
be sought in the scale of logical thought, the objective reference of which gives
rise to a prior question. They should rather be sought in the elucidation of certain data which are spiritual in their own right, such as fidelity, hope, and love,
where we may see man at grips with the temptations of denial, introversion,
and hard-heartedness. Here the pure metaphysical has no power to decide
whether the principle of these temptations lies in man's very nature, in the
intrinsic and invariable characteristics of that nature, or whether it lies rather
in the corruption of that same nature as the result of a catastrophe which gave
birth to history and was not merely an incident in history.

Perhaps on the ontological level it is fidelity which matters most. It is in
fact the recognition—not a theoretical or verbal, but an actual recognition—of
an ontological permanency; a permanency which endures and by reference to
which we endure, a permanency which implies or demands a history, unlike
the inert or formal permanency of pure *validity,* a law for example. It is the
perpetuation of a witness which could at any moment be wiped out or denied.
It is an attestation which is creative as well as perpetual, and more creative in
proportion as the ontological worth of what it attests is more outstanding.

An ontology with this orientation is plainly open to a revelation, which
however, it could not of course either demand or presuppose or absorb, or
even absolutely speaking understand, but the acceptance of which it can in
some degree prepare for. To tell the truth, this ontology *may* only be capable
of development *in fact* on a ground previously prepared by revelation. But on
reflection we can see that there is nothing to surprise us, still less to scandalise
us, in this. A metaphysic can only grow up within a certain situation which
stimulates it. And in the situation which is ours, the existence of a Christian
datum is an essential factor. It surely behooves us to renounce, once for all,
the naively rationalist idea that you can have a system of affirmation valid for
thought *in general,* or for *any consciousness whatsoever.* Such thought as this
is the subject of scientific knowledge, a subject which is an idea but nothing
else. Whereas the ontological order can be only recognised personally by the
whole of a being, involved in a drama which is his own, though it overflows
him infinitely in all directions—a being to whom the strange power has been
imparted of asserting or denying himself. He asserts himself in so far as he

asserts Being and opens himself to it; or he denies himself by denying Being and thereby closing himself to It. In this dilemma lies the very essence of his freedom.

STUDY AIDS FOR PART TWO

Review Questions

1. What three principles of metaphysical procedure does von Hildebrand single out for censure?

2. What does von Hildebrand consider to be the major evils inherent in premature classification?

3. Does von Hildebrand make a distinction between the terms "system" and "systematic"? In what way?

4. Does von Hildebrand believe that the "reconciliation" of fundamental facts is impossible? Explain.

5. What are the "universal constants" that Hall calls the basic concepts of metaphysics? Give examples of at least three such constants.

6. What three kinds of propositions containing "universal constants" does Hall say metaphysics deals with?

7. What reason does Hall give for saying that metaphysical concepts cannot be translated into predictions?

8. What does Hall mean by "verificatory instances" of hypothesis? By "illustrative instances"? By "disverificatory instances"? What is the only type of disverificatory instance of a hypothesis that Hall says is valid?

9. Why does Whitehead say that the relevance of evidence is dictated by theory?

10. What does Whitehead mean by "the attitude of strained attention"? What specific "errors" of former metaphysical procedure does Whitehead single out for comment?

11. What does Lonergan mean when he says that "every insight is an a priori"?

12. Why does Lonergan deny that all analytic principles are indubitable?

13. What does Lonergan mean by saying that knowing is not just "taking a look"? What confusion does he say that the "observational method" is based on?

14. Why does Lonergan say that "one man's common sense is not another's"? What makes the difference between kinds of common sense?

15. Why does Hegel say that the "beginning" of metaphysics must be an absolute?

16. What does Hegel mean by saying that "the line of scientific advance becomes a circle"?

17. How does Hegel explain that pure being is both "absolutely immediate" and "absolutely mediated"?

18. Why does Hegel reject any beginning of metaphysics with the ego?

19. Why does Bergson say that the metaphysical image behaves like the demon of Socrates in practical life?

20. What two means of expression, according to Bergson, can the metaphysical intuition take?

21. What reasons does Bergson either state or imply for contending that no philosopher has said "more than a single thing"? What degree of success does he allow in the philosopher's expression?

22. In what way does Weiss assert that sceptical honesty ends in uncritical dogmatism? What example does he give of this assertion?

23. What are the four final modes of Weiss's analysis of reality? In what way do they imply each other?

24. Why does Weiss say that specialization requires a grasp of the whole of things?

25. In what two ways does Lieb contend that philosophers have chosen to begin metaphysics?

26. Why do both methods, according to Lieb, tend to be arbitrary? In what way does he say that they are arbitrary? What special science does each of these methods adopt as its model?

27. Why does Marcel say that there is no datum for "consciousness in general" or "for any consciousness whatsoever"? What does he mean by this statement?

28. Why does Marcel say that self-assertion is an assertion of being? What reasons does he give for this statement?

Discussion Topics

1. Facts are not given, says Lewis Hahn (*Philosophical Review*, LXII [1952], 184), "innocent of interpretation." Nor can they be analyzed, observes W. T. Stace (*Philosophical Review*, LII [1943], 123), without implying the presence of speculative doctrines. In short, as Bradley has asserted (*Collected Essays*, I, [1935], p. 10), "the exercize of criticism requires a canon." Do all of these statements confirm Whitehead's assertions in the foregoing section? Lonergan's assertions? How? How might Bergson respond to the statements? How might Marcel? C. W. Churchman (*Theory of Experimental Inference*, [1946], p. 14) seems to imply that statistical technique can avoid the problem of "interpretation." Can it? Would Lonergan concede it? Would Whitehead?

2. The ideal of a rational system, observes Morris R. Cohen (*Nature and Reason*, [1931], p. 107), is in the "connectedness" of its parts. Science, he says, "views facts not as isolated or separate events, but as connected in essence." Would Hegel approve of this remark? How? Why? Would Weiss? Why?

3. Hegel once said that "the truth is the whole," or the totality of being. Does this remark have anything to do, do you think, with his "circular" method? Why do you think that he chose the circle as the fitting analogy for his explanation? Can you think of any more appropriate geometrical figure—for instance, a spiral? What geometrical figure would Lieb choose? Why? Is there any similarity between Lieb's method and Hegel's?

4. Whitehead said that theory dictates method; Lonergan, that method anticipates the goal of theory; Bergson, that theory corrects theory. Are they all saying the same thing in different ways? Explain your answers.

5. What specific traits do the methods of Hegel and Weiss have in common? Of Bergson and Hegel? Of Bergson and Marcel?

6. What difference, do you think, would be made in one's metaphysics by beginning with such ontological facts as "fidelity" and "hope," as opposed to "geometry" and "physics"? What sort of philosopher would most likely choose the former? The latter?

7. Bergson contended that metaphysics seeks to penetrate temporal and empirical realities in order to discover their "real structure." This structure he considered to be hidden from scientific methods, and in no way to be confused with Kantian categories. In what specific ways do the following statements from his *Introduction to Metaphysics* indicate his methodology? In what way do you believe that Hegel would agree or disagree with these statements? In what way would Marcel?

§ "Either metaphysics is only [a] play of ideas, or else, if it is a serious occupation of the mind, if it is a science and not simply an exercize, it must transcend concepts in order to reach intuition. . . . It is only truly itself when it goes beyond the concept, or at least when it frees itself from rigid and ready-made concepts in order to create a kind very different from those which we naturally use. . . ."

§ "Metaphysics . . . is the science which claims to dispense with symbols."

Research Themes

1. Analyze the article "Phenomenology and Speculation" (*Philosophy Today*, III [1959], 43–64) by Hedwig Conrad-Martius on the phenomenological method. Do you find any similarities between her description of phenomenology and the methods employed by any of the authors in this section—say, Hegel? To what extent? Develop your findings in a 1,000-word essay.

2. Make a précis of the article "A Note on the Method of Metaphysics" by Béla Freiherr von Brandenstein (*International Philosophical Quarterly*, I [1961], 264–72), and compare it with the views expressed by Hall in the foregoing section. What question do these authors share in common? What different lines of development does each follow? Write up your conclusions in a 1,000-word essay.

SELECTED BIBLIOGRAPHY
FOR PART TWO

1. Anderson, J. F. "On Demonstration in Thomistic Metaphysics," *New Scholasticism*, 32 (1958), 476–94.
2. Anderson, F. "Metaphysics as a Science," *Journal of Philosophy*, 35 (1938), 57–66.
3. Bergson, Henri. *Introduction to Metaphysics*. New York: Liberal Arts Press, 1949.
4. Born, Max. "Physics and Metaphysics," *Scientific Monthly*, 82 (1956), 229–35.
5. Carmichael, P. A. "The Metaphysical Matrix of Science," *Philosophy of Science*, 20 (1953), 208–16.
6. Hahn, L. E. "Metaphysical Interpretation," *Philosophical Review*, 61 (1952). 176–87.

7. Henle, R. J., S.J. *Method in Metaphysics*. Milwaukee: Marquette University Press, 1951.
8. Hocking, W. E. "Fact, Field and Destiny," *Review of Metaphysics*, 11 (1958), 525–49.
9. ———, Lamprecht, S. N., and Randall, Jr., J. H. "Metaphysics: Its Function, Consequences and Criteria," *Journal of Philosophy*, 43 (1946), 365–78; 393–412.
10. Kennick, W. E. "Metaphysical Presuppositions," *Journal of Philosophy*, 52 (1955), 769–80.
11. Levi, A. W. "Substance, Process, Being," *Journal of Philosophy*, 55 (1958), 749–61.
12. Lowe, Victor. "Empirical Method in Metaphysics," *Journal of Philosophy*, 44 (1957), 225–33.
13. McKeon, Richard. "Principles and Consequences," *Journal of Philosophy*, 56 (1959), 385–401.
14. McKian, J. D. "The Metaphysics of Introspection According to St. Thomas," *New Scholasticism*, 15 (1941), 89–117.
15. Maritain, Jacques. *Science and Wisdom*. London: Geoffrey Bles, 1940.
16. Marvin, W. T. "The Emancipation of Metaphysics From Epistemology," in *The New Realism*. New York: Macmillan, 1912, pp. 45–83.
17. Pepper, S. C. "Metaphysical Method," *Philosophical Review*, 52 (1943), 252–69.
18. Rieser, M. "Noetic Models of Mythology and Metaphysics," *Journal of Philosophy*, 59 (1958), 909–11.
19. Schipper, E. W. "Existence and Common Sense," *Journal of Philosophy*, 41 (1944), 298–302.
20. Smith, V. E. "Wisdom and Science," *Proceedings of the American Catholic Philosophical Association*, 30 (1956), 3–15.
21. Weinberg, Y. L. "Dynamic and Static Aspects of Existence and Their Significance for the Problem of Method," *Journal of Philosophy*, 41 (1944), 617–26.
22. Wright, H. W. "Note on Communication as a Principle of Metaphysical Synthesis," *Journal of Philosophy*, 56 (1959), 730–33.

Three   METAPHYSICAL
PERSPECTIVES

NOT TOO MANY PEOPLE DRAW A DISTINCTION BETWEEN METAPHYS-
ical conceptions and the conceptions of metaphysics—that is theories of metaphysics as opposed to theories about it. But the distinction should certainly be
made, especially if we are to explain the reason for the often profound disagreements among metaphysicians. In fact, it is usually the differences in the
way a philosopher conceives the functions of metaphysics that eventually determine the content of his metaphysical theories. In this section, then, we shall
consider some of these differences, and the bearing they have on any answer
to the question, "What is metaphysics, and what is it about?"

I

There is no doubt that, in some ways at least, metaphysics literally encourages partisanship. It can make friends or enemies on the same issues, and
either divide or strengthen its alliances from the very beginning. For metaphysicians, the beginning of differences, or agreements, in theory usually
centers around the particular viewpoint taken toward the extent of metaphysical business. The question that is framed at the beginning is, therefore,
"To *what* is metaphysics applicable, and what is its range of applicability?" To
this question, three general answers can be distinguished, and they can be expressed in the following propositions:

    1. Metaphysics is universally applicable, having propositions that,
though drawn from particular instances of reality, can be assigned universal
scope.

    2. Metaphysics is either actually or hypothetically applicable to only
some kinds of reality, having propositions of purely limited scope.

    3. Metaphysics, if at all applicable, is concerned with strictly pro-
cedural questions.

Let us try to make these differences a little clearer.

    1. When Aristotle characterized metaphysics as a "universal science,"
dealing with the ultimate principles of whatever *is* or *can be,* he gave voice

to the classical view, which has dominated the history of metaphysics until comparatively recent times—though even today, its adherents are numerous. Such a modern thinker as Whitehead, for instance, indicates that he holds with some form of this view, since he believes that comprehension provides the basic theme of metaphysics.

In thinkers of the classical schools, this general view, however, is supported by certain dependent beliefs—for example, that there is (*a*) a cohesive and coherent character to all true knowledge, (*b*) a hierarchic structure to knowledge and reality, and (*c*) an attainable world view that is the theoretic goal of knowledge. According to this view, the science of metaphysics gives a single and indisputable knowledge of reality, and is theoretically attached to subaltern sciences, which both derive meaning *from* it and are assigned meaning *by* it. It seeks "a general view which will satisfy the intellect" by providing a theoretic container for all knowledge and by making possible a comprehension of the universe as a whole. For Aristotle, this would mean that metaphysics is concerned with being as such, rather than with fragmentary studies about various kinds of beings. For a modern classicist, such as F. H. Bradley, metaphysics is concerned with Absolute Reality, as opposed to mere "appearances."

2. The second viewpoint, considerably less ambitious than the first, cautions metaphysics to concentrate its attention on the explication of either some kinds of things or on one kind of knowledge about things. The British thinker G. E. Moore is one representative of this view. He believes that the function of metaphysics is to deal with possible or suprasensible things, rather than with actual or "natural" objects.

Proponents of this view invariably bridle at the terms "all" and "everything." They prefer to say "some" and "several"—but they never go beyond "many." They reason that any attempt to "universalize" statements indicates a certain *naïveté* in one's attitude toward knowledge. For example, S. N. Hampshire, another British thinker, contends that knowledge, of its very nature, is oriented to *individual* things. It is therefore not only unwise but impossible to "extrapolate" individuals into universals, and to say that, since there is a knowledge of "some" things, there *must* be a knowledge of "all" things.

We may point out, however, that adherents of this view often forget that the use of universal adjectives is not always an attempt to finalize thought or to inhibit its further development. It may simply indicate that "all" and "every" are at least legitimate references. The physicist, for instance, does not consider his world view incorrigible. Nonetheless, he makes statements about "all" electrons and "every" species of vertebrate. In short, he "extrapolates" to the "top of the scale" with at least some justification.

3. The third view of metaphysical business bases its case on the fact that metaphysical statements have not, either logically or historically, received

universal accord. Its adherents, therefore, conclude that metaphysics is a suspect term. Their view might thus be called anti-metaphysical. For example, A. J. Ayer considers that a metaphysical proposition is nothing more than "a sentence which purports to express a genuine proposition, but does, in fact, express neither a tautology nor an empirical hypothesis." For this reason, the metaphysician "produces sentences which fail to conform to the conditions under which alone a sentence can be literally significant."

In saying this, Ayer assumes that only tautologies (what Kant had called analytic a priori) and empirical hypotheses (Kant's synthetic a posteriori) can be genuine propositions, because only these can be actually or theoretically "verifiable." A realist logician might wonder whether Ayer commits the fallacy of false assumption in making this statement. Or a realist metaphysician might say that Ayer represents the view, not of *anti*-metaphysics, but of *un*-metaphysics. Now, however true either of these contentions might be, we cannot avoid the fact that Ayer's ideas have a certain amount of historical precedent, and point back to the views of a predecessor and fellow-anti-metaphysician—David Hume.

Hume contended that any metaphysics that posed as a science of absolute certitude was either poetry or nonsense. A metaphysical proposition that contained neither analyses (tautologies) nor "experimental reasonings" should be committed to the flames; "for it can contain nothing but sophistry and illusion."

The reason Hume was opposed to his contemporary "school" metaphysics was that he regarded it as an effort to prove, by logic alone, the existence of supraempirical realities, such as God and the personal self. Hume did not disbelieve in such realities; he simply denied that there could be absolutely demonstrable knowledge about them. That they exist and truly exist, he nowhere denied. But that one could prove or disprove them, he refused to accept. We are convinced of their existence, he contends, not on rational, but on habitual and instinctual grounds. He contended that a true metaphysics rightfully restricts its knowledge to phenomena, while metaphysics in a pejorative sense is fool's play, in that it attempts to demonstrate supraphenomenal realities by appeal to causal relations. But this is impossible because we have no idea—which could be traceable to a direct sense-impression—of cause or causality.

We have already mentioned in Part One the way in which Kant tried to deal with this difficulty. Kant said that the human mind comes to experience already provided with certain basic meanings, or categories, such as "causality," "relation," "quantity." Must we conclude, then, that metaphysical explanations are either to be explained by Kant's transcendental categories, or else to be dismissed, as Hume put it, as unexplainable? Three examples may help us to decide.

Consider the statement, "There is no truth," or its rephrasing in logical language, "All claims to truth are false claims." How shall we establish whether this is an acceptable or an unacceptable proposition? Some might reply that on grounds of universal belief it is not an acceptable statement, since by universal agreement there is truth. But, we must ask, does such an answer do anything more than carry the burden of demonstration to what men believe? And would we then not have to inquire whether this belief was itself acceptable?

It would seem, however, that the "logical" question to ask of such a statement is this: Is it, as a statement, true or false? If it is a false statement, we have no problem. It may be a "meaningful," "significant," and, in one sense of the term, "genuine" proposition, but admittedly false. On the other hand, however, if the proposition is true, then it would claim its truth on the grounds of denying truth. It is certainly obvious that if the statement is true, then here at least is one truth, even though its content is a denial of truth. It would be, in the first place, a true denial; and, in the second place, it would maintain such a denial to be "true." And it is no use to admit that this would constitute an exception to prove its own rule, because a single lapse of a universal statement is as good as a total lapse.

As the second example, consider a sceptical statement, such as, "I'm not sure of anything." One would have to insist that this statement itself must also take its place as a member of the "anything" class. Can one be sure of this statement? To say, "I'm not sure of anything, including this statement," would cut the very ground from under it. On the other hand, the statement as originally given implies that there is one thing that *is* certain: namely, this statement—which, however, claims total uncertainty.

In both of these examples, an obvious contradiction shows up. Though "logic" or mental categories seem to dictate these contradictions, it seems that something more than logic is at stake, something that is below even logic; for these examples indicate something about reality and about the mind. St. Augustine dealt with such examples under the title *veritates aeternae,* or eternal truths, which the mind does not arbitrate, but which govern the mind. The essential meanings at stake here bring one to a frontier of the mind, where something other than the mind is present. We are saying, "This is how reality is."

There is, however, a further example that, in the light of the *veritas aeterna,* may help to illustrate one of the weaknesses in Kant's explanation, as well as in the Hume-Ayer position. Consider the statement, "Only empirical propositions are true." The statement is clearly self-referable, and we would therefore have to ask, "On what empirical grounds is this statement advanced?" Is it, or is it not, itself empirical? If it is not empirical, it is self-destructive. If it is empirical, it must be empirically verifiable. But clearly, this cannot be the case. Moreover, such a statement is not equivalent to the proposition, "Empirical sentences can be verified, and therefore are true statements," because the original statement—though applicable to "lab-oratory" propositions—is not itself a laboratory proposition. It is only a uni-versalized statement about such propositions. How then is it to be verified? Clearly, one cannot pretend that verifying particular instances of a generaliza-tion is the same as verifying the generalization.

In each of these foregoing three examples, we find "meaningful" state-ments that are neither tautologies nor empirical hypotheses. Does this then mean that such statements fall into the class—the only class left—of meta-physical statements? More precisely, do they fall into the class of anti-metaphysical statements? If the answer to these questions is "yes," then it would appear that, although anti-metaphysicians dismiss metaphysics, they are playing at it.

This contention may become more evident if we select an example con-cerning metaphysics from one of their spokesman. Let us consider the early work of a logical positivist, Rudolf Carnap, who has contended that "meta-physical statements assert nothing at all." Now the question is, if this is to stand as a significant and genuine proposition, it must be either an analysis of meaning or an empirical proposition. Obviously, it is neither. But if, as Fr. Copleston has pointed out, the only other class of statements is "metaphysical," then, apparently, we have here a metaphysical statement, wittingly or not. Thus Ayer (though he denies it), Carnap, and others are, in Bradley's still relevant phrase, "brother metaphysicians." Perhaps anti-metaphysics, then, is related to metaphysics as an antilogism is to a syllogism. That is to say, anti-metaphysics substantiates the relevance of metaphysics.

From our previous discussion, one fact seems to emerge: it is that mean-ing transcends merely tautological and empirical confines. Even the act of empirical identification implies that an object (a that) must be turned into an object-known (a what) in order for the identifying statement to have any meaning whatsoever. Plato understood this very well and was therefore—long before Kant—emboldened to suggest the myth of *anamesis,* or remembrance (as he did in the dialogue *Meno*), to explain how meaning is "superimposed" upon a datum to make it a meaningful-datum. Plato tried to say that knowl-edge is helpless without class-concepts or categories.

II

It is necessary at this point, however, to move more fully into the problem of describing metaphysical viewpoints. The three divisions, which we have al-ready suggested as distinguishing the conceptions about metaphysics, are con-fessedly a rough approximation of a complex problem. At closer view, it becomes apparent that there are additional ways in which distinctions may be drawn between various views, especially in the light of specific questions. Questions like these: What does metaphysics do; is it concerned with the character of things or of language, or both; in what way does metaphysics affect other philosophical tasks, and in what way is it self-restrictive; is the aim of metaphysics the creation of a world view that is universally applicable, and does this therefore imply the assertion of a mathematically-modeled system of references; how valid are metaphysical systems; are they ultimately self-destructive; what kind of conditions must they meet for validity?

In order to take account of such questions, the following essays have been divided into two categories: (A) the one is concerned with general viewpoints toward metaphysics, and (B) the other, with specific contentions about metaphysical business. The first is entitled "Universes of Discourse," the second, "Representative Schools."

(A) If we choose the question: "What is the metaphysical task?" we obviously have a general rather than a specific question. Answers to this question develop under the category "Universes of Discourse" and, if put in tabular form, might be read this way:

(a) Lazerowitz: It is the pursuit of nonsensical statements and problems.
(b) Copleston: On the contrary, there are meaningful statements and problems that are also metaphysical.
(c) Woodbridge: It deals with the whole of reality.
(d) Moore: It deals with only parts of reality.
(e) Whitehead: It deals with the whole of reality *and* all of its parts.
(f) Hampshire: It couldn't possibly.

Though it would be naive to imagine that each of the above authors simply puts forward an alternative to the original question, it is still useful to consider such statements as though they were elements of a dialogue.

In the table, for example, (a) and (b) represent exclusive alternatives: Lazerowitz maintains that there is no such thing as "genuine metaphysics" because metaphysics is simply another name for "linguistic confusion," while Copleston points out that metaphysical problems cannot be condemned out of hand without first being formulated. When they are formulated, Copleston says, it appears that at least some metaphysical statements are also meaningful in a linguistic sense. The alternatives expressed by (a) and (b) thus suggest the competition of negative and positive statements. In contrast, statements (c), (d), and (e) compete in different ways, each of them positive, and not expressly exclusive. Woodbridge believes that metaphysics deals with the whole of reality, but only in so far as metaphysics accounts for the enormous variety-in-union that the "whole" represents. Moore, conversely, is interested not in the union but in the variety of things—but only in specific kinds of that variety—treatment of which precedes the question of what the "whole" is; Whitehead believes that metaphysics can combine positions (c) and (d) by achieving both theoretical coherence (system) and empirical adequacy. Hampshire contends, however, that statements (c) and (e) are illusory, since no systematic account of things can meet all the conditions, but only some of the conditions of expression.

(B) Now if we shift the ground of comparison to the second category, "Representative Schools," we can expose more specific differences in meta-physical viewpoints by asking more specific questions. At the same time, we will notice that differences and similarities, which would not show up in the first category, (A), now become more apparent. For instance, Thomists also contend that metaphysics is concerned with "the whole of reality," but their position is not, except superficially, the same as that of Woodbridge or White-head. The same distinction would hold, generally speaking, for the other five schools selected for comparison.

For example, if we were to put a question, such as, "What is metaphysics about?" to the members of the six following schools, the answers could be divided by a line drawn inclusively from Maritain to Emmet, and another drawn inclusively from Pepper to Lieb. In the first division, the answers would all agree, in general terms, that metaphysics is concerned with being; in the second, that metaphysics is concerned with delusive or procedural problems, which are engendered by appeals to being. But if an even more specific question is posed, the lines of distinction narrow. Suppose we put the question, "What is the metaphysical object?" In this case, the lines of distinction can be drawn properly along the frontiers that separate each school. Thomists would tend to reply to this question by asserting that the metaphysical object is being *qua* being; existentialists, by asserting that the metaphysical object is concrete being as affirmed by the knowing "subject"; analogists, by asserting that it is reality perceived through metaphors. Linguists, heurists, and naturalists, on the other hand, deny that there is any such thing as a metaphysical object, and consider the problem of metaphysics as a puzzle, a procedure, or a meth-odology either to be worked out or to be modernized.

III

If we wish to achieve more accurate information on the various positions set forth here, we will find it necessary to formulate more explicit questions. As we do, we will notice that in the same school, answers show certain differ-ences that do not show up in a general survey. At the same time, a certain amount of development and dialectic motion among the views becomes evi-dent. We can indicate this more adequately by surveying the essential char-acter of the schools listed below.

The Thomist view of metaphysics, to begin with, is that, while it does deal with the whole of reality insofar as it considers being *qua* being, it does so by means of a finite and abstractive intellectual intuition issuing from the direct existential judgment about the concrete existent. The emphasis here is on a sensory origin of concepts and on the assertion that metaphysical state-ments are grounded in experience. Always guiding the knowing mind are certain first principles of knowledge, which are antecedently principles of being itself.

These views are made more explicit by the three essays reprinted below. Maritain stresses that being (or intelligible reality), which is attained in a genuine and profound intuition, is the true subject of metaphysics. Father Phelan distinguishes the concept of being in everyday experience from that formed after arduous reflection—a distinction corresponding to the difference between the material and formal objects of metaphysics. Father Garrigou-Lagrange emphasizes that the principles of knowledge and of reality emerge from reflection upon the first concept formed by the intellect in its contact with being.

Existentialists, on the other hand, tend to perceive more mystery in the process of contact with being. For thinkers such as Heidegger, mystery occludes any penetration into reality, while for others, such as Marcel and Lavelle, mystery is the condition of such penetration. Berdyaev serves as a useful guide to the existentialist view in that he puts all his weight on the side of the being of the subject, or person knowing reality, rather than on the side of object-reality. For the existentialists, generally speaking, it is not abstractive being that is primary but the being of the existent and affective person. It is the anxiety-haunted and insecure reality that is "I" that asks the question of being. And in the question of being, as Heidegger points out, there is suspended the being of the questioner. Man, in the concrete, is the proper place to begin the inquiry into being, which is concerned not only with the existence of "anything," but especially with the meaning of the existence of the affective self. Being is a problem only because it is posed by an existent who understands the problem as a personal issue. All other reals, save the person, are submerged passively in the being of objectivization (where everything is a "thing," and never advances to the stage of self-questioning being). Rather than a science of abstractions, of possibility, or even of the external existent, metaphysics becomes, in the words of Jean-Paul Sartre, an effort on the part of the existential knower "to embrace being from within the human condition in its totality" and "to resolve as nearly as possible the fundamental question which is that of the existence of the existent."

Berdyaev appeals against any "objective" knowledge of being by intellectual abstraction, in favor of a "creative," communitarian knowledge of reality. To Marcel, being is known through an affirmation within being, which is equivalent to the ontological status of the inquirer. Heidegger accepts the importance of the ontological status of the inquirer but denies that it can be understood except against the background of nothingness. Lavelle affirms the entry into being by means of a development from the being-that-is-I, to absolute-being, and, finally, to the being-of-the-world.

The views of the analogical school can be divided roughly between those thinkers who believe that reality can be understood only by means of symbols, analogies, and metaphors, and those who believe that analogies are the methodological key that best unlocks the conceptions about metaphysics. Emmet believes that only "intra-experiential" analogies can hypothesize about reality with any amount of success. From the same position—with the difference, however, that the technique is aimed at talking about theories that talk about reality—Pepper considers that analogies or metaphors hold the key, first, to an understanding of systems, and only secondly to an understanding of the concerns of the systems.

As previously suggested, the line separating Emmet from Pepper separates answers to the question, "What is metaphysics about?" On the one hand (Maritain to Emmet), interest centers around a "factual" answer to a "factual" question. On the other hand (Pepper to Lieb), interest is essentially centered around procedural answers to procedural questions. The school of language analysis is a perfect example of the tendency to establish a procedure concerned with other procedures. Ayer and Lazerowitz, in their essays, give voice to this view in their outright denials of the authenticity of metaphysics—principally because it does not conform to the procedures allegedly required for meaningful discourse. Lazerowitz moves farther ahead, however, and agrees with such thinkers as John Wisdom and Wittgenstein in attributing metaphysical statements to the psychological perversions of metaphysicians. Metaphysical statements are considered to be symptomatic of a mental "crack-up," and to indicate more about the *idée fixe* of a metaphysical "patient" than about the state of reality. This is how John Wisdom puts the point in his two-part essay "Metaphysics and Verification," in which he asserts that metaphysics uncovers paradoxes that can be clarified only by understanding them as bizarre language-usage with a hidden meaning.

Proceduralist views are to be found in the essays by Carnap, Burtt, and Collingwood. Since in certain respects language analysts agree with logical positivists (the two, however, are not completely the same), their statement that metaphysics is spurious seems to indicate that both have much in common. Thus Carnap's views follow naturally from the remarks suggested by Ayer and Lazerowitz. Carnap adds, however, that if metaphysical statements did have any relevance, their relevance would be purely logical and methodological. The chief difference is that Carnap maintains that the proper metaphysical task is limited to questions that arise around the framework of scientific procedure, as opposed to questions within the framework itself. These latter are handled according to empirical canons. Metaphysics, he says, therefore comprises those theories "whose object is to arrange the most general propositions of the various regions of scientific knowledge in a well-ordered system"—hence, his early distinction between the claims of any "unscientific" metaphysics "to represent knowledge about something which is over and beyond all experience," and of any "verifiable" metaphysics, which attempts to study methodological statements about the theory of empirical procedures.

Burtt's procedural views, in contrast, represent a milder position. He takes his cue from the fact that a stalemate exists in the battle between what we might call "being-ists" and proceduralists—that is, between those who contend that metaphysics actually deals with reality and those who say that it deals with questions about questions. Burtt is a sort of compromise candidate. To settle the dispute, he contends that metaphysical discourse requires some kind of gauge of its identity. Its gauge, he believes, is that it estimates all other "gauges" relevant to its own inquiry. Collingwood suggests that the only kind of procedure that metaphysics can rightfully be engaged in is historical, or "archeological," inquiry. Its job is to find out what, in historical terms, lies behind the "scientific" statements made by different societies in the past.

Though Dewey is hardly a mere proceduralist in the precise sense, his great interest in methodological questions has brought him considerable attention. His insistence on what metaphysics should do, however, is (for present purposes) his ticket to the school of proceduralists. Dewey's remarks are based on the assertion that a chasm separates our "ideal" formulation from our "real" practice—what can be explained from what can be actualized, what can be intuitively known from what can be achieved. He felt that in a processive world, exhibiting interactions between nature and experience in and of it, theories have to earn their keep. He would agree with William James that theories are also "instruments, not answers to enigmas in which we can rest." Hence, Dewey insists that metaphysics be made "concrete" by aiming toward a conscious and aesthetic development of the meaning present in concrete experience.

Lieb's ideas, more strictly procedural than Dewey's, are based on the belief that the "ideal" and the "actual" have to be worked at in tandem. Metaphysics, he says, should therefore seek explicitly to elucidate the meaning inherent in our being and activity. Like Morris R. Cohen—also considered a proponent of American naturalism, though he describes his views in the term "rationalistic realism"—Lieb believes in an essentially circular method, which frames what is implicit in terms of what is explicit. Similarly, Cohen conceived the circular path of procedure to move from data to confirming-theory, and from theory to confirming-data. Employing one version of the reciprocity view, Cohen said that "we obtain evidence for principles by appealing to empirical material, to what is alleged to be 'fact'; and we select, analyze and interpret empirical material on the basis of principles. In virtue of such give and take between facts and principles, everything that is dubitable falls under careful scrutiny at one time or another."

The following selections should provide sufficient evidence of the fact, as we said earlier, that metaphysics can hardly be considered a completely peaceful art—perhaps one of the most painful lessons to be learned about the study.

UNIVERSES OF DISCOURSE

Morris Lazerowitz

1. THE LIMITS OF METAPHYSICS

Many charges have been leveled against metaphysics. But at the same time, many defenses have been given in its behalf. In this and in the following selection by Father Copleston, we have the opportunity of witnessing a "quarantined" dialogue made up of such charges and defenses. Though neither speaker actually questions the other, both speak unmistakably on opposite sides of the same issue.

In the present essay, Morris Lazerowitz contends that metaphysics, though a remarkable phenomenon in Western history, is totally deceptive. Wearing the garments of science, it never really acts like a science. Science has its own procedures, and guarantes its own results. Metaphysics has none. In fact, says Lazerowitz, metaphysics has so far produced nothing but idle, aimless, and endless debate. The reason for this is that metaphysics pretends that its problems are soluble; whereas, by their very nature they are not. Many people may not like to hear metaphysics spoken of in this way, he asserts, but this is what it comes to. And anyone with courage enough to master his own emotions will see this.

For Lazerowitz, metaphysics is rather like a sick cat playing Egyptian deity. We may understand the cat's problem, try to help it with medicine or diet, but beyond humoring it, there is little we can do for it. The "grand illusion" that makes the cat sick would also be responsible for making the metaphysician a clinical problem. The metaphysician is "sick with words," and dreams unrealistically of impossible feats of cognition. Where the cat pretends he is an Egyptian god with power over every householder, the metaphysician dreams he has found the secrets at the heart of the world. But actually, he has discovered only the secret illusions of his own words. Criticism shows that metaphysics is therefore only "a verbal dream, the linguistic substructure of which has to be uncovered before we see what it comes to. . . ." Those who defend what Lazerowitz might very well call the Egyptian-cat theory of metaphysics assert that it is (a) a set of empirical propositions about one fundamental fact of the universe; or (b) a priori statements that can be both discovered about, and applied to, the world; or (c) disguised claims about the uses of language; or, finally, (d) ultimately unintelligible (though perhaps emotionally moving) strings of words.

From *The Structure of Metaphysics*, by Morris Lazerowitz. Reprinted by permission of the publisher, Routledge & Kegan Paul Ltd., London.

Metaphysics, Lazerowitz holds, does not fall in the category of (*a*) through (*c*) Nor, on the other hand, as in (*d*), is it wholly unintelligible. A psychotic's dream is intelligible to a psychiatrist; and a metaphysician's to the critically-oriented inquirer. The difference between psychotic and metaphysician, he implies, is that while one is institutionalized, the other runs free.

M ETAPHYSICS PRESENTS US with an intellectual phenomenon that is both remarkable and mystifying. It is without doubt one of the highest of man's cultural achievements, combining in itself both the grandeur of conception and subtlety of thought. But what it is, its nature, remains unknown to us. It looks to be the deepest of the sciences, in which the attempt is made to arrive at an understanding of the ultimate constitution of the world, its basic material and structure, and of the nature and limits of our knowledge. Further, metaphysics has a scope, by comparison with which the ordinary sciences, with their laboratory techniques, appear to comprehend only the surface mechanics of the material universe, while, moreover, resting on tremendous assumptions that are the proper province of metaphysics, e.g., that nature is uniform.

But although metaphysics looks like science, it differs from science in an important respect, a respect which is overlooked by philosophers but which is a source of profound disturbance to intelligent outsiders. No one, except a person who must for some reason blind himself to the facts, can fail to contrast the special sciences, with their imposing edifices of sound results, and metaphysics, with its chronic condition of endless and unresolved debates. Theories which are accepted as undeniably true by many philosophers are rejected as certainly false by others. And what is perhaps even more perplexing, demonstrations, which, according to the considered opinion of some philosophers, are absolutely conclusive are, according to the considered opinion of other and equally able philosophers, inconclusive or mistaken. This is a state of affairs which is an enigma to our understanding. How is it to be explained?

Is the source of the condition to be discovered in the complexity and difficulty of the problems dealt with? Or is it to be found in the incompetence of philosophers? Neither of these alternatives is an impressive possibility, and the evidence against them need not detain us. There remains another possible explanation which, however unacceptable it may be to us emotionally, has to be faced and examined. This is that the irresolvability of the disagreements flows from the very nature of the problems, which is to say that the problems are *intrinsically* insoluble, in the sense that no *new fact* will finally establish one answer and lead to the discarding of other possible answers as false. This is an explanation which places a hardship on us, for it requires that we change our way of thinking about metaphysical problems. The difficulty of doing this can be put into its proper perspective if we imagine ourselves in the position of a person living in the sixteenth century who is told that the earth revolves around the sun, or, to use a more homely example, if we imagine ourselves trying to look at our wonderful children through the eyes of our annoyed guest. However that may be, the last explanation is one that can no longer be ruled out of court; for it must be realized that the condition of metaphysics is chronic and pervasive. Until the permanence of the disagreements has been satisfactorily explained a metaphysical theory remains an intellectual creation which we do not understand, or perhaps it would be better to diagnose it as a linguistic symptom for which there exists no diagnosis.

The traditional idea of metaphysics is that its theories are perfectly well understood and that the debates about them are debates over whether they are true or false. This idea is so entirely natural that it is difficult to think that it could be subject to question. Descartes's dissatisfaction with the intellectual anarchy he found everywhere in philosophy was based on the unquestioned acceptance of this idea, and he conceived his task to be one of devising a reliable method for determining the truth-values of theories. This was also the problem of the empiricists, from Locke on. But metaphysics, and in fact the whole field of technical philosophy still remains in dispute. If we take the long history of philosophy into consideration, it becomes not altogether unreasonable to question whether there is a theoretical procedure for ending the disagreements by "solving" the problems. It is worth calling attention to William James's observation, which he himself did not elaborate, that "philosophical theories are not refuted; they are only outmoded."

There is reason indeed, for suspecting that the disputes are, *by their very nature,* not resolvable by scientific means of any sort, *a priori* or empirical, and that the real method, whatever that may be, which is employed for accepting or rejecting theories is effectively concealed in the deceptive façade of demonstrations and refutations. It may well be the case that the proofs and refutations are not what we take them to be, that the theories, unlike those of the natural sciences and of mathematics, are not open to proof or disproof, and that the disputes cannot be resolved, although it may be possible that we may find *insight* into their nature to *dissolve* them. It may quite well be that *understanding,* not solving, is the real intellectual problem. In fact, I shall argue that metaphysical problems *have no solutions,* though this does not mean that we cannot understand them. Only because we *fail* to understand them do we *seek* for solutions, and to understand them is to rid ourselves of the feeling that there *must be* solutions.

This is a possibility which needs now to be investigated. To question the assumption that philosophers are engaged in the task of trying to discover the truth-values of metaphysical views, which brings into question the idea that the views are understood, is to initiate a new Copernican revolution. But there can no longer be any hesitation about investigating this assumption. The curious fact that there are no established results in metaphysics needs to be explained; and any path which gives any promise whatever of leading to an explanation is to be followed, however emotionally disturbing it may be to do this. It must, of course, be admitted that we take the risk of following an intellectual will-o'-the-wisp.

It will be my purpose in these pages to pursue the consequences of supposing that metaphysical theories have no truth-values and that controversies about them are not debates over whether they are true or false. I shall try to show that the sentences used to express metaphysical theories are not understood, not because they lack intelligibility, but because we simply are not cognizant of what the words which express the theories and their fortifying or refuting arguments come to. We are not consciously aware of what we are doing with language when we imagine ourselves to be expressing and demonstrating or refuting profound and important views about the limits of human knowledge, the nature of space or the will. We do not understand our own linguistic creations. Like a dream, a metaphysical theory is a production of the unconscious and has both sense and motivation. We enjoy it or are repelled by it, it gives us pleasure or pain, a feeling of security or one of danger; but its meaning is hidden from us. Just as in our sleep we dream with images, so many of us in our waking intellectual life dream with words. A metaphysical theory, I shall try to show, is a verbal dream, the linguistic substructure of which has to be uncovered before we can see what it comes to and how it produces its last effect. The main problem is to expose to clear view the linguistic machinery which is used to create the illusion that metaphysics gives us views about pervasive and fundamental phenomena and that arguments for or against these views are demonstrations of their truth or falsity. But it is necessary first to see that none of the explanations of the nature of metaphysics so far advanced, explicitly or by implication, is correct. And above all it is important to see that none of them gives a satisfactory account of the disconcerting fact that metaphysical differences of opinion never get resolved, though interest in various problems may pass out of fashion.

Four important hypotheses, classical and contemporary, have been either assumed or explicitly proposed and argued for as answers to the question, "What is the nature of metaphysical theories?" According to one hypothesis they are empirical propositions about the world, about its fundamental aspects and ultimate nature, and are to be confirmed or discarded by experience. Another describes them as being *a priori* propositions about reality, i.e., as being propositions about reality which are arrived at or refuted *a priori*, without the help of any experimentation or observation. A third hypothesis construes them to be disguised linguistic claims about the proper or correct or established usage of expressions. And still a fourth has it that metaphysical statements are meaningless strings of words, that they are sentences which conform to the rules of grammar but are lacking in literal intelligibility, even though they arouse strong emotional reactions in people.

These hypotheses, it seems to me, have been in part the result of the fact that different philosophers have been impressed by and have concentrated their attention mainly on different aspects of metaphysics or on particular classes of views. If a philosopher is especially interested and impressed by the appearance metaphysics has of being about phenomena, their existence or nature, he will be likely to think that the theories are open to empirical testing of some sort. If, instead, he is impressed by the demonstrations that are adduced, he will tend to think that the views are *a priori* descriptions of reality. And if he has insight into the nature of both *a priori* and empirical propositions and concentrates his attention mainly on theories which, at least in appearance, go against the beliefs of common sense, he will hold that they are concealed linguistic statements about proper usage. Or if he concentrates mainly on theories which refer to the suprasensible, he will hold them to be nonsensical counterfeits which philosophers have, somehow, been duped into taking for the real thing. . . .

There are those propositions which, like "Everything flows" and "There are no material things," seem to go against the most fundamental beliefs of a common sense. These strike practical-minded people with a well-developed sense of reality as being bizarre and shocking, to be dismissed as intellectual chimeras; but they hold great fascination for people with mystical tendencies, who, moreover, may be subtle reasoners. The list contains other propositions which seem consistent with, or even to fortify, the beliefs of common sense. Thus, the view that there are two distinct kinds of substance, minds and bodies, which can produce changes in each other, agrees with the most common conception we have of ourselves. And the statement "It is possible for one person to know that another person exists," when maintained by a philosopher, fortifies a belief against the attacks of many metaphysicians, a belief we should all say we had, if asked. Then there are those propositions which state the existence of transcendent objects, objects which lie beyond the limits of the ordinary, everyday sense-experience. A philosopher who maintains that there are suprasensible universals, entities which he can only apprehend with his mind's eye, gives one the idea that he is acquainted with objects which would not be accessible to him were he limited to his five senses. And a philosopher who claims that in addition to the various experienced qualities of things, such as a pebble, there is an unknowable substratum in which the qualities inhere, gives the impression of having discovered evidence for the existence of an object which he is prevented from examining, from knowing as it is "in itself" by some sort of insurmountable barrier. The important proposition that a transcendent, absolutely perfect Being exists belongs only to this last group.

The propositions of all three groups have the look of being about the world; they represent the conclusions of attempts "To know reality as against mere appearance." Whether in fact they are about the world, they undeniably have the appearance of making factual claims. That the sentence

"Motion is impossible," for example, has empirical descriptive sense seems entirely clear; and though the proposition it expresses may strike many readers as odd and certainly false, it must strike them as even more odd that anyone should wish to assert that the literal meaning of the sentence actually is unknown. What else could the sentence be saying except the startling thing that objects are incapable of moving, that rivers do not flow and that my pen, which appears now to be moving, is really stationary? It may be absurd to say that the motion does not exist; but it would seem even more absurd to maintain that the sentence does not deny that rivers flow and birds fly, and to maintain, moreover, that we have no ideas of what it does state. It is the same with the other statements in the list. What could the sentence "It is possible for one person to know that another person exists" mean, be saying, except something reassuring about human knowledge? And what could the statement "In addition to the gross things of sense, there are suprasensible universals" be saying except that objects exist which cannot be seen or felt but require a higher faculty than any used in sense experience? What the statements of this list are about, regardless of whether we agree with them or not, seems undeniably plain, at least on the surface. And unquestionably, a great part of the fascination they have for most people lies in their being believed to be about the world, sensible or suprasensible. . . .

Frederick C. Copleston, S.J.   ## 2. A REALIST'S REJOINDER

In this essay Father Copleston takes up the issue of metaphysical validity at much the same point that Lazerowitz left it. Viewed historically, he says, metaphysics "arises out of the natural desire to know the world or the historical situation." Yet it has been condemned by non-metaphysicians as nothing but a linguistic satire, developed from pseudo-problems, or as an attempt to answer meaningless questions.

The initial problem to be dealt with, says Father Copleston in defense of metaphysics, is the problem of analysis. Metaphysical questions cannot be condemned out of hand unless they are first formulated. Only then can they be analyzed for meaning. We want to know, first, not simply whether our answers are valid or mistaken but whether metaphysical questions have been raised. Among anti-metaphysicians, he says, it has been assumed that

From *Contemporary Philosophy* by Frederick C. Copleston, S.J. Reprinted by permission of the publisher, The Newman Press, Westminster, Maryland.

meaningful questions can be answered only by the sciences—for these produce "answers" in the form of practical results. Scientific questions grow out of the same desire to know that metaphysics has grown out of. Indeed, at one time these desires were identical. Sciences prospered and progressed by means of "their gradual purification of metaphysics." Questions once asked by metaphysician-scientists, such as Aristotle or Plato, are now answered by the physicists or astrophysicists. But there have been questions raised which cannot be answered by scientists and are best described as *metaphysical* questions. However, not all non-scientific questions are automatically metaphysical (for instance, moral questions are not scientific questions, neither are they metaphysical).

The crucial point against anti-metaphysicians is gained when it can be shown that there are some *meaningful* questions that are also metaphysical questions. This can be done on the very ground occupied by linguistic analysts who, when describing material objects—such as chairs and tables—as "logical constructs," are actually posing metaphysical theories. To say that statements about any phenomenon—say, a table—are simply the equivalent of statements about sense-data is to propose a metaphysical thesis, since "it is the result of a philosophical analysis of meaning." It is "sibling" metaphysics. Moreover, language analysts seem to assume that metaphysicians are most likable when they are silent. For such allegedly naive, exaggerative men, silence would be more than golden.

Now it should be understood, Copleston points out, that even the understanding of empirical realities involves "at the end, if not at the beginning" an attempt to fathom the "givenness" of finite reals. As Copleston puts it in a paraphrase of a Wittgenstein dictum: "Not *how* the world is, is the metaphysical [question], but *that* it is." Thus, the meaningful metaphysical problem of being is necessarily raised. Yet "the question of the ultimate Ground of empirical existence would never be raised were there not a primary implicit awareness of existing against a background of Being."

It is not easy, Copleston concludes, to speak of metaphysical issues, for they are never without their expressional difficulties, and are bound to involve problems of meaning. But to choose silence because there is not universal and absolute clarity in every metaphysical discussion is to choose a false alternative.

ARISTOTLE STATED THAT philosophy began with "wonder" and that men continue to philosophize because and in so far as they continue to "wonder." Philosophy, in other words, is rooted in the desire to understand the world, in the desire to find an intelligible pattern in events and to answer problems which occur to the mind in connection with the world. By using the phrase "the world" I do not mean to imply that the world is something finished and complete at any given moment: I use the phrase in the sense of the data of outer and inner experience with which any mind is confronted. One might say just as well that philosophy arises out of the desire to understand the "historical situation," meaning by the last phrase the external material environment in which a man finds himself, his physiological and psychological make-up and that of other people, and the historic past. One might discuss the question whether the desire to understand ought to be interpreted or analyzed in terms of another drive or other drives. Nietzsche, for example, suggested in the notes which have been published under the title "The Will to Power" that the desire to understand is one of the forms taken by the will to power. Or it might be suggested by some that the desire to understand is subordinate to the life-impulse, in the sense that it is the necessity of acting in given historic situations which drives us to attempt to attain clarity concerning this situation. But I do not propose to discuss these psychological questions. I am concerned at the moment to point out that philosophy—and I include metaphysical philosophy—had its origin on the conscious level in the desire to understand the world. We are all familiar with children asking for explanations without any other obvious motive than that of resolving some perplexity, solving some difficulty or understanding some event or set of events; and I suggest that philosophy, as far as its original motive is concerned, is inspired by the same sort of desire which is observable in children.

What I have been saying may appear very obvious and trivial. But the original drive behind philosophical inquiry may possibly become obscured owing to the contention of some contemporary anti-metaphysicians that metaphysical problems are pseudo-problems which have their origin in linguistic confusion and error. Metaphysicians, it is said, were misled by language; they did not understand the proper use of terms; and they thus came to utter a lot of unintelligible sentences—or rather sentences which, though *prima facie* intelligible, can be shown by analysis to lack any definite meaning. That some metaphysical theories were due in part at least to linguistic confusion I should not attempt to deny, though I do not think that this can properly be said of metaphysics in general. But I am not now concerned with assessing the part played by linguistic confusion in the genesis of metaphysical theories. What I should like to point out is that we are not entitled to say of any question or theory that it is meaningless until it has been formulated. Otherwise we do not know what we are calling "meaningless." The questions must first be raised before analysis of them is possible. And they were raised in the first place because the people who raised them wanted to understand something, because they wanted answers; and this fact remains true even if it could be shown that they were mistaken in thinking that there was anything to understand or that any answers to their questions were possible. I think that it is as well to have drawn attention to this point, even if it appears to be a trivial point. For acquaintance with detailed disputes between metaphysicians may give the impression that metaphysics is a mere verbal game and obscure the fact that in its origin metaphysics arises simply out of a natural desire to understand the world or the historical situation.

It is evident that science, too, owes its birth to the desire to understand. Francis Bacon emphasized the practical function of scientific knowledge, and living as we do in a highly technical civilization we are not likely to forget this aspect of science. We are also aware today of the part played by hypothesis in scientific theory, while the development of mathematical physics in particular has led thinkers like Eddington to lay great emphasis on the role of *a priori* mental construction in the framing of physical hypothesis. But though on the one hand technics obviously has a practical function while on the other hand we are now aware of the hypothetical character of scientific theory, it is not, I think, unreasonable to say that philosophy and science had a common origin in the natural desire to understand the world. However much anyone may be inclined to stress the practical function of science, he can hardly maintain that astronomy proper, as distinct from astrology, had any other origin than the desire to understand.

Originally, of course, there was no clear distinction between philosophy and science. Nor, indeed, could there have been. The distinction could not be drawn until science had developed far enough for the distinction to be brought clearly before the mind. It is sometimes difficult to say, therefore, whether a particular theory of a Greek philosopher should be classed as a metaphysical theory or as a scientific hypothesis, a primitive scientific hypothesis, that is to say. In a state of affairs when philosophy and science are not yet distinguished, it is a tautology to say that contours are vague and outlines obscure. For example, any philosopher today who wished to defend the Aristotelian hylomorphic theory must of necessity present it as a metaphysical theory; for it would be absurd to present it as a rival physical hypothesis to, say, the atomic theory. And he will probably also wish to maintain that it was propounded by Aristotle as a metaphysical theory. If he does not maintain this, he lays himself open to the charge of holding the theory merely out of respect for tradition. He is determined to keep the theory, it would be said, because it was Aristotle's theory; but since he sees that it cannot now be put forward as a rival physical hypothesis he changes what he admits to have been originally a physical hypothesis into a metaphysical theory in order to preserve it from attack on scientific grounds. A person, on the other hand, who does not wish to maintain the hylomorphic theory and who regards Aristotle's idea of "form," for example, as having been given definite content by the concepts of structure developed at a much later date by the various empirical sciences, may be inclined to speak of the Aristotelian theory as a primitive scientific hypothesis. And arguments could be adduced both for and against this way of speaking. One might say against it, for instance, that the theory involves mention of entity, or rather of an essential constituent of entities, which is in principle unobservable. I refer to "first matter." On the other hand, an alchemist might say in favor of calling the theory a primitive scientific hypothesis that one could derive from it the testable conclusion that the so-called "baser"

METAPHYSICAL PERSPECTIVES   166

metals can ultimately be turned into gold. But it might also be claimed that the whole dispute is superficial. It is only to be expected, it might be said, that at a time when the sciences had not yet taken shape speculative theories should have been put forward which it is difficult to classify in terms of distinctions which were made at a later date; and one should not attempt to make any rigid classification of this sort. To do so serves no useful purpose. All that one can profitably do is to distinguish, or to attempt to distinguish, those early speculative theories which represent answers to questions which have proved to be or are thought to be answerable by some branch of science from those other theories which represent answers to questions which are not answerable, or which we cannot see to be answerable, by any branch of science. This latter type of theory is properly called a "metaphysical" theory. As for the former type of theory, it does not matter much whether one calls it a metaphysical theory which has been succeeded by scientific theories or a primitive scientific theory, though the latter way of speaking may involve a misuse of the term "scientific." The main point is to recognize that theories of this type have been succeeded in the course of time by fruitful scientific theories which have formed the basis for further research, hypothesis, and experiment. It is a matter of minor importance whether we say that the movement was from metaphysics to science or from "primitive science" to science proper. On the whole, however, it is preferable to speak in the first way, since the development and progress of the sciences have involved their gradual purification from metaphysics.

I do not want to discuss the terminological question any further or to make any definite recommendation about the proper way of speaking. But it seems to me undeniable that at least some lines of inquiry were once pursued by philosophers in a speculative manner which are no longer pursued in this way. It is significant that when Aristotle stated that philosophy began with wonder he went on to state that people wondered first about the more obvious difficulties and that they then gradually advanced and stated difficulties about greater matters like the phenomena of the moon and sun and stars and about the genesis of the universe. Astronomical inquiries were once regarded as pertaining to philosophy. But this is not so today. If we want information about the sun or the moon, we do not turn to philosophers for that information. Again, if we want information about the physical constitution of matter, we turn to physicists. Questions about these matters are now classed as scientific questions, not as philosophical questions. And this is not simply an affair of terminology. The point is that we do not think that questions of this sort can be answered by means of the pure reason, that is, by armchair reflection alone. We see that another method, or other methods, are required. (I say "we see"; but as a matter of fact it was more or less clearly recognized in the late Middle Ages that if we want to learn empirical facts, *a priori* deduction will not enable us to do so.)

It seems to me, then, that it is undeniable that the empirical sciences have gradually taken over some tracts of the territory which was once supposed to belong to philosophy. And in this sense it is true to say that the field of philosophy has been narrowed. On the other hand, it is undeniable that philosophers have asked questions which cannot be answered by any particular science. Some might, perhaps, take exception to the use of the word "cannot" in an absolute sense. They might prefer to say of these questions that we do not see how they can be answered by any particular science. But I fail to see how a question about the origin of all finite beings, for example, could conceivably be answered by an empirical science. So I am content to say quite simply that philosophers have asked a number of questions which cannot be answered by any particular science. And if anyone chooses to say that these questions are the proper philosophical questions and that questions about the sun and moon were never proper philosophical questions, he can go on to say that philosophy proper has *not* in fact been narrowed.

I do not mean to imply that all questions which cannot be answered by the empirical sciences are "metaphysical" questions. For I think that there are moral questions which cannot be answered by empirical science but which one would not normally call "metaphysical" questions. But I confine my attention in this chapter to metaphysical questions. And I think that both metaphysicians and anti-metaphysicians would agree that as far as words are concerned a number of questions are properly called "metaphysical" questions. Some anti-metaphysicians would then go on to say that these questions cannot be answered scientifically because they are unanswerable and that they are unanswerable because no intelligible question has been asked. Speculative questions about the "Absolute" or about the "Cause" of "the world" or about the "spiritual soul" would be classified as questions of this sort. But I want to leave aside for the moment this type of difficulty and to ask whether there are any inquiries which the anti-metaphysician would concede to be meaningful and which at the same time can sensibly be called "metaphysical."

A good deal of attention has been paid by modern philosophers to the analysis of statements about material things like chairs, tables, and so on. And some have argued that objects like these are "logical constructions" out of sense-data or sense-contents. This might be taken to mean that a table, for example, is a fictitious entity, in the sense that there is no existent entity denoted by the word "table" but only a multiplicity of entities called "sense-data" or "sense-contents." We should then presumably have a form of idealistic phenomenalism, arrived at by philosophic reflection rather than scientific hypothesis and verification. For it would be as difficult to prove scientifically that a table consists of sense-data as it would be to prove scientifically Berkeley's theory that material objects are "ideas" presented to us by God. In this case the theory might well be called a "metaphysical" theory. What other name could one give it?

But those analysts who maintain the truth of this theory refuse to allow that it means that a table, for example, is a fictitious entity. The statement that a table is a "logical construction" out of sense-data or sense-contents is a linguistic statement, not a statement about the constitution of material things. What it says is that sentences which name a material thing like a "table" can be translated into sentences which refer to sense-data or sense-contents but which do not contain the word "table." This interpretation of the theory of "logical constructions" as a purely linguistic theory is highly ingenious; but I feel some misgivings about it. A table is a "phenomenon" in the sense that it is an object appearing to us; and if we say that statements about this phenomenon can be translated into statements of equivalent meaning about sense-data, it is difficult to avoid the impression that what we are saying is that this phenomenon is a collection of sense-data. I am not concerned with the truth or falsity of the contention that a table is a collection of sense-data. What I want to remark is this. The contention is not a metaphysical contention in the sense that anything is said about a substance in Locke's sense of the word "substance"; but it seems to me to be metaphysical in another sense, namely in the sense that it is not the result of any physical or chemical analysis of the table. It is the result of a philosophical analysis of meaning, and in this sense it can be called "linguistic"; but it is not linguistic in the sense that it concerns words exclusively. Philosophical analysis is not the same thing as grammatical analysis. I suggest, then, that the theory of "logical constructions" can sensibly be called a metaphysical theory and that what it does is to replace the metaphysic of substance by a phenomenal metaphysic. Possibly this is felt by those analysts who tend to exclude the sense-datum theory and the theory of "logical constructions" in the name of "ordinary language."

Perhaps one can apply the same line of reflection to the analysis of causality. This is often represented as an instance of linguistic analysis. So it is in a sense. But in what sense? If it is simply an analysis of the meaning of the term as used by scientists, or by a number of them, or if it is simply an analysis of the meaning of the term as used by certain social groups at certain periods, it is linguistic analysis in a strict sense. But if it is possible by means of this analysis to establish what people "ought" to mean by causality, the procedure involved does not seem to me to be radically different from the procedure followed by those philosophers who would have regarded the analysis of causality as an instance of metaphysical analysis.

It may be objected that metaphysicians have imagined that they could find out fresh information about the world by reflective analysis, whereas in point of fact we cannot do this. We can analyze the way in which people speak about the world, but any facts we learn in this way are linguistic facts. But I think that a distinction ought to be made. There is certainly a sense in which philosophical analysis gives no fresh knowledge of "facts." For example, by analyzing relation-sentences we do not obtain fresh knowledge of actual relations: that is obvious. Nor do we obtain knowledge that things stand in relation to one another in some sense. For this knowledge is presupposed by the ordinary use of language involving relation-sentences. But we can obtain information of what it "means" to say that one thing stands in relation to another thing. As this knowledge concerns "meaning" it can be said to concern linguistic usage; but it can also be called a knowledge of what relations "are"; it is not knowledge simply of what A or B thinks is the meaning of relationsentences. And it seems to me that this kind of analysis can sensibly be called "metaphysical" analysis. It is certainly not physical or chemical analysis. It may be objected that it is precisely in order to distinguish it from physical and chemical analysis that it is called "linguistic" analysis; but what I am suggesting is that what is called by philosophers "linguistic" analysis is not radically different from what in the past has been known as "metaphysical" analysis.

There is, of course, an obvious comment which can be made about what I have been saying. An anti-metaphysician might reply as follows. "Leaving aside the question whether your account of analysis is correct or incorrect, I am quite prepared to admit that if you choose to call analysis 'metaphysics,' metaphysics is possible and has a useful function. But to call analysis 'metaphysics' does nothing at all toward justifying metaphysics in the sense in which I reject metaphysics. If an astronomer rejects astrology, it would be futile to select some part of astronomy and call it 'astrology' under the impression that astrology in the sense in which the astronomer rejects it was thus being justified."

There is obviously truth in this line of reply. I entirely agree that to call analysis as practiced by the modern analyst "metaphysics" does little to justify metaphysics in the sense in which the anti-metaphysical analyst rejects metaphysics. At the same time I do not think that my line of argument is as futile as the analogy about astronomy and astrology might suggest. In the first place I have maintained that some at least of what passes for "analysis" bears a marked resemblance to what used to be called "metaphysics." The analyst might reply, of course, that he does not deny the resemblance but that the kind of inquiry referred to should be called "analysis" and not "metaphysics" whether it is practised by Plato or by Berkeley or by a modern analyst. The point is, however, that the phrase "linguistic analysis" may be misleading; and to draw attention to resemblances of the kind mentioned may help to show how it can be misleading. In the second place it is not, I think, futile to point out that the interpretation of the word "metaphysics" which is fairly common today, that is, as a study of or talk about transcendent and unobservable entities, has not been the sense in which the word has been exclusively understood by metaphysicians themselves. If one analyzes, for example, the meaning of the word "thing," one is, I suggest, engaging in precisely one of those pursuits which metaphysicians have not infrequently engaged in and which they have regarded as pertaining to metaphysics. And it is just as well to realize this.

However, as I have said, the classification of analysis, or some of it, as "metaphysics," does little or nothing to rescue what the anti-metaphysical analysts call "metaphysics." And I want to now turn to this subject.

(1) If one looks at the history of metaphysical theories which involve reference to a being or to beings in some sense transcending empirical reality, one will see that in some of them the transcendent being is postulated in order to explain or to account for the world being in some respect like this rather than like that. In the myth of the *Timaeus* the divine craftsman is postulated (with what degree of seriousness it is unnecessary to discuss here) to account for the intelligible structure of the world, that is, for what Plato took to be the world's intelligible structure. Again, in Aristotle's *Metaphysics* the first unmoved mover is postulated as the ultimate explanation of "movement." In Whitehead's philosophy eternal objects and God seem to have the function of explaining how the pattern of the world comes to be what it is, while in Bergson's *Creative Evolution* the idea of the evolutionary process leads on to the idea of a creative power at work in the world. In the case of metaphysical theories of this kind their function seems to be that of explaining what may be called the *how* of the world rather than the *that* of the world. This distinction certainly cannot be rigidly applied to philosophies like those of Whitehead and Bergson; but it applies very well in the case of Aristotle, who did not postulate the first unmoved mover in order to explain the existence of things, but rather in order to explain a feature of things, namely "movement" or becoming.

It is obvious, I think, that a metaphysical theory of this kind can claim to be taken seriously only if it is based on the conviction that any non-metaphysical explanation must be regarded as insufficient. An anti-metaphysician may think that all metaphysical theories are gratuitous hypotheses; but one could not expect him to give serious consideration to a metaphysical theory which even for its author was a gratuitous hypothesis. It is indeed unlikely that agreement will be reached in all cases whether a given feature of the world or a given set of empirical data can be adequately accounted for without the introduction of metaphysics. And I fail to see that the anti-metaphysician is entitled to issue a kind of advance prohibition against the introduction of metaphysics if he is unable to shake the conviction of another philosopher about the inadequacy of any non-metaphysical explanation. He is entitled, of course, to challenge the metaphysician to show that a metaphysical theory is required; for when any feature of the world can be adequately accounted for in terms of phenomenal causes, one should not drag in a metaphysical entity or theory to account for it. But, as I have said, agreement about the adequacy of non-metaphysical explanations is unlikely to be reached in all cases; and the metaphysician has as much right to his convictions on this matter as the anti-metaphysician has to his. In my opinion, there could be only one cogent ground for ruling out all metaphysical theories. This ground would obtain if it could be shown that the questions asked and theories propounded by metaphysicians are all meaningless, in the sense that to one or more of the terms no definite meaning can be assigned. But, as I said earlier in this paper, linguistic criticism of metaphysical questions and theories has to await their formulation. One has to allow the desire for understanding full play and permit it to lead to the formulation of questions and problems. Once a question has been asked, it is legitimate to ask what it means; but one is hardly entitled to say in advance: "Be silent! For if you speak, you will utter nonsense." One does not know *a priori* that nonsense will be uttered.

(2) Some metaphysicians might perhaps comment that I have misrepresented what they try to do. They do not take some isolated or selected feature of reality and build up a speculative theory on a narrow basis; they are more concerned with working out a general theoretical standpoint from which empirical data of various types can be seen as forming a coherent pattern. It is true that one type of metaphysician has tried to work out a system of philosophy, a comprehensive world-view, in a purely deductive manner, and that a procedure of this sort involves the application to empirical reality of a preconceived scheme, with the result that inconvenient data are slurred over or explained away. And it is true that some metaphysicians have emphasized one aspect of reality at the expense of other aspects. Schopenhauer is a case in point. But it is an exaggeration to suggest that metaphysicians in general attempt to force empirical data into a preconceived scheme or that they attend exclusively to one aspect of empirical reality. A philosopher like Bergson was not concerned with elaborating a "system." He considered problems separately, moving from one problem to another. And though his conclusions certainly converged on the formulation of a unified world-view, this was the result, rather than a presupposition, of his reflections.

It is doubtless quite true that metaphysics does not stand or fall with the validity of Spinoza's method. And it is, I think, an exaggeration to depict all metaphysicians as endeavoring to prove a preconceived system. But a full understanding of reality has surely been the limiting goal of speculative metaphysics, even with those who have recognized from the start the practical unattainability of the goal. And though this does not involve the *a priori* assumption of any definite answers to questions, it does involve the assumption that reality is intelligible. But we should never attempt to understand anything unless we believed that there was something to understand. Whether subsequent confirmation of our initial belief is forthcoming is another question.

(3) The attempt to understand empirical reality involves at the end, even if not at the beginning, an attempt to understand the *that* of finite beings. In the *Tractatus* Wittgenstein has said, "Not *how* the world is, is the mystical, but *that* it is." I should not care to use the word "mystical" here. But, provided that I am not understood as contradicting what I have said earlier about metaphysics and analysis, one might perhaps say, "Not *how* the world is, is the

metaphysical, but *that* it is." I should be inclined to say at least that the more prominent this existential problem is in a philosophy, the more metaphysical the philosophy is. The attempt might be made to dress up some metaphysical theories in the guise of scientific hypotheses, but it would be difficult to pass off any answer which might be given to the problem of the existence of finite beings as a scientific hypothesis in the common understanding of the term.

What I am concerned with is the question why this problem constantly recurs. Its prominence in Western philosophy may be connected in part with Judaeo-Christian theology; but it is not peculiar to Western philosophy. It is, indeed, easy to say that the problem is a pseudo-problem, which has its origin in linguistic confusion. We should ask, it may be said, only precise questions. If we ask for the cause or the causes of a given phenomenon, we can be given, in principle at least, a definite answer in terms of other phenomenon. If we do not ask precise questions, we shall find ourselves talking about "all phenomena" or "all finite things" or "all empirical reality" or about "finite being as such." And all these phrases give rise to logical difficulties. The metaphysician trades on linguistic confusion, vagueness and imprecision; he is able to impress other people only in so far as they are already involved in the same confusion as himself or in so far as he can involve them by the use of obscure and probably emotively-charged language in this confusion. Yet the fact remains that the problem of which I am speaking continues to be raised. Indeed, if the more important metaphysical problems are excluded from academic philosophy in a given period or in a certain region, what happens is that they are raised and discussed outside the confines of academic philosophy. It may be said that this is largely due to the fact that human beings are prone to wishful thinking, and that there are always a large number of them who endeavor to find some rational or pseudo-rational justification for what they believe or want to believe on other grounds. But what is the origin of this wishful thinking? That metaphysical speculation, when it is indulged in, is the fulfilment of a desire of some sort is obvious enough: nobody would practise it otherwise. But more than this can be said on the subject. And I want to suggest what seems to me a possible origin of the problem of existence of finite beings.

The primary datum is not, I think, either subject or object but the self as existing in an undefined and unarticulated situation. Man finds himself "there," within the area of Being. The consciousness of the self as a reflectively apprehended centre and of definite external objects, a consciousness which grows with experience, presupposes a pre-reflective awareness of existing in emcompassing Being. As empirical knowledge grows and as definite objects are marked off within a general field, that is, as "my world" is gradually constructed, these objects are still conceived, perhaps in a very vague way, as existing against a background of Being or as within encompassing Being. And accompanying the building-up, as it were, of a definite empirical world there is an articulation, an expression to the self, of the nature of this background.

By a great many people it is thought of as "the world" or "the universe." There are, I think, many people who, perhaps without clearly recognizing the fact, conceive themselves and other things as existing within the "world" as though all definite things were phenomena existing within an all-encompassing and meta-phenomenal "world." In this sense there is an implicit metaphysic in the outlook of many people who are far from being metaphysicians. Again, the pre-reflective awareness (perhaps one might say the "felt" awareness) of things as standing in relation to an obscure Ground of existence may be expressed in the way in which we find it expressed in the writings of some poets. On the other hand, there may be an attempt to render explicit on the reflective level this pre-reflective awareness. And this attempt gives rise to various metaphysical systems. The attempt to state the "felt" dependence on finite things may give rise to a system like that of Spinoza or to a theistic philosophy or even to a philosophy like that of Sartre, with its conception of the *en-soi*. I do not want to argue here in favor of any particular philosophy or type of philosophy; but I do suggest that the question of the ultimate Ground of empirical existence would never be raised, were there not a primary implicit awareness of existing against a background of Being. To avoid misunderstanding I had better say that by using the word "Being" with a capital letter I do not mean to imply a direct awareness of God. A pre-reflective awareness of dependence or what used to be called "contingency" is not the same thing as a direct awareness of God. If it were, there could hardly be those disputes between rival metaphysical systems of different types, to which we are accustomed in the history of philosophy.

It may be said that I have been putting forward a purely gratuitous hypothesis. I do not think that this is the case. I think that my hypothesis helps to explain a prominent feature of certain types of poetry, the origin, in part at least, of speculative metaphysics, a good deal of natural religion, and even the common though perhaps implicit conviction that things exist in "the world." I am perfectly well aware, of course, that what I have been saying is extremely vague: it could hardly be anything else when one attempts to discuss a matter of this sort within the limits of a few sentences. In any case, though one certainly ought to strive after clarity, language can be used to draw attention to what lies on the pre-reflective level; and one function of speculative metaphysics is to make explicit the pre-reflective awareness of which I have been speaking and to state its implications. Once the attempt to do this is made linguistic difficulties arise, and the philosopher must consider them honestly. But one should not allow oneself to be paralysed by Wittgenstein's dictum that "what can be said at all can be said clearly." It is indeed obvious that "whereof one cannot speak, thereof one must be silent"; but one is not compelled to choose between absolute clarity on the one hand and silence on the other. Language can have various functions: it can be used to "draw attention to." And when one has drawn attention, one can then endeavour to express in clear language, so far as this is possible, what one has drawn attention to. This, I think, is what speculative metaphysics tries to do in regard to the primary awareness of Being. One cannot bypass linguistic analysis, but one must first strive to state. Otherwise there can be no analysis.

What I have been saying will be regarded by some as a relapse into "mysticism," as an exhibition of the inherent weakness of metaphysics, as confirmation of the theory that metaphysical propositions possess no more than emotive significance, and even perhaps as an indication that metaphysicians stand in need of psychoanalysis. But many quite ordinary people possess an implicit metaphysic; and the real reason why the central metaphysical problem constantly recurs in different forms in spite of critical analysis is, I think, that it springs from man's existential situation, accompanied by an awareness of dependence or "contingency," and not from linguistic confusion. It is open to anyone, of course, to deny this. But one might, perhaps, reverse Wittgenstein's saying, "The limits of my language mean the limits of my world," and say, "The limits of my world mean the limits of my language," "my world" signifying here the experience which I am willing to acknowledge. Inability to find any value in metaphysics may very well be an indication of the limits of a man's "world."

F. J. E. Woodbridge   3. THE SCOPE OF
                                            METAPHYSICS

There is nothing wrong, Professor Woodbridge points out, in the fact that metaphysics has adjusted its interest to the investigation of the general character of things—in their union together, as well as in their specific and variety-laden nature. He concedes that metaphysics has often been maligned and consigned to the role of purveyor of insoluble problems. This, he feels however, is an injustice.

Metaphysics is concerned, as Aristotle had put it, with reality. For Woodbridge, it is concerned with no less. But Woodbridge feels that it is concerned with reality-in-general under the form of variety. It is the business of metaphysics, says Woodbridge, to undertake examination of points of view from which certain questions about reality can be asked and answered, since reality is "shot through and through with variety."

This lecture, originally entitled "Metaphysics," was first published in 1908 and later reprinted in *Nature and Mind* in 1937. Reprinted by permission of the publisher, Columbia University Press, New York.

As Woodbridge sees it, reality gains in relation to the variety it displays. The world is not static but filled with variables. This fact indicates for him the importance of "structural differences." Any metaphysical scheme, he observes, that attempts to reduce reality to a simple type is destined to failure because it overlooks the question of differences.

Woodbridge's "naturalism" envisions metaphysics as directed toward the question of existence. But it shows existence as "a process motivated by the variety of its factors, as an evolution characterized not by indifference but by selection based on the relative importance of its factors for the maintenance of natural goods. . . ." On the one hand, then, we cannot avoid systems of metaphysics because we like to see things together, integrated, and unified in their variety. Nor shall we abandon such systems as have been produced because they are inadequate. "Protests against metaphysical systems," he observes, are, consequently, "apt to be proofs of an impatient temper rather than a sound judgment." On the other hand, systems that are unwisely put forth are iniquitous.

The principal feature of metaphysical statements, Woodbridge concludes, is a concern with general characteristics of existence-in-its-variety, not with specific aspects. Hence, he feels that Aristotle was more right than not in his attitude toward the scope and function of metaphysics.

EITHER BECAUSE ARISTOTLE developed his science of existence with so much skill or because the science is to be reckoned, as he reckoned it, among those intellectual performances which are excellent, its unfortunate name has never completely obscured its professed aims and restrictions. Too often, indeed, metaphysics has been made the refuge of ignorance, and inquirers in other fields have been too ready to bestow upon it their own unsolved problems and inconsistencies. Many have thus been led to refuse discussion of certain difficulties for the reason that they are metaphysical, a reason which may indicate that one is tired rather than that one is wise. It has even been suggested that so long as problems are unsolved they are metaphysical. Even so, the study, on account of the comprehensiveness thus given to it, might advance itself, imposing and commanding, a guarantor of intellectual modesty. Yet metaphysicians, as a rule, have not regarded their work as that of salvation. They have viewed their problems as the result of reflection rather than emergency. And their reflection has ever seized upon the fact that nature's great and manifold diversities do, none the less, in spite of that diversity, consent to exist together in some sort of union, and that, consequently, some understanding of that unity is a thing to attempt. Metaphysics, therefore, may still adopt the definition and limitations set for it by Aristotle. We may, indeed, define it in other terms, calling it, for instance, the science of reality, but our altered words still point out that metaphysical interest is in the world as a world of connected things, a world with a general character in addition to those specific characters which give it its variety and make many sciences necessary for it comprehension.

The term "reality," however, is intellectually agile. It tends to play tricks with one's prejudices and to lead desire on a merry chase. For to denominate anything real is usually to import a distinction and to consign, thereby, something else to the region of appearance. Could we keep the region of appearance from becoming populated, it might remain nothing more than the natural negative implication of a region of positive interest. But reality, once a king, makes many exiles who crave and seek citizenship in the land from which they have been banished. The term "reality," therefore, should inspire caution instead of confidence in metaphysics—a lesson which history has abundantly illustrated, but which man is slow to learn. Contrast those imposing products of human fancy which we call materialism and idealism, each relegating the other to the region of appearance, and what are they at bottom but an exalted prejudice for matter and an exalted prejudice for mind? And had not their conflict been spectacular, as armies with banners, what a pitiable spectacle it would have presented, since a child's first thought destroys the one, and every smallest grain of sand the other? No; everything is somehow real; and to make distinctions within that realm demands caution and hesitation.

Thus it is that the concept of reality has become an important theme in a great part of metaphysical inquiry, and that a keen appreciation of its varieties is essential to the historian of metaphysics. That science has been thought to suffer from a too close scrutiny into the idiosyncrasies of its past; but being somewhat ancient and robust, and, withal, decidedly human, it may consult the reflection that more youthful sciences have not always walked in wisdom's path, and so bear its own exposure with some consequent consolation. Yet what it has to reveal in the light of the shifting concept of reality is significant indeed. For we have come to learn that to call anything real exclusively, is to imply a preference, and that preference is largely a matter of the time in which it is born. It reflects an age, an occasion, a society, a moral, intellectual, or economic condition. It does not reflect an absolute position which knows no wavering. For me, just now, metaphysics is the most real thing imaginable, more real than chemistry or the stock exchange. In displaying some enthusiasm for it, I care not if the elements revert to ether or how the market goes. To be invited just now to consider the periodic law of the latest market quotations would irritate me. An altered situation would find me, doubtless, possessed of an altered preference, indifferent no longer to another science or to the Street. So much does occasion determine preference, and preference reality.

The historical oppositions in metaphysics present themselves, therefore, not as a mass of conflicting and contradictory opinions about the absolutely real, but as a too exclusive championship of what their exponents have believed to be most important for their times. In such metaphysicians the enthusiasm of the prophet has outrun the disinterestedness of the scientist. We may describe them as men of restricted vision, but we may not, therefore, conclude that their vision was not acute. Plato was an idle dreamer, assigning to unreality the bed on which you sleep in order that he might convince you that the only genuinely real bed is the archetype in the mind of God, the ideal bed of which all others are shadows. Undoubtedly he converses thus about beds in his *Republic*, but he does not advise you, as a consequence, to go to sleep in heaven. He tells you, rather, that justice is a social matter which you can never adequately administer so long as your attention is fixed solely on individual concerns. You must seek to grasp justice as a principle, in the light of which the different parts of the body politic may find their most fruitful interplay and co-ordination. His metaphysics of the ideal was born in Athens' need, but his dialogues remain instructive reading for the modern man. We may confound him by pointing out the obvious fact that men, not principles, make society, and yet accept his teaching that men without principles make a bad society, exalting principles thus to the position of the eminently real.

Similarly, he who reads Fichte's *Science of Knowledge* should not forget that Fichte spoke to the German people, calling them a nation. And the response he met must have seemed, in his eyes, no small justification of his view that reality is essentially a self-imposed moral task. And Spencer, influenced by social and economic reorganization and consolidation, could force the universe into a formula and think that he had said the final word about reality. Thus any exclusive conception of reality is rendered great, not by its finality for all times, but by its historical appropriateness.

Such questions, therefore, as, What is real? Is there any reality at all? Is not everything illusion, or at least part of everything? and such statements as, Only the good is real, Only matter is real, Only mind is real, Only energy is real, are questions and statements to be asked and made only by persons with a mission. For reality means either everything whatsoever or that a distinction has been made, a distinction which indicates not a difference in the fact of existence, but a difference in point of view, in value, in preference, in relative importance for some desire or choice. Yet it is doubtless the business of metaphysics to undertake an examination and definition of the different points of view from which those questions can be asked and those statements made. Indeed, that undertaking may well be regarded as one of the most important in metaphysics. The outcome of it is not a superficial doctrine of the relativity of the real, with the accompanying advice that each of us select his own reality and act accordingly. Nor is it the doctrine that since nothing or everything is absolutely real, there is no solid basis for conduct and no abiding hope for man. That individualism which is willful and that kind of agnosticism which is not intellectual reserve, but which is intellectual complacency, have no warrant in metaphysics. On the contrary, the doctrine of metaphysics is much more obvious and much more sane. It is that existence, taken comprehensively, is an affair of distinctions; that existence is shot through and through with variety.

But this is not all. Metaphysics discovers in the fact of variety a reason for the world's onward movement. For a world without variety would be a world eternally still, unchanged and unchanging through all the stretches of time. We might endow such a world with unlimited power, capable, if once aroused, of a marvelous reaction; but unless there existed somewhere within it a difference, no tremor of excitement would ever disturb its endless slumber. All the sciences teach this doctrine. Even logic and mathematics, the most static of them all, require variables, if their formulations are to have any significance or application. Knowledge thus reflects the basal structure of things. And in this fact that differences are fundamental in the constitution of our world, we discover the reason why all those systems of metaphysics eventually fail which attempt to reduce all existence to a single type of reality devoid of variety in its internal make-up.

The variety in our world involves a further doctrine. While all varieties as such are equally real, they are not all equally effective. They make different sorts of differences, and introduce, thereby, intensive and qualitative distinctions. The onward movement of the world is thus, not simply successive change, but a genuine development or evolution. It creates a past the contents of which must forever remain what they were, but it proposes a future where variety may still exercise its difference-making function. And that is why we human beings, acting our part in some cosmic comedy or tragedy, may not be indifferent to our performance or to the preferences we exalt. The future makes us all reformers, inviting us to meddle with the world, to use it and change it for our ends. The invitation is genuine and made in good faith, for all man's folly is not yet sufficient to prove it insincere. That is why it has been easy to believe that God once said to man: "Be fruitful and multiply, and replenish the earth, and subdue it; and have dominion over the fish of the sea, and over the fowl of the air, and over every living thing that moveth upon the earth." That is why, also, willful individualism and complacent agnosticism have no warrant in metaphysics. Since all things are equally real, but all not equally important, the world's evolution presents itself as a drift towards results, as something purposeful and intended. While we may not invoke design to explain this relative importance of things, the world's trend puts us under the natural obligation of discovering how it may be controlled, and enforces the obligation with obvious penalties. Thus willfulness receives natural punishment and the universe never accepts ignorance as an excuse.

It seems difficult, therefore, not to describe evolution as a moral process. By that I do not mean that nature is especially careful about the kinds of things she does or that she is true and just in all her dealings. But evolution is movement controlled by the relative importance of things. We consequently find such terms as "struggle," "survival," "adaptation," useful in the description of it. And although these terms may appear more appropriate to the development of living things than to that of inorganic nature we may not overlook the fact that the physical world also begets varieties and has its character determined by their relative importance.

Thus it is that the metaphysical doctrine of final causes appears to be fundamentally sound. It is easy to render it ridiculous by supposing that things were once made on purpose to exhibit the features and manners of action which we now discover in them, or by conceiving adaptation as an efficient cause of events, as if the fact that we see were the reason why we have eyes. So conceived the doctrine of final causes is justly condemned. On the other hand, however, how superficial is the opinion that in nature there is entire indifference to results, and that there are no natural goods! Today is not simply yesterday rearranged or twenty-four hours added to a capricious time; it is yesterday reorganized, with yesterday's results carried on and intensified. So that we might say that nature, having accidentally discovered that the distinction between light and darkness is a natural good, stuck to the business of making eyes. We should thus express a natural truth, but should not thereby free ourselves from the obligation of discovering how nature had achieved so noteworthy a result. That obligation the doctrine of final causes most evidently does not discharge, because final causes have never been found adequate to reveal the method of nature's working. Again and again, some investigator, impressed by the undoubted fact of nature's continuity, by her preservation of forms, by that character of hers which we can properly describe only by calling it preferential or moral, impressed by these things he has attempted to turn them into efficient causes, factors operative in the mechanism of the world. And he has repeatedly failed. It is, consequently, not prejudice which leads many students of nature's processes to insist that these are ultimately what we call mechanical. It is metaphysical insight. Yet that insight may readily degenerate into the most superficial philosophy, if it leads us to forget that mechanism is the means by which the ends of nature are reached. For nature undoubtedly exists for what she accomplishes, and it is that fact which gives to mechanism its relevancy, its importance, and its high value. Thus metaphysics, true to its early formulations, finds the world to be both mechanical and teleological, both a quantitative relation of parts and a qualitative realization of goods. Some indication that this finding is correct may be discovered in our instinctive recognition that nature is appropriately described both in the formulations of science and in the expressions of poetry.

Metaphysical analysis tends thus to disclose existence as a process motivated by the variety of its factors, as an evolution characterized, not by indifference, but by selection based on the relative importance of its factors for the maintenance of natural goods, as a development executed through an elaborate mechanism. It is natural that metaphysics should become speculative and attempt the construction of a system of things wherein its obvious disclosures may be envisaged with coherence and simplicity, and thus be rationally comprehended and explained. It is in such attempts that metaphysics has historically scored its greatest successes and its greatest failures. The lesson to be derived from a survey of them is, doubtless, one of grave caution, but it would be idle to affirm that we have seen the last of great systems of metaphysics. Democritus, Plato, Aristotle, Bruno, Descartes, Hobbes, Spinoza, Newton, Leibniz, Berkeley, Kant, Laplace, Hegel, Spencer—to mention only the greatest names—each has had his system of the world which still has power to affect the thought and lives of men. System is beloved of man's imagination and his mind is restless in the presence of unconnected and unsupported details. He will see things *sub specie aeternitatis* even while time counts out his sands of life. It is a habit begotten of nature, to be neither justified nor condemned. It would be absurd consequently, to regard any system of metaphysics as absolutely true, but it would be more absurd to refuse to make one on that account. For such systems constitute the supreme attempts of intelligence at integration. They propose to tell us what our world would be like if our present restricted knowledge were adequate for its complete exposition. They are not, therefore, to be abandoned because they are always inadequate, incomplete, and provisional; they are rather to be pursued, because, when constructed by the wise, they are always ennobling and minister faithfully to the freedom of the mind.

Protests against metaphysical systems are, consequently, apt to be proofs of an impatient temper rather than of sound judgment. Yet such systems often grow arrogant, and become, thereby, objects of justified suspicion. Being the crowning enterprise of intelligence, to be worn, one might say, as an indication of a certain nobility of mind, they forfeit the claim to be thus highly regarded if they are made the essential preliminaries of wisdom. Yet the too eager and the too stupid have often claimed that the only possible foundation for the truth and value of science, and the only possible warrant for morality and human aspiration, are to be found in a system of metaphysics. If such a claim meant only that with a perfect system, could we attain it, would riddles all be solved and life's darkness made supremely clear, it would express an obvious truth. But made with the intent of laying metaphysics down as the foundation of science, of morality, and of religion, it is obviously false and iniquitous. In our enthusiasm we may indeed speak of metaphysics as the queen of all the sciences, but she can wear the title only if her behavior is queenly; she forfeits it when, ceasing to reign, she stoops to rule.

Yet there is justice in the notion that metaphysics, especially in its systematic shape, should contribute to the value of science, and be a source of moral and religious enlightenment. Its greatest ally is logic. In the systematic attempt to reduce to order the business of getting and evaluating knowledge, in distinguishing fruitful from fruitless methods, and, above all, in attempting to disclose the sort of conquest knowledge makes over the world, the aims and achievements of science should become better appreciated and understood. It is still true, as Heraclitus of old remarked, that much information does not make a man wise, but wisdom is intelligent understanding.

The disclosures of metaphysics are equally significant for ethics. The great systems have usually eventuated in a theory of morals. And this is natural. Metaphysics, disclosing the fact that behavior is a primary feature of things, raises inevitably the question of how to behave effectively and well. Emphasizing the relative importance of the factors of evolution, it encourages the repeated valuation of human goods. It can make no man moral, nor give him a rule to guide him infallibly in his choices and acts; but it can impress upon him the fact that he is under a supreme obligation, that of living a life controlled, not by passion, but by reason, and of making his knowledge contribute to the well-being of society. It will still preach its ancient moral lesson, that, since with intelligence has arisen some comprehension of the world, the world is best improved, not by passion or by parties, not by governments or by sects, but by the persistent operation of intelligence itself.

After a somewhat similar manner, metaphysics in its systematic character has significance for theology. To speak of existence as a riddle is natural, because so much of its import can be only guessed. That it has import most men suspect, and that this import is due to superior beings or powers is the conviction of those who are religious. Metaphysics is seldom indifferent to such suspicions and convictions. As it has a lively sense of the unity of things, it is led to seek ultimate reasons for the world's stability. And as it deals with such conceptions as "the infinite" and "the absolute," it has a certain linguistic sympathy with faith. Consequently, while it has never made a religion, it has been used as an apology for many. This fact witnesses, no doubt, more profoundly to the adaptability of metaphysics than it does to the finality of the ideas it has been used to sustain. Yet metaphysics, tending to keep men ever close to the sources of life, fosters a whole-hearted acceptance of life's responsibilities and duties. It is thus the friend of natural piety. And in superimposing upon piety systematic reflection on what we call the divine, it follows a natural instinct, and seeks to round out man's conception of the universe as the source of his being, the place of his sojourning, the begettor of his impulses and his hopes, and the final treasury of what he has been and accomplished.

Such, then, are the general nature and scope of metaphysical inquiry. With Aristotle we may define metaphysics as the science of existence and distinguish it from other departments of knowledge by its generality and its lack of attention to those specific features of existence which makes many sciences an intellectual necessity. Existence, considered generally, presents itself as an affair of connected varieties and, consequently, as an onward movement. Because the varieties have not all the same efficacy, the movement presents those selective and moral characters which we ascribe to a development or evolution. While the efficient causes of this evolution appear be mechanical, the mechanism results in the production of natural goods, and thus justifies a doctrine of final causes. Upon such considerations metaphysics may superimpose speculative reflection, and attempt to attain a unified system of the world. It may also attempt to evaluate science in terms of logical theory, to enlarge morality through a theory of ethics, and to interpret natural piety and religion in terms of theological conception. Metaphysics proposes thus both an analysis and a theory of existence; it is descriptive and it is systematic. If metaphysicians often forget that theory is not analysis, that system is not description, it is not because they are metaphysicians, but because they are human. For my part, therefore, I do not see why they should not be allowed to entertain at least as many absurdities as the average reflective inquirer. Greater indulgence is neither desired nor necessary. And while metaphysicians may be hard to understand, they do not like to be misunderstood. So I emphasize again the fact that it appears to be the greatest abuse of metaphysical theories to use them to justify natural excellence or to condone natural folly. It is their business to help clarify existence. It is not their business to constitute an apology for our prejudices or for our desires.

G. E. Moore   4. THE TASKS OF
METAPHYSICS

In contrast to the "wide-open" naturalism of Woodbridge, G. E. Moore emphasizes a type of British realism, which is set against what he once called the "naturalistic fallacy" of donating teleological arguments to Nature.

Certainly, Moore agrees, the philosophic problem has always been an attempt to give a general description and account of the universe. He discourages, however, the "visionary" approach to such a task and recommends, instead, a careful investigation of "the sorts of things you hold to be in the Universe." The difficulty with establishing one view of the universe, he says, is that not only must it offer reasonable proof of itself, but it must also disprove every investigation of other views. Moore therefore proposes investigation of a subordinate class of "entity" questions as the proper metaphysical task, because the answer to such questions has a main bearing on any answer to the question of "the Universe as a whole."

This selection is extracted from *Some Main Problems of Philosophy* by G. E. Moore, and is reproduced here through the kind permission of George Allen & Unwin Ltd., London, and The Macmillan Company, New York.

Consider, he says, the problem of knowledge. On its solution hinges a great deal in one's view of "the Universe as a whole." Yet the problem of knowledge is not one problem, but several. For example, in asking how one knows a particular something—an object, a fact, a statement—three different questions are involved. They are: (*a*) What kind of entity is our knowledge? (*b*) What is its relation to truth? (*c*) What verification have we for making a claim to its truth? Then, too, the stake in such questions belongs not only to metaphysics, but also to logic and psychology.

Furthermore, Moore says, the attempt to give a general account of the universe involves answers not only to metaphysical but to ethical problems. How can we say whether the universe is "good" or "bad," "right" or "wrong," unless we first ascertain the meaning and scope of such ethical adjectives? For this reason, Moore advocates a piecemeal approach to metaphysics, whereby it investigates varieties in their individual variousness, rather than in their togetherness.

To BEGIN WITH it seems to me that the most important and interesting thing which philosophers have tried to do is no less than this; namely: To give a general description of the *whole* of the Universe, mentioning all the most important kinds of things which we *know* to be in it, considering how far it is likely that there are in it important kinds of things which we do not absolutely *know* to be in it, and also considering the most important ways in which these various kinds of things are related to one another. I will call all this, for short, "Giving a general description of the *whole* Universe," and hence will say that the first and most important problem of philosophy is: To give a general description of the whole Universe. Many philosophers (though by no means all) have, I think, certainly tried to give such a description and the very different descriptions which different philosophers have given are, I think, among the most important differences between them. And the problem is, it seems to me, plainly one which is peculiar to philosophy. There is no other science which tries to say: Such and such kinds of things are the *only* kinds of things that there are in the Universe, or which we know to be in it. . . .

This, then, is the first and most interesting problem of philosophy. And it seems to me that a great many others can be defined as problems bearing on this one.

For philosophers have not been content simply to express their opinions as to what there is or is not in the Universe, or as to what we know to be in it. They have also tried to prove their opinions to be true. And with this, you see, a great many subordinate problems are opened up.

In order to prove, for instance, that any one of these views I have mentioned are true, you must both prove *it* and *also* refute all the others. You must prove either that there is a God, or that there is not, or that we do not know whether there is one or not. And so on with all other kinds of things I have mentioned: matter and space and time; and the minds of other men;

and other minds, *not* the minds of men or animals. In order to prove that any particular view of the Universe is correct, you must prove, in the case of each of these things, either that they do exist, or that they do not, or that we do not know whether they do or not. And all these questions you see, may be treated separately for their own sakes. Many philosophers, indeed, have not tried to give any general description of the *whole* Universe. They have merely tried to answer some one or more of these subordinate questions.

And there is another sort of subordinate question, which ought, I think, to be specially mentioned. Many philosophers have spent a good deal of their time in trying to define more clearly what is the difference between these various sorts of things: for instance, what is the difference between a material object and an act of consciousness, between matter and mind, between God and man, etc. And these questions of definitions are by no means so easy to answer as you might think. Nor must it be thought that they are mere questions of words. A good definition of the sorts of things you hold to be in the Universe, obviously adds to the clearness of your view. And it is not only a question of clearness either. When, for instance, you try to define what you mean by a material object, you find that there are several different properties which a material object might have, of which you had never thought before; and your effort to define may thus lead you to conclude that whole classes of things have certain properties, or have *not* certain others, of which you would never have thought, if you had merely contented yourself with asserting that there are material objects in the Universe, without inquiring what you meant by this assertion.

We may, then, say that a great class of subordinate philosophical problems consist in discussing whether the great classes of things I have mentioned do exist or do not, or whether we are simply ignorant as to whether they do or not; and also in trying to define these classes and considering how they are related to one another. A great deal of philosophy has consisted in discussing these questions with regard to God, a future life, matter, minds, Space and Time. And all these problems could be said to belong to that department of philosophy which is called Metaphysics.

But now we come to a class of questions which may be said to belong to other departments of philosophy, but which also have an evident bearing on the first main problem as to the general description of the Universe. One of the most natural questions to ask, when anybody asserts some fact, which you are inclined to doubt, is the question: "How do you know that?" And if the person answers the question in such a way as to show that he has not learnt the fact in any one of the ways in which it is possible to acquire real knowledge, as opposed to mere belief, about facts of the sort, you will conclude that he does *not* really know it. In other words, we are constantly assuming in ordinary life that there are only a limited number of ways in which it is possible to acquire real *knowledge* of certain kinds of facts; and that if a person asserts a fact, which he has not learnt in any one of these ways, then, in fact, he does not *know* it. Now philosophers have also used this argument very largely. They have tried to classify exhaustively all the different kinds of ways in which we can know things; and have then concluded that, since certain things, which other philosophers have asserted or which they formerly believed, are *not* known in any of these ways, therefore these things are not known at all.

Hence a large part of philosophy has, in fact, consisted in trying to classify completely all the different ways in which we can *know* things; or in trying to describe exactly particular ways of knowing them.

And this question—the question: How do we *know* anything at all?—involves three different kinds of questions.

The first is of this sort. When you are asked: How do you know that? it may be meant to ask: What sort of a thing *is* your knowledge of it? What sort of a process goes on in your mind when you *know* it? In what does this event, which you call a *knowing,* consist? This first question as to what sort of a thing knowledge is—as to what happens when we *know* anything—is a question which philosophy shares with psychology; but which many philosophers have tried to answer. They have tried to distinguish the different kinds of things, which happen in our minds, when we all know different things; and to point out, what, if anything, is common to them all.

But there is, secondly, something else which may be meant; when it is asked what knowledge *is.* For we do not say that we *know* any proposition, for instance, the proposition that matter exists, unless we mean to assert that this proposition is *true*: that it is *true* that matter exists. And hence there is included in the question what knowledge *is,* the question what is meant by saying any proposition is *true.* This is a different question from the psychological question as to what happens in your mind, when you know anything; and this question as to what *truth* is has generally been said to be a question for *Logic,* in the widest sense of the term. And Logic, or at least parts of it, is reckoned as a department of philosophy.

And, finally, there is still another thing that may be meant, when it is asked: How do you know that? It may be meant, namely, what reason have you for believing it? or in other words, what *other* thing do you know, which *proves* this thing to be *true?* And philosophers have, in fact, been much occupied with this question also: the question what are the different ways in in which a proposition can be proved to be true; what are all the different sorts of reasons which are good reasons for believing anything. This is also a question which is reckoned as belonging to the department of Logic.

There is, therefore, a huge branch of philosophy which is concerned with the different ways in which we know things; and many philosophers have devoted themselves almost exclusively to questions which fall under this head.

But finally, if we are to give a complete account of philosophy, we must mention one other class of questions. There is a department of philosophy called Ethics or ethical philosophy; and this department deals with a class of questions quite different from any which I have mentioned yet. We are all constantly in ordinary life asking such questions as: Would such and such a result be a good thing to bring about or would it be a bad thing? Would such and such an action be a right action to perform or would it be a wrong one? And what ethical philosophy tries to do is to classify all the different sorts of things which *would* be good or bad, right or wrong, in such a way as to be able to say: Nothing would be good unless it had certain characteristics, or one or other of certain characteristics; and similarly nothing would be bad, unless it had certain properties or one or other of certain properties: and similarly with the question of what sort of actions would be right, and what would be wrong.

And these ethical questions have a most important bearing upon our general description of the Universe in two ways.

In the first place, it is certainly one of the most important facts about the Universe that there are in it these distinctions of good and bad, right and wrong. And many people have thought that, from the fact that there are these distinctions, other inferences as to what is in the Universe can be drawn.

And in the second place, by combining the results of Ethics as to what *would* be good or bad, with the conclusion of Metaphysics as to what kinds of things there are in the Universe, we get a means of answering the question whether the Universe is, on the whole, good or bad, and how good or bad, compared with what it might be: a sort of question which has in fact been discussed by many philosophers. . . .

Alfred North Whitehead   5. THE AIM OF
SPECULATIVE THOUGHT

Though sometimes considered a "realist," and widely known as co-author with
   Bertrand Russell of the three-volume *Principia Mathematica*, Whitehead
   has little in common with G. E. Moore. In contrast to Moore's restricted
   analysis, Whitehead makes a case here for metaphysics as both visionary
   and factual—as being "a voyage toward the larger generalities" as well as

"the description of the generalities which apply to all the details of practice."

Though no label adequately applies to Whitehead's point of view—he himself used the term "organic philosophy"—he systematically combines Woodbridge's vision of variety-in-union with Moore's feeling for concrete and factual instances of real things. In one of his most celebrated sentences, Whitehead defines metaphysics (or speculative philosophy) as "the endeavor to frame a coherent, logical, necessary system of general ideas in terms of which every element of experience can be interpreted." He sees metaphysical vision, therefore, in empirical terms, and its factuality in rational terms. Each element in the metaphysical system is "a particular instance of the general scheme," while the general scheme is exemplified in each concrete factuality; the system's fundamental ideas must "presuppose each other so that in isolation they are meaningless," while the system itself should bear "its own warrant of universality throughout all experience."

Whitehead compares metaphysical discovery to an airplane flight, which starts from the ground of empirical observation, soars skyward for a larger view of things in imaginative generalization, and finally "lands again for renewed observation rendered acute by rational interpretation."

Admittedly, says Whitehead, previous philosophies have been one-sided. They have undoubtedly suffered deposition under the shock of criticism, motivated by coherence and logical perfection. Yet the "bundle of philosophic systems" simply await the coordination of their various truths in a larger framework, which would prevent the plague of "overstatement" that continually threatens philosophy. Several fallacies have joined to increase the viability of this plague: the use of restricted categories ("misplaced concreteness"); overblown logic; belief in the irreformability of working hypotheses ("dogmatic fallacy"); and the avoidance of all systematization ("discarding method").

No metaphysical system, Whitehead concludes, can ever hope entirely to satisfy the demands of pragmatic tests of its assertions. At best it can hope only for approximation. But at least it may hope realistically. There are no precisely stated axiomatic certainties to begin with, and there is no invulnerable language to frame them in. But there is the possibility of working theory against practice, and practice against theory. The metaphysical task, therefore, must be cured of its excesses. It must both abide by the judgment of selections taken from reality and "recover the totality obscured by selection."

SPECULATIVE PHILOSOPHY is the endeavour to frame a coherent, logical, necessary system of general ideas in terms of which every element of our experience can be interpreted. By this notion of "interpretation" I mean that everything of which we are conscious, as enjoyed, perceived, willed, or thought, shall have the character of a particular instance of the general scheme. Thus the philosophical scheme should be coherent, logical, and, in repect to its interpretation, applicable and adequate. Here "applicable" means that some items of experience are thus interpretable, and "adequate" means that there are no items incapable of such interpretation.

"Coherence," as here employed, means that the fundamental ideas, in terms of which the scheme is developed, presuppose each other so that in isolation they are meaningless. This requirement does not mean that they are definable in terms of each other; it means that what is indefinable in one such notion cannot be abstracted from its relevance to the other notions. It is the ideal of speculative philosophy that its fundamental notions shall not seem capable of abstraction from each other. In other words, it is presupposed that no entity can be conceived in complete abstraction from the system of the universe, and that it is the business of speculative philosophy to exhibit this truth. This character is its coherence.

The term "logical" has its ordinary meaning, including "logical" consistency, or lack of contradiction, the definition of constructs in logical terms, the exemplification of general logical notions in specific instances, and the principles of inference. It will be observed that logical notions must themselves find their places in the scheme of philosophic notions.

It will also be noticed that this ideal of speculative philosophy has its rational side and its empirical side. The rational side is expressed by the terms "coherent" and "logical." The empirical side is expressed by the terms "applicable" and "adequate." But the two sides are bound together by clearing away an ambiguity which remains in the previous explanation of the term "adequate." The adequacy of the scheme over every item does not mean adequacy over such items as happen to have been considered. It means that the texture of observed experience, as illustrating the philosophic scheme, is such that all related experience must exhibit the same texture. Thus the philosophic scheme should be "necessary," in the sense of bearing in itself its own warrant of universality throughout all experience, provided that we confine ourselves to that which communicates with immediate matter of fact. But what does not so communicate is unknowable, and the unknowable is unknown; and so this universality defined by "communication" can suffice.

This doctrine of necessity in universality means that there is an essence to the universe which forbids relationships beyond itself, as a violation of its rationality. Speculative philosophy seeks that essence.

Philosophers can never hope finally to formulate these metaphysical first principles. Weakness of insight and deficiencies of language stand in the way inexorably. Words and phrases must be stretched towards a generality foreign to their ordinary usage; and however such elements of language be stabilized as technicalities, they remain metaphors mutely appealing for an imaginative leap.

There is no first principle which is in itself unknowable, not to be captured by a flash of insight. But, putting aside the difficulties of language, deficiency in imaginative penetration forbids progress in any form other than that of an asymptotic approach to a scheme of principles, only definable in terms of the ideal which they should satisfy.

The difficulty has its seat in the empirical side of philosophy. Our datum is the actual world, including ourselves; and this actual world spreads itself for observation in the guise of the topic of our immediate experience. The elucidation of immediate experience is the sole justification for any thought; and the starting point for thought is the analytic observation of components of this experience. But we are not conscious of any clear-cut complete analysis of immediate experience, in terms of the various details which comprise its definiteness. We habitually observe by the method of difference. Sometimes we see an elephant, and sometimes we do not. The result is that an elephant, when present, is noticed. Facility of observation depends on the fact that the object observed is important when present, and sometimes is absent.

The metaphysical first principles can never fail of exemplification. We can never catch the actual world taking a holiday from their sway. Thus, for the discovery of metaphysics, the method of pinning down thought to the strict systematization of detailed discrimination, already effected by antecedent observation, breaks down. This collapse of the method of rigid empiricism is not confined to metaphysics. It occurs whenever we seek the larger generalities. In natural science this rigid method is the Baconian method of induction, a method which, if consistently pursued, would have left science where it found it. What Bacon omitted was the play of a free imagination, controlled by the requirements of coherence and logic. The true method of discovery is like the flight of an aeroplane. It starts from the ground of particular observation; it makes a flight in the thin air of imaginative generalization; and it again lands for renewed observation rendered acute by rational interpretation. The reason for the success of this method of imaginative rationalization is that, when the method of difference fails, factors which are constantly present may yet be observed under the influence of imaginative thought. Such thought supplies the differences which the direct observation lacks. It can even play with inconsistency; and can thus throw light on the consistent, and persistent, elements in experience by comparison with what in imagination is inconsistent with them. The negative judgment is the peak of mentality. But the conditions for the success of imaginative construction must be rigidly adhered to. In the first place, this construction must have its origin in the generalization of particular topics of human interest; for example, in physics, or in physiology, or in psychology, or in aesthetics, or in ethical beliefs, or in sociology, or in languages conceived as storehouses of human experience. In this way the prime requisite, that anyhow there shall be some important application, is secured. The success of the imaginative experiment is always to be tested by the applicability of its results beyond the restricted locus from which it originated.

In default of such extended application, a generalization started from physics, for example, remains merely an alternative expression of notions applicable to physics. The partially successful philosophic generalization will, if derived from physics, find applications in fields of experience beyond physics. It will enlighten observation in those remote fields, so that general principles can be discerned as in process of illustration, which in the absence of the imaginative generalization are obscured by their persistent exemplification.

Thus the first requisite is to proceed by the method of generalization so that certainly there is some application; and the test of some success is application beyond the immediate origin. In other words, some synoptic vision has been gained.

In this description of philosophic method, the term "philosophic generalization" has meant "the utilization of specific notions, applying to a restricted group of facts, for the divination of the generic notions which apply to all facts."

In its use of this method natural science has shown a curious mixture of rationalism and irrationalism. Its prevalent tone of thought has been ardently rationalistic within its own borders, and dogmatically irrational beyond those borders. In practice such an attitude tends to become a dogmatic denial that there are any factors in the world not fully expressible in terms of its own primary notions devoid of further generalization. Such a denial is the self-denial of thought.

The second condition for the success of imaginative construction is unflinching pursuit of the two rationalistic ideals, coherence and logical perfection. . . .

Logical perfection does not here require any detailed explanation. An example of its importance is afforded by the role of mathematics in the restricted field of natural science. The history of mathematics exhibits the generalization of special notions observed in particular instances. In any branches of mathematics, the notions presuppose each other. It is a remarkable characteristic of the history of thought that branches of mathematics developed under the pure imaginative impulse, thus controlled, finally receive their important application. Time may be wanted. Conic sections had to wait for eighteen hundred years. In more recent years, the theory of probability, the theory of tensors, the theory of matrices are cases in point.

The requirement of coherence is the great preservative of rationalistic sanity. But the validity of its criticism is not always admitted. If we consider philosophical controversies, we shall find that disputants tend to require coherence from their adversaries, and to grant dispensations to themselves. It has been remarked that a system of philosophy is never refuted; it is only abandoned. The reason is that logical contradictions, except as temporary slips of the mind—plentiful, though temporary—are the most gratuitous of errors; and usually they are trivial. Thus, after criticism, systems do not exhibit mere illogicalities. They suffer from inadequacy and incoherence. Failure to include some obvious elements of experience in the scope of the system is met by boldly denying the facts. Also while a philosophical system retains any charm of novelty, it enjoys a plenary indulgence for its failures in coherence. But after a system has acquired orthodoxy, and is taught with authority, it receives a sharper criticism. Its denials and its incoherences are found intolerable, and a reaction sets in. . . .

In its turn every philosophy will suffer a deposition. But the bundle of philosophic systems expresses a variety of general truths about the universe, awaiting coordination and assignment of their various spheres of validity. Such progress in coordination is provided by the advance of philosophy; and in this sense philosophy has advanced from Plato onwards. According to this account of the achievement of rationalism, the chief error in philosophy is overstatement. The aim at generalization is sound, but the estimate of success is exaggerated. There are two main forms of such overstatement. One form is what I have termed elsewhere, the "fallacy of misplaced concreteness." This fallacy consists in neglecting the degree of abstractions involved when an actual entity is considered merely so far as it exemplifies certain categories of thought. There are aspects of actualities which are simply ignored so long as we restrict thought to these categories. Thus the success of a philosophy is to be measured by its comparative avoidance of this fallacy, when thought is restricted within its categories.

The other form of overstatement consists in a false estimate of logical procedures in respect to certainty, and in respect to premises. Philosophy has been haunted by the unfortunate notion that its method is dogmatically to indicate premises which are severally clear, distinct, and certain; and to erect upon those premises a deductive system of thought.

But the accurate expression of the final generalities is the goal of discussion and not its origin. Philosophy has been misled by the example of mathematics, and even in mathematics the statement of the ultimate logical principles is beset with difficulties, as yet insuperable. The verification of a rationalistic scheme is to be sought in its general success, and not in the peculiar certainty, or initial clarity, of its first principles. In this connection the misuse of the *ex absurdo* argument has to be noted; much philosophical reasoning is vitiated by it. The only logical conclusion to be drawn, when a contradiction issues from a train of reasoning, is that at least one of the premises involved in the inference is false. It is rashly assumed without further question that the peccant premise can at once be located. In mathematics this assumption is often justified, and philosophers have been thereby misled. But in the absence of a well-defined categoreal scheme of entities, issuing in a satisfactory metaphysical system, every premise in a philosophical argument is under suspicion.

Philosophy will not regain its proper status until the gradual elaboration of categoreal schemes, definitely stated at each stage of progress, is recognized as its proper objective. There may be rival schemes, inconsistent among themselves; each with its own merits and its own failures. It will then be the purpose of research to conciliate the differences. Metaphysical categories are not dogmatic statements of the obvious; they are tentative formulations of the ultimate generalities.

If we consider any scheme of philosophic categories as one complex assertion, and apply to it the logician's alternative, true or false, the answer must be given to a like question respecting the existing formulated principles of any science.

The scheme is true with unformulated qualifications, exceptions, limitations, and new interpretations in terms of more general notions. We do not yet know how to recast the scheme into a logical truth. But the scheme is a matrix from which true propositions applicable to particular circumstances can be derived. We can at present only trust our trained instincts as to the discrimination of the circumstances in respect to which the scheme is valid.

The use of such a matrix is to argue from it boldly and with rigid logic. The scheme should therefore be stated with the utmost precision and definiteness, to allow of such argumentation. The conclusion of the argument should then be confronted with circumstances to which it should apply. . . .

Rationalism never shakes off its status of an experimental adventure. The combined influences of mathematics and religion, which have so greatly contributed to the rise of philosophy, have also had the unfortunate effect of yoking it with static dogmatism. Rationalism is an adventure in the clarification of thought, progressive and never final. But it is an adventure in which even partial success has importance. . . .

If we may trust the Pythagorean tradition, the rise of European philosophy was largely promoted by the development of mathematics into a science of abstract generality. But in its subsequent development the method of philosophy has also been vitiated by the example of mathematics. The primary method of mathematics is deduction; the primary method of philosophy is descriptive generalization. Under the influence of mathematics, deduction has been foisted onto philosophy as its standard method, instead of taking its true place as an essential auxiliary mode of verification whereby to test the scope of generalities. This misapprehension of philosophic method has veiled the very considerable success of philosophy in providing generic notions which add lucidity to our apprehension of the facts of experience. The depositions of Plato, Aristotle, Thomas Aquinas, Descartes, Spinoza, Leibnitz, Locke, Berkeley, Hume, Kant, Hegel, merely mean that ideas which these men introduced into the philosophic tradition must be construed with limitations, adaptations, and inversions, either unknown to them, or even explicitly repudiated by them. A new idea introduces a new alternative; and we are not less indebted to a thinker when we adopt the alternative which he discarded. Philosophy never reverts to its old position after the shock of a great philosopher.

Every science must devise its own instruments. The tool required for philosophy is language. Thus philosophy redesigns language in the same way that, in a physical science, pre-existing appliances are redesigned. It is exactly at this point that the appeal to facts is a difficult operation. This appeal is not solely to the expression of the facts in current verbal statements. The adequacy of such sentences is the main question at issue. It is true that the general agreement of mankind as to experienced facts is best expressed in language. But the language of literature breaks down precisely at the task of expressing in explicit form the larger generalities—the very generalities which metaphysics seeks to express.

The point is that every proposition refers to a universe exhibiting some general systematic metaphysical character. Apart from this background, the separate entities which go to form the proposition, and the proposition as a whole, are without determinate character. Nothing has been defined, because every definite entity requires a systematic universe to supply its requisite status. Thus every proposition proposing a fact must, in its complete analysis, propose the general character of the universe required for that fact. There are no self-sustained facts, floating in nonentity. . . .

The technical language of philosophy represents attempts of various schools of thought to obtain explicit expression of general ideas presupposed by the facts of experience. It follows that any novelty in metaphysical doctrines exhibits some measure of disagreement with statements of the facts to be found in current philosophical literature. The extent of disagreement measures the extent of metaphysical divergence. It is, therefore, no valid criticism on one metaphysical school to point out that its doctrines do not follow from the verbal expression of the facts accepted by another school. The whole contention is that the doctrines in question supply a closer approach to fully expressed propositions. . . .

Whatever is found in "practice" must lie within the scope of the metaphysical description. When the description fails to include the "practice," the metaphysics is inadequate and requires revision. There can be no appeal to practice to supplement metaphysics, so long as we remain contented with our metaphysical doctrines. Metaphysics is nothing but the description of the generalities which apply to all the details of practice.

No metaphysical system can hope entirely to satisfy these pragmatic tests. At the best such a system will remain only an approximation to the general truths which are sought. In particular, there are no precisely stated axiomatic certainties from which to start. There is not even the language in which to frame them. The only possible procedure is to start from verbal expressions which, when taken by themselves with the current meaning of their words, are ill-defined and ambiguous. These are not premises to be immediately reasoned from apart from elucidation by further discussion; they are endeavours to state general principles which will be exemplified in the subsequent description of the facts of experience. This subsequent elaboration should elucidate the meanings to be assigned to the words and phrases employed. Such meanings are incapable of accurate apprehension apart from a correspondingly accurate apprehension of the metaphysical background which the universe provides for them. But no language can be anything but elliptical, requiring a leap of the imagination to understand its meaning in its relevance to immediate experience. The position of metaphysics in the development of culture cannot be understood without remembering that no verbal statement is the adequate expression of a proposition. . . .

It has been an objection to speculative philosophy that it is overambitious. Rationalism, it is admitted, is the method by which advance is made within the limits of particular sciences. It is, however, held that this limited success must not encourage attempts to frame ambitious schemes expressive of the general nature of things.

One alleged justification of this criticism is ill-success: European thought is represented as littered with metaphysical systems, abandoned and unreconciled.

Such an assertion tacitly fastens upon philosophy the old dogmatic test. The same criterion would fasten ill-success upon science. We no more retain the physics of the seventeenth century than we do the Cartesian philosophy of that century. Yet within limits, both systems express important truths. Also we are beginning to understand the wider categories which define their limits of correct application. Of course, in that century, dogmatic views held sway; so that the validity both of the physical notions, and of the Cartesian notions, was misconceived. Mankind never quite knows what it is after. When we survey the history of thought, and likewise the history of practice, we find that one idea after another is tried out, its limitations defined, and its core of truth elicited. . . . The proper test is not that of finality, but of progress.

But the main objection, dating from the sixteenth century and receiving final expression from Francis Bacon, is the uselessness of philosophic speculation. The position taken by this objection is that we ought to describe detailed matter of fact, and elicit the laws with a generality strictly limited to the systematization of these described details. General interpretation, it is held, has no bearing upon this procedure; and thus any system of general interpretation, be it true or false, remains intrinsically barren. Unfortunately for this objection, there are no brute, self-contained matters of fact, capable of being understood apart from interpretation as an element in a system. Whenever we attempt to express the matter of immediate experience, we find that its understanding leads us beyond itself, to its contemporaries, to its past, to its future, and to the universals in terms of which its definiteness is exhibited. But such universals, by their very character of universality, embody the potentiality of other facts with variant types of definiteness. Thus the understanding of the immediate brute fact requires its metaphysical interpretation as an item in a world with some systematic relation to it. When thought comes upon the scene, it finds the interpretations as matters of practice. Philosophy does not initiate interpretations. Its search for a rationalistic scheme is the search for more adequate criticism, and for more adequate justification, of the interpretations which we perforce employ. Our habitual experience is a complex of failure and success in the enterprise of interpretation. If we desire a record of uninterpreted experience, we must ask a stone to record its autobiography. Every scientific memoir in its record of the "facts" is shot through and through with interpretation. The methodology of rational interpretation is the product of the fitful vagueness of consciousness. Elements which shine with immediate distinctness, in some circumstances, retire into penumbral shadow in other circumstances, and into black darkness on other occasions. And yet all occasions proclaim themselves as actualities within the flux of a solid world, demanding a unity of interpretation. . . .

There is no justification for checking generalization at any particular stage. Each phase of generalization exhibits its own peculiar simplicities which stand out just at that stage, and at no other stage. There are simplicities connected with the motion of a bar of steel which are obscured if we refuse to abstract from the individual molecules; and there are certain simplicities concerning the behaviour of men which are obscured if we refuse to abstract from the individual peculiarities of particular specimens. In the same way, there are certain general truths, about the actual things in the common world of activity, which will be obscured when attention is confined to some particular detailed mode of considering them. These general truths, involved in the meaning of every particular notion respecting the actions of things, are the subject matter for speculative philosophy.

S. N. Hampshire   6. METAPHYSICAL SYSTEMS

Whereas Whitehead admits the possibility of a logical, coherent, and necessary system that does justice to both theory and practice, Oxonian analyst Stuart Hampshire flatly denies any such possibility. Like his opposite number from Cambridge, G. E. Moore, Hampshire is little encouraged by great metaphysical systems. The Grand Metaphysicians (Aristotle, Aquinas, Spinoza, Leibniz), he says, can no longer hold up their heads under the critical blows of Kant, who showed the impossibility of any transcendental

From *The Nature of Metaphysics*, edited by D. F. Pears. Reprinted by permission of the publishers, Macmillan & Company Ltd., London, and St. Martin's Press, Inc., New York.

and deductive metaphysics. System-builders, he alleges, are not concerned with reality or knowledge as "it actually is," but ambitiously "try to set limits to it, to determine what it should be."

Hampshire believes that the most devastating rejoinder to metaphysical systems is to be found in the relation between any system and the elements it allows. "The meaning of any expression," he asserts, "is determined by the conditions under which one can claim certainty in the application of it." There could not therefore be any single set of conditions in which certainty "can properly be claimed in respect of all expressions, whatever they may be."

Great metaphysical systems avoid "the actual human situation which conditions all our thought and language," and "culminate in a picture of ideal knowledge"—representative, he says, of the "complete knowledge which an eternal mind would enjoy," unhampered by the actual limitations of knowledge, or point of view. The distinction between subject and object, knower and known, is thereby denied. Then knowledge takes "no particular viewpoint," but is extrapolated "to the top of the scale" where a comprehensive knower is substituted for the actual, finite knower.

Hampshire consequently argues that "there can be no sense in the notion of complete knowledge." Knowledge is, in its very nature, limited, and must always be incomplete. Since reality is inexhaustible, and since the concrete conditions of statements cannot be removed, such extrapolated knowledge, as claimed by system-builders, is thus impossible.

UNDERNEATH ALL THE particular grammars of particular languages, there is a deeper grammar which reflects the universal features of human experience, that is, the position of persons as observers in space and time of a succession of events. For instance, we have to think of our experience as an experience of things, existing in space and persisting as the same things through time with changing qualities. This is part of the unavoidable grammar of our thought, equally part of the unavoidable nature of experience. We cannot think it away. But at the same time we are aware of this limitation on our thought and experience as a limitation; and this is why we are tempted, hopelessly, into metaphysical speculation, trying to break the bonds, as it were, where the bonds are the necessary forms of experience as we know it. All we can do, as philosophers, is to penetrate to this deeper grammar, which reflects the presuppositions of all our thought and experience; and then we shall realize why it is that our knowledge can never be complete, and why we never have unconditional explanations of the nature of things, as they are in themselves, apart from the conditions of our experience of them.

Deductive metaphysics, system-building of the old kind, has never recovered from Kant's criticism, and I do not think that it ever will. The old idea that a philosopher might deduce by pure reason what must have been the origin of things, and what must be the structure of the universe, at least in outline, seems to me to have been killed stone dead. Certainly there have been some flickers of life in deductive metaphysics since: McTaggart's *Nature of Existence,* for instance, or Samuel Alexander's *Space, Time, and Deity,* which is more tentative and less deductive in method than McTaggart's was. But they have not held the interest of philosophers, who have generally been working out the implications of Kant's argument, either pressing it further or in some way qualifying it or amending it. I can think of only one later attempt at a metaphysical system which does take account of Kant's criticism and which therefore does still hold the attention of philosophers: that is Wittgenstein's *Tractatus Logico-Philosophicus,* published in England in 1922. And it is a very odd attempt at a system, since it disavows itself, the author showing that his own system precludes the possibility of any systematic philosophy. He makes it plain that he is attempting the impossible, and the reasons he gives against any systematic metaphysics are almost the same as Kant's. He says, for instance, that we cannot significantly ask questions, or make statements, which involve only formal concepts. We cannot therefore ask about the origin of things or of events, unless we specify things or events of a particular kind. The words "thing" and "event" stand for formal concepts, and such concepts are empty or vacuous unless some empirical concept is added to them. This distinction between the material and formal elements of our speech and thought is Kant's distinction; Kant also insisted that concepts are empty if considered apart from all possible application to experience. In his later work, the *Philosophical Investigations,* Wittgenstein went as far as anyone could in repudiating the possibility of any systematic philosophy. The lesson of his later work is that we fall into nonsense, mere idle words, if we consider questions or statements apart from the actual context of human life in which the questions would ordinarily be asked or the statements made. In order to achieve sense in thought and language, it is not enough merely to observe the dictionary definitions of words, the rules of grammar and the laws of logic. The significance of any statement whatever, together with its grammar and its logic, presupposes some constant background of ordinary human interests and purposes and of ordinary human experience. If we try to use ordinary forms of words in some context where this background of ordinary experience is lacking, we find ourselves merely playing with words in a void. For example, if I talk of the feelings and memories of disembodied spirits, I do not necessarily offend against the dictionary definitions of words or against the rules of grammar or of logic. There need be nothing wrong with my words and sentences considered merely as English words and sentences. But when I reflect on what I could mean by hopes and feelings and memories in this extraordinary context, I may find myself unable to say what I could mean; for the ordinary meaning of "hope" or "feeling" or "memory" is so inextricably tied up with the ordinary background of physical existence that I cannot say how I would, or even could, apply these words if persons did not exist as recognizable physical bodies. Perhaps I could give some strange sense to these words in this strange context: I do not know. But at least, it is not obvious what the meaning would be, or what analogy it would bear to the meaning of these words as they are ordinarily used. A systematic metaphysician need not speculate on the immortality of the soul; but he will always, I think, need to use some variant of ordinary language in a context in which the ordinary limitations of human experience are somehow removed. If in his speculations he accepts the limitations of human observers, as persons existing in time, and makes no claim to go beyond them, he would not be called a metaphysician at all; he would simply be a very speculative scientist, or perhaps a speculative historian, and we should wait to see whether any evidence was forthcoming to confirm his speculations. He steps over the limits into the kind of metaphysics which Kant condemned when he starts to tell us about timeless realities and tries to explain the existence of the universe, or the purposes of human life, by reference to them. At this point he should come to a stop and remain silent; that was Wittgenstein's advice. In Kant's phrase, we should realize that we are trying to comprehend the incomprehensible.

But having followed Kant so far, I must now say that it does not seem to me that he has proved that there is no such thing as metaphysics: only that there is no such thing as transcendental and deductive metaphysics. The difficulty here is not to quarrel about a word, a label. Kant is himself often referred to as a metaphysician. He is prepared to make statements about the necessary presuppositions of all thought and experience; and this may earn him the title of metaphysician, even though he does not try to deduce from them some system of ultimate reality, as, for example, Spinoza and Leibniz did. A strict empiricist philosopher of the contemporary kind would certainly not say anything about the necessary presuppositions of all thought and experience; for he would ask how such statements are to be proved or otherwise established as true. If he were very strict indeed, he would not say anything at all of an even remotely metaphysical kind; he would confine himself to showing metaphysicians that they had not so far attached a sense to their words. But let us forget labels. There is in fact a tradition of philosophical writing which effectively begins with Aristotle and passes through Aquinas and others in the Middle Ages, comes to life again in Descartes, Spinoza and Leibniz, suffers an enormous change in Kant, and continues in this century in the early work of Russell and in Wittgenstein's *Tracatus Logico-Philosophicus*. This is the tradition of systematic philosophy, that is, of philosophy trying to give an account of the necessary structure of human knowledge and of the limits of human knowledge.

In doing this, philosophy finds itself circling round and round certain key notions, which are the organizing notions on which all thought and knowledge depends; here are some of these organizing notions—Exist, True, Same, Possible and Impossible, Certain and Uncertain, Like and Unlike. It seems, on the

evidence of history, that systematic philosophy must come back to these notions and to exploring the relations between them. For they are the most general notions in our language and enter into every kind of discourse. When therefore we enquire into the varying conditions of their application, we get a view of the whole range of our discourse. But if we have the ambitions of a system-builder, we will try to do more than get a view of the range of our thought: we will try to set limits to it, to determine what it should be, or must be, not merely what it actually is. If, for example, we lay down under what conditions we can properly claim to be certain that a statement is true, we are already on the way to constructing a metaphysical system; for we have picked out one type of statement of which we can say that the subject-terms stand for something that certainly exists. And then we shall have to explain the existence of everything else in terms of this privileged type of entity, whatever it may be. This is the classical path by which the theory of knowledge has always, since Plato, led directly into system-building. Spinoza and Leibniz both used this argument from the nature of knowledge and of truth in constructing their metaphysical systems; and so did Russell, when he argued that, outside mathematics, we can only be certain of the truth of statements which describe our own sensations, and therefore that all scientific knowledge must ultimately refer to the order of our sensations. But there is a devastating reply which can be made to system-building of this deductive kind. In the last thirty years philosophers have seen more clearly why the conditions of application of "certain" and "uncertain," as of "same," "true," "exist," must vary with every type of term, and with every type of statement, with which they are combined. For the meaning of any expression is determined by the conditions under which we can claim certainty in the application of it. There could not therefore be any single set of conditions in which certainty can properly be claimed in respect of all expressions, whatever they may be. And for the same reason it must be impossible to find some general criterions of identity or of existence or of truth. I think that no philosopher now could follow Descartes, Spinoza and Leibniz in looking for such general criteria. Therefore I do not think that any philosopher now would try to found a metaphysical system on the basis of pure deduction—deduction, that is, from what knowledge must be, or what truth must be, where this is decided by *a priori* reasoning. But the general subject-matter of deductive metaphysics remains, even if the method of handling it must be different, no longer the deductive method. We still want some general view of the scope of human knowledge, of its divisions into different types, and of its outer limits, as far as we can determine them now. And exploring the relations between these most general notions—existence, truth, identity and so on—will provide us with the outlines of the map of human knowledge, and will show what the limits of knowledge are. But as Kant and Wittgenstein suggested, we have to start on this explanation from the actual human situation which conditions all our thought and language, the situation, that is, of men observing and acting from a particular position in time and space, referring to particular things in their environment, identifying and classifying them, and trying to find ways to alter them. It is characteristic of the great metaphysical systems—Spinoza, Leibniz, for instance—that they culminate in a picture of ideal knowledge which escapes all these limitations; actual knowledge is seen as an approximation to the complete knowledge which an eternal mind would enjoy, subject to no limitations of viewpoint. F. H. Bradley, writing after Kant and in the critical age of philosophy, admits that ideal and perfect knowledge would not be anything like what we now mean by knowledge; it would be more like feeling, in that the distinction between the knower and the known would have disappeared altogether, and knowledge would no longer be mediated through the forms of language or through our limited categories of thought. It would be direct and intuitive, an identification of the mind with reality. One may think that these are entirely mystical phrases, devoid of literal sense, except possibly as descriptions of some special mystical experiences. But history shows that this is not so; the use of just these phrases is the necessary consequence of following an entirely rational line of argument. For this reason they occur again and again as the culminating point, and as a kind of last chapter, of metaphysical systems: even in the most hard-headed philosophers, such as Spinoza, who certainly was not describing mystical experiences. We have to account for this recurrence, if we are to understand what metaphysical systems are: and not account for them only in William James's way, as the expression of psychological needs, but as the conclusions of severely rational men pushing clear reason to its limits, its limit being just a kind of apparent mysticism and obscurity.

The rational argument, I suggest, goes like this: We distinguish different levels of comprehensiveness and objectivity in our actual knowledge. Knowledge becomes more genuinely knowledge the more comprehensive it is and the less it reflects the viewpoint of the knowing subject. Therefore, at the top of the scale, perfect knowledge would be absolutely comprehensive and it would not reflect the viewpoint of the knowing subject even to the smallest degree; indeed the knowing subject would have no particular viewpoint; he would know things as they are in their own true, objective order. Any actual human knowledge, even of the most comprehensive scientific kind, does still reflect the limitations of the knowing subject. It is not therefore real knowledge of things as they are, in their own true order, but knowledge of things as they appear to us: it is the best we can do, but it is not ideal knowledge. This was Spinoza's argument, and it can be found in various forms in almost all metaphysical systems of the strictly deductive kind.

This argument has only one crucial step: The step of extrapolating to the top of the scale: it is just this step which makes metaphysical systems. Because we know what it is to know something about something, and to know more and more about more and more, it seems that we must be able to say what it would be like to know everything about everything. As we can in fact learn what is the cause of this or that being, so we can say what it would be like to know the cause of each and everything. It is this unrestricted use of "all" and "everything" that is characteristic of the metaphysician. It therefore seems that, if we reject his claims, we must be saying that knowledge is in its very nature limited and must always be incomplete, and that what remains to be known must always be inexhaustible. And this is indeed exactly what I would say. This seems to me to be the real ground for the impossibility of a metaphysical system of a deductive kind: that there can be no sense in the notion of complete knowledge. The objection to deductive metaphysics is not some more or less technical objection of logic; nor do we need to refer to some special philosophical principle, such as the principle that all statements must be verifiable, in some technical meaning of "verifiable." We need only appeal to the conditions in which statements are made and are understood and are known to be true or false. If we suppose these conditions removed, we find that we no longer know what could be meant by "statement" or "understanding" or "knowledge" and "truth." And this would not be a mere discovery about words; we would have advanced towards that general view of the nature of knowledge at which philosophers are always aiming. But we have to begin from the actual situation of persons, situated at a certain point relative to other things in space and time, using signs to refer and to identify, to ask questions and give orders, and to calculate possible changes in their environment. Given that this is the situation and that these are the needs, various forms of thought and speech may be traced back to these primary needs. But to many contemporary philosophers it seems that Kant was still too dogmatic in picking out just one set of categories or formal elements in our thought. It is rightly said that we can distinguish the formal elements in our thought, and also the human needs which they reflect, in many different ways. Nor can we assume that there is just one universal grammar, consisting of all the elements common to all the grammars of all human languages. But, while admitting this, it still seems to me that Kant was right in looking for some few categories, or elements of grammar, which are the most fundamental of all, and is trying to show some systematic connection between them. Perhaps no one would now claim that there is just one, finally correct way of exhibiting this systematic connection. Rather there is room for a variety of different tentative systems, none of them claiming finality, but each bringing into prominence some very general feature of our discourse. There is no reason why systematic philosophy should also be dogmatic and claim finality for itself; and there is no reason also why it should assume the form of pre-Kantian metaphysics, that is, why it should claim to represent the ultimate nature of reality independent of actual human knowledge.

Thomist

Jacques Maritain

7. THE TRUE SUBJECT OF METAPHYSICS

For nearly half a century, Jacques Maritain has remained one of the most articulate of Neo-Thomists. In this essay, he sets forth in a modern statement the traditional view on the material and formal objects of metaphysics. Traditionally, it has been held that the material object, or general subject matter, of metaphysics is *being*—that is, all reality, actual or possible—while its formal object is *being insofar as it is being,* or *being as such.* For the purpose of indicating the metaphysical theme, however, he does not at this point formally distinguish material from formal, but combines both terms under the title "subject of metaphysics."

Maritain asserts that the authentic subject matter of metaphysics is not the being treated by either the empirical or logical sciences. Rather it is "real being in all the purity of its distinctive intelligibility . . . as transobjectively subsistent, autonomous and essentially diversified." He then proposes two *lumines,* or lights, which properly pertain (*a*) to the object known in its own objective intelligibility, and (*b*) to the knowing mind which "grasps the object and conforms to it." Being "exposes" itself to a knower, but a knower in turn must "open" himself to being. It is this opening of himself to being, and the proportioning of his intellect to a given object, that constitutes the metaphysical *habitus*—a *lumen* in the effective, rather than the objective, order. Without such *habitus,* the actual intuition into being as such (*ens in quantum ens*) is frustrated.

Being is known by a genuine intuition, "a perception direct and immediate," which follows upon the natural capacity of mind. The mind, as he states elsewhere, is "cut out to conquer reality." Only being can produce the profound response generated by such an intuition. Unlike Bergson's, Heidegger's, and Marcel's explanation for the entry into being, says Maritain, authentic intuition is intellectual, rather than sympathetic, emotional, or "moralist." The metaphysical threshold is crossed only when this abstractive intuition, or "eidetic visualization," into being, is present—that is, when "the intellect by the very fact that it is spiritual, proportions its

From *A Preface to Metaphysics* by Jacques Maritain, published 1939 by Sheed & Ward, Inc., New York.

objects to itself, by elevating them within itself to diverse degrees, increasingly pure, of spirituality and immateriality."

THE BEING WHICH is the subject matter of metaphysics, being as such, is neither the particularised being of the natural sciences, nor the being divested of reality of genuine logic nor yet the pseudo-being of false logic. It is real being in all the purity and fullness of its distinctive intellibility or mystery. Objects, all objects, murmur this being; they utter it to the intellect, but not to all intellects, only to those capable of hearing. For here also it is true: He that hath ears to hear let him hear. *Qui habet aures audiendi audiat.* Being is then seen in its distinctive properties, as trans-objectively subsistent, autonomous and essentially diversified. For the intuition of being is also the intuition of its transcendental character and analogical value. It is not enough to employ the word being, to say "Being." We must have the intuition, the intellectual perception of the inexhaustible and incomprehensible reality thus manifested as the object of this perception. It is this intuition that makes the metaphysician.

As you know, to each science there belongs a distinctive intellectual virtue. There is, therefore, an intellectual virtue proper to the metaphysician. And this virtue, or habitus, corresponds to being as the object of the intuition just mentioned. We must therefore distinguish two "Lights" in the scholastic parlance, one pertaining to the object, the other to the habitus, or intellectual virtue. The characteristic mode of intellectual apprehension or eidetic visualisation—the degree of immateriality, of spirituality in the manner in which the mind grasps the object and conforms to it, demanded by the very nature of trans-objective reality as it presents to the mind as its object a particular intelligible facet—constitutes what the ancients termed the *ratio formalis sub qua,* the objective light in which at a given degree of knowledge objects are knowable by the intellect. At the same time proportionate to this objective light there is a subjective light perfecting the subjective activity of the intellect, by which the intellect itself is proportioned to a given object, fitted to apprehend it. That is why Thomists say that the habitus is a *lumen,* a light, not in the objective but in the *effective* order. For it is concerned with the production or effectuation of the act of knowing.

Hence the metaphysical habitus is requisite, if we are to have the intuition of being as such, *ens in quantum ens.* Yet on the other hand it is this intuition that effects, causes, the metaphysical habitus. This reciprocal causation simply means that the metaphysical habitus, the intellectual virtue of the metaphysician, comes to birth at the same time as its proper and specific object is disclosed to it. Nevertheless the object is prior, not in time but in ontological rank. In the order of nature the intuition of being as such takes precedence of the inner habitus of the metaphysician. It is this perception of being that determines the first moment at which the habitus comes to birth, and it is by the operation of this same habit thus developed that the being which is the metaphysician's distinctive object is more and more clearly perceived.

Enough of this digression. We are confronted here with a genuine intuition, a perception direct and immediate, an intuition not in the technical sense which the ancients attached to the term, but in the sense we may accept from modern philosophy. It is a very simple sight, superior to any discursive reasoning or demonstration, because it is the source of demonstration. It is a sight whose content and implication no words of human speech can exhaust or adequately express and in which in a moment of decisive emotion, as it were, of spiritual conflagration, the soul is in contact, a living, penetrating and illuminating contact, with a reality which it touches and which takes hold of it. Now what I want to emphasize is that it is being more than anything else which produces such an intuition. The characteristics of intuition as I have just described them may seem at first sight those of M. Bergson's intuition. They seem so, in truth, but with the important difference that he denies that his intuition is intellectual. I, on the other hand, have just maintained that the object *par excellence* of intuition is being, but that that intuition is intellectual. This is remote indeed from the Bergsonian philosophy. Being does not produce the intuition such as I have described it, by means of that species of sympathy which demands a violent return of the will upon itself of which M. Bergson speaks, but evokes it from the intellect and by means of a concept, an idea. The concept, or notion, of being corresponds with this intuition. The term being is the correct term to express it, though obviously we cannot display by this poor word nor for that matter by the most skillful devices of language all the wealth contained in the intuition. It requires all the metaphysics hitherto elaborated or to be elaborated hereafter in its entire future development to know all the riches implicit in the concept of being. It is by producing in conjunction with reality a mental word within itself that the intellect immediately attains being as such, the subject matter of metaphysics.

Thus we are confronted with objects and as we confront them, the diverse realities made known by our senses or by the several sciences, we receive at a given moment, as it were, the revelation of an intelligible mystery concealed in them. Nor is this revelation, this species of intellectual shock, confined to metaphysicians. It is sometimes given to those who are not metaphysicians. There is a kind of sudden intuition which a soul may receive of her own existence, or of "being" embodied in all things whatsoever, however lowly. It may even happen that to a particular soul this intellectual perception presents the semblance of a mystical grace. I have quoted elsewhere (*Degrés du Savoir,* p. 552) a personal experience communicated to me.

"I have often experienced in a sudden intuition the reality of my being, the profound first principle which makes me exist outside nonentity. It is a powerful intuition whose violence has sometimes frightened me and which first revealed to me a metaphysical absolute."

A similar intuition is described in the autobiography of Jean-Paul Richter. "One morning when I was still a child, I was standing on the threshold of the house and looking to my left in the direction of the woodpile when suddenly there came to me from heaven like a lightning flash the thought: I *am a self,* a thought which has never since left me. I perceived my self for the first time and for good."

There are, therefore, metaphysical intuitions which are a natural revelation to the soul, invested with the decisive, imperious and dominant character of a "Substantial word" uttered by reality. They reveal the intelligible treasure, the unforgettable trans-objective fact, which is either her own subsistence, the "Self" that she is, or being either her own or the being apprehended in objects. Evidently this intuition of which I am speaking does not necessarily present this appearance of a species of mystical grace. But it is always, so to speak, a gift bestowed upon the intellect, and beyond question it is in one form or another indispensable to every metaphysician. But we must also observe that although it is indispensable to the metaphysician, it is not given to everybody, nor to all those who engage in philosophy, nor even to all philosophers who desire to be or are believed to be metaphysicians. Kant never had it. What is the explanation of this? That it is difficult. It is not indeed difficult like an operation which it is hard to perform, whose successful performance demands expert skill. For there is nothing simpler. It was precisely because he sought it by a technique, an intellectual technique of extreme subtlety, that Kant failed to attain it.

Moreover, it is as true to say that this intuition produces itself through the medium of the vital action of our intellect. I mean as vitally receptive and contemplative, as to say that we produce it. It is difficult, inasmuch as it is difficult to arrive at the degree of intellectual purification at which this act is produced in us, at which we become sufficiently disengaged, sufficiently empty to *hear* what all things whisper and to *listen* instead of composing answers.

We must attain a certain level of intellectual spirituality, such that the impact of reality upon the intellect—or to use a less crude metaphor, the active attentive silence of the intellect, its meeting with the real—gives the objects received through our senses (whose *species impressa* is buried in the depths of the intellect) a new kind of presence in us: they are present in a mental word, another life, a living content which is a world of trans-objective presence and intelligibility. Then we are confronted within ourselves with the object of this intuition, as an object of knowledge, living with an immaterial life, with the burning translucence of intellectual nature in act.

It is worth remarking at this point that there are concrete approaches which prepare for this intuition and lead up to it. They are different *paths* which, however, it is important to observe, are radically insufficient if we stop short at them, but which may prove useful to particular individuals if they will transcend them, if they will go further. Here I will mention three of these. One is the Bergsonian experience of duration. Within limits it is a genuine experience.

Duration is apprehended by an experience of motion in which, on a level deeper than that of consciousness, our psychic states fuse in a potential manifold which is, notwithstanding, a unity, and in which we are aware of advancing through time and enduring through change indivisibly, yet that we are growing richer in quality and triumphing over the inertia of matter. This is a psychological experience which is not yet the metaphysical intuition of being, but is capable of leading us up to it. For involved in this psychological duration and implicitly given by it there is indeed existence, the irreducible value of being, *esse*.

This intuition is therefore a path, an approach, to the perception of existence. The latter, however, is not yet nakedly displayed in its own intelligible form.

The German philosopher, Heidegger, assures us that no man can become a metaphysician who has not first experienced anguish, this anguish being understood not only psychologically but also as metaphysically as possible. It is the feeling at once keen and lacerating of all that is precarious and imperilled in our existence, in human existence. As the effect of this feeling, of this anguish, our existence loses its commonplace and acquires a unique value, its unique value. It confronts us as something saved from nothingness, snatched from nonentity.

Certainly such a dramatic experience of nothingness may serve as an introduction to the intuition of being, provided it is taken as no more than an introduction.

My third example is not a thesis fully worked out, but suggestions put forward in preliminary sketches or in the course of conversation. Therefore I must speak of it with all due reserve and without committing its author to my interpretation. It would seem that M. Gabriel Marcel is seeking a method of approach to metaphysical being by deepening the sense of certain moral facts, such as fidelity. As Heidegger attaches himself to a personal experience, a psychological experience such as anguish, while warning us that he is not concerned with psychology, so the notion of fidelity is here understood in a sense which does or should transcend ethics and conveys strictly metaphysical value and content. We may observe that the consistency, *steadfastness,* firmness and victory over disintegration and oblivion contained in this virtue and suggested by the word fidelity are strictly dependent upon a certain *steadfastness* in reality itself in virtue of which I dominate the flux of my own life and possess my metaphysical consistence. Therefore, if I rightly understand M. Marcel's thought, if we follow its direction we shall conclude that a philosophy of life which confuses my *self* with the flux of my life is inconsistent with the experience of fidelity. The experience, the irreducible reality of what I experience and know as fidelity, is pregnant with an ontological realism.

In these three instances we are, you see, confronted with so many concrete approaches to being. The first of these experiences, that of duration, belongs to the speculative order, and is at once psychological and biological. The two others belong to the practical and moral order, the psychological factor being invested with the ethical. If we stop here, we have not, I maintain, crossed the threshold of metaphysics. These philosophic explorations are certainly not to be despised or refused. They can perform most valuable service by directing towards being many minds hidebound by idealist prejudices or repelled by some textbook of so-called scholasticism. They can prepare them to recover the sense of being. But they can do this, only if we will travel further; cross the threshold; take the decisive step. Otherwise, whatever we do, we shall remain in psychology and ethics, which we shall then work up, swell out, enlarge or rarefy to make them mimic metaphysics. We shall then have, not genuine metaphysics, but a substitute which may certainly possess a very considerable philosophic interest, but is nothing but a substitute all the same. The utmost that can be achieved along these lines are solutions obtained by an indirect route which skirts the essential issue or by definitions based on external criteria, not the genuine solutions demanded by a science worthy of the name, by philosophic knowledge. Even if psychology and ethics enrich their own speech with metaphysical echoes or undertones, they will be but echoes.

But the most serious danger which all these methods of approaching being involve is the danger of remaining imprisoned in one or other of the concrete analogues of being, whichever one has chosen as a path to it. The experience in question gives information only of itself. This is indeed the drawback of pure experience in philosophy and the pitfall of every metaphysical system which attempts to be empirical. The experience, though valid for the domain covered by the particular intuition, cannot, save by an arbitrary procedure, be extended to a wider province of the intelligible world, and be employed to explain it. On the other hand, as I have just said, such experiences bring us to the threshold which it is then for us to cross by taking the decisive step. We do this by letting the veils—too heavy with matter and too opaque—of the concrete psychological or ethical fact fall away to discover in their purity the strictly metaphysical values which such experiences concealed. There is then but one word by which we can express our discovery, namely being. Let us have the courage to require our intellect, acting as such, to look the reality signified by the term in the face. It is something primordial, at once very simple and very rich and, if you will, inexpressible in the sense that it is that whose perception is the most difficult to describe, because it is the most immediate. Here we are at the root, at last laid bare, of our entire intellectual life. You may say, if you please, for I am here attempting to employ a purely descriptive terminology as a preliminary to the formation of a philosophic vocabulary, that what is now perceived is, as it were, a pure activity, a subsistence, but a subsistence which transcends the entire order of the imaginable, a living tenacity, at once precarious—it is nothing for me to crush a fly—and indomitable—within and around me there is growth without ceasing. By this subsistence, this tenacity, objects come up against me, overcome possible disaster, endure and possess in themselves whatever is requisite for this. These are metaphors, lamentably inadequate, which attempt to express not so much what my intellect sees, which is superempirical, as my experience of the vision, and do not themselves enter the domain of metaphysics but which may make us aware that to the word "being," when it expresses a genuine metaphysical intuition, there must correspond a primary and original datum, of its essence above the scope of observation. . . .

This metaphysical content, of which we are speaking, covers the entire domain of intelligibility and reality. It is a gift bestowed upon the intellect by an intuition which infinitely exceeds, I do not say in the intensity of its experience but in its intelligible value, the experiences which may have led up to it.

I have spoken briefly of the intuition of being and of the paths which may lead to its threshold. I must add that it is both possible and necessary to show analytically that to arrive at this point is inevitable. We are now dealing with something totally different from these concrete approaches to being which I have just discussed. We are now concerned with a rational analysis establishing the necessity of being as such, *ens in quantum ens,* as the supreme object of our knowledge. Such an analytic proof presupposes, as taken for granted by common sense or as scientifically confirmed by the criticism of knowledge, what in general terms we may call the objective or rather trans-objective validity of understanding and knowledge, a non-idealist position. . . .

In the second place it is easy to prove, as St. Thomas proves in the first article of his *De Veritate,* that all our notions, all our concepts, are resolved in the concept of being. It is therefore the first of all our concepts, of which all the rest are determinations. Being is determined by the differences which arise within, not outside, itself. It is then to being that we inevitably reascend as to the fountainhead. It is being which the intellect perceives first and before anything else. It is, therefore, being which the metaphysical intellect must disengage and know in its distinctive mystery. . . .

It is, however, important to observe that the intuition of which I was speaking just now and the analysis with which I am at present concerned should accompany each other. Were we content with the intuition without the rational analysis we should risk being landed with an intuition unconfirmed by reason, whose rational necessity therefore would not be manifest. Were we content with the analysis—as we are able to be when we teach philosophy— though the analysis would indeed prove that we must arrive at the intuition of being as the goal of a necessary regress, it would not of itself furnish the intuition. Thus the analysis is in the same case as the approaches of which I spoke earlier. The latter led up concretely, *in via inventionis,* to the metaphysical intuition of being. But it still remained to cross the threshold to which they had led us. It is the same with rational analysis. It leads us by logical necessity, and *in via judicii,* to the threshold which an intuitive perception alone enables us to cross, the perception of being as such. When the mind once has this intuition it has it for good.

Observe what an unforgettable event in the history of philosophy was Parmenides' discovery, imperfect though it still was, of being as such. It was on that account that Plato called him the father of philosophy, and when obliged to criticise him accused himself of parricide. Parmenides was, it would seem, the first western philosopher to have the perception, though still very imperfect as I have said, of being as such. It was imperfect, for he does not seem to have disengaged it in its naked metaphysical value. He appears, as his theory of the sphere indicates, to have amalgamated the metaphysical intuition of being with a physical perception of sensible reality and to have misunderstood or misinterpreted his intuition of being, when the inevitable moment arrived for him to explain it in terms of philosophic concepts, by understanding it univocally and thus falling into monism.

You will also see why the intuition of the principle of identity, every being is what it is, being is being, can possess such value for the metaphysician, can become the object of his enraptured contemplation. Common sense—and therefore the man in the street—makes use of the principle without scrutinising it. "A cat is a cat," says common sense—what more could it say?—so that, if the philosopher comes on the scene and enunciates the principle of identity in front of common sense, the latter will not see it, but will merely have the impression that an insignificant commonplace has been affirmed, in fact a tautology. The philosopher, on the other hand, when he enunciates the principle of identity enunciates it as an expression of the metaphysical intuition of being, and thus sees in it the first fundamental law of reality itself, a law which astounds him because it proclaims *ex abrupto,* the primal mystery of being, its combination of subsistence and abundance, a law which is exemplified by objects in an infinite number of different modes, and applied with an infinite variety. It is not as the result of a logistic process that the metaphysician perceives and employs the principle of identity, so that it compels him to reduce everything to a pure identity, that is to say to obliterate all the diversities and varieties of being. For it is with its mode of analogical realisation that he apprehends the principle. When he apprehends being as such, being according to its pure intelligible nature, he apprehends the essentially analogous value of the concept of being which is implicitly manifold and is realised in diverse objects in such fashion as to admit differences of essence between them, complete and vast differences. The principle of identity secures the multiplicity and variety of objects. Far from reducing all things to identity, it is, as I have explained elsewhere, the guardian of universal multiplicity, the axiom of being's irreducible diversities. If each being is what it is, it is not what other beings are.

It follows that the metaphysical intuition of being is an abstractive intuition. Abstraction, however, is an antique term rendered suspect to modern ears by the distortion of long use and by errors and misconceptions of every sort. Therefore instead of *abstraction* I propose to speak of *eidetic* or *ideating visualisation*. I maintain then that the metaphysical intuition of being is an ideating intuition, that is an intuition producing an idea, and this in a preeminent degree. How could it be otherwise with the pure speculative operation of our human intellect? This intuition is at the summit of eidetic intellectuality. What do I mean by the phrase eidetic visualisation, *abstractio?* I mean that the intellect by the very fact that it is spiritual proportions its objects to itself, by elevating them within itself to diverse degrees, increasingly pure, of spirituality and immateriality. It is within itself that it attains reality, stripped of its real existence outside the mind and disclosing, uttering in the mind a content, an interior, an intelligible sound or voice, which can possess only in the mind the conditions of its existence one and universal, an existence of intelligibility in act. If being were the object of a concrete intuition like that of an external sense or of introspection, of an intuition centred upon a reality grasped concretely in its singular existence, philosophy would be compelled to choose, as it gave this intuition an idealist or a realist value, between a pure ontological monism and a pure phenomenalist pluralism. If, however, being is, as I have said, analogous and if the principle of identity is the axiom of reality's irreducible diversities, it is because extramental being is perceived in the mind under the conditions of the eidetic existence which it receives there, and the imperfect and relative unity it possesses in the mind must be broken up, as also must be the pure and unqualified unity of the objects of univocal concepts, when we pass from its existence in the concept to its real existence. The higher degree in which the intuition of being as such "ideates" is precisely the condition and guarantee of its correct metaphysical employment. . . .

Gerald Phelan

8. ONTOLOGY AND
ACTUS ESSENDI

Father Phelan, well-known commentator on, and teacher of, the thought of St. Thomas, makes further distinctions in this essay on the object of meta-

From *Essays in Modern Scholasticism* (in honor of John F. McCormick, S.J.), ed. by A. C. Pegis. Reprinted by permission of the publisher, The Newman Press, Westminster, Maryland.

physics. Although it is true, says Father Phelan, that "the first concept which the intellect forms is the concept of being," there is a crucial difference between the concept formed in ordinary experience by everyone, and that formed by a veteran metaphysician "after long and arduous reflection." This distinction may be stated roughly as the difference between being considered *materially* and being considered *formally*. It is this last which is the formal object of metaphysical intuition.

What then, asks Father Phelan, constitutes being formally *as* "being"? Such a formal constituent cannot itself be a species of being, or a mode of being; nor can it fit any other restricted category involving restrictions of itself. It must apply universally to being as being, not to being particularly conceived.

Now when the metaphysician thinks of being, says Phelan, he thinks first of the act by which all being is (id quod *est*), and secondarily of the thing (*id quod* est), or quiddity, which effects this act. Phelan therefore defines metaphysics as "a philosophy of whatever is or can be . . . considered specifically in the light of the ultimate existential actuality of all reality, the act of being (*esse*)." Thus, analyzing the celebrated definition of the act of being—*ens in quantum ens*—he observes that the first term (*ens*) designates the material object of metaphysics, which is being, "in the sense of whatever is or can be"; while the second *ens*, modified by *in quantum*, formally sets off being as the object of metaphysics from all other aspects of *ens* shared by other types of knowing.

B ORROWING A PHRASE from Avicenna, Saint Thomas Aquinas states that the first concept which the intellect forms is the concept of being. This statement is important in metaphysics as, indeed, it is in every philosophical inquiry. It would be ridiculous, however, to imagine that the concept of being alluded to in this connection is identical with that concept of being which the metaphysician achieves only after long and arduous reflection.

Being as known in the initial act of intellectual conception is conceived at that first moment when the intellect becomes aware of a vaguely and indefinitely understood somewhat, enveloped in the trappings of sensible appearances, concerted, so to speak, in the qualities which the senses perceive but not as yet differentiated from those qualities nor abstracted from them to be viewed and considered in and for itself. Were one to speak a word or term in which to express this first concept of being it could only be such a term as would signify, at once and undistinguished, both the sense quality perceived and its being. Such a term would be what the logician calls "connotative." Latin words like "album," "nigrum," "dulce" for instance express, at once and undistinguished, the sensible qualities of whiteness, blackness, sweetness and the subject in which these qualities are; when their signification is rendered explicit "album" becomes "ens album" or "res alba" (and likewise for the other terms "nigrum" and "dulce").

The concept of being formed by the spontaneous impulse of rational nature in this first instant of intellectual contact with what is sensibly apprehended thus contains the germ from which the metaphysical concept of being must develop (if and when it does develop); but that initial concept is only the beginning, the starting-point, from which the intellect sets out to achieve the term of its abstractive activity, which is the full-blown concept of being as being in the plenitude of its transcendental value, its thoroughgoing analogical character and the essential variety of its modes.

Just as the habitus of first principles is born of the notion of being thus formed within the intellect in its first encounter with what is sensed, and of the spontaneous judgment which follows that conception, so the habitus of metaphysical wisdom comes into existence at the moment when its specific object, the being of whatever is, stands revealed before the intellect. For metaphysics is a habitus, an accident of a rational suppositum, a quality of the speculative intellect, and, like all habitus, is constituted in its specific character by its proper object. That which the habitus of metaphysics renders the speculative intellect apt to know is the very being of whatever is, the formal constituent of being as such. What is it that formally constitutes being as being? It cannot be any species or kind or mode of being, else it could not extend to all species, kinds and modes of being. It must obviously be something which in itself is devoid of all such limiting determinations, free from all restrictions of form, species, essence or whatever else may involve potentiality, the source of all limitation, and thereby circumscribe it within the boundaries of quidditative being. In other words, what is ultimately formal in all that is does not belong to the order of essence or quiddity but is the very act of being as such, the act by which whatever is in any way, shape or form whatever, exercises the act of being, of existing, according to its nature.

It is this ultimate formal constituent of being as such, namely, the act of being (*esse*) which, when grasped by the intellect, specifies the habitus of metaphysical wisdom and differentiates it from every other habitus of knowledge. The act of being (*esse*) in itself cannot strictly speaking be conceived by any finite mind. It needs to be linked with some, at least vague, notion of a thing which exercises this act. But when the metaphysician thinks of being, he thinks primarily of the act by which all being is (*esse*) and only secondarily of the thing or the quiddity which exercises this act and which is, as it were, but the vehicle by which the knowledge of that act (*esse*) is transported to his mind and the staff or stay or prop which upholds it in conception. Just as, in the initial act of the intellect whereby the first notion of being is attained, the concept of being is wrapped up in the concrete apprehension of sensible qualities and only vaguely grasped while the quidditative aspect of the sensed object predominates, so in the peak of metaphysical abstraction wherein the concept of being as being is elaborated, something like the reverse of this takes place. The quidditative substream of the act of being (*esse*) is but vaguely and implicitly conceived while the act of being itself (*esse*) is explicitly envisaged and stands at the focus of intellectual intuition.

The habitus of metaphysics is specified, of course, by its formal object; for all habitus are specified by the formal constituent of their respective objects. When, therefore, the question is asked, "What is the formal object of metaphysics?" there can be but one answer, namely, that which formally constitutes its object, being (ID QUOD est), as being (id quod EST); and this is the act of being (*esse*).

Metaphysics cannot, consequently, be regarded as a philosophy of form or a philosophy of essence. It is a philosophy of whatever is or can be in any manner whatsoever, considered specifically in the light of the ultimate existential actuality of all reality, the act of being (*esse*). Metaphysics is definitely existential.

The existential character of the metaphysical thought of Saint Thomas Aquinas is strikingly manifested in two short sentences which he wrote in answer to an objection in the first article of the first question of his *Quaestio Disputata de Veritate*. The objection is drawn from a statement of Boethius to the effect that *esse* and *quod est* are diverse in all created things. This statement is used to support the contention that in creatures the true is diverse from being (*ens*) on the ground that the true follows from the *esse* of things, not from the *quod est*. Since *esse* is diverse from *quod est* and *quod est* is the same as being (*ens*), it should follow that the true must be diverse from being (*ens*).

In dealing with this objection, Saint Thomas states first, that when it is said that *esse* and *quod est* are diverse in creatures, a distinction is drawn between the act of being and that to which the act of being belongs; second, that the constitutive intelligibility of being (*ratio entis*) arises from the act of being, not from that to which the act of being belongs. The argument in question is therefore inconclusive; in fact it is a *non sequitur*.

Considering this statement in conjunction with the well-known description of the object of metaphysics, *ens in quantum ens,* it would appear that the first *ens* in this phrase designates the material object of the science of metaphysics, being, in the sense of whatever is or can be (which, because it is the material object, requires a formality in order to differentiate it from *ens* as the object of any and every other habitus of knowledge) and the second *ens,* qualified by *in quantum,* designates this very formal determination and sets off *ens,* object of metaphysics, from any and every other aspect of *ens* which may specify a cognitive habitus. It is this second *ens* which characterizes being formally as the object of metaphysics, since in designating the *esse* of what is as that which formally constitutes being as the object of metaphysics, it expresses the ultimate in the order of formal constituents. In other words, being (*ens*) which is the object of metaphysics, the specific constituent of the most perfect habitus of the speculative intellect, is being (*ens*) considered according to its intrinsic intelligibility as being (*ratio entis*) which is the act of being (*actus essendi*) or *esse* of what is. Paraphrasing the famous dictum *ens in quantum ens* one may say *ens,* i.e., *quod est* (with the emphasis upon *id quod*) *in quantum ens* i.e., *id quod est* (with emphasis upon *est*). . . .

Reginald Garrigou-   9. THE DERIVATION OF
Lagrange, O.P.   FIRST PRINCIPLES

The first act of the intellect, asserts Father Garrigou-Lagrange—re-echoing the
words of St. Thomas—is to know being, or reality. Thus the first and most
evident idea that the intellect conceives is the idea of being. From such
knowledge proceeds the understanding of the "first principles," which are
the immediate consequences of that idea, and which pertain to the intellect
because they pertain first to reality. The first of these principles is the
principle of *contradiction* ("Being is not nothing"), which arises immediately from the idea of being, and is a "declaration of opposition between being and nothing." Considered positively, it is the principle of
identity ("Being is not non-being," or "Being is being"). Following this
is the principle of *sufficient reason* ("Everything that is has its *raison
d'être* in itself, if of itself it exists; in something else, if of itself it does not
exist"). Various levels of this principle, however, must be distinguished.
Finally, there are the principles of *substance* ("That which exists as the
subject of existence is substance, and is distinct from its accidents or
modes"); *efficient causality* ("Every contingent being . . . needs an efficient
cause"); and *finality* ("Every agent acts for an end or purpose"). Dependent on these principles of the speculative reason is the first principle
of practical reason ("Do good and avoid evil").

St. THOMAS, following Aristotle, teaches that the intelligible being, the intelligible reality, existing in sense objects is the first object of the first act of
our intellect, i.e. that apprehension which precedes the act of judging. Listen
to his words: "The intellect's first act is to know being, reality, because an
object is knowable only in the degree in which it is actual. Hence being, entity,
reality, is the first and proper object of understanding, just as sound is the first
object of hearing." Now being, reality, is that which either exists (actual being) or can exist (possible being): "being is that whose act is to be." Further,
the being, the reality, which our intellect first understands, is not the being of

From R. Garrigou-Lagrange, O.P., *Reality* (St. Louis: B. Herder Book Co., 1950), 31–36.
Reprinted by permission of the publisher.

God, nor the being of the understanding subject, but the being, the reality, which exists in the sense world, "that which is grasped immediately by the intellect in the presence of a sense object." Our intellect, indeed, is the lowest of all intelligences, to which corresponds, as proper and proportioned object, that intelligible reality existing in the world of sense. Thus the child, knowing by sense, for example, the whiteness and the sweetness of milk, comes to know by intellect the intelligible reality of this same sense object. "By intellect he apprehends as reality that which by taste he apprehends as sweet."

In the intelligible reality thus known, our intellect seizes at once its opposition to non-being, and an opposition expressed by the principle of contradiction: Being is not non-being. "By nature our intellect knows being and the immediate characteristics of being as being, out of which knowledge arises the understanding of first principles, of the principle, say, that affirmation and denial cannot coexist (opposition between being and non-being), and other similar principles." Here lies the point of departure in Thomistic realism.

Thus our intellect knows intelligible reality and its opposition to nothing, before it knows explicitly the distinction between me and non-me. By reflection on its own act of knowledge the intellect comes to know the existence of that knowing act and its thinking subject. Next it comes to know the existence of this and that individual object, seized by the sense. In intellective knowledge, the universal comes first; sense is restricted to the individual and particular.

From this point of departure, Thomistic realism is seen to be a limited realism, since the universal, though it is not formally, as universal, in the individual sense object, has nevertheless its foundation in that object. This doctrine rises thus above two extremes, which it holds to be aberrations. One extreme is that of absolute realism held by Plato, who held that universals (he calls them "separated ideas") exist formally outside the knowing mind. The other extreme is that of Nominalism, which denies that the universal has any foundation in individual sense objects, and reduces it to a subjective representation accompanied by a common name. Each extreme leads to error. Platonist realism claims to have at least a confused intuition of the divine being (which it calls the Idea of Good). Nominalism opens the door to empiricism and positivism, which reduce first principles to experimental laws concerning sense phenomena. The principle of causality, for example, is reduced to this formula: every phenomenon presupposes an antecedent phenomenon. First principles then, conceived nominalistically, since they are no longer laws of being, of reality, but only of phenomena, do not allow the mind to rise to the knowledge of God, the first cause, beyond the phenomenal order.

This limited moderate realism of Aristotle and Aquinas is in harmony with that natural, spontaneous knowledge which we call common sense. This harmony appears most clearly in the doctrine's insistence on the objective validity and scope of first principles, the object of our first intellectual apprehension. These principles are laws, not of the spirit only, not mere logical laws, not laws merely experimental, restricted to phenomena, but necessary and un-limited laws of being, objective laws of all reality, of all that is or can be.

Yet even in these primary laws we find a hierarchy. One of them, arising immediately from the idea of being, is the simple first principle, the principle of contradiction; it is the declaration of opposition between being and nothing. It may be formulated in two ways, one negative, the other positive. The first may be given either thus: "Being is not nothing," or thus: "One and the same thing, remaining such, cannot simultaneously both be and not be." Positively considered, it becomes the principle of identity, which may be formulated to saying: "Being is not non-being." Thus we say, to illustrate: "The good is good, the bad is bad," meaning that one is not the other. According to this principle, that which is absurd, say a squared circle, is not merely unimaginable, not merely inconceivable, but absolutely irrealizable. Between the pure logic of what is conceivable and the concrete material world lie the universal laws of reality. And here already we find affirmed the validity of our intelligence in knowing the laws of extramental reality.

To this principle of contradiction or of identity is subordinated the principle of sufficient reason, which in its generality may be formulated thus: "Everything that is has its *raison d'être* in itself, if of itself it exists; in something else, if of itself it does not exist." But this generality must be understood in senses analogically different.

First: The characteristics of a thing, e.g., a circle, have their *raison d'être* in the essence (nature) of that thing.

Secondly: The existence of an effect has its *raison d'être* in the cause which produces and preserves that existence, that is to say, in the cause which is the reason not only of the "becoming," but also of the continued being of that effect. Thus that which is being by participation has its reason of existence in that which is being by essence.

Thirdly: Means have their *raison d'être* in the end, the purpose, to which they are proportioned.

Fourthly: Matter is the *raison d'être* of the corruptibility of bodies.

This principle, we see, is to be understood analogically, according to the order in which it is found, whether that order is intrinsic (the nature of a circle related to its characteristics), or extrinsic (cause, efficient or final, to its effects). When I ask the reason why, says St. Thomas, I must answer by one of the four causes. Why has the circle these properties? By its intrinsic nature. Why is this iron dilated? Because it has been heated (efficient cause). Why did you come? For such or such a purpose. Why is man mortal? Because he is a material composite, hence corruptible.

Thus the *raison d'être,* answering the question "why" (*propter quid*), is manifold in meaning, but these different meanings are proportionally the same, that is, analogically. We stand here at a central point. We see that the efficient cause presupposes the very universal idea of cause, found also in final cause, and in formal cause, as well as in the agent. Thus the principle of sufficient reason had been formulated long before Leibniz.

We come now to the principle of substance. It is thus formulated: "That which exists as the subject of existence is substance, and is distinct from its accidents or modes." Thus in everyday speech we call gold or silver a substance. This principle is derived from the principle of identity, because that which exists as subject of existence is one and the same beneath all its multiple phenomena, permanent or successive. The idea of substance is thus seen to be a mere determination of the idea of being. Inversely, being is now conceived explicitly as substantial. Hence the conclusion: The principle of substance is simply a determination of the principle of identity: accidents then find their *raison d'être* in the substance.

The principle of efficient causality also finds its formula as a function of being. Wrong is the formula: "Every phenomenon presupposes an antecedent phenomenon." The right formula runs thus: "Every contingent being, even if it exists without beginning, needs an efficient cause and, in last analysis, an uncreated cause." Briefly, every being by participation (in which we distinguish the participating subject from the participated existence) depends on the Being by essence.

The principle of finality is expressed by Aristotle and Aquinas in these terms: "Every agent acts for a purpose." The agent tends to its own good. But that tendency differs on different levels of being. It may be, first, a tendency merely natural and unconscious, for example, the tendency of the stone toward the center of the earth, or the tendency of all bodies toward the center of the universe. Secondly, this tendency may be accompanied by sense knowledge, for example, in the animal seeking its nourishment. Thirdly this tendency is guided by intelligence, which alone knows purpose as purpose, that is, knows purpose as the *raison d'être* of the means to reach that purpose.

On this principle of finality depends the first principle of practical reason and of morality. It runs thus: "Do good, avoid evil." It is founded on the idea of good, as the principle of contradiction on the idea of being. In other words: The rational being must will rational good, that good, namely, to which its powers are proportioned by the author of its nature.

All these principles are the principles of our natural intelligence. They are first manifested in that spontaneous form of intelligence which we call common sense, that is, the natural aptitude of intelligence, before all philosophic culture, to judge things sanely. Common sense, natural reason, seizes these self-evident principles from its notion of intelligible reality. But this natural common sense could not yet give these principles an exact and universal formulation.

Existentialist

Nikolai Berdyaev   10. THE EXISTENTIALIST
                                 VIEW

For Thomists, the cognitive act *par excellence* or the intuition into being, is a
purely intellectual act. For many existentialist thinkers, on the other hand,
"cognition" is a considerably broader term. Berdyaev—who sometimes
accepted, and sometimes rejected, the label "existentialist"—denounced
the notion that knowledge is "abstractive bare-bones," and vehemently
defended the notion that it is thoroughly concrete, passionate, and even
visceral in character—yet he believed it is always "a spiritual struggle for
meaning." The Promethean cast of his language, however, leaves little
doubt that he shares with many other existentialist thinkers a feeling for
the concrete "situation" of the knower.

Knowing, Berdyaev believes, cannot be abstracted from the person-knowing, and the person-knowing cannot be wrenched from "a corporate experience of his brothers in spirit." True knowledge is therefore not mere
objectivization—which means, for Berdyaev, a construct "thing" with
no real relation to spiritual reality—a passive reflection. It is a "creative
penetration into meaning," and a transcendent act out of the closed circle
of mortality.

Metaphysics is not a science, notes Berdyaev, because as "the apprehension
of spirit, in spirit, and through spirit," it can never be equated with the
objectivization of the sciences. It is not so much being that philosophical
knowledge pursues as the knowledge of truths, which is "an uplifting
movement of the spirit" and "a spiritual ascent." Knowledge is both personal and social. It is a function of what Berdyaev has called "solitude" and
"society." Each of these terms has two faces, however: the one objectivized
and thing-ridden; the other communicative, person-conscious, subjective,
and existentialist. Berdyaev uses the terms "subjective" and "objective"
after the fashion of Kierkegaard. Objective means dispassionate, un-
serious, bourgeois, abstract, and spiritless; subjective means committed,
authentic, concrete, serious, and passionate. Hence, philosophy's knowledge, he says, is really devoted to the passionate penetration, by a concrete
person, of spiritual meaning. It is always subjective, and cannot—without
losing its identity—become part of the objective order of things.

Extracted from Berdyaev's *The Beginning and the End* (New York, 1952), this selection
is here reprinted with the kind permission of Harper & Brothers and Geoffrey Bles Ltd.

THE DISCOVERY of reason by Greek philosophy was an important event in the history of knowledge. Man brought into the light forces which had hitherto been in a dreamlike state within him. He took possession of his reason and reason became independent. The emotional life of man had depended upon his impressions of the world of sense and his thought was entirely under the sway of mythological feelings about the world and tradition. Reason, however, is both itself free and it is a liberating agent; it both enriches man and impoverishes him.

The philosopher believed that reason lifted him up to the world of ideas, to the noumenal world. This opinion Kant subjected to criticism. But almost throughout the history of philosophy the apprehending mind remained faithful to the conviction that cognition is a purely intellectual act, that there exists a universal reason and that reason is always one and the same and remains true to its nature. But in reality cognition is emotional and passionate in character. It is a spiritual struggle for meaning, and it is such not merely in this or that line of thought or school, but in every true philosopher even although he may not recognize the fact himself. Cognition is not a dispassionate understudy of reality. The significance of a philosophy is decided by the passionate intensity of the philosopher as a man, as one who is present behind his effort to know. It is decided by the intensity of the will to truth and meaning; it is the whole man who takes knowledge of a thing. Dilthey, who was one of the forerunners of existential philosophy, says with truth that thinking is a function of life. The whole man, not reason, constructs metaphysics; it is not the autonomy of the intellect which needs to be asserted, but the autonomy of spirit, the autonomy of the knowing person as a complete being.

The process of thinking cannot be separated from the person who thinks and the person who thinks cannot be separated from the corporate experience of his brothers in spirit. The knowing person may, as an effect of his cognition, attain to an objective coolness of expression, but this is a secondary process of objectification. What is primary is the man's intuition as one who exists in the fullness of existence. Man apprehends emotionally to a greater extent than intellectually, and the view that emotional cognition is "subjective" in the bad sense of the word while intellectual cognition is "objective" in the good sense of the word is entirely wrong, and in any case it is expressed in terms which are inaccurate. To quicken the subject matter of knowledge into life is in any case a process which is emotional rather than intellectual in character. The intuitivism of Bergson and Scheler as well as of Schelling, to say nothing of Nietzsche, is non-intellectualist.

Purely intellectual discursive knowledge constructs an objectified world out of touch with reality. What is decisively important in knowledge is not the logical process of thought, which ranks as an instrument, and which takes control only in the centre of the path, but the emotional and volitional tension which is attributable to the spirit as a whole. Knowledge is a creative activity, not a passive reflection of things, and every act of creation includes knowledge. Intuition is not only the perception of something; it is also a creative penetration into meaning; and more than that, the very existence of meaning presupposes a creative condition of spirit.

Phenomenological philosophy requires passivity on the part of the subject. Existential philosophy, on the other hand, requires activity and passion in the subject. The world of ideas, the noumenal world, assumes this activity and passion of the spirit; it is not a congealed world which is devoid of the movement of life. An act of cognition is an act of transcendence; it is a way out from the closed circle and a way which opens out upwards. It is possible to conceive of the transcendent only because of the existence of such a transcending act. But the transcending act is an intense effort of the whole being. It is its uplifting power and its state of exaltation.

The pursuit of a metaphysics which is completely scientific in form, of metaphysics as a strict and objective science is the pursuit of a will-o'-the-wisp. Metaphysics can only be the apprehension of spirit, in spirit, and through spirit. Metaphysics is in the subject, which creates spiritual values and makes a transcending act, not into the object but into its own self-revealing depth. Metaphysics is empirical in the sense that it is based upon spiritual experience. It is a symbolism of that experience. Philosophical knowledge is knowledge attained by means of images to a greater extent than knowledge reached through concepts. The concept is important only as playing a secondary part. In Hegel the concept does not possess its traditional logical significance; it acquires not only a metaphysical but even an almost mystical meaning.

The principal and decisive thing about the philosopher has not by any means been the assertions which he has contributed for the objective use. The apprehending mind has never discovered truth by the assistance of the logical apparatus by which he endeavours to convince others. Philosophical knowledge is the knowledge of truth, of what is true and right, not of being, for the apprehension of truth is an uplifting movement of the spirit towards truth; it is a spiritual ascent, an entering into truth. There is, however, a social aspect of knowledge and too little attention has been paid to it. Knowledge is a form of communication and intercourse among human beings. At the same time knowledge is above all a gesture on the part of him who seeks it, which places him face to face not with some other, or others in general, but face to face with truth. It is to stand facing the primary reality which philosophers have been fond of calling "being." Human knowledge, and philosophical knowledge in particular, depends upon the spiritual condition of men, upon the scope of their minds, and the forms of communion and community which exist among men have an enormous part to play in this.

Philosophical knowledge is personal in character and the more personal it is the more important it is. But the personal character of knowledge doe<

not mean the isolation of personality. Personality gets to know things in com-munion and community with the world and with men; it enters into union with world experience and world thought. Knowledge is at the same time personal and social. The degrees of spiritual community which hold among men are here of very great importance. All this leads to the fundamental truth, that knowledge is anthropological, but this will not by any means denote relativism.

There is one very important truth which must be recognized in the theory of knowledge, and that is that the person who knows is himself existent, that he himself is "being," and that the recognition of the meaning of the world is possible only in the subject, not in the object, that is to say in human existence. It is indeed in this that the truth of existential philosophy is to be found. If it is not to be naively and unconsciously anthropocentric, philosophy must be consciously and critically anthropocentric. Philosophy is anthropocentric but the philosopher ought to be theocentric.

Comprehension of the mystery of the world in human existence is a pos-sibility only because man is a microcosm and a microtheos. There is no cos-mos in the object world of phenomena. There is no God in the objective world, but there is a cosmos in man. God is in man, and through man there is a way out into another world. That protagonist of the humanist theory of knowledge, F. S. Schiller, says with trust that a depersonalization and dehumanization of knowledge has taken place and that the personalizing and humanizing of it is imperative. Man is the measure of things, but there is a higher measure than man. St. Augustine was perhaps the first to turn to the existential phi-losophy of the subject. He set forth the principle of interior experience and of the credibility of the mind to itself. He recognized doubt as a source of cred-ibility and as a proof of one's own existence. To him the soul was the whole personality.

The theory of orderly and regular development in knowledge does not settle accounts with the invasion of individuality. It may be taken as beyond doubt that the act of appraisal, which has such an immense part to play in cognition, is performed above all by feeling, not by the intellect. Nietzsche, who did his philosophizing with a sledge hammer, said that the philosopher ought to be one who gives instructions and imposes commands. This means that in philosophical knowledge a rearrangement of values and the creation of values takes place. Philosophy seeks to break out from the slavery of this world into another world, towards a perfect free life, and deliverance from the suffering and ugliness of the world as we have it. To strive after objective knowledge is an illusion and in any case it is a mistake in terminology. Dis-passionate knowledge there cannot be and never has been among real phi-losphers; it can only exist in dissertations which are devoid of any creative gift. Even in Spinoza himself knowledge was nothing if not passionate. In-tellectual passion may be a source of perceptual transcendence. Plato, the greatest of all philosophers, was an erotic philosopher. There was an erotic pull in the rationalist Spinoza, and in the panlogist Hegel, to say nothing of such philosophers as Kierkegaard and Nietzsche.

The philosopher has fallen in love with wisdom. In real true-born philosophy there is the eros of truth; there is the erotic attraction of infinite and the absolute. Philosophical creativity is intoxicated with thought. Philosophical cognition can only be based upon experience, upon spiritual experience, and within that it is the spirit as one whole which accomplishes the act of cognition. There is bitterness in knowledge. But knowledge is by nature a liberating agent. Philosophical knowledge is called upon to set man free from the power of the objectified world and from his intolerable servitude to it. Not the will to power but the will to meaning and to freedom is the driving force of philosophical knowledge. As a system of concepts metaphysics is an impossibility, it is possible only as the symbolism of spiritual experience.

The conflict between subject and object, between freedom and necessity, between meaning and the lack of it is, in the language of metaphysics, a symbolic conflict which in "this" provides symbols of "another." Behind the finite the infinite is concealed, and it gives signs of its presence. The depth of my ego is steeped in infinity and eternity and it is only a superficial layer of my ego which is illuminated by the mind, rationalized, and recognized on the basis of the antithesis between subject and object. But out of the depth signs are given, whole worlds are there, and there is all our world and its destiny. Hartmann is right when he says that the problem of cognition is a metaphysical problem, and Heidegger is right when he says that we understand the EXISTENZIELE as an interpretation of our own selves. But what is truth? That is the eternal question. The answer that the Gospels give to this question has its importance even in philosophy.

Gabriel Marcel   # 11. THE ONTOLOGICAL
                                                      MYSTERY

In agreement with Berdyaev, Marcel emphasizes in this essay the importance of the spiritual state of human society for the knowledge of reality. And he contrasts a situation from which being is "erased" to one in which it is "exposed."

This selection is extracted from the initial chapter of Marcel's *The Philosophy of Existence,* titled "On the Ontological Mystery." Reproduced by courtesy of the author; Harvill Press Ltd., London; and Philosophical Library, Inc., New York.

Modern man, he points out, lacks the sense of being—the sense of ontological mystery—because he lives in an untragic, functionalized, spectator-like world. When modern man breaks down under the pressure of a time-tabled, mechanical existence, he turns for salvation to the aseptic hospital. In such a despairing world, consisting of those "who have retired from life," the ontological need "is exhausted in exact proportion to the breaking up of personality on the one hand, and, on the other, to the triumph of the category of the 'purely natural' and the consequent atrophy of the faculty of wonder."

But the *way into being* is through one's own personhood. This implies turning one's back on abstractions and theoretics, and recognizing that "the ontological status of the investigator assumes a decisive importance" in the recovery of the sense of the real. For "I" who frame the problem of being cannot remain outside of it.

Marcel indicates that the process of thought suffers infinite regression. A recognition of this fact gives support to the attempt to transcend thought and to see that "this process takes place within an affirmation of being—an affirmation which I am rather than an affirmation which I utter." The investigator is consequently the stage rather than the subject of any investigation into being.

It is at this point of transcension, Marcel notes, that the *meta-problematical,* or mystery, occurs. This is located in an overcoming of the difference between "the subject who asserts the existence of being" and "being as asserted by that subject." Being thereupon demonstrates its primacy over knowledge. For knowledge is "quarantined" by being, or "environed" by being. All epistemology presupposes this fact.

The vantage point on being, Marcel asserts, is recollection, which is "an inward hold, an inward reflection, . . . the ontological basis of memory." Rather than the term "intuition into being," then, he suggests the term "assurance." Such assurance, however, is not one-dimensional and untragic, but precisely tragic because it is exposed to the realities of despair, suicide, and betrayal. Marcel concludes that it is only through recognition of the drama and conflict within personality "that metaphysical thought grasps and defines itself."

RATHER THAN TO begin with abstract definitions and dialectical arguments which may be discouraging at the outset, I should like to start with a sort of global and intuitive characterisation of the man in whom the sense of the ontological—the sense of being—is lacking, or, to speak more correctly, of the man who has lost the awareness of this sense. Generally speaking, modern man is in this condition; if ontological demands worry him at all, it is only dully, as an obscure impulse. Indeed I wonder if a psychoanalytical method, deeper and more discerning than any that has been evolved until now, would not reveal the morbid effects of the repression of this sense and of the ignoring of this need. . . .

Travelling on the Underground, I often wonder with a kind of dread what can be the inward reality of the life of this or that man employed on the railway—the man who opens the doors, for instance, or the one who punches the tickets. Surely everything both within him and outside him conspires to his functions as worker, as trade-union member or as voter, but with his vital functions as well. The rather horrible expression "timetable" perfectly describes his life. So many hours for each function. Sleep too is a function which must be discharged so that the other functions may be exercised in their turn. The same with pleasure, with relaxation; it is logical that the weekly allowance of recreation should be determined by an expert on hygiene; recreation is a psycho-organic function which must not be neglected any more than, for instance, the function of sex. We need go no further; this sketch is sufficient to suggest the emergence of a kind of vital schedule; the details will vary with the country, the climate, the profession, etc., but what matters is that there is a schedule.

It is true that certain disorderly elements—sickness, accidents of every sort—will break in on the smooth working of the system. It is therefore natural that the individual should be overhauled at regular intervals like a watch (this is often done in America). The hospital plays the part of the inspection bench or the repair shop. And it is from this same standpoint of function that such essential problems as birth control will be examined.

As for death, it becomes, objectively and functionally, the scrapping of what has ceased to be of use and must be written off as total loss.

I need hardly insist on the stifling impression of sadness produced by this functionalised world. It is sufficient to recall the dreary image of the retired official, or those urban Sundays when the passers-by look like people who have retired from life. In such a world, there is something mocking and sinister even in the tolerance awarded to the man who has retired from his work.

But besides the sadness felt by the onlooker, there is the dull, intolerable unease of the actor himself who is reduced to living as though he were in fact submerged by his functions. This uneasiness is enough to show that there is in all this some appalling mistake, some ghastly misinterpretation, implanted in defenceless minds by an increasingly inhuman social order and an equally inhuman philosophy (for if the philosophy has prepared the way for the order, the order has also shaped the philosophy).

I have written on another occasion that, provided it is taken in its metaphysical and not its physical sense, the distinction between the full and the empty seems to me more fundamental than that between the one and the many. This is particularly applicable to the case in point. Life in a world centred on function is liable to despair because in reality this world is empty, it rings hollow; and if it resists this temptation, it is only to the extent that there come into play from within it and in its favour certain hidden forces which are beyond its power to conceive or to recognise. . . .

In such a world the ontological need, the need of being, is exhausted in exact proportion to the breaking up of personality on the one hand and, on the other, to the triumph of the category of the "purely natural" and the consequent atrophy of the faculty of wonder.

But to come at last to the ontological need itself; can we not approach it directly and attempt to define it? In reality this can only be done to a limited extent. For reasons which I shall develop later, I suspect that the characteristic of this need is that it can never be wholly clear to itself.

To try to describe it without distorting it we shall have to say something like this:

Being is—or should be—necessary. It is impossible that everything should be reduced to a play of successive appearances which are inconsistent with each other ("inconsistent" is essential), or, in the words of Shakespeare, to "a tale told by an idiot." I aspire to participate in this being, in this reality—and perhaps this aspiration is already a degree of participation, however rudimentary. . . .

As for defining the word "being," let us admit that it is extremely difficult. I would merely suggest this method of approach: being is what withstands—or what would withstand—an exhaustive analysis bearing on the data of experience and aiming to reduce them step by step to elements increasingly devoid of intrinsic or significant value. . . .

When the pessimist Besme says in *La Ville* that nothing is, he means precisely this, that there is no experience that withstands this analytical test. And it is always towards death regarded as the manifestation, the proof of this ultimate nothingness, that the kind of inverted apologetic which arises out of absolute pessimism will inevitably gravitate.

A philosophy which refuses to endorse the ontological need is, nevertheless, possible; indeed, generally speaking, contemporary thought tends towards this abstention. . . .

These preliminary reflections on the ontological need are sufficient to bring out its indeterminate character and to reveal a fundamental paradox. To formulate this need is to raise a host of questions: Is there such a thing as being? What is it? etc. Yet immediately an abyss opens under my feet: I who ask these questions about being, how can I be sure that I exist?

Yet surely I, who formulate this problem, should be able to remain outside it—before or beyond it? Clearly this is not so. The more I consider it the more I find that this problem tends inevitably to invade the proscenium from which it is excluded in theory: it is only by means of a fiction that Idealism in its traditional form seeks to maintain on the margin of being the consciousness which asserts it or denies it.

So I am inevitably forced to ask: Who am I—I who question being? How am I qualified to begin this investigation? If I do not exist, how can I succeed in it? And if I do exist, how can I be sure of this fact? . . .

It should be noted that this difficulty never arises at a time when I am actually faced with a problem to be solved. In such a case I work on the data, but everything leads me to believe that I need not take into account the I who is at work—it is a factor which is presupposed and nothing more.

Here, on the contrary, what I would call the ontological status of the investigator assumes a decisive importance. Yet so long as I am concerned with thought itself I seem to follow an endless regression. But by the very fact of recognising it as endless I transcend it in a certain way: I see that this process takes place within an affirmation of being—an affirmation which I am, rather than an affirmation which I utter: by uttering it I break it, I divide it, I am on the point of betraying it.

It might be said, by way of an approximation, that my inquiry into being presupposes an affirmation in regard to which I am, in a sense, passive, and of which I am the stage rather than the subject. But this is only at the extreme limit of thought, a limit which I cannot reach without falling into contradiction. I am therefore led to assume or to recognise a form of participation which has the reality of a subject; this participation cannot be, by definition, an object of thought; it cannot serve as a solution—it appears beyond the realm of problems: it is meta-problematical.

Conversely, it will be seen that, if the meta-problematical can be asserted at all, it must be conceived as transcending the opposition between the subject who asserts the existence of being, on the one hand, and being as asserted by that subject, on the other, and as underlying it in a given sense. To postulate the meta-problematical is to postulate the primacy of being over knowledge (not of being as asserted, but of being as asserting itself); it is to recognise that knowledge is, as it were, environed by being, that it is interior to it in a certain sense—a sense perhaps analogous to that which Paul Claudel tried to define in his *Art Poétique*. From this standpoint, contrary to what epistemology seeks vainly to establish, there exists well and truly a mystery of cognition; knowledge is contingent on a participation in being for which no epistemology can account because it continually presupposes it. . . .

It will be said: The meta-problematical of which you speak is after all a content of thought; how then should we not ask ourselves what is its mode of existence? What assures us of its existence at all? Is it not itself problematical in the highest degree?

My answer is categorical: To think, or, rather, to assert, the meta-problematical is to assert it as indubitably real, as a thing of which I cannot doubt without falling into contradiction. We are in a sphere where it is no longer possible to dissociate the idea itself from the certainty or the degree of certainty which pertains to it. Because this idea is certainty, it is the assurance of itself; it is, in this sense, something other and something more than an idea. As for the term content of thought which figured in the objection, it is deceptive in the highest degree. For content is, when all is said and done, derived from experience; whereas it is only by a way of liberation and detachment from experience that we can possibly rise to the level of the meta-problematical and of mystery. This liberation must be real; this detachment must be real; they must not be an abstraction, that is to say, a fiction recognized as such.

And this at last brings us to recollection, for it is in recollection and in this alone that this detachment is accomplished. I am convinced, for my part, that no ontology—that is to say, no apprehension of ontological mystery in whatever degree—is possible except to a being who is capable of recollecting himself, and of thus proving that he is not a living creature pure and simple, a creature, that is to say, which is at the mercy of its life and without a hold upon it.

It should be noted that recollection, which has received little enough attention from pure philosophers, is very difficult to define—if only because it reconciles in itself these two aspects of the antinomy. The word means what it says—the act whereby I re-collect myself as a unity; but this hold, this grasp upon myself, is also relaxation and abandon. Abandon to . . . relaxation in the presence of . . . —yet there is no noun for these prepositions to govern. The way stops at the threshold.

Here, as in every other sphere, problems will be raised, and it is the psychologist who will raise them. All that must be noted is that the psychologist is no more in a position to shed light on the metaphysical bearing of recollection than on the noetic value of knowledge.

It is within recollection that I take up my position—or, rather, I become capable of taking up my position—in regard to my life; I withdraw from it in a certain way, but not as the pure subject of cognition; in this withdrawal I carry with me that which I am and which perhaps my life is not. This brings out the gap between my being and my life. I am not my life; and if I can judge my life—a fact I cannot deny without falling into a radical scepticism which is nothing other than despair—it is only on condition that I encounter myself within recollection beyond all possible judgment and, I would add, beyond all representation. Recollection is doubtless what is least spectacular in the soul; it does not consist in looking at something, it is an inward hold, an inward reflection, and it might be asked in passing whether it should not be seen as the ontological basis of memory—that principle of effective and non-representational unity on which the possibility of remembrance rests. The double meaning of "recollection" in English is revealing.

We are here at the most difficult point of our whole discussion. Rather than to speak of intuition in this context, we should say that we are dealing with an assurance which underlies the entire development of thought, even of discursive thought; it can therefore be approached only by a second reflection—a reflection whereby I ask myself how and from what starting point I was able to proceed in my initial reflection, which itself postulated the ontological, but without knowing it. This second reflection is recollection in the measure in which recollection can be self-conscious.

It is indeed annoying to have to use such abstract language in a matter which is not one of dialectics *ad usum philosophorum*, but of what is the most vital and, I would add, the most dramatic moment in the rhythm of consciousness seeking to be conscious of itself.

It is this dramatic aspect which must now be brought out.

Let us recall what we said earlier on: that the ontological need, the need of being, can deny itself. In a different context we said that being and life do not coincide; my life, and by reflection all life, may appear to me as forever inadequate to something which I carry within me, which in a sense I am, but which reality rejects and excludes. Despair is possible in any form, at any moment and to any degree, and this betrayal may seem to be counselled, if not forced upon us, by the very structure of the world we live in. The deathly aspect of this world may, from a given standpoint, be regarded as a cease-less incitement to denial and to suicide. It could even be said in this sense that the fact that suicide is always possible is the essential starting point of any genuine metaphysical thought.

It may be surprising to find in the course of this calm and abstract reason-ing such verbal star turns—words so emotionally charged—as "suicide" and "betrayal." They are not a concession to sensationalism. I am convinced that it is in drama and through drama that metaphysical thought grasps and de-fines itself *in concreto*. Two years ago, in a lecture on the "Problem of Chris-tian Philosophy" which he delivered at Louvain, M. Jacques Maritain said: "There is nothing easier for a philosophy than to become tragic, it has only to let itself go to its human weight." The allusion was doubtless to the specu-lation of a Heidegger. I believe, on the contrary, that the natural trend of phi-losophy leads it into a sphere where it seems that tragedy has simply vanished, evaporated at the touch of abstract thought. This is borne out by the work of many contemporary Idealists. Because they ignore the person, offering it up to I know not what ideal truth, to what principle of pure inwardness, they are unable to grasp those tragic factors of human existence to which I have alluded above; they banish them, together with illness and everything akin to it, to I know not what disreputable suburb of thought outside the ken of any philosopher worthy of the name. But, as I have stressed earlier on, this attitude is intimately bound up with the rejection of the ontological need; in-deed, it is the same thing.

If I have stressed despair, betrayal and suicide, it is because these are the most manifest expressions of the will to negation as applied to being.

Let us take despair. I have in mind the act by which one despairs of reality as a whole, as one might despair of a person. This appears to be the result, or the immediate translation into other terms, of a kind of balance sheet. Inasmuch as I am able to evaluate the world of reality (and, when all is said and done, what I am unable to evaluate is for me as if it were not), I can find nothing in it that withstands that process of dissolution at the heart of things which I have discovered and traced. I believe that at the root of despair there is always this affirmation: "There is nothing in the realm of reality to which I can give credit—no security, no guarantee." It is a statement of complete insolvency.

As against this, hope is what implies credit. Contrary to what was thought by Spinoza, who seems to me to have confused two quite distinct notions, fear is correlated to desire and not to hope, whereas what is negatively correlated to hope is the act which consists in putting things at their worst—an act which is strikingly illustrated by what is known as defeatism, and which is ever in danger of being degraded into the desire of the worst. Hope consists in asserting that there is at the heart of being, beyond all data, beyond all inventories and all calculations, a mysterious principle which is in connivance with me, which cannot but will that which I will, if what I will deserves to be willed and is, in fact, willed by the whole of my being.

We have now come to the centre of what I have called the ontological mystery, and the simplest illustrations will be the best. To hope against all hope that a person whom I love will recover from a disease which is said to be incurable is to say: It is impossible that I should be alone in willing this cure; it is impossible that reality in its inward depth should be hostile or so much as indifferent to what I assert is in itself a good. It is quite useless to tell me of discouraging cases or examples: beyond all experience, all probability, all statistics, I assert that a given order shall be re-established, that reality is on my side willing it to be so. I do not wish: I assert; such is the prophetic tone of true hope.

No doubt I shall be told: "In the immense majority of cases this is an illusion." But it is of the essence of hope to exclude the consideration of cases; moreover, it can be shown that there exists an ascending dialect of hope, whereby hope rises to a plane which transcends the level of all possible empirical disproof—the plane of salvation as opposed to that of success in whatever form.

It remains true, nevertheless, that the correlation of hope and despair subsists until the end; they seem to me inseparable. I mean that while the structure of the world we live in permits—and may even seem to counsel—absolute despair, yet it is only such a world that can give rise to an unconquerable hope. If only for this reason, we cannot be sufficiently thankful to the great pessimists in the history of thought; they have carried through an inward experience which needed to be made and of which the radical possibility no apologetics should disguise; they have prepared our minds to understand that despair can be what it was for Nietzsche (though on an infra-ontological level and in a domain fraught with mortal dangers) the springboard to the loftiest affirmation.

At the same time, it remains certain that, for as much as hope is a mystery, its mystery can be ignored or converted into a problem. Hope is then regarded as a desire which wraps itself up in illusory judgments to distort an objective reality which it is interested in disguising from itself. What happens in this case is what we have already observed in connection with encounter and with love; it is because mystery can—and, in a sense, logically must—be degraded into a problem that an interpretation such as that of Spinoza, with all the confusion it implies, had to be put forward sooner or later. It is important and must be stressed that this attitude has nothing against it so long as our standpoint is on the hither-side of the realm of the ontological. Just as long as my attitude towards reality is that of someone who is not involved in it, but who judges it his duty to draw up its minutes as exactly as possible (and this is by definition the attitude of the scientist), I am justified in maintaining in regard to it a sort of principle of mistrust, which in theory is unlimited in its application; such is the legitimate standpoint of the workman in the laboratory, who must in no way prejudge the result of his analysis, and who can all the better envisage the worst, because at this level the very notion of worst is empty of meaning. But an investigation of this sort, which is just like that of an accountant going through the books, takes place on the hither-side of the order of mystery, an order in which the problem encroaches upon its own data.

It would indeed be a profound illusion to believe that I can still maintain this same attitude when I undertake an inquiry, say, into the value of life; it would be paralogism to suppose that I can pursue such an inquiry as though my own life were not an issue.

Hence, between hope—the reality of hope in the heart of the one whom it inhabits—and the judgment brought to bear upon it by a mind chained to objectivity there exists the same barrier as that which separates a pure mystery from a problem.

Martin Heidegger

12. THE FUNDAMENTAL QUESTION OF METAPHYSICS

The title of this essay, Heidegger himself points out, is deliberately ambiguous, in that it implies an erroneous relation between metaphysics and being. He believes that "being *as such* is precisely hidden from metaphysics."

It is true, he says, that the question of the "disclosure of being" casts a light on the essence of metaphysics hitherto hidden. But before any answer can be given regarding the task of metaphysics, one must first ask: "What is the fundamental question about being?" Such a question indicates not only the function of metaphysics but, more importantly, the meaning of the ground of being itself.

Heidegger proposes such a question in the form: "Why are there essents [i.e., "beings"]* rather than nothing?" Under examination, he says, the question consists of two parts: (a) "Why are there essents?" and (b) "Rather than nothing?" At first glance, he argues, the second part is a seemingly useless appendage, since allegedly to speak of *nothing* is to turn it into something. But, that tradition has paired the essent with its contrary, nothing, is for Heidegger an important fact.

Once such a question with its obvious extremes ("either essents—or nothing") is expressed, the whole foundation under the question is washed away. For "with our question we place ourselves in the essent in such a way that it loses its self-evident character *as the essent.*"

There is a crucial ambiguity in the term "essent": there is that which applies to a *that,* an object, a *this-particular,* and that which applies to a foundational character—to "that which 'brings it about,' so to speak, that this thing is an essent rather than a nonessent." The contrast is therefore between a *thing-which-is* (*ónta*) and *is-ness* (*einái*).

Certainly, Heidegger continues, "we encounter the essent everywhere; it sustains and drives us, enchants and fills us, elevates and disappoints us." Yet essent remains an empty term. One must still ask, Heidegger suggests, "where is, and wherein consists, the being of the essent?" He answers his own question by the return to a meditation on the second part ("rather than nothing?") of the question he called fundamental.

Being is nowhere, he says. It "remains unfindable, almost like nothing, or ultimately *quite* so. Then, in the end, the word 'being' is no more than an empty word." When we ask the question of being—"How does it stand with being?"—we find that being is not sufficient ground of itself. In more than a manner of speaking, it requires *nothing* as a "backdrop."

Heidegger does not leave the matter, however, by a denial of the difference between *is* and *is-not.* What matters ultimately, he says, "is not that the word 'being' remains a mere sound and its meaning a vapor, but that we have fallen away from what this word says and for the moment cannot find our way back."

IN THE CURRENT INTERPRETATION the "question of being" signifies the inquiry into the essent as such (metaphysics). But from the standpoint of *Sein und Zeit,* the "question of being" means the inquiry into being as such.

---

* "Essents" is a term coined by the translator of this passage for Heidegger's term *die Seienden.* It means "existents" or "things that are"—ED. NOTE.

This signification of the title is also the appropriate one from the standpoint of the subject matter and of linguistics; for the "question of being" in the sense of the metaphysical question regarding the essent as such does *not inquire* thematically into being. In this way of asking, being remains forgotten.

But just as ambiguous as the "question of being" referred to in the title is what is said about "forgetfulness of being." It is pointed out—quite correctly—that metaphysics inquires into the being of the essent and that it is therefore an obvious absurdity to impute a forgetfulness of being to metaphysics.

But if we consider the question of being in the sense of an inquiry into being as such, it becomes clear to anyone who follows our thinking that being *as such* is precisely hidden from metaphysics, and remains forgotten—and so radically that the forgetfulness of being, which itself falls into forgetfulness, is the unknown but enduring impetus to metaphysical questioning.

If for the treatment of the "question of being" in the indeterminate sense we choose the name "metaphysics," then the title of the present work is ambiguous. For at first sight the questioning seems to remain within the sphere of the essent as such, yet at the very first sentence it strives to depart from this sphere in order to consider and inquire into another realm. Actually the title of the work is deliberately ambiguous.

The fundamental question of this work is of a different kind from the leading question of metaphysics. Taking what was said in *Sein und Zeit* (pp. 21f. and 37f.) as a starting point, we inquired into the "*disclosure of being.*" Disclosure of being means the unlocking of what forgetfulness of being closes and hides. And it is through this questioning that a light first falls on the *essence* of metaphysics that had hitherto also been hidden.

"Introduction to metaphysics" means accordingly: an introduction to the asking of the fundamental question. But questions and particularly fundamental questions do not just occur like stones and water. Questions are not found ready-made like shoes and clothes and books. Questions *are,* and are only as they are actually asked. A leading into the asking of the fundamental questions is consequently not a going to something that lies and stands somewhere; no, this leading-to must first awaken and create the questioning. The leading is itself a questioning advance, a preliminary questioning. It is a leading for which in the very nature of things there can be no following. When we hear of disciples, "followers," as in a school of philosophy for example, it means that the nature of questioning is misunderstood. Such schools can exist only in the domain of scientific and technical work. Here everything has its definite hierarchical order. This work is also an indispensable part of philosophy and has today been lost. But the best technical ability can never replace the actual power of seeing and inquiring and speaking.

"Why are there essents rather than nothing?" That is the question. To state the interrogative sentence, even in a tone of questioning, is not yet to question. To repeat the interrogative sentence several times in succession does not necessarily breathe life into the questioning; on the contrary, saying the sentence over and over may well dull the questioning. . . .

"Why are there essents rather than nothing?" In what direction can it be asked? First of all the question is accessible in the interrogative sentence, which gives a kind of approximation of it. Hence its linguistic formulation must be correspondingly broad and loose. Let us consider our sentence in this respect. "Why are there essents rather than nothing?" The sentence has a caesura. "Why are there essents?" With these words the question is actually asked. The formulation of the question includes: 1) a definite indication of what is put into question, of what is *questioned;* 2) an indication of what the question is about, of what is asked. For it is clearly indicated what the question is about, namely the essent. What is asked after, that which is asked, is the why, i.e. the ground. What follows in the interrogative sentence, "rather than nothing," is only an appendage, which may be said to turn up of its own accord if for purposes of introduction we permit ourselves to speak loosely, a turn of phrase that says nothing further about the question or the object of questioning, an ornamental flourish. Actually the question is far more unambiguous and definite without such an appendage, which springs only from the prolixity of loose discourse. "Why are there essents?" The addition "rather than nothing" is dropped not only because we are striving for a strict formulation of the question but even more because it says nothing. For why should we go on to ask about nothing? Nothing is simply nothing. Here there is nothing more to inquire about. And above all, in talking about nothing or nothingness, we are not making the slightest advance toward the knowledge of the essent.

He who speaks of nothing does not know what he is doing. In speaking of nothing he makes it into a something. In speaking he speaks against what he intended. He contradicts himself. But discourse that contradicts itself offends against the fundamental rule of discourse (*logos*), against "logic." To speak of nothing is illogical. He who speaks and thinks illogically is unscientific. But he who goes so far as to speak of nothing in the realm of philosophy, where logic has its very home, exposes himself most particularly to the accusation of offending against the fundamental rule of all thinking. Such a speaking about nothing consists entirely of meaningless propositions. Moreover: he who takes the nothing seriously is allying himself with nothingness. He is patently promoting the spirit of negation and serving the cause of disintegration. Not only is speaking of nothing utterly repellent to thought; it also undermines all culture and all faith. What disregards the fundamental law of thought and also destroys faith and the will to build is pure nihilism.

On the basis of such considerations we shall do well, in our interrogative sentence, to cross out the superfluous words "rather than nothing" and limit the sentence to the simple and strict form: "Why are there essents?"

To this there would be no objection if . . . if in formulating our question, if altogether, in the asking of this question, we were as free as it may have seemed to us up to this point. But in asking this question we stand in a tradition. For philosophy has always, from time immemorial, asked about the ground of what is. With this question it began and with this question it will end, provided that it ends in greatness and not in an impotent decline. Ever since the question about the essent began, the question about the nonessent, about nothing, has gone side by side with it. And not only outwardly, in the manner of a by-product. Rather, the question about nothing has been asked with the same breadth, depth, and originality as the question about the essent. The manner of asking about nothing may be regarded as a gauge and hallmark for the manner of asking about the essent.

If we bear this in mind, the interrogative sentence uttered in the beginning, "Why are there essents rather than nothing?" seems to express the question about the essent far more adequately than the abbreviated version. It is not looseness of speech or prolixity that leads us to mention nothing. Nor is it an invention of ours; no, it is only strict observance of the original tradition regarding the meaning of the fundamental question. . . .

It is perfectly true that we cannot talk about nothing, as though it were a thing like the rain outside or a mountain or any object whatsoever. In principle, nothingness remains inaccessible to science. The man who wishes truly to speak about nothing must of necessity become unscientific. But this is a misfortune only so long as one supposes that scientific thinking is the only authentic rigorous thought, and that it alone can and must be made into the standard of philosophical thinking. But the reverse is true. All scientific thought is merely a derived form of philosophical thinking, which proceeded to freeze into its scientific cast. Philosophy never arises out of science or through science and it can never be accorded equal rank with the sciences. No, it is prior in rank, and not only "logically" or in a table representing the system of the sciences. Philosophy stands in a totally different realm and order. Only poetry stands in the same order as philosophy and its thinking, though poetry and thought are not the same thing. To speak of nothing will always remain a horror and an absurdity for science. But aside from the philosopher, the poet can do so—and not because, as common sense supposes, poetry is without strict rules, but because the spirit of poetry (only authentic and great poetry is meant) is essentially superior to the spirit that prevails in all mere science. By virtue of this superiority the poet always speaks as though the essent were being expressed and invoked for the first time. Poetry, like the thinking of the philosopher, has always so much world space to spare that in it each thing— a tree, a mountain, a house, the cry of a bird—loses all indifference and commonplaceness. . . .

It is already becoming clearer that this "rather than nothing" is no superfluous appendage to the real question, but is an essential component of the whole interrogative sentence, which as a whole states an entirely different question from that intended in the question "Why are there essents?" With our question we place ourselves in the essent in such a way that it loses its self-evident character *as the essent*. The essent begins to waver between the broadest and most drastic extremes: "either essents—or nothing"—and thereby the questioning itself loses all solid foundation. Our questioning being-there is suspended, and in this suspense is nevertheless self-sustained.

But the essent is not changed by our questioning. It remains what it is and as it is. Our questioning is after all only a psycho-spiritual process in us which, whatever course it may take, cannot in any way affect the essent itself. True, the essent remains as it is manifested to us. But it cannot slough off the problematic fact that it might also not be what it is and as it is. We do not experience this possibility as something that we add to the essent by thinking; rather, the essent itself elicits this possibility, and in this possibility reveals itself. Our questioning only opens up the horizon, in order that the essent may dawn in such questionableness. . . .

The main thing is not to let ourselves be led astray by overhasty theories, but to experience things as they are on the basis of the first thing that comes to hand. This piece of chalk has extension; it is a relatively solid, grayish white thing with a definite shape, and apart from all that, it is a thing to write with. This particular thing has the attribute of lying here; but just as surely, it has the attribute of potentially not lying here and not being so large. The possibility of being guided along the blackboard and of being used up is not something that we add to the thing by thought. Itself, as this essent, is in this possibility; otherwise it would not be chalk as a writing material. Correspondingly, every essent has in it this potentiality in a different way. This potentiality belongs to the chalk. It has in itself a definite aptitude for a definite use. True, we are accustomed and inclined, in seeking this potentiality in the chalk, to say that we cannot see or touch it. But this is a prejudice, the elimination of which is part of the unfolding of our question. For the present our question is only to open up the essent in its wavering between nonbeing and being. Insofar as the essent resists the extreme possibility of nonbeing, it stands in being, but it has never caught up with or overcome the possibility of nonbeing.

We suddenly find ourselves speaking of the nonbeing and being of the essent, without saying how this being or nonbeing is related to the essent. Are the two terms the same? The essent and its being? What, for example, is "the essent" in this piece of chalk? The very question is ambiguous, because the word "the essent" can be understood in two respects, like the Greek *to on*. The essent means first that which is at any time, in particular this grayish white, so-and-so-shaped, light, brittle mass. But "the essent" also means that which "brings it about," so to speak, that this thing is an essent rather than a nonessent, that which constitutes its being if it is. In accordance with this two-fold meaning of the word "the essent," the Greek *to on* often has the second significance, not the essent itself, not that which is, but "is-ness," essentness, being. Over against this, "the essent" in the first sense signifies all or particular essent things themselves, in respect to themselves and not to their is-ness, their *ousia*.

The first meaning of *to on* refers to *ta onta* (entia), the second to *to einai* (esse). We have listed what the essent is in the piece of chalk. This was relatively easy to do. It was also easy to see that the object named can also not be, that this chalk need ultimately not be here and not be. What then is being in distinction to the essent? Is it the same as the essent? We ask the question once again. But in the foregoing we did not list being; we listed only material mass, grayish-white, light, so-and-so-shaped, brittle. But where is the being situated? It must belong to the chalk, for this chalk *is*.

We encounter the essent everywhere; it sustains and drives us, enchants and fills us, elevates and disappoints us; but with all this, where is and wherein consists, the being of the essent? One might reply: this distinction between the essent and its being may occasionally have an importance from the standpoint of language and even of meaning; this distinction can be effected in mere thought, i.e. in ideas and opinions, but is it certain that anything essent in the essent corresponds to the distinction? And even this merely cogitated distinction is questionable; for it remains unclear *what* is to be thought under the name of "being." Meanwhile it suffices to know the essent and secure our mastery over it. To go further and introduce being as distinct from it is artificial and leads to nothing.

We have already said a certain amount about this frequent question: What comes of such distinctions? Here we are going to concentrate on our undertaking. We ask: "Why are there essents rather than nothing?" And in this question we seemingly stick to the essent and avoid all empty brooding about being. But what really are we asking? Why the essent as such is. We are asking for the ground of the essent: that it is and is what it is, and that there is not rather nothing. Fundamentally we are asking about being. But how? We are asking about the being of the essent. We are questioning the essent in regard to its being.

But if we persevere in our questioning we shall actually be questioning forward, asking about being in respect to its ground, even if this question remains undeveloped and it remains undecided whether being itself is not in itself a ground and a sufficient ground. If we regard this question of being as the first question in order of rank, should we ask it without knowing how it stands with being and how being stands in its distinction to the essent? How shall we inquire into, not to say find, the ground for the being of the essent, if we have not adequately considered and understood being itself? This undertaking would be just as hopeless as if someone were to try to bring out the cause and ground of a fire, and yet claim that he need not worry about the actual course of the fire or examine the scene of it.

Thus it transpires that the question "Why are there essents rather than nothing?" compels us to ask the preliminary question: "How does it stand with being?"

Here we are asking about something which we barely grasp, which is scarcely more than the sound of a word for us, and which puts us in danger of serving a mere word idol when we proceed with our questioning. Hence it is all the more indispensable that we make it clear from the very outset how it stands at present with being and with our understanding of being. And in this connection the main thing is to impress it on our experience that we cannot immediately grasp the being of the essent itself, either through the essent or in the essent—or anywhere else.

A few examples may be helpful. Over there, across the street, stands the high school building. An essent. We can look over the building from all sides, we can go in and explore it from cellar to attic, and note everything we encounter in that building: corridors, staircases, schoolrooms, and their equipment. Everywhere we find the essents and we even find them in a very definite arrangement. Now where is the being of this high school? For after all it is. The building is. If anything belongs to this essent, it is its being; yet we do not find the being inside it. . . .

But we must take a wider look around us and consider the lesser and greater circle within which we spend our days and hours, wittingly and wittingly, a circle whose limits shift continuously and which is suddenly broken through.

A heavy storm coming up in the mountains "is," or what here amounts to the same thing, "was" during the night. Wherein consists its being?

A distant mountain range under a broad sky . . . It "is." Wherein consists the being? When and to whom does it reveal itself? To the traveler who enjoys the landscape, or to the peasant who makes his living in it and from it, or to the meteorologist who is preparing a weather report? Who of these apprehends being? All and none. Or is what these men apprehend of the mountain range under the great sky only certain aspects of it, not the mountain range itself as it "is" as such, not that wherein its actual being consists? Who may be expected to apprehend this being? Or is it a non-sense, contrary to the sense of being, to inquire after what is in itself, behind those aspects? Does the being lie in the aspects?

The door of an early romanesque church is an essent. How and to whom is its being revealed? To the connoisseur of art, who examines it and photographs it on an excursion, or to the abbot who on a holiday passes through this door with his monks, or to the children who play in its shadow on a summer's day? How does it stand with the being of this essent?

A state—*is*. By virtue of the fact that the state police arrest a suspect, or that so-and-so-many typewriters are clattering in a government building, taking down the words of ministers and state secretaries? Or "is" the state in a conversation between the chancellor and the British foreign minister? The state *is*. But where is being situated? Is it situated anywhere at all?

A painting by Van Gogh. A pair of rough peasant shoes, nothing else. Actually the painting represents nothing. But as to what is in that picture, you are immediately alone with it as though you yourself were making your way wearily homeward with your hoe on an evening in late fall after the last potato fires have died down. What is here? The canvas? The brush strokes? The spots of color?

What in all these things we have just mentioned is the being of the essent? We run (or stand) around in the world with our silly subtleties and conceit. But where in all this is being?

All the things we have named *are* and yet—when we wish to apprehend being, it is always as though we were reaching into the void. The being after which we inquire is almost like nothing, and yet we have always rejected the contention that the essent in its entirety is not.

But being remains unfindable, almost like nothing, or ultimately *quite* so. Then, in the end, the word "being" is no more than an empty word. It means nothing real, tangible, material. Its meaning is an unreal vapor. Thus in the last analysis Nietzsche was perfectly right in calling such "highest concepts" as being "the last cloudy streak of evaporating reality." Who would want to chase after such a vapor, when the very term is merely a name for a great fallacy! "Nothing indeed has exercised a more simple power of persuasion hitherto than the error of Being. . . ."

"Being"—a vapor and a fallacy? What Nietzsche says here of being is no random remark thrown out in the frenzy of preparation for his central, never finished work. No, this was his guiding view of being from the earliest days of his philosophical effort. It is the fundamental support and determinant of his philosophy. Yet even now this philosophy holds its ground against all the crude importunities of the scribblers who cluster round him more numerous with each passing day. And so far there seems to be no end in sight to this abuse of Nietzsche's work. In speaking here of Nietzsche, we mean to have nothing to do with all that—or with blind hero worship for that matter. The task in hand is too crucial and at the same time too sobering. It consists first of all, if we are to gain a true grasp of Nietzsche, in bringing his accomplishment to a full unfolding. Being a vapor, a fallacy? If this were so, the only possible consequence would be to abandon the question "Why are there essents as such and as a whole, rather than nothing?" For what good is the question if what it inquires into is only a vapor and a fallacy?

Does Nietzsche speak the truth? Or was he himself only the last victim of a long process of error and neglect, but as such the unrecognized witness to a new necessity?

Is it the fault of being that it is so involved? is it the fault of the world that it remains so empty? or are we to blame that with all our effort, with all our chasing after the essent, we have fallen out of being? And should we not say that the fault did not begin with us, or with our immediate or more remote ancestors, but lies in something that runs through Western history from the very beginning, a happening which the eyes of all the historians in the world will never perceive, but which nevertheless happens, which happened in the past and will happen in the future? What if it were possible that man, that nations in their greatest movements and traditions, are linked to being and yet had long fallen out of being, without knowing it, and that this was the most powerful and most central cause of their decline? . . .

The spiritual decline of the earth is so far advanced that the nations are in danger of losing the last bit of spiritual energy that makes it possible to see the decline (taken in relation to the history of "being"), and to appraise it as such. This simple observation has nothing to do with *Kulturpessimismus,* and of course it has nothing to do with any sort of optimism either; for the darkening of the world, the flight of the gods, the destruction of the earth, the transformation of men into a mass, the hatred and suspicion of everything free and creative, have assumed such proportions throughout the earth that such childish categories as pessimism and optimism have long since become absurd. . . .

To ask "How does it stand with being?" means nothing less than to recapture, to repeat, the beginnings of our historical-spiritual existence, in order to transform it into a new beginning. This is possible. It is indeed the crucial form of history, because it begins in the fundamental event. But we do not repeat a beginning by reducing it to something past and now known, which need merely be imitated; no, the beginning must be begun again, more radically, with all the strangeness, darkness, insecurity that attend a true beginning. Repetition as we understand it is anything but an improved continuation with the old methods of what has been up to now.

The question "How is it with being?" is included as a preliminary question in our central question "Why are there essents rather than nothing?" If we now begin to look into that which is questioned in our preliminary question, namely being, the full truth of Nietzsche's dictum is at once apparent. For if we look closely, what more is "being" to us than a mere word, an indeterminate meaning, intangible as a vapor? Nietzsche's judgment, to be sure, was meant in a purely disparaging sense. For him "being" is a delusion that should never have come about. Is "being," then, indeterminate, vague as a vapor? It is indeed. But we do not mean to side-step this fact. On the contrary, we must see how much of a fact it is if we are to perceive its full implication.

Our questioning brings us into the landscape we must inhabit as a basic prerequisite, if we are to win back our roots in history. We shall have to ask why this fact, that for us "being" is no more than a word and a vapor, should have arisen precisely today, or whether and why it has existed for a long time. We must learn to see that this fact is not as harmless as it seems at first sight. For ultimately what matters is not that the word "being" remains a mere sound and its meaning a vapor, but that we have fallen away from what this word says and for the moment cannot find our way back; that it is for this and no other reason that the word "being" no longer applies to anything; that everything, if we merely take hold of it, dissolves like a tatter of cloud in the sunlight. Because this is so—that is why we ask about being. And we *ask* because we know that truths have never fallen into any nation's lap. The fact that people still cannot and do not wish to understand this question, even if it is asked in a still more fundamental form, deprives the question of none of its cogency.

Louis Lavelle   13. HOW BEING IS
                                                   ENCOUNTERED

The "perspectives"—as Lavelle often called his remarks—that comprise this essay provide an interesting contrast to the previous essays by Marcel and Heidegger. With Heidegger, Lavelle proposes the notion of an "access to being"; with Marcel, he uncovers the "Cartesian" fact that "being is self-born."

Lavelle asserts that being is brought to an affirmation through three stages, which roughly correspond to the terms, "I," "absolute," and "world." The first ontological affirmation is the affirmation of self—or "The power I have to say I"—which begins in the discovery of self-consciousness and self-activity. This discovery uncovers not being, but its "situation," since being is recognized not *by* consciousness but *in* consciousness. As Lavelle says, ". . . in the act of consciousness I give myself being: I cannot say I, except *by* and *in* that very act."

Consciousness is not outside being—over and opposed to it, spectator-fashion—but enveloped in the *being of the inquirer:* ". . . there can be actual presence of being only in that being which is mine." Thus, "my awareness of the totality of being is not different from my own being," for there is no distinction between "the ego who gives the awareness and the ego to whom it gives it."

Refusing the position of most schools of "objective realism," which believe that being is "attached" through discrete and objective contemplation, Lavelle holds that being—absolute being—is reached only in the *subjectivity* of the person, and only when this is "most complete and most

This selection was originally entitled "The Three Stages of Metaphysics" in *Philosophic Thought in France and the United States,* edited by M. Farber. Reprinted by permission of the publisher, University of Buffalo Press, Buffalo, New York.

unadorned." "Being in itself consists, therefore," he asserts, "in utmost subjectivity and not in utmost objectivity."

As opposed to all forms of subjectivist idealisms, Lavelle distinguished between what might be called a relative-absolute and the absolute-absolute—that is, betwen the "absolute" character of a contingent being and the Absolute itself. The absolute that we *are* introduces us into the Absolute of Being in a participative way, since "every act is in a way an act of participation." Such participation is provided as intermediary by the real world, which "comes as an immense datum between the infinite act and the finite ego, filling the interval which separates them."

All consciousnesses share in this world in so far as it is defined by three properties: (*a*) its appearance; (*b*) its "trial for each consciousness," and (*c*) its instrumentality as a mediator "among different consciousnesses." The world is therefore instrumental being to the ego-being in its attachment to absolute being. It is "a tool for it, not a place to stay."

IT IS USELESS to try to define metaphysics and to inquire into its possibility before undertaking to *make* it. These preliminary investigations merely delay and confuse reflection: by questioning the legitimacy of an object to which we have not yet given existence, we necessarily conclude in the negative. Here as always, there is no other method than to push thought as far as it can go. It will soon appear what results it obtains, and whether the term "metaphysics" is suitable to cover them. Here as always it is by moving that we prove movement; we show its possibility by making it actual.

Now in the affirmation of being there seem to be three different stages for (1) being reveals itself to me at the outset by the *very power I have to say I,* which bears within it, from the moment that it begins to operate, the very act which causes me to be. But, (2) in this very experience which I have of it, my being is infinitely overwhelmed by a being which contains it and exceeds it, from which I derive my own power to be and hence to say I, in which I continually participate, which can never be considered as an object, which on the contrary should be defined as *pure inwardness,* that is, as an act free from all passivity and from which all particular acts derive the very possibility of being accomplished. (3) Between the act of participation which enables me to say I and the omnipresent and absolute subject which is its basis and continually supports it, there is *an infinite interval which nothing other than the world comes to fill up:* it can only present itself to me in the form of an outwardness which I always seek to penetrate and to reduce.

I. The Power I Have to Say I

From Descartes to Husserl it can be said that the indivisibly ontological and gnosiological primacy of the self-affirmation of the subject has always been recognized. It has been taken for granted and forgotten rather than disputed. And the objections directed against it bear against its sterility when the attempt is made to isolate it from an object to which it applies and yet with respect to which it can define itself only by opposition, or against the possibility of objectivizing itself, which, despite the prejudice which links existence to objectivity, strengthens its originality rather than weakens it. For *the first stage of metaphysical thought lies precisely in the discovery of oneself as consciousness and as act, and in uniting the two terms as genesis of oneself.* Whereas we almost always consider consciousness as being merely the condition of our access to being, which it acquaints us with, we should say with respect to access to being that it is not only *by consciousness* but primarily *in consciousness* that it is realized. We can make no assertions regarding being as such, where it differs from us who think it, and where consequently, insofar as being, it has an existence independent of us which we can only know as external to us: we can only reach it, then, as image or as concept, that is, by a representation which aims at it, but without containing it. On the contrary, in the act of consciousness I give myself being: I cannot say I, except *by* and *in* that every act. And the basic error into which common sense and philosophy continually relapse is to believe that that act of consciousness is nothing more than a power to think things different from myself and, among other things, the thing which is yet myself. But if being consists in outwardness, we need not be surprised that, of all the objects in the world, the ego is the only one which always eludes us. The essence of philosophical invention is continually to re-climb this slope: to recognize, as happens in the most lucid and secret moments of my personal existence, that for me there can be actual presence of being only in that being which is mine, that this being consists in a presence to itself which gives me an incomparable emotion, which does not conceal an unknown being whose reactions can surprise me; (for such a being is a part of nature; I only undergo it; it is so far from being identical with me that it is in relation to it, with it, for it or against it, that I define what I am;) whereas the ego consists in a being always being born, with the very consciousness it has of itself, and which, at every instant, assumes the responsibility of what it is going to be.

In such a discovery the ego grasps itself as pure activity, that is, as an activity which before giving rise to any effect first gives rise to itself. Now, if such an activity is constitutive of the ego, if we do not have the right to pronounce the word I except at the point where this activity comes into play, then we can say that the ego is really heterogeneous to every object and that we should never hope, therefore, to obtain any sort of representation of it; but if there is no representation except in relation to it, the reason is that it posited itself at the outset as a real being which is not the representation of anything. And despite appearances, the paradox here is on the part of common sense, which considers as the model of being that being which I have in my purview, of which I know only that it is not my being, and of which I can have only an image, instead of seeing that the being which I myself am constitutes the only domain in which being is really present to me in its own genesis. On the contrary, I posit an *object* of knowledge only where I discover that I am not myself coextensive with the totality of being. It appears then that it should be an undisputed result of metaphysics that it is by the ego that we have access to being, but to a being such that it is never a being-object because it can never be distinguished from the act which causes it to be and that, far from being alien to knowledge, it should be considered as being the very source of knowledge.

This analysis succeeds in eliminating the classic notion of substance considered by a sort of contradiction as a *transcendent object,* that is, a term which by definition is the point of application of our experience and which yet is intrinsically outside of every possible experience. But the object is always before us and never behind; and this objectivizing procedure of consciousness must be very essential to it if it prefers to expel itself from being rather than accept its inability to convert itself into an object. This is seen not only in the materialists but in all those who wish to reduce the subject to a purely formal existence.

Nevertheless, if on the contrary self-consciousness is the only road which enables us to enter into being, that means not, as is thought, that it gives us merely the means of knowing being, but that it is already the very presence of being, or again that my awareness of the totality of being is not different from my own being. I cannot, where I am concerned, make the distinction between the ego who gives the awareness and the ego to whom it gives it, as when my awareness of a thing is involved; but this impossibility is instructive. It shows that the awareness consists in an act of attention which always revives, which gives rise to myself in giving rise to the show of things, which cannot give way without my existence giving way, in which I continually accept the responsibility of making myself in the double and invisible power of thinking whatever is and of willing what I am.

It will be said: this is the extremity of being, but it requires an immense substructure. At the least it must be recognized that the being we are seeking, the only one which merits the name of being, the one to which metaphysics gives the name of absolute, since it is necessarily internal to itself, can only be grasped in the form of inwardness. *Absolute and interior to itself have the same meaning.* Kant made a mistake in introducing the name of "thing in itself" into philosophy, for metaphysical being is almost always represented to oneself under the form of the thing in itself; but the expression is a contradiction in terms. A thing is what is never in itself, which has no self, which is never itself. It is what never is, except for a subject or an "in itself" which, positing it outside of itself, although in relation with itself, defines it precisely as a thing. In other words, entering into being is entering into a world which, since it is self-interiority, is the basis of my interiority to myself; and if this is the world which precisely we call the spiritual world, we must say that there is an *identity between the discovery of being and the discovery of spirituality.*

One thus realizes that the direction of metaphysical thought is just the opposite of that in which it is almost always used, but which is seen at once to be a blind alley. For, in meditating on the nature of the object which is held to furnish us with the very type of being, one sees very soon that it is subject to certain conditions which the subject places on it: we try to separate it from those conditions and thus one comes to imagine a being which should be a pure object, liberated from all the subjective conditions which enable one to think of it as object. But this is a chimera. It is not enough to say with regard to such an object that it is unknowable: it is impossible; it is still I the subject who posits it as beyond all knowledge, as self-sufficient without me. This is what was formerly called an imaginary entity (*être de raison*), but one which is equally alien to all intelligibility and to any experience. The only way which is open to metaphysics is the opposite one: since in subjectivity itself, even though it is often impure, being is always present as "self," absolute being can be reached only where subjectivity is most complete and most unadorned. *Being in itself consists, therefore, in utmost subjectivity and not in utmost objectivity.* The more thought objectifies itself, the more it turns away from being toward the spectacle, the image, or the concept; the more it concentrates on its own subjectivity, the nearer it comes to the source where being is constantly being born to itself and to the multiplicity of its modes. The objection should not be made that we are as unable to find pure subjectivity as pure objectivity, for these two contraries cannot be compared. For if the object can only be posited in its relation to us, an absolute object deprived of all relation with us is nothing. Whereas if the subject is our self, the absolute subject is an awareness which goes beyond us, but into which we penetrate and which becomes ours as we increasingly participate in it.

However, the word "subjectivity" acquires a more insidious connotation, and one more in accordance with the common prejudice, when it is reduced to the states which we experience, which we feel as ours and which each of us knows by himself alone. The observation could already be made that this does not diminish their reality, as is believed, but on the contrary means "living" them, experiencing their being at the precise point where it is one and the same thing to say that they are and that we feel them. But this is not possible unless I feel them as mine. At any rate, true subjectivity consists only in the very act which enables me to say I, that is to experience my states and to say of this representation that it is mine, while the object it represents is not mine. Now this power consists in a pure initiative which is inseparable from its exercise, which can always be more or less blocked but which for this reason continually contrasts itself to objects which appear to it, to states which affect it; but it is the only experience we have of true being where it becomes our own being, i.e., its own beginning, without there being anything whose modality or phenomenon it can be, even though there is nothing which goes beyond it and in relation to it does not become modality or phenomenon. All objects, all states express the limitation of the being which is I, which consists exclusively in the act which causes it to be, without one's being able, however, to ignore the fact that whatever limits it also brings it the experience of what it lacks: all the objects I find in front of me form a world which precisely in going beyond me discloses to me the richness of being, all the states which I experience within myself from the content of my life, continually developing and growing with its contact with the world.

II. Pure Inwardness

It is not for exclusively logical reasons that I am compelled to grant that there is no contact with being except in the being which I am, where being asserts itself as ego. There is no emotion comparable to that given, not exactly by the discovery of the states which I feel are mine, through which I pass in succession, but by the power I have to call them mine, which is inseparable from an initiative in which I enlist all my responsibility and which is the being which I call "I." Of the ego I shall say that it is the only place where I can deal with the "in itself" or the "self" of being, at least if the universe which surrounds me only exists in relation to it, that is to say, is for it only a phenomenon, whereas the ego who thinks this universe makes me enter, by the fact of its existence, into absolute existence, which is the existence of pure inwardness. We like to speak of the limits of subjectivity as if the real world of the object and subjectivity were nothing but a perspective we have of it, from which we do not succeed in escaping and yet which we should have to surmount in order to meet being as it really is. Thus subjectivity would shut us up in a solitude which would forever separate us from being. Yet it is our very being. *It is an absolute of our own which introduces us into the absolute of being.* And it is for that reason that, once the field of subjectivity is opened to us, we see it immediately as susceptible of being indefinitely extended. We should not say that it turns us in upon ourselves, but on the contrary that it enables us to penetrate everywhere. For the being which it discloses to us is the univalent being which puts us on the same plane with all of being, where we unendingly move and expand.

Here however the difficulties begin. If there is a universality of the *self* into which the ego constantly gives us entry, the comparison inevitably arises of the ego with the body which occupies a determinate place in the immense universe. But the comparison does not hold, for, in enlarging subjectivity beyond our own limits, I am not dealing with a spiritual immensity of which I represent a small corner, but with an infinite power which I put in operation at the very point where I can say I. It is in this sense alone that one has the right to say of the ego that it can only assert itself in the interior and by means of a subjectivity which infinitely exceeds it, whence it unendingly draws its nourishment, as Fichte says of this *Ichheit,* from which it continually draws the power of saying I. But for this reason, as I penetrate further into the intimacy of the pure Ego, I unceasingly go into the depths of my own intimacy. I enlist my body in the universe, but it always remains a body exterior to me; on the contrary, as I go further down into that primeval subjectivity from which I draw the subjectivity which is my own, I increasingly divest myself of all that in any way was exterior to me, of all that was only appearance or state in respect to me, I coincide more and more rigorously with what I am, and in the act which causes me to be, I recognize the presence of the same act which gives being to whatever is.

But then the difficulties redouble, instead of disappearing. What right could I still have to say I beyond the very act that I perform? And beyond that act how could everything not be exterior for me, that is, object? Nevertheless exteriority, objectivity is precisely that in which I do not participate, which I continually put away from me, even though I cannot define them except in their relationship to me. But subjectivity, intimacy, on the contrary, constitute the essence of what I am, even though, in the experiences I have of them, they are never pure and are always subject to some limitation, that is to say, some contamination with the external. But there the word "participation" will find its adequate connotation. For this word seems to express the only means by which particular being can act, that is to say, enter into communication with what exceeds it, but in order to make it its own. Thus, every act is in a way an act of participation. Inversely, participation is always effected by an act; and this is so true that, in order to say of being that it does not act or remains inert, we say merely that it no longer participates in anything. But the nature of participation is to presuppose an activity rightfully common to all and offered to everyone, which can be engaged in without us, but also with us and by us and which is always available to all, although everyone may take it up in his own way. If all our acts are imperfect and unfinished, or, what comes to the same thing, if they always enclose within themselves an object to which they apply, that is no obstacle to their having a common origin from which they draw that which makes them acts, which is the very power of acting. And it will readily be granted even that, in activity as such, it is impossible to conceive any particular determination, so that it may equally be said of it that it does not apply to anything and that it can be applied to everything: which explains why we cannot define ourselves as act without setting ourselves equal to the all, not actually no doubt, but potentially and in that infinite ambition which forms man's ambiguous essence and the source at once of his greatness and his wretchedness.

One could justify this analysis in another way, and show that the experience we have of ourselves is the experience of an activity which unendingly supplies us and which we never use more than partially, that is the experience of an infinite possibility which we can make use of up to a certain point. And just as our body, the only one we experience as real, is inserted into a universe which is present to us in its entirety, but only in the form of representation, the act which we perform is itself inserted into a universe which is the universe of possibility that each one makes actual according to his powers. But, as there is a being of representation, there is also a being of possibility, far from possibility's being a pure chimera or an unintelligible middle term between being and nothing. No doubt the possible can be reduced to a pure object of thought, but its secret is only grasped in the act which causes it to be in us: *it is this act which, in being performed, reveals to us the very intimacy of being.* For, first of all, what does our being itself, which is never a thing, consist in except in the being of something possible, which is in process and which it is up to us to realize? I have no right, it is true, to consider this possible thing as something determined in advance, entrusted exclusively to me and to which I would have the sterile task of giving a form in the visible world. The word "possible" has meaning only in the plural. The infinitude of the possible is an infinite multiplicity of possibles among which I always have to choose that possible which shall be mine. It must be said too that this world of possibles is the totality of being insofar as that totality is the basis of the existence of an ego whose destiny it is to realize itself by an act of participation, just as the world of represented things is the totality of being insofar as it is the basis of the existence of my own body, that is of a body by which the ego is unceasingly affected. But that does not mean that possibilities, any more than things, ever have a separate existence. For if there is always, as Bergson believed, an artifice, based on the nature of my physical needs, in the division of the world into an infinity of different objects, there is the same artifice based on the internal requirements of participation, in the division of pure activity into an infinite diversity of possibles.

Thus, I could maintain in a sense that all possibles derive from my invention. It is still necessary that this invention should not be arbitrary, that the very constitution of the all should have certain characters which justify my invention and correspond to it. It is still necessary that there should be in us a power to produce it which we feel belongs to us, since it is we who exercise it, and that it comes nevertheless from higher up, since we have received it. Actually, we cannot say that we originate possibility; it imposes itself on us with the same rigor as does objectivity. Like the object, but better than the object, which it always surpasses, it bears witness to that sort of omnipresent infinity which is the very mark of the absolute, whose exterior and given manifestation only is disclosed to us by the object, and the internal and creative power by the possible. It is the possible, not as pure object of thought, but as a proposal for our activity which discloses to us, in its relations with us, the very intimacy of the being in which we participate. The word "possibility," like the word "representation," seems to express a diminished existence which is only in its relation to us, but it is in order that by their mediation we may form, in the totality of being, precisely that double corporal and spiritual existence which is ours.

It will be said again that if the possible is before us without being us, if it is unceasingly offered us and set before us, even though there is nothing, even as possible, outside of our thinking, we must at least consider the act which realizes it as our own act, so that if the intimacy of being, precisely insofar as it goes beyond us internally, is enclosed to us only as the infinite of possibility, the operation by which we make a choice among possibles in order to adopt that possible of which we will make our very being belongs to us alone. Participation would then play a part in the evocation of possibilities, but not in their actualization. However matters are much less simple. For one thing, possibility is not, as one might suppose, a pure object of contemplation: it is itself an active possibility, or at least one which has meaning only with relation to the act which realizes it: it already invites me, and if I have the power to repress it, it is always a virtualness in waiting, never a spectacle given to me. Finally, at the very moment I act, that act by which I actualize it puts into motion a power which is not mine, or at least one which notably exceeds mine, whose efficacy fills me with astonishment and admiration when I think back to it, but which becomes mine as soon as I grant it my consent. This consent can never be forced: it alone constitutes my own being and bases my personal subjectivity in the total subjectivity.

At the point we have reached we have not only discovered in the intimacy of the ego our first encounter with being, but we have shown that if that intimacy is always imperfect it participates in a pure intimacy which itself consists in an act which creates itself rather than anything exterior to itself, which is consequently the eternal beginning of oneself, from which too I draw that power of being the first beginning of myself, that is of discerning that possibility out of which I, by consenting to actualize it, will make an existence which is mine.

III. The Externality of the World, or the Interval Between the Ego and Pure Inwardness

This metaphysical analysis has thus far remained acosmic: it is a dialectic of intimacy, that is, of correlation within the intimacy between the individual and the universal. However, the world continues to be present to us. In following our analysis we have continually used comparisons drawn from the relations of our body with the world. And it would be rash to think that it is the characteristic of metaphysical thought to abolish the world in behalf of a spirituality which it would never succeed in isolating, whatever its efforts toward purification or *askesis*.

We must now prove finally that the real world comes as an immense datum between the infinite act and the finite ego, filling the interval which separates them, that the ego always tries to fill up this interval without ever succeeding, but that the efforts it makes toward that goal explain at once both the evolution of the world and the progress of humanity, for the world is continually being humanized and spiritualized; I penetrate it gradually by knowledge. I constantly reform it to make it conform to my purposes, that is, not only the most pressing needs of my body but also the most delicate requirements of my thought. It is understandable then how *from within being should appear to me as a system of possibilities and from without as a system of things*. But not all possibility is actualized. Yet it must be capable of actualization; and it never finishes the process; thus the world will never have finished its course. It can be said of all these possibilities that they can never be considered as given; otherwise their actualization would not add anything. In this sense they are perpetually invented, that is, isolated from each other within the sovereign act which contains them all, and that is the proper object of our intelligence; but we continually choose among them, and that is the object of our will. That explains also why the world of possibilities not only appears legitimately as infinitely more ample than the world of things but also how there is in it a dynamic power which uplifts the world of things and continually moves it onward. Finally, we realize that, if the secret of existence comes down for us to the relation between the pure act and the act which participates, the former supplying the latter with all the possibilities it actualizes, we still do not succeed in explaining the shape of the world unless we also realize, first, that all these free actions fit into each other, that is, have to limit each other in order to come together, which is an adequate explanation of the degree of necessity which reigns in the world; and secondly, that the very exercise of liberty requires, as its precondition, the actualization of certain possibilities which it continually makes use of and goes beyond, which is an adequate explanation of why there is an evolution of the world, whose liberty at each point can never be regarded as anything but the utmost point. Thus we can say of liberty that it governs the world because it is liberty which draws out of infinite possibility, as the condition of its own elevation, those first sketches of existence on which it has to rely in order to go beyond them by means of denying them.

We shall now show that the world possesses three properties which suffice to define it: for it is at once an appearance and a trial for each consciousness, and an instrument of mediation among different consciousnesses.

(1) *The world is an appearance.* The act which lies at the basis of my interiority to myself does not coincide with the infinite act, that is, with the inwardness of whatever is, although it participates in it; but yet it cannot be separated from it. And the very indivisibility of the all requires it to be present to me, even though it always exceeds me. I can neither confuse it with myself, nor *know* it as it is in itself. This amounts to saying that it can only be present

to me in its relation to me, which may be expressed by saying that it is for me an object, a phenomenon or an appearance. All of being must therefore become for me a spectacle or an immense datum which as such is linked to inwardness only by my own thought, without which no spectacle would ever be presented to me. I should add that I have to make myself a part of this world of objects, that is, I must be able to become an object for others, but also for myself to the extent that the act which creates me, although always unfinished, should still at every instant be present to itself. I express this by saying that I have a body. From this analysis can be deduced the nature of attachment, which superadds itself to the representation which I have of my body, and by continually setting a limit to the very act by which I make myself as I, will enable me to say that it is mine. Thus the ego is legitimately reduced to the body by all those who think that there is no other existence than that of the object.

From the fact that each being has its own characteristic representation of the world, it cannot be inferred that the world in which it lives has existence only for it: for that representation is of a non-ego which is common to all consciousness, precisely because it expresses them all in going beyond them, that is, changing itself into a datum for them, the act from which each of them borrows precisely the power to say I. We cannot yield to a certain realism which seems to be inseparable from scientific research, and according to which it is the characteristic of the spirit to go behind the layer of appearance as it takes form under the action of our senses, to reach the objects that in themselves they are. There can be no object with which knowledge will coincide one day: for knowledge is knowledge only if it is distinguished from its object. But we can easily understand that the part played by an ever deeper and more delicate experience, the use of tools, the very artifices which thought continually uses to obtain more and more precision and coherence, continually change the representation we form of things, but still do not take from them the character of being a representation. The conception which science forms of the world does not do away with the image which the senses give us. The image remains when we consider the immediate relation which things have to our body: it is on these things that the acts of our most accustomed life are based. The image seems to vanish, but what we should say is only that it opens when we bring new means of investigation into play; then our action requires more power and finesse. But all these successive representations are equally true: we pass from one to the other as method and point of view change: they admirably express the infinite multiplicity of possibilities which the all continually offers for participation.

However, it will be observed that as our knowledge becomes more complex the role of the spirit's operations continually increases. Whereas if we thought we could reach the thing as it is, it would seem that we should on the contrary break off all those operations and break them down in a sort of receptivity toward the thing itself with which consciousness would mysteriously come to coincide. On the contrary, when we come to the highest degree of knowledge, the thing itself seems to have evaporated, to have resolved itself into a pure object of thought: which would favor a return to Platonism, that is, to the conception which identifies the real with the idea. We should moreover try to show that the idea is never a thing which the spirit just runs up against; there is in it, it is true, a certain opacity which always remains and which is like an irreducible residue of sensible experience; but as it becomes more transparent, it is no longer distinct from the operation of the spirit which thinks it, that is, from a pure relation between the finite and the infinite in the very act which causes us to be.

(2) *The world is a trial.* It is sometimes thought that by saying of the world that it is an appearance, we attenuate its existence: and it is held that every appearance is an illusion. But that is impossible. The appearances are in fact things. Or in words, things only subsist in the very appearance they give us. One would like then to know what it is they are appearances of; but the word "appearance" indicates only that they have no existence except for a subject capable of saying I as the inwardness of his being enlists itself in the inwardness of all of being which, beyond the limits in which the ego continually confines itself, takes on the character of externality and turns into a world which seems to come to it from without. Hence the density and depth which such a world has for us. At each instant it is only a vanishing appearance. Yet it is always reborn and has an immense reserve. It never fails to provide for me; it brings me a revelation which continually astonishes and enriches me. I always begin to discover it anew. I shall never succeed in exhausting it. It has eternal novelty for me. It comes about then that my existence may seem poor and pale by comparison, being only a pure possibility. Once my existence turns in upon itself, once it suspends its relations with the world, it is as nothing. My existence always needs to be actualized, and that can only take place through and by means of the world. And not only is it thanks to the world that my being ceases to be a secret being and becomes a manifest being, but it must also be said that this becoming manifest is essential to my secret being, which without it would be rather as aspiration to being than a veritable being.

Here we grasp in the profoundest manner the relation between the being which is and the being which appears; here we can give the world which appears its true meaning. We should in no way impair the principle that being is internal to itself, but this inwardness consists in the very power it has to make itself. Now if we admit that such a proposition can be conceded by all, it seems possible to draw from it two opposite consequences, against each of which we must defend ourselves: the first is that externality is an illusion we must learn to free ourselves from; the second that it alone enables inwardness to realize itself. But in both cases the meaning of the world escapes us. We cannot say that the ego should give its attention principally to never going outside of itself, nor that it is only in the world that it finds its existence. *The world is a tool for it, not a place to stay*. For (a) we have no right to despise the world as a phantasmagory which takes the ego away from itself: to the extent that it is a given, not a created presence, it is all the being which I feel infinitely exceeds me and continually instructs me. I find in myself only a virtual infinity; but it can only actualize itself by the stimulus which the world brings it and to which I constantly respond. (b) Inversely, it would be a contradiction to desire, as often happens, that the destiny of the ego should be achieved outside of the ego, namely in the world where all its actions come to receive a material form. For, on the contrary, it is well known that all the efforts of knowledge, will, and love aim, by means of the world, at giving us a spiritual satisfaction without which the world would have no sense for us. This is a conclusion which the most hardened materialist, who asks only one thing, to change the world, cannot avoid. This is the reason why the shape of the world constantly passes away, as we so often complain; but the world must pass in order to be at once passed through and surpassed. The material world is the place where the conversion of my spiritual possibility into my spiritual existence continually takes place; it is the place where the spirit realizes itself.

(3) *The world is an instrument of mediation among consciousnesses.* Up to now we have considered each consciousness as if it were alone over against the world. And it is from this relation with the absolute that we have derived the existence of the world. It will be readily understood that we do not have the immediate experience of any other finite existence than our own. But perhaps we can show that the existence of only one finite being implies the existence of an infinity of finite beings, as if the infinity of the multiple were nothing more than a manner of putting the infinity of the one to work.

However, it is through the world that we learn of the existence of other consciousnesses, that is, of other existences internal to themselves from which we remain separated, but yet with which we can communicate. It will be said that this experience is indirect and hypothetical, for it takes place by means of the manifestation, that is of the body behind which we imagine a secret life comparable to ours. But that is not enough. For one thing, if the ego is always a possibility of realizing itself, we cannot ignore the fact that there are still of right within each ego all the possibilities at once, so that what you are I am too, or at least could be in some way; which confirms the view that all being is present in every point, and that still it is by liberty, that is by the actualization of different possibilities, that particular beings come to establish their separate existence. And again, it is illegitimate, as the objectivist prejudice so often leads us to do, to consider the ego as capable of entering into relation only with things and not with beings. For, as has been shown, outside the ego there is nothing but things whose relations with me constitute what we call representations. But the relations of the ego with another ego are of a different nature. The being that I am and the being that you are, in the degree that each of them on its own initiative assumes the existence proper to it, are infinitely farther apart than the subject and the object of knowledge can be. And yet between these two beings there is a much greater affinity than between the ego and a thing. The difference there is between you and me, the debate I have with you, are also a difference that exists between me and myself and a debate I have with myself. And as there is in me a part of myself which only has meaning by its relations with an object which is at once external and represented, there is also a part of myself of which I can say that instead of confining me within myself, it gets me out of myself, not, it is true, in order to set before me a thing which I contemplate as a spectacle, but in order to set before me another being I set myself up against, but with which I communicate.

We now see that there is the closest unity between the affirmation of the existence of the world and the affirmation of an infinite plurality of beings who, like me, can say I. But it is on condition of not limiting oneself to saying that these other beings are a part of this world that I see, because in that case they would be nothing more than things among other things. Like me they think the world and they contribute to modifying it, but it is thanks to it that they constitute what they are. They are therefore not simply a fragment of it. It is as ego in this world that they have to express themselves, that is to manifest themselves; and that expression or that manifestation is indispensable for their entering into relationship with each other and with me. This no doubt is the reason why Hegel considered as the motive force of the development of consciousness and perhaps even of the evolution of the world *the desire to be recognized*. But that is not enough. The relation which two beings have with each other and with the world is much deeper. The world brings them the presence of the all, which is a unique presence, but only a given presence, in the face of which each one remains unequal, but which applies each one with the career in which his destiny is involved. They find there a source of material which continually enriches them, provided that they themselves continually spiritualize it. Each one of them has a perspective of its own on the world. Nevertheless all these perspectives must be in agreement. They are only perspectives. We say that they open out on the same world: it would be truer to say that they open out on the same being, which, to the extent that it goes beyond all particular beings, presents itself to them in the form of a world. Therefore it is because there is a world that consciousnesses are separated from each other instead of fusing in the unity of the pure spirit, and it is also because there is a world that they can enter into communication with each other; but it is because it is an instrument of mediation among them that it has become the foundation of human society.

Metaphoric

Dorothy Emmet   # 14. THE ANALOGICAL
                                   ## MANNER

By her own confession, Professor Emmet has attempted to deal with the problem of the analogy of being "outside the frontiers of the *philosophia
perennis.*" Somewhat like poetry, she says, metaphysics is an *analogical*
way of thinking, in that "it takes concepts drawn from some form of
experience or some relation within experience, and extends them either
so as to say something about the nature of reality, or so as to suggest a
possible mode of co-ordinating other experiences."

By "analogy," she means neither Kantian, Scholastic, Euclidean, or Millsian
forms of the term. This is to say that analogy for her (*a*) does not
emanate from the "form-creating activity of mind," as in Kant's category
of *relation* whose three principles (substantiality, reciprocity, and causality)
effected "analogies of experience"; (*b*) it is not the predication, in different
senses, of a common term, as distinguished by the Scholastics into analogy of attribution, proportion, and proportionality; (*c*) it is not the
equality of ratios (as in Euclid's *Elements,* VII), or "the repetition of the
same fundamental pattern in two different contexts"; or (*d*) it is not
"argument from parallel cases," as in the inductive canons of J. S. Mill or
Francis Bacon.

As Emmet sees it, there are five senses in which the term "metaphysical
analogy" may be used—only the last of which she considers legitimate.
These are (1) the "deductive" or matrix type, which starts with some
pattern of the universe and then deduces "the patterns of empirical
things"; (2) a kind of ideograph analogy, which argues from the supposition that there is similarity between concept and reality; (3) the
"probable hypothesis," which argues from particular instances to a universal fact; (4) the "co-ordinating hypothesis," which extends key ideas
to all parts of reality; and (5) the "intra-experiential" or "existential
analogy," which argues from what is experienced to what is not experienced.

"Existential analogies," Emmet says, are properly called "analogies of
being" and are "drawn from elements within experience to the nature of
that in relation to which the experience is constituted."

This selection constitutes a portion of the introductory chapter to *The Nature of Metaphysical Thinking* and appears through the courtesy of the author, the Macmillan Company
Ltd., London, and St. Martin's Press, Inc, New York.

... THE VIEW we shall try to develop is that metaphysics is an analogical way of thinking. That is to say, it takes concepts drawn from some form of experience or some relation within experience, and extends them either so as to say something about the nature of "reality," or so as to suggest a possible mode of co-ordinating other experiences of different types from that from which the concept was originally derived. We shall look at the considerations which lie behind the judgments of significance or importance which lead to the selection of particular concepts as providing key ideas capable of extended use. We shall have to ask with what justification concepts may be drawn from some particular type of experience and extended analogically to say something about "reality," "God," "the external world" or "the world as a whole." Are such analogies not in the end products of the form-creating activity of mind, constructing pictures of the world (whether we call these pictures metaphysical or theological) seen through the medium of a particular kind of experience? And if we have to concede a substantial truth in this, have we any warrant to suppose that such theories can be more than expressions of particular ways of feeling about the world which, because of some maybe personal or traditional associations, have seemed to people significant?

But first let us clarify the sense in which we are suggesting that metaphysical theories are analogical. An analogy in its original root meaning is a proportion, and primarily a mathematical ratio, e.g. 2:4::4:x. In such a ratio, given knowledge of three terms, and the nature of the proportionate relation, the value of the fourth term can be determined. Thus analogy is here the repetition of the same fundamental pattern in two different contexts. 2:4 and 4:8 exhibit the same relational pattern. Mathematical thinking has developed from the discovery that identities of pattern can be abstracted from different contexts, *e.g.* the number of a group of days abstracted from the days, and of a group of fishes from the fishes, and the analogous function which the number performs in each context can be considered by itself.

In the logic of induction, analogy means argument from parallel cases. We argue from some resemblance either of relation or of properties that resemblance of further relations or of properties is probable. The argument thus points to a hypothesis to be further tested. A famous example is Darwin's hypothesis of Natural Selection, which was suggested by analogy by considering the development of certain varieties of plants and animals as a result of selective breeding. Analogy may also be used to bring out a relation by exhibiting it in a different context, which may be either more familiar, or one in which the significance of the relation may be seen without prejudice: parables are instances of analogies of this kind. Such an analogy is contained in a Rabbinic parable illustrating the relation between soul and body and the responsibility of the whole person, comprised of soul and body, for his sin. "R. Ismael said that the matter resembled a king who had a garden with fine early figs. He put two keepers in it, one was blind, and one was lame, and he bade them to look well after the figs. After a time the lame man said to the blind man, 'I see some fine figs in the garden.' The blind man said, 'Bring me to them and we will eat.' The lame man said, 'I cannot walk.' The blind said, 'I cannot see.' Then the lame man got on the shoulders of the blind man and they went and ate the figs. After a time the king came to the garden, and he asked, 'Where are the figs?' The blind man said, 'Can I see?' The lame man said, 'Can I walk?' But the king was clever; he set the lame man on the shoulders of the blind man, and made them walk a little, and he said, 'Even so have you managed and you have eaten the figs.' "

Whether such analogies can be *arguments* as well as *illustrations* of something known or partly known on other grounds depends on whether the relation illustrated is sufficiently alike in both cases for it to be possible to draw further conclusions from the one case to the other. An example of a doubtful argument from analogy of this type is that brought forward by Hume in support of his contention that virtue and vice are not attributes of an act or agent, but describe feelings which an act may arouse in a spectator. "To put the affair, therefore, to this trial, let us choose any inanimate object, such as an oak or elm; and let us suppose, that by dropping of its seed, it produces a sapling below it, which, springing up by degrees, at last overtops and destroys the parent tree: I ask if in this instance there be wanting any relation, which is discoverable in parricide or ingratitude? Is not the one tree the cause of the other's existence; and the latter the cause of the destruction of the former, in the same manner as when a child murders his parent? 'Tis not sufficient to reply, that a choice or will is wanting. For in the case of parricide, a will does not give rise to any *different* relations, but is only the cause from which the action is derived; and consequently produces the *same* relations, that in the oak or elm arise from some other principles." The force of this argument turns on whether the relation is only the similar relation of physical parenthood; or whether in the case of the human father and child additional elements of a psychological or spiritual kind enter in and make a relevant difference to the relationship.

A metaphysical analogy is clearly not an argument based on mathematical proportion, nor is it an inductive argument from parallel cases of a homogeneous type. It is more likely to resemble an illustrative analogy, but it will probably turn out to be an illustrative analogy of a very special kind. There seem to be at least five senses in which it might be said that metaphysical theories are analogies.

1. There is first what I shall call the "deductive" sense. The term "metaphysical analogy" may suggest that we can start from knowledge of the pattern of the universe, and can deduce the patterns of empirical things or events within the universe from this. This is the principle behind many ancient and mediaeval allegorizings, bestiaries, number mysticisms and the like. An ex-

ample is Irenaeus' argument as to why the number of canonical Gospels must be four. The argument is based on a tradition widespread in antiquity (and probably of Pythagorean origin) that the basic pattern of the world was four-square. "As there are four corners of the world in which we live, and four winds throughout the world, and as the Church is sown over the whole world and the breath of its life, consequently the world must have four pillars inspiring it with incorruptibility and reviving man. Thus it follows that the Logos, the architect of the world, who is enthroned on the Cherubim and supports the world, when He became manifest among men gave us the Gospel in four forms. . . . For the Living Creatures are quadriform, and the Gospel also is quadriform."

Dante argues for the political unity of the world under the Emperor by saying that man is the child of heaven, and that therefore his proper form of political organization can be deduced from the order of heaven, "Wherefore the human race is best disposed when it follows the track of heaven in so far as its proper nature allows. And since the whole heaven in all its parts, motions and movers is regulated by a single motion (to wit of the *primum mobile*) and a single motor, God, it follows that the human race is then best disposed when it is ruled in its motors and motions by a single prince as single motor, and by a single law as single motion. Wherefore it appears necessary to the well-being of the world that there should be a monarchy or single princedom which is called empire."

Metaphysical analogies of this type depend on the belief that there is a predominant pattern of being. Their use depends on two questionable assumptions; first that we know the basic pattern of the macrocosm, and secondly, that it is repeated in the sub-patterns of mirocosmic events.

2. The second way in which metaphysics might be called analogical could be by claiming that there is an analogy between concepts derived from experience and the "reality" to which these are referred. Such a view would start from something like a phenomenalist view of experience. That is to say, it would analyse experience in terms of sensations and ideas derived therefrom, and, saying that we can only be aware of appearances—signs within phenomenal experience,—would define the "transcendent" as standing beyond and outside experience. If it does not then go all the way with the positivist conclusion that assertions about "noumenal reality" behind phenomena are meaningless, it might suggest that the intrinsic nature of the transcendent reals (*e.g.* physical objects) should be conceived *by analogy* with the constructions built out of phenomenal experiences. But this is to suggest something like a representative theory of ideas. It would only hold if it were possible to maintain that the relation between the conception of a thing and the thing itself could be that of some kind of copy, or at least of structural identity. We shall have to examine this theory later, and shall see reason to question whether the relation between our sensations and whatever non-phenomenal objects they

may be connected with can be that of repetition or structure, and *a fortiori* whether the relation of signs to that which they signify can be so conceived. But although there are philosophical objections to be brought against a "representative" theory of ideas, it is probably the theory most generally and popularly assumed, once people give up the naïvely realist conception that our ideas give us direct knowledge of things just as they are in themselves. It is perhaps equally natural to assume that our ideas are somehow duplicates of things, copying their essential characters. If this were true, the idea might be described as the analogue of a thing, reproducing its properties, and perhaps particularly its structural relations, in a different medium. We can sometimes point to such a structural relation between something we experience, *e.g.* the perceived lines on a map, and something else we can experience, *e.g.* the measured roads on a landscape, so that the former could be referred to the latter as an analogical symbol. But can we jump from phenomenal experiences and ideas to the nature of *transcendent objects,* except by assuming the "representational" character of the former? If the transcendent is defined as that which is entirely "beyond" or "outside" our experience, we have no grounds for assuming that the latter can even give us analogical knowledge of its nature. For this would mean that we could compare a phenomenon with something which is not a phenomenon, which is obviously impossible since it is only in so far as anything enters experience that we are aware of it to do the comparing. So, if "metaphysical analogies" are of this nature, we can only say that they are attempts to *imagine* the noumenal by analogy with the phenomenal. Such analogies as we construct from intra-experiential ideas would then be "projections" of these ideas upon what is intrinsically unknowable. Hence it could be argued that to speak of physical objects as causes, or of God as "Father," is merely to make an analogical projection of ideas drawn from familiar intra-experiential relations without any grounds for the analogy. The conclusion we must draw is that, if we start from an analysis of experience which exhibits a complete break between the "phenomenal" and the "noumenal," no significant analogies can be drawn from the former to the latter. Such pseudo-analogies would only be projections of a phenomenal relationship on to a transcendent real which was strictly unknowable. We may call them "projective analogies."

It might be suggested that metaphysical analogies are, in fact, pseudo-analogies of this kind. It will be difficult to contravert this, unless we can find some sense in which there can be some direct, non-analogical relation to the "transcendent" which our analogies may then serve to illustrate and express. Hence it will be necessary for us to examine the phenomenalist view of the nature of experience and see whether any such relation is precluded.

3. Certain metaphysical theories have claimed to be *probable hypotheses* about the nature of the world as a whole, for instance the teleological argument as stated by Paley. The discovery of a watch points to a watchmaker as its

designer; the signs of intelligent order in the world point to a designing mind behind it. Arguments of this type presuppose that we can draw analogies between the nature of the world as a whole and some class of phenomena within it. Though speciously like inductive analogical arguments from parallel cases, they are not so in fact. For the world as a whole cannot be an object of experience, hence the hypothesis is unverifiable; and, as Hume and Kant pointed out, the analogy is drawn in terms of certain selected phenomena. There are some phenomena in the world which look like the result of intelligent contrivance, others which do not. So the question must be asked why this particular type of relation is selected. Hence we might have a teleological view of the world, interpreted in terms of the experience of purposive action; or a mechano-morphic view of the world, interpreted in terms of the structure of a machine. Those who hold such views are not generally conscious of their analogical character; they are prepared to present an intepretation of the nature of the world as a whole in terms of some intra-mundane or intra-experiential relationship and use the conception univocally. The possibility of doing this successfully would depend on there being in fact some unitary character in the world, whereas there may be real breaks and diversities which cannot be brought under the same categories, so that the univocal use of terms derived from one kind of experience may be misleading when applied to the whole.*

On these counts, such metaphysical theories are not best described as "probable hypotheses" concerning the world as a whole. For the procedure of applying to the world as a whole concepts drawn from some relation within the world can only be undertaken, if at all, with every recognition of the analogical character of such concepts, not pressing them so far as to distort real and relevant diversities. And this is slurred over by the term "probable hypothesis." Moreover, the term suggests that some method of verification should be possible in a sense appropriate to the inductive study of parallel cases.

4. From metaphysical analogies as "probable hypotheses" we should therefore distinguish "co-ordinating analogies." These would be attempts to co-ordinate different kinds of experience in terms of an analogical extension of a key idea derived from one type. I shall suggest that some of the great metaphysical systems of the past have been analogical in this sense. They start out from an idea drawn from some form of intellectual or spiritual experience which for some reason is judged to be especially significant or im-

---

* I would not foreclose the possibility that there may be a unitary categorical character or relation within the world which could be formulated univocally. We should then have a non-analogical metaphysics. But *de facto* attempts to formulate such a character or relationship are made by analogical extensions of certain selected characters or relationships. Moreover, if the metaphysical nature of the world should be that of the relation of finite existents to an *absolute* existent, the absolute existent would be *sui generis* and *in principle* could only be described analogically.

portant, and then extend this idea so as to achieve some wider co-ordination in terms of it.

5. A metaphysical analogy might express a relation to an object in part experienced and in part not experienced, describing it in concepts drawn from intra-experiential relations. In this case it would be necessary to understand "transcendent" not as meaning "beyond" or "outside" any possible experience (spatial metaphors which may for that reason be misleading, since it is not clear that the relation between our minds and what is other than our minds is a spatial one). We should need to understand the word "transcendent" as standing for that which is "other" than our minds—"being" or "existence" apart from our interpretations. But this would not preclude our interpretations from arising within some situation in which we are related to that which is "other" than our minds. Then we should have to see whether analogies might not be drawn between our various relationships to other being; and whether through these analogies anything might be said about distinctions in the character of being itself. Such analogies must of necessity be indirect attempts to say something about being through our judgments concerning the relationships in which we find ourselves. We must ask to what extent our experience can be held to be constituted by relations to what is other than ourselves, and whether a study and comparison of such relationships in different types of experience might enable us to say anything analogically about the nature of that to which we are related. Such a conception of metaphysical analogies would be difficult to sustain. To defend it, it would be necessary to show that there must be relationships in which we stand to that which is other than our ideas, and that the nature of that other or others could be suggested indirectly by drawing analogies between the feelings and the judgments evoked in such relationships, in order to suggest possible characterizations in that which evokes them. This would be a peculiar type of analogy, but it is not obviously a pseudo-analogy, such as would be an analogy between phenomenal and noumenal when the latter is regarded as standing completely outside experience. Hence "God is Light" would be an analogical expression drawn from the discovery that an experience described as religious is an intellectual and spiritual experience analogous to the sensory experience evoked by physical light. So God would be thought of as the source of such intellectual and spiritual "illumination." I shall call analogies of this kind, drawn from elements within experience to the nature of that in relation to which the experience is constituted, "existential analogies" or "analogies of being."

But before we can proceed, some defence of the use of the word "being" is called for. If we would use it, we must make both our defence and our apology. Our apology is due to the Thomist writers, since the term "Analogy of Being" might be said to have become the special property of their great tradition. I have tried in Chapter VIII to indicate my debt to and my divergence from the Thomist philosophy of the *Analogia Entis;* the divergences are mainly due to epistemological differences of a fairly far-reaching kind. A Thomist will, no doubt, detect signs of metaphysical relativism in my view. If so, I accept the rebuke, and ask that my use of the plural *"analogies"* be taken to indicate that I acknowledge this, and am trying to develop a view of the analogical element in kinds of metaphysical thinking outside the frontiers of the *philosophia perennis.*

I must also defend the use of the word "being." I am using it to refer to "that which exists."* But the path of existential propositions has been fraught with pitfalls ever since Kant's attack on the Ontological Argument showed that whatever is meant by "existence," it is not a logical predicate. Russell's well-known analysis of the logical use of the existential "is" makes it apply properly to descriptions and mean that values can be assigned to propositional functions. So "Men exist" means that the propositional function "x is a man" is sometimes true.

Russell's method of substituting a statement about the truth value of propositional functions is of service in so far as we are concerned to distinguish logic from epistemology and metaphysics. But if we do not confine ourselves to logic as a study of relations between propositions, but go on to raise epistemological and metaphysical questions, we can still ask, when confronted by Russell's analysis, "Why should the propositional function 'x is a man' sometimes be true?" And the answer might be that it would be possible to point to an instance—"*This* is a man"—and it would not be true unless "this" *is* a man. That is to say, what makes a true proposition true is something other than another proposition to which reference may be made. Russell himself does not seem to be concerned to deny that "existence" is significant in some such sense, when he is concerned with epistemology as well as with logic. So in *The Analysis of Mind* he says "the feeling of reality" belongs primarily to whatever can have effects on us, without our voluntary co-operation, and the content of the feeling of reality is best expressed by the words "existence of this." This description obviously needs further expansion. A nightmare can have effects on us without our voluntary co-operation, and it can of course be said that the nightmare *qua* nightmare "exists," though it might be said also that it was "unreal." The nightmare exists in the sense that it is the case that we are dreaming, and having certain beliefs, but it is "unreal" in that our belief that we are being entertained by Hitler dressed as Julius Caesar refers to what is not the case. The distinction between "reality" and "existence," if such can be drawn, seems to consist in the way the word "reality" is used in

* The attempt of certain philosophers, notably the critical realists, to distinguish "being" and "existence" by saying that "being" includes subsisting possibilities, such as universals, and even subsisting impossibilities, such as round squares and hallucinations, does not seem to me convincing. I agree with Professor Laird's observations on this point in *Mind*, N.S. Vol. LI, No. 203.

an evaluative sense with reference to some interpretation. So the real is the genuine, the authentic, as opposed to the spurious, or the misleading ("That is not a real door," or "a real pound note"). Hence "reality" has come to have emotional associations which make it something of a "blessed word" (we remember Eddington's remark about "Reality! Loud cheers!"). In this discussion we shall use "reality" as meaning that which is needed over and above other propositions in order to make true categorical propositions true, and in this sense it will be synonymous with our use of "existence" or "being."* I take it to be implied in the notion of truth that to say a proposition is true is to refer it to something other than itself. The difficulty in stating the truth relationship satisfactorily (a difficulty to which we shall return) need not at this stage deter us from saying that to call a proposition true is to refer it in some sense to something beyond itself. The possibility of this something being only other propositions will be considered later on in our criticism of the coherence theory. We shall find reason to question the adequacy of this; and so shall be brought to hold that what makes true propositions true cannot in the end be merely other propositions. Hence we shall hold that there must be in some sense "matter of fact" beyond propositions, and we shall enquire whether this can be exhaustively described in phenomenalist terms. Our warrant will be largely, to use Russell's description, "a feeling of reality aroused primarily by whatever can have effects on us without our voluntary co-operation." We shall, however, need to distinguish the "feeling of reality," which gives impetus to our interpretation, from that which is not "feeling of reality," but, by being what it is, makes our feelings trustworthy or non-trustworthy. "That which is what it is" apart from our interpretations is, we suggested above, the meaning we should give to the word "transcendent." Yet we shall maintain

---

* The statement that reality may be defined as that which makes true categorical propositions true might be challenged by those who maintain that propositions are true with reference to the context of a "universe of discourse." So "Othello killed Desdemona in jealousy" is said to be true *in Shakespeare's play,* and we need not hold that Othello was a "real" man, or "existed." But the existential reference is to the play as Shakespeare in fact constructed it, as a story in which Othello killed Desdemona in jealousy. In another sense we should say that the proposition was not "true" but "fictitious."

Hypothetical propositions are true within a defined system of relations; hence it may be said that "if *p,* then *q*" can be true without postulating the "existence" of *p.* But if hypothetical propositions are to be said to be true in any sense other than as statements of possible formal connections, it will be with reference to some categorical proposition which states that the relation is sustained. "If it rains, the grass will be wet" depends on a categorical proposition that the nature of physical conditions is such that. . . . And this categorical basis of the hypothetical proposition will only be true if reality *is* such. Mathematical propositions are either hypothetical; if you assume the axioms and definitions, then the statements follow as their necessary implications; or, if they are said to be true in so far as they are applied, there is implicit reference to a categorical proposition, and so to "existence" (*e.g.* the nature of space within this defined field is such that the angles of a triangle equal two right angles). But pure mathematical propositions would be hypotheticals; if you take Euclidean axioms, it is true that the angles of a triangle equal two right angles; if you take Riemannian axioms, then it is not true that they equal two right angles.

that we have no direct apprehension of the intrinsic properties of "that which is" in itself. We have only indirect apprehensions, arising out of relations in which we stand to it.

Stephen C. Pepper   15. SEARCH FOR THE
                                       ROOT METAPHOR

Hypothesis, Professor Pepper insists, is the only shelter for critical thought. With this contention squarely at stake, he undertakes in this essay an explanation of the origin and development of metaphysical hypotheses. He concludes by putting forward his own solution to metaphysical problems and disputes.

Three presuppositions frame his treatment. First he believes that, since metaphysics involves only metaphors (and no metaphor can be absolute), it does not give certain knowledge. Hence, dogmatism of any variety is an illegitimate form of metaphysical thought. This implies, in the second place, that the only legitimate form of metaphysical thought is hypothesis. Lastly, the only proper form of hypothesis, he supposes, is that derived "through the analysis of selected facts (which I call the root metaphor) and the expansion of that analysis among other facts."

The root metaphor theory of metaphysics involves a comparative study of different kinds of metaphysical systems and presentations. These Pepper calls "world hypotheses." His theory, consequently, is less a theory about metaphysics and more a theory about other theories of metaphysics.

A world hypothesis to cover all the facts, says Pepper, "is framed in the first instance on the basis of a rather small set of facts. The set of facts which inspired the hypothesis is the original root metaphor." Since there are different root metaphors, there are different "world hypotheses"—each one of which must by definition suffer from some inadequacy, from "some internal ulcer of self-contradiction."

But there is good reason, Pepper argues, to retain *all* world hypotheses, since any selectivity would necessitate dogmatism. Each one will give a different description of the same "facts," but each will be "autonomous." No single one should ever be used as an instrument to judge another world hypothesis. Such a view, Pepper protests, does not constitute a form

Entitled "The Root Metaphor Theory of Metaphysics," this selection was published originally in *The Journal of Philosophy*, Vol. 32 (1935), pages 365–74. Reprinted by permission of the author and the Directors of *The Journal of Philosophy*.

of eclecticism, because eclecticism can never be a metaphysical solution. Eclecticism is nothing more than a confusion of categories from different and irreconcilable theories. In short, eclecticism is a "mixed metaphor."

THE ROOT METAPHOR THEORY of metaphysics is a theory of the origin and development of metaphysical hypotheses. If correct, it entails certain conse-sequences clarifying not only to the field of metaphysics but to other cognitive fields as well. It involves first (1), the proposition that dogmatism is illegitimate and unnecessary in cognitive procedure; second (2), that the method of hypothesis is legitimate, and so far as we can see, the only available undogmatic method; and third (3), that one way, and perhaps the only way, in which metaphysical hypotheses can be derived is through the analysis of a selected group of facts (which I call the root metaphor) and the expansion of that analysis among other facts. The third proposition presupposes the first two, and the second the first; but the first proposition does not involve the other two, nor the second the third. One may eschew dogmatism and not champion a method of hypothesis, provided one can think of any other undogmatic cognitive method, but one may accept the method of hypothesis and not champion the root metaphor method, provided one can think of any other better hypothetical method by which metaphysical hypotheses may be derived. I will take the first two propositions up very briefly, for a thorough discussion of them would lead far beyond the bounds of a single paper, and I will spend my time mainly on the third. This paper, then, is an argument in the form: If the first two propositions are true, let me show you that the third proposition also is true—namely, that one way and perhaps the only way of legitimately developing a metaphysical hypothesis is by the root metaphor method.

The objection to dogmatism as a cognitive procedure is that it is a refusal to submit cognitive materials to cognitive scrutiny. It is an assertion that such and such is true, or such and such is a fact, with an implicit or explicit threat of "hands off." Or it is similar assertions accompanied with a set of restrictions as to the sort of criticisms acceptable, such that automatically no hostile criticisms are acceptable. When brought out into the light in this way and plainly described, the position of dogmatism is seen to be intrinsically self-contradictory, for it is a way of attributing to materials cognitive values which these materials could receive only upon the application to them of cognitive criteria, and a refusal to permit these criteria to be applied.

The symptom of dogmatism is a refusal to permit certain materials to be doubted, and the subterfuge by means of which this refusal is legitimatized is to convert the particular form of refusal into a cognitive criterion. For example, the criterion suggested may be self-evidence—a term extraordinary enough in itself, for how could anything be evidence for itself? Evidence in that sense is a genuine cognitive criterion (indeed, a whole set of criteria). But "self-evidence" is a way at once of acquiring the prestige of the criteria of evidence, and of dispensing with the need of applying them. Self-evidence is thus not a cognitive criterion at all, but precisely a refusal to permit a cognitive criterion to be applied.

One would think the exposure of such a subterfuge would be sufficient to banish it from use, but experience has shown otherwise. The more effective means is to show in the history of thought or in our own day contradictory facts (?) or principles which eminent men have asserted were self-evident or the equivalent. But there is not time to stop for this. On the basis of what I have said already, I must hope that you will agree with me that no dogmatic method is a legitimate cognitive method in metaphysics or anywhere else.

Now, if dogmatism is rejected, then any specific appeals by theories to self-evidence, certainty, indubitability, inconceivability, meaninglessness, and the like, are also rejected. The consequence of these rejections is to wipe the slate of cognitive methods amazingly clean. The traditional deductive method of discovering truths from the implication of self-evident axioms is obviously wiped away. But so, also, is the traditional inductive method of discovering reliable truths by generalizations from indubitable or stubborn facts. So, also, is the Descartian method of doubt, with its residue of indubitable facts, or the extension of his method to that limit known as the solipsism of the present moment. So, also, is the Kantian method of molding phenomena from *a priori* categories and forms of intuition. So also, the mystic method of dubbing unreal whatever is not a specific sort of feeling. And so, also, the positivistic method of dubbing meaningless whatever falls outside of an arbitrary definition of definition and meaning, or can not be stated in the form of atomic propositions. These are all methods of refusing to submit cognitive materials to cognitive scrutiny.

But it must not be thought that because all these methods are dogmatic and cognitively illegitimate, excellent cognitive results have been attained by men employing these methods. On the contrary. And this fact brings out the point that even if dogmatic methods were legitimate, they are unnecessary. Perhaps the best way to exhibit this point is by reference to the two thoroughly intuitive views of traditional philosophy—mysticism, and solipsism of the present moment. Incidentally, the two views are mutually contradictory, and yet both are generally dogmatically supported on grounds of indubitable immediacy. But all I wish to point out here is that the substance of the two views is not changed an iota if the claims of indubitability are dropped. Offered as descriptions of the nature of things, a mystic or solipsistic *hypothesis* does not differ a bit from a mystic or solipsistic *dogma*. If either hypothesis is true, the corresponding intuition will be straight, of course. If the hypothesis is false, the intuition is illusory. There is no cognitive gain in insisting on the intuition. Dogmatism is, therefore, unnecessary. In fact, dogmatism has always in the history of thought been obstructive to cognitive advance, and the cognitive drive has come from a method of hypothesis. It is this method working beneath the dogmatisms of the great thinkers that has produced the advances in philosophy and science.

From the method of dogmatism I turn to the method of hypothesis, simply because I am not aware of any other undogmatic method. Though this method can be observed in its concrete operation through the whole history of thought, I am not sure that men have noticed what it involves when all dogmatic elements are cleared away.

In the first place, it involves the frank acceptance of the situation that the origin of hypotheses is among uncriticized and therefore alterable facts. If anyone objects to the term "facts" denoting such entities, he may use any other term he pleases, but he must remember that facts denoting unalterable entities are at our present stage of knowledge purely ideal goals. Not that our perceptions, feelings, and immediacies may not be just what we perceive, feel, and intuit them to be, but that to assume certainty on these matters is dogmatic, and has frequently been shown to be unjustified in the history of thought. If we desire to be undogmatic, and unexposed in the rear of our cognitive endeavors, we must be prepared to change our minds about the reliability of any evidence whatever. Facts do not guarantee our hypotheses. Facts and hypotheses cooperate to guarantee the factuality and the truth of each other. Cognitive enterprises open in a field of uncriticized fact. How much of this field will remain unaltered as a result of critical scrutiny, one can not risk stating in advance. A constant recollection of this field of uncriticized fact, which quite correctly every hypothesis tries to abandon, is the greatest insurance against the fallacies of dogmatism. This field was called by Plato "opinion," by others it has been called common sense, or middle-sized fact, or pre-analytical fact.

In the second place, the method of hypothesis involves the acceptance of the criteria of scope and adequacy as the only general criteria for the factuality of fact or the truth of hypothesis. And the two criteria mutually support each other. By adequacy is meant the power of an hypothesis to give a description that apparently fits a fact or set of facts. The precise mode of fitting is at the discretion of the hypothesis and is part of the hypothesis. It may be correspondence, or coherence, or workability, or what you will. But whatever the mode of fitting is, the fit itself must be a good fit. It is not a good fit if some of the fact or some of the facts of the set are not included in the description; nor is it a good fit if two or more descriptions, both equally consistent with the hypothesis, can be given.* The fact itself, since it is not dogmatic or stub-

---

* I am assuming here that the cause of the alternative mutually inconsistent descriptions is some indeterminateness in the governing concepts of the hypothesis, not an insufficiency of facts. In the latter case, it is not the hypothesis that is inadequate, but the facts; and the proper cognitive thing to do in the absence of sufficient facts is to make as many alternative descriptions of sub-hypotheses as one can, consistent with the main hypothesis and such facts as one has. Then one knows as much as one can know, under the circumstances.

born, can of course, be molded or even disintegrated and distributed among other facts—whatever an hypothesis may demand. But a fact can not be ignored. An adequate hypothesis may explain a fact away, but it may not leave a fact unexplained.

Adequacy alone, however, is not sufficient to determine the reliability of an hypothesis and its descriptions. For since it is dogmatic to assume that any limited description will be unaffected by outlying facts not included in that description, the determination of the reliability of that description can be reached only by obtaining descriptions of these outlying facts and observing whether or not the given description is affected. The greater the range of consistent descriptions the greater the assurance as to the adequacy of any given description. All of these mutually consistent and apparently adequate descriptions become evidence for one another, and render the fit of each particular description more firm. In short, scope increases adequacy. It follows, that the maximum of adequacy will be reached with the maximum of scope, namely, when the scope is all available facts whatever and the theory a world theory or a metaphysics.

In the third place, it must be apparent from the consequences already gleaned that a world hypothesis is informative of the nature of our world, or nothing is. There are notions prevalent that if judgments are derived from hypotheses they are merely hypothetical in a derogatory sense. Such notions, I believe, can only be held by people who retain a dogmatic faith in immediacies and stubborn facts. That faith, as I suggested, is cognitively quite unjustifiable, and once that faith is shaken, where can one turn for critical information about facts except to hypotheses and in the end to world hypotheses. Even utter scepticism is not an escape from this conclusion, for unless this doctrine is dogmatically held (and a dogmatic scepticism is no different from any other sort of dogmatism), the doctrine is subject to the same cognitive criticism as any other hypothesis and could not justify itself short of an examination of all available facts, in which case it becomes itself a world hypothesis.

So much, then, for the method of hypothesis. In the course of the foregoing discussion the prominent role of world hypotheses as our ultimate source for the discovery of the nature of facts comes to light. Now I want to ask: How do world hypotheses arise? And in answer to this question, I wish to suggest an hypothesis about world hypotheses, in order to glean therefrom a few more consequences relevant to the cognitive enterprise.

I will state the hypothesis without more ado. What I call the root metaphor theory is the theory that a world hypothesis to cover all facts is framed in the first instance on the basis of a rather small set of facts and then expanded in reference so as to cover all facts. The set of facts which inspired the hypothesis is the original root metaphor. It may be a ghost, or water, or air, or mutability, or qualitative composition, or mechanical push and pull, or the life history of youth, maturity, and age, or form and matter, or definition and similarity, or the mystic experience, or sensation, or the organic whole or temporal process. Some of these facts in the course of expansion may prove adequate, others not. At first, they are accepted as they are found in uncriticized fact. How else could they be found? They are generally dogmatically assumed to be self-evident and indubitable. They are cognitively digested and analyzed. Their structure is usually found capable of rather wide extension through uncriticized facts not at first supposed to be of their nature. This structure is then elevated into an hypothesis for the explanation of other uncriticized facts, as a result of which these become critically interpreted in terms of the root metaphor. In the course of this interpretation, the root metaphor itself may undergo critical analysis and refinement which reciprocally increases its range and power of interpretation. When it assumes unlimited range, or world-wide scope, then it is a metaphysical hypothesis, and a catalogue of its principal descriptive concepts is a set of metaphysical categories.

That is the theory. Now, let me draw from this theory a number of consequences, which are not only interesting in themselves, but also the natural elaboration of the theory.

First, there develop alternative world theories based on different root metaphors. For while many root metaphors fail, a few expand into hypotheses of world-wide scope and great adequacy. These relatively fruitful root metaphors with their corresponding relatively adequate world hypotheses, I believe to be the following: similarity, which generates immanent realism; form and matter, which generates transcendent realism; push and pull, which generates mechanism; organic whole, which generates objective idealism; and temporal process, which generates contextualism (metaphysical pragmatism). None of these hypotheses is fully adequate. Whether in the hands of future ingenious philosophers one of them may turn out to be, nobody can very well say in advance. But it seems unlikely, since the inadequacies that arise within these philosophies are all of the form of self-contradictions. That is to say, the categories of each hypothesis lead to descriptions which both assert and deny something of certain facts. Such is the basis of the difficulty in the so-called problem of mind and matter in mechanism, and of the problem of the relation of the absolute to its fragments in objective idealism. There is always, of course, the chance that with refinement of the categories, the contradictory descriptions may disappear. But in such cases as the above where the difficulties are traceable directly back to the categories, and where the theories have been worked over by many men for many years, the chance seems slight of ironing out the source of the difficulties. The point is that we now have, and are likely to continue to have, no fully adequate world theory, but a number of alternative rather highly adequate world theories, each of which is able to describe or interpret any presented fact, criticized or uncriticized, but each of which contains some internal ulcer of self-contradiction.

Second, the foregoing situation does not justify anyone in rejecting any or all of these theories in default of a better. The rejection of all but one of these theories and the retention of that, is too obviously dogmatic to need exhibition. Yet this method of exclusion is one of the commonest methods for justifying a preferred theory. The inadequacies of theories *A, B,* and *C* are carefully shown. That leaves only theory *D,* which is then sympathetically exposed. The unwary reader may never suspect that the inadequacies of *D* are as great as those of *A, B,* and *C.* The inadequacies of other world theories are no evidence for a given world theory.

Moreover, a sweeping rejection of all world theories as cognitively worthless because they are all demonstrably somewhat inadequate, is also dogmatic. It must not be forgotten that the denial of a theory, in so far as the denial has any cognitive significance, is also a theory. And this theory that no world theories have any cognitive value, has, in view of the several relatively adequate world theories we know, very little adequacy—only as much, to be precise, as any one of these theories has inadequacy. It is as weak as the strongest world theory is strong. The only facts this theory can describe adequately are the facts the most adequate theory can not describe adequately. As a theory, then, in competition with relatively adequate theories, this theory is not tenable—a result which merely indicates in an abstract way the concrete fact that utter scepticism in the face of the large amount of corroborative knowledge we possess is a ridiculous theory. And a scepticism which refuses to examine the evidences of knowledge is sheer dogmatism.

The second point, then, is that the admitted inadequacies of the several relatively adequate world hypotheses is not a good reason for the rejection of all or any of them; but, on the contrary, since they are all in the same condition, a reason for the retention of them all. Presumably each gives some sort of information about the world the others garble.

Third, each of the alternative relatively adequate theories gives a different and irreconcilable description from the others of the "same" fact. Let the fact be any uncriticized fact—say, voluntary action, this fact is critically described in one way by a mechanist, in quite another way by an idealist. There can be no question about the difference between the two descriptions. And the more the reasons for the discrepancies are looked into the more obvious appears the irreconcilability of the descriptions, for the differences have their source in the categories of the two world theories, and these two sets of categories show no sign of ever converging into a single set of categories. Moreover, neither of these descriptions can be discarded in favor of the other, since, so far as we can see, the two world theories are about equally adequate.

Can we avoid the difficulty by saying that the two descriptions cover different facts, or cover different aspects or relations of a fact? Two people describe different sides of the same coin, or, having different esthetic interests, describe different features of the same painting. Each description is true but partial, and all are reconcilable because, strictly speaking, every description was of a different fact. At first, and to a degree, this explanation would seem to apply to our metaphysical situation. It is admitted that the uncriticized fact, from which the two metaphysical descriptions start, is not certain or stubborn, and is to a degree molded and metamorphosed by the two categorial interpretations. By the time the analyses are finished, the facts intended as well as the descriptions may be totally different.

But this explanation is weakened, when we realize that a relatively adequate world theory describes not only uncriticized facts but also the criticized facts of other world theories, for its adequacy depends on its capacity to interpret any facts whatever. The idealist will, then, have his explanation of the error in the mechanist's description of voluntary action, and vice versa. If either description has so far transformed the uncriticized fact that the latter is unrecognizable in the former, the critic is sure to bring this out and gloat over the discovery. Rarely, he succeeds in doing this, as when a mechanist is caught identifying the quality of a sound with air waves, but the greatness of the jubilee when this does occur is evidence that it does not often occur. Clearly, it could not occur often without jeopardizing the adequacy of the theory that did it, for it amounts to a failure to describe a fact. But the point I am here making is that even if the two descriptions of the uncriticized fact so far diverged from each other as to become descriptions of different facts, the divergence would be filled in as soon as each of the theories described each other's descriptions, for an adequate description of a description involves consideration of what that description was about.

And whatever plausibility may yet remain for the idea that alternative metaphysical descriptions supposedly of the same fact are actually about different facts, evaporates when one considers the alternative theories as total descriptions. The total mass of facts presented for description to each world theory is the same total mass on any interpretation of "same." Any fact, part, aspect, or relation which may have escaped description in considering a theory problem by problem, does not escape in the total systematic consideration of a theory. Take the spread of description wide enough and two relatively adequate world theories are bound to cover any given field of fact, and their descriptions of this field will be different and irreconcilable.

Fourth, alternative equally adequate world theories are autonomous. One world theory can not legitimately judge a description of another world theory as wrong simply because the description of the latter is not such as the former would have made. For this kind of judgment assumes that one set of categories is right and other sets wrong, which is, without a sympathetic consideration of the other theory, a dogmatic assumption. The justification for such general legislative powers is often claimed on the basis that a given world theory can explain or include in itself the other theories. But so can and must any relatively adequate world theory. Other theories are among the most important facts that any world theory must interpret. Failure in interpreting would constitute a great inadequacy in an interpreting theory, but success in interpreting has no effect upon an interpreted theory. The adequacy of a theory can not, therefore, be judged by any alien theory.

Neither can it be judged by any other external agency—unless facts be regarded as external to a theory, and even these are not stubborn. Is there not truth and logic? Every world theory has its own theory of truth and its own logic. `.. at about a logical calculus, such as a calculus of propositions? As a fact, of course, every world theory must accept such a calculus and interpret it; but as an ultimate canon of right reasoning, such a calculus is far from acceptable to many theories. Even such general logical principles as identity and contradiction acquire quite different concrete interpretations from theory to theory, and if anything strictly unaltered remains over for these principles in all theories, this is simply due to the fact that each set of categories generates them. The validity of these principles depends on the fruitfulness of the hypotheses which employ them, not the reverse. To assert their self-evidence or their validity independent of their function in hypotheses, would be dogmatic.

Each world theory develops its own cognitive canons out of its own categories, and by these canons judges its own adequacy. That is to say, the contradictions which develop in a theory, are contradictions in the theory's own terms. Idealistic logic itself, for instance, offers no means of harmonizing the finite and the absolute. A world theory is autonomous in its interpretations of facts and autonomous in its criticism of its interpretations. This does not mean that an idealist is always the best critic of idealism, but that, whoever the critic may be, the only legitimate criticism of idealism is in idealistic terms.

Fifth, eclecticism is confusing. By the root metaphor conception we are able to give a precise definition of eclecticism. It is an attempt to interpret facts by means of incompatible sets of categories, categories generated from different root metaphors. Eclecticism is, therefore, mixed metaphor. A specious richness of connotation is obtained thereby at the sacrifice of clarity. I hesitate to say that it is always fallacious. In cases where the inadequacy of a world theory lies in its inability to describe a certain type or group of facts, it may well be claimed that a more complete total theory is obtained by borrowing for this group of facts the categories of another root metaphor. But it must be remembered that the adequacy of the descriptions of this borrowed set can only be determined by the scope (that is, range of descriptive power) of that set. In other words, the borrowed set of categories can be relied upon to furnish a relatively adequate description of the limited group of facts only because it has a capacity of describing a much larger group of facts than the group it is called on to describe; it may even be able to describe all facts. Why not, then, go over to the descriptions of the borrowed set throughout, and abandon the descriptions of the first set, which lack scope? The only plausible reason why this should not be done is that the second set may lack scope in a region of fact where the first set appears to be adequate. But even then, the intermediate regions of fact, which both theories claim to describe with adequacy, will be permeated with ambiguity and confusion. Is it not better to keep the two theories well apart, study the descriptions which each give separately, and note the regions which each is able to describe but the other not?

Actually, however, such considerations as these, as to what should be done in cases where theories lack scope, are of little more than academic interest, for we possess several theories of worldwide scope, and, the dogma of the stubborn fact being set aside, these world theories automatically supplant hypotheses of limited scope. This must not, incidentally, be interpreted to mean that hypotheses applying to a limited number of facts are necessarily hypotheses of limited scope. Every world hypothesis generates a nest of sub-hypotheses for the purpose of describing limited ranges of fact. But since these sub-hypotheses are all derivable from the main hypothesis, they possess indirectly the scope of that main hypothesis. They are not hypotheses of limited scope.

Sixth and last, as the reverse of eclectic confusion, the root metaphor conception offers a means of obtaining clarity in metaphysics. Once the few fruitful root metaphors have been intuited and the characteristic behavior of their sets of categories in description noted, then it is possible to untangle complex philosophic writings, to judge the feasible mode of solution or the very solubility of given problems, and to determine the bearing and validity of philosophic criticisms.

I offer this theory in the first place as a description of fact, as a statement of what philosophers consciously or unconsciously always have done in their attempt to understand the world in which they live. The method expounded by this theory underlies, I maintain, all dogmatisms, and is presupposed by all eclecticisms. And in the second place, whether the theory be correct in fact or not, I offer it as a useful instrument for the clarification of a confused field.

Linguistic

A. J. Ayer

16. THE SCIENCE OF GRAMMATIC FALLACY

Ayer's attempt to introduce a new "realism" into metaphysics is presumably based on the assumption that a transcendent knowledge of reality is at

This selection is extracted from the initial chapter of Ayer's *Language, Truth and Logic* and is reprinted by permission of Dover Publications, Inc., New York.

best spurious, and at worst a hoax. All so-called metaphysical utterances, he says, are due to the commission of logical errors.

To establish this contention, Ayer puts two questions to metaphysicians. He asks: (1) From what premises could transcendent propositions be deduced? (2) On what grounds could intellectual intuition be justified?

Answering his own questions, he asserts that, in the first place, metaphysicians must begin, "as other men do," with empirical evidence. This being so, they could not possibly deduce supraempirical realities from empirical evidence. Second, no proof (and no disproof) can be advanced for intellectual intuition. For these reasons, "no statement which refers to a 'reality' transcending the limits of all possible sense-experience can possibly have any literal significance; from which it must follow that the labours of those who have striven to describe such a reality have all been devoted to the production of nonsense."

The criterion of literal significance, says Ayer (who, incidentally, denies being a "brother metaphysician"), is to be found in the principle of "verifiability." This requires that certain observational conditions follow upon a genuine proposition, so as to lead one to accept or reject that proposition. If a proposition cannot be verified by empirical or logical methods, it is no proposition. "Practically verifiable" is distinguished from verifiable "in principle"; and verifiable in the "strong," or conclusive, sense is distinguished from verifiable in the "weak," or probable, sense.

The "principle of verifiability" for any statement whatsoever, Ayer contends, is used to seek out some experiential proposition that can be deduced from the original statement. This search is determined by the answer to a single question: "Would any observations be relevant to the determination of this proposition's truth or falsehood?" Since a metaphysical statement cannot qualify under such conditions, Ayer contends that it simply "purports to express a genuine proposition, but does in fact express neither a tautology nor an empirical hypothesis." Because only tautologies and empirical hypotheses constitute for Ayer the class of genuine propositions, he concludes that metaphysical statements are necessarily nonsensical.

THE TRADITIONAL DISPUTES of philosophers are, for the most part, as unwarranted as they are unfruitful. The surest way to end them is to establish beyond question what should be the purpose and method of a philosophical enquiry. And this is by no means so difficult a task as the history of philosophy would lead one to suppose. For if there are any questions which science leaves it to philosophy to answer, a straightforward process of elimination must lead to their discovery.

We may begin by criticising the metaphysical thesis that philosophy affords us knowledge of a reality transcending the world of science and common sense. Later on, when we come to define metaphysics and account for its existence, we shall find that it is possible to be a metaphysician without believing in a transcendent reality; for we shall see that many metaphysical utterances are due to the commission of logical errors, rather than to a conscious desire on the part of their authors to go beyond the limits of experience. But it is convenient for us to take the case of those who believe that it is possible to have knowledge of a transcendent reality as a starting-point for our discussion. The arguments which we use to refute them will subsequently be found to apply to the whole of metaphysics.

One way of attacking a metaphysician who claimed to have knowledge of a reality which transcended the phenomenal world would be to enquire from what premises his propositions were deduced. Must he not begin, as other men do, with the evidence of his senses? And if so, what valid process of reasoning can possibly lead him to the conception of a transcendent reality? Surely from empirical premises nothing whatsoever concerning the properties, or even the existence, of anything super-empirical can legitimately be inferred. But this objection would be met by a denial on the part of the metaphysician that his assertions were ultimately based on the evidence of his senses. He would say that he was endowed with a faculty of intellectual intuition which enabled him to know facts that could not be known through sense-experience. And even if it could be shown that he was relying on empirical premises, and that his venture into a non-empirical world was therefore logically unjustified, it would not follow that the assertions which he made concerning this non-empirical world could not be true. For the fact that a conclusion does not follow from its putative premise is not sufficient to show that it is false. Consequently one cannot overthrow a system of transcendent metaphysics merely by criticising the way in which it comes into being. What is required is rather a criticism of the nature of the actual statements which comprise it. And this is the line of argument which we shall, in fact, pursue. For we shall maintain that no statement which refers to a "reality" transcending the limits of all possible sense-experience can possibly have any literal significance; from which it must follow that the labours of those who have striven to describe such a reality have all been devoted to the production of nonsense.

It may be suggested that this is a proposition which has already been proved by Kant. But although Kant also condemned transcendent metaphysics, he did so on different grounds. For he said that the human understanding was so constituted that it lost itself in contradictions when it ventured out beyond the limits of possible experience and attempted to deal with things in themselves. And thus he made the impossibility of a transcendent metaphysic not, as we do, a matter of logic, but a matter of fact. He asserted, not that our minds could not conceivably have had the power of penetrating beyond the phenomenal world, but merely that they were in fact devoid of it. And this leads the critic to ask how, if it is possible to know only what lies within the bounds of sense-experience, the author can be justified in asserting that real things do exist beyond, and how he can tell what are the boundaries beyond which the human understanding may not venture, unless he succeeds in passing them himself. As Wittgenstein says, "in order to draw a limit to thinking, we should have to think both sides of this limit," a truth to which Bradley gives a special twist in maintaining that the man who is ready to prove that metaphysics is impossible is a brother metaphysician with a rival theory of his own.

Whatever force these objections may have against the Kantian doctrine, they have none whatsoever against the thesis that I am about to set forth. It cannot here be said that the author is himself overstepping the barrier he maintains to be impassable. For the fruitlessness of attempting to transcend the limits of possible sense-experience will be deduced, not from a psychological hypothesis concerning the actual constitution of the human mind, but from the rule which determines the literal significance of language. Our charge against the metaphysician is not that he attempts to employ the understanding in a field where it cannot profitably venture, but that he produces sentences which fail to conform to the conditions under which alone a sentence can be literally significant. Nor are we ourselves obliged to talk nonsense in order to show that all sentences of a certain type are necessarily devoid of literal significance. We need only formulate the criterion which enables us to test whether a sentence expresses a genuine proposition about a matter of fact, and then point out that the sentences under consideration fail to satisfy it. And this we shall now proceed to do. We shall first of all formulate the criterion in somewhat vague terms, and then give the explanations which are necessary to render it precise.

The criterion which we use to test the genuineness of apparent statements of fact is the criterion of verifiability. We say that a sentence is factually significant to any given person, if, and only if, he knows how to verify the proposition which it purports to express—that is, if he knows what observations would lead him, under certain conditions, to accept the proposition as being true, or reject it as being false. If, on the other hand, the putative proposition is of such a character that the assumption of its truth, or falsehood, is consistent with any assumption whatsoever concerning the nature of his future experience, then, as far as he is concerned, it is, if not a tautology, a mere pseudo-proposition. The sentence expressing it may be emotionally significant to him; but it is not literally significant. And with regard to questions the procedure is the same. We enquire in every case what observations would lead us to answer the question, one way or the other; and, if none can be discovered, we must conclude that the sentence under consideration does not, as far as we are concerned, express a genuine question, however strongly its grammatical appearance may suggest that it does. . . .

In the first place, it is necessary to draw a distinction between practical verifiability, and verifiability in principle. Plainly we all understand, in many cases believe, propositions which we have not in fact taken steps to verify. Many of these are propositions which we could verify if we took enough trouble. But there remain a number of significant propositions, concerning matters of fact, which we could not verify even if we chose; simply because we lack the practical means of placing ourselves in the situation where the relevant observations could be made. A simple and familiar example of such a proposition is the proposition that there are mountains on the farther side of the moon. No rocket has yet been invented which would enable me to go and look at the farther side of the moon, so that I am unable to decide the matter by actual observation. But I do know what observations would decide it for me, if, as is theoretically conceivable, I were once in a position to make them. And therefore I say that the proposition is verifiable in principle, if not in practice, and is accordingly significant. On the other hand, such a metaphysical pseudo-proposition as "the Absolute enters into, but is itself incapable of, evolution and progress," is not even in principle verifiable. For one cannot conceive of an observation which would enable one to determine whether the Absolute did, or did not, enter into evolution and progress. Of course it is possible that the author of such a remark is using English words in a way in which they are not commonly used by English-speaking people, and that he does, in fact, intend to assert something which could be empirically verified. But until he makes us understand how the proposition that he wishes to express would be verified, he fails to communicate anything to us. And if he admits, as I think the author of the remark in question would have admitted, that his words were not intended to express either a tautology or a proposition which was capable, at least in principle, of being verified, then it follows that he has made an utterance which has no literal significance even for himself.

A further distinction which we must make is the distinction between the "strong" and the "weak" sense of the term "verifiable." A proposition is said to be verifiable, in the strong sense of the term, if, and only if, its truth could be conclusively established in experience. But it is verifiable, in the weak sense, if it is possible for experience to render it probable. In which sense are we using the term when we say that a putative proposition is genuine only if it is verifiable?

It seems to me that if we adopt conclusive verifiability as our criterion of significance, as some positivists have proposed, our argument will prove too much. Consider, for example, the case of general propositions of law—such propositions, namely, as "arsenic is poisonous"; "all men are mortal"; "a body tends to expand when it is heated." It is of the very nature of these propositions that their truth cannot be established with certainty by any finite series of observations. But if it is recognised that such general propositions of law are designed to cover an infinite number of cases, then it must be admitted that they cannot, even in principle, be verified conclusively. And then, if we adopt conclusive verifiability as our criterion of significance, we are logically obliged to treat these general propositions of law in the same fashion as we treat the statements of the metaphysician.

In face of this difficulty, some positivists have adopted the heroic course of saying that these general propositions are indeed pieces of nonsense, albeit an essentially important type of nonsense. But here the introduction of the term "important" is simply an attempt to hedge. It serves only to mark the authors' recognition that their view is somewhat too paradoxical, without in any way removing the paradox. Besides, the difficulty is not confined to the cause of general propositions of law, though it is there revealed most plainly. It is hardly less obvious in the case of propositions about the remote past. For it must surely be admitted that, however strong the evidence in favour of historical statements may be, their truth can never become more than highly probable. And to maintain that they also constituted an important, or unimportant, type of nonsense would be unplausible, to say the very least. Indeed, it will be our contention that no proposition, other than a tautology, can possibly be anything more than a probable hypothesis. And if this is correct, the principle that a sentence can be factually significant only if it expresses what is conclusively verifiable is self-stultifying as a criterion of significance. For it leads to the conclusion that it is impossible to make a significant statement of fact at all.

Nor can we accept the suggestion that a sentence should be allowed to be factually significant if, and only if, it expresses something which is definitely confutable by experience. Those who adopt this course assume that, although no finite series of observations is ever sufficient to establish the truth of a hypothesis beyond all possibility of doubt, there are crucial cases in which a single observation, or series of observations, can definitely confute it. But, as we shall show later on, this assumption is false. A hypothesis cannot be conclusively confuted any more than it can be conclusively verified. For when we take the occurrence of certain observations as proof that a given hypothesis is false, we presuppose the existence of certain conditions. And though, in any given case, it may be extremely improbable that this assumption is false, it is not logically impossible. We shall see that there need be no self-contradiction in holding that some of the relevant circumstances are other than we have taken them to be, and consequently that the hypothesis has not really broken down. And if it is not the case that any hypothesis can be definitely confuted, we cannot hold that the genuineness of a proposition depends on the possibility of its definite confutation.

Accordingly, we fall back on the weaker sense of verification. We say that the question that must be asked about any putative statement of fact is not, Would any observations make its truth or falsehood logically certain? but simply, Would any observations be relevant to the determination of its truth or falsehood? And it is only if a negative answer is given to this second question that we conclude that the statement under consideration is nonsensical.

To make our position clearer, we may formulate it in another way. Let us call a proposition which records an actual or possible observation an experiential proposition. Then we may say that it is the mark of a genuine factual proposition, not that it should be equivalent to an experiential proposition, or any finite number of experiential propositions, but simply that some experiential propositions can be deduced from it in conjunction with certain other premises without being deducible from those other premises alone.

This criterion seems liberal enough. In contrast to the principle of conclusive verifiability, it clearly does not deny significance to general propositions or to propositions about the past. Let us see what kinds of assertion it rules out.

A good example of the kind of utterance that is condemned by our criterion as being not even false but nonsensical would be the assertion that the world of sense-experience was altogether unreal. It must, of course, be admitted that our senses do sometimes deceive us. We may, as the result of having certain sensations, expect certain other sensations to be obtainable which are, in fact, not obtainable. But, in all such cases, it is further sense-experience that informs us of the mistakes that arise out of sense-experience. We say that the senses sometimes deceive us, just because the expectations to which our sense-experience give rise do not always accord with what we subsequently experience. That is, we rely on our senses to substantiate or confute the judgments which are based on our sensations. And therefore the fact that our perceptual judgments are sometimes found to be erroneous has not the slightest tendency to show that the world of sense-experience is unreal. And, indeed, it is plain that no conceivable observation, or series of observations, could have any tendency to show that the world revealed to us by sense-experience was unreal. Consequently, anyone who condemns the sensible world as a world of mere appearance, as opposed to reality, is saying something which, according to our criterion of significance, is literally nonsensical.

An example of a controversy which the application of our criterion obliges us to condemn as fictitious is provided by those who dispute concerning the number of substances that there are in the world. For it is admitted both by monists, who maintain that reality is one substance, and by pluralists, who maintain that reality is many, that it is impossible to imagine any empirical situation which would be relevant to the solution of their dispute. But if we are told that no possible observation could give any probability either to the assertion that reality was one substance or to the assertion that it was many, then we must conclude that neither assertion is significant. We shall see later on that there are genuine logical and empirical questions involved in the dispute between monists and pluralists. But the metaphysical question concerning "substance" is ruled out by our criterion as spurious.

A similar treatment must be accorded to the controversy between realists and idealists, in its metaphysical aspect. A simple illustration, which I have made use of in a similar argument elsewhere, will help to demonstrate this. Let us suppose that a picture is discovered and the suggestion made that it was painted by Goya. There is a definite procedure for dealing with such a question. The experts examine the picture to see in what way it resembles the

accredited works of Goya, and to see if it bears any marks which are characteristic of a forgery; they look up contemporary records for evidence of the
existence of such a picture, and so on. In the end, they may still disagree, but
each one knows what empirical evidence would go to confirm or discredit his
opinion. Suppose, now, that these men have studied philosophy, and some of
them proceed to maintain that this picture is a set of ideas in the perceiver's
mind, or in God's mind, others that it is objectively real. What possible experience could any of them have which would be relevant to the solution of this
dispute one way or the other? In the ordinary sense of the term "real," in
which it is opposed to "illusory," the reality of the picture is not in doubt.
The disputants have satisfied themselves that the picture is real, in this sense,
by obtaining a correlated series of sensations of sight and sensations of touch.
Is there any similar process by which they could discover whether the picture
was real, in the sense in which the term "real" is opposed to "ideal"? Clearly
there is none. But, if that is so, the problem is fictitious according to our
criterion. This does not mean that the realist-idealist controversy may be dismissed without further ado. For it can legitimately be regarded as a dispute
concerning the analysis of existential propositions, and so as involving a logical
problem which, as we shall see, can be definitely solved. What we have just
shown is that the question at issue between idealists and realists becomes
fictitious when, as is often the case, it is given a metaphysical interpretation.

There is no need for us to give further examples of the operation of our
criterion of significance. For our object is merely to show that philosophy, as
a genuine branch of knowledge, must be distinguished from metaphysics. We
are not now concerned with the historical question how much of what has
traditionally passed for philosophy is actually metaphysical. We shall, however, point out later on that the majority of the "great philosophers" of the
past were not essentially metaphysicians, and thus reassure those who would
otherwise be prevented from adopting our criterion by considerations of piety.

As to the validity of the verification principle, in the form in which we
have stated it, a demonstration will be given in the course of this book. For
it will be shown that all propositions which have factual content are empirical
hypotheses; and that the function of an empirical hypothesis is to provide
a rule for the anticipation of experience. And this means that every empirical
hypothesis must be relevant to some actual, or possible, experience, so that
a statement which is not relevant to any experience is not an empirical hypothesis, and accordingly has no factual content. But this is precisely what
the principle of verifiability asserts.

It should be mentioned here that the fact that the utterances of the metaphysician are nonsensical does not follow simply from the fact that they are
devoid of factual content. It follows from that fact, together with the fact
that they are not a priori propositions. And in assuming that they are not a
priori propositions, we are once again anticipating the conclusions of a later

chapter in this book. For it will be shown there that a priori propositions, which have always been attractive to philosophers on account of their certainty, owe this certainty to the fact that they are tautologies. We may accordingly define a metaphysical sentence as a sentence which purports to express a genuine proposition, but does, in fact, express neither a tautology nor an empirical hypothesis. And as tautologies and empirical hypotheses form the entire class of significant propositions, we are justified in concluding that all metaphysical assertions are nonsensical. Our next task is to show how they come to be made.

The use of the term "substance," to which we have already referred, provides us with a good example of the way in which metaphysics mostly comes to be written. It happens to be the case that we cannot, in our language, refer to the sensible properties of a thing without introducing a word or phrase which appears to stand for the thing itself as opposed to anything which may be said about it. And, as a result of this, those who are infected by the primitive superstition that to every name a single real entity must correspond assume that it is necessary to distinguish logically between a thing itself and any, or all, of its sensible properties. And so they employ the term "substance" to refer to the thing itself. But from the fact that we happen to employ a single word to refer to a thing, and make that word the grammatical subject of the sentences in which we refer to the sensible appearances of the thing, it does not by any means follow that the thing itself is a "simple entity," or that it cannot be defined in terms of the totality of its appearances. It it true that in talking of "its" appearances we appear to distinguish the thing from the appearances, but that is simply an accident of linguistic usage. Logical analysis shows that what makes these "appearances" the "appearances of" the same thing is not their relationship to an entity other than themselves, but their relationship to one another. The metaphysician fails to see this because he is misled by a superficial grammatical feature of his language.

A simpler and clearer instance of the way in which a consideration of grammar leads to metaphysics is the cause of the metaphysical concept of Being. The origin of our temptation to raise questions about Being, which no conceivable experience would enable us to answer, lies in the fact that, in our language, sentences which express existential propositions and sentences which express attributive propositions may be of the same grammatical form. For instance, the sentences "Martyrs exist" and "Martyrs suffer" both consist of a noun followed by an intransitive verb, and the fact that they have gramatically the same appearance leads one to assume that they are of the same logical type. It is seen that in the proposition "Martyrs suffer," the members of a certain species are credited with a certain attribute, and it is sometimes assumed that the same thing is true of such a proposition as "Martyrs exist." If this were actually the case, it would, indeed, be as legitimate to speculate about the Being of martyrs as it is to speculate about their suffering. But, as Kant pointed out, existence is not an attribute. For, when we ascribe an attribute to a thing, we covertly assert that it exists: so that if existence were itself an attribute, it would follow that all positive existential propositions were tautologies, and all negative existential propositions were self-contradictory; and this is not the case. So that those who raise questions about Being which are based on the assumption that existence is an attribute are guilty of following grammar beyond the boundaries of sense.

A similar mistake has been made in connection with such propositions as "Unicorns are fictitious." Here again the fact that there is a superficial grammatical resemblance between the English sentences "Dogs are faithful" and "Unicorns are fictitious," and between the corresponding sentences in other languages, creates the assumption that they are of the same logical type. Dogs must exist in order to have the property of being faithful, and so it is held that unless unicorns in some way existed they could not have the property of being fictitious. But, as it is plainly self-contradictory to say that fictitious objects exist, the device is adopted of saying that they are real in some non-empirical sense—that they have a mode of real being which is different from the mode of being of existent things. But since there is no way of testing whether an object is real in this sense, as there is for testing whether it is real in the ordinary sense, the assertion that fictitious objects have a special non-empirical mode of real being is devoid of all literal significance. It comes to be made as a result of the assumption that being fictitious is an attribute. And this is a fallacy of the same order as the fallacy of supposing that existence is an attribute, and it can be exposed in the same way.

In general, the postulation of real non-existent entities results from the superstition, just now referred to, that, to every word or phrase that can be the grammatical subject of a sentence, there must somewhere be a real entity corresponding. For as there is no place in the empirical world for many of these "entities," a special non-empirical world is invoked to house them. To this error must be attributed, not only the utterances of a Heidegger, who bases his metaphysics on the assumption that "Nothing" is a name which is used to denote something peculiarly mysterious, but also the prevalence of such problems as those concerning the reality of propositions and universals whose senselessness, though less obvious, is no less complete.

These few examples afford a sufficient indication of the way in which most metaphysical assertions come to be formulated. They show how easy it is to write sentences which are literally nonsensical without seeing that they are nonsensical. And thus we see that the view that a number of the traditional "problems of philosophy" are metaphysical, and consequently fictitious, does not involve any incredible assumptions about the psychology of philosophers.

Among those who recognise that if philosophy is to be accounted a genuine branch of knowledge it must be defined in such a way as to distinguish it from metaphysics, it is fashionable to speak of the metaphysician as a kind of mis-

placed poet. As his statements have no literal meaning, they are not subject to any criteria of truth or falsehood: but they still serve to express, or
arouse, emotion, and thus be subject to ethical or aesthetic standards. And it
is suggested that they may have considerable value, as means of moral inspiration, or even as works of art. In this way, an attempt is made to compensate
the metaphysician for his extrusion from philosophy.

I am afraid that this compensation is hardly in accordance with his
deserts. The view that the metaphysician is to be reckoned among the poets
appears to rest on the assumption that both talk nonsense. But this assumption is false. In the vast majority of cases the sentences which are produced
by poets do have literal meaning. The difference between the man who
uses language scientifically and the man who uses it emotively is not that the
one produces sentences which are incapable of arousing emotion, and the other
sentences which have no sense, but that the one is primarily concerned with
the expression of true propositions, the other with the creation of a work of
art. Thus, if a work of science contains true and important propositions, its
value as a work of science will hardly be diminished by the fact that they are
inelegantly expressed. And similarly, a work of art is not necessarily the worse
for the fact that all the propositions comprising it are literally false. But to say
that many literary works are largely composed of falsehoods is not to say that
they are composed of pseudo-propositions. It is, in fact, very rare for a literary
artist to produce sentences which have no literal meaning. And where this
does occur, the sentences are carefully chosen for their rhythm and balance. If
the author writes nonsense, it is because he considers it most suitable for
bringing about the effects for which his writing is designed.

The metaphysician, on the other hand, does not intend to write nonsense.
He lapses into it through being deceived by grammar, or through commiting
errors of reasoning, such as that which leads to the view that the sensible world
is unreal. But it is not the mark of a poet simply to make mistakes of this
sort. There are some, indeed, who would see in the fact that the metaphysician's utterances are senseless a reason against the view that they have
aesthetic value. And, without going so far as this, we may safely say that it
does not constitute a reason for it.

It is true, however, that although the greater part of metaphysics is merely
the embodiment of humdrum errors, there remain a number of metaphysical
passages which are the work of genuine mystical feeling; and they may more
plausibly be held to have moral or aesthetic value. But, as far as we are concerned, the distinction between the kind of metaphysics that is produced by
a philosopher who has been duped by grammar, and the kind that is produced by a mystic who is trying to express the inexpressible, is of no great
importance: what is important to us is to realise that even the utterances of
the metaphysician who is attempting to expound a vision are literally sense-

less; so that henceforth we may pursue our philosophical researches with as little regard for them as for the more inglorious kind of metaphysics which comes from a failure to understand the workings of our language.

Morris Lazerowitz   17. LINGUISTIC

                                      INNOVATION

Going a step beyond Ayer, Professor Lazerowitz seeks to inquire into the "reason" behind the "nonsensical statements" of metaphysics. That they are nonsensical, he has no doubt. How else, he asks, can we explain the intellectual stalemate which has too long settled upon the playing board of irreconcilable and irresolvable systems? Since "all the facts . . . are perfectly well known" and "no new fact will settle it either way," dispute is not merely idle but is simply a symptom of the linguistic pathology that affects the "metaphysical mind." Metaphysicians alter customary language, witlessly or not, and therefore their metaphysical formulations "cannot be refuted or established, be proved false or proved true."

What, then, characterizes the metaphysician, Lazerowitz's argument runs, more than the advantage he takes of the ambiguity in language, or the free use he makes of hyperbole? Where there are no clear-cut rules for language, the metaphysician feels most at home. Consider, for example, the manner in which the term "change" is used by Parmenides and Bradley, and the way it is used by Heraclitus and Bergson. Each pair of thinkers uses a series of ambiguities to "prove" its case against a competing set of ambiguities used by the other pair.

Furthermore, all talk of "proofs" is meaningless, since "proofs" are *facts about language*. When such facts about language are then used as justification for altering everyday language into private meanings, the metaphysician simply demonstrates that he "speaks with the vulgar and thinks with the learned." If one were then to put the problem of metaphysics in concrete terms, one would say that it is "language gone on a holiday" or a "game played with language."

Nonetheless, the "game" has for Lazerowitz "a deep purpose." The "startling announcements" of metaphysics, he charges, are very much like the distorted dreams of the mentally disturbed. But where Freud would say that "a dream frequently has the profoundest meaning in the places where

This selection constitutes a portion of *The Structure of Metaphysics* by Morris Lazerowitz (London, 1955), and is reprinted through the courtesy of the publisher, Routledge and Kegan Paul, Ltd., London.

it seems most absurd," Lazerowitz would simply substitute the term "meta-physics" for "dream." The deeper meaning and "deep purpose" of a meta-physics thus become indications of the state of a metaphysician's mental health. And he could be said to suffer from the "metaphysical syndrome."

WHEN SOME METAPHYSICIANS, with complete conviction, maintain that "everything is constantly changing" and other metaphysicians, with equal conviction, maintain that "nothing changes," there results an unbreakable in-tellectual stalemate, an undecidable disagreement, the nature of which can be explained satisfactorily in only one way. It is not difficult to see what makes the dispute *intrinsically* irresolvable, i.e., irresolvable in the sense that no *new fact* will settle it one way or the other: all the facts, material or linguistic, that are relevant to the solution of the problem are perfectly well known by the metaphysicians who take part in the dispute. There is no question of a super fact-finder breaking the deadlock. This makes it clear that the disagree-ment is not factual, not about what is or is not the case. What has happened is that metaphysicians, who divide on the question as to whether things change or not, have decided to alter customary language: some have decided to alter it in one direction and others in the opposite direction. And perhaps their de-cisions are dictated by concealed psychological motives. Regardless of this, it is easy to see that each side can go its own linguistic way *securely,* because what each side maintains is not open to possible refutation. The positions taken *have no theoretical refutations.* One cannot refute, nor for that matter establish by proof, a language innovation. One can only like it or dislike it. It can attract or repel, become popular, lose its popularity, be forgotten, be revived, be forgotten again and revived again. But it cannot be refuted or established, be *proved* false or *proved* true.

One of the "proofs" for the view that everything remains unchanged might be looked at briefly. It is the case that in ordinary language there are no sharp criteria, or rules, for the application of the expressions "has not changed" and "has changed," just as there are no sharply defined rules for the applica-tion of the words "rich" and "poor." By making use of this lack of criteria an eminent logician once "proved" to me that there is no real difference be-tween being rich and being poor. There are, of course, clear cases of a thing having changed or of someone being poor, and there are clear cases of a thing not having changed or of someone being rich: a piece of granite and a burning twig, Oliver Twist and Rockefeller. But there are penumbral cases with regard to which we are at a loss as to what to say, "changed" or "unchanged," "rich" or "poor." And we are at a loss as to what to say, not, as may of course hap-pen, because we are not fully aware of the condition of an object, but because no rules exist for the application or non-application of the word "changed" to all cases which we conceivably might encounter. C. D. Broad's words of warning might well be remembered: ". . . in the absence of clear knowledge of the meanings and relations of the concepts that we use, we are certain sooner or later to apply them wrongly or to meet with exceptional cases where we are puzzled as to how to apply them at all. For instance, we all know pretty well the place of a certain pin which we are looking at. But suppose we go on to ask: Where is the image of that pin in a certain mirror; and is it in this place (whatever it may be) in precisely the sense in which the pin itself is in its place? We shall find the question a very puzzling one, and there will be no hope of answering it until we have carefully analysed what we mean by being *in a place.*"

According to Broad, terminologically undecidable situations can only be avoided with the help of logical analysis. But this is a mistake and a misplaced faith in the magical efficacy of logic. For no analysis of the *actual* meaning of a word can make the meaning, or the word's use, sharper and more exact than it is. I think that no one is likely to be tempted to argue that the meanings of words have *hidden* sharpness and exactness. The ordinary meaning of a word is not more precise than its ordinary use, and to make its use more exact than its actual, everyday use is to alter its meaning.

Now the penumbral, undecidable cases, whether actual or imaginable, *connect by continuity* the opposite clear and decidable cases. And it is this fact that metaphysicians take advantage of. It is this linguistic fact that underlies the "proofs" for the opposite positions of Heraclitus and Parmenides. If, and perhaps for an unconscious reason, a metaphysician wants to maintain that everything is constantly changing, he points to the fact that there is no sharp, and therefore no real, difference between changing and remaining unchanged; and if he is attracted to the phrase "constantly changes" and is repelled by the expression "remains unchanged" he can argue that, since some things do constantly change and since there is not a difference in *kind* but only a difference *in degree* between changing and not changing, everything really is changing. What he has done is to strike "unchanged" out of his philosophical vocabulary; but in doing this, he has deprived "constantly changing" of its descriptive use. A Parmenidean or a Bradleian metaphysician uses the same linguistic fact to "prove" that nothing *really* changes, that change is an illusion, a bare appearance. To generalize, a metaphysician uses a fact about language as a *justification* (his "proof") for changing the language, not, to be sure, for practical everyday use, but only for contemplation, for the pleasure his revision gives him. In Berkeley's words, he speaks with the vulgar and thinks with the learned.

It needs no great amount of intellectual penetration to see that the meta-hypothesis which tells us that the sentences for metaphysical theories use familiar words in deliberately altered ways connects the theories with their proofs in a way that is intelligible. No other meta-explanation does this. What the metaphysician does is concealed from us at two different levels. At the linguistic level it is concealed by the form of language the metaphysician uses to express himself, i.e., by the ontological idiom, in which familiar words seem to be used descriptively. At a deeper, psychological level our emotional needs blind us to what is being done with language.

A metaphysical theory may be described as a two-layer structure. Uppermost is the *illusion* of a theory about the nature or real existence of a phenomenon, the illusion, that is to say, that a metaphysical sentence states a view of some sort about reality. And this is produced by altering the use of a word or an expression. The changed use is not explicitly and openly declared, and it remains concealed by the mode of speech in which it is formulated. There is still a further and even deeper and less accessible layer in the total structure of a metaphysical "theory," and I find that it is impossible for me to refrain from hinting here and there at its existence. It will, perhaps, only be cryptic at this point to say that metaphysical sentences express empirical beliefs which are held unconsciously; but if it is not a mistake to think this, then we have an explanation of the deeply rooted feeling that metaphysical sentences are about reality. The "realities" referred to by them are subjective, the unconscious contents of our minds, not the physical world. We also have at hand an explanation of the position, which remains unshaken by the claim of logical positivism, that metaphysical sentences are not pieces of literal nonsense and, in particular, that expressions which refer to "suprasensible" realities are perfectly intelligible.

Ludwig Wittgenstein has made the colourful and penetrating observation that "a philosophical problem arises when language goes on holiday," and there is truth in this. Metaphysics may be justly described as a game played with language; but there is nothing frivolous about the game. It does not consist in cutting verbal capers, though this is what in an unclear way it seems to be to some intelligent outsiders; nor is it, as it perhaps was with Lewis Carroll, merely having a good time at the expense of ordinary language. Metaphysics is linguistic play with a deep purpose, just as a dream may be said to be mental play with a hidden psychic purpose. Thus, the philosophical sentence "Nothing really changes" constitutes a fantasied, holiday rejection of the word "change," which because it is not made consciously, creates the illusion of being a startling pronouncement about things—and in doing this it perhaps indulges our wish to be able to do magical things with words, our wish, as one of Freud's patients phrased it, for "omnipotence of thought." But more specifically than this, the make-believe rejection of the word "change" indicates that the word has become charged with special meeting. The rejection must play an important and serious role in the drama of our unconscious life.

Heuristic

Rudolf Carnap   18. THE LOGIC OF SCIENCE

Professor Carnap, in this statement from an early work, provides what he believes to be a cure for the "metaphysical syndrome."

The first fact to determine about any scientific discourse, he states, is the
degree to which it supports both authentic *object-questions* and genuine
logical-questions. Object-questions are concerned with the concrete objects
of a specific domain; logical-questions are concerned with the referents of
such objects—that is, terms, sentences, theories, and so forth.

While philosophy, he says, exhibits both types of questions, metaphysics has
becomes especially infamous for its "supposititious" objects which are not to
be found in "the object-domains of the sciences." Thus, metaphysics is
concerned with pseudo-questions because its object-problems do not show
up in the empirical sciences. As he puts the point, "The supposititious
sentences of metaphysics . . . are pseudo-sentences."

Though Carnap denies *object-status* to metaphysical questions, he does
admit that they have *logical-status*. The "supposititious" metaphysical questions are really logical-questions "in a misleading guise," since they emanate
from an illusory "philosophical viewpoint."

Suffering dementia, he seems to say, philosophy has not untangled itself
from the sort of problems that for so long have disturbed it. Only by
untangling itself will it attain the dignity it cannot now claim. But when
"philosophy is purified of all unscientific elements, only the logic of science
remains."

THE QUESTIONS dealt with in any theoretical field—and similarly the corresponding sentences and assertions—can be roughly divided into *object-
questions* and *logical questions*. (This differentiation has no claim to exacti-
tude; it only serves as a preliminary to the following non-formal and inexact
discussion.) By object-questions are to be understood those that have to do with
the objects of the domain under consideration, such as inquiries regarding their

From *The Logical Syntax of Language* by Rudolf Carnap (Humanities Press, New York,
1953, and Routledge & Kegan Paul Ltd., London, 1954), pages 277–80. Reprinted by permission of the publishers.

properties and relations. The logical questions, on the other hand, do not refer directly to the objects, but to sentences, terms, theories, and so on, which themselves refer to the objects. (Logical questions may be concerned either with the meaning and content of the sentences, terms, etc., or only with the form of these; of this we shall say more later.) In a certain sense, of course, logical questions are also object-questions, since they refer to certain objects—namely, to terms, sentences, and so on—that is to say, to objects of logic. When, however, we are talking of a non-logical, proper object-domain the differentiation between object-questions and logical questions is quite clear. For instance, in the domain of zoology, the object-questions are concerned with the properties of animals, the relations of animals to one another and to other objects, etc.; the logical questions, on the other hand, are concerned with the sentences of zoology and the logical connections between them, the logical character of the definitions occurring in that science, the logical character of the theories and hypotheses which may be, or have actually been, advanced, and so on.

According to traditional usage, the name "philosophy" serves as a collective designation for inquiries of very different kinds. Object-questions as well as logical questions are to be found amongst these inquiries. The object-questions are in part concerned with supposititious objects which are not to be found in the object-domains of the sciences (for instance, the thing-in-itself, the absolute, the transcendental, the objective idea, the ultimate cause of the world, non-being, and such things as values, absolute norms, the categorical imperative and so on); this is especially the case in that branch of philosophy usually known as metaphysics. On the other hand, the object-questions of philosophy are also concerned with things which likewise occur in the empirical sciences (such as mankind, society, language, history, economics, nature, space and time, causality etc.); this is especially the case in those branches that are called natural philosophy, the philosophy of history, the philosophy of language, and so on. The logical questions occur principally in logic (including applied logic), and also in the so-called theory of knowledge (or epistemology), where they are, however, for the most part, entangled with psychological questions. The problems of the so-called philosophical foundations of the various sciences (such as physics, biology, psychology, and history) include both object-questions and logical questions.

The logical analysis of philosophical problems shows them to vary greatly in character. As regards those object-questions whose objects do not occur in the exact sciences, critical analysis has revealed that they are pseudo-problems. The supposititious sentences of metaphysics, of the philosophy of values, of ethics (in so far as it is treated as a normative discipline and not as a psycho-sociological investigation of facts) are pseudo-sentences; they have no logical content, but are only expressions of feeling which in their turn stimulate feel-

ings and volitional tendencies on the part of the hearer. In the other departments of philosophy the psychological questions must first of all be eliminated;
these belong to psychology, which is one of the empirical sciences, and are to
be handled by it with the aid of its empirical methods. [By this, of course, no
veto is put upon the discussion of psychological questions within the domain
of logical investigation; everyone is at liberty to combine his questions in the
way which seems to him most fruitful. It is only intended as a warning against
the disregard of the difference between proper logical (or epistemological)
questions and psychological ones. Very often the formulation of a question,
does not make it clear whether it is intended as a psychological or a logical
one, and in this way a great deal of confusion arises.] The remaining questions,
that is, in ordinary terminology, questions of logic, of the theory of knowledge
(or epistemology), of natural philosophy, of the philosophy of history, etc., are
sometimes designated by those who regard metaphysics as unscientific as questions of scientific philosophy. As usually formulated, these questions are in
part logical questions, but in part also object-questions which refer to the objects of the special sciences. Philosophical questions, however, according to
the view of philosophers, are supposed to examine such objects as are also investigated by the special sciences from quite a different standpoint, namely,
from the purely philosophical one. As opposed to this, we shall here maintain
that all these remaining philosophical questions are logical questions. Even
the supposititious object-questions are logical questions in a misleading guise.
The supposed peculiarly philosophical point of view from which the objects
of science are to be investigated proves to be illusory, just as, previously, the
supposed peculiarly philosophical realm of objects proper to metaphysics disappeared under analysis. Apart from the questions of the individual sciences,
only the questions of the logical analysis of science, of its sentences, terms,
concepts, theories, etc., are left as genuine scientific questions. We shall call
this complex of questions the *logic of science*. [We shall not here employ the
expression "theory of science"; if it is to be used at all, it is more appropriate
to the wider domain of questions which, in addition to the logic of science,
includes also the empirical investigation of scientific activity, such as historical,
sociological, and, above all, psychological inquiries.]

According to this view, then, once philosophy is purified of all unscientific
elements, only the logic of science remains. In the majority of philosophical
investigations, however, a sharp division into scientific and unscientific elements is quite impossible. For this reason we prefer to say: *the logic of
science takes the place of the inextricable tangle of problems which is known
as philosophy.* Whether, on this view, it is desirable to apply the term "philosophy" or "scientific philosophy" to this remainder, is a question of expedience
which cannot be decided here. It must be taken into consideration that the
word "philosophy" is already heavily burdened, and that it is largely applied

(particularly in the German language) to speculative metaphysical discussions. The designation "theory of knowledge" (or "epistemology") is a more neutral one, but even this appears not to be quite unobjectionable, since it misleadingly suggests a resemblance between the problems of our logic of science and the problems of traditional epistemology; the latter, however, are always permeated by pseudo-concepts and pseudo-questions, and frequently in such a way that their disentanglement is impossible.

E. A. Burtt   # 19. THE ASSESSMENT
                                 OF CRITERIA

In this selection, E. A. Burtt acts the role of umpire in the dispute over metaphysics that is initiated by positivist criticism. He takes this position because he feels that the stalemate created by those defending and those assaulting metaphysics requires the calm clarification of impartial analysis. The problem for such arbitration is "to choose wisely between various proposed definitions (explicit and implicit) of metaphysics." To do this, the arbitrator must "line up . . . available definitions and by systematic comparison . . . discover the essential virtues and defects of each."

What we are looking for, Burtt says, is an experimentally-oriented criterion of the kind of knowledge that metaphysics gives. In fact, the search for it constitutes the key problem of metaphysics.

Since every knowledge has its own context, metaphysics must likewise have *its* context. For example, when one asks whether railroad tracks do or do not converge in the distance, one asks a question about the *appearance* and *reality* of a specific situation. In such a question one really seeks a solution to a specific instance of the general paradox of appearance and reality—that is, that the tracks appear to converge but really do not.

Now in each field of knowledge, Burtt continues, there are specific distinctions that in fact do solve the paradox of appearance and reality. It is the realization of all such equivalent terms that is crucial for a solution to the metaphysical problem. For instance, the equivalent terms for "real" and "apparent" in ethics are "good-bad"; in law, "legitimate-illegitimate"; in methodology, "true-false." In all such cases, the contrast is between

From the article entitled "What is Metaphysics?" originally published in *The Philosophical Review*, Vol. 54, No. 6 (November, 1945). Reprinted by permission of the author and the publisher.

"a less adequate and the most adequate perspective which emerges in rational consideration as relevant to the determination of what is real and its distinction from what is to be pronounced merely apparent."

What, then, is the equivalent term proper to metaphysics itself, and what criterion does it seek? It seeks, he says, "an adequate criterion of criteria . . . by whose aid we may reasonably tell . . . what other criteria are relevant . . ." to metaphysical inquiry.

THE POSITIVIST ATTACK on metaphysics has forced philosophers to call a moratorium on system-making while they attempt to satisfy themselves, more seriously than had for some time been necessary, as to whether the word "metaphysics" stands for any legitimate enterprise or not. For two decades the debate remained for the most part on the level of pontifical repartee rather than that of constructive analysis, the primary aim of the positivists being to damn metaphysics into the Cimmerian darkness of obvious irrationality, while those in the opposite party feverishly laid about with all the weapons in their arsenal in the hope of rescuing their speculative darling from this threatened catastrophe.

Today the smoke of battle has dissipated enough so that the discussion seems capable of rising from the level of heated partisanship to that of relatively impartial clarification. It is in the hope of contributing toward such clarification that the present paper is written. From sparring with dogmatic contentions thinkers first turned to orderly debate, in which they gradually became aware of the presuppositions of their opponents. The next constructive step in dealing with this as with any philosophic issue is taken when some participants in the argument gain sufficient detachment so that their own presuppositions as well as those of their rivals become objectively visible, and can be critically analyzed in that more inclusive perspective. It seems to me that this stage has now been reached in dealing with the basic problems of metaphysics, and that the discussion initiated by modern positivism may be profitably expanded on this more promising basis.

When one views the situation in these terms it becomes tolerably clear that in this issue we are trying, at bottom, to choose wisely between various proposed definitions (explicit and implicit) of metaphysics. If, then, discussion is to be carried forward hopefully, what is now needed is to line up our available definitions and by systematic comparison to discover the essential virtues and defects of each. Only to the confirmed, dogmatic partisan is it apparent in advance which definition is the wisest one to adopt; others will view all proposed definitions as philosophical hypotheses to be accepted or rejected, revised or synthesized, in the light of searching analysis of what they commit us to if we adopt them. Whether there is any legitimate quest which may be called "metaphysics" is a question whose answer waits, for them, on the outcome of such an investigation; it cannot be settled beforehand by mere fiat. This paper is addressed to those who are ready to consider metaphysical proposals in such an experimental orientation.

The positivists wish us to define metaphysics as consisting of nonempirical assertions about facts. Now in the course of history many influential systems of metaphysics have proffered such assertions, so there is much to justify this proposed definition. Moreover, the proposal is justified for another reason; it has forced their opponents to consider carefully, as they would not have done otherwise, whether they really believe that knowledge can be derived from assertions of this kind. And it is instructive to observe that under the stress of the challenge most opponents have been unwilling to defend the claim to nonempirical knowledge of fact—at least, without serious qualifications with respect to the meaning of the terms "knowledge" and "nonempirical." This is a most important occurrence in the history of Western philosophy; it shows that all influential schools have now adopted a fundamental empiricism—a viewpoint not long since accorded far from universal acceptance. They still differ as to what empiricism means, but the older apriorism, respectable in one form or another for many centuries, seems to be gone.

What lines of defense have the critics of positivism, confronted by this definition, followed? Well, the less bold among them have been content to point out that the positivist rejection of metaphysics means the abandonment of certain problems which are attacked by none of the sciences and apparently belong to none of the other branches of philosophy, but which are significant and important. One is the problem, how are the sciences to be properly classified, so that their relations with each other will be clearly brought out? Scientists as such do not engage in this task, and yet the explanations of different sciences often converge upon the same data and thus inevitably stand in relation. How is the relation to be construed? Another is the problem of mind; in view of the radical differences between the various schools of psychology a question seems pressing that can only be adequately answered by systematic comparative analysis, namely: What conception of mind would permit all the facts that seem relevant to be brought together and to be studied in the most promising way? But few psychologists take it as their responsibility to perform this sort of analysis. The more bold men are carrying the issue even into the adversaries' camp. They endeavor to show that positivism itself implies, in any given statement of its position, certain presuppositions which may not unfairly be called metaphysical. Any theory which talks about language, and fact, and the relation between symbol and its referent, is assuming some criterion by which one discriminates facts from what are not facts and symbols from what are not symbols. But there is no agreement among philosophers as to the proper criteria to employ for such purposes; and so far as the criterion of fact, at least, is concerned, the major key to the differences between traditional schools of metaphysicians has lain in their adoption of different principles on this point. The idealist champions a criterion in virtue of which his "systematic wholes" become facts; the realist a criterion in virtue of which they are denied the status of fact. And so, these bolder critics claim, the positivist becomes a metaphysician in spite of himself; he offers an answer to a problem which has from time immemorial been regarded as a metaphysical one.

But our present-day antipositivists are as yet rather reluctant when it comes to proposing their own definitions of metaphysics, and to giving them sufficient elaboration so that constructive critics can determine with some assurance what they really amount to and can proceed to assess their points of strength and of weakness. This responsibility cannot be evaded if discussion is to advance beyond the stage now reached. . . .

What is the key problem of metaphysics? [We] . . . would suggest that it is this: What is the criterion by which we may reasonably distinguish between the real and the unreal?—or, since what is unreal would never have to be taken into account unless, under some conditions, it appears to be real—by what criterion do we properly distinguish between reality and appearance? "Reality" is traditionally the basic category of metaphysics, in terms of which all its other categories gain their meaning; they refer (so it has been assumed) to universal aspects of reality. . . . What does metaphysics become when approached in terms of this orientation, and how are we to understand the meaning of its basic categories "reality" and "appearance"?

. . . Appearance contrasts with reality as its opposite category, for whatever is mere appearance is not real, and whatever is real is for that reason more than mere appearance. And yet appearance could not be at all unless it had some sort of reality. How is this puzzle to be straightened out? Well, its key, in terms of the present approach, lies in the distinction between reality and agreement with reality. Consider the analogous puzzle in the less complex field of factual science. There is no opposite to "fact," but there is an opposite to "truth," namely, "falsity." Falsity is not a fact, just as truth is not a fact; it is a value, the value of disagreement with fact, just as truth is not a fact; it is a value, the value of disagreement with fact, even as truth is the contrasting value of agreement with fact. Let us carry this lesson over to the more complex field of metaphysics. There is no opposite to "reality," since everything is real in some sense, but there is an opposite to "agreement with reality," namely, "disagreement with reality." And when we brand anything as mere appearance, we mean that it disagrees with the relevant reality. The opposite of "appearance" is thus not "reality" *simpliciter* but "agreement with reality"; the apparent contradiction is solved.

. . . once the meaning of the ideas of agreement and disagreement with reality have been apprehended in terms of this approach, we find that they can be applied significantly in simpler contexts too. Their meaning is primarily determined by the situations in which heterogeneous realities* are involved. But the general criterion by whose aid one decides which judgments agree and which disagree with reality in these heterogeneous forms prove applicable without ambiguity to less complicated situations, e.g., situations in which only one of the three kinds of reality is concerned. The contrast verifiably appears, in short, at all levels of complexity. But the best way to clarify this contention, and likewise the rather abstract relationships which have been discussed, is to examine a number of illustrative uses of the categories "reality" and "appearance." It will be well to begin with the simple common sense situations in which they are used, and to advance gradually to cases of their distinctively metaphysical employment; by following this order we shall be able to see most readily the connecting link between their unsophisticated meaning and their meaning when applied to the traditional metaphysical issues.

Take a situation in which we are dealing with one species of reality alone, and let it be the familiar field of facts. Does this pair of railroad tracks "really" converge in the distance, or do they only "appear" to do so? Well, what do these key words mean here? On examination, their intent in this situation is simply: When we view this problem in the widest perspective that is relevant, is it or is it not the case that the tracks are closer together in the distance than they are near at hand? To direct, uncorrected vision it is the case; when that perception is placed in its proper context, is its testimony confirmed or are we forced to a different conclusion? And what is the proper context here, the widest relevant perspective? The answer is: It is the field of physical facts, as studied by science, with its techniques of measurement which can correct direct perception by applying a common standard to distant objects and to objects in the immediate vicinity. Hence, in this context, we may replace the terms "real" and "apparent" by "true" and "false"; the criterion of reality is here the same as the criterion of truth. Instead of answering the initial question by saying: The tracks only appear to converge, they are really the same distance apart everywhere; we may say: It is false to suppose that the tracks converge, and true that they are everywhere equidistant. However, it is also clear that reality is not simply identical with truth, nor appearance with falsity; when the metaphysical rather than the methodological categories are used one always has in mind the contrast between a more and a less adequate

---

* The author defines "reality" as "whatever is independent of our individual opinion, and therefore exercises coercion upon individual opinion so far as the latter seeks to conform to the nature of its object." On the basis of this definition he holds that there are three species of reality: formal relations, facts, and values (the latter being distinguished from transitory individual satisfactions). A "homogeneous" reality involves only one of these species, while a "heterogeneous" reality is complex, involving two or more of them. Cases of both homogeneous and heterogeneous reality are discussed in the paragraphs that follow. [Professor Burtt added this footnote especially for this edited version of his original article. —EDITOR.]

perspective. The criterion is the same, but it is now considered as playing its role in terms of this contrast, which we know to be applicable elsewhere as well as in the field of facts; whereas, when the concepts "true" and "false" are employed, one is thinking simply of the methodological norms of factual science without reference to anything further.

Is democracy really a good form of social organization, or does it only appear to be so, because of our American traditions and the associated ideals and habits that to us have become familiar? What do the notions of reality and appearance mean in this situation? Well, analysis leads to exactly the same conclusions as were adopted in the preceding instance, except that now the relevant context is that of social ethics rather than that of factual science. Their meaning in this question is: When we face the problem of the validity of democracy in terms of all the considerations that are appropriate, does the judgment that this social institution is better than any competing alternative maintain itself as sound, or does it in that perspective give way to a different judgment? Hence here we may restate the questions thus: Is democracy as a form of social organization ethically good or ethically bad?; the criterion of reality in this realm of discourse is the same as the criterion of moral goodness. However, it is likewise clear that "real" is not simply identical with "good" or "right," nor "apparent" with "bad" or "wrong." When the metaphysical rather than the ethical concepts are chosen we again always have in mind the contrast between a broader and a narrower orientation; and the fact that what is actually bad sometimes seems to be good because it is seen in a more limited orientation than is relevant. . . .

An act of Congress has been pronounced unconstitutional by one of the lower Federal courts. When it is appealed to the Supreme Court, the question faced by the latter may be thus expressed: Is this act really contrary to the constitutional rights of Congress, or did it only appear to be so to the members of the lower court? And what do the categories "real" and "apparent" mean here? On due consideration, they mean once more: When this issue is viewed in terms of the broadest relevant orientation, must the verdict that the act is unconstitutional be sustained or not? To the judgment of the lower court it was the warranted verdict; when that judgment is reviewed by the court of last resort, with the ultimate authority which appeal to it secures, is the decision approved or set aside? Now the appropriate context here is that of our fundamental American law, in its distinctive way of deciding how regard for supreme ethical ends is to be reconciled with regard for the traditionally accepted limitations on the ways in which those ends may be pursued. Hence, in this context, we may replace "real" and "apparent" by "legitimate" and "illegitimate"; the criterion of reality is here the same as the criterion of constitutional legitimacy. Instead of saying: The act is really constitutional, although it appeared to the lower court not to be so; we may say: The act is constitutionally legitimate, as determined by the court of last resort. However, here too, reality is not simply identical with legitimacy. When the metaphysical categories are preferred to the legal ones, we have in mind the contrast between a less authoritative perspective and an ultimately authoritative one. We are not considering the legal categories in their universe of discourse alone, but are reminding ourselves of the fact that an act which is constitutional, like a proposition that is true or an institution that is good, may appear not to be so when taken in too limited an orientation.

Let us take one more illustration, this time from the field of religion. Here our categories combine reference to all the three types of reality, but the problem still lacks the quite unlimited generality that is possible in metaphysics, for reasons that will soon come to light. Does God really exist, or does He only appear to do so to the wishful thinking of seekers after cosmic protection? Following the analogy with the illustrations already discussed, our first question is: What do the words "really" and "appear" mean when thus employed? And the answer will be: When we view this problem in the full perspective that is relevant—that is, with due regard to the light thrown upon it from the field of ethics and from our experiences of beauty as well as from the various branches of science—does the conviction that God exists maintain itself, and, if so, with what meaning to be assigned to the concept "God"? And here there is no generally accepted equivalent for "real," such as we have found in "true" or "good" or "legitimate" in the preceding illustrations; this shows that when we reach the more complex situations in which the category is employed we have come to the sort of context that primarily determines its meaning. There is no satisfactory translation of the question: Is God real, or is He not real? into other terms.

Now let us briefly generalize from these illustrations. We have examined the way in which the concepts "real" and "apparent" are naturally employed in contexts which vary from relatively narrow and specific ones to the very broad and composite context of religion. Just what is in common to all these modes of employment? The answer is: the contrast between a less adequate and the most adequate perspective which emerges on rational consideration as relevant to the determination of what is real and its distinction from what is to be pronounced merely apparent. With this generalization in mind, we can proceed to the next step, and the decisive one so far as concerns the distinctive role of metaphysics.

Are these categories naturally and intelligibly employed in situations which are even more complex than any thus far illustrated? And if so, what do they mean in contexts of such unlimited generality? How are they applied in such cases, and what positive value does their employment there contribute to man's intellectual and cultural life?

The answer to the first of these questions is clearly yes, and when we see why it is so, the way to an answer to the others becomes clear. Frequent and seriously perplexing situations arise in which two or more judgments, claiming to agree with reality in more than one of these fields, conflict with each other, and where a reasonable solution therefore requires us to find a perspective wide enough to include, impartially, all of them. That is, there are cases in which our highest moral ideal and our ultimate esthetic standard are alike relevant but in which they point toward contrary judgments; there are cases in which the moral ideal similarly conflicts with the clearest criterion of truth which we have been able to reach, or with the supreme legal norm, or with our deepest religious intuitions; there are cases in which, in the same way, the demands of religion, or morals, or law conflict with those of science. In these situations, as well as in the less complex ones earlier considered, we find it natural and appropriate to employ the categories "real" and "apparent" when seeking guidance in the endeavor to reach a rational solution of the conflict. And these categories have the same meaning here that we have found them to have in these simpler problems, except for the differences inevitably arising from the more intricate and inclusive context that is now involved. I proceed to illustrate this abstract description of such situations by a brief analysis of several of them.

Take the case in which esthetic values conflict with a moral ideal. Artists are frequently inspired to realize an envisioned beauty in forms that violate the moral sensibilities of their contemporaries, as in the treatment of sex by many present-day novelists. Or esthetic values which were quite consistent with the moral conceptions of an earlier day become inconsistent with the revised ideals established after a period of ethical progress; one thinks of the classic discussion of this theme in the third book of Plato's *Republic*. Confronted by such a conflict, different thinkers propose different principles for its resolution; there is, for example, the puritanical principle championed by Plato himself, that the demands of art are subordinate to the moral ends involved, and there is the principle that artists naturally incline to accept, expressed in the formula "Art for art's sake." Which of these is the sound principle to apply in such situations, or is some third principle a sounder one than either, and if so what would it be? In other words—to put this question in a form which brings out its metaphysical significance—is art really subordinate to morals, or morals to art, or do such principles only appear to be sound guides in the presence of these conflicts? And what is the meaning of the words "really" and "appear" here? An answer is responsible to bring out the common core of significance which this use of the words shares with the cases above analyzed, and also the essential difference. As for the former, it is clear that, once more, our meaning in essence is: When we view the conflict in the wide perspective that is now relevant and necessary, what principle is capable of giving dependable guidance so that the best combination of ethical and esthetic values that is feasible in any such situation will be realized? As for the latter, what is the relevant and distinctive perspective here? Must we not reply: It is the total experience of men and women, as beings both capable of moral excellence and responsive to visions of beauty, and therefore always seeking, so far as they understand themselves aright, the richest possible synthesis of the values in these two fields—the synthesis in terms of which both morals and art can make the fullest contribution that, with due regard to each other's presence, each might make to the enterprise of human living?

Take the case in which moral ideals conflict with the supreme demands of religion. The classic instances here are reflected in the ethical criticisms of the religion of their day given by the Hebrew prophets and by the Greek dramatists and philosophers. Here, too, the main principles that have been championed are familiar to all of us. On the one hand there is the principle that God is not to be judged by man—that if man's moral thinking leads to conclusions at variance with those of the current theology, his thinking is thereby shown to be fallacious and the values envisioned delusive. On the other hand, there is the principle expressed so vividly by Euripides: "If the gods do aught that is base, they are no gods." Which of these is valid, or is some third principle superior to either valid? Again, let us formulate the question so as to bring out its metaphysical bearing: Are man's moral ideals really subordinate to what God is now conceived to approve, or should man's conceptions of God be revised so that they will harmonize with his clearest attainable vision of what is good and right? Or does any such principle only appear to be adequate? Well, the meaning of "really" and "appear" here is to be understood in the way that analogy with our earlier instance would suggest. When the conflict is viewed as impartially as possible, in a perspective wide enough to include all that moral sensitivity and religious insight contribute to the growth of humanity in realizing its fullest potentialities, what principle is capable of guiding us toward the wisest solution? . . .

In terms of this orientation, just how is metaphysics to be properly defined, and how is it related to the other main branches of philosophy? Let us answer the first of these questions by way of the second. It was said in an early paragraph that each of these other branches finds its major problem in determining the criterion that is ultimately applicable within its field. The major problem of ethics concerns the criterion of rightness or moral goodness, that of methodology the criterion of truth, that of law the criterion of legitimacy, etc. What, then, is the major problem of metaphysics? Formally, it is of course to determine the criterion of reality. But what does this mean more concretely, in the light of all the factors brought out in the above discussion? In a relatively brief and precise statement, it means that metaphysics is concerned to establish an adequate criterion of criteria—that is, a criterion by whose aid we may reasonably tell, in any complex situation, what other criteria are relevant, in what form each should be applied, what context is necessary and sufficient to give them appropriate meaning, and how they should be weighted when two or more are alike relevant but point in incompatible directions. In a more lengthy statement, bringing out less technically the human considerations involved, it means that metaphysics is the intellectual enterprise whose task it is to enlighten creative progress in the sciences and the arts, in morals, social statesmanship, law, and religion, i.e., in all the varied phases of expanding human culture; and to enlighten it by providing the most comprehensive attainable vision of the totality of man's powers in relation to the totality of his environment, so that each of these other great enterprises may contribute the maximum value that in this unlimited context is possible to the enrichment of human experience.

R. G. Collingwood   20. METAPHYSICS AND

                                       HISTORICAL SCIENCE

One of the leading spokesmen for modern British historicism was Robin G. Collingwood, who gained fame as both a philosopher and a critical historian. His philosophy envisions the presence of empirical history at work everywhere—not only in politics and economics but also in nature, society, and mind. For Collingwood nothing—not even metaphysics— can transcend or get outside of history. As he sees it, metaphysics is "the science of absolute presuppositions." Hence, the task of metaphysics is a *scholar's* task. It devotes its attention to an ideological scrutiny of the presuppositions, ideas, loyalties, beliefs, and convictions of all societies. It is, in short, a study in the history of ideas.

He illustrates what he means by citing a series of three different propositions about the notion of causation. These he labels *Newtonian, Kantian,* and *Einsteinian.* For Newton, he observes, some events have causes; for Kant, all events; for Einstein, no events. Each of the statements about causation therefore indicates a difference in the set of presuppositions that prompt their framing. The truth or falsity of each of the propositions cannot be discussed in the abstract, but must be immersed in the question of its truth or falsity to the proponents of each proposition. Truth-falsity is, consequently, a question of historical context, and it is the work of metaphysics to discover what such a context is—or in other words, to discover "what absolute presuppositions are made" by thinkers.

Each realm of knowledge brings with it a certain "rubric," or way of expressing itself. As fairy tales always begin: "Once upon a time . . ." so too,

From *An Essay on Metaphysics* by R. G. Collingwood, pages 94–97. Reprinted by permission of the publisher, The Clarendon Press, Oxford.

metaphysics always begins: "In such and such a phase of scientific thought it is . . . absolutely presupposed that . . . " This is the rubric of a historical inquiry, and such precisely, he concludes, is what metaphysics is.

ALL METAPHYSICAL QUESTIONS are historical questions, and all metaphysical propositions are historical propositions. Every metaphysical question either is simply the question what absolute presuppositions were made on a certain occasion, or is capable of being resolved into a number of such questions together with a further question or further questions arising out of these.

This is the central point of the present essay. I will try therefore to put it, even at the risk of repeating myself, as clearly as I can. For this purpose I will go back to the example of causation, and remind the reader of three familiar facts.

(a) In Newtonian physics it is presupposed that some events (in the physical world; a qualification which hereinafter the reader will please understand when required) have causes and others not. Events not due to the operation of causes are supposed to be due to the operation of laws. Thus if a body moves freely along a straight line p_1, p_2, p_3, p_4 . . . its passing the point p_3 at a certain time, calculable in advance from previous observation of its velocity, is an event which is not according to Newton the effect of any cause whatever. It is an event which takes place not owing to a cause, but according to a law. But if it had changed its direction at p_3, having collided there with another body, that change of direction would have been an event taking place owing to the action of a cause.

(b) In the nineteenth century we find a different presupposition being made by the general body of scientists: namely that all events have causes. . . . I do not know any explicit statement of it earlier than Kant; and accordingly I shall refer to the physics based upon it as the Kantian physics. The peculiarity of Kantian physics is that it uses the notion of cause and the notion of law, one might almost say, interchangeably: it regards all laws of nature as laws according to which causes in nature operate, and all causes in nature as operating according to law.

(c) In modern physics the notion of cause has disappeared. Nothing happens owing to causes; everything happens according to laws. Cases of impact, for example, are no longer regarded as cases in which the Laws of Motion are rendered inoperative by interference with one body on the part of another; they are regarded as cases of "free" motion (that is, motion not interfered with) under peculiar geometrical conditions, a line of some other kind being substituted for the straight line of Newton's First Law.

It might seem, but wrongly, as I shall try to show, that the metaphysician is here confronted by a rather embarrassing problem. It might seem that there are three schools of thought in physics, Newtonian, Kantian, and Einsteinian, let us call them, which stand committed respectively to the three following metaphysical propositions:

(i) Some events have causes.

(ii) All events have causes.

(iii) No events have causes.

It might seem that these three propositions are so related that one of them must be true and the other two false; and that the metaphysician's duty is to say which of them is true: an important duty, because when we know which of the three propositions is true, we shall know which of these three schools of physicists is on the right lines, and we shall know that the others are doomed from the start to a career of illusion and error owing to faults in their metaphysical foundations.

I call it an embarrassing problem for the metaphysician because I assume him to be a conscientious man. If he is an irresponsible and dogmatic person it will not embarrass him at all. He will pronounce loudly and confidently in favor of one alternative, whichever he fancies, expressing the fact that he fancies it by calling it "self-evident" or the like, and will pour scorn on any one who hesitates to agree with him; and this will give him a good deal of satisfaction. But if he is a conscientious man, who thinks that the right way of dealing with problems is to solve them, the problem will embarrass him because there is no way in which he or for that matter any one else can solve it. This is because it is what at the end of the preceding chapter I called a pseudo-metaphysical problem: a problem in the form "Is AP true?" What I have now to explain is that the reason why it is not a metaphysical problem is that it is not an historical problem.

The sentences numbered (i), (ii), (iii), above, express absolute presuppositions made respectively in three different schools of physical science. Each is important, and fundamentally important, to the science that makes it, because it determines the entire structure of that science by determining the questions that arise in it, and therefore determining the possible answers. Thus every detail in these respective sciences depends on what absolute presuppositions they respectively make. But this does not mean that it depends on these presuppositions' being thought true, or that the truth of the conclusions arrived at depends on the presuppositions' being in fact true. For the logical efficacy of a supposition does not depend on its being true, nor even on its being thought true, but only on its being supposed . . . . It is a mistake, therefore, to fancy that by investigating the truth of their absolute presuppositions a metaphysician could show that one school of science was fundamentally right and another fundamentally wrong. That "embarrassing problem" does not arise.

A reader may reply: "I see that you have proved metaphysics to be perfectly useless for the purpose for which it is generally thought useful, namely assisting the progress of science by showing which presuppositions, and therefore which schools of scientific thought, are justified in the light of meta-physical criticism and which are not. But whereas I draw from this conclusion the inference that metaphysics is a futile occupation and had better be stopped, you seem to be inferring that metaphysics is not, for example, the attempt to decide whether it is true or false that all events have causes, but an attempt to do something different. This seems to me perverse."

There is no need to repeat the grounds upon which I am assuming meta-physics to be the science of absolute presuppositions, because the point at issue between myself and the reader I have just quoted lies in the interpretation we put upon the phrase "science of absolute presuppositions." He thinks that there are two things you can do with absolute presuppositions: you can pre-suppose them, which is what the ordinary scientist does with them; or you can criticize them in order to find out whether they are true or false, which is what the metaphysician does with them, though actually it is of no use. I deny this, because the second thing (the thing which my reader calls metaphysics) is one which simply cannot be done, whether usefully or uselessly. To inquire into the truth of a presupposition is to assume that it is not an absolute presuppo-sition but a relative presupposition. Such a phrase as "inquiry into the truth of an absolute presupposition" is nonsense. . . .

But I agree with my hypothetical reader that there are two things you can do with absolute presuppositions, and I agree that one of them is what the ordinary scientist does, and the other what the metaphysician does. You can presuppose them, which is what the ordinary scientist does; or you can find out what they are, which is what the metaphysician does. When I speak of finding out what they are, I do not mean finding out what it is to be an absolute presupposition, which is the work for a logician; I mean finding out what absolute presuppositions are in fact made. When I say that this is what meta-physicians do, I mean that this is what I find them doing when I read their works from Aristotle onwards. . . .

Let us return to my three numbered sentences. The business of an or-dinary scientist relatively to these three sentences is to presuppose in his scientific work:

(AP i)* if he is a Newtonian, that some events have causes;

(AP ii) if he is a Kantian, that all events have causes;

(AP iii) if he is an Einsteinian, that no events have causes.

The business of a metaphysician is to find out:

(M i) that Newtonian scientists presuppose that some events have causes;

(M ii) that Kantian scientists presuppose that all events have causes;

(M iii) that Einsteinian scientists presuppose that no events have causes.

I have marked these last three propositions with an M, by way of indicat-

---

* AP stands for absolute presupposition—ED. NOTE

ing that they are metaphysical propositions. These three are true metaphysical propositions; their contradictories would be false metaphysical propositions. It will be clear that the true metaphysical propositions are true historical propositions and the false metaphysical propositions, false historical propositions. It is the proper business of a metaphysician to answer the question what absolute presuppositions are or were made by Newtonians, Kantians, Einsteinians, and so forth. These are historical questions.

This historical nature of the metaphysician's inquiries is at once evident when the propositions he makes it his business to state are stated as they are above in the examples (M i), (M ii), (M iii). What makes it evident is that the wording of each statement includes the formula "So-and-so presupposes (or presupposed) that . . ." Since the presupposition alleged to be made is an absolute presupposition and since the question whether it is made is not a personal one but one concerning the peculiarities of a certain phase of scientific thought, the formula would be more accurately rendered: "In such and such a phase of scientific thought it is (or was) absolutely presupposed that . . ." This formula I call the "metaphysical rubric."

In a long discussion about the absolute presuppositions of any one phase of thought it would not only be intolerably wearisome to introduce every sentence expressing such presupposition by prefixing to it the metaphysical rubric; it would also be an insult to the reader; and in such cases, therefore, it is omitted on the assumption that the reader is intelligent enough and enough accustomed to this kind of literature to put it in for himself.

This is common form. History has its own rubric, namely, "the evidence at our disposal obliges us to conclude that" such and such an event happened. What I call scissors-and-paste history has the rubric "we are told that" such and such an event happened. There is also a rubric for use in narrating legends, which in some kinds of legendary literature is here and there explicitly inserted: "the story says that . . ." or "now the story goes on to say that . . ." Where the reader is assumed to know the ropes these rubrics are left out.

There may be an alternative reason for leaving them out: namely because the writer himself does not see that they are required. It is only when a man's historical consciousness has reached a certain point of maturity that he realizes how very different have been the ways in which different sets of people have thought. When a man first begins looking into absolute presuppositions it is likely that he will begin by looking into those which are made in his own time by his own countrymen, or at any rate by persons belonging to some group of which he is a member. This, of course, is already an historical inquiry. But various prejudices current at various times which I will not here enumerate have tended to deceive such inquirers into thinking that the conclusions they have reached will hold good far beyond the limits of that group and that time. They may even imagine that an absolute presupposition discovered within these limits can be more or less safely ascribed to all human beings everywhere and always. In that case, mistaking the characteristics of a certain historical milieu for characteristics of mankind at large, they will leave out the metaphysical rubric on purpose, and present a piece of purely historical research as if it were a research into the universal nature of understanding. But their mistaking it for something else does not alter the fact that it is history.

Naturalist

John Dewey

21. EXPERIENTIAL
RELEVANCE

Despite obvious differences, Dewey and Collingwood are not quite so far apart as might be expected. Both had high regard for the empirical business of history and society. Both were deeply conscious of the evolutionary fluid that social forces injected into human experience. Dewey's viewpoint, however, was perhaps the larger, since he placed human ideological events not only in the lap of socio-history, but—perhaps because he never completely forsook Hegelian aims—on the cushion of nature and life.

The metaphysical business, he asserts, is not to delve into Being. Metaphysics has, after all, no private stock of knowledge from which it makes perceptual investments. The belief that it has, has made it stiff-necked and narrow-minded. Its true business "is to accept and utilize for a purpose the best available knowledge of its own time and place. And this purpose is criticism of beliefs, institutions, customs, policies with respect to their bearing on good." Its eventual concern is not to define and analyze the generic traits of existences of all kinds, but "to render goods more coherent, more secure, and more significant in appreciation." Metaphysics does not legislate insight but is contextually and naturally given it. Metaphysics "is a recipient, not a donor." The goods that metaphysics must attach itself to are born out of human experience, which is engendered in the concrete confinement of nature and life. Experience is not private but public—even cosmic. And metaphysical assertions are part of that wider experience. "Nothing but the best, the richest and fullest experience possible, is good enough for man."

The experiential orientation of metaphysics thus makes its job more complicated than would be so if everything existed in bookish categories that merely awaited an accountant's pen to assign universal values. But the

From *Experience and Nature* by John Dewey. Reprinted by permission of the publisher, The Open Court Publishing Company, La Salle, Illinois.

fact is, Dewey insists, things are "intermixed," not separated. This is the main reason why he feels that metaphysical discourse must join in the experiential task already undertaken by its partner, philosophy. That is, it must "comment on nature and life in the interest of a more intense and just appreciation of the meanings present in experience." The metaphysical and philosophic aim is experiential vision. Both must therefore "clarify, liberate, and extend the goods which inhere in the naturally generated function of experience."

P HILOSOPHIC DISCOURSE partakes both of scientific and literary discourse. Like literature, it is a comment on nature and life in the interest of a more intense and just appreciation of the meanings present in experience. Its business is reportorial and transcriptive only in the sense in which the drama and poetry have that office. Its primary concern is to clarify, liberate and extend the goods which inhere in the naturally generated functions of experience. It has no call to create a world of "reality" *de novo,* nor to delve into secrets of Being hidden from common-sense and science. It has no stock of information or body of knowledge peculiarly its own; if it does not always become ridiculous when it sets up as a rival of science, it is only because a particular philosopher happens to be also, as a human being, a prophetic man of science. Its business is to accept and to utilize for a purpose the best available knowledge of its own time and place. And this purpose is criticism of beliefs, institutions, customs, policies with respect to their bearing upon good. This does not mean their bearing upon *the* good, as something itself attained and formulated in philosophy. For as philosophy has no private store of knowledge or of methods for attaining truth, so it has no private access to good. As it accepts knowledge of facts and principles from those competent in inquiry and discovery, so it accepts the goods that are diffused in human experience. It has no Mosaic nor Pauline authority or revelation entrusted to it. But it has the authority of intelligence, of criticism of these common and natural goods.

At this point, it departs from the arts of literary discourse. They have a freer office to perform—to perpetuate, enhance and vivify in imagination the natural goods; all things are forgiven to him who succeeds. But philosophic criticism has a stricter task, with a greater measure of responsibility to what lies outside its own products. It has to appraise values by taking cognizance of their causes and consequences; only by this straight and narrow path may it contribute to expansion and emancipation of values. For this reason the conclusions of science about matter-of-fact efficiencies of nature are its indispensable instruments. If its eventual concern is to render goods more coherent, more secure and more significant in appreciation, its road is the subject-matter of natural existence as science discovers and depicts it.

Only in verbal form is there anything novel in this conception of philosophy. It is a version of the old saying that philosophy is love of wisdom, of wisdom which is not knowledge and which nevertheless cannot be without knowledge. The need of an organon of criticism which uses knowledge of re-lations among events to appraise the casual, immediate goods that obtain among men is not a fact of philosophy, but of nature and life. We can conceive a happier nature and experience than flourishes among us wherein the office of critical reflection would be carried on so continuously and in such detail that no particular apparatus would be needed. But actual experience is such a jumble that a degree of distance and detachment are a pre-requisite of vision in perspective. Thinkers often withdraw too far. But a withdrawal is necessary, unless they are to be deafened by the immediate clamor and blinded by the immediate glare of the scene. What especially makes necessary a generalized instrument of criticism, is the tendency of objects to seek rigid non-communicating compartments. It is natural that nature, variegatedly qualified, should exhibit various trends when it achieves experience of itself, so that there is a distribution of emphasis such as are designated by the adjectives sci-entific, industrial, political, religious, artistic, educational, moral and so on.

But however natural from the standpoint of causation may be the in-stitutionalizing of these trends, their separation effects an isolation which is unnatural. Narrowness, superficiality, stagnation follow from lack of the nourishment which can be supplied only by generous and wide interactions. Goods isolated as professionalism and institutionalization isolate them, petrify; and in a moving world solidification is always dangerous. Resistant force is gained by precipitation, but no one thing gets strong enough to defy every-thing. Over-specialization and division of interests, occupations and goods create the need for a generalized medium of intercommunication, of mutual criticism through all-around translation from one separated region of experi-ence into another. Thus philosophy as a critical organ becomes in effect a messenger, a liaison officer, making reciprocally intelligible voices speaking provincial tongues, and thereby enlarging as well as rectifying the meanings with which they are charged.

The difficulty is that philosophy, even when professing catholicity, has often been suborned. Instead of being a free messenger of communication it has been a diplomatic agent of some special and partial interest; insincere, because in the name of peace it has fostered divisions that lead to strife, and in the name of loyalty has promoted unholy alliances and secret understand-ings. One might say that the profuseness of attestations to supreme devotion to truth on the part of philosophy is matter to arouse suspicion. For it has usually been a preliminary to the claim of being a peculiar organ of access to highest and ultimate truth. Such it is not; and it will not lose its esoteric and insincere air until the profession is disclaimed. Truth is a collection of truths; and these constituent truths are in the keeping of the best available methods of inquiry and testing as to matters-of-fact; methods, which are, when collected under a single name, science. As to truth, then, philosophy has no pre-eminent status; it is a recipient, not a donor. But the realm of meanings is wider than that of true-and-false meanings; it is more urgent and more fertile. When the claim of meanings to truth enters in, then truth is indeed pre-eminent. But this fact is often confused with the idea that truth has a claim to enter everywhere; that it has monopolistic jurisdiction. Poetic meanings, moral meanings, a large part of the goods of life are matters of richness and freedom of meanings, rather than of truth; a large part of our life is carried on in a realm of mean-ings to which truth and falsity as such are irrelevant. And the claim of philos-ophy to rival or displace science as a purveyor of truth seems to be mostly a compensatory gesture for failure to perform its proper task of liberating and clarifying meanings, including those scientifically authenticated. For, as-suredly, a student prizes historic systems rather for the meanings and shades of meanings they have brought to light than for the store of ultimate truths they have ascertained. If accomplishment of the former office were made the avowed business of philosophy, instead of an incidental by-product, its posi-tion would be clearer, more intelligent and more respected.

It is sometimes suggested, however, that such a view of philosophy dero-gates from its dignity, degrading it into an instrument of social reforms, and that it is a view congenial only to those who are insensitive to its evils. Such a conception overlooks outstanding facts. "Social reform" is conceived in a Philistine spirit, if it is taken to mean anything less than precisely the liberation and expansion of the meanings of which experience is capable. No doubt many schemes of social reform are guilty of precisely this narrowing. But for that very reason they are futile; they do not succeed in even the special reforms at which they aim, except at the expense of intensifying other defects and creating new ones. Nothing but the best, the richest and fullest experience possible, is good enough for man. The attainment of such an experience is not to be con-ceived as the specific problem of "reformers" but as the common purpose of men. The contribution which philosophy can make to this common aim is criticism. Criticism certainly includes a heightened consciousness of defi-ciencies and corruptions in the scheme and distribution of values that obtains at any period.

No just or pertinent criticism in its negative phase can possibly be made, however, except upon the basis of a heightened appreciation of the positive goods which human experience has achieved and offers. Positive concrete goods of science, art and social companionship are the basic subject-matter of philosophy as criticism; and only because such positive goods already exist is their emancipation and secured extension the defining aim of intelligence. The more aware one is of the richness of meanings which experience possesses, the more will a generous and catholic thinker be conscious of the limits which prevent sharing in them; the more aware will he be of their accidental and arbitrary distribution. If instrumental efficacies need to be emphasized, it is not for the sake of instruments but for the sake of that full and more secure distribution of values which is impossible without instrumentalities.

If philosophy be criticism, what is to be said of the relation of philosophy to metaphysics? For metaphysics, as a statement of the generic traits manifested by existences of all kinds without regard to their differentiation into physical and mental, seems to have nothing to do with criticism and choice, with an effective love of wisdom. It begins and ends with analysis and definition. When it has revealed the traits and characters that are sure to turn up in every universe of discourse, its work is done. So at least an argument may run. But the very nature of the traits discovered in every theme of discourse, since they are ineluctable traits of natural existence, forbids such a conclusion. Qualitative individuality and constant relations, contingency and need, movement and arrest are common traits of all existence. This fact is source both of values and of their precariousness; both of immediate possession which is casual and of reflection which is a precondition of secure attainment and appropriation. Any theory that detects and defines these traits is therefore but a ground-map of the province of criticism, establishing base lines to be employed in more intricate triangulations.

If the general traits of nature existed in water-tight compartments, it might be enough to sort out the objects and interests of experience among them. But they are actually so intimately intermixed that all important issues are concerned with their degrees and the ratios they sustain to one another. Barely to note and register that contingency is a trait of natural events has nothing to do with wisdom. To note, however, contingency in connection with a concrete situation of life is that fear of the Lord which is at least the beginning of wisdom. The detection and definition of nature's end is in itself barren. But the undergoing that actually goes on in the light of this discovery brings one close to supreme issues: life and death.

The more sure one is that the world which encompasses human life is of such and such a character (no mattter what his definition), the more one is committed to try to direct the conduct of life, that of others as well as of himself, upon the basis of the character assigned to the world. And if he finds that he cannot succeed, that the attempt lands him in confusion, inconsistency and darkness, plunging others into discord and shutting them out from participation, rudimentary precepts instruct him to surrender his assurance as a delusion; and to revise his notions of the nature of nature till he makes them more adequate to the concrete facts in which nature is embodied. Man needs the earth in order to walk, the sea to swim or sail, the air to fly. Of necessity he acts within the world, and in order to be, he must in some measure adapt himself as one part of nature to other parts.

In mind, thought, this situation, this predicament becomes aware of itself. Instead of the coerced adaptation of part to part with coerced failure or success as consequence, there is search for the meaning of things with respect to acts to be performed, plans and policies to be formed; there is search for the meaning of proposed acts with respect to objects they induce and preclude. The one cord that is never broken is that between the energies and acts which compose nature. Knowledge modifies the tie. But the idea that knowledge breaks the tie, that it inserts something opaque between the interactions of things, is hardly less than infantile. Knowledge as science modifies the particular interactions that come within its reach, because it *is* itself a modification of interactions, due to taking into account their past and future. The generic insight into existence which alone can define metaphysics in any empirically intelligible sense is itself an added fact of interaction, and is therefore subject to the same requirement of intelligence as any other natural occurrence: namely, inquiry into the bearings, leadings and consequences of what it discovers. The universe is no infinite self-representative series, if only because the addition within it of a representation makes it a different universe.

By an indirect path we are brought to a consideration of the most far-reaching question of all criticism: the relationship between existence and value, or as the problem is often put, between the real and ideal.

Philosophies have usually insisted upon a wholesale relationship. Either the goods which we most prize and which are therefore termed ideal are identified completely and throughout with real Being; or the realms of existence and of the ideal are wholly severed from each other. In the European tradition in its orthodox form the former alternative has prevailed. *Ens* and *verum, bonum* are the same. Being, in the full sense, is perfection of power to be; the measure of degrees of perfection and of degrees of reality is extent of power. Evil and error are impotences; futile gestures against omnipotence—against Being. Spinoza restated to this effect medieval theology in terms of the new outlook of science. Modern professed idealisms have taught the same doctrine. After magnifying thought and the objects of thought, after magnifying the ideals of human aspiration, they have then sought to prove that after all these things are not ideal but are real—real not *as* meanings and ideals, but as existential being. Thus the assertion of faith in the ideal belies itself in the making; these "idealists" cannot trust their ideal till they have converted it into existence—that is, into the physical or the psychical, which since it lacks the properties of the empirically physical and psycho-physical becomes a peculiar kind of existence, called metaphysical.

There are also philosophies, rarer in occurrence, which allege that the ideal is too sacredly ideal to have any point of contact whatever with existence; they think that contact is contagion and contagion infection. At first sight such a view seems to display a certain nobility of faith and fineness of abnegation. But an ideal realm that has no roots in existence has no efficacy nor relevancy. It is a light which is darkness, for shining in the void it illumines nothing and cannot reveal even itself. It gives no instruction, for it cannot be translated into the meaning and import of what actually happens, and hence it is barren; it cannot mitigate the bleakness of existence nor modify its brutalities. It thus abnegates itself in abjuring footing in natural events, and ceases to be ideal, to become whimsical fantasy or linguistic sophistication.

These remarks are made not so much by way of hostile animadversion as by way of indicating the sterility of wholesale conceptions of the relation of existence and value. By negative implication, they reveal the only kind of doctrine that can be effectively critical, taking effect in discriminations which emanicipate, extend, and clarify. Such a theory will realize that the meanings which are termed ideal as truly as those which are termed sensuous and generated by existences; that as far as they continue in being they are sustained by events; that they are indications of the possibilities of existences, and are, therefore, to be used as well as enjoyed; used to inspire action to procure and buttress their causal conditions. Such a doctrine criticizes particular occurrences by the particular meanings to which they give rise; it criticizes also particular meanings and goods as their conditions are found to be sparse, accidental, incapable of conservation, or frequent, pliant, congruous, enduring; and as their consequences are found to afford enlightenment and direction in conduct, or to darken counsel, narrow the horizon of vision, befog judgment and distort perspective. A good is a good anyhow, but to reflection those goods approve themselves, whether labelled beauty or truth or righteousness, which steady, vitalize and expand judgments in creation of new goods and conservation of old goods. To common-sense this statement is a truism. If to philosophy it is a stumbling-block, it is because tradition in philosophy has set itself in stiff-necked fashion against discriminations within the realm of existence, on account of the pluralistic implications of discrimination. It insists upon having all or none; it cannot choose in favor of some existences and against others because of prior commitment to a dogma of perfect unity. Such distinction as it makes are therefore always hierarchical; degrees of greater and less, superior and inferior, in one homogeneous order. . . .

Fidelity to the nature to which we belong, as parts however weak, demands that we cherish our desires and ideals till we have converted them into intelligence, revised them in terms of the ways and means which nature makes possible. When we have used our thought to its utmost and have thrown into the moving unbalanced balance of things our puny strength, we know that though the universe slay us still we may trust, for our lot is one with whatever is good in existence. We know that such thought and effort is one condition of the coming into existence of the better. As far as we are concerned it is the only condition, for it alone is in our power. To ask more than this is childish; but to ask less is a recreance no less egotistic, involving no less a cutting of ourselves from the universe than does the expectation that it meet and satisfy our very wish. To ask in good faith as much as this from ourselves is to stir into motion every capacity of imagination, and to exact from action every skill and bravery.

While, therefore, philosophy has its source not in any special impulse or staked-off section of experience, but in the entire human predicament, this human situation falls wholly within nature. It reflects the traits of nature; it gives indisputable evidence that in nature itself qualities and relations, individualities and uniformities, finalities and efficacies, contingences and necessities are inextricably bound together. The harsh conflicts and the happy coincidences of this interpenetration make experience what it consciously is; their manifest apparition creates doubt, forces inquiry, exacts choice, and imposes liability for the choice which is made. Were there complete harmony in nature, life would be spontaneous efflorescence. If disharmony were not in both man and nature, if it were only between them, man would be the ruthless overlord of nature, or its querulous oppressed subject. It is precisely the peculiar intermixture of support and frustration of man by nature which constitutes experience. The standing antitheses of philosophic thought, purpose and mechanism, subject and object, necessity and freedom, mind and body, individual and general, are all of them attempts to formulate the fact that nature induces and partially sustains meanings and goods, and at critical junctures withdraws assistance and flouts its own creatures.

The striving of man for objects of imagination is a continuation of natural processes; it is something man has learned from the world in which he occurs, not something which he arbitrarily injects into that world. When he adds perception and ideas to these endeavors, it is not after all he who adds; the addition is again the doing of nature and a further complication of its own domain. To act, to enjoy and suffer in consequence of action, to reflect, to discriminate and make differences in what had been but gross homogeneous good and evil, according to what inquiry reveals of causes and effects; to act upon what has been learned, thereby to plunge into new and unconsidered predicaments, to test and revise what has been learned, to engage in new goods and evils is human, the course which manifests the course of nature. They are the manifest destiny of contingency, fulfillment, qualitative individualization and generic uniformities in nature. To note, register and define the constituent structure of nature is not then an affair neutral to the office of criticism. It is a preliminary outline of the field of criticism, whose chief import is to afford understanding of the necessity and nature of the office of intelligence.

Irwin C. Lieb   22. THE USE OF
                                  RECIPROCAL INQUIRY

A logic capable of assessing "intermixed" experience is suggested in this essay
by Irwin Lieb, as a means of clarifying the kind of inquiry he feels is
proper to metaphysics.

> Inquiry, he says, is not linear. It does not travel straight to the question of
> existence or straight to the problem of knowledge. Rather, it must combine
> and alternate both problems, like a pendulum sweeping from one extreme
> to another. Any explicit question about knowledge presupposes certain
> implicit commitments about the meaning of existence; explicit questions
> about existence presuppose implicit solutions to the problem of knowledge.
> These questions are intermixed in theory because they are intermixed in
> fact. And as these components become more and more complex, more and
> more detailed, inquiry must work more dependently from side to side in
> order to "replace what is implicit on one side with what is explicit on the
> other. We check the implicit with the explicit, and necessarily alter the
> side upon which we are working."

> The problem for metaphysics is therefore to articulate implicit solutions—
> which "are far richer than the explicit ones"—into explicit solutions, even
> though implicit insights will never be rendered wholly explicit. It is for this
> reason that "inquiry into metaphysical problems is . . . in principle con-
> tinuous." Metaphysics, in principle, is never done. It can thus never right-
> fully succumb to mere dogmatism, since it is "forever open to correction,
> emendation, and refinement."

> Because we are working in a wide-open context, Lieb observes, there is
> constant need to keep open the lines between the implicit and explicit sides
> of our inquiry—that is, between what we *say,* and what we *are* and *do.*
> "What we have to see is whether or not our metaphysics properly and ade-
> quately isolates and interprets the suppositions which are ingredient in our
> being and acting," because metaphysics is nothing more than "an explica-
> tion of what is implicit in our being and activity." The reason metaphysics
> can investigate itself is that it also is something we *do.*

W E DO NOT and cannot begin our inquiries into the problem of metaphysics
by doubting everything, by stating the most pervasive nature of the real, or by

---

This selection is excerpted from *American Philosophy,* edited by R. W. Winn and published by Philosophical Library, Inc., New York, 1955. It is reprinted with the permission of
the publisher.

pledging confidences in a universally efficient method. We begin in fact and
theory where we are—usually with some familiar observation about what we
know or the way in which we know it. Suppose, for example, that I bump into
someone while I'm walking on a street. Suppose, even though I don't find this
to show my suppositions failing or conflicting, that I begin to wonder just what
are my suppositions about people, walking, and streets. Granting that I know
I've bumped into a person, I may ask just what the evidences are that it is a
person I've bumped into. There is no doubt that I have the evidences. But I
want to examine them, to see what their strength consists in, and to see what
other sorts of things similar evidences would entitle me to acknowledge. When
I recognize that something is a tree, do I give the same sort of reasons to
justify my judgment as when I recognize something as a person? Perhaps I
do, and perhaps doing so does not cause conflict with other of my suppositions.
But do I know anything about past or future persons or trees in the way in
which I know that it is a person or tree I now bump into? Hardly, I have
to bring in other things. I have fully to use remembering and anticipating, and
to settle the accuracy these instruments have.

Perhaps I am more concerned about what I know than the way in which
I know it. If I bump into a person, I may be led to wonder, for example, how
two persons can differ from one another; or whether there are responses appropriate to persons that are not appropriate to trees; or whether the responses appropriate to one person are appropriate to all others, regardless
of their differences.

Such questions as these raise themselves in floods. But we do not answer
them best by answering them indiscriminately. Were we to do that we would
make our metaphysics random, and would have no notion of the incomplete-
ness of our answers. Our questions and our answers should be organized,
though not necessarily on a linear plan. To avoid the difficulties of a linear
plan, what we may do is go back and forth between the problem of knowledge
and the problem of existence. This will give us, perhaps, the least compromising ideal we can have. The order the ideal provides is so general, though, that
it can be specified in many ways. We might, for example, begin by saying
what range and reliability the senses have. Then we could turn to questions
about the characters objects must have if they are to be sensed. However, we
might prefer a larger sweep: before we turn to the problem of existence, we
might want answers to questions about the senses and mind and their relations; or we may even wait until we've given all our views about the ways in
which we know things. Comparable starts, with wide or narrow sweeps, could
just as easily be made from the side of questions about existents.

Our ideal is nevertheless not simply a back and forth, or line upon line,
model. If we remember the way in which the problems of knowledge and existence intertwine, I think we will see that our model is more like a spiral or

vortex. Even more important, we will see a plausible way to do metaphysics without prejudging one or the other of its problems.

Solutions to the problems of knowledge and existence, as we saw, presuppose one another. No fitting and final answer to one can be given without a fitting and final answer being given to the other as well. The model of the spiral or vortex accommodates these interrelationships.

If we are to go back and forth between the problems of knowledge and the problem of existence, we have to have answers to questions about our ways of knowing and about the sorts of objects we believe there are. If we are to work back and forth between the problems of knowledge and existence, that is, we must have provisional solutions to go back and forth between. But here the intertwining of the problems, and their answers, becomes important. If we have made articulate our first answers to questions about knowing, we already presuppose answers to questions about existents. The answers we presuppose, however, are not articulated. If we begin from the side of the problem of knowledge, we begin with explicit answers to questions about ways of knowing and implicit answers to questions about existents. The same is true of the problem of existence. If we make articulate our answers to questions about the sorts of things there are, we will presuppose answers to questions about knowing. From the side of the problem of existence, then, we have explicit answers about kinds of objects and inexplicit answers to questions about ways of knowing. The two sides between which we work thus have explicit and implicit parts. On the one side, answers about ways of knowing are explicit while answers about existents are implicit. On the other side, answers about existents are explicit while answers about ways of knowing are implicit. What is explicit on one side is implicit on the other, and vice versa.

To work back and forth between the problems of knowledge and existence is therefore not simply to double back upon a line we have already drawn. For in working back and forth, we partly replace what is implicit on one side with what is explicit on the other. We check the implicit with the explicit, and necessarily alter the side upon which we are working. For example, if we are using our answers to questions about knowing to mediate our answers about existents, we have to check our explicit doctrines on knowledge with those implicitly supporting our answers to questions about existence. We have, of course, to see that our explicit solutions to both problems support one another. For we cannot claim to have a way of knowing something that couldn't be; and we can't claim that there is something we have absolutely no way of knowing about. But the substitution of the explicit for the implicit, and the mutual check they give to one another are far more interesting. They lead to changes in the side we are working on. They have to lead to changes because the explicit and implicit are not structurally the same and cannot be substituted as equal for equal. To justify the substitution we have to see whether our explicit answers to questions about ways of knowing are fair elucidations of those implicit answers which support our provisional solution to the problem of existence. The explicit answers don't, so to speak, reproduce the implicit ones out loud. The implicit ones are far richer than the explicit ones. They can and perhaps should have many elucidations. However, if the decree of our act of judgment is that the explicit answers are revealing explications of the implicit answers which support our solution to the problem of existence, the explicit answers can be taken as partial articulations of what was before wholly implicit. The explicit answers do not wholly replace the implicit ones. Being richer, the implicit answers can be further articulated, and no amount of articulation will ever render them wholly explicit. To render them even in part articulate, though, is to change the base for our solution to the problem of existence. And so far as that solution really presupposes and rests on that now changed base, the explicit part of our solution to the problem of existence will itself be modified, more or less slightly. When we move from the problem of knowledge to check and support our answers to the questions about the sorts of existents there are, we therefore necessarily modify and deepen those answers. The modified and deepened answers should themselves be used to check and to support our answers to the questions about our ways of knowing. To check and support those answers, we not only have to use our explicit solution to the problem of existence to articulate the implicit solution presupposed by our solution to the problem of knowledge. This check and support in turn necessarily lead to modifications to our solution to the problem of knowledge.

Going back and forth between the problems of knowledge and existence thus seems to generate a vortex of inquiry. The solution to the problem of knowledge causes refinements in our solution to the problem of existence. In turn, the refined solution to the problem of existence causes further refinements in our solution to the problem of knowledge. And these further refinements in their turn can lead to still further refinements. Inquiry into metaphysical problems is therefore in principle continuous. In principle, our metaphysics is never done. It is forever open to correction, emendation, and refinement. As individual inquirers we naturally have our inquiries ended—because we don't have patience, wit, or strength to continue them further, or because we die. Our metaphysics is incomplete in this interesting way: it is incompletely articulated. All it could reveal articulately is there implicitly at any level of the spiral-like inquiry. Our inquiries thus stand whole, subject at any stage to evaluation.

In judging the correctness of our metaphysics, the back and forth pattern of our inquiry is of great help. We can check our solution to the problem of knowledge against our solution to the problem of existence. When we do this, we certify that our ways of knowing are adequate to the things we believe there are, and vice versa. Doing this is, however, not quite enough. For it assures us only that our solutions to the problems of knowledge and existence do not contradict one another: it assures us that we don't claim to know something which is held to be such that it could not be known, and that we don't claim something can't be known which we hold is there to be known. We have to meet the test of consistency. But from the fact that our solutions do not contradict one another, it does not necessarily follow that they are true. If our solutions were related to one another as are the axioms and the theorems of a geometrical system, and if the primary solution were known to be true, the other solution would also be true. But the relations between the solutions are not of that deductive kind, and there seems no privileged way to know that one of the two solutions is in fact true. No matter how favorably the relations between the solutions be conceived, their consistency cannot be a sufficient test of their truth. For limited sets of beliefs, the test of consistency is plainly not strong enough. For the most comprehensive set, for a set that embraces all the true beliefs there could be, the case is admittedly not so plain. But even if it were in principle correct that consistency could insure the truth of the beliefs embraced by a comprehensive set, the difficulty of using the test would be insurmountable. For we would first have to solve the problem of whether the beliefs whose truth we are interested in are embraced by a comprehensive enough set. And to use the test to solve the problems, seems beyond human capacity. Even if we could solve the problem, there would be this integral peculiarity: the belief that a set of beliefs embraces the totality of consistent beliefs is itself included in that totality, but is not made true simply by being consistent with the others. Such a belief would be true if the set embraces all the true beliefs there could be; but whether it does is not shown by the beliefs themselves. Something else is required. To find it out we have no recourse, it seems, but to turn from the test of consistency to face that about which we hold our beliefs to be true.

What we have to turn to is the world in which we live and act. What we have to see is whether or not our metaphysics properly and adequately isolates and interprets the suppositions which are ingredient in our being and acting. What we have to do makes it clear, I think, that methods of testing for truths are of secondary use in metaphysics. They find their use only after we isolate what we think are the pervasive, underlying suppositions revelatory of the world as men engage it. If we succeed in isolating those suppositions, there would be no question of establishing their adequacy in the usual ways. For they are not only the source for all our less comprehensive suppositions, but also the ground for all the principles used in examining beliefs. For anything we in fact isolate, there is always the question whether it concerns what is genuinely pervasive, general and fundamental enough. To settle that question methods of evaluation are needed. The ultimate test is, unfortunately, not a simple, formal one. Ultimately, we have to see whether the metaphysics we explicitly formulate is an adequately revealing explication of the pervasive but implicit suppositions embodied in us as beings and knowers. We do this only partially by inspection. We can do it best through actions which are subject to evaluation by ideals. The ideals for our action find their place in our metaphysics. And in our criticizable actions, our explicit metaphysics meets our ingredient suppositions face to face. Here, the adequacy of the first to the second has its measure. To find our metaphysics inadequate is not to disprove it. It is to give it up, turn away from it, get over it, and perhaps to begin construction of another. To find it adequate is not to find it fully revealing, for the metaphysics makes explicit but does not exhaust what is supposed in being and acting.

The test of being and action enables us, I think, to approach and answer the last peculiarity of metaphysics: the peculiarity of a subject that treats itself as part of its subject matter. The test shows us, I think, how metaphysics is self-reflective. For just as we deal with solutions to the problems of knowledge and existence by measuring the adequacy of explicit answers with implicit ones, so we deal with the whole metaphysics. The whole activity of doing metaphysics is reproduced in the special activities of solving the problems of knowledge and existence. Our metaphysics, at any stage of its development, is an explication of what is implicit in our being and activity. Thus the very activities that justify us in measuring the explicit part of our solution to one problem with the implicit part of our solution to the other, justify us in doing metaphysics, in measuring our explicit metaphysics with the suppositions implicit in us as beings and knowers.

These last remarks are, of course, metaphysical remarks. They would have to be, if metaphysics is concerned with the sorts of questions I have suggested it is, and if it can deal with these best in the ways I have described. Whether my remarks are correct is not settled, I think, by appeal to historical texts or metaphysics. Their correctness is best tested by considering whether the sort of inquiry I have described is the sort of inquiry we engage in when we think persistently about the sorts of things there are in the world and about the ways in which we know them.

STUDY AIDS FOR PART THREE

Review Questions

1. Why does Lazerowitz call metaphysics "totally deceptive"?

2. What is the task of "honest criticism," according to Lazerowitz, vis-à-vis metaphysics?

3. What four chief defenses of metaphysics does Lazerowitz give account of?

4. Why does Copleston say that, before condemning metaphysics, it is first necessary to formulate its questions? Does he make a distinction between "meaningful questions" and "meaningful answers"? If so, what is it?

5. Why does Copleston say that all scientifically unanswerable questions are not *ipso facto* metaphysical? Give an example of one such type of question?

6. What is the difference, according to Copleston, between a metaphysics of substance and a phenomenal metaphysics?

7. What criticism of the linguist's alternative, "clarity or silence," does Copleston make?

8. In what ways does Woodbridge believe that reality is "shot through and through with variety"? Does he believe that this fact bears any consequences in metaphysical theories?

9. To what specific questions does Woodbridge believe metaphysics should turn to? To what other branches of philosophy does its inquiry have significance? In what ways?

10. Why does Moore believe that, in order to prove any one view of the universe, the metaphysician must disprove all others?

11. What specific task, according to Moore, should metaphysics undertake?

12. Why is it necessary, does Moore believe, to handle specific questions before undertaking an account of the whole universe?

13. What does Whitehead say is the "aim" of speculative philosophy?

14. In what sense does Whitehead say that a metaphysical system must be coherent?

15. What does Whitehead mean by the terms "coherent," "logical," "necessary," "adequate," and "applicable," in regard to a metaphysical system?

16. What "faults" of systematic philosophy does Hampshire single out for criticism?

17. What "devastating reply" does Hampshire suggest can be made to the deductive system-builders?

18. In what sense does Hampshire contend that system-builders leap from "actual" to "ideal" knowledge?

19. What, according to Maritain, is the express subject matter of metaphysics? What, does he say, is *not* the true subject of metaphysics?

20. What does Maritain consider to be the "distinctive properties" of the subject of metaphysics?

21. Between what two "lights" on metaphysics does Maritain distinguish?

22. What does Maritain mean by "eidetic visualization"?

23. What difference does Phelan draw between the common experience of being and the metaphysician's experience?

24. What does Phelan mean by "the habitus of metaphysical wisdom"?

25. What formal distinction does Phelan suggest to describe the object of metaphysics? What does it mean?

26. What does Garrigou-Lagrange consider to be the first intuition of the mind?

27. How many "first principles" does Garrigou-Lagrange distinguish? What are they?

28. What is the relation, drawn by Garrigou-Lagrange, between the principles of theoretic and practical reason?

29. What does Berdyaev mean when he says that reason "both enriches man and impoverishes him"?

30. What does Berdyaev mean by "knowledge of reality"? What relation does knowledge have to "logical apparatus"? To "creativity"?

31. What does Berdyaev mean by "subject" and "object"? In the knowledge of reality which of these does he emphasize? In what way?

32. What relevance does Marcel's distinction between "full" and "empty" have for the knowledge of metaphysics?

33. How does Marcel define "Being"? What relation does he draw between the knowledge of Being and "the ontological status of the investigator"? What is the importance of this relation?

34. What does Marcel mean by the "meta-problematical"? What is its relation to "the ontological mystery"?

35. How does Marcel use the terms "recollection" and "assurance"?

36. What is the fundamental question of metaphysics for Heidegger? In what way does he divide the question? Why does he divide it?

37. What two levels of meaning of the term "essent" does Heidegger derive?

38. What three stages in the affirmation of being does Lavelle distinguish? What relations does he draw between these stages?

39. What three properties define the "world" for Lavelle?

40. How does Emmet define metaphysics? What does she mean by it?

41. What five senses of the term "analogy" does Emmet classify? In which sense does she accept the term?

42. What three assumptions on metaphysical practice does Pepper make? What justification, if any, does he offer for these assumptions?

43. What does Pepper mean by the "root metaphor theory"? What solution to metaphysical problems does he claim for it?

44. What criticism of "eclecticism" does Pepper make? How does he defend his own position against the charge of eclecticism?

45. What principal charge against metaphysics does Ayer make? What arguments does he use to substantiate his thesis?

46. By what series of arguments does Ayer conclude that metaphysicians have been "devoted to the production of nonsense"?

47. What does Ayer mean by the "principle of verifiability"? What does he mean by "practical verifiability" and "verifiability in principle"? By verifiable in the "strong sense" and the "weak sense"? What is the minimal criterion of verifiability?

48. What does Ayer mean by "a genuine proposition"? How many kinds of "genuine propositions" does he admit?

49. Why does Lazerowitz say that "no new fact" will settle the conflicting propositions of metaphysics? How does he characterize metaphysics? Metaphysicians?

50. How does Lazerowitz define "proof"?

51. What does Carnap mean by the terms "object-questions" and "logical questions"?

52. What proper role does Carnap assign to metaphysics?

53. What does Carnap mean by "the logic of science"?

54. What solution does Burtt offer to minimize the conflict between logical positivism and traditional metaphysics?

55. What is the criterion of metaphysics according to Burtt?

56. What, according to Collingwood, is the function of metaphysics?

57. What does Collingwood mean by the phrase "the science of absolute presuppositions"?

58. What is the "rubric" of metaphysics, as Collingwood sees it?

59. What does Dewey consider to be "the business" of metaphysics?

60. What does Dewey mean by "experiential orientation"?

61. What reasons does Lieb advance to explain why "in principle, our metaphysics is never done"?

62. What role does Lieb assign to metaphysics?

63. What, according to Lieb, does metaphysics explicate?

Discussion Topics

1. In what way do the following statements agree that metaphysics has "universal scope"? What specific interpretations of "universal scope" does each one contain?

§ ". . . the object of metaphysics is to find a general view which will satisfy the intellect, and I have assumed that whatever succeeds in doing this is real and true and that whatever fails is neither."—F. H. Bradley, *Appearance and Reality*.

§ "Speculative philosophy is the endeavor to frame a coherent, logical, necessary system of general ideas in terms of which every element of our experience can be interpreted."—A. N. Whitehead, *Process and Reality*.

§ ". . . the more comprehensive a science becomes, the closer it comes to philosophy, so that it may be difficult to say where the science leaves off and philosophy begins."—S. Alexander, *Space, Time and Deity*.

§ "Metaphysics . . . tries to include all facts. It has for its subject matter the totality of things and understandably has greater difficulty in working out precise knowledge. . . ."—Lewis Hahn, "Metaphysical Interpretation," *Philosophical Review*.

§ ". . . it is a binding or unifying function which metaphysics aspires to perform."—W. P. Montague, *The Ways of Things*.

2. Do you find any similarity beween Whitehead's views on the functions of speculative philosophy and those of Aristotle? If so, how? If not, why? Can you establish any relationship between Aristotle's "ultimate causes" and Whitehead's terms "coherent," "logical," "necessary," "adequate," and "applicable"? Whitehead says that the philosopher can never hope fully to formulate metaphysical first principles. Why does he say this? What does he mean by it? Would Plato concur? Would Aristotle? In what ways?

3. On what front does Whitehead say that metaphysics faces its greatest difficulties? Compare his view on the problem with that given in Part One by Aristotle. By Plato. Are they all talking about the same problem? What makes you think so?

4. The mathematician Kurt Gödel demonstrated, in what is known as Gödel's theorem, that a complete logical system remains inconsistent, while a consistent system must remain incomplete. Do you feel that Gödel's theorem substantiates Hampshire's arguments against the use of "all" and "every"? In what way? Does G. K. Chesterton's famous critical paradox (*Heretics* [New York, Garden City Publishing Co., 1927], p. 13) that "everything matters—except everything" clarify Hamphire's position? Does the paradox strengthen or weaken Hampshire's case?

5. Philosophical decisions, says David Hume (*Enquiry Concerning Human*

Understanding, XII, 3), "are nothing but the reflections of common life, method-ized and corrected." He concludes that when we take in hand any volume of "divinity or school metaphysics," we must ask: *"Does it contain any abstract reasoning concerning quantity or number? No. Does it contain any experimental reasoning concerning matter of fact or existence? No.* Commit it then to the flames: for it can contain nothing but sophistry and illusion." In what specific ways do the following statements by Carnap and Ayer reflect Hume's viewpoint?

§ "Metaphysical statements assert nothing at all."—Rudolf Carnap, *Philosophy and Logical Syntax.*

§ "Tautologies and empirical statements form the entire class of significant propositions; hence metaphysics is nonsense."—A. J. Ayers, *Language, Truth and Logic.*

How would these writers account for the continuing popularity of metaphysics, as W. H. Walsh ("True and False in Metaphysics," *Cross Currents,* XI [1961], p. 270) points out in his summary of analytic conceptions of metaphysics?

6. Maritain's assertion (see *Discussion Topics,* Part One) that metaphysics "bakes no bread" appears to substantiate Lazerowitz's claim that it can boast no "tangible results." Does it actually do so? What differences, if any, can you enumerate in their respective attitudes toward the "unproductive" character of metaphysics? Does Copleston's assertion that "philosophy gives no new facts" support both or either of their views?

7. Can you discover any link between Woodbridge's remarks on great metaphysical systems and Pepper's remarks on the same topic? What specific differences can you draw in their viewpoints on the subject? Cite specific comparative passages.

8. To Copleston, moral questions are not metaphysical matter. To Moore, such questions have metaphysical relevance. Does Moore, then, ignore Copleston's distinction? If so, how? Does Moore's specific tasks of analysis of "the sort of things you hold to be in the universe" amount to "specialization"? How can you explain his point of view in the light of Weiss' remark in his essay (Part Two) that specialization "requires a grasp of the whole?"

9. Does Copleston's essay lend any weight to Bradley's assertions in his essay in Part One? In what ways?

10. Contrast the way in which Garrigou-Lagrange explains how "first principles" are framed with Whitehead's views on the same subject. Are they speaking about the same kind of "first principles"?

11. Fulton J. Sheen once wrote that "the only two things which pre-exist first principles are the mind and sensible experience, and these two suffice for the formation of first principles." Interpret this statement in the light of the specific views expressed in Garrigou-Lagrange's essay. What criticisms do you imagine could be brought against the statement by Marcel and Heidegger? By Ayer? By Collingwood?

12. Existentialism is reputed to trace its heritage to the thought of many thinkers in the ancient and medieval world. Socrates and Heraclitus believed that man is a reality in search of itself; St. Augustine said that man walks about insecurely with a "glass heart." What comment on these remarks do you suppose would be made by Berdyaev, Marcel, Heidegger, and Lavelle? Which statements —those by Heraclitus, Socrates, or St. Augustine—would be most revealing to which of the existentialists mentioned?

13. Does Marcel agree with Maritain, Phelan, and Garrigou-Lagrange, in giving the primacy to being or to knowledge? In what way?

14. Maritain, Phelan, and Garrigou-Lagrange agree with Aristotle and St. Thomas in maintaining that the object of metaphysics is "being as such." Heidegger says that "being as such" is precisely hidden from metaphysics. Is this a difference of terminology or of meaning? Can you account for this difference? On which side would Marcel stand? Would Lavelle stand?

15. Do you perceive any similarity between Lavelle's contention that "the world is a tool for [the ego], . . . not a place to stay," and Thomas Browne's remark (*Religio Medici*, I, xiii) that the world is "not an Inn, but an Hospital. . . ."

16. Moore suggests that, to establish a theory of the universe, one must disprove all other theories. What rejoinder would Pepper make to such an assertion? What rebuttal, in turn, might Moore make?

17. According to Bradley's essay in Part One, any thinker who denies the validity of metaphysics is a "brother metaphysician." Ayer however, denies metaphysics and also refuses to accept the label "brother metaphysician." What reason does Ayer give for this refusal? Are both his refusal and reason justified? How might Bradley answer this denial?

18. "The essential act of thought," A. D. Ritchie once wrote, "is symbolization." Suzanne Langer has added that experiential statements are achieved only through symbolization. What specific criticism of these positions would Maritain make? Do you think that "symbolization," in the analogical sense, has anything to do with Maritain's "eidetic visualization"? Explain.

19. Literary scholar J. Middleton Murray once said that every "transcendentalism" (or indication of a reality that is more than an appearance) is "only the name for a prodigious metaphor." Identify the authors in this section who might agree with the statement. How many would disagree? Would it be just as fair to say that "every metaphor is only the name for a prodigious transcendentalism"? Would Aristotle's remark that metaphors imply "the intuitive perception of the similarity in dissimilars" tend to substantiate Murray's view? Why?

20. "Metaphor," says Kenneth Burke (*Rhetoric of Motives* [New York, Prentice-Hall, 1952], p. 503), "is a device for seeing something in terms of something else. It brings out the thisness of a that or the thatness of a this." Would Pepper accept his statement? Does it add to, or detract from, his "root metaphor" theory? In what way?

21. According to William Empson (*Seven Types of Ambiguity* [New York, Noonday, 1955], p. 1), an ambiguity is a verbal nuance "which gives room for alternative reactions to the same piece of language." It can mean "an indecision as to what you mean, an intention to mean several things, probability that one or other or both of two things has been meant, and the fact that a statement has several meanings" (pp. 5–6). What comments do you believe Ayer and Carnap would make to these statements? Burtt and Collingwood?

22. Ayer contends that his principle of "verifiability" ("Would any observations be relevant to the determination of this proposition's truth or falsehood?") is the only valid method of assessing the relevance of data. Is Burtt's "principle of relevance" the same method in a different guise? If so, is his claim to be an independent umpire, in the dispute between logical positivism and its critics, colored by methodological bias? In what way? What connection do you find between Ayer's principle of verifiability and Hall's remarks in Part Two on "verificatory instances"?

23. Both Pepper and Lieb seem to feel that dogmatism is the chief sin of metaphysics. From what positions do they reach this "conclusion"? Are they the same or different positions?

24. "The supposititious sentences of metaphysics," observes Carnap, ". . . are pseudo-sentences." Is this a tautology in the clothing of a synthetic statement? Is it an empirical statement? Does it, as a definition, follow the rules of a good definition? Why?

25. What common denominator can you discover in the following quotations about the function of metaphysics? Under what "school" would you place these statements?

§ Metaphysics constitutes those theories "whose object is to arrange the most general propositions of the various regions of scientific knowledge in a well-ordered system."—Rudolf Carnap, *Philosophy and Logical Syntax.*

§ "The task of philosophy is to form as consistent as possible a general conception of [the] apparently confused collection of experiences, so that we can guide our conduct in accordance with the general conception."—J. B. S. Haldane, *The Sciences and Philosophy.*

§ ". . . it is the business of philosophy to correlate the evidence collected by the special sciences and to try to fit it into a coherent scheme of the universe as a whole. . . ."—C. E. M. Joad, *Philosophical Aspects of Modern Science.*

§ "The enterprise of metaphysics emerges as, above all, an attempt to re-organize the set of ideas with which we think about the world. . . . It is supremely a kind of conceptual revision which the metaphysician undertakes. . . ."—H. P. Grice, *et al., The Nature of Metaphysics.*

§ ". . the logic of science teaches us no new facts; its function being rather to put the facts we already know in a new light; and in this new light they may be said to reveal the nature of mind. . . ."—H. R. Smart, *The Logic of Science.*

§ "The particular task of philosophy has been to establish a general theory of the world. Philosophy aims to be such a theory; its method consists in the generalization of the generalizations of science."— A. Riehl, *Introduction to the Theory of Science and Metaphysics.*

§ Ontology is unobjectionable if it means the general theory of objects, which is developed "in a purely empirical way, and which differs from other empirical sciences only by its generality."—Alfred Tarski, "The Semantic Conception of Truth," *Readings in Analytic Philosophy.*

26. In the following quotes what views on the role of science and metaphysics do you find implied?

§ "No scientific result, no scientific theory, in short no science in the exercise of its own proper means, can ever adequately cut the knot of a philosophical problem, for those problems depend both in their origin and their solution on a light which is not in the reach of science."— Jacques Maritain, *The Degrees of Knowledge.*

§ "To take the generally accepted results of the various sciences and to weave them together into a picture of reality, seems to many the readiest and safest way of philosophizing."—M. R. Cohen, *Reason and Nature*.

Heidegger has said that "all scientific thought is merely a derived form of philosophical thinking." What comment on this remark do you believe is implied in each of the foregoing statements? What comment on Heidegger's statement can you discover in Copleston's essay?

Research Themes

1. Marcel believes that metaphysical inquiry must "bring one back" to the situation of the inquirer. (*a*) Does "retrogression" to the existential subject appear to be related to Descartes's fundamental axiom in his *Discourse on Method*, IV? Marcel also speaks of modern man being "repaired" in hospitals. (*b*) Does he here refer implicitly to the distinction drawn by Plato between physician-judges and trainer-legislators, and the societies represented by each? Check Plato's *Republic* (405a) and *Gorgias* (464b) for details of this distinction. Assemble your conclusions for both (*a*) and (*b*) in statements of about 200 words each.

2. Analyze the chapters in Whitehead's *Symbolism* (New York, Macmillan, 1927) on "presentational immediacy" and "causal efficacy." What relation do these terms have to Emmet's "intra-experiential analogy"? Reduce your findings to a statement of about 500 words.

3. Metaphysics, B. A. O. Williams (*The Nature of Metaphysics* [New York, St. Martin's Press, 1957], p. 124) observes, "invites the taking of sides." What explanation of this remark can you discover in the following statement by Herbert W. Schneider from his essay "Metaphysical Vision" (*Philosophical Review*, LVIII [1949], 403)?

> § "Whereas any ordinary philosopher is systematically contentious, the metaphysical philosopher is contentiously systematic; for he insists on putting the whole of human experience into scientific form and at the same time putting the whole of science into the form of human experience."

Is this an adequate explanation? Does the following quote from Schneider explain why metaphysicians must choose sides, or why they should avoid choosing sides?

> § "The . . . task of philosophical metaphysics is to get a binocular view of whatever subject matter happens to be central to the field of vision. . . . [It is] a peculiar method of binocular vision which can be applied to any subject matter, not for the sake of integrating knowledge systematically, but for the sake of illuminating by its plurality of perspective those aspects of a particular being which no one science or any other art can reveal."

Write up your conclusions in a statement of 300 words.

4. In everyday experience, most of us speak metaphors to simplify complex situations. Instead of saying that our friend's brusque and assertive appearance hides "timidity" and "insecurity," we say something like: "What a lion—but he's got the heart of a churchmouse." (Kenneth Burke has called this an "informative anecdote.") Think of five other examples, based on everyday experiences, and analyze each one. Do you find that you thought of each example, *as a metaphor*

and then translated each into abstract terms? Or conversely? Or did you think in neither metaphoric nor abstract terms? Write up your analysis in a 300-word paper.

5. Analyze the arguments given by John Wisdom in his article "Metaphysics and Verification, I" (*Mind* [N. S.], XLVII [1938], 452–98) on the character of the metaphysical quest. Metaphysical theories, he remarks with Wittgenstein, are signs of the "mental crack-up" of philosophers who suffer from an *idée fixe*. Would this imply that Schopenhauer's "itching point of metaphysics," Socrates' *aporia,* Heidegger's *Dasein,* and Plato-Aristotle's *thaumázein* are signs of "mental crack-up" or intellectual neurosis? Would it also imply that such "natural" activities as wonder, and so forth, are deliberate frustrations? What ultimate view of the universe would this suggest? Does Wisdom's view make of metaphysics a kind of "psychology"? If so, what relation would it have to Bergson's contentions (*Creative Mind* [New York, 1946]) that the function of metaphysical thought is "principally the intimate knowledge of the mind by the mind" (p. 306, n. 26); that metaphysical intuition is "the direct vision of the mind by the mind" (p. 35), and "represents the attention that the mind gives to itself" (p. 92)? Does it have any relation to J. S. Mill's contention (*J. S. Mill's Philosophy of Scientific Method,* ed. E. Nagel [New York, 1950], p. 10) that metaphysics is "that portion of mental philosophy which attempts to determine what part of the furniture of the mind belongs to it originally, and what part is constructed out of materials furnished to it from without"? What contribution does Marcel's distinction between *problem* and *mystery* make to a solution of John Wisdom's difficulties? Summarize your findings in a 1,500-word paper.

6. Make a tabulation on file cards of all definitions of the term "metaphysics" which have appeared in these readings, marking each with its appropriate author. Stack the cards of similar character, labeling each with some descriptive term (e.g., Thomist, existentialist, and so forth). How many groups have you been able to distinguish? Compare each file card with every other card so that each definition of the term "metaphysics" appears with agreements and disagreements, vis-à-vis other views, clearly stated. Tabulate the differences and similarities that show up. Are the similarities basic or only superficial? Are the disagreements irreconcilable. Or do you think that they could be negotiated? Based upon the number of irreconcilable views left, how many interpretations of the term show up? (*a*) Write a paper of 1,500–2,000 words, outlining your findings and stating both major and minor conflicts and agreements between views investigated; and (*b*) construct a chart visually illustrating these findings.

SELECTED BIBLIOGRAPHY FOR PART THREE

Universes of Discourse

1. Bernadete, J. A. "Analytic Aposteriori and the Foundations of Metaphysics," *Journal of Philosophy,* 55 (1958), 503–14.

2. Burnheim, J. "The Modern Attack on Metaphysics," *Philosophical Studies*, 2 (1952), 3–17.
3. Copleston, F. C., S.J. "Flight from Metaphysics," *Month*, 185 (1948), 150–65.
4. ———. *Contemporary Philosophy*. Westminister, Md.: Newman, 1956.
5. Gotshalk, D. W. *Metaphysics in Modern Times*. Chicago: University of Chicago Press, 1940.
6. Hartshorne, Charles. "Metaphysical Statements as Nonrestrictive and Existential," *Review of Metaphysics*, 12 (1958), 35–47.
7. McMahon, F. E. "Thomistic Metaphysics," *New Scholasticism*, 8 (1934), 240–59.
8. Martin, W. O. *Metaphysics and Ideology*. Milwaukee: Marquette University Press, 1959.
9. Osgniach, A. J. *The Analysis of Objects*. New York: J. F. Wagner, 1938.
10. Pears, D. F. (ed). *The Nature of Metaphysics*. New York: St. Martin's Press, 1957.
11. Scheuer, Pierre, S.J. "Notes on Metaphysics," *Cross Currents*, 7 (1957), 337–46.
12. Sheldon, W. H. "The Task of Present-day Metaphysics," in *American Philosophy Today and Tomorrow*, ed. Kallen and Hook. New York: Furman, 1935.
13. Wick, W. A. *Metaphysics and the New Logic*. Chicago: University of Chicago Press, 1942.

Thomist Metaphysics

1. Anderson, J. F. "On Being: Its Meaning and Its Role in Philosophy," *Thomist*, 4, (1941), 579–87.
2. ———. *The Bond of Being*. St. Louis: B. Herder, 1949.
3. Bourke, V. J. "Experiences of Extramental Reality as the Starting Point of St. Thomas' Metaphysics," *Proceedings American Catholic Philosophical Association*, (1934), 134–48.
4. ———. "On the Being of Metaphysics," *New Scholasticism*, 20 (1946), 72–84.
5. Eslick, L. J. "What is the Starting Point of Metaphysics?" *Modern Schoolman*, 34 (1957), 247–63.
6. Glutz, M. A. "Being and Metaphysics," *Modern Schoolman*, 35 (1958), 271–85.
7. Griesbach, M. F. "Judgment and Existence," *Proceedings American Catholic Philosophical Association*, 30 (1956), 205–11.
8. Henle, R. J., S.J. "Existentialism and the Judgment," *Proceedings American Catholic Philosophical Association*, 26 (1946), 40–53.
9. Kane, W. H., O.P. "The Subject of Metaphysics," *Thomist*, 18 (1955), 503–21.
10. McMahon, F. E. "Being and the Principles of Being," *New Scholasticism*, 17 (1943), 322–39.
11. Maritain, Jacques. *A Preface to Metaphysics*. New York: Sheed and Ward, 1939.

12. O'Neill, C. J. "Is the Point of Departure a Choice?" *Proceedings American Catholic Philosophical Association,* 33 (1959), 118–126.
13. Owens, Joseph, C.Ss.R. "A Note on the Approach to Metaphysics," *New Scholasticism,* 28 (1954), 454–76.
14. Renard, Henri. "Metaphysics of the Existential Judgment," *New Scholasticism,* 23 (1949), 387–94.
15. Smith, V. E. "On the Being of Metaphysics," *New Scholasticism,* 20 (1946), 72–84.
16. Wild, John. "What is Realism?" *Journal of Philosophy,* 44 (1947), 148–58.
17. Ziegelmeier, E. H., S.J. "The Discovery of First Principles According to Aristotle," *Modern Scholasticism,* 22 (1945), 132–38.

Existentialist Metaphysics

1. Blackman, H. J. *Six Existentialist Thinkers.* New York: Macmillan, 1952.
2. Collins, James. *The Existentialists.* Chicago: Henry Regnery, 1952.
3. ———. "The German Neo-Scholastic Approach to Heidegger," *Modern Schoolman,* 21 (1944), 143–52.
4. Copleston, F. C., S.J. "What is Existentialism?" *Mind,* 183 (1947), 13–21.
5. ———. *Existentialism and Modern Man.* Oxford: Blackfriars, 1948.
6. Conrad-Martius, Hedwig. "Phenomenology and Speculation," *Philosophy Today,* 3 (1959), 43–64.
7. Heinemann, F. H. *Existentialism and the Modern Predicament.* New York: Harper, 1958.
8. Kuhn, Helmut. "Existentialism and Metaphysics," *Review of Metaphysics,* 1 (1947), 37–60.
9. McInnery, R. M. "Metaphysics and Subjectivity," *Proceedings American Catholic Philosophical Association,* 32 (1958), 172–182.
10. Maritain, Jacques, "From Existential Existentialism to Academic Existentialism," *Sewanee Review,* 56 (1948), 210–29.
11. Mounier, Emmanuel. *Existentialist Philosophies.* New York: Macmillan, 1949.
12. Van Peurson, C. A. "Phenomenology and Ontology," *Philosophy Today,* 3 (1959), 35–42.
13. Sanford, H. W. "The Search of Man for Himself," *Sewanee Review,* 50 (1942), 515–23.
14. Rickey, C. W. "On the Intentional Ambiguity of Heidegger's Metaphysics," *Journal of Philosophy,* 55 (1958), 1144–48.
15. Schrader, G. A. "Existential Psychoanalysis and Metaphysics," *Review of Metaphysics,* 13 (1959), 139–63.
16. Smith, J. E. "The Revolt of Existence," *Yale Review,* 43 (1954), 364–71.
17. Tillich, Paul. "The Conception of Man in Existential Philosophy," *Journal of Religion,* 19 (1939), 201–15.
18. Troisfontaines, Roger. *Existentialism and Modern Thought.* London: Blackfriars, 1949.
19. Wilhelmsen, F. D. "Meditation on Nothing," *Downside Review,* 72 (1954), 135–45.
20. Yanitelli, V. R. "Types of Existentialism," *Thought,* 24 (1949), 495–508.

Metaphoric Metaphysics

1. Ballard, E. G. "Metaphysics and Metaphor," *Journal of Philosophy*, 45 (1948), 208–14.
2. Pepper, S. C. *World Hypotheses*. Berkeley, California: University of California Press, 1942.
3. Reardon, B. U. G. "Myth, Metaphysics and Reality," *Hibbert Journal*, 55 (1957), 124–30.
4. Slattery, M. P. "Metaphor and Metaphysics," *Philosophical Studies*, 5 (1955), 88–99.
5. Strong, E. W. "Metaphors and Metaphysics," *International Journal of Ethics*, 47 (1937), 461–71.

Linguistic Metaphysics

1. Alexander, H. G. "Language and Metaphysical Truth," *Journal of Philosophy*, 34 (1937), 645–52.
2. Alston, W. P. "Are Positivists Metaphysicians?" *Philosophical Review*, 63 (1954), 43–57.
3. Ayer, A. J. "The Genesis of Metaphysics," in *Philosophy and Analysis*, ed. M. Macdonald. Oxford: Blackwell, 1954.
4. Bakan, M. B. "Logical Influence and Seeing," *Journal of Philosophy*, 49 (1952), 713–22.
5. Carnap, Rudolf. "The Elimination of Metaphysics," in *Logical Positivism*, ed. A. J. Ayer. New York: The Free Press of Glencoe, 1957.
6. Copilowish, I. M. "Language Analysis and Metaphysical Inquiry," *Philosophy of Science*, 16 (1949), 65–74.
7. Copleston, F. C., S.J. "A Note on Verification," *Mind*, 59 (1950), 522–29.
8. Dineen, J. A., S.J., "The Course of Logical Positivism," *Modern Schoolman*, 34 (1956), 1–21.
9. Erickson, R. W. "Metaphysics of a Logical Empiricist," *Philosophy of Science*, 8 (1941), 320–28.
10. Esser, G. "Metaphysics is Concerned With Tautology or Nonsense Statements," *Proceedings American Catholic Philosophical Association*, 29 (1955), 176–95.
11. Joad, C. E. M. *A Critique of Logical Positivism*. Chicago: University of Chicago Press, 1950.
12. Körner, S. "The Meaning of Some Metaphysical Propositions," *Mind*, 57 (1948), 275–93.
13. Lewis, C. J. "Logical Positivism and Metaphysics," *New Scholasticism*, 16 (1942), 242–56.
14. Miller, R. G. "Linguistic Analysis and Metaphysics," *Proceedings American Catholic Philosophical Association*, 34 (1960), 80–109.
15. Nagel, Ernest. *Logic Without Metaphysics*. New York: The Free Press of Glencoe, 1957.
16. Pap, Arthur. "The Semantic Examination of Realism," *Journal of Philosophy*, 44 (1947), 561–75.

17. ———. *Elements of Analytic Philosophy*. New York: Macmillan, 1949.
18. Ryan, C. "Metaphysics and Language," *Blackfriars Review*, 32 (1951), 462–68.
19. Slattery, M. P. "Thomism and Positivism," *Thomist*, 20 (1957), 447–69.
20. Somerville, J. M., S.J. "Language as Symbolic Function," *Proceedings American Catholic Philosophical Association*, 34 (1960), 139–51.
21. Whiteley, C. H. *An Introduction to Metaphysics*. London: Metheun, 1950.
22. Wisdom, John. "Metaphysics and Verification," *Mind*, 47 (1938), 452–98.

Heuristic Metaphysics

1. Cartwright, R. L. "Ontology and the Theory of Meaning," *Philosophy of Science*, 21 (1954), 316–25.
2. Collingwood, R. G. *An Essay on Metaphysics*. Oxford: Oxford University Press, 1940.
3. Dingle, R. J. "Metaphysics: History or Science?" *Nineteenth Century*, 128 (1940), 289–94.
4. Feibleman, J. K. "The Range of Dyatic Ontology," *Journal of Philosophy*, 51 (1954), 117–24.
5. ———. *Ontology*. Baltimore, Md.: Johns Hopkins Press, 1951.
6. Frankel, Charles. "Seeing Things in Double Focus," *Saturday Review*, 36 (1953), 7–8.
7. Hart, J. N. "Metaphysics, History and Civilization," *Journal of Religion*, 33 (1953), 198–211.
8. Hartshorne, Charles. "Some Empty Though Important Truths," *Review of Metaphysics*, 8 (1955), 553–68.
9. Lee, H. N. "Metaphysics as Hypothesis," *Journal of Philosophy*, 45 (1948), 208–14.
10. Levi, A. W. "The Quixotic Quest for Being," *Ethics*, 66 (1956), 132–36.
11. Merlan, Philip. "Metaphysics and Science—Some Remarks," *Journal of Philosophy*, 56 (1959), 612–18.
12. Parker, D. H. *Experience and Substance*. Ann Arbor, Mich.: University of Michigan Press, 1941.
13. Rickman, H. P. "Metaphysics as the Creation of Meaning," *Hibbert Journal*, 52 (1954), 166–74.
14. Schneider, H. W. "Metaphysical Vision," *Philosophical Review*, 58 (1949), 399–411.

Naturalist Metaphysics

1. Hofstadter, Albert. "The Conception of Empirical Metaphysics," *Journal of Philosophy*, 45 (1948), 421–35.
2. Eames, E. R. "Quality and Relation as Metaphysical Assumptions in the Philosophy of John Dewey," *Journal of Philosophy*, 55 (1958), 166–69.
3. Hook, Sidney. "The Quest for Being," *Journal of Philosophy*, 50 (1953), 709–31.

4. Lamont, Corliss, *et al.* "A Humanist Symposium on Metaphysics," *Journal of Philosophy*, 56 (1959), 45–64.
5. Miller, R. G. "The Empiricists' Dilemma," *Proceedings American Catholic Philosophical Association*, 29 (1955), 151–76.
6. Morris, V. C. "An Experimentalist on Being," *Modern Schoolman*, 35 (1958), 125–33.
7. Pollock, R. C. "Process and Experience: Dewey and American Philosophy," *Cross Currents*, 9 (1959), 341–66.
8. Sleeper, R. W. "Dewey's Metaphysical Perspective," *Journal of Philosophy*, 57 (1960), 100–115.

Four   METAPHYSICAL
ISSUES

U P TO THIS POINT WE HAVE BEEN CONCERNED WITH QUESTIONS THAT either precede or accompany the practice of metaphysics. At most, we have used metaphysical questions to illustrate certain conceptions about metaphysics. We might call them pre-metaphysical and para-metaphysical questions.

In this section, however, our attention will be drawn to issues of a formal metaphysical character. We have chosen eight such issues, to which both classical and contemporary speculation have been drawn. These are: being, essence-existence, value, time-space, the person, knowledge, freedom, and God.

Since we assume that the question of *being* constitutes the proper metaphysical business, all of these issues fall either explicitly or implicitly, within the "circle of being." They propose for consideration either some situation or character of being, or some kind of being. They are, in short, a set of variations on ontological themes.

For instance, the human person is a specific kind of being. But we cannot ask what kind of being the person is without being conscious of the fact that we are also referring to its relation to other ontological issues—not only to the question of being as such, but also to situational and characterological questions about being; namely, essence-existence, value, space-time, knowledge, freedom—and even God. Or again, when we turn our attention to questions about the being of "desks" or "cabbages," we are conscious that only about half of these same issues apply. And so it will be with anything else—things, or the relations of things—all will fall somewhere within this circle of being.

In order to bring this out more clearly, the following essays have been selected to develop eight questions on ontological themes. These questions are:

1. What is being, and what does it mean?
2. Which aspect of being has primacy?
3. What is value?

4. What is the nature of space and time?
5. What is the person?
6. What is the nature of knowledge?
7. What is freedom?
8. What is the nature of metaphysical knowledge about God?

In this introduction, comments on each question will include a "table of discourse" to show how the statements of each of the following authors relates to the original question.

I

To begin with, we must consider the first question: What is being, and what does it mean? It is clear, however, that this is not a single question, but implies at least two questions about being. There is on the one hand, the question of the *identity* of being (What is being?) and the question of the *implications* of being (What does being mean?).

If we ask, "What *is?*" we might immediately reply, "Things are." This would at first appear to be a reputable answer, of course. But it would leave out one essential element of things as we perceive them—which is that they seem to "lean" on one another and come together in our thought. Notice, we say that a thing is, or that things are; and it is this term ("is"—or its pluralization) that applies to all things, and in which all things seem to share.

The relation between things and their "is-ness," or being, may appear to be very much like the relation between cities or countries and the world. A friend may tell me that he plans to see the world, or to take a trip around the world. But we both know that he will not see the world, only the countries and cities *of* the world. Even if the kind of trip he meant is an orbital flight around the world, he would not see the world all at once; he would simply pass over various parts of it at any one time. Still, both of us assume that there is a community of all these geographical places. We call that community the world.

Now is it possible that this is what we mentally do when we say *being* rather than *things?* Do we make a "geographical community" of things, called "being"? But perhaps we have left out an important difference. Reflection on the problem indicates that we do not simply pile things together in our mind, and call this pile being—as we pile together all geography, and call it the world. The something extra we have added in speaking about being appears when we talk about the being of things. Of course, it is true that we use such expressions as "the Parisian world," or "the world of New York artists." But this is just because we mentally make "Paris" or "New York artists" a restrictive term, and imagine that nothing more than either actually exists. We also speak about "the private world of Walter Mitty," as though there were no other world, and no one else except Mr. Mitty and his aliases. But when we say "the being of cabbages and desks," we assert something non-restrictive about cabbages and desks. In so speaking, we have not narrowed these terms; we have extended them. Hence, in one respect, we speak about all the things of our experience, as so many individualities; and, in another, we speak about the togetherness of all things; and, in still a third, about what each thing is that makes it both itself and an instance of a sort of "everything." Three separate elements, then, can be distinguished: things; the togetherness of things; and the being of things. What then is this being, and what is the being of each thing?

If we think about it, we will notice that our life is made up of a long series of collisions with things, although, apparently, we do not collide either with being or with the being of things. For example, we stub our foot painfully on a warped board jutting from a step. Surely we would not say we stubbed our foot on being, but rather on the step (or its defective board). However, this does not stop us from talking about the being of this step, of our foot, and of our pain. Does this, then, mean that we are only performing a kind of "ontological bookkeeping," by giving a generic name to all these things—step, foot, pain? If so, then we must also account for our habit of applying this generic term "everything" to each thing, and not simply to all of them.

It was an attempt to answer just such a question that brought Greek thinkers to what has since been called the problem of the one and the many. How they went about this task can be judged in the light of the following essays by Parmenides, Plato, and Aristotle. Adding the essay by Descartes gives us not only a sense of contrast between ancients and moderns but also a sense of continuity. Thus if we make a "table of discourse" to the question "What is being?" as it is handled by these four philosophers, we get the following results:

What is being?

Parmenides: It is One.
Plato: It is, through the Ideas, One and Many.
Aristotle: It is Substance, or that which *particularly* persists; and thus, both one and many.
Descartes: It is Substance, but according to the modes of thought and extension.

Let us consider the question in somewhat more detail.

Parmenides, an Eleatic thinker of the late sixth century, B.C., is considered to be the greatest of pre-Socratic philosophers and, in many ways, the "father of metaphysics." It was he who announced the question of being in a deceptively simple fashion. He simply said: *estí,* it is. Now we might wonder what this sentence "says." But so have all subsequent metaphysical practitioners, and we must join in the enterprise of inquiry to understand some of the sentence's implications.

If it seems obvious that Parmenides' *is* refers to an *it,* it is not at all obvious what the *it* refers to. Could this *it* be a shorthand reference to everything? If so, then perhaps Parmenides' mystic proclamation means that things *are*, that they are in the "situation" of "is-ness" or being, and that this "situation" is One. This kind of reasoning may seem to leave a lot unanswered, but it is at least a beginning. Let us see how much further we can go by inquiring into how this sentence influences speculation.

The influence of Parmenides can be seen in the fact that he set up a way of thinking to which all metaphysicians after him have been drawn. In the first place, his proclamation has a logical—even technological—character to it. This is to say, he subjects what he says to investigation and submits it to a procedure. He points out that there are three possibilities inherent in any assertion about *it*. Either *it is* (as the sentence says); or it *is not* (the opposite of what the sentence says); or it both *is* and *is not*. If we translate this into later terminology, we get the formulations: Only being exists; Only nonbeing exists; or, Being and nonbeing simultaneously exist.

In the second place, Parmenides argues through these three possibilities by eliminating what can be thought from what cannot be thought. He immediately questions the last two possibilities for consistency. Nonbeing, he argues, cannot be thought, and it would be contradictory to say that it exists, since being cannot come from nothing; hence, nonbeing is not. If being and nonbeing exist simultaneously, contradiction also results since there can be no discontinuity in being and no introduction of nonbeing into it; hence, being and nonbeing cannot both exist. Therefore, only one possibility remains: Being exists. This assertion is equivalent to the "parsimonious sentence," *it is*.

In the third place, Parmenides draws out the implications of this type of logical procedure—which has much in common with the legal practice of the time—and concludes that there can be no real change, no real coming-to-be. Hence, he condenses the results of his thought: A thing is either in being, or it is not a thing; there can be no growth out of nothing; indeed, no such thing as real growth.

In the fourth place, Parmenides must account for evidences against his results. Do not things appear to grow or change? So much the worse for appearances, he answers. Appearances are not that important. The important thing is to see deeper than what appears. "See with thy mind," he says, and you will understand what *is*.

This means, in the fifth place, that one must be critical, and must judge (*krineín*) of things, not in an untutored way, but by reason (*krineín tòu logóu*).

The over-all result of Parmenides' speculation is called *monism,* which simply means, in Parmenides' case, that he believes in the irrevocable oneness of things. But this does not deny that the way he thinks (by reason) and the conclusions he reaches are necessarily inseparable. Plato illustrates for us why this is so.

To Plato, Parmenides' position seemed all but unanswerable—except for the fact, that is, that Plato was convinced that there are different kinds of things or "is-nesses" some of which change, others of which do not. Plato does not, in short, start from the same set of facts as did Parmenides; that is, he gives some facts—notably, those of change—a more important place in his thought. What most truly is, he argues, certainly cannot change, and is one. But how about the coming-to-be and passing-away of things in our experience? A man is born and dies; a flower blooms and fades away. Surely, these are not only deception—they *are,* although they *are* in a different sense than justice *is,* or beauty *is.* Hence, Plato explains how things are, by suggesting that there are two realms of being: the one, a realm of authentic and intelligible being (the *eídē*); the other, of sense-felt things that come to be and pass away—that is, those that indicate a mixture of being and nonbeing. Thus, on the one hand, there is a realm of the trans-sensuous real, the really real; on the other hand, there is a realm of sense-data, which get their meaning from their relation with—or participation in—the "really real," or *eídē.* We call this solution Plato's "Theory of Ideas," although we should probably call it his theory of realities.

Every sense-object, Plato says, finds its model in the *eídos* after which it is patterned. Hence *what is,* is both one (in terms of the *eídē*) and many (in terms of things that participate in the *eídē*). Change, he concludes, is consequently not a deception but a fact about sense-objects. What changes, what comes to be and passes away, are sense-objects; their authentic models, however, do not change. Plato contends that Parmenides was only partially correct and that Parmenides accounted for only half of things by reducing—against good evidence—everything to the same kind of being. Parmenides missed the fact that things themselves are not self-explanatory, but need a trans-sensuous explanation. On the other hand, in every object there is something that, as it were, speaks to us, and our business with things shows that we can communicate this something. What we can communicate is its participation in intelligibility, or its *eídos.*

Plato's explanation seems acceptable enough. It accounts for the unity and plurality of *what is* and also for the fact of change in *what is.* However, it leaves both Plato and us with a difficult problem—perhaps even more difficult than the original problem of unity-plurality and change: it leaves us with two types of *reals:* a really real (the *eídē*) and a sensuous real. Every thing is then in two different places at the same time. There is, on the one hand for instance, a just constitution; and, on the other hand, there is justice itself, against which the justice of the constitution is judged. What then is the relation between these two worlds, and how can these worlds be unified?

Plato tried to solve this theoretic problem by indicating that these two realms were related by the participation (*methéxis*) of things in an *eídos,* or by the imitation (*mímesis*) of an *eídos* in things. It is improbable that Plato was ever really satisfied with these answers, but he doubtless felt that they gave a certain amount of theoretic satisfaction. As he put it in the *Timaeus* (29c): In philosophizing, one ought to be content with a high degree of probability, even if it means speaking in myths.

To Plato's disciple, Aristotle, however, there was little satisfaction in any thinking on being that ended up by separating the world of sense from the world of meaning, or by making objects mere shadows of reality. Hence, Aristotle set to work on the question "What is being?" where Plato had left it—not in the way Plato had done, but in a new way.

The *Metaphysics* seems to make this new way plain, yet its relation to Plato's work should not be lost sight of. Just as Parmenides' problems gave rise to Plato's answers, so Plato's problems engendered Aristotle's views, conclusions, and procedures. These are meaningful only in the light of Plato's thought—only as a *dialogue* with Plato.

What Aristotle apparently wanted to do was to make a "phenomenological" analysis of experience, and to scientize Plato—to rid Plato of myths and "likely accounts." It would therefore be naive of us to interpret Aristotle in the *Metaphysics* as presenting a fully-formed system or to read his work as a closed book written by a sort of Delphic Oracle. Rather, Aristotle's work is filled with new starts, and with the intuitions and reasonings of a thinker "making philosophy." After all, it was his editors, not he, who categorized the corpus of his work under pedagogical headings. Lest we end up with a caricature of Aristotle—clothed in a sort of *toga praetexta,* legislating answers to "how it is"—we should be mindful that he is in this work still thinking, still inquiring.

Aristotle thus sets to work on the problem of how things are in the light of what has been said about "how things are." He is so much influenced by the literature of the problem that he begins the first book of the *Metaphysics* with a critique of his metaphysical forebears. None of them supplies a satisfactory answer—not even his master, Plato. So he starts afresh.

Looking at the question concretely, Aristotle observes that what a thing *is,* marks it off unmistakably from what it is *not;* and what it can become is essentially restricted. For instance, a seed can become a zinnia or a tomato, but it cannot become a man. Furthermore, only a zinnia seed can become a zinnia, and a tomato seed, a tomato. What a being becomes is confined within certain limitations of possibility. Looked at empirically (and this is the way Aristotle usually looked at things), a being is in action or in process; and its process is to become *this* rather than *that*—say, a zinnia, rather than a tomato or a man. Everything that *is,* consequently, is a composite of what it *is* and what it can *become*. What it becomes, furthermore, is always in relation to what it already is. Its becoming is intrinsically related to its being, and is limited by that being. Being takes place within the limits of possibility.

As an explanation of the duality in beings—their being and becoming—

Aristotle proposed the solution of *act* and *potency*, of *energéion* and *dýnamis*. In each thing, he said, there is a principle of its actuality and a principle of its possible capacity—this latter, however, always being restricted by actuality. Act precedes potency, and potency indicates the alteration of this act that a being is; that is, chickens come before eggs, not after them.

Thus, for Aristotle, there is an eternal world of things realizing themselves in a continuous unfolding of potency out of act. Hence, he explained the problem of change as an activity occurring within a single realm of being. He did not deny change—as Parmenides had done—nor did he create a double realm of beings to explain it—as Plato had done.

Since every being is a composite of act and potency, Aristotle understood how a being can both be and come to be something, over and above what it is—a seed becomes a rose, wood becomes ash, a child becomes a man—all the while remaining within being. But he did not seem to be satisfied simply with an explanation of change. He asked more. He wanted to know the answers to other questions: What *is* a being? What is the fundament of being? What is behind every change in a being? The fundament of a being, Plato had said, is its *éidos;* but for Plato the *éidos* existed separately from a concrete being. For Aristotle, on the other hand, true being is concretely *in* actual being, not *outside* of it.

To Aristotle, the search for the answer to the fundament of being was a search for the "firsts." "What," he asks, "is first in a being?" What is the *prótē ousía?* The eventual answer, which he gives in that baffling book, *Metaphysics,* is substance, or that which stands below all other characteristics of a thing. He reaches this conclusion after many turns and detours. Let us see how.

Every thing has a structure, Aristotle argues. There is (*a*) a material substratum, which is stamped by (*b*) the *déutera ousía,* or form. But in the thing there is also that which makes it move; that is, (*c*) its efficient cause. (This is the typical Aristotelian touch, and should remind us that Aristotle began his speculation in the light of the relation between being and motion.) At the terminus of motion, moreover, Aristotle suggests that there is that which a thing should become, or that which moves it toward its end and final determinant, the Good. This he called (*d*) the final cause. These four "causes" (*aitíe*) Aristotle considered to be the four ultimate perspectives or viewpoints that explain how a thing is, though they did not explain for him what a thing is.

In the first book of the *Metaphysics,* Aristotle enters into a historical account of the way in which his predecessors explained "how a thing is." Clearly, however, his inquiry is different from those of his antecessors—most of whom asked where things come from, and what things are made of. We should not then assume that Aristotle is simply illustrating the "historical approach" to the ideas that precede him. Rather, he appears to be interrogating and passing judgment on his philosophical forebears to see if they were aware of what he is aware of—that is, the specifying elements, or causes of things. Like a prosecuting attorney, he seems to cross-examine them, asking how much they saw and what answers they gave. Plato, he notes, was aware of the formal cause, the *déutera ousía;* but, unfortunately Plato "located" this cause outside the thing, whereas (says Aristotle) it is *in* the thing. All others who have inquired about "how things are" have said nothing of any importance.

Aristotle concentrates his attention on the individual thing, the *this* being because only individual things *are*. But this leads to ticklish problems. For instance, how are things related to the "universal," which Plato (and Aristotle) believed to be the clearest reality that we know? Such a question makes Aristotle shift gears and begin anew. There seem, he observes, to be four claimants to the title of being: matter, essence, universal, and genus. Matter, or *hýlē*, he immediately eliminates because it has no "thisness"; it is a principle of pure passivity and is unspecified. What exists is eminently specified. Hence, matter must be excluded as the answer to what a thing is. For similar reasons of either specification or actual concrete existence, he excludes, in turn, essence, the universal, and the genus.

At this point he is also reminded that a thing is one, and what makes it one has to do with that toward which it strives. Its essence, therefore, cannot be understood apart from its purpose or end, which is present in the organization of the thing's elements. At length, Aristotle reaches his firmest conclusion: to be a being is (*a*) to be active, (*b*) to be this individual being, and (*c*) to be this kind of thing. The fundament of these three facts of existence, individuality, and essence is none other than substance.

For Aristotle, the term substance is the basic category of being, and cuts across all divisions—act-potency, matter-form, existence-essence, and substance-accident—in which being can be understood. It is substance that is the subject of all qualifications or accidents. It is substance that "contains" the existence of a specific essence. It is substance that is composed of matter (the unspecified) and form (the specifying). And it is substance that is *in act,* and has the capacity to *become* (potency).

Thus, Aristotle seems to make a clean sweep of the problem of being by seeing it from many angles—but, more particularly, by choosing one term, substance, as the title of true being. For example, in explaining corruption, or passing-away, he can point to the fact that in this process *this* being loses a form; in explaining generation, or coming-to-be, he can assert that *this* being gains a potential form. But, with this solution, he exposes some new difficulties. For instance, where *is* the form that a being gains or loses? A form cannot be produced, but must precede the process in which it is stamped on matter. Yet, whence does it precede? And whither does it return? It cannot have a substantial existence (as Plato had contended). Aristotle is baffled. Or again, what is it that "individuates" a thing? Is it matter, as some passages in the *Metaphysics* suggest? Is it matter-form, as other passages suggest? We find no unqualified answer to these questions in Aristotle. And it may be that he had none.

When Descartes turns his attention to Aristotle's substance, he is forced once again to set up a new kind of division in being, which will split substance into two realms, or modes—that is, extended, or material, substance (*res extensa*) and thinking, or spiritual, substance (*res cogitans*). Between these two modes, says Descartes, no real communication can take place. What then is to be said of man, who is both a material and a spiritual being? Descartes seems to hesitate on this question, but ultimately, he suggests an *ad hoc* solution, which locates the joint between these two realms in man's pineal gland (*epiphysis*). The pineal gland, an outgrowth of the third ventricle of the brain, is classed as one of the body's endocrine, or ductless, glands, which pour their secretion directly into the blood and the lymph. The actual function of the gland remains obscure even to this day, although it is thought that its secretions probably inhibit production of anterior pituitary hormone. To Descartes, the mysterious gland doubtless seemed an appropriate peg on which to hang his own mysterious question regarding the realms of substance. Even today, this *ad hoc* solution stands as one of the chief curiosities in the annals of speculation.

But what is perhaps most instructive in Descartes's solution is its appearance of completing the swing of a pendulum that begins its oscillation with Parmenides. Parmenides had said that being is one; Plato swung this answer in the opposite direction, where being became not one but two. Aristotle seemed to restore the unity of being by calling upon substance as the unifying force. And Descartes once again swung in an opposite direction, and split substance into two irreconcilable elements—extension and thought. Hence, from Parmenides to Descartes the pendulum of speculation completes two full arcs from unity to duality.

The question, What is being?—as we have said—does not stand alone. Even if we give being an identity (for example, Parmenides' One, Plato's *éidos*, Aristotle's *ousía*, or Descartes's *res cogitans-res extensa*), we must still ask the meaning of this identity. Hence, we must now turn to the second part of the question, What is being? and ask, What does being mean? Once again, we can make a "table of discourse" to indicate how the philosophers in the following section are brought together on this problem:

What does being mean?

Moeller: It means *grounding*.
Pieper: It means created-being and uncreated-being.
Phelan: It means that which is analogated.
De Raeymaeker: It means participation through causality, in infinite act.
Somerville: It means "action."

Rousselot: It means that which is *for* mind.
Royce: It means the community of interpretation.
Clarke: It means both real and intentional being.
Bergson: It means that which is made possible.

Let us inquire into these assertions in more detail.

Being, as Joseph Moeller understands it, is a term that refers to the fundament of all things. It is a ground that is illuminated in beings and that, in turn, illuminates all beings. No single being, therefore, can be explained apart from this ground. Similarly, Josef Pieper indicates that there is a radical difference between the beings of our empirical experience and being. The being of finite beings can be known by us because it is created-being; but what is not known to us is the order of the being of being itself, or uncreated-being.

But how is it possible that we can, nevertheless, speak of these two different orders of being? It is because, Father Phelan points out, we employ "being" as an analogical term, which applies, in the analogy of proper proportionality, to each being in direct proportion to its essence or nature. The primary analogate of being is being itself, whose essence is the act of existence. The importance of analogy is also apparent in Monsignor De Raeymaeker's essay, in which he says that being implies both a "horizontal" and a "vertical" participation in the infinite act of being. The key to this intuition is to be found, he observes, in the fact of causality. Once again, this viewpoint is suggested—although from a different angle—in Father Somerville's essay on Blondel's metaphysics of "action."

The question of being's meaning for mind is investigated in the essays by Father Rousselot and Josiah Royce. For Rousselot, the character of being is its intelligibility, which at its widest means its intelligibility for Divine Mind; whereas, for Royce, being's intelligibility is always judged in terms of a set of ideas that make up what he calls a "community." Being, he says, needs interpretation, and is never identical with being-known.

The final pair of essays, concerned with the meaning of being, approaches the problem in terms of possibility and actuality. Real being, says Father Clarke, is *existential* being. How then shall we explain *possible* being? Clarke answers this question by showing the relationship between possible being and intentional being, which takes its status as being-known by God. Bergson, on the other hand, though he agrees that being is always *actual* being, explains the question of possibility as consequent upon, rather than antecedent to, actual being.

II

As we have seen, Aristotle suggested that every being is not only a *that,* or objective presence, but a *what,* or meaningful presence. It is a thing's *that,* or existence, and its *what,* or essence, that make it *this* being. In terms of this distinction, then, we might ask which of these elements—essence or existence —has, in contingent things, the primary title to being. A table of the views in this section would give these answers:

What aspect of being has primacy?

Aquinas: Existence, because contingent being is governed by the composition of act of existing and potentiality.

Santayana: Essence, because contingent being is governed by the stability of essence.

Pontifex: Neither separately, because there can be no separation between them in concrete being.

Dewey: Neither, since what is real is both "hazardous," or impermanent, like existences, and "stable," or permanent, like essences.

In this section, St. Thomas tells us that everything in experience is a combination of *what-it-is* and *act-of-being-what-it-is*. Although the proper object of the intellect (he tells us in *De Veritate*) is *whatness*, or essence (*quidditas*), the fundamental fact about a thing is its *act-of-existing*. The existence of a thing, he points out, is related to its essence in a manner similar to that by which act is related to potency. The essence of a thing comes to us, however, in a concrete situation of act-of-existing. It is this, therefore, that is fundamental.

Santayana disagrees with this analysis, however, by making a distinction between the world of natural facts and events, and a world of possible beings or essences—somewhat reminiscent of Plato's distinction. Through clear and imaginative insight, says Santayana, we reach this realm of ideal external objects, and it is this that makes our lives bearable. Cleansed by "scepticism," we pierce through to this solitude where things lose urgency and venom.

To Dom Pontifex and Dewey, neither St. Thomas's nor Santayana's solution is adequate. For Pontifex, the inadequacy of their solutions is laid at the doorstep of any distinction that would break up a being into component parts of existence and essence, which he deems unjustified. For Dewey, the inadequacy is due to the fact that things are, in reality, neither essences nor existences, nor components of essences and existences.

III

We must turn now to a consideration of one of the "faces" of being— value. Any analysis of being will indicate that being—whether material or immaterial—is not neutral and inconsequential, but that it has a positive character (worth) from which certain consequences follow. In the first place, we are drawn to speak about it, so we can see that it has a motivating power for us. This indicates that it cannot be neutral. Secondly, if it motivates us, or at least our inquiry, its own character must be otherwise than neutral. Of things (and, therefore, of being) we use value- or disvalue-words; and we are

able to say of things that they are good-bad, right-wrong, true-false, beautiful-ugly. Plato and Aristotle believed that there is a transcendent relation of being to the good, true, and beautiful. Indeed, if one were to trace a line through every major metaphysical conception from Plato to Whitehead, one would see unmistakably that each one has considered value as a prime factor in the question of being. What then, we can ask at this point, is the relation between being and value? A "table of discourse" drawn from the essays in this section shows the following propositions:

What is value?

Aquinas: The value "goodness" has a transcendental relation to being, and is convertible with it.

Hawkins: Value, or goodness, is an objective character of a being, insofar as value resides in the development of a being's potentialities.

von Hildebrand: Value is the important-in-itself and is the objective title of being; but, it is utterly opposed to any mere development of a being's potentialities.

Alexander: Value is objective in the sense that it is standard satisfaction; that is, satisfaction of certain natural sentiments for a standard individual.

IV

We have said that value is a prime characteristic of being—whether material or nonmaterial. But material beings share in something over and above this character. That is, they inhabit an ontological "situation," which we can call time and space. We must now ask, What is the character of this situation?

Most types of "realism" contend that space and time are not themselves beings but are "ideal" situations of being—that is, products of the mind with a foundation in reality. Space is thus considered a kind of receptacle for things, while time is considered a mental measure of change. This is somewhat the way Aristotle thought of the problem.

Modern scientific thought and Christian historical consciousness, however, find this version of the problem unacceptable. Modern science, for which Whitehead speaks, considers space and time as "vectors" of objects, and as "constitutive of entities." For some contemporary Christian thinkers, such as Monsignor de Solages and Father Johann, such a historical, processive view not only is scientifically important but also is in keeping with Christian perspective. To the question, then, of time and space the following essays give these answers:

What is the nature of space and time?

McWilliams: Space is an "ideal" receptacle of things and is a product of the mind, having a foundation in external reality.

Wild: Time is a measure of change, conceived according to mental relations, but inherent in extramental change.

Whitehead: Time and space are intrinsic to the events of nature; they are internal, not external, relations.

de Solages: Time is evolutionary, not cyclic; and traditional philosophy must take this fact seriously.

Johann: The modern notion of processive time is best understood in the light of charity.

V

In the scale of finite material things, which share in the existential-essential, valuative, and space-time character of all such beings, only one kind of being is able to reflect on its ontological situation. This kind of being is the human person. In the first place, there resides in man not only the ontological value of his status in being but other values as well—moral, intellectual, and aesthetic. Secondly, man's person is situated in the paradox between "self-identity" and "community." That is, he is both alone, and impelled toward contact with other persons. The essays in this section bring out both of these facts. In the two following sections, the situations—that is, knowledge and freedom—of this kind of being will be developed. At this point, however, it is necessary to set out a "table of discourse" on the question:

What is the person?

Maritain: The person is a suppositum, which knows itself as a subject, but knows others only as objects.

de Finance: The person is an ipseity of being, whose affirmation of being is his existence.

Johann: The person is a unique reality that, in seeking love, testifies to the participation of multiple reality in Divine Being.

Berdyaev: Personality is a spiritual category, distinguished from the individual and the ego, and situated within the sphere of tragedy.

VI

The situation of the person is, perhaps above all, one of knowledge. It is knowledge, in its many forms, which puts human personality reflectively and consciously in contact with reality—and, indeed, makes reality an inescapable question for it. As Father de Finance has already pointed out, when man makes an affirmation of reality, he makes an affirmation about himself, and conversely. These affirmations are rooted in knowledge. Similarly, as Jean Wahl once suggested, any affirmation about knowledge is also an affirmation about reality, and conversely. This is so, because the business between being and knowing centers around truth or "how things are." This section therefore treats the question:

What is the nature of knowledge?

Plato: Knowledge, as opposed to opinion, is ordered according to an ontological scale; and only the knowledge of the highest principles is, strictly speaking, knowledge.

Martin: There is only one knowledge which is, humanly speaking, regulative of all others; this knowledge is theoretic, autonomous, and nonpositive, and is called metaphysics.

Sturzo: Knowledge is given in a cognitive situation that makes possible an obscure intuition of total reality and the Absolute.

VII

The second fact about personal being is its freedom which, together with knowledge, constitutes the central ontological issue of man's "situation." In it, many of the themes of metaphysics are brought together.

What, then, is freedom? Is it the ability in man to choose a *this* rather than a *that?* Is it "reason," as Milton suggested in his *Areopagitica?* And what is its relation to truth and value?

We can say that freedom—whether it is free choice or something more—implies, first, a context and, second, a proclamation. Its context is valuative, because even choice demands something over and above a mere neutrality. If everything were neutral, there could be no choice and, hence, no freedom. Secondly, its proclamation is of that which is either for or against a value or disvalue. Freedom thus presupposes a conflict between value and its opposite. Were there no good-evil, freedom would be meaningless. Moreover, if man were determined to either good or evil, there would be no freedom, because, then, not only would value have no significance for man but freedom, too, would lose all significance. Just as to one who is blind, color is meaningless—for it is only in terms of sight that color is a meaningful datum—so too, to one who is determined, and not free to act, value is without meaning.

In the next place, there is a price to be paid for freedom: insecurity. This fact may be illustrated dramatically in "The Legend of the Grand Inquisitor," a chapter in Fyodor Dostoevsky's novel *The Brothers Karamazov.* The "Legend," which is a poem read by Ivan Karamazov to his brother Aloysha, recounts the story of the appearance of Christ in sixteenth-century inquisitorial Seville. The aged Cardinal Inquisitor has Christ arrested and brought to a dungeon. There, in a midnight meeting, the Inquisitor accuses Christ of having needlessly weighed down man with freedom. Christ, he says scornfully, has expected of man the same heroic and free response which He Himself gave to suffering and crucifixion. Freedom, he argues, is too high a price to pay for humanity; for man has a right to security, unfettered by questions and doubts and choices. The result of freedom in man's experience, he claims, is "unrest, confusion, and unhappiness—that is the present lot of man after Thou didst bear so much for their freedom."

It is doubtless true, as the Inquisitor complained, that freedom involves risks, uncertainties, and insecurities. But without freedom, as Augustine and Kierkegaard—and even Dostoevsky—point out, could man choose God? Before we turn to the question of God, our final question about being, we must set down how the essays in this section answer the question:

What is freedom?

Augustine: Freedom, as distinguished from free will—which is the instrument of freedom—is attained in right action, or in the right use of free will.

Aquinas: Free choice, or freedom, denotes an act of election; hence, it is an intellectual appetite.

James: The belief in free will is substantiated by consideration of a pluralistic universe.

Jaspers: Freedom is placed before man as a consciousness of risk, finitude, and transcendence.

VIII

The final implication of the question of being, to which we now turn, is to be found in the question of God. For only God, says St. Augustine, can claim the title of "true being, pure being, real being"; only God "is, and truly and supremely is."

In this section, three themes will claim our attention. They are: What metaphysics can say (*a*) about God, (*b*) about God's existence, and (*c*) about the relation between religious knowledge and its own knowledge of God. Each of these three themes will be treated by two of the concluding six essayists. Let us at this point, however, consider in somewhat more detail the second of these themes—the question of God's existence.

In metaphysical speculation, the question of God has always been linked with the problem of the proofs of God's existence, as attained by the natural light of human reason. The term "proof" is, of course, a thorny term, since it is often used in ambiguous ways. In mathematics and logic, it becomes an instrument used to substantiate procedures already employed. In legal practice, it is usually thought of as a method to supply missing pieces of evidence. For example, a courtroom is concerned, first with certain evidence—People's Exhibits A, B, and so on. With this evidence, and testimony elicited under questioning and cross-examination, a prosecutor's case is either "proved" or not. The prosecutor does not, of course, try to prove the evidence, although he may question the admissibility of certain evidence, as may the defense attorney. In a murder trial, for instance, the prosecutor does not try to prove that the alleged murder weapon is a .45-caliber revolver. This, it evidently is. What he does try to establish by inference is that *this* .45 is the murder weapon; that it was used by the defendant at such-and-such a time and place;

that there is motivation and circumstance and testimony sufficient to link the defendant with the crime. Within these limits he proves, or fails to prove, his case. It is understood by all parties, moreover, that this procedure is not absolute, but is an attempt to achieve only a high degree of probability.

Traditionally, the so-called proofs for the existence of God have not taken this form. In the first place, such proofs—or rather arguments—were framed not so much to initiate belief in God's existence as to amplify the knowledge already held by believers. These arguments were meant not to inaugurate faith—this is a question of grace, and therefore outside the purview of metaphysics—but to deepen faith by natural means.

A clear example of this kind of rational argument for the existence of God was developed by St. Anselm of Canterbury some time after 1078 when he became Abbot of the Priory at Bec. As he expressed it in his work *Proslogium,* the argument for God's existence was based upon an attempt to penetrate the doctrines of Christian faith. His motivation for demonstrating God's existence is summed up in the phrase, *Credo, ut intelligam (I believe in order that I may understand).* The argument, which he considered more decisive than those used in his earlier *Monologium,* was intended for his co-religionists at the Abbey of Bec in order to help them to understand more comprehensively what they already believed. It later became known as Anselm's "ontological argument."

The argument takes the form of a meditation on the meaning of the term God. Anselm assumes that "to exist in the mind"—which is of a different order than "to exist outside the mind"—is to exist truly. He expresses the argument in this form: I can conceive that than which a greater cannot be conceived; therefore, It exists. He then points out that if this conception were merely an *ens rationis,* or a being of the mind, it would not, by definition, be "that than which a greater cannot be conceived," since a greater yet—that is, an existent outside the mind—could still be conceived. Furthermore, this being cannot be thought not to exist, for then it would not be "that than which a greater cannot be conceived." Hence, he adds, the fool who in Scripture denies God in his heart, knows full well what it is he denies; namely, that which cannot be thought not to exist.

A contemporary, the monk Gaunilon, chided Anselm for what seemed to be an obvious loophole in the argument. In his tract *Pro Insipiente (On Behalf of the Fool),* Gaunilon pointed out that what exists *in* the mind need not necessarily exist *outside* the mind. Simply because one conceives, for example, the greatest green isle that can be conceived does not imply that in reality there is such an isle. In his *Defense* against Gaunilon, Anselm pointed out that Gaunilon's example held a fair comment, although he, Anselm, was not talking about green isles, but about God—references to Whom are not of the same order as references to any kind of contingent, or non-self-explained, realities. God's Being, Anselm goes on to say, is *sui generis* and necessary; His

Essence is absolutely to exist; whereas, the essence of any contingent reality is not to exist absolutely. Hence, he says, "if such a Being [as God] can be conceived to exist, necessarily it does exist." His argument continues: We refer to God as the Necessary, Absolute, and Perfect Being; He cannot therefore be a merely possible-necessity, an almost-perfect-perfection (that is, if He is all-perfect, He cannot lack the perfection of existence), or a contingent-absolute. In the very act of thinking of God, says Anselm, we understand the reason of His necessary existence. Anselm thus believes that he is giving a new viability to the traditional words of St. Augustine: Could we seek Him unless we had already found Him?

Anselm, it should be made clear, is not saying in this argument that we have a right to jump from the logical order to the real order, but rather that the recognition of God's existence is in the real order. Or, as Professor Collins points out below, the assertion of God's existence is based on both experiential and inferential grounds. It should also be made clear that Anselm is not arguing for an immediate intuition of God's existence. The point is rather that God's existence as a fact is rationally attainable. Nonetheless, neither St. Thomas nor Immanuel Kant accepted Anselm's reasoning, whether because each of them misinterpreted it (as some critics contend) or not is, at the moment, unimportant.

Now in the light of what we have already said about the difference between proof and evidence, it might be asked: "Should arguments for God's existence be considered as evidences or as proofs?" To St. Anselm, the proper function of such arguments was apparently one of illuminating evidence, rather than of proving a point in a legal or mathematical sense. Subsequent analysis, by those who find Anselm's argument acceptable, brings out that we do not prove facts but only prove something about facts. Such critics thus agree that if God's existence is a fact, we cannot prove it to be such but can only say something about it.

To say this, however, is also to leave ajar the door into various forms of scepticism and denials of all rational attempts to demonstrate the Divine Existence. Such a negative approach to the question is illustrated in the essay by W. T. Stace, who denies that argumentation can carry us to any rationally warranted proposition about God's existence. God's being, says Stace, cannot be proved any more than it can be disproved. And this is so, he argues, because the order of God's being is absolutely cut off from the order of man's being. No logic can leap such an inferential chasm.

In order to put Stace's difficulties into the proper light, we should make it plain at this point that a necessary distinction has traditionally been drawn between the reasonability of arguments for the existence of God and the range of these arguments. Even St. Thomas, often condemned as the arch-rationalist in this respect, did not mean that his "five ways" gave out the secrets of the *Deus absconditus*, or hidden God. St. Thomas did not intend that his arguments, or indeed any others of such nature, could capture or penetrate into the Divine Existence. Rather, he asserted that such arguments simply indicated the validity of a knowledge of the *fact* of God's existence, but not the *meaning* of God's existence. The human mind, he was saying, can apprehend God; it cannot, however, comprehend God. And even the apprehensions of rational argument lead inquiry out of the boundaries of metaphysical finitude (to adapt Whitehead's phrase used at the beginning of this book) and into the realms of sacred theology. To those who flatly deny the relevance of all metaphysical arguments for God's existence, we must then put two questions: What do you intend such a proof to produce? and What range do you demand that such proof possess?

The point of such questions becomes clearer when we consider the relation between man's ability to understand God metaphysically and his actual religious life in God. Is there, indeed, an antagonism between metaphysics and religion? The final pair of essays in this section holds answers to this question. There is, says Martin Buber, an intrinsic antagonism between the "way" of religion and the "way" of speculation. Metaphysics is devoted to the abstract, and its knowledge of God is therefore lifeless; whereas, true religious contact with God is always concrete and personal. Father Lotz, on the other hand, submits that there is, in fact, no antagonism between metaphysics and religion. Metaphysics and religion, he says, share in common the question of being. Each in its own way implicitly embraces the true intuitions of the other. Between them there can be no dispute; between them a firm bond exists, for each adds strength to the experiences of the other.

If we set out a final "table of discourse" to indicate the contentions of the philosophers in this section, we find that it looks like this:

What is the nature of metaphysical knowledge about God?

Aquinas: Speculation shows that all things seek God in proportion to their rank in being, because they seek their own self-perfection.

Gilson: God, in St. Thomas's thought, is properly known by rational demonstrations as *He Who Is,* because His essence is to be the existential act.

Stace: Metaphysics cannot find God, because God exists in the eternal order, and his existence cannot be demonstrated by inferential argument, which begins from the natural order of man's finite experience.

Collins: Metaphysics does not prove the divine act of existing; but it can prove in an experiential-and-inferential manner the truth of the propositions affirming the Divine Existence.

Buber: Metaphysics cannot meet God, because He is met only in a living and concrete religious contact between our "I" and His "Thou," and not as a metaphysical "It."

Lotz: God is met both through the loving knowledge of metaphysics and the knowing love of religion; both develop their contact with being in different, but not inimical, ways.

Being

Parmenides   ## 1. BEING AND THE ONE

It is commonly remarked that Plato considered Parmenides a man to be both
feared and respected. Why he was to be feared may become more apparent in the Platonic portrait that follows this selection. But why he was
to be respected is surely indicated in this present selection in which he
lays down the law of being.

This is the first such philosophical work to appear in poetic form. Entitled
On Nature (a common enough title at the time), it has been given to us in
three parts—the first two of which are reprinted here. Although it is only
a guess, Parmenides probably chose the poetic form to emphasize his
right to replace the two great Hellenic poet-ideologists, Hesiod and Homer.
As Hesiod had supplanted Homer in telling the "way of things," Parmenides would replace Hesiod. Certainly Parmenides makes claims for
his own message similar to those made by Hesiod. They are that what
he says has been given him by the gods (Hesiod had his Muses), and
that what he speaks is true—let no man deny it! But Parmenides does
something else: he casts away the wrappings of myth and presents his
message in the cloth of logical consistency.

He pictures himself as the philosopher traveling along a road leading from
the palace of Night to the palace of Day where he is introduced to the goddess of light. He is told by the goddess that he will be given the knowledge of all things. The positive truth, she tells him, is that "Being is" and
"Non-Being is not"; it is therefore wrong to believe that "Being is not, and
Non-Being must be." The goddess says that thinking and being are one
and the same. It would follow that what cannot be thought cannot be.
Nonbeing cannot be thought and, hence, cannot be.

In dialectical fashion, Parmenides' poem then shows the impossibility of
change and motion, which are simply ascribed to the deception of the senses.
Being is one. It suffers no alterations. It cannot be thought to come to *be*
(because then it would not have been "being" in the first place); it cannot
be thought of as anything other than eternal; it is "void of beginning,
without any ceasing." Conversely, nonbeing cannot, by definition, come
to *be*. The goddess warns Parmenides to avoid the error—some have
thought this an oblique reference by Parmenides to the thought of Heraclitus—of believing that being and nonbeing equally exist. The character of
being is, therefore, that it is one, eternal, indivisible, motionless, boundless, and perfect.

This translation of Parmenides' fragmentary poem was made by Dr. W. T. Harris.

Proem

Soon as the coursers that bear me and drew me as far as
extendeth

Impulse, guided me and threw me aloft in the glorious
pathway,

Up to the Goddess that guideth through all things man
that is conscious,

There was I carried along, for there did the coursers
sagacious,

Drawing the chariot, bear me, and virgins preceded to
guide them—

Daughters of Helios leaving behind them the mansions of
darkness—

Into the light, with their strong hands forcing asunder
the night-shrouds,

While in its socket the axle emitted the sound of a syrinx,

Glowing, for still it was urged by a couple of wheels well-
rounded,

One upon this side, one upon that, when it hastened its
motion.

There were the gates of the paths of the Night and the
paths of the Day-time.

Under the gates is a threshold of stone and above is a
lintel.

These too are closed in the ether with great doors guarded
by Justice—

Justice the mighty avenger, that keepeth the keys of
requital.

Her did the virgins address, and with soft words deftly
persuaded,

Swiftly for them to withdraw from the gates the bolt
and its fastener.

Opening wide, they uncovered the yawning expanse of
the portal,

Backward rolling successive the hinges of brass in their
sockets,—

Hinges constructed with nails and with clasps; then onward
the virgins

Straightway guided their steeds and their chariot over
the highway.

Then did the goddess receive me with gladness, and
taking my right hand

Into her own, thus uttered a word and kindly bespake
me:

Youth that art mated with charioteers and companions
immortal,

Coming to us on the coursers that bear thee, to visit our
mansion,

Hail! for it is not an evil Award that hath guided thee
hither,
Into this path—for, I ween, it is far from the pathway of
mortals—
Nay, it is Justice and Right. Thou needs must have
knowledge of all things,
First of the Truth's unwavering heart that is fraught
with conviction,
Then of the notions of mortals, where no true conviction
abideth;
But thou shalt surely be taught this too, that every
opinion
Needs must pass through the ALL, and vanquish the test
with approval.

On Truth

Listen, and I will instruct thee—and thou, when thou
hearest, shalt ponder—
What are the sole two paths of research that are open to
thinking.
One path is: That Being doth be, and Non-Being is not:
This is the way of Conviction, for Truth follows hard in
her footsteps.
Th' other path is: That Being is not, and Non-Being must
be;
This one, I tell thee in truth, is an all-incredible pathway.
For thou never canst know what is not (for none can
conceive it),
Nor canst thou give it expression, for one thing are
Thinking and Being. . . .

. . . And to me 'tis indifferent
Whence I begin, for thither again thou shalt find me
returning. . . .

Speaking and thinking must needs be existent, for IS is
of being.
Nothing must needs not be; these things I enjoin thee to
ponder.
Foremost of all withdraw thy mind from this path of
inquiry,
Then likewise from that other, wherein men, empty of
knowledge,
Wander forever uncertain, while Doubt and Perplexity
guide them—
Guide in their bosoms the wandering mind; and onward
they hurry,
Deaf and dumb and blind and stupid, unreasoning cattle—

Herds that are wont to think Being and Non-Being one
and the self-same,
Yet not one and the same; and that all things move in a
circle. . . .

Never I ween shalt thou learn that Being can be of what
is not;
Wherefore do thou withdraw thy mind from this path of
inquiry,
Neither let habit compel thee, while treading this pathway
of knowledge,
Still to employ a visionless eye or an ear full of ringing,
Yea, or a clamorous tongue; but prove this vexed
demonstration
Uttered by me, by reason. And now there remains for
discussion
One path only: That Being doth be—and on *it* there are
tokens
Many and many to show that what is birthless and
deathless,
Whole and only-begotten, and moveless and ever-
enduring:
Never it was or shall be; but the ALL simultaneously
now is,
One continuous one; for of it what birth shalt thou
search for?
How and whence it hath sprung? I shall not permit
thee to tell me,
Neither to think: 'Of what is not,' for none can say or
imagine
How Not-Is becomes Is; or else what need should have
stirred it.
After or yet before its beginning, to issue from nothing?
Thus either wholly Being must be or wholly must not be.
Never from that which is will the force of Intelligence
suffer
Aught to become beyond itself. Thence neither production
Neither destruction doth Justice permit, ne'er slackening
her fetters;
But she forbids. And herein is contained the decision of
these things;
Either there is or is not; but Judgment declares, as it
needs must,
One of these paths to be uncomprehended and utterly
nameless,
No true pathway at all, but the other to be and be real.
How can that which is now be hereafter, or how can it
have been?
For if it hath been before, or shall be hereafter, it is
not:

Thus generation is quenched and decay surpasseth
  believing.
Nor is there aught of distinct; for the All is self-similar
  alway.
Nor is there anywhere more to debar it from being
  unbroken;
Nor is there anywhere less, for the All is sated with
  Being;
Wherefore the All is unbroken, and Being approacheth
  to Being.
Moveless, moreover, and bounded by great chains' limits
  it lieth,
Void of beginning, without any ceasing, since birth and
  destruction
Both have wandered afar, driven forth by the truth of
  conviction
Same in the same and abiding, and self through itself it
  reposes.
Steadfast thus it endureth, for mighty Necessity holds
  it—
Holds it within the chains of her bounds and round doth
  secure it.
Wherefore that that which IS should be finite is not
  permitted;
For it is lacking in naught, or else it were lacking in all
  things. . . .

Steadfastly yet in thy spirit regard things absent as
  present;
Surely thou shalt not separate Being from clinging to
  Being,
Nor shalt thou find it scattered at all through the All of
  the Cosmos,
Nor yet gathered together. . . .

One and the same are thought and that whereby there is
  thinking;
Never apart from existence, wherein it receiveth expression,
Shalt thou discover the action of thinking, for naught is
  or shall be
Other besides or beyond the Existent; for Fate hath
  determined
That to be lonely and moveless, which all things are but
  a name for—
Things that men have set up for themselves, believing as
  real
Birth and decay, becoming and ceasing, to be and to
  not-be,
Movement from place to place, and change from color
  to color.

But since the uttermost limit of Being is ended and
   perfect,
Then it is like to the bulk of a sphere well-rounded on all
   sides,
Everywhere distant alike from the centre; for never there
   can be
Anything greater or anything less, on this side or that
   side;
Yea, there is neither a non-existent to bar it from coming
Into equality, neither can Being be different from Being,
More of it here, less there, for the All is inviolate ever.
Therefore, I ween, it lies equally stretched in its limits
   on all sides.

Plato

2. THE ANTINOMY OF
BEING AND THE ONE

In the selection from the Platonic dialogue reprinted here, it has been suggested
   by some critics that the aged figure of Parmenides represents Plato's
   criticism of his own Doctrine of Ideas—which Socrates here sets forth
   as an explanation of what *really is*. Certainly, Plato drew the portrait
   with a light hand, for he makes Parmenides chide Socrates on the doctrine's difficulties. You are young, Parmenides is made to say, to put
   forward such a bold notion; "the time will come . . . when philosophy
   will have a firmer grasp on you." There have been few people—indeed,
   if any at all—on whom philosophy has had a surer grasp; but the difficulties, which Plato makes Parmenides point out in the dialogue, were
   never to be erased from Platonic thought.

The question of the dialogue begins from the point of view of Parmenides'
   conception that what exists is *one*. But how can this be? Socrates charges
   that such a view does not square with experience, which evidences the
   existence of many individual things. He also submits that the thesis of
   Parmenides' disciple, Zeno of Elea, is essentially (though not apparently)
   the same as that of his master. Parmenides affirms the *unity* of what
   is; Zeno denies the *plurality* of what is. This, says Socrates, comes to the
   same thing.

Experience, Socrates continues, evidences plurality, even though thought
   demands that this plurality be conceived as one. Socrates suggests a solution

   This selection, excerpted (127b–135b) from the dialogue *Parmenides,* and translated by
Benjamin Jowett, is used with the kind permission of the copyright holder, The Clarendon
Press, Oxford.

to the paradox. The unity of what is, is to be found in the *éidē,* or ideas, while plurality is seated in things that participate in these *éidē.* Does every class of objects, then, Parmenides interjects, have its own idea? Are there absolute ideas of the just, the good, the beautiful? Socrates believes so. And what of man? Is there a single idea in which all men participate? Socrates is undecided. And what of hair, mud, dirt? Is there an idea for each of these? Socrates believes not—yet, he admits that he is disturbed at the thought of denying it. Perhaps, after all, there is nothing that does not have its corresponding idea.

At this point, Parmenides follows a line of questioning that concludes in the paradoxical assertion that the one is at the same time many. And this, he says, is absurd. But could not, Socrates suggests, the ideas be "thoughts" existing only in our minds? "For in that case each idea will still be one, and not experience this infinite multiplication." The ideas, he finally presses forward, are "patterns" fixed in nature, "and other things are like them, and resemblances of them."

Parmenides pounces on this, however, and asserts that if this were so, there would be an infinite regress. For if the idea and the individual objects are alike, they must be so by some further idea of likeness; and this likeness in turn would be "like" through another idea of likeness, and so on. No, no, Parmenides warns Socrates, your theory must be discarded for one more adequate to explain the difficulties. Furthermore, he says, if the ideas are absolute, how could they exist in us who are not absolute? Socrates admits the problem but concludes that to deny the absolute character of the ideas is finally to do away with the very notion of true knowledge.

[ED. NOTE: The dialogue, recounted from memory by one of its minor figures, takes place when Socrates as a young man meets the aged and whitened Parmenides and his forty-year-old disciple Zeno during a visit to Athens. Zeno has just finished a recitation of some of his writings.]

WHEN THE RECITATION was completed. Socrates requested that the first thesis of the first argument might be read over again, and this having been done, he said: What is your meaning, Zeno? Do you maintain that if being is many, it must be both like and unlike, and that this is impossible, for neither can the like be unlike, nor the unlike like—is that your position?

Just so, said Zeno.

And if the unlike cannot be like, or the like unlike, then according to you, being could not be many; for this would involve an impossibility. In all that you say have you any other purpose except to disprove the being of the many? and is not each division of your treatise intended to furnish a separate proof of this, there being in all as many proofs of the not-being of the many as you have composed arguments? Is that your meaning, or have I misunderstood you?

No, said Zeno; you have correctly understood my general purpose.

I see, Parmenides, said Socrates, that Zeno would like to be not only one with you in friendship but your second self in his writings too; he puts what you say in another way, and would fain make believe that he is telling us something which is new. For you, in your poems, say The All is one, and of this you adduce excellent proofs; and he on the other hand says There is no many; and on behalf of this he offers overwhelming evidence. You affirm unity, he denies plurality. And so you deceive the world into believing that you are saying different things when really you are saying much the same. This is a strain of art beyond the reach of most of us.

Yes, Socrates, said Zeno. But although you are as keen as a Spartan hound in pursuing the track, you do not fully apprehend the true motive of the composition, which is not really such an artificial work as you imagine; for what you speak of was an accident; there was no pretense of a great purpose; nor any serious intention of deceiving the world. The truth is, that these writings of mine were meant to protect the arguments of Parmenides against those who make fun of him and seek to show the many ridiculous and contradictory results which they suppose to follow from the affirmation of the one. My answer is addressed to the partisans of the many, whose attack I return with interest by retorting upon them that their hypothesis of the being of many, if carried out, appears to be still more ridiculous than the hypothesis of the being of one. Zeal for my master led me to write the book in the days of my youth, but some one stole the copy; and therefore I had no choice whether it should be published or not; the motive, however, of writing, was not the ambition of an elder man, but the pugnacity of a young one. This you do not seem to see, Socrates; though in other respects, as I was saying, your notion is a very just one.

I understand, said Socrates, and quite accept your account. But tell me, Zeno, do you not further think that there is an idea of likeness in itself, and another idea of unlikeness, which is the opposite of likeness, and that in these two, you and I and all other things to which we apply the term many, participate—things which participate in likeness become in that degree and manner like; and so far as they participate in unlikeness become in that degree unlike, or both like and unlike in the degree in which they participate in both? And may not all things partake of both opposites, and be both like and unlike, by reason of this participation?—Where is the wonder? Now if a person could prove the absolute like to become unlike, or the absolute unlike to become like, that, in my opinion, would indeed be a wonder; but there is nothing extraordinary, Zeno, in showing that the things which only partake of likeness and unlikeness experience both. Nor, again, if a person were to show that all is one by partaking of one, and at the same time many by partaking of many, would that be very astonishing. But if he were to show me that the absolute one was many, or the absolute many one, I should be truly amazed. And so of all the rest: I should be surprised to hear that the natures or ideas themselves had these opposite qualities; but not if a person wanted to prove of me that I was many and also one. When he wanted to show that I was many he would say that I have a right and a left side, and a front and a back, and an upper and a lower half, for I cannot deny that I partake of multitude; when, on the other hand, he wants to prove that I am one, he will say, that we who are here assembled are seven, and that I am one and partake of the one. In both instances he proves his case. So again, if a person shows that such things as wood, stones, and the like, being many are also one, we admit that he shows the coexistence of the one and many, but he does not show that the many are one or the one many; he is uttering not a paradox but a truism. If however, as I just now suggested, some one were to abstract simple notions of like, unlike, one, many, rest, motion, and similar ideas, and then to show that these admit of admixture and separation in themselves I should be very much astonished. This part of the argument appears to be treated by you, Zeno, in a very spirited manner; but, as I was saying, I should be far more amazed if any one found in the ideas themselves, which are apprehended by reason, the same puzzle and entanglement which you have shown to exist in visible objects.

While Socrates was speaking, Pythodorus thought that Parmenides and Zeno were not altogether pleased at the successive steps of the argument; but still they gave the closest attention, and often looked at one another, and smiled as if in admiration of him. When he had finished, Parmenides expressed their feelings in the following words:—

Socrates, he said, I admire the bent of your mind towards philosophy; tell me now, was this your own distinction between ideas in themselves and the things which partake of them? and do you think that there is an idea of likeness apart from the likeness which we possess, and of the one and many, and of the other things which Zeno mentioned?

I think that there are such ideas, said Socrates.

Parmenides proceeded: And would you also make absolute ideas of the just and the beautiful and the good, and of all that class?

Yes, he said, I should.

And would you make an idea of man apart from us and from all other human creatures, or of fire and water?

I am often undecided, Parmenides, as to whether I ought to include them or not.

And would you feel equally undecided, Socrates, about things of which the mention may provoke a smile?—I mean such things as hair, mud, dirt, or anything else which is vile and paltry; would you suppose that each of these has an idea distinct from the actual objects with which we come into contact, or not?

Certainly not, said Socrates; visible things like these are such as they appear to us, and I am afraid that there would be an absurdity in assuming any idea of them, although I sometimes get disturbed, and begin to think that there is nothing without an idea; but then again, when I have taken up this position, I run away, because I am afraid that I may fall into a bottomless pit of nonsense, and perish; and so I return to the ideas of which I was just now speaking, and occupy myself with them.

Yes, Socrates, said Parmenides; that is because you are still young; the time will come, if I am not mistaken, when philosophy will have a firmer grasp of you, and then you will not despise even the meanest things; at your age, you are too much disposed to regard the opinions of men. But I should like to know whether you mean that there are certain ideas of which all other things partake, and from which they derive their names; that similars, for example, become similar, because they partake of similarity; and great things become great, because they partake of greatness; and that just and beautiful things become just and beautiful, because they partake of justice and beauty?

Yes, certainly, said Socrates, that is my meaning.

Then each individual partakes either of the whole of the idea or else of a part of the idea? Can there be any other mode of participation?

There cannot be, he said.

Then do you think that the whole idea is one, and, yet, being one, is in each one of the many?

Why not, Parmenides? said Socrates.

Because one and the same thing will exist as a whole at the same time in many separate individuals, and will therefore be in a state of separation from itself.

Nay, but the idea may be like the day which is one and the same in many places at once, and yet continuous with itself; in this way each idea may be one and the same in all at the same time.

I like your way, Socrates, of making one in many places at once. You mean to say, that if I were to spread out a sail and cover a number of men, there would be one whole including many—is not that your meaning?

I think so.

And would you say that the whole sail includes each man, or a part of it only, and different parts different men?

The latter.

Then, Socrates, the ideas themselves will be divisible, and things which participate in them will have a part of them only and not the whole idea existing in each of them?

That seems to follow.

Then would you like to say, Socrates, that the one idea is really divisible and yet remains one?

Certainly not, he said.

Suppose that you divide absolute greatness, and that of the many great things, each one is great in virtue of a portion of greatness less than absolute greatness—is that conceivable?

No.

Or will each equal thing, if possessing some small portion of equality less than absolute equality, be equal to some other thing by virtue of that portion only?

Impossible.

Or suppose one of us to have a portion of smallness; this is but a part of the small, and therefore the absolutely small is greater; if the absolutely small be greater, that to which the part of the small is added will be smaller and not greater than before.

How absurd!

Then in what way, Socrates, will all things participate in the ideas, if they are unable to participate in them either as parts or wholes?

Indeed, he said, you have asked a question which is not easily answered.

Well, said Parmenides, and what do you say of another question?

What question?

I imagine that the way in which you are led to assume one idea of each kind is as follows:—You see a number of great objects, and when you look at them, there seems to you to be one and the same idea (or nature) in them all; hence you conceive of greatness as one.

Very true, said Socrates.

And if you go on and allow your mind in like manner to embrace in one view the idea of greatness and of great things which are not the idea, and to compare them, will not another greatness arise, which will appear to be the source of all these?

It would seem so.

Then another idea of greatness now comes into view over and above absolute greatness, and the individuals which partake of it; and then another, over and above all these, by virtue of which they will all be great, and so each idea instead of being one will be infinitely multiplied.

But may not the ideas, asked Socrates, be thoughts only, and have no proper existence except in our minds, Parmenides? For in that case each idea may still be one, and not experience this infinite multiplication.

And can there be individual thoughts which are thoughts of nothing?

Impossible, he said.

The thought must be of something?

Yes.

Of something which is or which is not?

Of something which is.

Must it not be of a single something, which the thought recognizes as attaching to all, being a single form or nature?

Yes.

And will not the something which is apprehended as one and the same in all, be an idea?

From that, again, there is no escape.

Then, said Parmenides, if you say that everything else participates in the ideas, must you not say either that everything is made up of thoughts, and that all things think; or that they are thoughts but have no thought?

The latter view, Parmenides, is no more rational than the previous one. In my opinion, the ideas are, as it were, patterns fixed in nature, and other things are like them, and resemblances of them—what is meant by the participation of other things in the ideas, is really assimilation to them.

But if, said he, the individual is like the idea, must not the idea also be like the individual, in so far as the individual is a resemblance of the idea? That which is like, cannot be conceived of as other than the like of like.

Impossible.

And when two things are alike, must they not partake of the same idea? They must.

And will not that of which the two partake, and which makes them alike, be the idea itself?

Certainly.

Then the idea cannot be like the individual, or the individual like the idea; for if they are alike, some further idea of likeness will always be coming to light, and if that be like anything else, another; and new ideas will be always arising, if the idea resembles that which partakes of it?

Quite true.

The theory, then, that other things participate in the ideas by resemblance, has to be given up, and some other mode of participation devised?

It would seem so.

Do you see then, Socrates, how great is the difficulty of affirming the ideas to be absolute?

Yes, indeed.

And, further, let me say that as yet you only understand a small part of the difficulty which is involved if you make of each thing a single idea, parting it off from other things.

What difficulty? he said.

There are many, but the greatest of all is this:—If an opponent argues that these ideas, being such as we say they ought to be, must remain unknown, no one can prove to him that he is wrong, unless he who denies their existence be a man of great ability and knowledge, and is willing to follow a long and laborious demonstration; he will remain unconvinced, and still insist that they cannot be known.

What do you mean, Parmenides? said Socrates.

In the first place, I think, Socrates, that you, or any one who maintains the existence of absolute essences, will admit that they cannot exist in us.

No, said Socrates; for then they would be no longer absolute.

True, he said; and therefore when ideas are what they are in relation to one another, their essence is determined by a relation among themselves, and has nothing to do with the resemblances, or whatever they are to be termed, which are in our sphere, and from which we receive this or that name when we partake of them. And the things which are within our sphere and have the same names with them, are likewise only relative to one another, and not to the ideas which have the same names with them, but belong to themselves and not to them.

What do you mean? said Socrates.

I may illustrate my meaning in this way, said Parmenides:—A master has a slave; now there is nothing absolute in the relation between them, which is simply a relation of one man to another. But there is also an idea of mastership in the abstract, which is relative to the idea of slavery in the abstract. These natures have nothing to do with us, nor we with them; they are concerned with themselves only, and we with ourselves. Do you see my meaning?

Yes, said Socrates, I quite see your meaning.

And will not knowledge—I mean absolute knowledge—answer to absolute truth?

Certainly.

And each kind of absolute knowledge will answer to each kind of absolute being?

Yes.

But the knowledge which we have, will answer to the truth which we have; and again, each kind of knowledge which we have, will be a knowledge of each kind of being which we have?

Certainly.

But the ideas themselves, as you admit, we have not, and cannot have?

No, we cannot.

And the absolute natures or kinds are known severally by the absolute idea of knowledge?

Yes.

And we have not got the idea of knowledge?

No.

Then none of the ideas are known to us, because we have no share in absolute knowledge?

I suppose not.

Then the nature of the beautiful in itself, and of the good in itself, and all other ideas which we suppose to exist absolutely, are unknown to us?

It would seem so.

I think that there is a stranger consequence still.

What is it?

Would you, or would you not say, that absolute knowledge, if there is such a thing, must be far more exact knowledge than our knowledge; and the same of beauty and of the rest?

Yes.

And if there be such a thing as participation in absolute knowledge, no one is more likely than God to have this most exact knowledge?

Certainly.

But then, will God, having absolute knowledge, have a knowledge of human beings?

Why not?

Because, Socrates, said Parmenides, we have admitted that the ideas are not valid in relation to human things; nor human things in relation to them; the relations of either are limited to their respective spheres.

Yes, that has been admitted.

And if God has this perfect authority, and perfect knowledge, his authority cannot rule us, nor his knowledge know us, or any human thing; just as our authority does not extend to the gods, nor our knowledge know anything which is divine, so by parity of reason they, being gods, are not our masters, neither do they know the things of men.

Yet, surely, said Socrates, to deprive God of knowledge is monstrous.

These, Socrates, said Parmenides, are a few, and only a few of the difficulties in which we are involved if ideas really are and we determine each one of them to be an absolute unity. He who hears what may be said against them will deny the very existence of them—and even if they do exist, he will say that they must of necessity be unknown to man; and he will seem to have reason on his side, and as we were remarking just now, will be very difficult to convince; a man must be gifted with very considerable ability before he can learn that everything has a class and an absolute essence; and still more remarkable will he be who discovers all these things for himself, and having thoroughly investigated them is able to teach them to others.

I agree with you, Parmenides, said Socrates; and what you say is very much to my mind.

And yet, Socrates, said Parmenides, if a man, fixing his attention on these and the like difficulties, does away with ideas of things and will not admit that every individual thing has its own determinate idea which is always one and the same; he will have nothing on which his mind can rest; and so he will utterly destroy the power of reasoning, as you seem to me to have particularly noted.

Very true, he said.

But, then, what is to become of philosophy? Whither shall we turn, if the ideas are unknown?

I certainly do not see my way at present.

Aristotle   # 3. BEING AND SUBSTANCE

What really is, Plato suggested, is paradoxically one and many; one through the *éidē,* but many in existence. Aristotle was never satisfied with this answer. To ask any question about being, he says, is to ask about the primary, the first, the basic, the most fundamental. There can be only one thing that in every sense of the term is primary, and this is *substance.* Substance is the fundament of all beings, for it is "that which persists when all attributes are removed." It is that of which all others are predicated, but which itself is not predicated of anything. It is the subject of all accidents. Thus, asserts Aristotle, the ancient question about being —whether it is one or many, finite or not—is actually the question of substance.

There are at least four ways a being can be defined, and therefore four claims to the title of being: there is the substratum, the essence, the universal, and the genus. But of these four, only one holds rightful claim to the title, and that is: substratum, or substance. It is primary because it is the "receptacle" of all qualities and movements. None of the categories except substance can exist apart; hence, its rightful claim to the title of what is real. Neither matter, nor form has a rightful claim to this title—only substance.

We may also assert, Aristotle contends, that there are three kinds of substance: eternal substance, perishable substance, and immovable substance. The first two of these may be classified as "sensible" substance as opposed to the last, immovable. Hence there are really two chief kinds of substance; sensible and immovable, or motionate and non-motionate. Since substance is a source and cause of motion, we may therefore say that there are substances that move, but move by deriving their motion from another; and there is a substance that does not itself move but engenders movement in another. This last is the First Cause, or immovable substance, but its study "belongs to another science."

From Book Z

THE WORD "BEING" has a variety of senses which are listed in my treatise "On the Several Meanings of Words." It denotes first "what a thing is" (i.e.

This selection is excerpted from Book Zeta and Book Lambda of the *Metaphysics.* The first part is from the edition of the *Metaphysics* translated by John Warrington and published by E. P. Dutton & Co., Inc., New York, and J. M. Dent & Sons Ltd., London. The second part is from *The Works of Aristotle Translated into English,* edited by J. A. Smith and W. D. Ross, published by The Clarendon Press, Oxford. Both selections appear by permission of the publishers.

its individuality), and then its quality, quantity, or other category. Now of all these senses which "being" may have, the primary sense is clearly "what a thing is"; for this denotes substance, whereas nothing else is considered to exist unless by virtue of its being a quantity, quality, affection, or other determination of substance. Hence one might doubt whether or not such terms as "walking," "being in good health," "sitting," etc., signify each of these things *as* "*being*"; for none of them has an independent existence or can be separated from its substance. Rather, if anything it is the thing which walks or sits or is in good health that is existent, because its subject is something definite; i.e. the substance and individual which is clearly implied in the use of such a designation, since "the good" or "the sitting" has no meaning apart from it. Clearly, then, it is by virtue of substance that each of the other categories "exists." Therefore that which "is" primarily (i.e. not in any qualified sense, but absolutely) must be substance.

While there are several senses in which a thing may be described as "primary," substance is so in every one of them: in definition, in knowledge, and in time. It is primary in definition, because the definition of a substance is involved in the definition of everything else; in knowledge, because we know a thing (e.g. man, fire) best when we know *what* it is, and not simply its quantity, quality, position, etc.; and in time, because substance alone among the categories can exist apart.

The ancient and everlasting question "What is being?" really amounts to "What is substance?" It was substance that many of the earlier philosophers described as one or many, as numerically finite or infinite; so that it must be our first and principal, if not our *only,* subject. . . .

Four things at the very least have a special claim to be described as substance: (A) Substratum, (B) Essence, (C) the Universal, and (D) Genus.

(A) The substratum is that of which everything else is predicated, but itself is never predicated of anything. And so we must first determine its nature; for the primary substratum is considered to be in the truest sense substance. The *matter,* the *sensible form,* and the *compound* of these two are each in its appropriate sense described as the substratum. Thus, if the sensible form is prior to and more real than the matter, it is also prior to their compound. Such, in brief, is the nature of substance; but to describe it merely as "that which is always subject and never predicate" is quite inadequate. Apart from the statement itself being vague, it seems inevitably to imply that matter is substance, i.e. that which persists when all attributes are removed. For (1) the secondary qualities of a sensible thing are merely its actions, products, and potencies; (2) length, breadth, and depth are quantities and therefore not substances; (3) when length, breadth, and depth are removed, nothing is left except what is bounded by them—i.e. matter, which (4) must accordingly, on this view, be substance. But this is impossible; for it is agreed that separability and individuality belong especially to substance, so that the sensible form, and the compound of this and matter, are more truly substance than is matter itself. The compound may be dismissed as posterior in nature and familiar to sense; matter also is not very difficult to understand. We must therefore consider essence, which is the most perplexing of all three. . . .

(B) We began by distinguishing various ways in which substance is defined, and discovered one of them to be essence. This we have now to study, prefacing our inquiry with some abstract linguistic remarks.

(1) The essence of a thing is that which it is said to be *per se;* e.g. (*a*) "to-be-you" is not "to-be-musical," because you are not *by your very nature* musical. Your essence, then, is what you are *per se.* But not everything which a thing is *per se* constitutes its essence; e.g. (*b*) the essence of "surface" is not "whiteness," because "being a surface" is not identical with "being white." Nor (*c*) is the compound of both ("being a white surface") the essence of surface; for here "surface" itself is repeated in the definition. The formula of a thing's essence is that which defines the term but does not contain it; so that if "being a white surface" were "being a smooth surface," it would be implied that "white" and "smooth" are one and the same. Again (*d*), since there are compounds within the categories other than substance, we must inquire whether there is a formula of the essence of each of them, whether these compounds also (e.g. "white man") have an essence. Let the compound be denoted by X. What is the essence of X?

It may be objected that "essence of X" is not a thing that exists *per se.* We reply that there are two ways in which a predicate may fail to be *per se* true of its subject: (i) by an addition, and (ii) by an omission. In case (i) the predicate is not *per se* true, because the term which is being defined is combined with another determinant; as if, for example, in defining whiteness one were to state the definition of a white man. In case (ii) the predicate is not *per se* true, because the subject has a qualification which is omitted in the definition; as if, for example, X denoted "white man" and yet were defined as "white." "White man" is of course white; its essence, however, is not "to be white." But is "being-X" an essence at all? Surely not. The essence is an individual type; but where an attribute is predicated of an alien subject the complex is not an individual type. Thus "white man" is not an individual type, assuming that individuality belongs only to substance. Therefore there is an essence of those things whose account is a definition. There is no definition if you merely have an account which means the same as a name, but only if it is the account of a primary real, i.e. of one which does not imply the assertion of something about something else. So nothing except species of a genus will have essence; for in species, and only in species, the predicate is not considered as related to the subject by participation, or as an affection or accident. On the other hand, there can be an account of the meaning of *any* word (saying that X belongs to Y), or, instead of a vague formula, one more accurate, but no definition or essence.

It may be, however, that "definition" has more than one sense, just as "what a thing is" means in one sense the substance and individual, and in another sense one of the other categories—quantity, quality, etc. Just as "is" applies to everything (not in the same way, but primarily to one thing and derivatively to others), so "what a thing is" applies without qualification to substance, and to other things in a qualified sense. For we might well ask "what is" a quality; so that even quality is a "what it is"—not in an unqualified sense, but just as not-being is held by some (emphasizing the linguistic form) to "be" in so far as it *is* not-being.

(2) Although we must consider the proper use of words in any particular case, it is still more important to understand the facts. Therefore, having made clear the proper usage of the term "essence," we may say that in fact essence belongs (*a*) just as "what a thing is" does, primarily and simply to substance, and (*b*) secondarily to the other categories, being in their case not essence in the full sense, but the essence of a quantity, quality, etc. The other categories must be said to "be" either by equivocation, or by adding and subtracting qualifications, as we say that the unknowable is "known," i.e. is unknowable; or rather, they "are" neither in the same sense as substance nor in a merely equivocal sense, but just as various things are called surgical not because they *are* one and the same thing, not because the word "surgical" has more than one *meaning,* but by virtue of their relation to a single thing.

Anyway, it makes not a scrap of difference how we choose to describe the facts; this much is evident, that definition and essence belong primarily and simply to substance. It remains true of course that they belong to other categories as well, but not primarily. To assume this does not necessarily entail a definition of any word or phrase which means the same as any formula. Such a word or phrase must mean the same as a particular kind of formula; and this condition is satisfied only if it is a formula of something which is one not by continuity (like the *Iliad*) or by arbitrary combination, but in one of the proper senses of "one" which answer to the essential sense of "being," viz. to the categories—substance, quantity, quality, etc. Hence (*c*) there will be a definition even of "white man," but not in the sense in which there is a definition of "white" or of a substance. . . .

. . . We start with the fact that substance is an originative source and cause. The interrogative "why" is always used in the sense of "why does A belong to B?" The question "Why is the musical man a musical man?" is either (1) of the type just mentioned, i.e. "why is the man musical?" or (2) it is different therefrom. In this second case it is of the type "Why is a thing itself?" Now to ask why a thing is itself is no question at all; for when we ask *why* a thing is so, we must already know *that* it is so, e.g. that the moon is eclipsed. "Because a thing is itself" is the single answer to all such questions as "why the man is man" or "why the musical is musical," unless one prefers to put it in the form "because each thing is indivisible from itself, and this is what being one means." This is an answer which meets all such cases and is a "short and easy way" with them. However, the question "why is man such and such a kind of animal?" *is* one which may fairly be asked. It is not equivalent to asking why he who is a man is a man; it must therefore mean "why does A which is predicated of B belong to B?" e.g. "Why does it thunder (why is a noise produced in the clouds?)"; "why are these things, viz. bricks and stones, a house?"

Evidently, then, we are looking for the *formal* cause, i.e. (speaking abstractly) for the *essence*. This is in some cases (e.g. in that of a bed or a house) identical with the *final* cause, and in others with the prime mover or *efficient* cause. We look for the second only in cases of generation and destruction, but for the first in that also of being. The object of our search is particularly elusive when one term is not expressly predicated of another, e.g. in the question "what is man?" The interrogation is a simple one, not analysed into subject and attributes; we do not ask expressly "why do these parts form this whole?" We must first make our question articulate, otherwise it shares the character both of a genuine and of a meaningless inquiry. Now since one must know *that* a thing is before one asks *why* it is, the question must always be "why is the *matter* so-and-so?" *Q*. Why do these materials form a house? *A*. Because what-it-is-to-be-a-house, i.e. the *essence* of house, is present in them. Likewise certain matter, or rather certain matter having a certain form, is a man. Therefore what we are seeking is the cause, i.e. the *form,* whereby the matter is some definite thing; and this is the *substance* of the thing. Clearly, then, in the case of pure forms, which contain no matter, question and answer are impossible; there must be another method of inquiry than that described above.

Now as regards those compounds which form a unity, not in the sense of an aggregate but as a syllable is one. A syllable is not merely the sum total of its letters: BA is not just B + A; nor is flesh just fire + earth. For after dissolution, the compounds—flesh or the syllable—no longer exist; but the letters do, and so do fire and earth. The syllable, then, is something on its own—not merely the letters (vowel and consonant), but something else besides. Similarly, flesh is not merely fire and earth, hot and cold, but something else besides. Let us suppose that the principle of union must be either an element or a complex of elements. If (1) it is an element, this leads to an infinite regress; because flesh will then consist of fire and earth, and this element + something else, and so on *ad infinitum*. If (2) it is a complex, it must have more than one element (otherwise it will itself be that element), and the same difficulty will arise as in the case of flesh or the syllable. It would seem, however, that this "something else" is something which is not an element, and that it is the cause which makes one thing flesh, another thing a syllable, and so on. This is the substance of things, for it is the primary cause of their being. Some things of course are not substances at all, but only such as are held together according to nature and by nature. Therefore this "nature," which is not a material element but a principle, would appear to be substance. The elements, on the other hand, are the material consituents of things, into which the latter may be resolved; e.g. A and B are the element of a syllable.

From Book Λ

The subject of our inquiry is substance; for the principles and the causes we are seeking are those of substances. For if the universe is of the nature of a whole, substance is its first part; and if it coheres merely by virtue of serial succession, on this view also substance is first, and is succeeded by quality, and then by quantity. At the same time these latter are not even being in the full sense, but are qualities and movements of it—or else even the not-white and the not-straight would be being; at least we say even these are, e.g. "there is a not-white." Further, none of the categories other than substance can exist apart. And the early philosophers also in practice testify to the primacy of substance; for it was of substance that they sought the principles and elements and causes. The thinkers of the present day tend to rank universals as substances (for genera are universals, and these they tend to describe as principles and substances, owing to the abstract nature of their inquiry); but the thinkers of old ranked particular things as substances, e.g. fire and earth, not what is common to both, body.

There are three kinds of substance—one that is sensible (of which one subdivision is eternal and another is perishable; the latter is recognized by all men, and includes e.g. plants and animals), of which we must grasp the elements, whether one or many; and another that is immovable, and this certain thinkers assert to be capable of existing apart, some dividing it into two, others identifying the Forms and the objects of mathematics, and others positing, of these two, only the objects of mathematics. The former two kinds of substance are the subject of physics (for they imply movement); but the third kind belongs to another science, if there is no principle common to it and to the other kinds.

Sensible substance is changeable. Now if change proceeds from opposites or from intermediates, and not from all opposites (for the voice is not-white [but it does not therefore change to white]), but from the contrary, there must be something underlying which changes into the contrary state; for the contraries do not change. Further, something persists, but the contrary does not persist; there is, then, some third thing besides the contraries, viz. the matter. Now since changes are of four kinds—either in respect of the "what" or of the quality or of the quantity or of the place, and change in respect of "thisness" is simple generation and destruction, and change in quantity is increase and diminution, and change in respect of an affection is alteration, and change of place is motion, changes will be from given states into those contrary to them in these several respects. The matter, then, which changes must be capable of both states. And since that which "is" has two senses, we must say that everything changes from that which is potentially to that which is actually, e.g. from potentially white to actually white, and similarly in the case of increase and diminution. Therefore not only can a thing come to be, incidentally, out of that which is not, but also all things come to be out of that which is, but is potentially, and is not actually. And this is the "One" of Anaxagoras; for instead of "all things were together"— and the "Mixture" of Empedocles and Anaximander and the account given by Democritus—it is better to say "all things were together potentially but not actually." Therefore these thinkers seem to have had some notion of matter. Now all things that change have matter, but different matter; and of eternal things those which are not generable but are movable in space have matter—not matter for generation, however, but for motion from one place to another.

One might raise the question from what sort of non-being generation proceeds; for "non-being" has three senses. If, then, one form of non-being exists potentially, still it is not by virtue of a potentiality for any and every thing, but different things come from different things; nor is it satisfactory to say that "all things were together"; for they differ in their matter, since otherwise why did an infinity of things come to be, and not one thing? For "reason" is one, so that if matter also were one, that must have come to be in actuality which the matter was in potency. The causes and the principles, then, are three, two being the pair of contraries of which one is definition and form and the other is privation, and the third being the matter.

Note, next, that neither the matter nor the form comes to be—and I mean the last matter and form. For everything that changes is something and is changed by something and into something. That by which it is changed is the immediate mover; that which is changed, the matter; that into which it is changed, the form. The process, then, will go on to infinity, if not only the bronze comes to be round but also the round or the bronze comes to be; therefore there must be a stop.

Note, next, that each substance comes into being out of something that shares its name. (Natural objects and other things both rank as substances.) For things come into being either by art or by nature or by luck or by spontaneity. Now art is a principle of movement in something other than the thing moved, nature is a principle in the thing itself (for man begets man), and the other causes are privations of these two.

There are three kinds of substance—the matter, which is a "this" in appearance (for all things that are characterized by contact and not by organic unity are matter and substratum, e.g. fire, flesh, head; for these are all matter, and the last matter is the matter of that which is in the full sense substance); the nature, which is a "this" or positive state towards which movement takes place; and again, thirdly, the particular substance which is composed of these two, e.g. Socrates or Callias. Now in some cases the "this" does not exist apart from the composite substance, e.g. the form of house does not so exist, unless the art of building exists apart (nor is there generation and destruction of these forms, but it is in another way that the house apart from its matter, and health, and all ideals of art, exist and do not exist); but if the "this" exists apart from the concrete thing, it is only in the case of natural objects. And so Plato was not far wrong when he said that there are as many Forms as there are kinds of natural object (if there are Forms distinct from the things of this earth). The moving causes exist as things preceding the effects, but causes in the sense of definitions are simultaneous with their effects. For when a man is healthy, then health also exists; and the shape of a bronze sphere exists at the same time as the bronze sphere. (But we must examine whether any form also survives afterwards. For in some cases there is nothing to prevent this; e.g. the soul may be of this sort—not all soul but the reason; for presumably it is impossible that *all* soul should survive.) Evidently then there is no necessity, on this ground at least, for the existence of the Ideas. For man is begotten by man, a given man by an individual father; and similarly in the arts; for the medical art is the formal cause of health.

The causes and the principles of different things are in a sense different, but in a sense, if one speaks universally and analogically, they are the same for all. For one might raise the question whether the principles and elements are different or the same for substances and for relative terms, and similarly in the case of each of the categories. But it would be paradoxical if they were the same for all. For then from the same elements will proceed relative terms and substances. What then will this common element be? For (1) (a) there is nothing common to and distinct from substance and the other categories, viz. those which are predicated; but an element is prior to the things of which it is an element. But again (b) substance is not an element in relative terms, nor is any of these an element in substance. Further, (2) how can all things have the same elements? For none of the elements can be the same as that which is composed of elements, e.g. b or a cannot be the same as ba. (None, therefore, of the intelligibles, e.g. being or unity, is an element; for these are predicable of each of the compounds as well.) None of the elements, then, will be either a substance or a relative term; but it must be one or other. All things, then, have not the same elements.

Or, as we are wont to put it, in a sense they have and in a sense they have not; e.g. perhaps the elements of perceptible bodies are, as *form,* the hot, and in another sense the cold, which is the *privation;* and, as *matter,* that which directly and of itself potentially has these attributes; and substances comprise both these and the things composed of these, of which these are the principles, or any unity which is produced out of the hot and the cold, e.g. flesh or bone; for the product must be different from the elements. These things then have the same elements and principles (though specifically different things have specifically different elements); but all things have not the same elements in this sense, but only analogically; i.e. one might say that there are three principles—the form, the privation, and the matter. But each of these is different for each class; e.g. in colour they are white, black, and surface, and in day and night they are light, darkness, and air.

Since not only the elements present in a thing are causes, but also something external, i.e. the moving cause, clearly while "principle" and "element" are different both are causes, and "principle" is divided into these two kinds and that which acts as producing movement or rest is a principle and a substance. Therefore analogically there are three elements, and four causes and principles; but the elements are different in different things, and the proximate moving cause is different for different things. Health, disease, body; the moving cause is the medical art. Form, disorder of a particular kind, bricks; the moving cause is the building art. And since the moving cause in the case of natural things is—for man, for instance, man, and in the products of thought the form or its contrary, there will be in a sense three causes, while in a sense there are four. For the medical art is in some sense health, and the building art is the form of the house, and man begets man; further, besides these there is that which as first of all things moves all things.

Some things can exist apart and some cannot, and it is the former that are substances. And therefore all things have the same causes, because, without substances, modifications and movements do not exist. Further, these causes will probably be soul and body, or reason and desire and body.

And in yet another way, analogically identical things are principles, i.e. actuality and potency; but these also are not only different for different things but also apply in different ways to them. For in some cases the same thing exists at one time actually and at another potentially, e.g. wine or flesh or man does so. (And these two fall under the above-named causes. For the form exists actually, if it can exist apart, and so does the complex of form and matter, and the privation, e.g. darkness or disease; but the matter exists potentially; for this is that which can become qualified either by the form or by the privation.) But the distinction of actuality and potentiality applies in another way to cases where the matter of cause and of effect is not the same, in some of which cases the form is not the same but different; e.g. the cause of man is (1) the elements in man (viz. fire and earth as matter, and the peculiar form), and further (2) something else outside, i.e. the father, and (3) besides these the sun and its oblique course, which are neither matter nor form nor privation of man nor of the same species with him, but moving causes.

Further, one must observe that some causes can be expressed in universal terms, and some cannot. The proximate principles of all things are the "this" which is proximate in actuality, and another which is proximate in potentiality.

The universal causes, then, of which we spoke do not exist. For it is the individual that is the originative principle of the individuals. For while man is the originative principle or man universally, there is no universal man, but Peleus is the originative principle of Achilles, and your father of you, and this particular *b* of this particular *ba,* though *b* in general is the originative principle of *ba* taken without qualification.

Further, if the causes of substances are the causes of all things, yet different things have different causes and elements, as was said; the causes of things that are not in the same class, e.g. of colours and sounds, of substances and quantities, are different except in an analogical sense; and those of things in the same species are different, not in species, but in the sense that the causes of different individuals are different, your matter and form and moving cause being different from mine, while in their universal definition they are the same. And if we inquire what are the principles or elements of substances and relations and qualities—whether they are the same or different—clearly when the names of the causes are used in several senses the causes of each are the same, but when the senses are distinguished the causes are not the same but different, except that in the following senses the causes of all are the same. They are (1) the same or analogous in this sense, that matter, form, privation, and the moving cause are common to all things; and (2) the causes of substances may be treated as causes of all things in this sense, that when substances are removed all things are removed; further, (3) that which is first in respect of complete reality is the cause of all things. But in another sense there are different first causes, viz. all the contraries which are neither generic nor ambiguous terms; and further, the matters of different things are different. We have stated, then, what are the principles of sensible things and how many they are, and in what sense they are the same and in what sense different.

Since there were three kinds of substance, two of them physical and one unmovable, regarding the latter we must assert that it is necessary that there should be an eternal unmovable substance. For substances are the first of existing things, and if they are all destructible, all things are destructible. But it is impossible that movement should either have come into being or cease to be (for it must always have existed), or that time should. For there could not be a before and an after if time did not exist. Movement also is continuous, then, in the sense in which time is; for time is either the same thing as movement or an attribute of movement. And there is no continuous movement except movement in place, and of this only that which is circular is continuous.

But if there is something which is capable of moving things or acting on them, but is not actually doing so, there will not necessarily be movement; for that which has a potency need not exercise it. Nothing, then, is gained even if we suppose eternal substances, as the believers in the Forms do, unless there is to be in them some principle which can cause change; nay, even this is not enough; for if it is not to *act,* there will be no movement. Further, even if it acts, this will not be enough, if its essence is potency, for there will not be *eternal* movement, since that which is potentially may possibly not be. There must, then, be such a principle, whose very essence is actuality. Further, then, these substances must be without matter; for they must be eternal, if *anything* is eternal. Therefore they must be actuality.

Yet there is a difficulty; for it is thought that everything that acts is able to act, but that not everything that is able to act acts, so that the potency is prior. But if this is so, nothing that is need be; for it is possible for all things to be capable of existing but not yet to exist.

Yet if we follow the theologians who generate the world from night, or the natural philosophers who say that "all things were together," the same impossible result ensues. For how will there be movement, if there is no actually existing cause? Wood will surely not move itself—the carpenter's art must act on it; nor will the menstrual blood nor the earth set themselves in motion, but the seeds must act on the earth and *semen* on the menstrual blood.

This is why some suppose eternal actuality—e.g. Leucippus and Plato; for they say there is always movement. But why and what this movement is they do not say, nor, if the world moves in this way or that, do they tell us the cause of its doing so. Now nothing is moved at random, but there must always be something present to move it; e.g. as a matter of fact a thing moves in one way by nature, and another by force or through the influence of reason or something else. (Further, what sort of movement is primary? This makes a vast difference.) But again for Plato, at least, it is not permissible to name here that which he sometimes supposes to be the source of movement—that which moves itself; for the soul is later, and coeval with the heavens, according to his account. To suppose potency prior to actuality, then, is in a sense right, and in a sense not; and we have specified these senses. That actuality is prior is testified by Anaxagoras (for his "reason" is actuality) and by Empedocles in his doctrine of love and strife, and by those who say that there is always movement, e.g. Leucippus. Therefore chaos or night did not exist for an infinite time, but the same things have always existed (either passing through a cycle of changes or obeying some other law), since actuality is prior to potency. If, then, there is a constant cycle, something must always remain, acting in the same way. And if there is to be generation and destruction, there must be something else which is always acting in different ways. This must, then, act in one way in virtue of itself, and in another in virtue of something else—either of a third agent, therefore, or of the first. Now it must be in virtue of the first. For otherwise this again causes the motion both of the second agent and of the third. Therefore it is better to say "the first." For it was the cause of eternal uniformity; and something else is the cause of variety, and evidently both together are the cause of eternal variety. This, accordingly, is the character which the motions actually exhibit. What need then is there to seek for other principles?

Since (1) this is a possible account of the matter, and (2) if it were not true, the world would have proceeded out of night and "all things together" and out of non-being, these difficulties may be taken as solved. There is, then, something which is always moved with an unceasing motion, which is motion in a circle; and this is plain not in theory only but in fact. Therefore the first heaven must be eternal. There is therefore also something which moves it. And since that which is moved and moves is intermediate, there is something which moves without being moved, being eternal, substance, and actuality. And the object of desire and the object of thought move in this way; they move without being moved. The primary objects of desire and of thought are the same. For the apparent good is the object of appetite, and the real good is the primary object of rational wish. But desire is consequent on opinion rather than opinion on desire; for the thinking is the starting-point. And thought is moved by the object of thought, and one of the two columns of opposites is in itself the object of thought; and in this, substance is first, and in substance, that which is simple and exists actually. (The one and the simple are not the same; for "one" means a measure, but "simple" means that the thing itself has a certain nature.) But the beautiful, also, and that which is in itself desirable are in the same column; and the first in any class is always best, or analogous to the best.

That a final cause may exist among unchangeable entities is shown by the distinction of its meanings. For the final cause is (a) some being for whose good an action is done, and (b) something at which the action aims; and of these the latter exists among unchangeable entities though the former does not. The final cause, then, produces motion as being loved, but all other things move by being moved.

René Descartes   # 4. THE PRINCIPLE OF SUBSTANCE

Following, for some distance at least, in the footsteps of Aristotle, Descartes in this selection places strong emphasis on the subsistent or persistent character of reality. In the real world, he points out, there are either things or the "affections" of things. But here he leaves the path of Aristotle and

This selection is translated from the French edition of Descartes's *The Principles of Philosophy* (John Veitch, trans.), New York, Tudor Publishing Co. It consists of sections 48, 51–56, and 61–64 in Part I.

subjects the notion of substance to certain rationalist tests. By substance, he says, "we can conceive nothing else than a thing which exists in such a way as to stand in need of nothing beyond itself in order to exist." Substance is the seat of a thing's reality, because it is the subject of all the "affections" or qualities of a thing. We must of course, he adds, point out that there is a difference between created substances, which are only relatively absolute as seats of reality, and uncreated substance, or God, which is absolutely independent. The term substance does not, therefore, apply univocally to God and creatures.

Confining the discussion, however, to created substance—which stands in need of nothing except the concourse of God—Descartes maintains that there is a conceptual and fundamental division in the type of substance that can be conceived. Since there is only one principal property of every created substance that constitutes its essence or nature, substances can be divided into two clear and distinct conceptions. There is, first, a created substance that thinks, and, second, corporeal substance, which is extended. We also have, he adds, a clear and distinct idea of uncreated thinking substance, which is God. Descartes therefore believes that all substance—created and uncreated—is confined within the ideas of extension and thought. From the point of view of substance, however, he states that thought and extension are best conceived not simply as two kinds of substances but as two modes of substance itself.

WHATEVER OBJECTS fall under our knowledge we consider either as things or the affections of things, or as eternal truths possessing no existence beyond our thought. Of the first class the most general are substance, duration, order, number, and perhaps also some others, which notions apply to all the kinds of things. I do not, however, recognize more than two highest kinds (*summa genera*) of things: the first of intellectual things, or such as have the power of thinking, including mind or thinking substance and its properties; the second, of material things, embracing extended substance, or body and its properties. Perception, volition, and all modes as well of knowing as of willing, are related to thinking substances; on the other hand, to extended substance we refer magnitude, or extension in length, breadth, and depth, figure, motion, situation, divisibility of parts themselves, and the like. . . .

But with regard to what we consider as things or the modes of things, it is worth while to examine each of them by itself. By substance we can conceive nothing else than a thing which exists in such a way as to stand in need of nothing beyond itself in order to exist. And in truth, there can be conceived but one substance which is absolutely independent, and that is God. We perceive that all other things can exist only by help of the concourse of God. And, accordingly, the term substance does not apply to God and the creatures UNIVOCALLY, to adopt a term familiar in the schools; that is, no signification of this word can be distinctly understood which is common to God and them. . . .

Created substances, however, whether corporeal or thinking, may be conceived under this common concept: for these are things which, in order to exist, stand in need of nothing but the concourse of God. But yet substance cannot be first discovered merely from its being a thing which exists independently, for existence by itself is not observed by us. We easily, however, discover substance itself from any attribute of it, by this common notion, that of nothing there are no attributes, properties, or qualities; for, from perceiving that some attribute is present, we infer that some existing thing of substance to which it may be attributed is also of necessity present.

But, although any attribute is sufficient to lead us to the knowledge of substance, there is, however, one principal property of every substance, which constitutes its nature or essence, and upon which all the others depend. Thus, extension in length, breadth, and depth, constitutes the nature of corporeal substance; and thought the nature of thinking substance. For every other thing that can be attributed to body, presupposes extension, and is only some mode of an extended thing; as all the properties we discover in the mind are only diverse modes of thinking. Thus, for example, we cannot conceive figures unless in something extended, nor motion unless in extended space, nor imagination, sensation, or will, unless in a thinking thing. But, on the other hand, we can conceive extension without figure or motion, and thought without imagination or sensation, and so of the others; as is clear to anyone who attends these matters. . . .

And thus we may easily have two clear and distinct notions or ideas, the one of created substance, which thinks, the other of corporeal substance, provided we carefully distinguish all the attributes of thought from those of extension. We may also have a clear and distinct idea of an uncreated and independent thinking substance, that is of God, provided we do not suppose that this idea adequately represents to us all that is in God, and do not mix up with it anything fictitious, but attend simply to the characters that are comprised in the notion we have of him, and which we clearly know to belong to the nature of an absolutely perfect Being. For no one can deny that there is in us such an idea of God, without groundlessly supposing that there is no knowledge of God at all in the human mind. . . .

We will also have most distinct conceptions of duration, order, and number, if, in place of mixing up with our notions of them that which properly belongs to the concept of substance, we merely think that the duration of a thing is a mode under which we conceive this thing, in so far as it continues to exist; and, in like manner, that order and number are not in reality different from things disposed in order and numbered, but only modes under which we diversely consider these things.

And, indeed, we here understand by modes the same with what we else-

where designate attributes or qualities. But when we consider substances as
affected or varied by them, we use the term modes; when from this variation
it may be denominated of such a kind, we adopt the term qualities [to designate the different modes which cause it to be so named]; and finally, when
we simply regard these modes as in the substance, we call them attributes.
Accordingly, since God must be conceived as superior to change, it is not
proper to say that there are modes or qualities in him, but simply attributes;
and even in created things that which is found in them always in the same
mode, as existence and duration in the thing which exists and endures, ought
to be called attribute, and not mode or quality. . . .

There are two kinds of modal distinction, viz. that between the mode
properly so-called and the substnce of which it is a mode, and that between
two modes of the same substance. Of the former we have an example in this,
that we can clearly apprehend substance apart from the mode which we say
differs from it; while, on the other hand, we cannot conceive this mode without
conceiving the substance itself. There is, for example, a modal distinction
between figure or motion and corporeal substance in which both exist; there is
a similar distinction between affirmation or recollection and the mind. Of
the latter kind we have an illustration in our ability to recognize the one of
two modes apart from the other, as figure apart from motion, and motion apart
from figure; though we cannot think of either the one or the other without
thinking of the common substance in which they adhere. If, for example, a
stone is moved, and is withal square, we can, indeed, conceive its square figure
without its motion, and reciprocally its motion without its square figure; but
we can conceive neither this motion nor this figure apart from the substance
of the stone. As for the distinction according to which the mode of one substance is different from another substance, or from the mode of another substance as the motion of one body is different from another body or from
the mind, or as motion is different from doubt, it seems to me that it should
be called real rather than modal, because these modes cannot be clearly
conceived apart from the really distinct substance of which they are the
modes. . . .

Finally, the distinction of reason is that between a substance of some one
of its attributes, without which it is impossible, however, that we can have a
distinct conception of the substance itself; or between two such attributes of
a common substance, the one of which we essay to think without the other.
This distinction is manifest from our inability to form a clear and distinct
idea of such substance, if we separate from it such attribute; or to have a clear
perception of the one of two such attributes if we separate it from the other.
For example, because any substance which ceases to endure ceases also to
exist, duration is not distinct from substance except in thought (*ratione*); and
in general all the modes of thinking which we consider as in objects differ only

in thought, as well from the objects of which they are thought as from each other in a common object. . . .

Thought and extension may be regarded as constituting the natures of intelligent and corporeal substance; and then they must not be otherwise conceived than as the thinking and extended substances themselves, that is, as mind and body, which in this way are conceived with the greatest clearness and distinctness. Moreover, we more easily conceive extended or thinking substance than substance by itself, or with the omission of its thinking or extension. For there is some difficulty in abstracting the notion of substance from the notions of thinking and extension, which, in truth, are only diverse in thought itself (*i.e.,* logically different); and a concept is not more distinct because it comprehends fewer properties, but because we accurately distinguish what is comprehended in it from all other notions. . . .

Thought and extension may be also considered as modes of substance; in as far, namely, as the same mind may have many different thoughts, and the same body, with its size unchanged, may be extended in several diverse ways, at one time more in length and less in breadth or depth, and at another time more in breadth and less in length; and then they are modally distinguished from substance, and can be conceived not less clearly and distinctly, provided they be not regarded as substances or things separated from others, but simply as modes of things. For by regarding them as in the substances of which they are the modes, we distinguish them from these substances, and take them for what in truth they are: whereas, on the other hand, if we wish to consider them apart from the substances in which they are, we should by this itself regard them as self-subsisting things, and thus confound the ideas of mode and substance.

Joseph Moeller   5. THE GROUND OF BEING

Aristotle, as we have seen, inquired after the fundament of a being. In this essay Joseph Moeller attacks a similar problem by asking after the *ground* of a being.

Every being points to *being itself* as its ground, he asserts, and the question of being is intimately bound up with the question of grounds. The ques-

---

These extracts are from an essay entitled "The Ground of Thought," which appeared in the quarterly *Philosophy Today,* edited at Saint Joseph's College, Rensselaer, Indiana. Translated from the German by William J. Kramer, C.Pp.S.

tion is, in fact, crucial to the structure of metaphysics. By being, we mean "that which makes a being a being"; that is, being itself. Plato, Moeller observes, did not say, as the *Parmenides* shows, that being is the idea; Aristotle, by his assertion of substance, did not solve the difficulty of the relation between being and beings; St. Thomas, though he showed by the doctrine of analogy that "beings are characterized by a participation in being," did not completely answer the difficulty of grounds.

We must still understand, Moeller continues, that being "is that which is most known to us, yet in its ground the most hidden and inexhaustible." Being allows itself to be seen differently through "the inexpressible situations of thought, without allowing itself to be grasped by thought." As *that which encompasses,* being is the ultimate horizon of thought, but at the same time it is "that which bears both thought and horizon and makes them possible."

The actual thing, as Aristotle suggested, is being in the concrete—*a* being. But *a* being, according to Moeller, is simply a pointer to being, and "this pointer from everything to being is another word for grounding in being," which "leads directly to the ground of being." This simply means that being is ground to itself, that it is "self-standing." Otherwise it could not be conceived as "encompassing."

Metaphysics, Moeller continues, is the ultimate search for grounds; it does not seek merely relations, conditions, or environs, as empirical sciences do. It is the thought-movement "that investigates grounds and which must apply this ground as being, over beings." At the same time, "being itself surpasses metaphysics insofar as it does not and cannot merge with the questioning of metaphysics." Metaphysics "is not and cannot be final," since, like beings, it always points beyond itself. On the other hand, the "question of the pointer"—the interrogation of the meaning of beings—"opens up being," and shows that "passing being"—contingent being—is determined from being itself, and, hence, points beyond its limits in the direction of being. Thus, "beings" imply Being; contingents imply the Absolute. If there were only beings—and not being and the ground of being—then the unity of the world could be explained only through being itself, since beings by their limitation require a *raison d'être.* Thus the difference between being and beings is undeniable. To deny this difference is to make being merely a concept or to refuse to recognize every differentiation.

We are pointing then, says Moeller, to a cause of every being, which is nothing other than "showing the relationship of passing beings to being as their source." Pointing to finite beings is really a pointing to infinite being.

To pretend, he says, that this is a vicious circle—that is, pointing from finite being to infinite being by the aid of causality, which itself presupposes infinite being to point to—is unwarranted. For we understand by a vicious circle that the result is already the starting point: "But where I extract from data something that is implicitly bound up with it, there is no vicious circle." In the interrogation of beings, therefore, one does not end at the point of initiation, but travels beyond it to the meaning of its own initiation. The principle of causality is crucial to the investigation of being because it represents that connection by which "a being in its being points to the being of another being." This pointing means a grounding. Human thought shows this in an eminent fashion in that it points to something else, and is pointed to by something else. That is to say, it is determined by being.

THE QUEST FOR the ground of things is as old as man. But as this search becomes more intense, is there any real progress? It may seem at first sight that man is less prone in our day than in former times to the naive acceptance of things. We may be tempted to say that in modern times man investigates the reasons for things and distinguishes himself thereby from the simple belief in being that characterized the Middle Ages, when the principal aim was to examine and to ponder what was handed down.

Relational Explanations

But do we seek grounds more than formerly? Modern man would like to think so. We look for the grounds of man's varied behavior: in his physical make-up, in his surroundings, even in the weather. The historian examines the grounds of historical events, of political movements in the will to power combined with rare coincidence, of intellectual currents as a reaction against the status quo, of great deeds and progress as the result of the efforts of a few great men. The man who thinks in terms of technology sees the grounds of all functioning in the center-adjustment of various causes. No matter what we say about the leveling of the masses through technology, we cannot deny its impressive control of causes. We are not allowed to lose sight of the great progress man has made in the past few decades. No one would doubt this, unless it is someone who remembers two world wars and the present unrest. But there is a pat answer even to this objection: there have always been wars and unrest; it is only the form of human strife that has altered with technical progress.

But while we are searching for "grounds" for all these external events, for "causes," motives, occasions, conditions, situations and possibilities, the ground is getting farther and farther away. Thinking of the grounds is going out of style. There is a propensity to think of grounds as no more than a functional relationship or an observable and empirically demonstrable cause. If we mention thinking in terms of grounds we run the risk of being shouted down as unscientific. For science in the eyes of the many is nothing else than the method of figuring out functional relationship of the phenomena at hand. The question of why there are functional relations does not arise for them.

And the question of why there are phenomena at all is met with a blank stare. As we forget the quest for grounds, we forget true quest altogether.

It has been said that modern philosophy has succeeded in reducing what exists to a series of phenomena that tell of it. By such means antitheses that are hard to explain are replaced by phenomena. Is the phenomenon, therefore, the "determining" factor? Can it be determining at all? For many men it can be, for they do not see the phenomenon but only an appearance, an outward seeming. Of course this observation probably only bolsters what it would reject, for we can hardly understand the inside of those who chase after shadows. The anxiety, the unrest and doubt that lie crusted over them are not always brought to light, even with the best efforts of psychologists and psychiatrists.

The great vogue is relationships, conditions, influences, dependence, milieu, talent. We are interested in predispositions and production methods. The true grounds recede more and more into the background.

Since Kant discovered a limit to human understanding, we are lightly prone to accept his limit. The transformation of being into an objective something that refers back to us and yet points to itself (but only as an unknown) is the spawn of the modern mind. The question of grounds is on the one hand relegated to the subjectivity of the subject and on the other left in the gloom by the reference to the unknowable thing-in-itself. Since the time of Kant the questions of the ground of beings stands in a strangely ambiguous position: it points in one direction to thinking man, and in the other, to obscurity. With this the search for grounds comes to an end. For the subjectivity of the thinking subject cannot be given as basis. Nietzsche's "God is dead" and his reference to the creator are symptomatic for the present view of the problem of basis. The obscurity and confusion that surround this problem emphasize the difficulty of the question itself as well as the difficulty of thought which ever and anon dares to range beyond particular being to being itself. This thought we call metaphysics. The question of grounds is essentially bound up with the question of the structure of metaphysics.

Efforts of History

Being means grounding. Does this expression form the basis of the so-called principle of adequate ground? Such an assumption may seem at first to be ambiguous and even confusing. For is not the "clear principle" of adequate ground here made to depend upon a confusing and ambiguous expression?

The expression "being means grounding" is a metaphysical one. The metaphysics of the West contemplates beings, it is true; but since it considers being as beings, it necessarily points to that which makes a being a being, namely being. In Platonic thought, you cannot simply reduce being to the idea, since the question of being first comes to the fore in Plato with the *parousia* and *participation*. Plato did not solve our problem, but does not the *Parmenides* itself demonstrate the *aporia* of thus circumscribing the question of being? Neither is it true that this *aporia* was solved by Aristotle. Indeed, with the definition of *entelechy* the problem of the constitution of beings was brought into sharper focus than in Plato. But the relationship of the constitutive principles to the *noesis noeseos* was finally left unexplained by Aristotle. St. Augustine made some progress on the problem by proceeding to the one truth. St. Thomas Aquinas explains analogy in such a way that the analogy of being applies not only to beings but also to Being itself. In this analogy beings are characterized by a participation in Being. Being is that which is most known to us, yet in its ground the most hidden and inexhaustible. The question concerning being was shifted by Descartes to this extent, that being is brought into an inner relationship with the human *Cogito*, which itself is anchored only in the omnipotence of God. Thus it is that the new metaphysics is characterized by the relationship of beings to human thinking, a relationship that first came to the fore in the thought of Kant and with his interpretation of objectivity. It was not by accident that being became for Kant an empty term and that the most monumenal achievement of modern metaphysics, Hegel's *Logic*, is not a metaphysics of absolute being but a logic of the absolute concept.

The interpretation of being as *entelechy* and at the same time as *noesis noeseos*, interpretation as the one by Plotinus, truth by Augustine, interpretation of the *actus purus* as God by St. Thomas, interpretation of being from the standpoint of the thinking subject by Descartes, from the absolute spirit by Hegel, through the will to power by Nietzsche:—we watch the problem of metaphysics grow more and more confused. Is not being then that which as occasion arises might be seen differently through the inexpressible situations of thought, without allowing itself to be grasped by thought? Or might it be the imaginary something which cannot be understood at all and remains only a name or a figment of thought for the horizon of the historical expression as it runs along?

The All-Encompassing

Yet being is that which encompasses. It is the ultimate horizon of our thought and at the same time that which bears both thought and horizon and makes them possible. Any name that is given, be it "idea," "concept," "absolute spirit," or "will," or even the one and the all-encompassing, is but a hollow sound if it does not point to that which is.

The actual thing that is we call a being. That through which it is a being, is being. This pointer from everything to being is another word for grounding in being. For nothing could be if it were not grounded in being. The question of the grounding of beings leads directly to the ground of beings. Our thinking itself, which affirms this connection, could not even think out what is here expressed if itself *is* not, that is, if it does not point to being.

Being means grounding—this means that everything that subsists and is named, even our thinking itself, points to being. But this does not exhaust the meaning of the statement. For it means that that "which" ground conveys is necessarily bound up with being, so that this connection surpasses our thought. But this could imply that being is the ultimate, reverting to itself, sufficient to itself, that recognizes no recourse over itself. Then terms such as *actus purus, noesis noeseos,* absolute spirit, would be designations of being by our thought, and in each case the correctness of the term must be shown. Every one of these designations is basically encompassed by being. This encompassing is a movement of our thought; but it is at the same time an original "movement" of the self-standing of being, which penetrates and moves us. This encompassing cannot be understood unless being is ground to itself, that is, self-standing.

To allay the false impression that this is some sort of *a priori* proof for the existence of God, let it be said: What is expressed here is only the fact that nothing can go beyond being. Being as being can ultimately point to nothing else. How the relationship of beings to being is to be explained (as well as the relation of various forms of beings to one another) must remain an open question for the moment. It has of course already been said that being cannot be an empty stipulation of thought (otherwise it would again be something pointing beyond itself). Whether the relation to being is to be interpreted dialectically in the sense of participation, *parousia,* analogy, creation, is a question not yet answered. . . .

Inasmuch as metaphysics concerns itself with beings as beings, it gives basis to beings through being. Therefore in the observation "being means grounding," being shows itself to be the self-evident ground of all metaphysics, toward which it tends. Since metaphysics therefore sets up such a supposition, it also carries out what this supposition demands: that form of understanding which appears as *Denken des Grundes* points to being as the ground and is itself understood on this ground. Metaphysics is the thought-movement that investigates grounds and which must apply their ground as being, over beings. The return to grounds in metaphysics is necessary to give being its place. But since the thought-movement which appears here necessarily points beyond itself, being appears as the ultimate and the basis of the very inquiry of metaphysics. It is evident at the same time that being itself surpasses metaphysics insofar as it does not and cannot merge with the questioning of metaphysics. But being is not excluded from metaphysics. It is rather that which gives basis to the thought-movement of metaphysics and makes it possible.

Hence the statement "being means grounding" becomes the basic principle of the thought-movement of all metaphysics. And beyond all talk of principle, which can all too easily be misinterpreted in a "merely" logical fashion, being appears as the basis of human inquiry. At the same time the statement "being means grounding" reflects the provisional character of all metaphysics. For it is not the inquiry which is basic, but being. And this provisional character does find expression. For the grounding power of being must be expressed in metaphysics by way of a ground-statement or principle. This can easily lead to misunderstanding if we do not think of the dynamic structure of a statement, which as a thought-movement necessarily reaches beyond itself. Metaphysics therefore represents a thought-movement which is not and cannot be final, since it always points beyond itself. On the other hand, metaphysics itself is portrayed as the binding force of that which metaphysics is trying to do. The quest of metaphysics is shot through with an urgency over which thought has no control—which dominates thought. The founding of being in metaphysics presupposes the grounding of being. And since being as basis is the presupposition of metaphysical search, metaphysics can inquire after grounds. Metaphysics as inquiry is from the first directed to grounds, because the ground has so directed it, and therefore it cannot collapse into a mere chaotic darkness. In many a philosophic interpretation (think of modern philosophy from Descartes to Nietzsche) there is still more light than is acknowledge by those committed to another terminology and not open to the living character of the question.

Grounding Cause

All our thought, the principle of ground included, is but a pointer to that ground that is being, . . . What does such a pointer mean? We can first say that thought in asking the question opens up being. You can, therefore, explain this pointer as a thought-relationship which makes itself accessible in its being. In any case you thereby go in one step from finite beings to infinite being. Here we are concerned with grounding from being which is not just any being. Such a grounding we call causality. The criterion of causality is first the grounding of beings in another, or the affecting of another. In this the cause must be at least as strong in being as the effect, since nothing comes of nothing. (Since Leibniz the ontological distinction between ground and cause has been too little considered, with ill effect.) On the one hand the otherness can be swallowed up in the ground as necessary, so that the quest of ground then sinks to a calculating in the imagination. Or again—with equal right—the pointing to otherness in thought of the cause can disappear. Then God becomes the *causa sui*. Either way the basic question of metaphysics is betrayed.

The connection with which we are concerned here was already seen by Plato when he said, "Does not everything which comes into being, of necessity come into being through the cause?" (*Philebus* 26E) With Plato we cannot yet speak of a principle properly so called; there is only a discussion of the connection between becoming and cause, and the cause is considered as a fourth element along with the limited, the unlimited and the compounded. What cause is, is not yet stated. The relationship of the cause to the limited, the unlimited and the compound is still open. For "cause" appears on the one hand as the "creator of them" (27B), while on the other it is set down side by side with three of them as a fourth member. Cause indeed is set in a special rapport to mind (30E, 31A). The principle that anything finite has a cause is found in Plotinus (*Enn.* III, 1), and for St. Augustine the connection between becoming and cause (the expression *nihil fieri sine causa, De Ord.* I, 11) is not deducible. A causal problem existed, therefore, even before the proofs for the existence of God were formulated at the height of Scholasticism.

With all this we still have said nothing about what cause really is. Even in the well-known teaching on causes in Aristotle the connection between being and cause remains obscure, although in the teaching on actuality and potentiality we find an approach to a more proximate determination.

The question of the essence of cause is today often covered over by the question of the structure of the principle of causality. The latter usually follows this course: whether in this formulation a necessary connection between cause and effect can be shown without slipping into tautology. Without this necessary connection the principle of causality—so it is argued—would be either a purely empirical observation or a postulate.

The questions involved will not be brought up here. Even the distinction between causality in the sense of natural science (calculable functional connection) and metaphysical causality, which some years ago unleashed a flood of misunderstanding, need no longer be discussed. But has the battle been won when we have discovered that the principle of causality is sure? You may wish to go farther and show that the principle of causality is a special case of the principle of sufficient reason. But that would only—something not often noticed—give the principle of causality some of the unclear quality of the principle of ground. It is not enough just to compare "principles" with one another. It is more to the point to ask what these principles tell us and how what they tell us is bound together.

Ontological Ground

The principle of ground gains ontological significance only in the measure that being itself means grounding. And any thinking of ground, and the thought that grounds ground, can justify itself only when it has its ultimate source in grounding being. Otherwise the discussion of thinking of ground would be only a discussion of thinking which cannot give grounds for itself and yet talks of grounds. It is possible to talk of grounds only if thought is grounded in being. A philosophy that denies this slips into a formal method of thought, or it asks questions without answering them. But we must not over-simplify this idea. For it remains open for the moment how being itself is thought of and interpreted. For being is thought of wherever some compre-hension beyond a mere logic of thought is achieved. So it is not our intention to say that there is no genuine metaphysical point of departure in the thought of Kant and the Idealists. But beings are determined by being and are to be understood only from being. If the being is being itself, an encompassing is not possible. But the question of the ground will always remain, since the passing being is limited and does not represent the fullness of the answer.

Now if the passing being is determined from being, then every limited being points beyond its limits in the direction of being. This is neither an ex-pression of a proof for God nor a denial of the possibility of knowing absolute being. But it does insist on the decisive importance of the difference between beings and being. If there were only beings, then it would be hard indeed to explain the unity of the world otherwise than through beings. Then the al-ternative of the one or the many beings puts thought before a new *aporia*. Whoever fails to recognize the difference between beings and being must either make being a mere concept or call into question every differentiation. A difference of beings with respect to being necessarily means that the passing finite being is not being simply and yet is determined from being. If being means grounding, then the differentiation of beings to being also determines grounding, at least in the sense that grounding does not necessarily mean identity with self. On the other hand a differentiation of beings cannot be understood without an ultimate self-identity of being, since difference as such cannot be its own ground. There must be supposed a relation to beings which founds the passing beings from being. But this "relationship" can have its ground only in being itself. This manner of grounding we call cause. Pointing to a cause is nothing other than showing the relationship of passing beings to being as their source. Since being determines the passing beings, there is in the finite realm a genuine causality. But ultimately, causality can be explained only from being itself, which is all-embracing.

Finite Pointers

The observation that the principle of causality is the application of the principle of adequate ground in reference to finite beings is not false. Still the ontological connection of ground and cause remains obscure. The observation that not every ground is a cause but every cause is a ground can also be consistently justified; but in this way too the relationship between ground and cause becomes perilously formalized. For the difference is presented as a "not," and is in no way illumined ontologically. Let us not be satisfied here with pure postulates of thought, for it is presupposed in such an approach that we are able to understand a difference only from the difference between finite and infinite being. But causality shows itself thereby the necessary thought-presupposition for a finite expression of ground, a presupposition which is not limited to the realm of thought. It presupposes the ontological difference for the perfection of thought which remains finite. For thought which lives on being cannot be brought to completion. And thought which is not an expression of the ontological difference of being cannot be differentiated.

I can speak of ontological causality only when I presuppose that human understanding is of necessity directed to being, even that without this direction there would be no understanding. But this direction necessarily brings "causality" with it. For we can speak of a being as directed to something only because human understanding is determined through ontological differentiation. The pointing of understanding beyond itself therefore necessarily means the pointing of an effect to its cause, without meaning that the essence of cause and causality in such a question has already been clarified.

We must therefore say that any question in the finite realm is necessarily causally determined. This means that causality is expressed in the very question. The observation that we first come across causality in pondering the way of founding the finite does not say everything. Our life and thought in the finite is but the expression of an original causal structure. The indication of this is the structure of beings looking to being. It is not at once clear from this in what way being "effects" beings, or permits them to emerge. Grounding here appears at first as an ultimate horizon of being, one which no longer points to a further horizon, but which yet must ground in being which grounds. Therefore, from the necessarily causal situation of man, ground is at first disclosed as horizon, which itself points to an absolute grounding. It is not as if we were simply setting up being as grounding only on the grounds of certain *a priori* insights to explain the essence of causality with the help of experience. For causality determines as structure our entire life and thought, and there is no philosophy outside the thought of self-conscious man in the world.

The Circle of Being

But do we not have a vicious circle here? Do we not point from finite to infinite being with the help of causality? And do we not say that this causality is what stretches from the finite to the infinite? Does this not mean that metaphysical causality presupposes infinite being that is to be proved by its help?

And do we not define causality as a self-communication and go back to a grounding, while on the other hand we explain the question of ground itself by causality? Such questions can be multiplied at will with reference to the relation of the finite to the infinite, beings to being, and thought to being. A whole arsenal of conclusions, which always carry us back to where they began, can be collected here. (If a philosophy does not sufficiently expose these *aporia,* it is not a good sign. For it has either become encased in a naive belief in being, or it lives on the illusion that it can explain reality by going back to "clear" principles of thought whose ontological grounds remain obscure.)

We speak of a vicious circle. Is there really one here? First of all, we must ask whether being can ever be understood from the image of the vicious circle. Is it not rather the other way, that the content of expressions that bear with them, or seem to bear, a vicious circle must be understood from the being of beings? A vicious circle is present when the result as such is already the supposition and therefore the starting point. I can, therefore, speak of a vicious circle only with reference to a thought process leading to a conclusion, in which process the truth disclosed is already presupposed either expressly or in other words. But where I extract from data something that is implicitly bound up with it, there is no vicious circle. That is the whole purpose of the process: to work out the accompanying data that I at first do not observe.

When we put this question of ground, and when we want to explain what causality means, the first thing that comes to mind is to work with a scheme of concepts so that we can make a little progress. We easily slip up at this point, because this conceptual scheme is inwardly determined by what we want to investigate. It is man indeed that seeks grounds, and in this question man points beyond himself. In this question, then, transcendence shows itself as the pointing of man beyond himself. But the pointing first gains meaning when we understand man from that vantage point toward which he is pointing: from being. Causality, ground, thought, transcendence, being, all appear in the question of man who asks. All this has nothing to do with a vicious circle. For the being of beings is that to which every question is directed and from which alone it takes its meaning. Causality, ground and transcending thought are therefore ultimately to be pondered from the viewpoint of being.

From such a viewpoint causality becomes that faculty of being through which a being in its being points to the being of another being. This pointing means a grounding, for being itself means grounding. The principle of causality represents nothing else than the observation by thought of this primordial connection. Human thinking, which affirms this connection, is itself determined in its being through causality, since it points to something else, and is pointed to by something else. What causality really means, and what ground really implies, can be brought to light only to the extent that the relationship of beings to being is illumined and beings are pondered from the viewpoint of being. Therefore, causality itself "grounds" in being, insofar as it communicates itself to others. The step to the ultimate and highest being with the help of causal thinking means therefore nothing else than the illumination of an ultimate ground of beings and of thought as it is set up toward being. What "being" is remains obscure for the moment. It will become "clearer" only to the extent that being itself is recognized as the source of light.

Josef Pieper   # 6. CREATION:
                                                           ## THE HIDDEN KEY

Like Moeller, who suggested that the natural inclination of thought is to search for grounds, Josef Pieper asserts that "it is in the nature of the philosophical question to ask for the root of things." Like Moeller, too, he perceives that there is both an accessible and an inaccessible side to this search. Metaphysics thus looks for that which, ultimately, it cannot find but, at the same time, finds that which it is provisionally constituted to seek.

What then, asks Pieper, is the relation between these two elements of the search—the one positive, the other negative? The relation, he answers, is that between the double aspect of the truth of things that is to be found, especially in the writings of St. Thomas, in the idea of creation. This double aspect of the truth of things is constituted, first, by their thought-createdness by God and, second, by their intelligibility to the human mind. The fact that they are thought-created by God is the cause of their intelligibility to man: "Things are knowable *because* God has thought them into being." The knowability of things for man is therefore due to the fact that they are created.

Of this double aspect, only one aspect is made possible for human knowledge. The correspondence of things to the creative knowledge of God—which constitutes the truth of things—is beyond formal knowledge. "We can know the things, but not formally their truth; we know the image, but not its correspondence to the original, not the correspondence between the thought-creation and the thought-created." For this reason, truth and unknowability go together in man's knowledge.

This selection is part of an article that appeared in *Cross Currents,* Vol. 4 (1953), no. 1, under the title "On the Negative Element in the Philosophy of St. Thomas," and also forms a chapter in Pieper's *The Silence of St. Thomas,* published by Pantheon Books, Inc., New York, and Faber and Faber Ltd., London. It is reprinted through the courtesy of its publishers.

Everything that is, is itself luminous by virtue of being. But we must always distinguish: knowable to what—to finite or infinite intellect? It is of the essence of things, *as creatures, qua creatura,* that their knowability cannot be exhausted by a finite intellect. What we see in things is their being as image, as thought-created; we do not see their beings as original-being. We see in things the imitation of being, but cannot compare this imitation to the original from the eye of God. When we speak of the knowability of things, we must therefore understand this double implication of (*a*) true knowability, which is God's knowledge, and (*b*) limited knowability, which is man's knowledge.

Hence the being of things is bound to remain inaccessible to us because we are unable to grasp the image *qua image* of the Divine original. This, however, as St. Thomas points out, constitutes the meaning of human knowledge of things, which is underlined by a "hope-structure"—by a "not-yet-having." For this reason, Pieper concludes, the full answer to the philosophical question about being cannot be answered by the philosopher.

In THE PHILOSOPHY of Thomas Aquinas, an unexpressed basic idea, determining nearly every one of the structural concepts of his world view, is the idea of Creation—more precisely, the idea that there is nothing that is not *creatura* (except the Creator Himself); and that this createdness completely and entirely determines the inner structure of the *creatura.* . . .

St. Thomas' doctrine of truth can be grasped in its essential and profoundest meaning only if we formally take account of the concept of creation. And the connection of the concept of truth with the concept of unknowable, of mystery—the connection with which we propose to deal—this connection becomes visible only against the background of the idea that everything that can become object of human knowledge is either *creatura* or Creator. . . .

Things Are Knowable Because They Are Creatura

The basic tenet of St. Thomas' doctrine of the truth of things is found in the *Quaestiones Disputatae de Veritate* (1, 2): *Res naturalis inter duos intellectus constituta* [est]—"the natural thing [is] placed between two intellects," to wit, St. Thomas continues, between the *intellectus divinus* and the *intellectus humanus.*

With this situation of the real between the absolute, creatively thinking knowledge of God and the imitative, "conforming" knowledge of man, the constitution of the whole of reality presents itself as a structure of interconnected originals and imitations. St. Thomas here employs the concept of "measure" (which, in this non-quantitative sense, is age-old and presumably Pythagorean), of that which measures and that which is measured. The creative knowledge of God measures and is not measured (*mensurans non mensuratum*); natural things are both measured and measuring (*mensuratum et mensurans*); human knowledge is measured and not measuring (*mensuratum non mensurans*)—not, that is, the measure of the thing of nature, although it is the measure of the *res artificiales* (this is where distinction between created things and man-made things becomes important for St. Thomas).

In accordance with the double relatedness of things—so St. Thomas develops his doctrine—there is a double concept of the "truth of things." The first states their being thought-created by God, the second their intelligibility to the human intellect. "Things are true," then, signifies first that things are creatively known by God, and second that things are in themselves accessible and intelligible to human knowledge. But between the first and the second concept of truth there exists a relation of essential priority, *prioritas naturae.* This priority has a twofold meaning: *first,* that the core of the concept "truth of things" cannot be grasped, that it would simply be missed, if we do not explicitly think of things as *creatura*—brought forth by the thought-creating intellect of God, or, as early Egyptian ontology expressed the same thought, issued from the "eye of God"; and *second,* that the fact that things are thought-created by God is the *cause* of their intelligibility to man. These two relations, then, are to each other not like an older to a younger brother, so to speak, but like father to son: the first begot the second. What does this mean? It means that things are knowable *because* God has thought them into being; things, being thought-created by God, not only have *their* nature ("for themselves alone," so to speak), but, being thought-created by God, things also have an existence "for us." Things have their intelligibility, their inner lucidity, their luminosity, their manifestness because of the fact that God has thought-created them: because of this they are essentially intellectual. The lucidity and brightness which flows into things from the creative knowledge of God at the same time as their existence (nay, *as* their very existence)—this lucidity alone renders existing things visible to human knowledge. In a commentary to 1 *Tim.,* 6, 4, St. Thomas says: "As much actuality as a thing has, so much light it has." And in one of his late works, the Commentary to the *Liber de Causis* (1, 6), there is a deep statement that couches the same thought in something not unlike a mystical formula: *Ipsa actualitas rei est quoddam lumen ipsius*— the actuality of things is itself their light: the actuality of things understood as their createdness! And it is this light which makes the things visible to our eyes—which means that things are knowable because they are created! (At this point, we might express an objection to the epistemology, similar to the objection which Sartre raised against the philosophy of the eighteenth century and its talk about the nature of things: Let no one believe he could think away the thought-createdness of things by God and yet go on understanding how man's knowledge of things is possible!)

Things Are Unfathomable Because They Are Creatura

But we meant to speak about *un*knowability as an element of the very concept of truth. We found that, according to St. Thomas, one may in the realm of created natural reality speak of "truth" in two different senses. First, we may refer to the truth of *things,* which consists primarily in that the things, *qua creatura,* correspond to the original, creative knowledge of God: it is this very correspondence which formally constitutes the truth of things. Second, we may speak of truth with a view to human *knowledge;* this knowledge is true by virtue of corresponding "measure-receiving"—to the *a priori* given objective reality of things. And it is again this correspondence itself which formally constitutes the truth of human knowledge.

In the *Summa Theologiae,* these two concepts of truth are found formulated and juxtaposed within the same *articulus:* "If the things are the measure and yardstick of the intellect, truth consists in the intellect conforming to the things. . . . But if the intellect is the yardstick and measure of things, then truth consists in things conforming to the intellect." (I, 21, 2). These statements, again, express from a new viewpoint the structure of all created being, which is essentially placed between the thought-creative intellect of God and the imitating intellect of man—a thought of unsoundable depth!

Between the two correspondences (of intellect to reality, and of reality to intellect) which both, as "adaequatio," mean truth in their different ways— between the two correspondences there is this fundamental difference: that the one of them may become the object of human knowledge but not the other, that the one is humanly intelligible and the other is not. Man is fully capable of knowing not only the things, but also the correspondence between the things and his own idea of them. That is to say: beyond his naive perception of things, man is capable of knowing things in judgment and reflection. Human knowledge, in other words, not only can be true, it can also be a knowledge of the truth (*Summa Theologiae,* I, 16, 2).

But the correspondence of things to the creative knowledge of God, which primarily and most essentially constitutes the truth of things that in turn renders human knowledge possible (*cognitio est veritatis effectus*—this is another of those formulations in St. Thomas' *Quaestiones Disputatae de Veritate,* I, 1, which turns a customary formulation upside down: knowledge a fruit of truth, precisely of the truth of things)—this correspondence, I say, which constitutes the "truth of things"; the correspondence between natural reality and the original, creative knowledge of God; this correspondence itself is beyond our formal knowledge! We can know the things, but not formally their truth; we know the image, but not its correspondence to the original, not the correspondence between the thought-creation and the thought-created; this correspondence which formally constitutes the "truth of things" we cannot know. Here, then, it becomes clear how truth and unknowability belong together.

But this thought still needs to be expressed with greater precision. "Unknowability," in common usage, has several and at least two meanings. It may signify that something is of such a nature that in itself it is generally accessible to knowledge—but that a certain intellect, nonetheless, is incapable of grasping it because that intellect is not sufficiently penetrating. In this sense we speak of objects that are "not visible to the naked eye"—a failure of the eye rather than an objective peculiarity of the thing: the stars which we do not see are in "themselves" quite visible. "Unknowability" in this sense means that the intellect does not suffice to realize the objectively given possibility of knowing. But "unknowability" may also mean that no such possibility of knowing exists; that, in a manner of speaking, there is nothing to be known; it is not just that the knowing subject lacks sufficient power to perceive and penetrate—the object itself lacks intelligibility. But unknowability in this second sense—intrinsic unknowability of something real—is a notion which to St. Thomas is unthinkable. For since all that is is *creatura*—that is, thought-created by God—therefore all that is is in itself luminous, bright, manifest: luminous by virtue of *being!* Unknowability, therefore, can to St. Thomas never mean that there could exist something which is in itself inaccessible and dark; it can mean only that although there is light, it exceeds the power of comprehension, escapes the grasp of understanding.—This is the sense in which we here speak of unknowability, and we assert that this unknowability is part and parcel of the notion of the truth of things. In other words, we assert that it is of the essence of things, *qua creatura,* that their knowability cannot be exhausted by a finite intellect, because the cause of this knowability (manifestness, luminosity) has at the same time of necessity caused the unfathomable character of things!

Let us look more closely.

"Things are true"—that means, we have seen, primarily that things are thought-created by God. To begin with, this statement would be totally misunderstood if it were to be taken solely as a statement about God—for instance, as a mere statement about God's activity in respect of things. No, this sentence concerns the structure of *things:* it expresses the thought of St. Augustine that the things exist because God sees them (while we see the things because they exist); it states that the essence of things consists in their being thought-created by the Creator. As we have said, the statement is another name for "being," a synonym for "real"; *ens et verum convertuntur;* it is all the same to speak of "something real" and of "something thought-created by God." It is the essence of all existing things (*qua creatura*) that they are formed after an original which resides in the absolute creative knowledge of God. In his Commentary to John (1, 2) St. Thomas says: *"Creatura in Deo est creatrix essentia"*—"The created is in God creative essence," and in the

Summa Theologiae (I, 14, 12 ad 3): "Everything real possesses the truth of its essence insofar as it imitates the knowledge of God."

But to return to the problem at hand. The relation of correspondence between the original within God and the created imitation—which formally and primarily constitutes the truth of things—can never, we have said, be grasped as such by us directly. We can never occupy a point of vantage from which we could compare the original with the imitation: we are flatly incapable of witnessing, as onlookers, so to speak, the origin of things from "the eye of God." And because this is so, our understanding, as soon as it seeks to learn the essence of things, even the lowest and "simplest," enters upon a path which in principle has no end. It has no end because things are *creatura,* that is, because their inner lucidity has its original source in the boundless light of Divine knowledge. This fact is given, we have said, in the concept of the truth of being as St. Thomas formulated it—a concept whose full depth becomes visible, however, only when its connection with the concept of creation is understood: and this connection was to St. Thomas self-evident.

Philosophia Negativa

In this concept of truth, so understood, the element of unknowability— the element of *philosophia negativa* with which we now have to deal more specifically—has its legitimate locus and origin. To be sure, our interpretation does not blend into the traditional picture of the "scholastic" St. Thomas. For supposedly it is both characteristic of and essential for scholasticism and St. Thomas—and especially St. Thomas—that natural reason is deemed adequate not only to construct a self-sustaining philosophy, but even to bring the truths of faith by conclusive argument into a compelling and structurally perfect "system." How this misinterpretation and misunderstanding have come about historically cannot be explained in a few words. No doubt several causes contributed in a highly complex manner, beginning with the Augustinian (or, better, Augustinistic) distrust of nature and *ratio* which inspired the reformers of the 16th century, and ending with the concern of neo-scholasticism to keep the Master, Thomas, clear of any suspicion of "agnosticism." But whatever the causes and motives—there is a whole family of statements of St. Thomas which are hardly ever found in expositions of his doctrine: even the formulations of this negative element are rarely found.

We are dealing here only with the *philosophia negativa* of St. Thomas. He also formulated the principles of a *theologia negativa,* which are as a rule equally passed over in silence, not to say suppressed, in most expositions. Only rarely do we find it mentioned that the doctrine of God in the *Summa Theologiae* begins with the statement: "We cannot know what God is; we can know what He is *not*." I have not encountered one text-book on Thomistic philosophy which had found room for the thought St. Thomas expressed in his Commentary on Boethius' *De Trinitate* (1, 2, ad 1), that there are three degrees of human knowledge of God: the lowest, to know God as Him who is active in creation; the second, to know Him in the reflection of spiritual essence; and the highest, to know Him as the Unknown—*Deum tamquam ignotum!* Not to mention the statement in the *Quaestiones Disputatae de Potentia Dei* (7, 5, ad 14): "This is the ultimate of man's knowledge of God—to know that we do not know God"—*quod sciat se Deum nescire!*

Concerning, then, the negative element in the philosophy of St. Thomas, it is true, of course, that this statement about the philosopher (whose intellectual efforts had not sufficed even to understand the essence of a single fly) is found in the almost popularly written explanations of the *Symbolum Apostolicum,* and this may be the reason why it is hardly ever cited in learned treatises. But the statement is in a rather closely-knit connection with many other statements, all of which together circumscribe a concept of philosophy that, if formulated sharply, does in fact formally rule out the notion of a complete philosophical system. If a philosophical question can be defined by the fact that it asks for the deepest roots, the ultimate meaning, in short, for the "essence" of something ("What is this thing, ultimately and at bottom?")— then, according to St. Thomas' concept of philosophy, it is in the nature of the question that it cannot be answered in the same sense as it is asked; in a word, that it cannot be answered adequately. By a comprehensive knowledge, St. Thomas means this: to know a thing to the extent to which it is in itself knowable; to convert the knowability of the thing, without residue, into knowledge, so that there is nothing left in the thing, which is not *actu* known. Now what the philosophical question, by its very nature, aims for is an answer that is comprehensive in this sense; no other answer would be adequate. And such an answer is not possible—*because the knowability of being, which is here to be converted into knowledge, consists in the thought-createdness of that same being by the Creator!* Comprehensive knowledge, and thus an adequate answer to the question of the philosopher, is not possible because human knowledge, addressing itself to the essence of things, falls into a chasm of light, the bottom of which is God Himself.

Science is free to limit itself to the realm of that which can be positively known. As long as I ask for the chemical make-up of the cell-substance of this piece of wood, or for the structure of the atom, so long I remain within the realm of that which can in principle be answered definitively or which, at any rate, is not in principle unanswerable. But as soon as I ask "What is this thing?" and do not answer that it is a table, or a tool, or a piece of wood, but "This is matter," or "This is something real" (what does that mean, "something real"?)—as soon as I do so I am dealing formally with the unfathomable and unknowable. Philosophy does deal formally with the unknowable, because it is in the nature of the philosophical question to ask for the root of things, and thereby to penetrate to the dimension of their thought-createdness by the Creator, that is, to the dimension of creaturehood.

This explains how St. Thomas, in his Commentary to the *Metaphysics,* can say with Aristotle himself: The knowledge with which metaphysics is concerned, the knowledge of the essence of things, belongs to man not as a possession but as a loan: *non ut possessio, sed sicut aliquid mutuatum;* and why St. Thomas has no objection whatever to Aristotle's thesis (proclaimed with a most un-Aristotelian pomp) that the question of being is a question "raised since always and today and forever."

Yet there are some much more "negative" formulations in St. Thomas. There is, for instance, the following: "The essential principles of things are unknown to us"—"*Principia essentialia rerum sunt nobis ignota*" (Commentary to Aristotle's *De Anima* 1, 1; nr. 15). This statement is far less unusual and exceptional than might at first appear. It would be easy to match it with a dozen similar ones, from the *Summa Theologiae,* the *Summa contra Gentiles,* or from *De Veritate* and other *Quaestiones Disputatae.* All of them state that we do not really know the essence of things; which, St. Thomas says, is also the reason why we are unable to give things an essential name, but must take names from outward accidentals (in support of which St. Thomas then often offers those hopeless medieval etymologies, such as that *lapis* is derived from *laedere pedem*).

Why, after all—so St. Thomas once asks (*De Ver.* 5, 2 ad 11)—why is it impossible for us to know God perfectly through His creation? The answer has two parts, of which the second is of special interest for us here. The first part of the answer is: Creation reflects God only imperfectly. The second part: Owing to the dullness and stupidity of our intellect (*imbecilitas intellectus nostri*) we are incapable of drawing from things even what information about God they do indeed contain. To understand the full weight of this formulation, we must recall that, in St. Thomas' view, the special *essence* of a thing is the special manner in which it reflects Divine protection. This thought, which in turn points toward an entirely new and complex set of problems, has a very precise relation to our theme for it means that the essence of things themselves remains at bottom inaccessible to us just because we are incapable of grasping the image, *qua* image, of the Divine original.

This two-part answer has a plainly dialectical structure, reflecting the structure of the *creatura* itself (also made up of thesis and antithesis) which, by definition, has its origin both in God and in nothingness. (This is why St. Thomas says, not only that the reality of things is their light, but also: *creatura est tenebra in quantum est ex nihilo*—Creatures are darkness insofar as they are from nothing; this statement is *not* Heidegger's but St. Thomas', *Quaestiones Disputatae de Veritate,* 18, 2 ad 5.) And the answer to the question, Why can we not know God fully through creation? has the same recalcitrant structure. For how is it put? It is put: Things, through their essence, express God only imperfectly. Why? Because things are *creatura,* and *creatura* cannot express the Creator perfectly. Nonetheless, the answer continues, the luminosity of even this imperfect expression surpasses human understanding. Why? Because things, being thought-created by God, reflect in their being an infinite light—which means, again, because things are *creatura.*

The Hope-Structure of Creaturely Knowledge

We have spoken of the "negative" element in the philosophy of St. Thomas Aquinas. Now we become aware how and why this formulation is misleading, and that it stands in need of sharper expression, not to say correction. What is "negative" is not, at any rate, that human knowledge does not reach to the essence of things. "*Intellectus . . . penetrat usque rei essentiam*"—"the intellect penetrates to the essence of things": this statement of the *Summa Theologiae* (I, II, 31; 5) remains valid for St. Thomas, *in spite of* the other statement that the philosopher's intellectual effort did not suffice to understand a single fly. The two statements in fact belong together! That the power of the intellect does reach things is proved precisely by the fact that the intellect falls into the unfathomable chasm of light—this happens to the intellect *because* and *as* it reaches the essence of things.

There can then be no question of agnosticism in St. Thomas; and neo-scholasticism is right in saying so emphatically. But it is, I believe, impossible to make clear the true case of this situation without bringing the concept of creation formally into play, without speaking of the structure of things *qua creatura;* of this structure which means that things, being thought-created by the Creator, have *both* their essential luminosity and manifestness, and their unfathomableness and "inexhaustibility"; both their knowability and their "unknowability." Unless we go back to this foundation, it is not possible, I believe, to show why the "negative" element in the philosophy of St. Thomas has nothing to do with agnosticism. If we try to do without this basic idea, we shall needs be exposed to the danger—as the example of many a neo-scholastic attempt at systematization shows—of interpreting St. Thomas as a rationalist, and thus misinterpreting him altogether.

In fact, the position of St. Thomas cannot be reduced to any "ism." One might perhaps say that it gives expression to the—essentially forever elusive—*hope-structure* of the existence of man as a being who is capable of knowledge: neither simply knowing and "having," nor simply "not-having,"—but "not-yet-having." Man is conceived as a traveler, one who is on the way; that means, first, that his steps have meaning, they are not in principle futile, they do lead nearer the goal. And this, in turn, is unthinkable without that other element:

so long as man, in his existence, is "on the way," just so long the way of his knowledge is without an end. And this hope-structure of the quest for the essence of things, for philosophic knowledge, springs from the fact—let it be said again—that the world (the world and knowing man himself) is *creatura*.

Gerald Phelan   7. BEING AND ANALOGY

Father Phelan addresses himself in this essay to two antitheses of being, which have been explored in previous selections. They are: the accessible-inaccessible and the unitive-plural character of being. He suggests that these antitheses may best be understood in the light of St. Thomas's doctrine of the analogy of being, without which "it is impossible to acquire a knowledge of metaphysics."

Being dazzles the investigator. It is to be seen not directly but only in its analogical participation in things that *are*. Any attempt to look on naked being, to make it a clear and distinct idea (as in Descartes), brings on intellectual blindness and destroys metaphysics.

Though there is darkness in being (its excessive brightness—what Pieper has called "the negative element"—makes it appear so), there is also vision. This is attained in the realization that being belongs to all that is and to each thing analogically in proportion to its nature. This is a fundamental truth of being, says Phelan, and "he who has . . . understood that . . . truth has grasped the significance of analogy in the philosophy of St. Thomas."

Phelan uses the term "analogy," however, not in a popular but in a technical sense. The term does not indicate mere resemblance or metaphor, as inductive and rhetorical usage suggests. Certainly, there are resemblances that we mark out in experience; but we mark out resemblances against a background of dissimilarity, just as we mark out dissimilarity against a background of likeness.

If the term seems ambiguous, says Phelan, it must be placed first against its competitive terms, "univocal" and "equivocal." "Univocal" usage implies synonymity: the same meaning and the same characteristics (roses and geraniums are "flowers," and the term "flower" is used univocally of both); "equivocal" implies homonymity: different meanings and different characteristics (a handle is a "crank," and so is an irritable person). "Analogical," on the other hand, implies that the meaning of a term is

From Gerald Phelan, *St. Thomas and Analogy* ("Aquinas Lecture"—Milwaukee, Marquette University Press, 1941), pages 1–29. Reprinted by permission of the publisher.

neither exclusively the same nor exclusively different ("healthy" may be applied to both a food and a person).

There are three requirements that Phelan lays down for the strict use of the term "analogy." These are that a common character (*a*) belong to each and all participants, but in unequal degrees; (*b*) belong properly to only one of the participants, but be mentally attributed to the others; (*c*) belong to each and all participants in proportion to their being. The doctrine of the analogy of being is therefore stated: "Whatever perfection is analogically common to two or more beings is intrinsically (formally) possessed by each . . . in proportion to its being."

There are three types of analogy, but to Father Phelan and to St. Thomas only one is authentically applied to being. As opposed to the analogies of inequality and attribution, the analogy of *proper proportionality* requires that the analogated perfection is not univocal in being or concept, but that both being and concept exist intrinsically in all of the analogates according to a different mode.

Using the doctrine of analogy, therefore, to translate the problem of the relation between being and beings—between being as one and many— Phelan concludes that "it is in being . . . that all beings are one, yet the very being by which they are one is diverse in each, though proportionate to the essence of each." Furthermore, the doctrine of analogy accounts for our "accessible" knowledge of being but, at the same time, sets limits to that knowledge.

WHEN THE INTELLECT of man is confronted with *being as such,* it is dazzled, and can only hope to see by gazing upon its analogical reflections or participations in the things that are. Those who, in spite of all, have tried to look upon being naked and unadorned have been struck with intellectual blindness. And those who have attempted to express it in clear and distinct ideas have sinned against intelligence; for clear and distinct ideas banish mystery and bring death to metaphysics.

Nevertheless, in the realm of metaphysical abstraction, there is light and vision—the light and vision which come with that rush of understanding, that burst of insight, in which one knows and realizes, with sudden vivid intellectual joy, that being belongs intrinsically to all that is and to each and every thing *analogically,* that is, *in proportion to its nature.* He who has seen and understood that pregnant truth has grasped the significance of analogy in the philosophy of St. Thomas.

Analogy, therefore, although it cannot lay claim to be the master-key to the temple of Thomistic wisdom, lies, nevertheless, at the very heart of his philosophy, and, as Cajetan has truly said, without an understanding of analogy it is impossible to acquire a knowledge of metaphysics.

Before plunging into the depths of metaphysics, however, allow me to review the various meanings of the term analogy appropriate to the less profound levels of reflection. The word, analogy, itself is, of course, only Greek for proportion, and in the broadest and most general (non-technical) meaning of the term, an analogy means a comparison based upon any resemblance; a sameness of some sort among different things. Such, indeed, is the popular conception of what analogy is. Primitive mythologies are full of such analogies; the everyday conversation of the everyday man abounds in them and they often form the basis of his reasonings. This basic notion of likeness of diversity, however, clings to the concept of analogy wherever it is found, and carries with it the implication that analogous things are neither entirely the same nor utterly different. Philosophers (who never seem satisfied until they have rendered the simplest things unintelligible by their jargon), philosophers, I say, express this technically by saying that analogy is the mean between univocity and equivocity.

Of course, no two things can be exactly the same from every point of view, else they would not be *two* things but one and the same thing. Likewise, no two things can be completely other from every point of view else they could not be different *things,* for they are alike, at least, in that each is a thing. By an apparent paradox, only things which differ can be alike and only like things can differ. But likeness in difference extends over a wide range and consequently may be regarded as analogous in every manner of way. Some things are very much alike and other things are extremely different. The degrees to which two or more things may resemble or differ from each other are practically limitless.

The first obstacle encountered, then, in the attempt to understand the alleged importance of analogy in philosophy arises from the very vagueness of the term. How can a hopelessly ambiguous word like analogy be employed to good effect in the accurate context of philosophical discussion? For, after all, is it not true that analogy is one of those words which (like democracy) get bandied about in every conceivable sort of conversation and, more often than not, with a reckless abandon, a nonchalance and a looseness of expression which are, to say the least, disconcerting? A popular word, both in the sense of possessing a sufficiently vague and indefinite meaning to be useful in describing any observable likeness between things, and in the sense of enjoying a vogue among all kinds of writers and speakers, from journalists and platform orators to scientific authors and academic lecturers, analogy can be made to mean anything from the remotest or most superficial resemblance to the strictest and most technical relation of proportion.

The term analogy, as popularly used, designates all manner of comparisons between all sorts of things; the examples, parallels, resemblances which men naturally use to explain their thoughts are all more or less vaguely called analogies by most people who are able to pronounce the word. But, there are more precise meanings of the word which, while retaining the general connotation of resemblance, refine its signification and restrict it to particular kinds of resemblance. Biologists use it to describe organs which look like each other or discharge similar functions. Psychologists use it in the expression "analogies of sensation" as a synonym for synaesthesia. Philologists use it to denominate certain associations of linguistic forms. Logicians use it to characterize a primitive sort of reasoning from resemblance. Mathematicians use it to signify an identity or equality of relations. Philosophers use it in half-a-dozen different meanings, e.g. Kant speaks of the analogy of experience, Leibniz of the analogy of reason, Locke of the rule of analogy, Bosanquet discusses at length argument from analogy in order to dismiss it and F. C. S. Schiller does the same in order to maintain it. Yet even in these more refined meanings of the term there remains no little vagueness regarding the exact meaning of the term. Is it possible to rescue the term analogy from such confusion and give it any definite significance for the purposes of correct philosophical enquiry?

None of these meanings of the term analogy are in fact properly speaking metaphysical. They all indicate, indeed, a resemblance or likeness between things coupled with a difference, but all remain on the level of physical, logical or mathematical relations. In fact, as I hope to demonstrate, all of them are basically univocal meanings; none are strictly speaking truly analogical. But before proceeding, it is obviously necessary to compare and contrast analogical with univocal and equivocal meanings.

St. Thomas regards as univocal, things which possess a common characteristic, that is to say, things designated by terms which mean exactly the same thing when predicated of different things. E.g. in the two statements, an oak is a *tree,* an elm is a *tree,* the word *tree* designates an intrinsic formal constituent of both the oak and the elm which each equally possesses and by reason of which they are the same, although for other reasons they may differ. Equivocal terms, on the contrary, are those which, although identical in sound or in their written form, do not signify any such common formal constituent but mean something totally different when predicated of diverse things. E.g. the word *pen,* used to designate an instrument for writing and an enclosure for swine does not indicate anything common to those two objects. Analogical terms, however, have a meaning which is neither entirely the same nor entirely different when predicated of diverse objects. E.g. when I say that my dinner was *good* and my shoes are *good,* the word good does not signify any common constituent of both my dinner and my shoes, but it does indicate that the relation between *my* dinner and what a dinner ought to be, on the one hand, and *my* shoes and what shoes ought to be, on the other hand, is similar. *Proportionately speaking* both dinner and shoes may be called good.

Let us now examine the various resemblances which pass for analogies in popular parlance and in scientific, logical, mathematical and philosophical contexts, in order to reduce them if possible to certain general types and to appraise their claims to consideration as analogies properly so called.

The more or less universal propensity to compare one subject with another, to note their resemblances and their differences is a deep-seated habit of
the human mind and one which, no doubt, as Joseph Jastrow remarks, "characterizes undeveloped stages of human thought" and constitutes a kind of
primitive logic. But it is obvious that popular analogies of this sort designate
no more than certain undefined resemblances (sometimes real, sometimes
imaginary) between various objects upon the basis of which they may be
compared. Some of them may give rise to valid comparisons (i.e. when the resemblance or difference noted is real) and even be, strictly speaking, analogies.
However, there is nothing to prevent such analogies from signifying purely
univocal participations in a common formal constituent or even fictitious and
imaginary likenesses. In a word, any sort of resemblance may be called an
analogy in this popular sense of the word. It is practically the same with respect to the use of the term analogy in biology, psychology and philosophy.

Likeness in external form or function appears to be the basis upon which
certain resemblances are given the name of analogies in these sciences, and the
most the term indicates in respect to the objects studied by them is a similarity
mingled with a difference. No further refinement of the meaning of the term
is needed to cover the case. But it is perfectly evident that resemblances of
this kind may or may not be due to the univocal possession of the characteristics upon which the analogy is predicated.

In the logical order argument from analogy or reasoning by analogy is
simply what Aristotle calls the rhetorical method of persuasion by *example*.
It has nothing to do with analogical knowledge. It designates purely and simply
a way of arguing from observed resemblance to the *probability* of a conclusion
based upon that resemblance; it does not affect the character of the concepts
involved nor of the objects represented by those concepts. Valuable as such
a method may be in discovering relations between diverse phenomena—
Newton's apple, for instance, or any of a score of happy guesses about the
properties of things—it yields no knowledge of the inward constitution of the
objects upon which its *tentative inferences* are based.

Finally, mathematical analogy—although the word analogy was first used
to designate the proportion of one quantity to another—cannot be regarded as
a strict analogy since it is valid only within the genus of dimensive quantity.

In a word, none of the current meanings of the term analogy signify more
than a superficial resemblance between things, or at most a univocal participation in a generic, specific or accidental characteristic. None of them satisfy the
strict requirement of analogy proper.

Leaving aside, then, the myriads of popular "analogies" based upon superficial resemblances or imaginary likenesses, there appear to be only three ways
in which two or more different things may be said proportionately to participate in a common characteristic. *First,* the common character or *ratio* belongs
really and truly to each and all of the participants, in the same way but in

unequal degrees of intensity or under conditions of existence which are not identical. Men and dogs, for example, are *equally* animals but they are not *equal* animals, the common character which makes them both animals really and truly belongs to each, but it does not exist in dogs and men under the same conditions of existence. *Second,* the common character or *ratio* belongs properly to only one of the participants but is attributed by the mind to the others. Health, for instance, belongs properly speaking only to an organism but, because of the relation in some order of causality which other things like food, medicine, exercise, bear to the health of the organism, these too are called healthy. *Third,* the common characteristic or *ratio* belongs really and truly to each and all of the participants but to each and all in proportion to their respective being (*esse*). . . .

The basic proposition in the doctrine of Thomistic analogy, in its strict and proper meaning, is that whatever perfection is analogically common to two or more beings is intrinsically (formally) possessed by each, not however, by any two in the same way or mode, but by each in proportion to its being. Knowledge, for example, is possessed by men, by angels and by God, but not in the same way; the way in which men know is proportionate to the being which men have and likewise for angels and for God. There is thus a strict proportion of proportions in which the terms of one proportion are not proportionate to the terms of the other proportion, but the whole proportion between the terms on the one side of the relation is proportionate to the whole proportion between the terms on the other side of the relation. Thus, in the analogous statement knowledge is to the angel as knowledge is to man, knowledge in the first case (angelic knowledge) is not directly compared to knowledge (human knowledge) in the second case (in other words, the term knowledge does not mean the same thing when predicated of angel as it does when predicated of man); nor is "angel" directly compared with "man" (or in other words, man is not said to be an angel nor an angel to be a man).

What is stated is that the proportion between knowledge and angel *holds,* i.e. angels know *as* angels are; and that the proportion between knowledge and man *holds,* i.e. men know *as* men are; and further (and finally) that there is a proportion between the way the first proportion *holds* and the way the second proportion *holds.* Of course, the ultimate basis upon which such analogies rest is the proportion existing between the essence (*quod est*) and existence (*esse*) of every being that is; from which it follows that every metaphysical perfection, every metaphysical concept and every metaphysical term is of its very nature analogical. This is indeed a very far-reaching statement for it implies that whenever one uses such a common word as "is" or "true" or "good," or any other term expressing a metaphysical or transcendental object of thought, the meaning of that word never remains exactly the same but is always proportionate to the nature of the being of which it is said.

This type of analogy, the analogy of proper proportionality, is the only truly metaphysical analogy. All other analogies fail to fulfill the requirements of metaphysical analysis for one of two reasons:

1. Because the perfection or character which is predicated of two or more beings is possessed intrinsically by only one of the beings in question and is merely transferred by the mind to the others.
2. Because the perfection or character which is predicated of two or more beings, although possessed intrinsically by each of the beings in question, is possessed by all in the same manner or mode, albeit in unequal degrees.

Since Cajetan's *De Nominum Analogia* it is customary to deal with the doctrines of analogy in the philosophy of St. Thomas under the general headings of analogy of inequality, analogy of attribution and analogy of proportionality—which correspond exactly with the three types of analogy which St. Thomas himself distinguished in his commentary on the *Sentences* of Peter Lombard. Cajetan's terminology is, indeed, found elsewhere throughout the writings of St. Thomas, but in this particular passage he definitely describes each type. Given that in any analogical predication, as distinguished from univocal and equivocal predications, one term is predicated of another in a meaning which is neither entirely the same nor entirely different, the terms in which St. Thomas describes the three types of analogy just alluded to are more revealing than Cajetan's terminology.

Cajetan's analogy of inequality is described by St. Thomas as that in which there is a proportion in the *being* of the analogated perfection but not in the *concept* of it. That is to say, 1: that the concept of the analogated perfection is univocal and, since a concept is the intellectual representation of the quiddity of its object, the analogated perfection is itself univocal in its very quiddity; 2: that this univocal quiddity exists intrinsically in two or more beings in a more or less perfect manner according to (proportionate to) the nature of each. It is obvious that in this type of analogy we are dealing with a generic perfection unequally shared by the species within the genus. Not only is this a rather thin sort of analogy but may be regarded, as Cajetan regards it, as "utterly alien to analogy." Nevertheless it is to this type of analogy that many philosophers have had recourse in a vain endeavor to escape the inexorable logic driving them on to monism.

The second type of analogy which Cajetan calls the analogy of attribution is described by St. Thomas as that in which the analogated perfection exists intrinsically in only one of the analogates (and is, therefore, univocal), and is applied by the mind proportionately to others on the basis of some relation of causality existing between the prime analogate and the minor analogates. Here we have to deal once more with a case of ontological univocity coupled with a logical use of the univocal term after the manner of a true analogy. The procedure is, of course, logically valid and, no doubt, of considerable importance in dialectics; but, once more we have on our hands a type of analogy which is far too weak to bear the weight of metaphysical or transcendental predication.

It will not be surprising to find a number of idealists using arguments to maintain the necessary distinction between the Absolute and the Relative (by whatever names they may be called in different systems of idealism), for idealism always either explicitly or implicitly reduces metaphysics to logic and erroneously applies procedures valid in dealing with the *entia rationis* of logic to the *entia realia* of ontology.

St. Thomas' description of the third type of analogy—Cajetan's analogy of proportionality—demands that the analogated perfection be not univocal either in its *being* or in the *concept* of it, but, on the contrary, that it both exist intrinsically in all of the analogates and in each according to a different mode. This is, indeed, a difference in the very likeness and a likeness in the very difference; not merely a mingling of likeness and difference wherein likeness is based upon a formal identity and difference is based upon a formal diversity. This is true analogy; for it is *in being* (*essendo*) that all beings are one, yet the very *being* (*esse*) by which they are one is diverse in each, though proportionate to the essence of each.

The peculiar type of proportionality which is at the root of the metaphor and of symbolism cannot be regarded as a proper proportionality upon which metaphysical reasoning can be based because the perfection symbolically or metaphorically analogated is univocal and it is only *used* analogically to designate a certain likeness in relations. The analogated perfection is not of itself and intrinsically analogous and this is the essential requirement of a truly metaphysical analogy.

Louis De Raeymaeker   8. BEING AND CAUSALITY

The connection between being and causality, Joseph Moeller has already pointed out, is utterly crucial. In this essay Monsignor De Raeymaeker pursues the point further and amplifies it by the theme of creativity, as suggested in Pieper's essay.

De Raeymaeker's interest, as he states it, is not merely in the empirical bond suggested by the term "causality" but in "the ontological causal relationship connecting supposits" (what Aristotle would term substrata

Originally entitled "The Metaphysical Problem of Causality," this essay appeared in the quarterly *Philosophy Today,* edited at Saint Joseph's College, Rensselaer, Indiana. Translated from the French by Ambrose J. Heiman, C.Pp.S.

of being). By causality, De Raeymaeker means "the activity exercised by one being upon another being."

Selecting man as the starting point for an inquiry into the ontological relations between cause and effect, De Raeymaeker notes the link between human agent, or efficient causality, and purposive, or final causality. To the question "Is causality a fact, and where is it so?" he answers, first, that it *is* a fact, and is present at least in the realm of the spatio-temporal. Matter is passively enclosed within space and time, and a material being coming to be requires the influence of causal activity. Man, as a material being, accedes to this spatio-temporal demand in coming to be.

But what of man as a spiritual reality with the personal principle of free activity? Is he, as a spiritual being, also subject to causal influence? Taking much the same stand as Moeller, De Raeymaeker asserts that "you cannot basically explain any least reality without explaining reality as a whole, for in the order of being everything inseparably hangs together." No particular being—that is, either material or spiritual contingent—can furnish the reason for its own relation with the order of being, and, hence, for its own reality. All things, being totally dependent on the same creative act, bear the same ontological message even though as beings they differ; they "bear witness to the absolute stability of that single all-powerful act which puts and keeps them in being."

De Raeymaeker thereupon distinguishes two levels of causality: a "horizontal," or finite level, which forms a series, and a "vertical" level, which joins the order of finite and correlative causes to the infinite and absolute cause. "Thus the whole order of finite beings, of finite causes, taken together and in their content, 'participates' in the absolute perfection of subsistent being. Their entire content is immediately and continually in contact with the creative act which 'gives' it being."

CAUSALITY, like all philosophic problems, has been much discussed. But it seems to have run up against more misunderstanding than most problems. Before beginning our discussion, however, we must understand what is meant by causality and define the terms of the problem.

Meaning of Terms

The meaning of words is conventional. Anyone is free to use the words *activity* and *causality* as synonymous, but he should make this clear, for not everyone understands them as identical. Nor do we. The exact meaning we have for causality is the following: *the activity exercised by one being upon another being,* whether in giving it existence or only a new mode of being. There are indeed other kinds of activity, whereby a being is changed through self-determination, especially by an act of free will or judgment. There are problems involved both in immanent activity and in causality, but there is no reason for assuming that these problems are the same, so they should not be confused. We shall therefore not appeal exclusively to immanent activity to solve the problems of causality. And we particularly want to avoid accounting for the way an effect proceeds from its cause merely in terms of thinking and willing, useful though it may be to reflect on such activity.

We are concerned, then, with external causality. Surely you could also speak of an internal causality if you want to. But it seems to us that you run into confusion unless you separate questions concerning a being's internal structure from those concerning its causality—even though admittedly metaphysical problems are interdependent.

Fact of Causality

But on to our first question: *is causality a fact?* Can we empirically establish the influence of cause on effect? If so, its reality is beyond doubt. More precisely, *where is causality a fact?* In the physical world? Since Hume it has been the fashion to say that we see phenomena coming after each other, but not acting on each other. We see, for instance, the hammer hitting the nail and the nail becoming less visible but we do not see the hammer exercising a causal action whose effect is to drive the nail into the wall.

The trouble is that an atomistic view of pyschic data usually underlies the description of these phenomena of physical causality. We should rather appeal to Gestalt psychology, as Professor Michotte has shown. It has been experimentally established that all our verbs for physical causality (push, carry, pull, throw, etc.) are matched by a definite Gestalt or configuration. In each case the psychic configuration corresponds to a number of simultaneous or successive physical movements which stimulate the sense organs and give rise to that unified perception known as causality. This of course is only the organic side of perception as a whole. But our question is precisely whether it is right here, in the sense act, that we recognize the causal influence of one material being on another. Do we perceive a causal fact as we see colors or hear sounds? Rather, is it not strictly necessary for intelligence, which is also present in the psychic reaction as a whole, to take a hand here? If so, we must define its role precisely. Two possibilities come to mind: either intelligence grasps the causal relationship immediately, intuitively; or else it gets there by reasoning from the facts. If the latter, then we must pinpoint the principle of this reasoning.

In this connection it is interesting to note the direction that research takes in the experimental sciences. They aim at formulating "scientific laws," which express empirical functional relations among data. In other words, by using inductive methods we can show that two things are functionally connected, so that we do not experience one without the other. This is the meaning for instance, of water "boiling" at "one hundred degrees." Such laws let us single out and formulate precisely the physical conditions of our perceptive reactions, whether these conditions are a group of simultaneous factors or a series of antecedents and consequents. The experimental sciences try to calculate exactly these relationships of simultaneity or succession. And often they express these "laws" in terms of causality: the antecedent "causes" the consequent. But they do so without deciding the ontological value of the phenomenon. By no means do they deny this value. But it is not strictly their business, so they leave to others, especially philosophers, the task of reflecting on it.

Subject of Causality

To get back to our original question: on what grounds do we admit ontological relations between cause and effect? One preliminary clarification is essential. If (extrinsic) cause means a being that produces an effect in another being, then first we must know what realities to consider as beings, as active ontological units, as "supposits" (*actiones sunt suppositorum*).

We can take for granted that man is a supposit, existing in himself in virtue of an *esse proprium,* since he is a person, freely acting by himself. Autonomous action implies a subsistent agent. But beyond man the matter is not so simple. Where do you have supposits in the mineral world? Hard to say. We might wonder if the whole universe, ruled throughout by the same physical necessity, is not one single material supposit, with each mineral reality being, in a restricted sense, only a part. Vegetables and especially animals give a stronger impression of being subsistent units, acting by themselves. But even so, an animal never enjoys any least freedom, properly speaking. From every viewpoint he is always tied down to his surroundings. Whatever subsistence is here is highly precarious. So if we grant that an animal shows the characteristics of a "being-in-itself," this is true only in a limited sense. Such a "being-in-itself" is never more than a shadow of the subsistence man shows in an independent human act.

Thus everything points to taking man as our starting point in analyzing causality. But of course it is the real man, man as he is, that we must consider. This man is no doubt a *personal being,* but he is just as much a *being-in-the-world.* We must take both aspects, which are indissolubly united and correlative, into account. Man is endowed with activity that is strictly immanent; he "is alive" in the fullest sense of the word, for he displays personal intellectual and volitional activity. But he is naturally just as much a bodily, "mundane" reality, a part of the universe ruled by physical laws. In short, man's activity, which is as unified as man himself, is both material and spiritual, just as man is both body and spirit in his substantial unity. And just as man's spirit is a "soul," a form animating matter, so his immanent activity naturally embodies itself in material transient activity. However spiritual man's personal activity, it nonetheless has its bodily aspect and is influenced by the outer world.

Man therefore exercises causality properly so-called, since he acts upon an "outer" world from which he is "personally" distinct. Such interaction takes place between two distinct supposits. Our spontaneous impression of exercising causality on the outer world, as well as being influenced by it, is quite in accord with the facts.

Cause and Effect

Analyzing human activity should then enable us to discover the essential factors in causality.

Whether there is question of local motions, or qualitative modifications, or substantial changes such as those involved in the conception or death of a living being, causality is always a form of activity. It "makes something happen," so that reality is other than it was. In short, the upshot of any causal operation is a result, a product.

No doubt the same holds for immanent activity, but then the product stays in the agent, affecting and determining him. For example, when man thinks and wills, these acts come to an end right within the agent. Causal activity, on the contrary, comes to an end outside the agent; it begets a new determination in a being that is really distinct from the agent. Thus it is essential to causality to be fruitful, productive, efficient; it is the source of an external effect. We must not picture the cause producing its effect by breaking off a part of itself and handing it over to another reality. That would hardly be causality, or production, but at most a transfer of reality. Causal activity in itself does not formally modify the cause; it neither adds to it nor takes away from it. Rather, it implies that a cause, in act, brings about through this act a real product, an upheaval in being, outside itself.

If the cause is the ontological source of the effect, then cause and effect must belong to the same order, they must show a certain similarity (*causa agit sibi simile*) and share the same order of perfection. Moreover, the perfection of the effect cannot exceed that of the cause (*nemo dat quod non habet*).

Participation and Final Cause

Causality is best expressed in terms of participation. The act of being is a radiant perfection; it is itself a summons to being, *est diffusivum sui*. Simply through the perfection of its own reality it gives rise to perfection outside itself, so that another being now has, in its own original way, the perfection that the cause had. This very diffusiveness shows the fecundity of the act of being, —and justifies an optimistic view of reality.

Just as causality is related to participation, so efficiency goes hand in hand with finality. What we have here is a natural order, one that embraces the nature itself, the act of that nature, and the effect that is brought about. Any being whatever is always a definite reality, inwardly determined, "shaped." It expresses itself in an activity which is its own and which must be an extension of its own active nature. On the other hand, the effect must be in proportion to the efficient act, for it is simply a participation in that act. It would be nonsense to say that just any kind of act results in any kind of effect. The point of arrival is only where the road leads, and the road can only lead to its end, its final point. Now if action, in virtue of what it is, naturally leads to its terminus, then it must be pointed towards this terminus as to its end. The terminus must be a goal which attracts the action.

Consequently, there is no efficiency without finality, for the agent's nature governs its activity. Efficiency and finality are two aspects of one and the same causality. Problems indeed arise about the attraction exercised by the end and the relationship between the end and intelligence, but we have no time for them now.

The Material World

When is the intervention of a cause required? Can we formulate a law on this point? In other words, can we set down and justify a "principle of causality"? Many think so, though their view is still challenged.

Certain distinctions which are often neglected should be made here. In the first place, our concern is precisely with the ontological causal relationship connecting supposits, not simply with the "empirical bond" that the experimental sciences try to discover. Secondly, we have to be clear about where this causality applies. Are we thinking of being itself, whose extension is transcendental, or of just one category of beings—material beings for instance, whose extension is limited? What we may rightly assert about one category of beings cannot be extended to others without furnishing proof. This remark is worth making, for man's experience is of the material world, and the danger is only too real of applying to all of reality without restriction what has been proved for material reality only.

Let us first turn our attention to matter. It is characterized by extension. Every material thing is located in space; in its whole reality it is related spatially to other material things. In short, a material object is completely enclosed within the *spatial order*. That is why its movements sucessively go through points of space which are side by side. This assures them a continuous duration; they take place entirely in a *temporal order*.

An example. If I am writing, I am doing so "here" and "at this moment." This activity was preceded by other activities at other places. My life as a whole began at a certain place and moment; my death too will occur at a determined place and time. The beginning, the end, and all the intermediary points are necessarily located within a wider spatial and temporal whole. You cannot consider them without taking into account their relations with other material realities which precede or accompany or follow them.

This "extendedness" is responsible for matter's "passivity." Since things are necessarily located within the continua proper to space and time, they depend on each other. Together they form a solid whole without any break in continuity. Every place, province, country, is bounded by something else, without any break. Every moment, hour, year, rises out of a past and tends toward a future, without any interruption. If the past had not been as it was, the present could not be as it is. Similarly, the characteristics of each portion of matter are a function of its environment. In the long run you have to take into account the material order as a whole to explain any of its parts.

This fact is evidenced by the inertia of matter: its activity is conditioned by outside influences. Thus every material thing shows the *potentiality peculiar to passivity*. If you cut a thing off from all other material reality, it will remain inert, incapable of any activity whatsoever; it starts acting when you again bring it under the influence of neighboring realities. This means that these other realities give it a completion which it lacks, which it is radically incapable of giving itself and without which it could never begin to act.

In the material universe, therefore, the principle of causality is clearly necessary. *Quidquid movetur ab alio movetur*. That is, a material thing is active only when it is influenced from without. *Quod incipit esse causatur:* a material thing is always the outcome of an evolution, the result of pre-existing matter, the fruit of a change. *Generatio unius corruptio alterius*. Because of matter's passivity, such a coming into being can occur only under the influence of a causal activity.

Beyond the Material

Do these principles hold for all beings? Our experience is limited to matter. Yet we do have experience of beings which are neither purely material nor purely spiritual but both, namely, men. Since men are material, earmarked by passive potentiality, the above principles apply to them. But to the extent that they are spiritual they rise above this passivity; they need no further completion from without in order to be actually in operation. In other words, they move and determine themselves. They can lay hold of and possess themselves by a conscious and reflective act, and hence are personal principles of free and autonomous activity. This does not mean that man's activity is a pure act of freedom. Rather, in his substantial oneness man is the source of a single activity which is always both sensible and intellectual, material and spiritual. That is why human freedom, real though it is, is exercised only within the narrow limits of a living organic framework which is marked by passivity and is always subject to the influence of material surroundings. But personal activity still escapes this influence and rises above passivity, at least insofar as it implies consciousness of self, knowledge personally conceived, inclination ruled by free choice. Here then is an autonomous source of activity, a personal initiative, a self-determination, which cannot be adequately explained by material antecedents—even though there are such antecedents and they have their bearing on human activity as a whole, since it does contain organic elements.

Non-material Cause

To the extent that this autonomous domain escapes the law of causality proper to the material order (marked by passivity), is it then free of all causal influence? The question calls for a close look. We must note that man's purely immanent intellectual and volitional activity is not always in act in the same way, nor even always in act. It involves a coming into being, a passage from potency to act. Since such an act affects its very source it is a new and enriching factor for the agent himself. Must we not then admit the influence of a cause which does not operate in the spatio-temporal order and does not correspond to the insufficiency proper to passivity but which acts inwardly on the immanent source itself? But how could this inward causality be imposed upon something so personal and independent without nullifying the autonomous activity it is supposed to explain? If you consider man's origin you fall into the same dilemma. To the extent that human reality is spiritual, a "preceding moment" or a material evolution cannot adequately explain it. It transcends every relationship with such a moment and implies an origin that is independent of all pre-existing matter. Must we further conclude that this absolute beginning involves an absolute independence, a denial of every relationship of dependence?

An analogous problem comes up even with regard to the material universe. By definition this universe embraces all of material reality, all the relations established among things and making up the material order. Now what holds for a part as a part cannot be transferred to the whole as a whole. The principle of causality, we just defined it for material things by reason of their passivity, cannot be applied to the whole universe, since it is not located in an environment which acts on it from without. Nor does its origin imply a relation to some pre-existing matter from which it evolves since by universe we mean the whole material order. But if the universe as a whole does not depend on a preceding moment, is it thereby independent of every cause whatsoever? That is our question.

We readily admit that the problem is not so rudimentary as some people think. They are dazzled by the evidence for saying that what begins has a cause. No doubt there is such evidence for the origin of things within the material universe. But it is not quite so easy to account for the universe as a whole, or for man insofar as he is spiritual and above material evolution.

Being from Nothing

We must state the problem accurately. It is usually said that what does not come from pre-existing matter is made from nothing. Two termini are set in contrast: a purely negative one, nothing and a positive one, the reality in question. And the second would be reached by starting from the first. But in this case there can obviously be no passing from potency to act, no coming into being, since the first terminus, far from being a real potency is pure nothingness. To come from nothing means not coming, just as to go nowhere is not to go at all.

It is a figure of speech (and these are dangerous in philosophy) to think of being as wrested from nothingness. The same holds for considering nothingness an enemy that makes it hard for being to come on the scene and who is always dogging being like a menacing shadow. Such a menace is no menace at all; it offers not a shadow of danger. It is just as easy to escape the clutches of nothingness at the beginning of existence as it is later on. And indeed, there is small glory in defeating an enemy who does not exist. In this respect, then, the beginning of being presents no special difficulty. It is only being itself that we have to consider. Every efficiency, as every menace, comes only from being and applies only to being, for it alone is real. Only being has a reason for existence, for outside it there is nothing, and this reason is found within itself and nowhere else, since it is the only reality. No matter what you are explaining, it is foolishness to bring in either nothingness or some intermediary which you picture as a bridge between nothingness and being.

Absolute Beginning

But can we speak of a beginning without referring to what came before— or could have come before? Not if we are talking about a *relative* beginning, which by definition bespeaks a relation to a preceding moment, real or imaginary. But this is not true of an *absolute* beginning, especially the beginning of the material order as a whole, with all the possibilities that it implies. In this case we consider all moments, excluding none, so that any appeal to a preceding moment is impossible. But then how can we speak of a beginning? Only on condition that the moments which the universe has traversed can be counted, that their number is limited. The same is true of the origin of every reality insofar as it is spiritual—for instance, a man's personal soul.

With regard to any real order, the vegetative for example, we can raise questions about the units making it up and the relations among those units. There can also be questions about the relations between this and other orders such as the animal and mineral and human orders. But if we take all the orders together, the totality of finite beings beyond which, by definition, no other particular being is possible, then there can be questions only about the inner make-up of this whole, not about a bond between it and some particular terminus beyond it; for beyond this whole nothing is even conceivable. From this viewpoint the totality of finite beings is "absolutely" complete without any restriction.

Here then is the basic metaphysical problem about causality. In what sense is this absolutely complete whole an absolute that excludes every extrinsic relation? As we have just seen, it surely excludes every relation to a particular being outside itself. But does that mean it cannot be related to some reality radically different from every particular being? In other words, is it "relatively absolute"—with respect to every particular being; or is it "absolutely absolute"—in every respect?

Supposing that this totality of particular beings does not have its sufficient reason within itself, then we would have to admit a being distinct from the totality on which it would depend for its sufficient reason. But how to conceive a being that is not some particular being?

Sufficient Reason

Experience testifies that many realities do not have within them their sufficient reason, neither for what they are nor that they are; they are "effects," depending on extrinsic causality. As we saw before, such dependence is the rule in the material order because of the passivity that goes with spatial extension. In this spatial order mutually dependent material causes form a series which goes on indefinitely and transfers movements and qualitative changes from one spatial point to another in all directions.

In the spiritual realm it is another story. For example, the intellectual activity of knowing tends to assimilate, on the intentional level, all outward reality. It is indeed dependent on this outward reality, at least in the sense that such assimilation could not take place if this reality did not and could not exist. Nevertheless, it is not because of any causal action of exterior reality upon the spiritual faculty that a purely immanent intellectual act occurs. And all the more so no purely immanent act is due to the causality of material reality. No material cause can touch a faculty which transcends the material order and is free from any passivity in the proper sense. Hence you do not find in the spiritual realm those series of interdependent causes that are peculiar to the material order and that can act only within the perimeter of mutual passivity.

This, then, is the basic question: does the material order have its sufficient reason within itself, within the totality of material causes united to one another? Or again, does each particular spirit have its sufficient reason within itself, or can that reason perhaps ultimately be found in the community of spirits?

Part and Whole

As far as the material order is concerned, it is not uncommon to meet the following line of reasoning: every material thing is an effect; therefore the totality of material things is also an effect. But do we have any right to say that, because every part in a whole is a part, the whole also is only a part? What is proper to a part as such is not automatically proper to the whole as such. The formal characteristics of the members of an order cannot be attributed to the order as such. That dependence upon others which is so essential to each member of the material order cannot be transferred just as it stands to the order as a whole. For outside that whole there is by definition no material reality which could act on it. If anyone wants to assert that, because each material thing depends on an external cause (a material one, intrinsic to the universe), the whole material universe should also depend on an external (and hence non-material) cause, we can only reply that we will gladly admit it once proof is offered. And even after getting such proof we still would not know whether it applies also to the spiritual domain.

Causality and Being

As a matter of fact, these reflections rest on too narrow a basis. If we appeal only to the nature (whether material or spiritual) of things, we can never get down to bedrock. For a problem to be metaphysical in scope it has to be put on a transcendental level, which embraces everything without exception, including what is most basic. We must therefore formulate the problem in terms of *being,* the transcendental which is the formal object of metaphysics.

We experience being as a fact. "There is" being; we run into it at every moment. But we do more than just materially experience this fact and record it, we understand it. Being speaks to the intellect, it implies "reason" for being. What is more, it is proper to the intellect to lay hold of it; it is the formal object of the intellect.

First, last and always, being has a meaning which is "absolute," which obviously rules out any opposite; non-being is nothing and means nothing. Being thrusts itself on the mind unconditionally, decisively, unswervingly. And since being has no opposite, there is no limit to the scope of its meaning; it is transcendental.

No wonder then that St. Thomas declares that being is not just a certain perfection, one value among others, but that it is "the perfection of perfections," the basic perfection of which other perfections are but modes. Being is the one fundamental act of which everything else is a participation while being itself is a participation of nothing.

This means that being is at the root of all reality and all intelligibility; it is the stuff from which everything is made. It shows up under various forms, since there are different beings. Each particular being possesses the act of being in its own way, within the limits of its own nature. Every being participates in the perfection of being and it is precisely in this participation that its reality consists. Its essence is nothing else but a mode of being, wholly potential in relation to the act of being. The domain of being constitutes an order of participation that includes everything without exception, since its extension is transcendental.

Consistency of Being

In showing that being is transcendental we also show how all reality hangs together. Everything belongs to the domain of being and does so by reason of its whole content. Things belong to the order of being not through something added on to what they are but simply through what they are. In other words, they do not have some consistency of their own before entering the domain of being; rather, to be oneself and to be part of this domain is all the same.

Our question about each thing's basic reason for existence now takes on a precise meaning. A part as such is explained only by the whole that contains it. In order of participation the members are related to one another and are explained only by the order to which they belong. And if participation concerns the whole reality—the being—of these members, then an adequate explanation of them can be found only within an over-all explanation of the order itself. Consequently the sufficient reason for each being is the same as that for the order of beings. You cannot basically explain any least reality without explaining reality as a whole, for in the order of being everything inseparably hangs together.

Evidently then our previous question applies in exactly the same way to any particular reality whatsoever, whether we are thinking of its beginning or its continuation in being. Ultimately this question can be answered only with reference to our fundamental explanation of all reality.

The Order of Being

Order is unity in multiplicity; it implies a plurality of things which are so related to each other that they form a whole. The order finds its explanation in its principle of unity, which must be just as real as the order itself. Such is the case with the order of being.

The distinctive feature about this order is that its members belong to it by their entire reality, not by some relation added on to their *being-in-itself*. This means that belonging to the order (and hence being related to the other members of the order) can be completely reduced to a member's *being-in-itself*. Hence the sufficient reason for the whole order is the same as the sufficient reason for each being contained therein.

Now obviously no particular being can furnish the sufficient reason for its relation with the order of being. Indeed, relations are specified by their terminus, and so can be adequately explained only from the viewpoint of the terminus. Nor does any particular being have within itself the adequate reason for any other particular being; for two beings, mutually distinct by reason of their own limits, are radically irreducible to each other. A fortiori no particular being has within itself the sufficient reason for all the realities contained in the order of being. But if a being cannot find within itself the sufficient reason for its belonging to the order of being, then neither can it find there the sufficient reason for its own reality, since, as we said before, these two are the same.

Moreover we could not say that the sufficient reason for the whole is found partially in each particular being, so that by considering the sum of these beings we could find the adequate reason for the whole. A sufficient reason that is split up into as many parts as there are beings cannot have any real unity; and if it lacks unity it cannot be the principle of unity in the order of being. Consequently, the principle of unity in the order of being is not the *being-in-itself* of particular beings, and hence these beings are really distinct from their own sufficient reason.

Absolute Cause

What is such a reason like? It must be a reason which is real and external: a cause. It is the real reason for all the reality contained in the being it explains: the fundamental and total cause. It is the adequate reason for the whole order of particular beings: the absolute cause. It is the fully independent and free cause, since particular beings depend on it absolutely and totally, while it is absolutely independent of everything.

We cannot pattern our thinking about this absolute cause on particular beings, since they are distinct from other finite realities by their limits, their essence, their definition, while this cause is the total cause of all particular beings. Hence it is non-particular, non-finite Being, simply Being without restriction, pure subsistent Being. Since it is the reason for everything that is in particular beings, it must have all that they have, but virtually, unrestrictedly, eminently. It can receive from these creatures only what it gives them; a creature's perfection cannot be added as a new element to the divine perfection, for it is only a finite participation of the latter. The divine perfection of itself contains in an adequate and eminent way the creature's perfection.

The creative cause is always an immediate cause, for it is the total real cause of all reality. It belongs to no series, even as a first member, for an absolute cause cannot be the subject of relations which would put it among the members of an order. Moreover, when causes act in a series each has a share in the result. By reason of their limits particular causes are irreducible to each other, and therefore so are their acts, their products. Each acts in its own way, produces its own effect, and only when these acts are joined in a series does the complete effect come about. Thus each particular cause has its part, its share, in producing the effect. The absolute cause, on the contrary, is in no wise partial; it is the total cause of all reality.

The creative cause is the active source of the whole order of particular causes, of their existence and their nature, of their acts and their effects. It "touches" every reality in the most intimate and complete way, since it makes it to be. Were it to end this creative presence it would make the creature stop being.

Levels of Causality

Let us note our point of departure and point of arrival in these reflections on metaphysical causality.

Every reality reveals being's value and hence the absoluteness of that value; it shows that being can have no opposite (for that would be pure nothingness) and no correlative. All realities proclaim that undeniable truth by the fact that they are and by all that is in them. On this point there is no difference among realities; they are all the same. But how to reconcile this with the plain fact of experience that there is plurality of beings, each different from the other? How can they differ if their ontological message is exactly the same? How are differences possible on the level of the absolute? How is participation (which implies relativity) conceivable on the level of the absolute value of being?

The answer lies in the doctrine of absolute, fully independent, creative causality. If all things are totally dependent on the same creative act, it is not surprising that all of them, by the fact that they are, bear witness to the absolute stability of that single all-powerful act which puts and keeps them in being.

In this matter of causality, therefore, we have to distinguish two radically different levels. The first could be called "horizontal"; it is the level of finite causes, which in acting on one another form a series. (And we might raise the question whether this series contains a limited or infinite number of members.) The second level could be called "vertical"; it joins the order of finite and correlative causes to the infinite and absolute Cause.

These two levels are not juxtaposed as two territories bordering on each other. You cannot get to the infinite cause by extending the series of finite causes, for the Infinite transcends the finite. Nor is it necessary to take the very first member of the series as your steppingstone for leaping to the Infinite; any member at all will serve equally well, for they all depend on the creative cause in the same total way. Each single member and not just the first one needs the creative cause, not only to begin to be but simply "to be"—to keep on being as much as to start being. The need, the contingency, which characterizes all finite reality is always exactly the same: it is total, for it affects what this reality has as being—all that it has.

Thus the whole order of finite beings, of finite causes, taken together and in their entire content, "participates" in the absolute perfection of subsistent being. Their entire content is immediately and continually in contact with the creative act which "gives" it being.

First Cause

There is no objection to calling the creative cause "first," so long as we are clear that it is not the first in a series. And if by contrast we speak of "second" cause, it is with the understanding that this term applies in the same way to all finite causes, for they are all second causes. First and second cause are opposed as creative and created cause; the former transcends the latter. Consequently there cannot be a third or fourth cause, since beyond Creator and creature there is nothing.

These reflections make it plain that the creative act which is proper to the absolute cause is unique, for it transcends the whole order of finite causes. And since we cannot reach God by reason unless we start with creatures, with that radical dependence proper to finite reality, then this path which leads up to God must also be unique. It cannot be reduced to any path which leads from one creature to another, for it differs from them as the creative act differs from the created causality, as the Absolute and Infinite differ from the finite and relative.

James M. Somerville, S.J.   **9. ACTION AND THE SILENCE OF BEING**

What is the *act* by which being is? The answer to this question is cast in a new light in this essay by Father Somerville, who writes from the point of view of Maurice Blondel.

The term "action" in the philosophy of Blondel, Somerville indicates, implies a "transcendental reality which is co-extensive with the whole of life." It is "the manifestation or epiphany of the silence of being," which "is not static. . . . At its zenith it is Pure Act." Action is, consequently, to be understood in a manner reminiscent of the analogy of proper proportionality, for at its limit is "the primary analogate which is the action of an infinite being whose *to be* is *to act*, whose *esse* is *agere*."

Action opens up the "road to being." The road to being is through "an action which embraces wholeheartedly the entire hierarchy of actions without losing the essence of any of them. . . . Each level of action and value is like a string on a harp, and each string gives off its own peculiar sound." There is no one note, however, that utters the name of the source. Although we do not grasp being in its source, we do contact being in its concrete manifestations—that is, in action, because action is the epiphany of being.

As action is interiorized and taken upon oneself consciously, it becomes more universal and "seems to approximate the mysterious universality of being." Yet man is capable of displaying a new dimension to action. He lives "longitudinally," within the dimension of world action and self-conscious action, or exterior and interior action—that is, action that is non-self, and action that he himself as a human *being* inhabits. He also lives "latitudinally," where the action of personal will joins the action

This essay is reprinted with the kind permission of the author and the editors of *Spiritual Life*, in whose Spring, 1961, issue it originally appeared under the title "Maurice Blondel and the Philosophy of Action."

of "primordial," implicit will, which is God's will. Thus, "one's grasp of being is the more authentic to the extent that there is an increasing adequation between what the explicit will freely embraces and what the implicit will necessarily seeks."

Through reflection we become aware of the interior life and the possibilities of its explicit will, and thus of action's hidden roots in being. The deeper this message is carried within personal life, the more telling does the exterior action become, for "the being that we find outside is the echo of an abiding presence within"; while "the being within calls to the being without, and it is through the action of the subject that they are brought together." Through action, one, in one's own being, consciously and freely participates in the Being of Pure Act, and this is to realize that *to-be* means *to-be-from-God* and *toward-God.*

I T IS ALWAYS RISKY to attempt to sum up the thought of any writer in a word or a phrase since it tends to stress one facet at the expense of others which may be equally important. Maurice Blondel, the eminent French Catholic philosopher who died in 1949, was never entirely reconciled to the fact that his philosophy was called "The Philosophy of Action." The first time that the unwary reader comes upon this phrase he is apt to have visions of an action-packed western or of Teddy Roosevelt leading his Rough Riders into the thick of battle.

Those who have a little more acquaintance with philosophy may think of John Dewey or of William James, both of whom emphasize the importance of action and doing in contradistinction to abstract speculation. William James, who read quite a bit of Blondel, thought for a time that their philosophies were moving along the same lines. It is of some importance to note then that James finally concluded that such was not the case. But the fact that the great American Pragmatist was at first deceived into believing that Blondel was one of his tribe should be a warning to others. Maurice Blondel has been called a Pragmatist by those who were not nearly so perceptive as James and the confusion between Pragmatism and the Philosophy of Action still persists in some quarters. A more unfortunate and misleading identification can scarcely be imagined.

What then is action? Blondel never opposed thought to action since he always maintained that thought is the highest form of action. He considered that his own vocation as a philosopher was to act by thought; for thought is the soul of action. When faced with the dilemma of choosing between the two, between theory and practice, Blondel refused the option. Authentic human action is suffused with rationality, and thought itself is the most intense and interior form of action.

Blondel's reluctance to have the label "action" attached to his philosophy is easily explained. When he published *L'Action* in 1893, he considered that this book constituted only one chapter of his total philosophy. He said that it was rather like a treatise on the Trinity which deals explicitly with the Holy Spirit and does not provide any extended treatment of the other two Persons. Later on, in his Trilogy of Thought, Being and Action, the matter originally treated in his earlier book on action occupied only one of the five volumes.

The Meaning of Action

In spite of these protests, it must be allowed that "action" is the proper word to characterize Blondel's philosophy. No philosopher can completely escape the inevitable. Plato deals with the Good, Plotinus with Unity, St. Thomas with Existence. Since Blondel's philosophy is basically an ethical one and since he is a modern, we should not be surprised to find that he stresses the subjective counterpart of the Good, namely, human action.

Action expresses the inner dynamism of the spirit which is restless until it finds repose in the Absolute. Blondel believed that metaphysics is inseparable from the quest for the Good. However, it is not the abstract idea of the Good that interests him, but the concrete reality itself. Philosophy must treat of life and its moral exigencies, not simply of logical abstractions. Years before the first of the Existentialists began talking about "engagement" and man's need for confrontation and personal commitment to values, Blondel had already written:

I am involved; I must act. My actions carry with them the weight of an eternal responsibility and even at the price of blood I cannot purchase nothingness. Our acts follow us and they cannot be undone. The past is forever, and what I have done is a burden which I must bear to the end. What I shall know and the way I shall know it depends largely on what I am and have done.

Like Plotinus and Augustine, Blondel maintains that a moral purification is necessary if we are to see things as they are. Those who would come to the truth must do the good. *Fac et videbis.* Blondel has little patience with those who spend their time speculating about reality yet never have the courage to live the truths which they extol in the abstract. To be a philosopher, one must set one's own house in order so that the light may not meet the darkness of deep prejudices and inveterate habits of selfishness. One is reminded here of St. Augustine's advice to the pagan whom he invites to live as a Christian and see whether or not the truths of the Christian faith do not acquire a new lucidity and cogency.

If this seems like a pragmatic test for a doctrinal position, it must be remembered that virtue does not make doctrines true; it can only reveal their meaningfulness by removing impediments to clear vision. A condition is not a cause. The sincerity of a philosopher is not measured by the intensity with which he holds a speculative position, but by his willingness to commit himself to a way of life. Cornelia De Vogel in her recent article in *International Philosophical Quarterly* (Feb., 1961) shows that even for the Greeks the ultimate test for the true philosopher was not his dialectical ability but his living of the truths which he proclaimed in theory.

Thus, there is nothing particularly new about Blondel's position. What is new is his ability to convert the common belief that philosophers should practice what they preach into a *science* of action. Science is of the necessary, and if there is a connection between action and thought, between life and light, it is for the philosopher to show that it is a necessary one and that there are certain immanent laws, ultimately moral and metaphysical laws, which govern the degree of one's insight.

There are many ways of showing this necessary connection between action and thought. An artist cannot impose his ideas on matter without a long training in the techniques of sculpture and painting. He must first infuse a law into his own members learning through discipline how to hold the chisel or the brush. He must also learn the nature of the material substance that he is fashioning. It is by doing that one learns. To incarnate an idea in matter, to give a soul to stone, a certain asceticism is necessary. Someone has wickedly observed that artists who lack discipline become art critics. The fingers of the trained artist are instinct with reason. They seem almost to think. And as the project progresses, the half-formed matter speaks to the artist, revealing potentialities that may not have been envisioned in the original exemplary idea of the work to be done.

So it is with philosophy. It requires discipline, and not merely the discipline of logic and dialectics. What the philosopher knows he must do. And in doing he learns more about himself and his hidden potentialities. Thus, knowledge is not a superfluous luxury. It must be put to work by receiving a body in action. Nor is this enough: man is a social being who cannot find himself or know himself adequately until he finds and knows others. Since no man is an island, human action is not complete until it becomes co-action and co-operation with others. So action embraces the family, the nation, and the race.

The Levels of Action

Now if we turn within and trace human action back to its source, we find that interior action has various levels, beginning with the simplest sensation and perception, up through all of the terms that express action (the Latin *io*-nouns), and ending with volition and contemplation. These are all action in Blondel's sense; for action is a transcendental reality which is coextensive with the whole of life. It is, in fact, the manifestation or epiphany of the silence of being. Being in its silence is not static; it is not an eternal axiom of an unmoved mover, not a thing, nor a concept. At its zenith it is Pure Act.

One does not touch the intensity of Pure Act until one has spelled out, *per gradus debitos,* the lower manifestations of being. Each lower form of interior action fails to exhaust the dynamism of life. Those who would live on the level of the senses soon discover that they disappoint. Sensation is a form of inner action, of course, but it does not use up the quasi-infinite appetite for personal fulfillment that drives every man to seek something beyond it. Science seems to be the ultimate fulfillment for some; others make an idol of esthetic action or social action. But they are all fetishes the moment one tries to infinitize them by pretending that they satisfy man's hunger for the absolute. Something always remains over and above the energies devoted to these limited forms of action: *Aliquid superest.* Man seeks to coincide with a kind of infinite action which concentrates the whole of reality at a point; it would be the condensation of all of the beauty, truth, goodness, and unity in the world. While we are never able to reach back within ourselves and grasp this intense center of unifying action, its presence there is the motor and *arché* of every other form of action. It is immanent to us, yet it transcends everything else.

There is an analogy of action here which reminds us of the Thomistic analogy of proper proportionality. At the limit is the primary analogate which is the action of an infinite being whose *to be* is *to act,* whose *esse* is *agere.* The human spirit necessarily seeks to coincide with such an action, and unable to reach it or reproduce it within itself, it can only stand and wait. If man is to share the divine action in the fullest sense of the word, he must dispose himself for the gift. And this, too, is an action. Call it humility, devotion, "disponibility": it is only by recognizing the limits of our own action that we can hope to share in the plenary action of infinite being. And by a strange paradox, it is this attitude of passivity and openness to the influence of a higher action that enables man to be himself. For the human spirit cannot even be human without the divine.

The Road to Being

What then is the role of the inferior forms of action? Is man to flee from every lower manifestation of being by turning his back on the many-splendored aspects of life? Blondel's Platonism is not escapist; he does not look on the finite as evil. On the contrary, the spirit must constantly shuttle back and forth between the poles of its aspiration towards the fullness of being and its experience of being's more available manifestations. Action feeds on the concrete reflections of the pure white light that is differentiated and refracted through the prism of time and matter. These levels of life form a spectrum stretching from the most elementary sensation to the most sublime contemplation. The pity is that we so easily stall on one of the levels. Or if we are resolved to avoid this pitfall, we may go to the other extreme and attempt to leap completely off the spectrum into the void. The experience of transcendence is had by going *into* the spectrum, by grasping the whole panoply of its colors, and by seeing that each color is at the term of a ray that leads to and from the central focal point which is the mysterious source of light, the "hearth" of being.

From our point of view it might seem that being is the intense distillation of the various levels of life, just as white light is made up of many colors. But primordial being and action are not the totalization of their finite manifestations. The "infinite" is incommensurable with the finite. It encompasses all of the perfections of its limited expressions—and it is something more. Here the whole is greater than the sum of its parts: *Aliquid superest.*

The "road to being" then, to use Heidegger's expression, is not a blind leap off the spectrum, nor is being a totalization of all of the perfections of life. We approach it by an action which embraces wholeheartedly the entire hierarchy of actions without losing the essence of any of them. This synthetic or unifying action cannot objectivize being by turning it into a thing, but it does point the way towards the incommensurable source of all action. Each level of action and value is like a string on a harp, and each string gives off its own peculiar sound. No single note, however, can utter the name of the source. And if a giant wind were to set every string vibrating in unison, that is, if a man were to experience in succession or simultaneously every form of inner and outer action, he would still not hear the silence of being. "The wind blows where it will, and thou hearest its sound but dost not know where it comes from or where it goes." Yet the sound of creation elicits a sympathetic resonance within us; it touches an inner chord which reverberates like a high-frequency harmonic of what we experience in a low key on the phenomenal level. What is heard within is a very rare and very pure tremolo that stands between the full diapason of concrete experience and the silence of being.

The philosopher is the citizen of two worlds; or rather, an inner and an outer world live and act in him. Concrete experience, divorced from its hidden inner source, easily absorbs all of our energies; it encloses us within the specious present which we try to infinitize and eternalize. On the other hand, if we despise the world of sense and its particular instances, we retreat to a world of solemn abstractions and lose our vital contact with life. The road to being is in function of both poles. The concrete experiences of life must never become so absorbing that we cannot stand off from them and grasp their essence. We cannot possess beauty without putting a certain distance between it and ourselves. "Touch not beauty," says the poet. Let the rose *be* and do not try to *have* it, for it will wither the moment you touch it. There is a sadness or pathos in all contingent things, like Virgil's *lacrimae rerum,* and that is why he also says that memory, which is interiorization, tends to purify sensible experiences by creating perspective and by giving them a more delicate kind of existence in the inner spirit: *Haec olim meminisse juvabit.* Literal outer action must be interiorized; the letter must yield to the spirit, so that the mind is dilated; and once we have tasted this detachment which expands the soul, we begin to live on a new level of interior action. We do not need many experiences nor repeated instances to grasp the essence of things or the spirit that is enclosed in the letter. One instance can be enough. The more interior action becomes the more universal it becomes and the more it seems to approximate the mysterious universality of being.

Inner and Outer Action

There is an outer action which expands from man, as a center of source, into the world. It is expressed in art, institutions, and society. It draws its nourishment from the world and transforms what it receives before giving it back to the world. And there is a complementary inner action, ever deepening, which begins at the periphery of man's organism in sense life, and by a kind of ingathering or purification of one's spiritual forces, converges towards the total interiority of pure action without ever reaching it. But somewhere, deep within the spirit, action and being are one. As already noted, when the sound of creation is distilled in an intense, platinum thread of a melody, it almost seems to merge with the silence of being. But this is only the view that begins at the periphery and moves inward and upward. We must now shift our perspective and begin with that which is already within man, prior to all experience.

No one has ever seen the light. It shines in the darkness and does not become visible until it strikes an object. We see all things *in* the light; yet in another sense we do see the light in the luminosity reflected in the object. *In lumine videmus lucem.* Even if we do not grasp being in its source, we do contact it in its concrete manifestations, that is, in action and in the products of action. Here we might paraphrase the words applied to Eternal Wisdom: Action is an aura of being and a pure effusion of its glory; it is the refulgence of eternal light, the spotless mirror of its majesty.

There is a light which illumines every man coming into the world and it filters down from the inner recesses of our being towards the periphery. The deeper we go in, towards the hidden source of action, the more profound is our penetration of the outer world. The shadow of a man lengthens when the sun sets directly behind him, and the shadow moves out towards the infinite horizon. Similarly, our action, as our experience of its length and breadth and height and depth increases, reinforces our belief in the light of being which is directly back of our innermost self, even though it cannot be seen directly. All things are seen in the light; all action is an epiphany of being.

Our Free and Necessary Action

The world, then, is not without its lessons and one cannot dispense with the experience it provides, nor with the inner light. But action is divided not only longitudinally, as inner and outer action, it is also divided latitudinally. There are two parallel wills in man. The first is a deeper action or primordial will which seeks the infinite and cannot rest until it finds it. This action is necessary and it expresses the very essence of a finite, rational being. But there is also a conscious, explicit action or will; it is free and seeks to find an object equal to the *élan* of the deeper will. These two wills operate, as it were, side by side, and in order to bring the free and the necessary wills into equation, man travels through the whole world like a pilgrim in search of his identity. Symbolically, to find oneself it is necessary to embrace freely the world and the whole of reality. Outer reality becomes the bridge over which one must cross if one is to bring the conscious will into equation with the primordial will. Objectivity, or being in the traditional sense, lies at the point where these two wills arch towards one another in their parallel expansion. Reality is the keystone or stop-gap which is cradled in the arms of the subject's twofold action. One's grasp of being is the more authentic to the extent that there is an increasing adequation between what the explicit will freely embraces and what the implicit will necessarily seeks.

But if being is only that which fills the gap or cleft between two subjective loves, is not the world merely my representation? Now Blondel is no more an idealist than he is a pragmatist. Without the world there would be no representation of it, and without exteriority there would be no interiority. Being is both within and without. If it seems to lie at the juncture, between two subjective movements, this inner representation is the intentional translation and reflection in us of an outer reality. It is only because there is a world that we can interiorize it.

The genesis of action is analogous to the genesis of any living thing. A tree grows up only by laying its roots more firmly in the earth. We do not see the roots, and in the expansion of our action into the world we are only conscious of what appears in the movement outward. It is by reflection that we become aware of the interior life and of action's hidden roots in being. There is no expansion outward without an interior intensification and deepening. Therefore, if being lies at the point where man's free action is integrated into his necessary action, this centrifugal movement or exodus has its counterpart in an inverse or centripetal action of the subject which plunges from the periphery of the organism inwards towards the light of being. The being that we find outside is the echo of an abiding presence within. We would not find it or even seek for it were it not already vitally operative in us prior to our discovery of it in the world. "You would not seek me if you had not already found me."

The truth of Platonism lies in its acute realization of the fact that each particular experience of objectivity on the overt level is an embodiment and explication of the being that is already a secret presence within. Outer experience fills up those things that are lacking in the spirit's necessary orientation towards the absolute. But experience is not enough; when we have gone through the whole world, the being that we are seeking will be found waiting for us at the place where the journey began. The being within calls to the being without, and it is through the action of the subject that they are brought together. We analyse the world that we find, cutting it up into manageable morsels that can be assimilated. We synthesize and interiorize these fragments under the dominion of the regulative presence of being within. So it is not enough to find the world; we must reconstitute it on a higher level through the action of the subject under the inner rule of the light of being.

Creative Action

There is a unity that man puts into the world by his art and by his social action. But there is also a unity in the cosmos which exists quite independent of man's action. Wherever there is unity there is being, and wherever there is being there is a subject for which it is an object. Berkeley attributed the being of the world to the divine perception. But his *esse est percipi* left no place for action. If the world, as object, lies between the two phases of man's free and necessary action, may it not be said that, independent of man's perception of it, the real universe which we find and do not create stands at the apex of the double action of an infinite subject? Between the originative action of the Creator and the inborn instinct of all creatures to return to their source—at the turning point of God's action—lies the being of the world. It is the point where His efferent, efficient action ends and becomes an afferent movement of finality and return. To be, is to be from God and towards God. The world goes out from Him and it must boomerang back to His expectant hand. The impetus of its necessary return is proportional to the dynamism of His free production of it. Here there is adequation between the necessary and the free, that is, between the two faces of action.

Each man's action is a kind of recapitulation of the history of the universe. It is true that man does not create being or the world, but he must recreate it within himself by interiorizing it and by lifting it up to the level of the spirit. Action then introduces new meaning into the world as it fashions matter and molds it according to an ideal pattern. The temptation of naturalism and idealism is to suppose, each in its own way, that by inserting an infinitesimally small degree of meaning into the world man is the creator of all values and meaning. But the fact remains that beyond all human creativity lies a cosmic rationality that man does not put there but only finds. The difference between human action and the primordial action which constitutes the world is that the latter generates, not an ideal representation of the world, but its very being.

From this point of view, human action is the reverse of divine action. Man draws nourishment from the affluent waters of the cosmos that flow into him on the levels of sensation, perception, and science, and these same waters are returned to the world transformed by the unifying action of the spirit. Man breathes in the world and exhales it. He is at the turning point of the movement of assimilation and production. The world, on the contrary, is at the turning point of God's action, and among the things that have their being as the term of the divine action is man himself. So if man is the *vinculum* or bond of creation, in that the meaning of the world flows into him and out from him, he may be said to recapitulate the world in himself. Unfortunately, he is subject to the illusion that the being and unity which he discovers is his own creation. But if there were a man who was at once the creator of the world as well as its discoverer, he would indeed be the Substantial *Vinculum* in whom all things hold together: *in quo omnia constant.* He would truly recapitulate all things in himself. All creation would be from him and in him and unto him. He would learn by experience and discovery what he knew from the beginning, *in principio,* in the hearth of being. He would be patient of his own action: the high point of creation and the low point of the divine immanence and personal presence in the world. In him the twofold action of God descending would meet the twofold action of creation ascending. The apex of the action of a finite nature would be identical with the nadir of infinite action.

The Supernatural

For the philosopher such a consummation can only be suggested, not as a fact but as a possibility. The science of action deals with the necessary. It cannot deduce the fact of the Incarnation and of man's supernatural vocation from any of the exigencies of nature. To do so would be to deny that the supernatural is a gift. But if philosophy cannot establish, with regard to the supernatural, that "it is," it can at least show where the point of insertion of grace into nature would lie. The dynamism of human action in the concrete seems to go beyond man's power of realization. Can all the *élan* of human action be from nature? Reason can only show that this overplus of action may be the manifestation that there is something more in man than man himself. In any case, philosophy has no right to enclose man within the squirrel-cage of nature. It must leave open the question of an hypothetical higher vocation. It is enough if philosophy shows that reason necessarily asks questions which it cannot hope to answer on its own grounds. The answer, if it exists, will have to be provided by a higher science whose principles of verification transcend those of philosophy. And this too is a necessary and scientific conclusion; for if the science of action cannot explain all of the data which it uncovers, it is the sanity of reason to leave the question open.

But there is one more step which reason can take. Not being able itself to provide an answer as to whether or not man has been offered a gift which lies within the province of God's free choice, it can provide an outline of the conditions that would normally have to be realized on the part of man for him to receive the gift. If it is true that those who do the truth come to the light, then human action must surrender its idols. It must cease trying to infinitize any one of the levels of action. Detachment leads the way to moral purification and rectitude of will, and these are the conditions which must be introduced if one is to prepare the way of the Lord. So let not those who have never made the test complain if they have not found a speculative answer to a question which, after all, must be asked with one's whole being and action. If there is an answer, it will be discovered in and through an attitude that involves active expectancy rather than a determination not to receive. This expectancy is itself an action. And who can say that it comes entirely from man; for even the desire for a good desire may still be a grace.

The Problem of Christian Philosophy

Blondel's philosophy need not end with the hypothesis of the supernatural. It completes his thought, but even without it he has provided a rich framework within which one can work on the strictly philosophical level. It would be wrong, then, to condemn him, as some have done, for rigging up a kind of pre-established harmony between faith and reason. He is, of course, a "Christian" philosopher with a strong sense of historical realities. He would certainly not pretend that a separate philosophy is possible or desirable, nor does he think that one can develop a neutral physics or mathematics. Christianity is an historical fact which even unbelievers acknowledge, and many notions such as process, person, and creation have entered into the common fund of ideas which now constitute public knowledge.

Why then should Christians deny their own patrimony and enter the lists with one hand tied behind their backs so that they reason as though nothing had happened since Aristotle wrote the *Posterior Analytics?* Perhaps one of the reasons why philosophy has become so arid in nominally Christian circles is that too many are trying to keep the left hand from knowing what the right hand is doing. Phenomenology, and Blondel's phenomenology in particular, deals with every kind of human experience and action. It is freed from the need to abstract or extract the elements of a scientific philosophy from life as it is lived in the concrete. Action concerns everything in man that is in any way a datum of human existence: knowledge, love, volition, desire, and even faith.

The phenomenon of man living in the twentieth century is a rich area for investigation and analysis, and it is in his action that man reveals himself, and more than himself. That is why Blondel began his philosophical enterprise with a study of action and why, now more than ever, he will best be remembered as the philosopher of action.

Pierre Rousselot, S.J.

10. BEING AND INTELLIGIBILITY

Thought, says Father Rousselot, is for St. Thomas the "most intense and powerful form of action." The way into being is through thought, which is the faculty of being, "the faculty which most truly grasps, and attains, and holds being." For in a certain manner of speaking, thought becomes reality.

Contact with being and perfection of life, says Rousselot, is related for St. Thomas to the measure of immanence accorded a being's activity. The higher a being is in the scale of being, the greater its immanent activity, and hence its contact with being. "Radically complete immanence . . . is to be found in Him Whose being is identical with intelligence." Now the more intense the life of an intellectual being, the less limited it is to its own narrow circle of being, and the wider is its range and contact with being. With Father Somerville in the previous essay, Rousselot asserts that knowledge of the non-self increases in proportion to the depth of a being's immanence.

St. Thomas, Rousselot points out, regarded "activity" not so much as movement, or as a becoming from potency to act; he believed that, as a perfection already possessed "in that arising out of movement, which implies change and potentiality, it fixed its subject in the extra-temporal consistency of *act*." From this fact St. Thomas concluded that possession of "non-self being" was to be achieved not by means of material contact but in a spiritual contact brought about through thought and ideas. Without the condition of immanence, this intellectual possession of "otherness" would be impossible.

Material action cannot penetrate reality; only the spiritual action of a person can do this. And this penetration succeeds—in whatever way it does succeed—only through knowledge. "By definition, knowledge alone permits the ego while remaining itself to become the non-ego." The intensification

From *The Intellectualism of St. Thomas* by Pierre Rousselot, S.J., published by Sheed & Ward, Inc., New York, 1935.

of being therefore implies knowledge, which in turn implies immanence and interiorization as the condition of penetration into the non-self. For "it is necessary to know oneself in order to know truth as such." The higher a reality in the scale of being, the greater will be its possession, through thought, of other reality. Intellect in a special sense is *the* "road to being" (to use Heidegger's phrase once again).

An examination of the intellectual process, Rousselot contends, affirms the Existence of Absolute Mind. For it is the heart of St. Thomas's doctrine, he says, that God's knowledge is the cause of things.

The proper work of intelligence, he concludes, consists in directly grasping what is proper to things. The intellectual operation effects a real grasp of reality—a spiritual grasp—which is characterized by a living intimacy with reality and an illuminative clarity. Being, therefore, is that which is *to be known;* for nothing has a title to reality except in function of intelligibility. "Mind comes first and all being is for mind." Man grasps reality, understands it according to his place in the order of being, and pursues it only because he is endowed with intellect. And he both is, and is endowed with intellect, because of Absolute Mind.

CONTRARY TO THE popular idea of to-day, which regards the intellectual process as an "epiphenomenon" on the surface of true "life," St. Thomas looks upon it as the life-process *par excellence,* and sees in it the deepest and most intense activity of intellectual beings. In opposition to those who see in intellect something necessarily egocentric, he makes of it the faculty which emancipates men from mere subjectivity; it may aptly be called "the faculty of otherness" if we may employ the term. In a wider sense it is for him, as has been well said, the "faculty of being," the faculty which most truly grasps, and attains, and holds being. It unites in the highest degree subjective intensity and objective extension, because if it grasps reality it does so by *becoming* reality in a certain manner: and in that precisely consists its nature.

Of these two characteristics, immanence and exteriorisation, it is immanence which, on last analysis, imparts to the intellectual acts its perfection. The real reason of its superiority over will is that "speaking simply and absolutely it is better to be in possession of the nobility of another being than to have a relation to a noble being which remains beyond it." If, then, intelligence is perfect and supreme life, it is because it can reflect upon itself and because at one and the same time it can know reality and know itself. *Est igitur supremus et perfectus gradus vitae qui est secundum intellectum, nam intellectus in seipsum reflectitur et seipsum intelligere potest.* These words, taken from the last book of the *Summa Contra Gentes,* form the conclusion of a long exposition of the idea of "emanation" as it is realised in the different orders of Nature.

We find different modes of emanation [it is said] and further, we observe that from the higher natures things proceed in a more intimate way. Now, of all things the inanimate obtain the lowest place, and from them no emanation is possible except by the action of one on another: thus, fire is engendered from fire when an extraneous body is transformed by fire, and receives the quality and form of fire. The next place to inanimate bodies belongs to plants, whence emanation proceeds from within, in as much as the plants' intrinsic humour is converted into seed, which being committed to the soil grows into a plant. Accordingly, here we find the first traces of life: since living things are those which move themselves to act, whereas those which can only move extraneous things are wholly lifeless. It is a sign of life in plants that something within them is the cause of a form. Yet the plants' life is imperfect because, although in it emanation proceeds from within, that which emanates comes forth little by little, and in the end becomes altogether extraneous: thus the humour of a tree gradually comes forth from the tree and eventually becomes a blossom, and then takes the form of fruit distinct from the branch, though united thereto; and when the fruit is perfect it is altogether severed from the tree, and falling to the ground, produces by its seminal force another plant. Indeed, if we consider the matter carefully we shall see that the first principle of this emanation is something extraneous: since the intrinsic humour of the tree is drawn through the roots from the soil whence the plant derives its nourishment. There is yet above that of the plants a higher form of life, which is that of the sensitive soul, the proper emanation whereof, though beginning from without, terminates within. Also the further the emanation proceeds, the more does it penetrate within: for the sensible object impresses a form on the external sense, whence it proceeds to the imagination and further still, to the storehouse of the memory. Yet, in every process of this kind or emanation, the beginning and end are in different subjects; for no sensitive power reflects on itself. Wherefore this degree of life transcends that of plants in so much as it is more intimate; and yet it is not a perfect life, since the emanation is always from one thing to another. Wherefore the highest degree of life is that which is according to intellect: for the intellect reflects on itself and can understand itself.

A hundred other passages might be cited to the effect that perfection of life and reality must be gauged by the measure of immanence to be accorded to a being's activity; the text I have chosen has this in particular, that it excludes from immanent activity not only its consummation in an external object but also the reception of elements from without. This aspect, apparently so incompatible with the extension of mind to the knowledge of the non-self which we have regarded as the second chief attribute of intellectual activity, sends us back to the primal fact which dominates the entire intellectualism of St. Thomas, that is, to the living and personal existence of Absolute Mind. In the chapter cited, once the author has classified the natural powers of operation he goes on to arrange the different degrees of intellectual activity; in so doing he always assigns the lowest place to those forms of it that are most dependent on what comes from without. Radically complete immanence, he writes down as his conclusion, is to be found in Him Whose being is identical with intelligence and idea, that Mind, namely, which is the Measure of the truth of things.

The human intellect can know itself, but because it knows nothing without a sensible image the principle of its knowledge comes to it from without. The intellectual life of the angels is more perfect because their intelligence knows itself without having to make use of anything outside it. Yet, their life does not reach the highest point of perfection since their idea, which is within, is not identical with their essence, and their being and knowledge are distinct. The last perfection of life then belongs to God for Whom to know and to be are equivalent, and in Whom the idea, understanding by idea what the intellect conceives in itself of the object known, is identically the divine essence itself.

Thus perfect consciousness, which is the creative source of all truth, is at the same time exhaustive knowledge and perfect unity, and God is no less one for the fact of knowing; the thinker and his thought *do not add,* said St. Thomas. In the angelic world, that region which lies between God and man, degrees of reality and life are determined by comparative depth of immanence; that is the essential thing which remains while the unity of intelligible object is recognized as accidental and transitory. "In God the whole plenitude of intellectual knowledge is contained in one thing, that is to say, in the divine essence, by which God knows all things. This plenitude of knowledge is found in created intellects in a lower degree, and less simply."

No created mind could pretend to be the universal exemplar of all reality, since such a perfect similitude is necessarily infinite; the created intellect must therefore depend on a multiplicity of ideas for its knowledge. But "the higher a separate substance is, the more is its nature similar to the divine; and consequently it is less limited, as approaching nearer to the perfection and goodness of universal being . . . consequently, the intelligible species that are in the higher substances are less numerous and more universal," not indeed in virtue of generalisation, as we shall see, but by a process of condensation. By a multitude of thoughts the energy of a being is scattered and the less dependent it is on many thoughts the more intense does its life become.

Now the more intense is the life of an intellectual being, the less limited is it to the narrow circle of itself. Taking up the series of finite beings just mentioned, we realise that the second of the recognised perfections, that which has to do with the knowledge of the non-self, is also dependent upon the measure of immanent activity which a being posseses rather than being opposed to it; it increases and diminishes in direct proportion to depth of immanence.

A little reflection suffices to get beyond the popular opposition that is made between *thought* and *action;* but it is another thing to see that thought is the most intense and powerful form of action. The latter way of looking at things was, however, natural to St. Thomas. He regarded activity not so much as movement or as passage from potency to act, but as perfection already possessed in that arising out of movement, which implies change and potentiality; it fixed its subject in the extra-temporal consistency of *act*. Given that, he quickly concluded that the possession of the non-self was brought about more fully by means of ideas than by any material form of contact, and that immanence was an implied condition of this intellectual possession of "otherness."

Undoubtedly, "to have," "to possess," "to grasp," "to hold," are terms borrowed from the exercise of our corporeal powers. At first sight it would seem that to apply such terms to intellectual activity would be to empty them of their real meaning and to content ourselves with describing the shadow activity of intellectual possession working on a shadow of reality. Yet if action implies the passage of influence from one being to another, then it follows that such action will be all the more perfect according as it reaches the other being more fully, that is, the being's reality and intimacy and unity, and the more imperfect according as it leaves the more of that being untouched by its influence (*Ens et unum convertuntur*). Nothing, however, is more *abstractive* than a material action, and, as a result, nothing is more impotent and restricted. A stone-breaker smashes up his stones, a dog upsets a basket or entangles a reel of thread, the cow crushes the flowers beneath it, but such actions have merely the effect of altering reality; they reach it in one way only, abstractively if we may so speak they do not invade it, penetrate it, and conquer it whole and entire. By his activity man seeks to subordinate reality to himself, to enrich himself with it, and to saturate it with himself, but by material activity he merely succeeds in transforming some of the qualities of the object; he does not touch it in its real depths. There is in the permanency of matter a quiet opposition to the most furious animal, to the greatest machine; and, in addition, the time-duration which conditions their actions introduces an element of instability as an inevitable possibility, if not as a necessary eventuality. Condense it, extenuate it, rarefy it as you will, matter still subsists, overcome and beaten down for a time, the repugnance of the non-self to place itself indefinitely at the disposal of material self is never entirely vanquished. Generation is an almost creative modification, yet it produces merely the same type, and gives birth to a new being external to the first. Material capacity and nutritive assimilation really bring the non-self into subjection to the individual, yet for all that they do not bring about that coincident fusion which is the ideal of action, for the simple reason that the mere juxtaposition of parts and the agglomeration of matter which is impenetrable is opposed to such fusion. By definition, knowledge alone permits the ego while remaining itself to become the non-ego; and we cannot speak of real possession except where there is intimate penetration of two unifying principles and where a thing becomes the other in some sense. It was that precisely St. Thomas had in mind when he wrote: "The noblest way of possessing or having a thing is to possess it in a non-material manner, yet formally, which is the definition of knowledge."

In presence of this immanence of knowledge it is essential to notice that activity grows immeasurably in extent and, particularly, in intensity. The cow may crush one or two daisies simultaneously, but it sees and lives all the daisies of the field together. But this conquest of reality by the knower varies with the degree of immanent activity it enjoys. As there is increase of immanence there is a diminution of abstraction. St. Thomas places the oyster and such animals as are immersed in matter and possessed only of the sense of touch at the lowest stage of sensitive knowledge. With these, the most "dispersed of souls," there is not knowledge save of what is actually present to them; being devoid of phantasy they are without memory. Their psychic content is characterised as "imagination and confused desire"; it keeps before them, as in a kind of perpetual twilight of knowledge, what is good or harmful; wanting in "particular judgments," they are neither "prudent" nor teachable; of them it may well be said: *In nullo participant de contemplatione.* Now that which is particularly characteristic of them and which explains why they are lowest in the scale of knowers is precisely the extreme abstractiveness of their knowledge, or, which comes to the same thing, its extreme subjectivity. Out of all the stimuli that pass from objects to sense-faculties the oyster and the starfish do not grasp or store or transform save those which have to do with the sense of touch. This sense is the foundation of all the others, and can alone subsist without them. It has this peculiarity about it, that it cannot be entirely denuded of its proper object, and that, in its case, the "real transformation" is more intimately connected with the "knowing transformation" than in others, much in the same way, for instance, that the hand which registers cold and heat is itself necessarily warm or cold already. The oyster, then, has knowledge in so far as a vague unity of consciousness may be said to bring about a certain co-ordination of the milieu around it. In its world-system it is *quodammodo alia* if not *quodammodo omnia.* But the extreme abstraction noticeable in this extract of the universe is due to the defective immanence of a shallow consciousness that cannot unite in memory the successive stages of its unity. The higher animals, being endowed with five senses and with more differentiated organisms, furnish a more complete and complex perception of the world. In this respect those animals which possess the sense of sight enjoy a more objective perception than those endowed merely with the sense of touch because the eye is entirely stripped of "the nature of its object" being neither white nor black nor red, devoid, in fact, of colour, and susceptible merely to that of the coloured object. In this case, perception is less abstractive: the addition of the other senses to that of touch, and the mutual co-operation which follows, results in a greater grasp of reality, or at least in a view of it from a greater number of angles. The cow of the field not only has eyes to see the colours of the marguerites; its organs of touch, its snout and tongue tell of their height and resistance, while its sense of smell makes known their perfume. These different perceptions, or memories, are gathered together, according to St. Thomas, in a concrete synthesis by the *sensus communis* and the *sensus estimativus,* which is the organic power of perceiving particulars. In this way the more complicated organisms of the higher animals allow of a certain advance in the perception of "otherness."

As yet, however, we have not sufficiently emerged out of that subjectivism and abstractiveness of which we have been speaking. The faculty of "otherness," that is, of things distinct from the knower, is to be had in its full sense only in such beings as can apprehend "otherness" as "otherness" with as much facility as they perceive things distinct from them to be such and such. To be able consciously to discriminate between self and non-self one must be capable of judging one's own perception and also of self-reflection. *Omnis intelligens est rediens ad essentiam suam reditione completa.* By definition it is necessary to know oneself in order to know truth as such. It follows that the capacity for reflection on one's act is a condition of intellectual knowledge, and further that the only activity which is perfectly acquisitive of things distinct from the knowing subject is confined to the intellectual process which is the type of immanent action.

It is already clear to what principle we must refer for the proof of the contention that in intelligent beings immanence and knowledge of the non-self go hand in hand. For such beings to possess the non-self is to be in possession of the self. "The better a thing is understood the more intimate is its knowledge to the knowing subject and the nearer is it to being one with him." This notion of unity, so constantly on the lips of St. Thomas and which has just been introduced here, throws full light upon that correlation which exists between immanence on the one hand and the enriching extensiveness of intellectual activity on the other.

If the intellectual faculty, as a matter of fact, is essentially given to the harmonising of contraries, if it is its nature to be able to become all things, then its ideal will be to gather together whatever is apprehended into the unity of a common idea. If such an idea does not represent for a particular individual the non-self in its totality, the very exigencies of its nature require that it does not feel tied down once for all to merely one representation of reality, but that it is always at liberty to discover in its intrinsic indetermination something with which to form either new complementary unities or more embracing unities that will combine the present one with those even that are opposed to it. This representative unity (corresponding to the degree of immanence the perfection of which we have seen to be found in the identity of essence and idea) is indeed an essential condition of the idea; the latter being a second self, that is the self as thought, ought to possess unity like the thinking self with which for the moment it is identical. It follows that the strength of an intellect is to be estimated by the extent of the self as thought, of its idea, and it will be all the more powerful according as it can concentrate within the self a greater portion of the non-self without being impaired in its own living unity. Those intellects are lowest in the scale which depend on material objects for their knowledge, since these objects are limited to themselves and cannot therefore give rise to an idea which is representative of many. On the other hand, intellects that are endowed with greater immanence and whose ideas are consubstantial with their essence are free to gather together into a single mental content a vast category of objects. We have already said the degrees of natural perfection to be found in pure intuitive intellects must be fixed according to the decreasing number of their ideas. We find the same thing exemplified, adds

St. Thomas, in the case of men, because he that is endowed with greater intellectual acumen is able, by means of a small number of principles, to reach many conclusions at which the less gifted arrive only by means of many reasonings and examples and by reference to particular topics more immediately suggestive of the conclusions.

What is essential to notice here, however, is extent of knowledge and understanding, instead of being in inverse ratio to one another, really go hand in hand, where intuitive intellects are concerned. The universality of the ideal forms by which the higher angels obtain their knowledge makes rather for a deeper penetration of the unique and ineffable character of things than for indistinctness and vagueness. It would correspond rather to a process of condensation than of generalisation; and the reason of this is to be sought in the nature of intelligence which is the faculty of unity because it is the faculty of being, or, if it is preferred, of being unified in mind, as it is in reality. *Ens et unum convertuntur;* and particular or transcendental unity, carefully distinguished by St. Thomas from that unity which is the principle of number, must not be separated, either in the real or in the "intentional" order, from reality with which it is identical. It is therefore because the unity of every creature, like its reality, is imperfect that it is better known rather in conjunction with others than by means of others, and also that the process of isolation which cuts it off from the rest of things in the universe deprives it of some degree of reality. *Omnia se invicem perambulant.* For St. Thomas, intelligence, as one of his followers has said, is "the natural order in potency"; *per se,* therefore, and under normal circumstances of exercise the more reality it incorporates within itself, and the wider its range of interest, the more true is it to its own nature. To have full and exhaustive knowledge on any detail it would be necessary to have grasped the entire and absolute unity of things. "A thing is known more perfectly," says St. Thomas, "in the Word than itself, even as regards its own particular shape and form."

Once again, then, he has been led by his examination of the intellectual process to affirm Absolute Mind: this Mind alone can reconcile by its absolute unity the twofold perfection we have discovered in the idea. The Cause of all being is the true mirror of reality such as it is in itself; creative Source of things that exist by participation, "spreading about It all being and degrees thereof," Absolute Mind is at one and the same time perfect Immanence and perfect Extensiveness penetrating to the depths of things. He alone is at home everywhere by intelligence Who knows all things by His own Essence, the unique Source at once of reality and of truth. The human soul is intelligent because it has a "passive capacity" for all being; God is intelligent because He is the active Source of all being. "God's knowledge is the cause of 'things.'"

Those who are familiar with the writings of St. Thomas well know that we are here at the very heart of his whole doctrine. And it is not difficult to collect from every page of his writings certain formulae which epitomise his general notion of the process of intellectual knowledge. "The greatest among the perfections of things is that a thing is intellectual because thereby it is, after a fashion, all things, having within itself the perfection of all." "Intellectual apprehension is not limited to particular beings but extends to all." "By the fact that a substance is endowed with intelligence it is capable of possessing within itself all being." We may conclude, then, by saying that, far from characterising intelligence as the faculty of abstraction, we must, on the contrary, designate it the faculty of complete "intussusception."

From the foregoing principles it follows that the typical intellectual operation must be sought neither in the judgment (*enuntiabile*), which is the result of a triple abstraction, nor in the concept, which on the Scholastic conception presupposes a certain working up of reality owing to the soul's presence in a body, but in a real grasp of reality, given, however, in the form of ideas and principles. As far as we can judge from an inductive examination of our own defective intellectual capacities, this spiritual possession of reality possesses two characteristics: a living intimacy with reality such as we experience in the concrete perception by the self of its own acts, and an illuminative clarity which we associate with the perception of axioms. Did we apprehend the essence of the non-self as immediately as we do the act of thought, the cogito, and as clearly as the principle of contradiction, then we would enjoy a share in typically intellectual activity.

To express the matter in another way: Intelligence must not be defined as the faculty of discrimination or of linking up, of ordering or of deduction, of assigning the "causes" or "reasons" of things. Its work does not consist in isolating things from their surroundings, but directly of grasping what is proper to them, of assimiliating to itself that which is most intimate to things and which naturally is supposed to be diaphanous and limpid for mind.

And if *truth* is "reality brought into relation to mind," then perfect truth does not consist in the stable union of two concepts; its deep and ultimate meaning is less an *adequatio rei et intellectus* than an assimilation and union of mind with things. It is true to the infirmity of our minds that truth cannot be attained without recourse to the manipulation of many terms and to the process *componendi et dividendi*. The truth to be ascribed to any particular object of intellectual knowledge is not something unique and static. Just as the union of the thinking subject and the object thought allows of an infinite number of degrees of immanence according to the indefinitely various capacities of the spiritual faculties in question, so we must allow for a proportionate increase of truth according to these different degrees of "limpidity," "clarity" and penetration. So little is true knowledge indivisible that it varies necessarily with the nature of the thinking subject. The whole of a simple object might be known without for all that being known wholly or exhaustively, and fully to grasp the intelligibility of the created world, while at the same time positing it, one would need to be God, that is, subsisting Truth. For if a being is progressive, then, according to St. Thomas, there cannot be an idea corresponding to it which would be arresting and completely definitive; if a being is finite, there can be nothing exhaustive about its corresponding concept. The indivisible equality of true ideas among themselves and in their relations with things is as foreign to him as the idea of the primacy of discursive reasoning.

To what extent the view-point adopted by St. Thomas in his intellectualism goes beyond the theory of universal explanation is evident by this time. To say that all things are susceptible of explanation is to be satisfied with a certain equation of thought and reality. That is tantamount to maintaining the duality of the two terms intellect and the object of intellect, and it does not solve the further question whether reality which is intelligible for mind is radically final-ised in regard to mind. It is equivalent to arresting the movement of thought at the judgment and concept stage and to allowing or postulating something more ultimate than knowledge in the form of action or such like. To affirm, on the other hand, that the highest form of activity consists in the intellectual acquisi-tion of reality, which in its turn must be distinguished from judgments of fact regarding such and such qualities, is to suppose, if finality be admitted, that everything which possesses reality is also *eo ipso intelligible,* and further that nothing has a title to reality except in function of intelligibility and as object of, or preparation for, intellectual knowledge according to the varying capacities of intelligent beings. Mind comes first, and all being is for mind.

If there is not actual knowledge corresponding to this universal intelligi-bility, and if the given contains what is relatively opaque for thought side by side with what is perfectly transparent, yet it is clearly insinuated that the ma-terial world occupies a position of dependence in regard to mind: in relation to the world of intelligences it is looked upon as a kind of appendix. The true finality of Nature is mind and intelligibility; the realities "willed for their own sakes" are the subsisting intelligibles.

Josiah Royce

11. REALITY AND INTERPRETATION

A more radical interpretation of reality as that which is "*for* mind" is to be found in the American Idealism of Josiah Royce, whose thought on this point provides an interesting contrast to the ideas of Rousselot and St. Thomas.

This selection is excerpted from Volume II of Royce's *The Problem of Christianity,* copy-right 1913 by The Macmillan Company and used with their permission.

Envisioning reality as a community joined together through social, political, and ideological, as well as ontological relations, Royce considered that reality *"must be present to the Unity of the Infinite Thought,"* as he put it in his early work *The Religious Aspect of Philosophy.* "The Infinite Thought," he said, "must, knowing all truth, include also a knowledge of all wills, and of their conflict." What makes *a* reality, as well as *all* reality, he noted, is the fact that "true judgment can be made about it." Everything that exists—good and evil; truth and falsehood—is known in and to the absolute thought. There is thus an ideal nature to reality in that it is known, and it can be known only if it is akin to mind.

In the following selection from *The Problem of Christianity,* Royce addresses himself to the question of understanding the meaning of reality in all its forms. Borrowing from Charles Sanders Peirce, an American contemporary, he developed a theory of "signs." By "signs" Royce and Peirce meant the symbols invested by a community with meanings. A frown, a traffic light, a handshake, are all signs endowed by a community with meaning. Signs are neither conceptions nor perceptions, but symbols of accumulated communitarian experience. Both Peirce and Royce called the process of translating "signs" and things, and relations understood as signs, "interpretation." Interpretation involves three elements: (a) that which is interpreted (the sign); (b) one who interprets; and (c) one to whom the interpretation is made. Interpretation evidences the dimensions of a community, for it joins two or more together in common experience.

Being, understood as the community of things and relations, therefore requires an interpreter and an "interpretee." Since community is a co-operative entity, each member of the community can extend both the spirit and act of cooperation by asserting that "this activity which we perform together, this work of ours, its past, its future, its sequence, its order, its sense,—all these enter into my life, and are the life of my own self writ large."

The philosopher, therefore, who seeks to understand reality and its unity must proceed not by way of conception and perception but by means of interpretation. For the real world is *"simply the 'true interpretation' of this our problematic situation."* He who would understand reality must understand present experience and its teleological implications—its goal. Whatever the real world is, its reality must be expressed in an antithesis between contrasting terms, such as "actual-ideal," "flesh-spirit," "foolish-wise." Each of these terms needs an interpreter "to represent its cause to the other idea." The real world is thus the interpreter of its own infinite signs, and the interpretation is made in a community of ideas.

I HAVE ALREADY more than once asserted that the principal task of the philosopher is one, not of perception, not of conception, but of interpretation. This remark refers in the first place to the office which the philosophers have filled in the history of culture.

Common opinion classes philosophy among the humanities. It ought so to be classed. Philosophers have actually devoted themselves, in the main, neither to perceiving the world, nor to spinning webs of conceptual theory, but to interpreting the meaning of the civilizations which they have represented, and to attempting the interpretation of whatever minds in the universe, human or divine, they believed to be real. That the philosophers are neither the only interpreters, nor the chiefs among those who interpret, we now well know. The artists, the leaders of men, and all the students of the humanities, make interpretation their business; and the triadic cognitive function, as the last lecture showed, has its applications in all the realms of knowledge. But in any case the philosopher's ideals are those of an interpreter. He addresses one mind and interprets another. The unity which he seeks is that which is characteristic of a community of interpretation.

The historical proofs of this thesis are manifold. A correct summary of their meaning appears in the common opinion which classes philosophy amongst the humanities. This classification is a perfectly just one. The humanities are busied with interpretations. Individual illustrations of the historical office of philosophy could be furnished by considering with especial care precisely those historical instances which the philosophers furnish who, like Plato or like Bergson, have most of all devoted their efforts to emphasizing as much as possible one of the other cognitive processes, instead of interpretation. For the more exclusively such a philosopher lays stress upon perception alone, or conception alone, the better does he illustrate our historical thesis.

Plato lays stress upon conception as furnishing our principal access to reality. Bergson has eloquently maintained the thesis that pure perception brings us in contact with the real. Yet each of these philosophers actually offer us an interpretation of the universe. That is, each of them begins by taking account of certain mental processes which play a part in human life. Each asks us to win some sort of touch with a higher type of consciousness than belongs to our natural human existence. Each declares that, through such a transformation of our ordinary consciousness, either through a flight from the vain show of sense into the realm of pure thought, or else through an abandonment of the merely practical labors of that user of tools, the intellect, we shall find the pathway to reality. Each in his own way interprets our natural mode of dealing with reality to some nobler form of insight which he believes to be corrective of our natural errors, or else, in turn, interprets the supposed counsels of a more divine type of knowledge to the blindness or to the barrenness or to the merely practical narrowness of our ordinary existence.

Each of these philosophers mediates, in his own way, between the spiritual existence of those who sit in the darkness of the cave of sense, or who, on the other hand, wander in the wilderness of evolutionary processes and of intellectual theories;—he mediates, I say, between these victims of error on the one hand, and that better, that richer, spiritual life and the truer insight, on the other hand, of those who, in this philosopher's opinion, find the homeland— be that land the Platonic realm of the eternal forms of being, or the dwelling-place which Bergson loves—where the artists see their beautiful visions of endless change.

In brief, there is no philosophy of pure conception, and there is no philosophy of pure perception. Plato was a leader of the souls of those men to whom he showed the way out of the cave, and in whom he inspired the love of the eternal. Bergson winningly devotes himself to saying, as any artist says, "Come and intuitively see what I have intuitively seen."

Such speech, however, is the speech neither of the one who trusts to mere conception, nor of one who finds the real merely in perception. It is the speech of an interpreter, who, addressing himself to one form of personality or of life, interprets what he takes to be the meaning of some other form of life.

This thesis, that the philosopher is an interpreter, simply directs our attention to the way in which he is required to define his problems. And the universality of these problems makes this purely elementary task of their proper definition at once momentous and difficult. We shall not lose by any consideration which rightly fixes our attention upon an essential aspect of the process of knowledge which the philosopher seeks to control. For the philosopher is attempting to deal with the world as a whole, with reality in general.

Why is it that the philosopher has to be an interpreter even when, like Bergson or like Plato, he tries to subordinate interpretation either to conception alone or to perception alone? Why is it that when, in his loftiest speculative flights, he attempts to seize upon some intuition of reason, or upon some form of direct perception, which shall reveal to him the inmost essence of reality, he nevertheless acts as interpreter?

The answer to this question is simple.

If, as a fact, we could, at least in ideal, and as a sort of speculative experiment, weld all our various ideas, our practical ideas as well as our theoretical ideas, together into some single idea, whose "leading" we could follow wherever it led, from concept to percept, or from percept to concept; and if we could reduce our problem of reality simply to the question, Is this one idea expressive of the nature of reality?—then indeed some such philosophy as that of Bergson, or as that of Plato, might be formulated in terms either of pure perception or of pure conception. Then the philosopher who thus welded his ideas into one idea, and who then assured himself of the success of that one idea, would no longer be an interpreter.

Thus, let us imagine that we could, with Spinoza, weld together into the one idea of Substance, the totality of ideas, that is of pragmatic leadings, which all men, at all times, are endeavoring to follow through their experience, or to express through their will. Suppose that this one idea could be shown to be successful. Then our philosophy could assume the well-known form which Spinoza gave to his own:—

By Substance, Spinoza means that which is "in itself" and which needs no other to sustain or in any ideal fashion to contain it. Hereupon the philosopher finds it easy to assert that whatever is in any sense real must indeed be either "in itself" or "in another." No other idea need be used in estimating realities except the idea thus defined. The only question as to any object is: Is this a substance or not? A very brief and simple process of conceptual development, then, brings us to Spinoza's result that whatever is "in another" is not in the highest sense real at all. Therefore there remains in our world only that which is real "in itself." The one idea can be realized only in a world which is, once for all, the Substance. The tracks of all finite creatures that are observed near the edge of the cave of this Substance lead (as was long ago said of Spinoza's substance) only inwards. The world is defined in terms of the single idea, all other human ideas or possible ideas being but special cases of the one idea. The real world is purely conceptual, and is also monistic.

Suppose, on the other hand, that we indeed recognize with Bergson, and with the pragmatists, an endless and empirical wealth of ideas which in practical life, lead or do not lead from concepts to percepts, as experience may determine. Suppose, however, that, with Bergson, we first notice that all these ideal leadings of the intellect constitute, at best, but an endlessly varied using of tools. Suppose that hereupon, with Bergson and with the mystics, we come to regard all this life of the varied ideas, this mechanical using of mere tools, this mere pragmatism, as an essentially poorer sort of life from which nature has long since delivered the nobler of the insects, from which the artists can and do escape, and from which it is the loftiest ideal of philosophy to liberate those who are indeed to know reality.

Then indeed, though not at all in Spinoza's way, all the ideal leadings which the philosopher has henceforth to regard as essentially illuminating, will simply blend into a single idea. This idea will be the one idea of winning a pure intuition. We shall define reality in terms of this pure intuition. And hereupon a purely perceptual view of reality will result.

If, then, all the ideas of men, if all ideas of reality, could collapse or could blend or could otherwise be ideally welded into a single idea, then this idea could be used to define reality, just as pragmatism has come to define all the endless variety of forms of "truth" in terms of the single idea which gets the name "success" or "working" or "expediency" or "cash-value," according to the taste of the individual pragmatist.

As a fact, however, the genuine problem, whether of reality, or of truth, cannot be faced by means of any such blending of all ideal leadings into a single ideal leading.

We all of us believe that there is any real world at all, simply because we find ourselves in a situation in which, because of the fragmentary and dissatisfying conflicts, antitheses, and problems of our present ideas, an interpretation of this situation is needed, but is not now known to us. *By the "real world" we mean simply the "true interpretation" of this our problematic situation.* No other reason can be given than this for believing that there is any real world at all. From this one consideration, vast consequences follow. Let us next sketch some of these consequences.

Whoever stands in presence of the problem of reality has, at the very least, to compare two essential ideas. These ideas are, respectively, the idea of present experience and the idea of the goal of experience. The contrast in question has countless and infinitely various forms. In its ethical form the contrast appears as that between our actual life and our ideal life. It also appears as the Pauline contrast between the flesh and the spirit; or as the Stoic contrast between the life of the wise and the life of fools. It is also known to common sense as the contrast between our youthful hopes and our mature sense of our limitations. The contrast between our future life, which we propose to control, and our irrevocable past life which we can never recall, presents the same general antithesis. In the future, as we hopefully view it, the goal is naturally supposed to lie. But the past, dead as it is often said to be, determines our present need, and sets for us our ideal task.

In the world of theory the same contrast appears as that between our ignorance and our possible enlightenment, between our endlessly numerous problems and their solutions, between our innumerable uncertainties and those attainments of certainty at which our sciences and our arts aim. For our religious consciousness the contrasts between nature and grace, between good and evil, between our present state and our salvation, between God and the world, merely illustrate the antithesis.

One can also state this antithesis as that between our Will (which, as Schopenhauer and the Buddhists said, is endlessly longing) and the Fulfilment of our will. Plato, on the one hand, and the mystics on the other, attempt to conceive or to perceive some such fulfilment, according as Plato, or as some mystic, emphasizes one or the other of the two cognitive processes to which the philosophers have usually confined their attention.

This antithesis between two fundamental ideas presents to each of us the problem of the universe, and dominates that problem. For by the "real world" we mean the true interpretation of the problematic situation which this antithesis presents to us in so far as we compare what is our ideal with what is so far given to us. Whatever the real world is, its nature has to be expressed in terms of this antithesis of ideas.

Two such ideas, then, stand in contrast when we face our problem of reality. They stand as do plaintiff and defendant in court, or as do the ideas of the suffering patient and his hopes of recovery, or as do the wrongs which the litigant feels and the rights or the doom which the law allows him. The empirical shapes which the antithesis takes are simply endless in their wealth. They furnish to us the special topics which science and common sense study. But the general problem which the antithesis presents is the world-problem. *The question about what the real world is, is simply the question as to what this contrast is and means.* Neither of the two ideas can solve its own problem or be judge in its own case. Each needs a counsel, a mediator, an interpreter, to represent its cause to the other idea.

In the well-known metaphysical expression, this contrast may be called that between appearance and reality. The antithesis itself is in one sense the appearance, the phenomenon, the world-problem. The question about the real world is that furnished to us by our experience of this appearance. When we ask what the real world is, we simply ask what this appearance, this antithesis, this problem of the two contrasting ideas both is and means. So to ask, is to ask for the solution of the problem which the antithesis presents. That is, we ask: "What is the interpretation of this problem, of this antithesis?" The real world is that solution. Every special definition of reality takes the form of offering such a solution. Whether a philosopher calls himself realist or idealist, monist or pluralist, theist or materialist, empiricist or rationalist, his philosophy, wherever he states it, takes the form of saying: "The true, the genuine interpretation of the antithesis is such and such."

If you say that perhaps there is no solution of the problem, that hypothesis, if true, could be verified only by an experience that in itself would constitute a full insight into the meaning of the real contrast, and so would in fact furnish a solution. In any case, the real world is precisely that whose nature is expressed by whatever mediating idea is such that, when viewed in unity with the two antithetical ideas, it fully compares them, and makes clear the meaning of the contrast. *But an interpretation is real only if the appropriate community is real, and is true only if that community reaches its goal.*

In brief, then, the real world is the Community of Interpretation which is constituted by the two antithetic ideas, and their mediator or interpreter, whatever or whoever that interpreter may be. If the interpretation is a reality, and if it truly interprets the whole of reality, then the community reaches its goal, and the real world includes its own interpreter. *Unless both the interpreter and the community are real, there is no real world.*

After the foregoing discussion of the nature and the processes of interpretation, we are now secure from any accusation that, from this point of view, the real world is anything merely static, or is a mere idea within the mind of a finite self, or is an Absolute that is divorced from its appearances, or is any merely conceptual reality, or is "out of time," or is a "block universe," or is an object of a merely mystical intuition.

Interpretation, as we have seen in our general discussion of the cognitive process in question, demands that at least an infinite series of distinct individual acts of interpretation shall take place, unless the interpretation which is in question is arbitrarily interrupted. If, then, the real world contains the Community of Interpretation just characterized, this community of interpretation expresses its life in an infinite series of individual interpretations, each of which occupies its own place in a perfectly real order of time.

If, however, this community of interpretation reaches its goal, this whole time-process is in some fashion spanned by one insight which surveys the unity of its meaning. Such a viewing of the whole time-process by a single synopsis will certainly not be anything "timeless." It will not occur, on the other hand, at any one moment of time. But its nature is the one empirically known to us at any one moment when we clearly contrast two of our own ideas and find their mediator.

Nothing is more concretely known to us than are the nature, the value, and the goal of a community of interpretation. The most ideal as well as the most scientifically exact interests of mankind are bound up with the existence, with the fortunes, and with the unity of such communities.

The metaphysical doctrine just set forth in outline can be summed up thus: The problem of reality is furnished to us by a certain universal antithesis of two Ideas, or, if one prefers the word, by the antithesis of two Selves. The first thesis of this doctrine is that Reality—the solution of this problem—is the interpretation of this antithesis, the process of mediating between these two selves and of interpreting each of them to the other. Such a process of interpretation involves, of necessity, an infinite sequence of acts of interpretation. It also admits of an endless variety within all the selves which are thus mutually interpreted. These selves, in all their variety, constitute the life of a single Community of Interpretation, whose central member is that spirit of the community whose essential function we now know. In the concrete, then, the universe is a community of interpretation whose life comprises and unifies all the social varieties and all the social communities which, for any reason, we know to be real in the empirical world which our social and our historical sciences study. The history of the universe, the whole order of time, is the history and the order and the expression of this Universal Community. . . .

We have no ground whatever for believing that there is any real world except the ground furnished by our experience, and by the fact that, in addition to our perceptions and our conceptions, we have problems upon our hands which need interpretation. Our fundamental postulate is: *The world is the interpretation of the problems which it presents.* If you deny this principle, you do so only by presenting, as Bergson does, some other interpretation as the true one. But thus you simply reaffirm the principle that the world has an interpreter.

Using this principle, in your ordinary social life, you postulate your fellow-man as the interpreter of the ideas which he awakens in your mind, and which are not your own ideas. The same principle, applied to our social experience of the physical world, determines our ordinary interpretations of nature and guides our natural science. For, as we have seen, the physical world is an object known to the community, and through interpretation. The same principle, applied to our memories and to our expectations, gives us our view of the world of time, with all its infinite wealth of successive acts of interpretation.

In all these special instances, the application of this principle defines for us some form or grade of community, and teaches us wherein lies the true nature, the form, the real unity, and the essential life of this community.

Our Doctrine of Signs extends to the whole world the same fundamental principle. The World is the Community. The world contains its own interpreter. Its processes are infinite in their temporal varieties. But their interpreter, the spirit of this universal community—never absorbing varieties or permitting them to blend—compares and, through a real life, interprets them all.

The attitude of will which this principle expresses, is neither that of the affirmation nor that of the denial of what Schopenhauer meant by the will to live. It is the attitude which first expresses itself by saying "Alone I am lost, and am worse than nothing. I need a counsellor, I need my community. Interpret me. Let me join in this interpretation. Let there be the community. This alone is life. This alone is salvation. This alone is real." This is at once an attitude of the will and an assertion whose denial refutes itself. For if there is no interpreter, there is no interpretation. And if there is no interpretation, there is no world whatever.

In its daily form as the principle of our social common sense, this attitude of the will inspires whatever is reasonable about our worldly business and our scientific inquiry. For all such business and inquiry are in and for and of the community, or else are vanity.

In its highest form, this attitude of the will was the one which Paul knew as Charity, and as the life in and through the spirit of the Community. . . .

W. Norris Clarke, S.J.   12. WHAT IS REALLY REAL?

It is the actuality of being, as noted in so many of the previous selections, that is at the center of Thomistic metaphysics. If this is so, what provision is to be made for the meaning of the "possibles"? Are they not also part of reality? Have they not hitherto been included in the definition of real being as "that which is or can be"? In this essay, Father Clarke attacks these problems in order to show the relation between real, or existential, being and the possibles.

Three principal reasons supporting the inclusion of the possibles under the title "real being," says Clarke, have traditionally been recognized. These reasons are based upon (*a*) the example of Aristotle, who put forward

From *Progress in Philosophy* (The Bruce Publishing Company, Milwaukee), pages 61–63, and 79–89. Reprinted by permission of the publisher.

the conception of science as concerned only with essential predicates; (*b*) the necessity of maintaining the absolute—and therefore essence-character of metaphysical truths; and (*c*) the difference between nonbeing and *entia rationis,* or mental realities, on the one hand, and real being, on the other hand.

As St. Thomas viewed the problem, possible beings have no title to goodness or to any of the other transcendental marks of real being. It is only actuality that endows these titles. As Clarke puts it, "Essences themselves . . . draw their whole reality and intelligibility for St. Thomas from their role as modes of existence." Hence Thomistic metaphysics studies *real being* formally as *existent.* We need not, Father Clarke points out, retreat to the realm of essences to obtain absolute certitude for the main principles and theses of a general metaphysics, because absolute certainty can be attained from the analysis of beings as actually existent.

There is no doubt that the possibles, insofar as they are distinguishable from nonbeing and from mental beings (*entia rationis*), are *intelligible.* But this does not endow them with an ontological status. We must be aware that there is, on the plane of experience, an ultimate division between the "really real" and thought—between "to-be-real" and "to-be-thought."

What status, then, is finally to be accorded the possibles? Their status, says Clarke, is that of *esse intentionale.* Though not real in themselves, possibles have a relation toward reality. They differ from mental realities, not in regard to their intrinsic reality, but only in their intelligible content. An inseparable part of the intelligibility of a possible, he says, is its two rational relations toward the real: the one, of "analogous imitation of the uncreated Real, its model; the other, of potential exemplary ordination toward a created real terminus." The possible is not real in itself but is intelligibly ordered to be real. The possibles can then be accorded place in the existential science of metaphysics in the same way that their intelligibility is related to real being. "Their intelligibility has intentional existence entirely in and through the reality of God, His essence and His act of thought."

I T IS THE PURPOSE of this essay to present for discussion and further exploration one instance of a point of doctrine long current in the Thomistic school tradition but which seems to us—and to an increasing number of others—to have its roots in quite a different metaphysical tradition and to be seriously out of harmony with the basic premises of a metaphysics centered on existence. We refer to the traditional practice among Thomistic metaphysicians (tradition, that is, for the past three or four centuries) of describing the content of "real being," the object of metaphysics, as "that which is or can be," thereby including within its extension two classes of beings, actual and possible. Both of the latter are thus presumed to verify the note of real in some proper and intrinsic way and hence to stand opposed to the so-called "beings-of-reason" (*entia rationis*), which all Scholastic philosophers admit do not fall under the proper object of metaphysics. Inseparably linked with this inclusion of the possibles within the order of real being is the analysis of being taken as a noun (the object of metaphysics) as signifying essence with some relation to existence but prescinding from the actual exercise of this existence. The point at issue is therefore whether or not it is legitimate to characterize "real being," the object of metaphysics, as a noun signifying essence prescinding from the actual exercise of existence and thus including in a proper and intrinsic sense the possibles; and if not, what is the proper way to describe their ontological status and relate them to the object of metaphysics? . . .

Let us examine briefly, then, some of the deeper intrinsic reasons usually put forward as justifying the inclusion of the possibles under real being and the precision from actual existence.

The first is based on the Aristotelian conception of science as concerned only with essential predicates. Now being in the sense of existent essence cannot be predicated as essential predicate of any being save God. Hence it cannot be the object of the science of metaphysics; otherwise the latter would be dealing with a nonessential or accidental predicate.

This objection can be disposed of quite briefly. It is surprising, to say the least, that Thomists, who elsewhere expound so eloquently the importance and originality of the distinction between essence and existence, should lend any weight to this purely terminological difficulty based on the inadequate Aristotelian categories of essence and accident as exhaustive of reality. St. Thomas himself warns that the substantial act of existence in his theory cannot be fitted into either of these categories. It is neither accident nor essence in the strict sense of the word, but a new *sui generis* principle in the substantial order and distinct from both. The permanent core of truth in the Aristotelian principle is that a science should deal only with necessary and ultimately constitutive, or nonaccidental, predicates. Now if the proper object of metaphysics is precisely existent being as existent, and if the substantial act of existence is according to St. Thomas the most intimate and most fundamentally constitutive element of every real being as long as it remains existent and the object of metaphysics, then the legitimate requirements for a science are met in a genuine, though analogous, way. In other words, the true answer to this difficulty is simply to refuse to accept its premises in a rigid and univocal sense and to insist that the too narrow Aristotelian concept of Science be enlarged to make room for the new *sui generis* element of reality brought into focus for the first time by St. Thomas and for the *sui generis* character of the science of metaphysics resulting from the nature of its object.

The next argument is a considerably more serious one, in that its roots extend all the way back to the fountainheads of the *philosophia perennis* through the venerable Platonic-Augustinian tradition. It proceeds thus. The truths of metaphysics, the most ultimate of all sciences, must have the characteristics of absolute necessity and immutability. But the beings accessible to our experience are in their actual existence irremediably contingent and mutable. Therefore the necessary truths of philosophy in general, and above all of metaphysics, can find no solid foundation in this contingent world, but only in a realm of the eternally necessary and immutable essences of things. This is the order of the possibles. The metaphysical order as such, therefore, is the order of the possibles, not of contingent actual existence. Now since metaphysics is by very definition the science of the real as such, if the possibles themselves are not real then metaphysics will find itself in the embarrassing position of being in the last analysis a science of the unreal.

There are two latent premises on which this whole argument rests. The first is that because the world of actual existence around us is contingent and mutable, it cannot bear within itself any necessity or immutability whatever. The second is that only essences in the strict sense can be abstracted. Both of these premises, we believe, are unsound and inconsistent with an integral Thomism, first, because they manifest an inadequate view of reality itself; second, because they fail to take into account the peculiar resources of Thomistic epistemology and metaphysics.

As regards the first proposition, the belief that the existing world of sensible reality is so unstable that it cannot become the object or source of immutable philosophical truth was certainly the profound conviction of Plato, for whom the realm of the ideas alone was the "really real." It also deeply marked the thought of St. Augustine. It is in fact the hidden spring of all his arguments for the existence of God from necessary and eternal truths, whose "reality" and necessity can find no sufficient foundation in contingent existents and hence must be rooted directly in the immutable necessity of the divine mind. But it is precisely one of the most significant advances made by St. Thomas in the history of Christian philosophy that he swung the balance back from this exaggerated Platonic-Augustinian depreciation of the contingent by pointing out the genuine necessities (and he does not hesitate to say absolute necessities, though always participated) that lie hidden within the core of even the frailest and most transitory contingent existent. "There is nothing," he says, "so contingent that it does not contain within it something necessary." And he devotes an entire chapter of his *Contra Gentes* (II, 30) to the question: "In what ways can there be absolute necessity within created beings?" It is precisely from this higher estimate of the *intrinsic* in creatures, their intrinsic consistency, intelligibility, dignity, and adequate inner resources for action as fully equipped natures, that stem the radical optimism and rich, positive, humanism so characteristic of his world outlook.

Nor can it be maintained that these necessities lie exclusively, or even primarily (at least as regards the truths of general metaphysics), on the side of essence. If the act of existence is the most fundamental common element of all beings as such, must it not have some common intrinsic characteristics necessarily accompanying it in whatever being it is found? The fact is that the great majority of the basic principles and theses of the Thomistic metaphysical system contain necessary truths derived from the properties of existing beings considered formally as existent. Thus, for example, the most fundamental and absolute necessity of all in Thomistic metaphysics is the principle of contradiction taken in its existential sense, namely, that nothing can simultaneously be (exist) and not be at the same time. This is because even the humblest and most short-lived existent being, so long as it actually exists, even for one moment, and precisely in virtue of its act of existence, excludes nonbeing with the most absolute necessity, and thus makes it an unconditioned truth for all time and for all minds that at this moment of time this particular being was and can in no way be thought not to have been at the same moment.

The entire analysis of goodness as a transcendental property of every being is also based formally on the principle that the act of existence is the root of all perfection and that exactly in proportion as it possesses an act of actual existence can any being lay claim to goodness. Possible beings can have no goodness for St. Thomas. What we really desire when we desire a possible being is its actuality, not its possibility. So, too, the deduction of the fundamental ontological structure of every finite being, its composition of essence and existence, is based on the analysis of the act of existence as common perfection participated and limited by different essences. Essences themselves, in fact, draw their whole reality and intelligibility for St. Thomas from their role as modes of existence (*modi essendi*). Furthermore, even if we go beyond the theses peculiar to the Thomistic metaphysical system, is it not true that in any Scholastic metaphysics the analyses of action, change, efficient and final causality must necessarily be founded (whether acknowledged or not) on the characteristics of being as actually existent? For possible essences can neither change nor act nor cause nor be attracted or repelled nor have real compositions or real relations (which all admit can be had only in actual existents).

It cannot be true, then—and here we touch the second latent premise mentioned above—that concrete existents as such are so exclusively particular that they have no common traits among themselves as existent at all. Why, then, cannot these too be disengaged by the mind by some process of abstraction analogous to, but not identical with, the abstraction of essences properly so called? This is precisely the achievement of Thomistic epistemology applied to metaphysics, that it has found a way, by its theory of the special mode of abstraction of the notion of being through the judgment of separation and the reduction of particularities to confused presence, to disengage and retain for intellectual analysis not only the essential but the existential aspects of the real beings that are its object. Thomistic metaphysics, therefore, studies real being (essence-existing) formally as *existent* (that is, under the unifying formal object of the act of existence), which is not at all the same as to say formally as *particular*.

One last difficulty in connection with the above argument can be briefly disposed of. It is the objection that, if metaphysics is based on contingent existents as existent, then none of its propositions can be stated as unconditional absolute truths but must always be prefixed by the condition: "*If anything exists,* then it must be good, etc., etc." This is absolutely correct. But the objection seems to overlook the fact that if there is one condition about whose verification the metaphysician need not worry it is the proposition, "Something exists." The very fact that any metaphysician existentially puts such a question to himself is the absolutely unconditioned guarantee that at least one being exists, he can prove that some being must always of necessity exist. Such an objection, instead of weakening, only illuminates more deeply the nature and validity of an existence-centered metaphysics.

The conclusion of the foregoing analysis is that it is quite possible to construct a general metaphysics the main principles and theses of which can be established with absolute certainty directly from the analysis of beings as actually existent, with no need of recourse to the possibles to guarantee this certitude. In fact, it is difficult to see how any sound metaphysics which does not start off with the existence of God as already given by faith or intuition, but accepts its responsibility for providing an absolutely certain base for proving His existence, can possibly establish the certainty of its own basic theses by recourse to the possibles. Is it not evident that the very objectivity of the possibles themselves depends entirely on the prior certainty of the existence of God as already established by independently valid metaphysical principles? This is by no means to deny, it cannot too strongly be asserted, that the recourse to the possibles (and the divine will) becomes absolutely necessary when the metaphysician wishes to discover, not whether or not there is necessity in contingent things, but what is the ultimate source whence they derive these various necessities really within them, but whose presence they show themselves unable to explain of themselves.

There remains the last and perhaps the strongest argument of the reality of the possibles, that drawn from the direct analysis of the nature of the possibles in themselves and their objective foundation in God. It reasons thus. First of all, the possibles are endowed with positive intelligibility, each distinct from the other, hence from mere nonbeing. Second, the constitutive notes of each coalesce into a self-consistent intelligible unit. This unit is founded on the most real of all realities, the divine essence seen by the divine intellect as really and existentially imitable in this particular way. Hence this intelligible unit is seen as objectively capable of actual existence outside the divine mind, if the divine will wished to confer such actual existence on it. Such an intelligible unit cannot be classed among mere beings of reason, which of their very nature, do not have the *per se* unity of a genuine essence and are incapable of actual subsistence outside of the mind actually thinking them. In sum, that which in its objective intelligibility is distinguishable from, and irreducible to, pure nonbeing, as well as to mere beings of reason, must necessarily be identified with real being in some proper and intrinsic sense.

This argument is admittedly impressive and on outward appearance seems foolproof in its logical rigor. In fact, however, its conclusion goes beyond the content of its premises, with the help of a subtle and elusive, but nonetheless illicit, transition from thought to reality. Aside from the necessary, immutable, and objectively founded intelligibility of the possibles, what exactly does it prove? Simply this: that the *idea content* or *intelligibility* of a possible is not the same as that of pure nonbeing or of a being-of-reason; or it is not the same to *think* of a possible as to *think* of nonbeing or an *ens rationis*. Quite true. But it does not follow that what is being thought about thereby acquires any ontological status of its own as opposed to ontological or extramental nonbeing. Otherwise one would have proved too much, and "he who proves too much proves nothing." One would also have proved that, from the mere fact that one being-of-reason is intelligibly distinct from another and from nonbeing (e.g. $\sqrt{-1}$, $\sqrt{-2}$, or any two positive relations of reason), it therefore follows that the same beings-of-reason are really opposed to ontological nonbeing and hence must be called somehow real beings—a conclusion repudiated by everyone. It would also follow that just because one thought about nonbeing with a definite actual act of the mind, it would therefore ensue that nonbeing itself was somehow real just because it was the object of a real thought.

In other words we are here face to face with the ultimate abyss between the order of pure thought and the order of the ontologically real, the real in itself, the "really real." This abyss cannot be bridged by intellect alone but only by will; only love can call up being out of nonbeing. What we are asserting here is what seems to us the absolutely primary condition of any thoroughgoing and fully conscious realism of being: that to be a pure *esse intentionale,* or object of thought, in any intellect, even the divine, confers no proper or intrinsic reality of its own whatsoever on the object. In other words, the "being" or existence of a thought object or intentional real is not a "to-be-real" but a "to-be-really-thought by a real act of a real mind." The reality resides entirely in the real act of the mind thinking, not in the object of this thought.

There is admittedly a genuine mystery involved here, how the mind can spin an endless thought progeny out of its own substance, so to speak, without adding in the slightest bit to the real multiplicity of the universe. This order of *esse intentionale* is one that desperately needs rigorous ontological analysis by Thomists and has not yet received anything like the attention it deserves. This paper will have been well worth the effort if it at least has the effect of stimulating further research into this obscure and neglected area. But no theory of the intentional order can lead to anything but further confusion unless it preserves inviolate the absolute irreducibility of the "to-be-real" and the "to-be-thought."

This means, of course, that when the terms "being," "existence," "real" and the like are applied to the intentional order, as indeed they must since we have no more ultimate terms of reference, they at once take on a new distinct meaning, irreducible by any intrinsic analogy to their primary and proper meaning, just as the orders themselves are irreducible to any common denominator. There is an extrinsic link of dependence, however, between the two meanings, just as between the two orders, which permits the extension of the same term from one to the other according to the laws of the analogy of extrinsic attribution (not proper proportionality) but with a radical shift in intrinsic signification. Thus an object of thought can be called "a being," or "real," not because it is a real being in itself, but because it is thought by a real being, and, in the case of a possible, has an intelligible relation to the real order.

Why is it so necessary to insist that possibles can only have an *esse intentionale?* In order to safeguard the two most important truths of all: first, the absolute simplicity of God's entire essence, His "real being," which allows no real multiplicity within Him whatsoever, not even real relations (save those between the three divine Persons); and second, the doctrine of strict creation, which asserts the production of all finite beings entirely and unqualifiedly out of nothing, with no shred of pre-existing reality of their own at all. There is no more unequivocal expression of the common doctrine on this point than that of Suarez himself, when he says: "We must lay it down at the very start that the essence of the creature . . . before it is produced by God, possesses within itself no true real existence, and, in this sense, such an essence deprived of its existential being (*esse existentiae*) is not even a thing at all but absolutely nothing." It is a little disconcerting, however, to recall that some thirty disputations earlier the same author has told us that the possibles have a "real essence" which is directly and properly included in real being as the object of metaphysics, the science of the real precisely as real!

If all this is true, how then do the possibles differ at all from those other intentional beings called beings-of-reason? From the point of view of their intrinsic reality, not a whit. The difference is solely in their intelligible content. This is thought up by the divine mind precisely as an exemplar or blueprint (guaranteed to work) of one way in which He *could* (intellect and will together) imitate, in the real order, if He so wished, the supremely real subsistent act of existence that is His own essence. Hence, the possible has as an inseparable part of its very intelligibility a set of relations (rational, not real) toward the real, one of analogous imitation of the uncreated Real, its model, the other of potential exemplary ordination toward a created real terminus. These intelligible relations, not possessed by the *entia rationis,* distinguish the possible in its intelligible content from the latter and permit it to be called "real" by a special kind of extrinsic denomination or extrinsic attribution, which means: "that which is not real in itself but is intelligibly ordered to the real." It is possible in this way, if one so insists, to give a valid interpretation to the traditional classification of the possibles among real beings as opposed to beings-of-reason, but only on the condition that it be explicitly recognized that real covers two different and irreducible meanings, one primary, proper, and absolute, the other secondary, improper, and denominated by relation only, and that it is not a single meaning intrinsically verified in both actuals and possibles. However, it would be much clearer, more accurate, and more in accord with the strong meaning of real as opposed to idea in the modern languages, we think, to divide being first into two primary orders, real being and intentional being, and then subdivide the latter into its main classes, possible beings and beings-of-reason.

Finally, if real being as the object of metaphysics signifies directly and properly only existent being, how can the possibles come at all under the science of metaphysics, as indeed they should? The answer is very simple. They come under it in precisely the same way that their intelligibility is related to real being. Their intelligibility has intentional existence entirely in and through the reality of God, His essence and His act of thought, and can only be validly postulated and analyzed by us through the mediation of the divine reality, as a necessary consequence of the divine attributes. Therefore they enter necessarily into the science of metaphysics and are studied by it, not directly in themselves, but indirectly through its primary object, existing being, as inseparably linked with it by a relation of necessary intelligibility—a quasi projection of the Supreme Being's own necessary intelligibility as existent, intelligent, and all-powerful.

Henri Bergson

13. THE POSSIBLE
AND THE REAL

Just as Royce represents a more radical version of Father Rousselot's intellectualism, so Henri Bergson represents a more radical interpretation of Father Clarke's views on the possibles. The contrast between Bergson and Clarke, however, is a contrast not merely of competing views but of competing issues. Where Clarke inquired into the meaning and status of possibles *as* possibles, Bergson is interested in the "possible" implications of an *actual* real.

This selection is from *The Creative Mind* (New York, 1946) and appears through the courtesy of the publisher, Philosophical Library, Inc.

Reality, for Bergson, is in continuous procession and is continually un-folding novelties. It is "global and undivided growth, progressive invention . . . fullness constantly swelling out." Opposed to this view, says Bergson, philosophers have for the most part considered reality statically, and have thus been forced into the creation of pseudo-problems about reality, two of which have been especially "agonizing." The first consists in asking why there should be being (but this arises only on the assumption that nothing-ness precedes being); the second, in asking how thought recognizes itself in things (but this is just as illusionary as the first).

One of the most agonizing problems, Bergson continues, derives from the notion that possibility is less than reality, that the possibility of a thing precedes its existence. The truth is just the opposite: possibility is consequent upon existence, not anterior to it. It is a "future-perfect." "For the possible is only the real with the addition of an act of mind which throws its image back into the past, once it has been enacted." A work of art *will have been possible* only after its creation. Before its creation it is not yet possible. "The possible is therefore the mirage of the present in the past."

The possible is to be judged against a background of process; it is not "there" simply awaiting actuation; it is not ideally pre-existent. It is actua-tion that brings forward what has been made possible. Hence, says Bergson, "the idea immanent in most philosophies and natural to the human mind, of possibles which would be realized by an acquisition of existence, is there-fore pure illusion."

In an evolutionary world view, he suggests, possibility achieves a distinc-tively "existential" character, being always "after-the-fact." In the light of evolution, possibility is inherent only in the conception of facts, rather than in the process of facts. Once this is seen, he feels, evolution can be understood as something more than a mere working out of a pre-existent program. Hence, we must understand that "it is the real which makes itself possible, and not the possible which becomes real."

I SHOULD LIKE to come back to a subject on which I have already spoken, the continuous creation of unforeseeable novelty which seems to be going on in the universe. As far as I am concerned, I feel I am experiencing it constantly. No matter how I try to imagine in detail what is going to happen to me, still how inadequate, how abstract and stilted is the thing I have imagined in com-parison to what actually happens! The realization brings along with it an unforeseeable nothing which changes everything. For example, I am to be present at a gathering; I know what people I shall find there, around what table, in what order, to discuss what problem. But let them come, be seated and chat as I expected, let them say what I was sure they would say: the whole gives me an impression at once novel and unique, as if it were but now designed at one original stroke by the hand of an artist. Gone is the image I had conceived of it, a mere prearrangeable juxtaposition of things already known! I agree that the picture has not the artistic value of a Rembrandt or a Velasquez: yet it is just as unexpected and, in this sense, quite as original. It will be alleged that I did not know the circumstances in detail, that I could not control the persons in question, their gestures, their attitudes, and that if the thing as a whole provided me with something new it was because they produced additional factors. But I have the same impression of novelty before the unrolling of my inner life. I feel it more vividly than ever, before the action I willed and of which I was sole master. If I deliberate before acting, the moments of deliberation present themselves to my consciousness like the successive sketches a painter makes of his picture, each one unique of its kind; and no matter whether the act itself in its accomplishment realizes something willed and consequently foreseen, it has none the less its own particular form in all its originality.—Granted, someone will say; there is perhaps something original and unique in a state of soul; but matter is repetition; the external world yields to mathematical laws; a superhuman intelligence which would know the position, the direction, and the speed of all the atoms and electrons of the material universe at a given moment could calculate any future state of this universe as we do in the case of an eclipse of the sun or the moon.—I admit all this for the sake of argument, if it concerns only the inert world and at least with regard to elementary phenomena, although this is beginning to be a much debated question. But this "inert" world is only an abstraction. Concrete reality comprises those living, conscious beings enframed in inorganic matter. I say living and conscious, for I believe that the living is conscious by right; it becomes unconscious in fact where consciousness falls asleep, but even in the regions where consciousness is in a state of somnolence, in the vegetable kingdom for example, there is regulated evolution, definite progress, aging; in fact, all the external signs of the duration which characterizes consciousness. And why must we speak of an inert matter into which life and consciousness would be inserted as in a frame? By what right do we put the inert first? The ancients had imagined a World Soul supposed to assure the continuity of existence of the material universe. Stripping this conception of its mythical element. I should say that the inorganic world is a series of infinitely rapid repetitions or quasi-repetitions which, when totalled, constitute visible and previsible changes. I should compare them to the swinging of the pendulum of a clock: the swingings of the pendulum are coupled to the continuous unwinding of a spring linking them together and whose unwinding they mark; the repetitions of the inorganic world constitute rhythm in the life of conscious beings and measure their duration. Thus the living being essentially has duration; it has duration precisely because it is continuously elaborating what is new and because there is no elaboration without searching, no searching without groping. Time is this very hesitation, or it is nothing. Suppress the conscious and the living (and you can do this only through an artificial effort of abstraction, for the material world once again implies perhaps the necessary presence of consciousness and of life), you obtain in fact a universe whose successive states are in theory calculable in advance, like the images placed side by side along the cinematographic film, prior to its unrolling. When then, the unrolling? Why does reality unfurl? Why is it not spread out? What good is time? (I refer to real, concrete time, and not to that abstract time which is only a fourth dimension of space.) This, in days gone by, was the starting-point of my reflections. Some fifty years ago I was very much attached to the philosophy of Spencer. I perceived one fine day that, in it, time served no purpose, did nothing. Nevertheless, I said to myself, time is something. Therefore it acts. What can it be doing? Plain common sense answered: time is what hinders everything from being given at once. It retards, or rather it is retardation. It must therefore, be *elaboration*. Would it not then be a vehicle of creation and of choice? Would not the existence of time prove that there is indetermination in things? Would not time be that indetermination itself?

If such is not the opinion of most philosophers, it is because human intelligence is made precisely to take things by the other end. I say intelligence, I do not say thought, I do not say mind. Alongside of intelligence there is in effect the immediate perception by each of us of his own activity and of the conditions in which it is exercised. Call it what you will; it is the feeling we have of being creators of our intentions, of our decisions, of our acts, and by that, of our habits, our characters, ourselves. Artisans of our life, even artists when we so desire, we work continually, with the material furnished us by the past and present, by heredity and opportunity, to mould a figure unique, new, original, as unforeseeable as the form given by the sculptor to the clay. Of this work and what there is unique about it we are warned, no doubt, even while it is being done, but the essential thing is that we do it. It is up to us to go deeply into it; it is not even necessary that we be fully conscious of it, any more than the artist needs to analyze his creative ability; he leaves that to the philosopher to worry about, being content, himself, simply to create. On the other hand, the sculptor must be familiar with the technique of his art and know everything that can be learned about it: this technique deals especially with what his work has in common with other works; it is governed by the demands of the material upon which he operates and which is imposed upon him as upon all artists; it concerns in art what is repetition or fabrication, and has nothing to do with creation itself. On it is concentrated the attention of the artist, what I should call his intellectuality. In the same way, in the creation of our character we know very little about our creative ability: in order to learn about it we should have to turn back upon ourselves, to philosophize, and to climb back up the slope of nature; for nature desired action, it hardly thought about speculation. The moment it is no longer simply a question of feeling an impulse within oneself and of being assured that one can act, but of turning thought upon itself in order that it may seize this ability and catch this impulse, the difficulty becomes great, as if the whole normal direction of consciousness had to be reversed. On the contrary we have a supreme interest in familiarizing ourselves with the technique of our action, that is to say in extracting from the conditions in which it is exercised, all that can furnish us with recipes and general rules upon which to base our conduct. There will be novelty in our acts thanks only to the repetition we have found in things. Our normal faculty of knowing is then essentially a power of extracting what stability and regularity there is in the flow of reality. Is it a question of perceiving? Perception seizes upon the infinitely repeated shocks which are light or heat, for example, and contracts them into relatively invariable sensations: trillions of external vibrations are what the vision of a color condenses in our eyes in the fraction of a second. Is it a question of conceiving? To form a general idea is to abstract from varied and changing things a common aspect which does not change or at least offers an invariable hold to our action. The invariability of our attitude, the identity of our eventual or virtual reaction to the multiplicity and variability of the objects represented is what first marks and delineates the generality of the idea. Finally, is it a question of understanding? It is simply finding connections, establishing stable relations between transitory facts, evolving laws; an operation which is much more perfect as the relation becomes more definite and the law more mathematical. All these functions are constitutives of the intellect. And the intellect is in the line of truth so long as it attaches itself, in its penchant for regularity and stability, to what is stable and regular in the real, that is to say to materiality. In so doing it touches one of the sides of the absolute, as our consciousness touches another when it grasps within us a perpetual efflorescence of novelty or when, broadening out, it comes into sympathy with that effort of nature which is constantly renewing. Error begins when the intellect claims to think one of the aspects as it thought the other, directing its powers on something for which it was not intended.

I believe that the great metaphysical problems are in general badly stated, that they frequently resolve themselves of their own accord when correctly stated, or else are problems formulated in terms of illusion which disappear as soon as the terms of the formula are more closely examined. They arise in fact from our habit of transposing into fabrication what is creation. Reality is global, and undivided growth, progressive invention, duration: it resembles a gradually expanding rubber balloon assuming at each moment unexpected forms. But our intelligence imagines its origin and evolution as an arrangement and rearrangement of parts which supposedly merely shift from one place to another; in theory therefore, it should be able to foresee any one state of the whole; by positing a definite number of stable elements one has, predetermined, all their possible combinations. That is not all. Reality, as immediately perceived, is fullness constantly swelling out, to which emptiness is unknown. It has extension just as it has duration; but this concrete extent is not the infinite and infinitely divisible space the intellect takes as a place in which to build. Concrete space has been extracted from things. They are not in it; it is space which is in them. Only, as soon as our thought reasons about reality, it makes space a receptacle. As it has the habit of assembling parts in a relative vacuum, it imagines that reality fills up some absolute kind of vacuum. Now, if the failure to recognize radical novelty is the original cause of those badly stated metaphysical questions, the habit of proceeding from emptiness to fullness is the source of problems which are non-existent. Moreover, it is easy to see that the second mistake is already implied in the first. But I should like first of all to define it more precisely.

I say that there are pseudo-problems, and that they are the agonizing problems of metaphysics. I reduce them to two. One gave rise to theories of being, the other to theories of knowledge. The first false problem consists in asking oneself why there is being, why something or someone exists. The nature of what is, is of little importance; say that it is matter, or mind, or both, or that matter and mind are not self-sufficient and manifest a transcendent Cause: in any case, when existences and causes are brought into consideration and the causes of these causes, one feels as if pressed into a race—if one calls a halt, it is to avoid dizziness. But just the same one sees, or thinks one sees, that the difficulty still exists, that the problem is still there and will never be solved. It will never, in fact, be solved, but it should never have been raised. It arises only if one posits a nothingness which supposedly precedes being. One says: "There could be nothing," and then is astonished that there should be something—or someone. But analyze that sentence: "There could be nothing." You will see you are dealing with words, not at all with ideas, and that "nothing" here has no meaning. "Nothing" is a term in ordinary language which can only have meaning in the sphere, proper to man, of action and fabrication. "Nothing" designates the absence of what we are seeking, we desire, expect. Let us suppose that absolute emptiness was known to our experience: it would be limited, have contours, and would therefore be something. But in reality there is no vacuum. We perceive and can conceive only occupied space. One thing disappears only because another replaces it. Suppression thus means substitution. We say "suppression," however, when we envisage, in the case of substitution, only one of its two halves, or rather the one of its two sides which interests us; in this way we indicate a desire to turn our attention to the object which is gone, and away from the one replacing it.

We say then that there is nothing more, meaning by that, that what exists does not interest us, that we are interested in what is no longer there or in what might have been there. The idea of absence, or of nothingness, or of nothing, is therefore inseparably bound to that of suppression, real or eventual, and the idea of suppression is itself only an aspect of the idea of substitution. Those are the ways of thinking we use in practical life; it is particularly essential to our industry that our thought should be able to lag behind reality and remain attached, when need be, to what was or to what might be, instead of being absorbed by what is. But when we go from the domain of fabrication to that of creation, when we ask ourselves why there is being, why something or someone, why the world or God, exists and why not nothingness, when, in short, we set ourselves the most agonising of metaphysical problems, we virtually accept an absurdity; for if all suppression is a substitution, if the idea of a suppression is only the truncated idea of a substitution, then to speak of a suppression of everything is to posit a substitution which would not be one, that is, to be self-contradictory. Either the idea of a suppression of everything has just about as much existence as that of a round square—the existence of a sound, *flatus vocis*—or else, if it does represent something, it translates a movement of the intellect from one object to another, preferring the one it has just left to the object it finds before it, and designates by "absence of the first" the presence of the second. We have posited the whole, then made each of its parts disappear one by one, without consenting to see what replaced it; it is therefore the totality of presences, simply arranged in a new order, that one has in mind in attempting to total up the absences. In other words, this so-called representation of absolute emptiness is, in reality, that of universal fullness in a mind which leaps indefinitely from part to part, with the fixed resolution never to consider anything but the emptiness of its dissatisfaction instead of the fullness of things. All of which amounts to saying that the idea of Nothing, when it is not that of a simple word, implies as much matter as the idea of All, with, in addition, an operation of thought.

I should say as much of the idea of disorder. Why is the universe well ordered? How is rule imposed upon what is without rule, and form upon matter? How is it that our thought recognises itself in things? This problem, which among the moderns has become the problem of knowledge after having been, among the ancients, the problem of being, was born of an illusion of the same order. It disappears if one considers that the idea of disorder has a definite meaning in the domain of human industry or, as we say, of fabrication, but not in that of creation. Disorder is simply the order we are not looking for. You cannot suppress one order even by thought, without causing another to spring up. If there is not finality or will, it is because there is mechanism; if the mechanism gives way, so much the gain for will, caprice, finality. But when you expect one of these two orders and you find the other, you say there is disorder, formulating what is in terms of what might or should be, and objectifying your regret. All disorder thus includes two things: outside us, one order; within us, the representation of a different order which alone interests us. Suppression therefore again signifies substitution. And the idea of a suppression of all order, that is to say, the idea of an absolute disorder, then contains a veritable contradiction, because it consists in leaving only a single aspect to the operation which, by hypothesis, embraced two. Either the idea of an absolute disorder represents no more than a combination of sounds, *flatus vocis,* or else, if it corresponds to something, it translates a movement of the mind which leaps from mechanism to finality, from finality to mechanism, and which, in order to mark the spot where it is, prefers each time to indicate the point where it is not. Therefore, in wishing to suppress order, you find yourself with two or more "orders." This is tantamount to saying that the conception of an order which is superadded to an "absence of order" implies an absurdity, and that the problem disappears.

The two illusions I have just mentioned are in reality only one. They consist in believing that there is *less* in the idea of the empty than in the idea of the full, *less* in the concept of disorder than in that of order. In reality, there is more intellectual content in the ideas of disorder and nothingness when they represent something than in those of order and existence, because they imply several orders, several existences and, in addition, a play of wit which unconsciously juggles with them.

Very well then, I find the same illusion in the case in point. Underlying the doctrines which disregard the radical novelty of each moment of evolution there are many misunderstandings, many errors. But there is especially the idea that the possible is *less* than the real, and that, for this reason, the possibility of things precedes their existence. They would thus be capable of representation beforehand; they could be thought of before being realised. But it is the reverse that is true. If we leave aside the closed systems, subjected to purely mathematical laws, isolable because duration does not act upon them, if we consider the totality of concrete reality or simply the world of life, and still more that of consciousness, we find there is more and not less in the possibility of each of the successive states than in their reality. For the possible is only the real with the addition of an act of mind which throws its image back into the past, once it has been enacted. But that is what our intellectual habits prevent us from seeing.

During the great war certain newspapers and periodicals sometimes turned aside from the terrible worries of the day to think of what would happen later once peace was restored. They were particularly preoccupied with the future of literature. Someone came one day to ask me my ideas on the subject. A little embarrassed, I declared I had none. "Do you not at least perceive," I was asked, "certain possible directions? Let us grant that one cannot foresee things in detail; you as a philosopher have at least an idea of the whole. How do you conceive, for example, the great dramatic work of tomorrow?" I shall always remember my interlocutor's surprise when I answered, "If I knew what was to be the great dramatic work of the future, I should be writing it." I saw distinctly that he conceived the future work as being already stored up in some cupboard reserved for possibles; because of my long-standing relations with philosophy, I should have been able to obtain from it the key to the storehouse. "But," I said, "the work of which you speak is not yet possible."—"But it must be, since it is to take place."—"No, it is not. I grant you, at most, that it *will have been possible*."—"What do you mean by that?"—"It's quite simple. Let a man of talent or genius come forth, let him create a work: it will then be real, and by that very fact it becomes retrospectively or retroactively possible. It would not be possible, it would not have been so, if this man had not come upon the scene. That is why I tell you that it will have been possible today, but that it is not yet so."—"You're not serious! You are surely not going to maintain that the future has an effect upon the present, that the present brings something into the past, that action works back over the course of time and imprints its mark afterwards?"—"That depends. That one can put reality into the past and thus work backwards in time is something I have never claimed. But that one can put the possible there, or rather that the possible may put itself there at any moment, is not to be doubted. As reality is created as something unforeseeable and new, its image is reflected behind it into the indefinite past; thus it finds that it has from all time been possible, but it is at this precise moment that it begins to have been always possible, and that is why I said that its possibility, which does not precede its reality, will have preceded it once the reality has appeared. The possible is therefore the mirage of the present in the past; and as we know the future will finally constitute a present and the mirage effect is continually being produced, we are convinced that the image of tomorrow is already contained in our actual present, which will be the past of tomorrow, although we did not manage to grasp it. That is precisely the illusion. It is as though one were to fancy, in seeing his reflection in the mirror in front of him, that he could have touched it had he stayed behind it. Thus in judging that the possible does not presuppose the real, one admits that the realisation adds something to the simple possibility: the possible would have been there from all time, a phantom awaiting its hour; it would therefore have become reality by the addition of something, by some transfusion of blood or life. One does not see that the contrary is the case, that the possible implies the corresponding reality with, moreover, something added, since the possible is the combined effect of reality once it has appeared and of a condition which throws it back in time. The idea immanent in most philosophies and natural to the human mind, of possibles which would be realised by an acquisition of existence, is therefore pure illusion. One might as well claim that the man in flesh and blood comes from the materialization of his image seen in the mirror, because in that real man is everything found in this virtual image with, in addition, the solidity which makes it possible to touch it. But the truth is that more is needed here to obtain the virtual than is necessary for the real, more for the image of the man than for the man himself, for the image of the man will not be portrayed if the man is not first produced, and in addition one has to have the mirror."

That is what my interlocutor was forgetting as he questioned me on the

theatre of tomorrow. Perhaps too he was unconsciously playing on the meaning of the word "possible." *Hamlet* was doubtless possible before being realised, if that means that there was no insurmountable obstacle to its realisation.
In this particular sense one calls possible what is not impossible; and it stands
to reason that this non-impossibility of a thing is the condition of its realisation.
But the possible thus understood is in no degree virtual, something ideally pre-
existent. If you close the gate you know no one will cross the road; it does
not follow that you can predict who will cross when you open it. Nevertheless,
from the quite negative sense of the term "impossible" you pass surreptitiously,
unconsciously to the positive sense. Possibility signified "absence of hindrance"
a few minutes ago: now you make of it a "pre-existence under the form of an
idea," which is quite another thing. In the first meaning of the word it was
a truism to say that the possibility of a thing precedes its reality: by that you
meant simply that obstacles, having been surmounted, were surmountable.
But in the second meaning it is an absurdity, for it is clear that a mind in which
the *Hamlet* of Shakespeare had taken shape in the form of possible would by
that fact have created its reality: it would thus have been, by definition, Shakespeare himself. In vain do you imagine at first that this mind could have appeared before Shakespeare; it is because you are not thinking then of all the
the details in the play. As you complete them the predecessor of Shakespeare
finds himself thinking all that Shakespeare will think, feeling all he will feel,
knowing all he will know, perceiving therefore all he will perceive, and consequently occupying the same point in space and time, having the same body
and the same soul: it is Shakespeare himself.

But I am putting too much stress on what is self-evident. We are forced to
these considerations in discussing a work of art. I believe in the end we shall
consider it evident that the artist in executing his work is creating the possible
as well as the real. Whence comes it then that one might hesitate to say the
same thing for nature? Is not the world a work of art incomparably richer than
that of the greatest artist? And is there not as much absurdity, if not more, in
supposing, in the work of nature, that the future is outlined in advance, that
possibility existed before reality? Once more let me say I am perfectly willing
to admit that the future states of a closed system of material points are calculable and hence visible in its present state. But, and I repeat, this system is
extracted, or abstracted, from a whole which, in addition to inert and un-
organised matter, compromises organisation. Take the concrete and complete
world, with the life and consciousness it encloses; consider nature in its entirety, nature the generator of new species as novel and original in form as the
design of any artist: in these species concentrate upon individuals, plants or
animals, each of which has its own character—I was going to say its personality (for one blade of grass does not resemble another blade of grass any
more than a Raphael resembles a Rembrandt); lift your attention above and
beyond individual man to societies which disclose actions and situations com-

parable to those of any drama: how can one still speak of possibles which would precede their own realisation? How can we fail to see that if the event can always be explained afterwards by an arbitrary choice of antecedent events, a completely different event could have been equally well explained in the same circumstances by another choice of antecedent—nay, by the same antecedents otherwise cut out, otherwise distributed, otherwise perceived,—in short, by our retrospective attention? Backwards over the course of time a constant remodelling of the past by the present, of the cause by the effect, is being carried out.

We do not see it, always for the same reason, always a prey to the same illusion, always because we treat as the more what is the less, as the less what is the more. If we put the possible back into its proper place, evolution becomes something quite different from the realisation of a program: the gates of the future open wide; freedom is offered an unlimited field. The fault of those doctrines,—rare indeed in the history of philosophy,—which have succeeded in leaving room for indetermination and freedom in the world, is to have failed to see what their affirmation implied. When they spoke of indetermination, of freedom, they meant by indetermination a competition between possibles, by freedom a choice between possibles,—as if possibility was not created by freedom itself! As if any other hypothesis, by affirming an ideal preexistence of the possible to the real, did not reduce the new to a mere rearrangement of former elements! As if it were not thus to be led sooner or later to regard that rearrangement as calculable and foreseeable! By accepting the premiss of the contrary theory one was letting the enemy in. We must resign ourselves to the inevitable: it is the real which makes itself possible, and not the possible which becomes real.

But the truth is that philosophy has never frankly admitted this continuous creation of unforeseeable novelty. The ancients already revolted against it because, Platonists to a greater or less degree, they imagined that Being was given once and for all, complete and perfect, in the immutable system of Ideas: the world which unfolds before our eyes could therefore add nothing to it; it was, on the contrary, only diminution or degradation; its successive states measured as it were the increasing or decreasing distance between what is, a shadow projected in time, and what ought to be, Idea set in eternity; they would outline the variations of a deficiency, the changing form of a void. It was Time which, according to them, spoiled everything. The moderns, it is true, take a quite different point of view. They no longer treat Time as an intruder, a disturber of eternity; but they would very much like to reduce it to a simple appearance. The temporal is, then, only the confused form of the rational. What we perceive as being a succession of states is conceived by our intellect, once the fog has settled, as a system of relations. The real becomes once more the eternal, with this single difference, that it is the eternity of the Laws in which the phenomena are resolved instead of being the eternity of the

Ideas which serve them as models. But in each case, we are dealing with theories. Let us stick to the facts. Time is immediately given. That is sufficient for us, and until its inexistence or perversity is proved to us we shall merely register that there is effectively a flow of unforeseeable novelty.

Philosophy stands to gain in finding some absolute in the moving world of phenomena. But we shall gain also in our feeling of greater joy and strength. Greater joy because the reality invented before our eyes will give each one of us, unceasingly, certain of the satisfactions which art at rare intervals procures for the privileged; it will reveal to us, beyond the fixity and monotony which our senses, hypnotized by our constant needs, at first perceived in it, ever-recurring novelty, the moving originality of things. But above all we shall have greater strength, for we shall feel we are participating, creators of ourselves, in the great work of creation which is the origin of all things and which goes on before our eyes. By getting hold of itself, our faculty for acting will become intensified. Humbled heretofore in an attitude of obedience, slaves of certain vaguely-felt natural necessities, we shall once more stand erect, masters associated with a greater Master. To such a conclusion will our study bring us. In this speculation on the relation between the possible and the real, let us guard against seeing a simple game. It can be a preparation for the art of living.

Essence and Existence

Thomas Aquinas

14. THE COMPOSITION OF ESSENCE AND EXISTENCE

As previous selections indicate, the notions of *act* of existing (*esse*) and creation take first rank in the metaphysics of St. Thomas. In the following passage, St. Thomas investigates the relation between created reals and *esse*.

In any understanding of created realities, he points out, one must distinguish between essence and existence in the same manner that one distinguishes between potentiality and act. Essences can be known insofar as

From *An Introduction to the Metaphysics of St. Thomas*, edited by James F. Anderson. Copyright 1953. Reprinted by permission of the publisher, Henry Regnery Company, Chicago.

they are intelligible but in such knowledge there is no implication of existence. The act of existing is other than essence, nature, or form, for it enters
into composition with these. Since only in God is essence the act of existing, every created being participates in the act of existing, but does not
hold claim to it of itself. In created reals, the act of existing is participated;
whereas, in God it is His substance. Though the act of existing is not
diverse, but is one, it is still diversified among created reals.

For St. Thomas, the composition of potentiality and act therefore applies
to all created reals. This composition is more comprehensive than that of
matter and form, or that of substance and act of existing, for it includes
both. Matter is not substance, but a part of substance: if it were substance,
then form would be simply an accident. Furthermore, the act of existing is
not the proper act of matter, but of the whole substance. Conversely, form
is not the act of existing, for form is related to act of existing as essence
is to "actuation," as "whiteness" is to "the act of being white."

Three terms, therefore, must clearly be set apart: form, substance, and
act of existing. By form is meant that-by-which-a-thing-is, *quo est;* by
substance, that-which-is, *quod est;* and by act of existing, that-by-which-
the-substance-is-denominated-a-being.

In spiritual or intellectual substances there is a single composition of act
and potentiality: form is itself a subsistent, or substance, and is therefore
quod est; whereas act of existing is *quo est,* that by which the form is. In
such substances, there is a single composition of act and potentiality—
that is, of act of existing and substance. In nonintellectual substances, on
the other hand, there is a twofold composition of act and potentiality: in
the first place, there is substance itself, which is composed of matter and
form; and in the second place, there is substance and act of existing.

Hence, the composition of act and potentiality is the one comprehensive
character of created realities. Natural or material substance is divided
along the lines of matter and form, but all created being—material and
immaterial—is divided along the line of act and potentiality.

IT IS CLEAR from what has been said already that in every created thing essence is *distinct* from existence and is compared to the latter as potentiality to
act. Every created being participates in the act of existing; God alone is His
act of existing. The act of existing of every finite thing is participated, because
no thing outside God is its own act of existing.

Whatever is participated is related to the participator as its act. . . . But
participated act of existing is limited by the (receptive) capacity of the participator. Hence God alone, who is His own act of existing, is pure and infinite
act. In intellectual substances, indeed, there is a composition of act and potentiality; not, however, of matter and form, but of form and participated act
of existing.

Now, act of existing, as such, cannot be diverse; yet it can be diversified by something extrinsic to itself; for instance, a stone's act of existing is other than that of a man.

God's act of existing is distinguished and set apart from every other act of existing by the fact that it is self-subsistent, and does not come to a nature [or an essence] other than itself. Every other act of existing, being non-subsisting, must be individuated by the nature and substance which subsists in that act of existing. And regarding these things [namely all creatures] it is true to say that the act of existing of this one is other than the act of existing of that one, inasmuch as it belongs to another nature. So, if there were one color existing in itself, without matter, or without a subject, by this very fact it would be distinguished from every other color; since colors existing in subjects are distinguished only through those subjects.

Because the quiddity of an intelligence is that very intelligence itself, its quiddity or essence is that which it itself is, and its existence, received from God, is that by which it subsists in the nature of things. Some therefore have said that substances of this kind are composed of that-by-which-they-are [the *quo est*] and that-which-they-are [the *quod est*] or that-by-which-they-are and essence. . . .

Whatever does not belong to the concept of essence or quiddity comes from without and and enters into composition with the essence, for no essence can be understood without its essential parts. But every essence or quiddity can be understood without anything being known of its actual existence. For example, I can understand what a man or a phoenix is and yet be ignorant whether either one exists in reality. It is evident, then, that act of existing is other than essence or quiddity—unless, perhaps, there exists a reality whose quiddity is its very act of existing. And there can be only one such reality: the First Being. . . . In every other being, act of existing is other than quiddity, nature, or form.

The act of existing belongs to the First Agent, God, through His own nature; for God's act of existing is His substance. . . . But that which belongs to something according to its own nature, appertains to other things only by participation. . . . Thus the act of existing is possessed by other things, from the First Agent, through a certain participation. But that which a thing has by participation is not its very own substance. Therefore it is impossible that the substance of anything except the First Agent should be the act of existing itself.

Now, the composition of matter and form is not of the same nature as the composition of substance and act of existing, though both compositions are of potentiality and act. This is so, first of all, because matter is not the very substance of a thing. If it were, then all forms would be accidents, as the ancient Naturalists thought. Rather, matter is a part of the substance. Secondly, this is so because the act of existing itself is not the proper act of the matter, but of the whole substance. For *esse* is the act of that whereof we can say: it *is; esse* is not said of the matter, but of the whole. Matter, therefore, cannot be termed that-which-is. On the contrary, the substance itself is that-which-is. Thirdly, the aforesaid compositions are diverse, because the form is not the act of existing, though between the two there exists a certain order. Form is compared to the act of existing as light to the act of illuminating, for instance, or as whiteness to the act of being white. Finally, there is this consideration: existence is act even in relation to the form itself. For in things composed of matter and form, the form is said to be a principle of existing because it is what completes the substance, whose act is *esse* itself. . . .

To sum up: in things composed of matter and form, neither the matter nor the form can be designated as that-which-is, nor even can the act of existing be so designated. However, form can be called that-by-which-a-thing-is, or exists (*quo est*), inasmuch as it is a principle of existing. Nevertheless, it is the whole substance which is that-which-is (*quod est*), and the act of existing is that by which the substance is denominated a *being*.

In intellectual substances (which . . . are not composed of matter and form, but form in them is itself a subsisting substance) form is that-which-is (*quod est*), whereas *esse* is act and that-by-which the form is (*quo est*). So in them there is but one composition of act and potentiality, namely, the composition of substance and act of existing, which by some is called a composition of that-which-is (*quod est*) and act of existing (*esse*), or that-which-is (*quod est*) and that-by-which-it-is (*quo est*).

On the other hand, in substances composed of matter and form there is a twofold composition of potentiality and act: first, that of the substance itself, which is composed of matter and form; second, that of the substance, thus composed, and its act of existing. This composition also can be called one of that-which-is (*quod est*) and act of existing (*esse*), or of that-which-is (*quod est*) and that-by-which-it-is (*quo est*).

It is evident, therefore, that the composition of act and potentiality is more comprehensive than that of form and matter; matter and form divide natural substance, potentiality and act divide universal being. Accordingly, whatever follows upon potentiality and act, as such, is common to both material and immaterial created substances, as *to receive* and *to be received, to perfect* and *to be perfected*. Yet, all that is proper to matter and form, as such, as *to be generated* and *corrupted,* and the like, appertain to material substances only, and in no way belong to immaterial created substances.

George Santayana   **15. THE BEING PROPER**
TO ESSENCES

For St. Thomas, essence is real but not existent; it is ordered, however, to an existential status. For Santayana, in contrast, essence is more "real" than any existent could be, for essence stands continually and intelligibly in opposition to the irrational realm of natural entities.

Every essence, Santayana says, is at the same time *individual*—because the principle of its being is self-identity—and *universal*—because, while retaining its absolute identity, it can be recalled to mind, repeated, and reviewed any number of times: "I am not myself unless I re-enact now the essence of myself, which I may re-enact at all times and places."

Furthermore, essence is autonomous in its own realm and indestructible: "There . . . it stands, waiting to be embodied or noticed, if nature or attention ever choose to halt at that point or to traverse it." Essence is "always standing behind the door."

Natural or existent entities, in contrast, are measured against essence. Essence cannot be empirically investigated because it has its being in a non-material realm. It is "an inert theme, something which cannot bring itself forward, but must be chosen, if chosen, by some external agent." Where existence is irrational, essence is fully intelligible. It is the program for nature, and "tempts nature with openings in every direction; and in so doing it manifests its own inexhaustible variety."

The reality of essence is not an existential reality, but a reality of limitations, for essences are the "patterns" of all possibilities. While essence does not exist, it is nonetheless real and *in being*. "To deny the being of essence, because it may happen to be unrealized, is self-contradictory; for if it is not realized, it must have a quality, distinguishing it from realized forms." Indeed, says Santayana, essence "much more truly *is* than any substance or any experience or any event." Unchangeable and inevitable, its reality is classically real. Without essence there could be no existence, since essence "is just that character which any existence wears insofar as it remains identical with itself and as long as it does so." When an existent changes, it does so by an alteration in the essential clothing it wears: at every step, existence "casts off one essence and picks up another." Hence, only essence is the truly real.

This selection is reprinted by kind permission of Charles Scribner's Sons and Constable and Company Limited, from *The Realm of Essence*.

Each Essence Is by Being Identical and Individual

THE PRINCIPLE of essence, we have seen, is identity: the being of each essence is entirely exhausted by its definition; I do not mean its definition in words, but the character which distinguishes it from any other essence. Every essence is perfectly individual. There can be no question in the realm of essence of mistaken identity, vagueness, shiftiness, or self-contradiction. These doubts arise in respect to natural existences or the meanings or purposes of living minds: but in every doubt or equivocation both alternatives are genuine essences; and in groping and making up my mind I merely hesitate between essences, not knowing on which to arrest my attention. There is no possibility of flux or ambiguity within any of the alternatives which might be chosen at each step.

Also Universal

This inalienable individuality of each essence renders it a universal; for being perfectly self-contained and real only by virtue of its intrinsic character, it contains no reference to any setting in space or time, and stands in no adventitious relations to anything. Therefore without forfeiting its absolute identity it may be repeated or reviewed any number of times. Such embodiments or views of it, like the copies of a book or the acts of reading it, will be facts or events in nature (which is a net of external relations); but the copies would not be copies of the same book, nor the readings readings of it, unless (and in so far as) the same essence reappeared in them all. Physical obstacles to exact repetitions or reproductions do not affect the essential universality of every essence, even if by chance it occurs only once, or never occurs at all; because, in virtue of its perfect identity and individuality, it cannot fall out of the catalogue of essences, where it fills its particular place. If I try to delete it, I reinstate it, since in deleting *that* I have recognised and defined it anew, bearing witness to its possessing the whole being which it can claim as an essence. There accordingly it stands, waiting to be embodied or noticed, if nature or attention ever choose to halt at that point or to traverse it. Every essence in its own realm is just as central, just as normal, and just as complete as any other: it is therefore always just as open to exemplification or to thought, without the addition or subtraction of one iota of its being. Time and space may claim and repeat it as often or as seldom as they will: that is their own affair. The flux is free to have such plasticity as it has, and to miss all that it misses; and it is free to be as monotonous as it likes, if it finds it easier to fall again and again into the same form, rather than to run away into perpetual and unreturning novelties. The realm of essence is the scale of measurement, the continuum of variation, on which these repetitions or these novelties may be plotted and compared. Re-embodiments or re-surveys of an essence (if they occur) bind the parts of the flux together ideally, and render it amenable to description. The essential universality of these forms makes any fact, in so far as it exhibits them, distinct and knowable: the universal and the individual being so far from contrary that they are identical. I am not myself unless I re-enact now the essence of myself, which I may re-enact at all times and places.

Essences Are Infinite in Number

Since essences are universals not needing to figure in any particular place or time, but fit to figure in any, it is not possible to investigate the realm of essence by empirical exploration. You cannot go in search of that which is nowhere. Some essences will appear or occur to you, since whatever intuition life may awaken in you must light up some essence or other; but what further essences, if any, there may be is not discoverable by simply waiting for them to turn up. Nature is indeed very rich in forms, compared with the inertia and monotony of experience in home-keeping animals, revolving in their private circle of habits and ideas; but nature too is built on a single plan—all nuclei and planets, all life and death—and as much a slave of routine as any of her creatures. The unexemplified is not exemplified there, the unthought of is not thought of; not because in itself it resists being created or described, but because nature and thought happen not to bloom in any way but that in which they have taken to blooming. In part, indeed, this restriction may be due to local prejudice and ignorance in the observer, who draws the periphery of nature with his compass. Another man, a different animal, a spirit native to another world may even now be greeting the essences which it has not entered into my heart to conceive. Evidently my limitations cannot forbid them to rejoice in their different experience; nor can the limitations of any actual experience forbid the essences it leaves out to be just those which are absent. An essence is an inert theme, something which cannot bring itself forward, but must be chosen, if chosen, by some external agent; and evidently the choice made by this agent, contingent as it is and wholly arbitrary, cannot render unavailable the other inert themes which other agents, or itself in a different moment of its flux, might choose instead. The very contingency of existence, the very blindness of life, throws the doors wide open towards the infinity of being. Even if some philosopher or some god thought himself omniscient, surprises might be in store for him, and thoughts new to his thought; nay, even supposing that his whole experience and the entire history of his world lay synthesised before him under the form of eternity, and that he was not a victim of sheer egotism in asserting that nothing more could ever exist, still the wanton idiosyncrasy of that total fact, the enormity of that accident, could not be blustered away. Existence is irrational for a deeper and more intrinsic reason than because one part of it may not be deducible from another: any part, and all its parts together, are irrational in merely existing, and in being otherwise than as essences are, that is, identical with themselves and endowed with that formal being which it is impossible that anything, whatever it be, should not possess. Not that essence can resist or resent this irrational selection which existence makes of its riches: on the contrary, essence is a sort of invitation to the dance; it tempts nature with openings in every direction; and in so doing it manifests its own inexhaustible variety. Its very being is to set no limits to the forms of being. The multitude of essences is absolutely infinite.

But Non-existent; They Form an Indelible Background to All Transitory Facts

This assertion has an audacious sound, and I should not venture upon it, had it not a counterpart or corollary which takes away all its venom, namely, that essences do not *exist*. If I were in pursuit of substance (as I shall be in the Second Book) I should distrust any description of it not purely tentative, empirical, and scrupulously modest: but the bold definition which Spinoza gives of what he calls substance, that it is Being absolutely infinite, seems to me a perfect and self-justifying definition of the realm of essence: because in conceiving and defining such an object we prove it to possess the only being which we mean to ascribe to it. Denying it to be infinite, or denying that any supposed element in it existed, we should be designating these missing elements and that absent infinity; whereby we should be instituting them ideally, and recognising them to be essences. The realm of essence is comparable to an infinite Koran—or the Logos that was in the beginning— written in invisible but indelible ink, prophesying all that Being could ever be or contain: and the flux of existence is the magical re-agent, travelling over it in a thin stream, like a reader's eye, and bringing here one snatch of it and there another to the light for a passing moment. Each reader may be satisfied with his own verse, and think it the whole of Scripture: but the mere assertion of this limit, or suspicion that other readers might find other texts, is enough to show that the non-existent cannot be limited, since the limits of the existent might always be changed. To deny the being of essence, because it may happen to be unrealised, is self-contradictory: for if it is not realised, it must have a quality, distinguishing it from realised forms. Unrealised forms may not interest a sluggish mind: an arithmetician who was happy in the thought of whole numbers, might deprecate all mention of vulgar fractions or repeating decimals, and might swear to die without them, lest his safe and honest arithmetic should be complicated with unrealities. But unrealities of that sort nevertheless envelop his realities on every side; and it is his arrest at his realities that, if you like, is unreal; there is no reason in it, and no permanence; whereas the unrealities are unchangeable, inevitable, and always standing behind the door. Even if the whole realm of essence (as Spinoza assumed) were realised some-where at some time in the life of nature, essence would remain a different and a non-existent realm: because the realisation of each part could be only local and temporary, and for all the rest of time and in all the worlds that excluded it, each fact would fade into the corresponding essence, and would remain cer-tain and inevitable as an essence only, and as a fact merely presumptive.

Existence and Truth Borrow Their Individuality from Essence

Essence so understood much more truly *is* than any substance or any ex-perience or any event: for a substance, event, or experience may change its form or may exist only by changing it, so that all sorts of thngs that are proper to it in one phase will be absent from it in another. It will not be a unit at all, save by external delimitation. Perhaps some abstract constancy in quantity, energy, or continuity may be discovered to run through it, but this constant element will never be the actual experience, event, or substance in its living totality at any moment. Or perhaps all the phases of such an existence may be viewed together and synthesised into one historical picture; but this picture would again not be the existent substance, experience, or event unrolling itself in act. It would be only a description of that portion of the flux seen under the form of eternity; in other words, it would be an essence and not an existence. Essence is just that character which any existence wears in so far as it remains identical with itself and so long as it does so; the very character which it throws overboard by changing, and loses altogether when it becomes something else. To be able to become something else, to suffer change and yet endure, is the privilege of existence, be it in a substance, an event, or an experience; whereas essences can be exchanged, but not changed. Existence at every step casts off one essence and picks up another: we call it the same existence when we are able to trace its continuity in change, by virtue of its locus and proportions; but often we are constrained to give up the count, and to speak of a new event, a new thing, or a new experience. The essences or forms traversed in mutation render this mutation possible and describable: without their eternal distinctness no part of the flux could differ in any respect from any other part, and the whole would collapse into a lump without order or quality. So much more profound is the eternal being of the essences traversed in change than that of the matter or attention or discourse which plays with those essences at touch and go.

Notion of the Realm of Essence

Nothing, then, more truly *is* than character. Without this wedding garment no guest is admitted to the feast of existence: whereas the unbidden essences do not require that invitation (with which very low characters are sometimes honoured) in order to preserve their proud identity out in the cold. There those few privileged revellers will soon have to rejoin them, not a whit fatter for their brief surfeit of being. After things lose their existence, as before they attain it, although it is true of them that they have existed or will exist, they have no internal being except their essences, quite as if they had never broached Existence at all: yet the identity of each essence with itself and difference from every other essence suffices to distinguish and define them all in eternity, where they form the Realm of Essence. True and false assertions may be made about any one of them, such, for instance, as that it does not exist; or that it includes or excludes some other essence, or is included or excluded by it.

Its Eternity Is the Counterpart of Its Non-existence

Here is a further character inseparable from essence: all essences are eternal. No hyperbole or rhetorical afflatus is contained in this assertion, as if some prophet pronounced some law or some city to be everlasting. That any existing thing should be everlasting, though not impossible, is incongruous with the contingency of existence. God or matter, if they are everlasting, are so by a sort of iterated contingency and perpetual reproduction; for it is in the nature of existence to be here and perhaps not there, now and perhaps not then; it must be explored to discover how far it may stretch; it must wait and see how long it shall last. The assumption that it lasts or stretches for ever can be made only impetuously, by animal enthusiasm, when the feeling of readiness and omnipotence makes some living creature defy all threats of disaster. Yet so long as we live in time, the ghost of the murdered past will always fill the present with a profound uneasiness. If the eternity of essence were conceived after that fashion, it would indeed be a rash boast; no essence has an essential lien on existence anywhere, much less everywhere and always. Its eternity has nothing to do with such mortal hazards. It is merely the self-identity proper to each of the forms which existence may put on or off, illustrate always, or very likely never illustrate at all.

Dom Mark Pontifex,   16. WHAT IS EXISTENCE?
O.S.B.

In this essay, Dom Mark Pontifex criticizes the separation in real being that he feels is often implied by the terms "essence" and "existence," and attempts to understand being noncompositively. For him the term "existence" is synonymous with "being"; both entail "assertibility," since what is being can be "asserted of."

Existence, or being, indicates what is common or similar in every object known or knowable but what cannot be identified completely with each particular being. What is not expressed by any other term finds its apt expression, therefore, in these words.

Existence, taken in this sense, is not merely a subjective idea, but wholly objective. Its authentic meaning becomes clearer if it is contrasted with its inadequate interpretations. First, existence is not merely the most universal category, a *summum genus,* available to discourse, since it would be contradictory to consider it simply as an attribute when, in fact, it is a subject of attribution. Nor is it, second, some primordial "stuff," or possibility, out of which everything is formed, or made actual. In order to be such, it would have to be indeterminate; and clearly it cannot be indeterminate and being at the same time. Moreover, it does not stand as a composite term under which all particulars may be hung—a sort of "whole" as distinct from "parts"—because it would then be a diverse term, having the distinctness of so many parts added together. Fourth, it cannot refer to something other than the different objects we actually know because our assertions are always about objects and what they are, not about something other. Finally, we commonly do not intend that existential propositions be simply descriptive, or "characterizing," propositions, but that they be propositions touching the real.

With the Thomistic distinction between essence and existence analogically conceived, Pontifex is not entirely satisfied, for he finds it hard to imagine how essence and existence "can be distinct in such a way that really and objectively there can be a proportion between them." Once the relation of proportion is introduced, we have something external to existence, because it is not identified with existence. If essence and existence are distinct, he asks, how then can existence refer both to an element in the whole and to the relation between that element and another element, essence?

He believes that the Thomist theory, however, supplies the clue to a solution, because it considers existence in some way to refer to a double object.

Such a consideration "enables us to see how existence can have apparently contradictory meanings"—that is, how existence can refer to the same things as like and unlike. Existence must therefore refer (*a*) to each thing; (*b*) to a single thing that is other than each; and (*c*) to the relation of similarity that each has to that other thing—that is, to the relation between (*a*) and (*b*).

When we make assertions, Pontifex notes, we refer ultimately to something other than mere objects, say, X, Y, Z. Indeed, we in fact refer to the source from which X, Y, and Z derive their character of assertibility. In analyzing the terms "existence," "being," or "assertibility," we notice that we are involved in certain ideas which we can call active and passive. "Existence does not refer to each of many objects by themselves, but to each as connected with a single common object by the relationship of passive to active. X, Y, and Z exist, but existence is a characteristic to which they are passive, . . . and a single agent, other than themselves, acts upon them and makes them exist."

The relation present in any application of the term "existence" to objects X, Y, and Z is the relation of absolute dependence, in which the whole of each is relative. "The existence of X, Y, and Z simply is X, Y, and Z, but looked at as wholly dependent." Hence, existence is a term "which is used partly, but not wholly, in the same sense about every object; it refers to things which are unlike one another under a common aspect, which applies to each wholly and entirely."

The source from which each thing receives its being, Dom Pontifex concludes, will have the characteristic of being or assertibility, and no other, since as the source of assertibility, it cannot have any particularizing characteristics.

W E USE THE WORDS existence or being. Do these words express something peculiar to themselves, or are they quite unnecessary, so that their meaning could be expressed by other words? The fact that a language can be constructed without explicitly expressing existence is no proof that it is not referred to implicitly. Every language aims at expressing truth, and existence or being refers to an object as true. But may not existence or being simply mean the object known, so as to imply nothing more than white or red? If so every statement about an object would be true. Further, is there not a common aspect or element in everything that we know, since everything that we know is alike knowable: is not this what we mean by existence or being? But in that case, it may be said, existence or being is nothing more than the fact that every object we know is knowable, merely the subjective state of the knower, which to that extent is the same, whatever object he may know. To this objection we reply that in every expression of knowledge there is a similar kind of activity which we call assertion, and that this activity of assertion may be true or false, and therefore should reflect an aspect or element found in the object known, and common to every object, known or knowable.

This common object, namely assertibility, is what we mean by existence or being, at least in one sense of these words. Hence existence or being are words which indicate a common aspect or element in every object known or knowable, not therefore to be identified entirely with each particular object. They indicate what is not expressed entirely by any other words. The proof of this rests ultimately on our direct experience, since, if we examine our state of mind when we express our knowledge of some object, we find that there is a similarity in every expression of knowledge, and therefore a similarity in every object that we express.

Basing our argument on this conclusion, let us go on to inquire whether we can discover any more precisely what is meant by existence or being or assertibility. We have seen that it is not merely a subjective idea in the mind, but is that characteristic of every knowable object which justifies us in making an assertion or affirmation about it, in making and expressing that mental act which we can make whenever we are aware of an object. What, then, is this common characteristic; can we describe it any more fully or in any other terms? Probably it will be best to begin by discussing certain theories which will have to be rejected, and then, when this has been done, to propose a solution which seems the only one left in the field.

The first suggestion likely to be made by anyone who considers this question, is that existence is a universal term like animal or red, and only differs from other such terms in being the most general of all. We can start, for example, from Socrates and Plato, and then put them in the class of men, and go on to living beings, and then to substances, gradually including more and more in each wider class. May not existence or being be the widest class of all which includes everything that is assertible, that is, everything there is? Existence or being would thus be the *summum genus*. There is, however, a fatal objection to this. For every class, as it becomes wider, is formed by taking a partial aspect of the narrower class, and leaving aside some aspect which is not included in the wider class. Horses and dogs may be classified as animals by taking a partial aspect which is common to both, and leaving aside those more particular aspects which constitute the animal as a horse or a dog. Genus is narrowed to species by a differentia which is not included in the genus. But existence or being applies to absolutely everything, and therefore there can be no differentia which is outside existence or being. There cannot be an aspect or element which is common in the same sense to absolutely every object of knowledge, because this would involve contradiction; if it were so there would be no possibility of distinction between objects. If everything, and every aspect or element in everything, is included in the most general class which we reach when we classify things, then no aspect is left outside by which things can be distinguished. Hence, if there were an aspect or element common in the same sense to every object of knowledge, there could be only one single object with no distinction in it, but, since we cannot think, or express what we experience, without expressing distinctions, it follows that a supreme genus is a contradictory idea. In other words existence or being cannot be an attribute of things in the same sense that red or hard are attributes.

Let us take another suggestion. Might existence be the stuff or material out of which everything is formed, since this would account for its universal character without involving the contradiction mentioned above? We speak of different kinds of being, and is it conceivable that existence refers, so to speak, to the raw material which is made up into different kinds of finished things? Might it refer to the possible out of which the actual is formed? This theory, however, will not stand criticism any more than the former. The suggestion would imply that existence referred to an utterly indeterminate material, which was determined by something else. But this other thing which determined it would itself necessarily exist in order to determine the material, and hence we can see at once that existence cannot be merely the indeterminate.

Existence or being, therefore, cannot refer either to a particular aspect common to all things (because it is not particular, but common to all), or to the material out of which all things are formed (because that which forms or determines the material must itself have being), but yet being refers to everything that exists, to the whole of reality, so that each particular thing is a part of being or reality? The reason why this solution must be rejected is that existence or being, namely, that aspect in everything which makes assertion true of everything, is common to every object, and must indicate a similarity in each, so far as it applies. But it applies to every object, and to every aspect of every object, so that there would be nothing to differentiate the parts of being, if being meant the whole of reality, and each particular object was a part of being. There would need to be something other than being to divide it into parts, whereas there is nothing other than being. The various objects, X, Y, and Z, are distinct from one another, and how could what is different, when added together, make up a whole which is the same?

Nor, it is important to add, can existence refer simply to an object which is other than the different objects that we know. It cannot refer to something wholly outside the objects which we know, because the point of departure for inquiry into the meaning of existence or being is that it refers to what justifies assertion, and it is X, Y, or Z, which we assert. Being or existence must in some sense refer to a common aspect or element in each object, that we know, not merely to something other than them. Assertibility is in some sense a characteristic of each object that we know, and cannot be something wholly distinct from each.

At this point it seems worth mentioning the following. It has been emphasized in recent years that existential propositions and characterizing propositions are not logically of the same form, although they have the same grammatical form. Prof. Broad refers to this when maintaining that the grammatical similarity has probably been a cause of acceptance of the ontological argument. He explains that existential propositions cannot be analysed in the same way as characterizing propositions, and continues: "The right analysis, as is well known, is somewhat as follows. These propositions [i.e. existential propositions] are not about cats or dragons, i.e. about things which have the cat-characteristics or the dragon-characteristics. They are about these characteristics themselves. What they assert is that these characterisics do apply to something or that they do not apply to anything, as the case may be. 'Cats exist' is equivalent to 'The defining characteristics of the word "cat" apply to something.' Again 'Dragons do not exist' is equivalent to 'The defining characteristics of the word "dragon" do not apply to anything.' " All this is, of course, perfectly true, but it should not lead us to suppose that the word "exist" is a superfluous word which can be wholly translated into other words. We are told " 'cats exist' is equivalent to 'The defining characteristics of the word "cat" apply to something,' " but we have not got rid of the word "exist," because "something" means "something which exists"; "cats exist" is equivalent to "The defining characteristics of the word 'cat' apply to something which exists." It is perfectly true that existence is not a characteristic in the same way as "red" or "heavy"; this is only what we have argued above, when showing that existence or being cannot be the supreme genus, and it is because this is true that existential propositions cannot be analysed in the same way as characterizing propositions. But by saying " 'cats exist' is equivalent to 'The defining characteristics of the word "cat" apply to something which exists,' " we have only partially analysed an existential proposition, because we have not yet analysed the meaning of "something which exists." It has already been argued above that "existence" cannot be identified with "something," because it is common to everything. Therefore we are still left with the problem how to analyse an existential proposition, even though we have been very rightly warned that it cannot be analysed in the same way as a characterizing proposition. We shall not be able to analyse an existential proposition fully, until we have decided what is the object to which existence refers. So far all we have done is to reject a number of proposed explanations.

What, then, are we to say? Is it possible for us to analyse the idea of existence and express it in any way which avoids contradiction? It is common to all objects and to every part of them, yet it is not a partial element or aspect like white or substance, nor is it the sum total of all that we know or can know.

The Thomist theory, as usually explained, may be summed up very shortly as follows. There is, it maintains, a distinction between the characteristics of a given thing, which are called its essence or nature, and its existence or being. There is a proportion between the essence of each thing and its existence which is similar to the proportion between the essence and existence of every other thing. Thus existence or being, in the sense of "existing thing" or *ens*, is not used in precisely the same sense of each thing, nor in an entirely different sense, but in a sense which is called analogical, that is, partly the same and partly different. This theory avoids the various difficulties which have just been discussed. But, it may be objected, does not existence refer to the thing itself which exists, and not merely to a proportion between the two elements of which it is composed? The usual answer to this is that existence does not refer to any objective aspect of things which is a simple unity, but refers to things which in themselves are many and distinct. It does not refer to them distinctly and explicitly, but in a confused way and implicitly, and in so far as in some sense they are a single object, that is, in so far as they are a single object in virtue of this proportion between essence and existence. For, because existence or being does not abstract from the differences to be found in particular objects, it contains and expresses these differences, yet confuses them together in virtue of that aspect which they possess of "having being," which aspect is similarity of proportion. That is how Gredt explains it: "Ergo ens non enuntiat aliquam rationem objectivam simpliciter unam, sed significat immediate inferiora sua, quae sunt simpliciter multa et diversa. Non tamen significat ea distincte et explicite, sed confuse et implicite, et prout sunt unum secundum quid, i.e. prout sunt proportionaliter unum. Nam quia ens non abstrahit a differentiis inferiorum suorum, has differentias actu continet et enuntiat, confundendo eas tamen a ratione proportionaliter una habendi esse."* He goes on to give the example of a man seeing a flock of sheep in the distance, who sees them as a confused whole, yet as really containing a number of distinct sheep.

Now there are difficulties against this theory, which may be put as follows. In the first place there is the difficulty of seeing how essence and existence can be distinct in such a way that really and objectively there can be a proportion between them. What does not exist is nothing, and it is for this reason that existence cannot be the supreme genus. It may be said that essence can never in fact occur objectively without existence, but, if it is distinct from existence in such a way that there is an objective proportion between it and existence, it is hard to see how this answer avoids the difficulty. Surely there is nothing which can stand outside existence in this way.

Secondly, "existing thing," and therefore also "existence," undoubtedly refers, as Gredt admits, to the distinguishing elements which separate particular things, and not merely to a similar proportion to be found in each thing. But the method of dealing with the problem does not seem satisfactory. We see a flock of sheep in the distance as a single whole because we cannot look

---

* "Consequently, being does not directly disclose some sort of objective *ratio* as though it were a single entity; rather, it signifies the very things themselves, which are absolutely diversified and pluralized. Nevertheless, the term being does not signify things exactly and with precision, but rather indefinitely and implicitly, and only insofar as they are relatively one, i.e., insofar as they are analogically one. But because being is not abstracted from the differences between things themselves, it encompasses and discloses such differences in the very act of being, enabling one mentally to compound them analogically as possessing a relationship to the ground of existence"—ED. TRANSLATION.

sufficiently closely, but the question we want answered is: what does existence refer to objectively, when it *is* looked at closely? It refers to the differences in each thing, yet under a similar aspect, The similar proportion, however, between essence and existence in each case does not imply a similar aspect in each essence, but only a similar relation to existence, which belongs externally to each essence. The only way to avoid the difficulty is to say, as Gredt does, that when we conceive of "existing thing," we only look at the different essences from a distance, so to speak, and in a confused way. This, however, is not a satisfactory solution.

Thirdly, if "existing thing" means X, Y, and Z, as having a similar proportion to their existence, if, that is to say, the similarity lies in the proportion between essence and existence, it is difficult to see how we have explained the similarity and difference in the idea of existence itself. "Existing thing" or *ens*, it is claimed, is composed of essence and existence, which are distinct. The common notion "existing thing" refers to X, Y, and Z, because they are all similar in their relation to existence. But the question then arises: how can existence be a common notion? If it refers to something distinct from essence, how can the similarity of existing things consist in a similar proportion to essence? This relation of proportion must be something external to existence, since it is not to be wholly identified with it. In short, if essence and existence are distinct, how can existence refer both to an element in the whole, and to the relation between that element and another element (essence)?

If for these or other reasons we find ourselves unable to accept the Thomist theory as usually explained, or at least in the form just described, what theory can be suggested? The Thomist theory gives the clue, I think, to the solution, even though we must make use of it in a rather different way. Let us look again at the problem. It arises from the fact that existence refers to each thing, and to each part of each thing, and yet at the same time, while referring to what is different, refers to what is similar in each. It refers at the same time to the same objects as like one another and also as unlike—and not from entirely different aspects, because it refers to every aspect. How are we to explain this? The Thomist solution rests on the view that existence refers, not to one single object, but to a proportion between two elements which compose the object. Now this suggestion that existence refers in some way to a double object gives the clue, because it enables us to see how existence can have apparently contradictory meanings, how it can refer to the same things as alike and as unlike. It cannot, we have argued, refer to an element in the composition of each thing, nor to a proportion between two elements, because it must refer to every element in every thing. Therefore we conclude that it must refer to each thing, and to a single thing which is other than each, and to the similar relation which each has to that other thing. This would explain how it includes a reference to things both as being unlike and as being alike.

It will be objected: is not a relation a partial aspect of a thing, and, if we say that existence means the similar relation which every thing has to a single thing outside itself, are we not excluding X, Y, and Z, from existence, whereas it is precisely X, Y, and Z, which exist? Are we not back in the old difficulty of trying to make existence mean a part of reality whereas there can be nothing to which existence does not apply? We must see if we can discover more about the relation X, Y, and Z, have to this single object, before answering the question.

Now the reason why we postulated a single common object to which existence refers, external to X, Y, and Z, is that we thereby explained how it refers to X, Y, and Z, both as like and unlike one another. We can carry the argument further. Existence or being or assertibility is a characteristic which belongs to X, Y, and Z, because X, Y, and Z, are each and all assertible. But it cannot be wholly identified with X, Y, or Z nor limited to each of them because it is common to all, and to every aspect and part of them, unlike such characteristics as red or animal. Therefore it must be a characteristic which they derive from a source or principle outside of them, since it is not limited to each. Assertibility must refer ultimately to something other than X, Y, or Z, and they must derive their characteristic of assertibility from this source. X, Y, and Z, must be assertible because they are made assertible by this external principle; assertibility, as we know it in X, Y, or Z, must refer to each as receiving this characteristic from a common principle which is its source. How else are we to satisfy the conditions of the problem? We have to explain how a characteristic, which is common to all, applies to each different thing. How can we do so except by saying that it refers to each different thing under the common aspect of derivation from a common source? This explanation will account for the fact that assertibility refers to each different thing, X, Y, and Z, and also for the fact that it is common to all, since it refers to them as derived wholly and entirely from a single principle.

The solution is further supported if we put the argument in a slightly different form. X, Y, and Z, do not have assertibility as a characteristic which simply belongs to them like other characteristics because, since it applies to every aspect and element in them, each would be wholly identified with assertibility and there would be only one single thing, and one single aspect of this thing. There would be no principle of distinction, since there could be nothing which was other than the characteristic of assertibility. Nevertheless the fact remains, as a matter of direct experience, that X, Y, and Z, and every aspect of them, are assertible. Therefore, since they do not have this characteristic from themselves, not being identified with it, they must in some sense share in it, by deriving their assertibility from a common source, other than themselves. This means that they must in themselves be capable of being made assertible (for they are in fact assertible), but are not rendered actually assertible by themselves, since it is not a principle which is identified with each of them, or limited to each. They are capable of having this characteristic, but it is actually imparted from a common source outside, or other than, themselves. Thus we find that, when we analyse what is meant by existence or being or assertibility, we discover that certain ideas which we call "active" and "passive" are involved in the analysis. Existence does not refer to each of many objects by themselves, but to each as connected with a single common object by the relationship of passive to active. X, Y, and X exist, but existence is a characteristic to which they are passive, or in other words which they receive, and a single agent, other than themselves, acts upon them and makes them exist. We have not introduced fresh ideas into the analysis of existence, which we have no warrant to introduce; all we have done is to examine what we mean when we say a thing exists, to exclude certain explanations which lead to contradiction, and to reach a solution in which we find certain ultimate ideas apply.

To return to the objection which asked: is not a relationship a partial aspect of a thing, and not the whole thing, whereas existence refers to the whole thing? To answer this we must show that existence, as applied to X, Y, or Z, refers to a relation of absolute dependence, in which the whole of each is relative. The reason for saying that existence refers to such a relation is that it refers to every aspect of each thing, to the whole of each from every point of view, since every aspect is assertible. X, Y, and Z are wholly assertible, and their characteristic of assertibility is given from a common source. But a characteristic which applies to the whole of X, Y, or Z means X, Y, or Z and therefore, if they receive this characteristic from an external source, this means they receive their whole selves from an external source, or in other words, that they are wholly dependent upon, wholly relative to, an external source. It is true that here we find a unique kind of relationship, but this is no argument against it, because there is no contradiction in saying that analysis of reality leads to the discovery of something which is unique. We are trying to express what we find in reality and we find something which can be expressed by an idea not wholly unlike ideas which apply in other ways, e.g. not wholly unlike such a relation as exists between the pen and the hand which guides it. The relation to which existence refers may be called a relation, but it applies to the whole of the object which is related, and in this is unique. X, Y, and Z are relative wholly to something else. Thus we are not, when we advance this theory, in the same difficulty as we put against the Thomist view, namely, that existence would be the similar proportion of essence to existence, but would not include the different essences of X, Y, and Z. According to the view we are proposing existence means X, Y, and Z, precisely as wholly dependent. Existence is not something which belongs to, or characterises them; it applies to them wholly and entirely. The existence of X, Y, and Z simply is X, Y, and Z, but looked at as wholly dependent. Thus existence refers not only to an aspect in different objects, which is a similar aspect, but to the whole of the different objects under an aspect of similarity. Of course this raises its own problems, but these are nothing else than the relation of finite to infinite, which we shall discuss more fully later on.

Another objection is this. We have argued that existence means a characteristic which cannot have its source in each particular object, because it is common to all. But why does not the same argument apply to other characteristics, such as hard or red, which are common to many objects? It is important to bring out the difference between existence and such characteristics as hard or red. These latter refer to only partial aspects of things, not to every possible aspect. The same thing may be both hard and red, but hard and red are not the same. They are common to many things, but can be particularized by the special characteristics of particular things, which are not referred to by hard or red. Hard and red do not refer to every aspect of each thing, as does existence. Thus existence cannot be regarded as a characteristic like these other characteristics; it is unique, and can only be called a characteristic in a special sense. Existence cannot be regarded as characterizing something to which it does not itself refer, as can other characteristics. It must refer to the whole of each thing, but, as we have argued, under a common aspect which applies to the whole of each, namely, to each as wholly dependent.

To sum up: the view here proposed is that existence or being refers to every knowable object under that aspect which each has, of complete dependence on a source from which they are derived. Existence refers to what is dissimilar, the particular dissimilar objects, and also to what is similar, the similar relationship to a common source. Yet there is no contradiction in saying that a common term applies to what is not common, to what is dissimilar. The similarity is not a characteristic which belongs to, but does not include, what is dissimilar; since X, Y, and Z are wholly dependent, it is similarity which includes, or applies to, even the dissimilar. Thus existence is a term which is used partly, but not wholly, in the same sense about every object; it refers to things which are unlike one another under a common aspect, which applies to each wholly and entirely. The theory thereby avoids the various objections which have been raised against other theories. If it is asked whether this is what we really mean by existence, we must explain that it is intended to be an analysis of the meaning of existence, and existence is a unique idea. We can use other words, such as being, assertibility, and so on, but these refer to the same thing. Existence is an ultimate idea, which cannot be analysed into more ultimate ideas; all we can do is to distinguish the objects to which it applies. What we have attempted, is to show that it is not a superfluous term, which has no special meaning. As to whether the meaning we have suggested is the commonly accepted meaning of the word, all we can do is to appeal to direct experience. Do we not have the experience of finding a common aspect in all the things we are aware of, and is not this what we call assertibility, and is not this the same as existence or being? And, when we inspect more closely what we mean, do we not find that it must refer to each particular thing under a common aspect, which must be that of complete dependence? The suggestion is that the other terms we have used in the analysis are really contained in the idea of existence, e.g. active and passive.

Finally, can we say anything more about the source from which each thing receives its being? Plainly the source will have the characteristic of assertibility or being, since from it all particular things derive their own assertibility or being. Moreover there will be no other characteristic which we can apply to it. For we have seen that X, Y, and Z cannot be their own source of assertibility, because they are differentiated by those characteristics which make them X, Y, and Z, while assertibility is common to them all. Therefore the source of assertibility cannot have had any particularizing or limiting characteristics. If so it would not be the source, but would itself require a source. In so far as we merely assert, we express no limitations. This is surely a matter of direct experience. We express limitations by limiting our assertion to X, Y, or Z. Hence, since we can only express the source of assertibility by unqualified assertion, the source must be unlimited in its assertibility. In other words it must be absolutely perfect, that to which we give the name God. . . .

John Dewey

17. THE DOUBLE IMAGE OF EXISTENCE

The "essence" of the world, Dewey would say, is that it is an inextricable and inexplicable mixture of risk and stability, of peril and permanence, of conflict and provisional resolution. And he would emphasize that we cannot speak of the "essence" or "existence" of something without referring to the almost infinite conditions set to it by the "essence" and "existence" of something else.

To Dewey, essence and existence are consequently not irreformable terms which denote how the world is. His naturalist metaphysics maintains that experience is surely not divided between any such terms. Quite another way around, the only terms that can be experientially applied are those of "relative stability" and "precariousness."

We live in a world, he says, "which is an impressive and irresistible mixture of sufficiencies, tight completenesses, order, recurrences which make possible prediction and control, and singularities, ambiguities, uncreated

From *Experience and Nature* by John Dewey. Reprinted by permission of the publisher, The Open Court Publishing Company, La Salle, Illinois.

possibilities, processes going on to consequences as yet indeterminate."
Change is pitted against permanence; but either one alone would make the
other impossible. Both together form the basis of a naturalistic metaphysics. A purely stable world would permit neither illusions nor ideals; it
would just exist. A purely risky world, on the other hand, would make
adventure impossible. The concurrence of both elements make adventure
possible, because it forces thought into existence.

Doubtless we long, in a troubled and uncertain world, for perfect being,
Dewey suggests. Yet we forget that "what gives meaning to the notion of
perfection is the events that create longing, and that, apart from them, a
'perfect' world would mean just an unchanging brute existential thing."
Our experience is thus one of contingency, the exponents of which are need
and desire. A complete world would rob necessity of its meaning, for we
speak of necessity only against a background of contingency.

We cannot, he continues, retreat to the realm of thought and reason to
guarantee a world of perfect being, for the simple fact is that these are
not specific powers of being, but consist of "the procedures intentionally
employed in the application to each other of the unsatisfactorily confused
and indeterminate, on one side, and the regular and stable, on the other."
Thought is therefore instrumental to the business of finding one's way in
the world of confused fact. Thought does not bear inquiry from a world of
change to one of permanence. Thinking is a "continuous process of
temporal re-organization within one and the same world of experienced
things, not a jump from the latter world into one of objects constituted
once for all by thought."

Thus, thinking is never to be equated with being, and to make it so is
simply to convert a logic of reflection into an ontology of rational being
and to transform "an eventual natural function of unification into a causal
antecedent reality." Such a conversion is, in fact, based upon "the tendency
of imagination working under the influence of emotion to carry unification
from an actual, objective and experimental enterprise, limited to particular
situations where it is needed, into an unrestricted, wholesale movement
which ends in an all-absorbing dream."

Reflection can never be separated from its own situation, he concludes, as
"a natural event occurring in nature." It is no more nor less, therefore, than
any other event in nature, and takes on the same contingent garments as
other natural events. To speak of thought as absolute would then be to
deprive it of its rightful role as an event in nature along with every other
existence.

A FEATURE OF EXISTENCE which is emphasized by cultural phenomena
is the precarious and perilous. Sumner refers to Grimm as authority for the
statement that the Germanic tribes had over a thousand distinct sayings,
proverbs and apothegms, concerning luck. Time is brief, and this statement
must stand instead of the discourse which the subject deserves. Man finds
himself living in an aleatory world; his existence involves, to put it baldly, a

gamble. The world is a scene of risk; it is uncertain, unstable, uncannily unstable. Its dangers are irregular, inconstant, not to be counted upon as to their times and seasons. Although persistent, they are sporadic, episodic. It is darkest just before dawn; pride goes before a fall; the moment of greatest prosperity is the moment most charged with ill-omen, most opportune for the evil eye. Plague, famine, failure of crops, disease, death, defeat in battle, are always just around the corner, and so are abundance, strength, victory, festival and song. Luck is proverbially both good and bad in its distributions. The sacred and the accursed are potentialities of the same situation; and there is no category of things which has not embodied the sacred and accursed: persons, words, places, times, directions in space, stones, winds, animals stars.

Anthropologists have shown incontrovertibly the part played by the precarious aspects of the world in generating religion with its ceremonies, rites, cults, myths, magic; and it has shown the pervasive penetration of these affairs into morals, law, art, and industry. Beliefs and dispositions connected with them are the background out of which philosophy and secular morals slowly developed, as well as more slowly those late inventions, art for art's sake, and business is business. Interesting and instructive as is this fact, it is not the ramifications which here concern us. We must not be diverted to consider the consequences for philosophy, even for doctrines reigning today, of facts concerning the origin of philosophies. We confine ourselves to one outstanding fact: the evidence that the world of empirical things includes the uncertain, unpredictable, uncontrollable and hazardous.

It is an old saying that the gods were born of fear. The saying is only too likely to strengthen a misconception bred by confirmed subjective habits. We first endow man in isolation with an instinct of fear and then we imagine him irrationally ejecting that fear into the environment, scattering broadcast as it were, the fruits of his own purely personal limitations, and thereby creating superstition. But fear, whether an instinct or an acquisition, is a function of the environment. Man fears because he exists in a fearful, an awful world. The world is precarious and perilous. It is as easily accessible and striking evidence of this fact that primitive experience is cited. The voice is that of early man; but the hand is that of nature, the nature in which we still live. It was not fear of gods that created the gods.

For if the life of early man is filled with expiations and propitiations, if in his feasts and festivals what is enjoyed is gratefully shared with his gods, it is not because a belief in supernatural powers created a need for expiatory, propitiatory and communal offerings. Everything that man achieves and possesses is got by actions that may involve him in other and obnoxious consequences in addition to those wanted and enjoyed. His acts are trespasses upon the domain of the unknown; and hence atonement, if offered in season, may ward off direful consequences that haunt even the moment of prosperity—or that most haunt that moment. While unknown consequences flowing from the past dog the present, the future is even more unknown and perilous; the present by that fact is ominous. If unknown forces that decide future destiny can be placated, the man who will not study the methods of securing their favors is incredibly flippant. In enjoyment of present food and companionship, nature, tradition and social organization have cooperated, thereby supplementing our own endeavors so petty and so feeble without this extraneous reinforcement. Goods are by grace not of ourselves. He is a dangerous churl who will not gratefully acknowledge by means of free-will offerings the help that sustains him.

These things are as true today as they were in the days of early culture. It is not the facts which have changed, but the methods of insurance, regulation and acknowledgment. Herbert Spencer sometimes colored his devotion to symbolic experiences with a fact of direct experience. When he says that every fact has two opposite sides, "the one its near or visible side and the other its remote or invisible side," he expresses a persistent trait of every object in experience. The visible is set in the invisible; and in the end what is unseen decides what happens in the seen; the tangible rests precariously upon the untouched and ungrasped. The contrast and the potential maladjustment of the immediate, the conspicuous and focal phase of things, with those indirect and hidden factors which determine the origin and career of what is present, are indestructible features of any and every experience. We may term the way in which our ancestors dealt with the contrast superstitious, but the contrast is no superstition. It is a primary datum in any experience.

We have substituted sophistication for superstition, at least measurably so. But the sophistication is often as irrational and as much at the mercy of words as the superstition it replaces. Our magical safeguard against the uncertain character of the world is to deny the existence of chance, to mumble universal and necessary law, the ubiquity of cause and effect, the uniformity of nature, universal progress, and the inherent rationality of the universe. These magic formulae borrow their potency from conditions that are not magical. Through science we have secured a degree of power of prediction and of control; through tools, machinery and an accompanying technique we have made the world more conformable to our needs, a more secure abode. We have heaped up riches and means of comfort between ourselves and the risks of the world. We have professionalized amusement as an agency of escape and forgetfulness. But when all is said and done, the fundamentally hazardous character of the world is not seriously modified, much less eliminated. Such an incident as the last war and preparations for a future war remind us that it is easy to overlook the extent to which, after all, our attainments are only devices for blurring the disagreeable recognition of a fact, instead of means of altering the fact itself.

What has been said sounds pessimistic. But the concern is not with morals but with metaphysics, with, that is to say, the nature of the existential world in which we live. It would have been as easy and more comfortable to em-phasize good luck, grace, unexpected and unwon joys, those unsought for happenings which we so significantly call happiness. We might have appealed to good fortune as evidence of this important trait of hazard in nature. Comedy is as genuine as tragedy. But it is traditional that comedy strikes a more super-ficial note than tragedy. And there is an even better reason for appealing to misfortunes and mistakes as evidence of the precarious nature of the world. The problem of evil is a well recognized problem, while we rarely or never hear of a problem of good. Goods we take for granted; they are as they should be; they are natural and proper. The good is a recognition of our deserts. When we pull out a plum we treat it as evidence of the real order of cause and effect in the world. For this reason it is difficult for the goods of existence to furnish as convincing evidence of the uncertain character of nature as do evils. It is the latter we term accidents, not the former, even when their ad-ventitious character is as certain.

What of it all, it may be asked? In the sense in which an assertion is true that uncontrolled distribution of good and evil is evidence of the precarious, uncertain nature of existence, it is a truism, and no problem is forwarded by its reiteration. But it is submitted that just this predicament of the inextricable mixture of stability and uncertainty gives rise to philosophy, and that it is re-flected in all its recurrent problems and issues. If classic philosophy says so much about unity and so little about unreconciled diversity, so much about the eternal and permanent, and so little about change (save as something to be resolved into combinations of the permanent), so much about necessity and so little about contingency, so much about the comprehending universal and so little about the recalcitrant particular, it may well be because the ambigu-ousness and ambivalence of reality are actually so pervasive. Since these things form the problem, solution is more apparent (although not more actual), in the degree in which whatever of stability and assurance the world presents is fastened upon and asserted.

Upon their surface, the reports of the world which form our different philosophies are various to the point of stark contrariness. They range from spiritualism to materialism, from absolutism to relativistic phenomenalism, from transcendentalism to positivism, from rationalism to sensationalism, from idealism to realism, from subjectivism to bald objectivism, from Platonic realism to nominalism. The array of contradictions is so imposing as to sug-gest to sceptics that the mind of man has tackled an impossible job, or that philosophers have abandoned themselves to vagary. These radical opposi-tions in philosophers suggest however another consideration. They suggest that all their different philosophies have a common premise, and that their diversity is due to acceptance of a common premise. Variant philosophies may be looked at as different ways of supplying recipes for denying to the uni-verse the character of contingency which it possesses so integrally that its

denial leaves the reflecting mind without a clew, and puts subsequent philos-
ophising at the mercy of temperament, interest and local surroundings.

Quarrels among conflicting types of philosophy are thus family quarrels.
They go on within the limits of a too domestic circle, and can be settled only
by venturing further afield, and out of doors. Concerned with imputing complete, finished and sure character to the world of real existence, even if things
have to be broken into two disconnected pieces in order to accomplish the
result, the character desiderated can plausibly be found in reason or in mechanism; in rational conceptions like those of mathematics, or brute things like
sensory data; in atoms or in essences; in consciousness or in physical externality which forces and overrides consciousness.

As against this common identification of reality with what is sure, regular
and finished, experience in unsophisticated forms gives evidence of a different
world and points to a different metaphysics. We live in a world which is an
impressive and irresistible mixture of sufficiencies, tight completenesses, order,
recurrences which make possible prediction and control, and singularities, ambiguities, uncertain possibilities, processes going on to consequences as yet
indeterminate. They are mixed not mechanically but vitally like the wheat
and tares of the parable. We may recognize them separately but we cannot divide them, for unlike wheat and tares they grow from the same root. Qualities
have defects as necessary conditions of their excellencies; the instrumentalities
of truth are the cause of error; change gives meaning to permanence and recurrence makes novelty possible. A world that was wholly risky would be a world
in which adventure is impossible, and only a living world can include death
Such facts have been celebrated by thinkers like Heraclitus and Lao-tze; they
have been greeted by theologians as furnishing occasions for exercise of divine grace; they have been elaborately formulated by various schools under
a principle of relativity, so defined as to become itself final and absolute. They
have rarely been frankly recognized as fundamentally significant for the formation of a naturalistic metaphysics. . . .

The union of the hazardous and the stable, of the incomplete and the recurrent, is the condition of all experienced satisfaction as truly as of our
predicaments and problems. While it is the source of ignorance, error and
failure of expectation, it is the source of the delight which fulfillments bring.
For if there were nothing in the way, if there were no deviations and resist-
ances, fulfillment would be at once, and in so being would fulfill nothing, but
merely be. It would not be in connection with desire or satisfaction. Moreover
when a fulfillment comes and is pronounced good, it is judged good, distinguished and asserted, simply because it is in jeopardy, because it occurs
amid indifferent and divergent things. Because of this mixture of the regular
and that which cuts across stability, a good object once experienced acquires
ideal quality and attracts demand and effort to itself. A particular ideal may
be an illusion, but having ideals is no illusion. It embodies features of exist-

ence. Although imagination is often fantastic it is also an organ of nature, for it is the appropriate phase of indeterminate events moving toward eventualities that are now but possibilities. A purely stable world permits of no illusion, but neither is it clothed with ideals. It just exists. To be good is to be better than; and there can be no better except where there is shock and discord combined with enough assured order to make attainment of harmony possible. Better objects when brought into existence are existent not ideal; they retain ideal quality only retrospectively as commemorative of issue from prior conflict and prospectively, in contrast with forces which make for their destruction. Water that slakes thirst, or a conclusion that solves a problem has ideal character as long as thirst or problem persists in a way which qualifies the result. But water that is not a satisfaction of need has no more ideal quality than water running through pipes into a reservoir; a solution ceases to be a solution and becomes a bare incident of existence when its antecedent generating conditions of doubt, ambiguity and search are lost from its context. While the precarious nature of existence is indeed the source of all trouble, it is also an indispensable condition of ideality, becoming a sufficient condition when conjoined with the regular and assured.

We long, amid a troubled world, for perfect being. We forget that what gives meaning to the notion of perfection is the events that create longing, and that, apart from them, a "perfect" world would mean just an unchanging brute existential thing. The ideal significance of esthetic objects is no exception to this principle. Their satisfying quality, their power to compose while they arouse, is not dependent upon definite prior desire and effort as is the case with the ideally satisfying quality of practical and scientific objects. It is part of their peculiar satisfying quality to be gratuitous, not purchased by endeavor. The contrast to other things of this detachment from toil and labor in a world where most realizations have to be bought, as well as the contrast to trouble and uncertainty, give esthetic objects their peculiar traits. If all things came to us in the way our esthetic objects do, none of them would be a source of esthetic delight.

Some phases of recent philosophy have made much of need, desire and satisfaction. Critics have frequently held that the outcome is only recurrence to an older subjective empiricism, though with substitution of affections and volitional states for cognitive sensory states. But need and desire are exponents of natural being. They are, if we use Aristotelian phraseology, actualizations of its contingencies and incompletenesses; as such nature itself is wistful and pathetic, turbulent and passionate. Were it not, the existence of wants would be a miracle. In a world where everything is complete, nothing requires anything else for its completion. A world in which events can be carried to a finish only through the coinciding assistance of other transitory events, is already necessitous, a world of begging as well as of beggarly elements. If human experience is to express and reflect this world, it must be marked by needs; in becoming aware of the needful and needed quality of things it must project satisfactions of completions. For irrespective of whether a satisfaction is conscious, a satisfaction or non-satisfaction is an objective thing with objective conditions. It means fulfillment of the demands of objective factors. Happiness may mark an awareness of such satisfaction, and it may be its culminating form. But satisfaction is not subjective, private or personal: it is conditioned by objective partialities and defections and made real by objective situations and completions.

By the same logic, necessity implies the precarious and contingent. A world that was all necessity would not be a world of necessity; it would just be. For in its being, nothing would be necessary for anything else. But where some things are indigent, other things are necessary if demands are to be met. The common failure to note the fact that a world of complete being would be a world in which necessity is meaningless is due to a rapid shift from one universe of discourse to another. First we postulate a whole of Being; then we shift to a part; now since a "part" is logically dependent as such in its existence and its properties, it is necessitated by other parts. But we have unwittingly introduced contingency in the very fact of marking off something as just a part. If the logical implications of the original notions are held to firmly, a part is already as part-of-a-whole. Its being what it is, is not necessitated by the whole or by other parts: its being what it is, is just a name for the whole being what it is. Whole and parts alike are but names for existence there as just what it is. But wherever we can say if so-and-so, then something else, there is necessity, because partialities are implied which are not just parts-of-a-whole. A world of "ifs" is alone a world of "musts"—the "ifs" express real differences; the "musts" real connections. The stable and recurrent is needed for the fulfillment of the possible; the doubtful can be settled only through its adaptation to stable objects. The necessary is always necessary for, not necessary in and of itself; it is conditioned by the contingent, although itself a condition of the full determination of the latter.

One of the most striking phases of the history of philosophic thought is the recurrent grouping together of unity, permanence (or "the eternal"), completeness and rational thought, while upon another side full multiplicity, change and the temporal, the partial, defective, sense and desire. This division is obviously but another case of violent separation of the precarious and unsettled from the regular and determinate. One aspect of it, however, is worthy of particular attention: the connection of thought and unity. Empirically, all reflection sets out from the problematic and confused. Its aim is to clarify and ascertain. When thinking is successful, its career closes in transforming the disordered into the orderly, the mixed-up into the distinguished or placed, the unclear and ambiguous into the defined and unequivocal, the disconnected into the systematized. It is empirically assured that the goal of thinking does not remain a mere ideal, but is attained often enough so as to render reasonable additional efforts to achieve it.

In these facts we have, I think, the empirical basis of the philosophic doctrines which assert that reality is really and truly a rational system, a coherent whole of relations that cannot be conceived otherwise than in terms of intellect. Reflective inquiry moves in each particular case from differences toward unity; from indeterminate and ambiguous position to clear determination, from confusion and disorder to system. When thought in a given case has reached its goal of organized totality, of definite relations of distinctly placed elements, its object is the accepted starting point, the defined subject matter, of further experiences; antecedent and outgrown conditions of darkness and of unreconciled differences are dismissed as a transitory state of ignorance and inadequate apprehensions. Retain connection of the goal with the thinking by which it is reached, and then identify it with true reality in contrast with the merely phenomenal, and the outline of the logic of rational and "objective" idealisms is before us. Thoughtlike Being, has two forms, one real; the other phenomenal. It is compelled to take on reflective form, it involves doubt, inquiry and hypothesis, because it sets out from a subject matter conditioned by sense, a fact which proves that thought, intellect, is not pure in man, but restricted by an animal organism that is but one part linked with other parts, of nature. But the conclusion of reflection affords us a pattern and guarantee of thought which is constitutive; one with the system of objective reality. Such in outline is the procedure of all ontological logics.

A philosophy which accepts the denotative or empirical methods accepts at full value the fact that reflective thinking transforms confusion, ambiguity and discrepancy into illumination, definiteness and consistency. But it also points to the contextual situation in which thinking occurs. It notes that the starting point is the actually problematic, and that the problematic phase resides in some actual and specifiable situation.

It notes that the means of converting the dubious into the assured, and the incomplete into the determinate, is use of assured and established things, which are just as empirical and as indicative of the nature of experienced things as is the uncertain. It thus notes that thinking is no different in kind from the use of natural materials and energies, say fire and tools, to refine, re-order, and shape other natural materials, say ore. In both cases, there are matters which as they stand are unsatisfactory and there are also adequate agencies of dealing with them and connecting them. At no point or place is there any jump outside empirical, natural objects and their relations. Thought and reason are not specific powers. They consist of the procedures intentionally employed in the application to each other of the unsatisfactorily confused and indeterminate on one side and the regular and stable on the other. Generalizing from such observations, empirical philosophy perceives that thinking is a continuous process of temporal re-organization within one and the same world of experienced things, not a jump from the latter world into one of objects constituted once for all by thought. It discovers thereby the empirical basis of rational idealism, and the point at which it empirically goes astray. Idealism fails to take into account the specified or concrete character of the uncertain situation in which thought occurs; it fails to note the empirically concrete nature of the subject-matter, acts, and tools by which determination and consistency are reached; it fails to note that the conclusive eventual objects having the latter properties are themselves as many as the situations dealt with. The conversion of the logic of reflection into an ontology of rational being is thus due to arbitrary conversion of an eventual natural function of unification into a causal antecedent reality; this in turn is due to the tendency of the imagination working under the influence of emotion to carry unification from an actual, objective and experimental enterprise, limited to particular situations where it is needed, into an unrestricted, wholesale movement which ends in an all-absorbing dream.

The occurrence of reflection is crucial for dualistic metaphysics as well as for idealistic ontologies. Reflection occurs only in situations qualified by uncertainty, alternatives, questioning, search, hypotheses, tentative trials or experiments which test the worth of thinking. A naturalisic metaphysics is bound to consider reflection as itself a natural event occurring within nature because of traits of the latter. It is bound to inference from the empirical traits of thinking in precisely the same way as the sciences make inferences from the happening of suns, radio-activity, thunder-storms or any other natural event. Traits of reflection are as truly indicative or evidential of the traits of other things as are the traits of these events. A theory of the nature of the occurrence and career of a sun reached by denial of the obvious traits of the sun, or by denial that these traits are so connected with the traits of other natural events that they can be used as evidence concerning the nature of these other things, would hardly possess scientific standing. Yet philosophers, and strangely enough philosophers who call themselves realists, have constantly held that the traits which are characteristic of thinking, namely, uncertainty, ambiguity, alternatives, inquiring, search, selection, experimental reshaping of external conditions, do not possess the same existential character as do the objects of valid knowledge. They have denied that these traits are evidential of the character of the word within which thinking occurs. They have not, as realists, asserted that these traits are mere appearances; but they have often asserted and implied that such things are only personal and psychological in contrast with a world of objective nature. But the interests of empirical and denotative method and of naturalistic metaphysics wholly coincide. The world must actually be such as to generate ignorance and inquiry; doubt and hypothesis, trial and temporal conclusions; the latter being such that they develop out of existences which while wholly "real" are not as satisfactory, as good, or as significant, as those into which they are eventually re-organized.

The ultimate evidence of genuine hazard, contingency, irregularity and in-determinateness in nature is thus found in the occurrence of thinking. The traits of natural existence which generate the fears and adorations of super-stitious barbarians generate the scientific procedures of disciplined civiliza-tion. The superiority of the latter does not consist in the fact that they are based on "real" existence, while the former depend wholly upon a human na-ture different from nature in general. It consists in the fact that scientific in-quiries reach objects which are better, because reached by method which con-trols them and which adds greater control to life itself, method which miti-gates accident, turns contingency to account, and releases thought and other forms of endeavor.

The conjunction of problematic and determinate characters in nature renders every existence, as well as every idea and human act, an experiment in fact, even though not in design. To be intelligently experimental is but to be conscious of this intersection of natural conditions so as to profit by it in-stead of being at its mercy. The Christian idea of this world and this life as a probation is a kind of distorted recognition of the situation; distorted because it applied wholesale to one stretch of existence in contrast with another, re-garded as original and final. But in truth anything which can exist at any place and at any time occurs subject to tests imposed upon it by surroundings, which are only in part compatible and reinforcing. These surroundings test its strength and measure its endurance. As we can discourse of change only in terms of velocity and acceleration which involve relations to other things, so assertion of the permanent and enduring is comparative. The stablest thing we can speak of is not free from conditions set to it by other things. That even the solid earth mountains, the emblems of constancy, appear and disappear like the clouds is an old theme of moralists and poets. The fixed and un-changed being of the Democritean atom is now reported by inquirers to pos-sess some of the traits of his non-being, and to embody a temporary equilibrium in the economy of nature's compromises and adjustments. A thing may endure *secula seculorum* and yet not be everlasting; it will crumble before the gnaw-ing tooth of time, as it exceeds a certain measure. Every existence is an event.

This fact is nothing at which to repine and nothing to gloat over. It is something to be noted and used. If it is discomfiting when applied to good things, to our friends, possessions and precious selves, it is consoling also to know that no evil endures forever; that the longest lane turns sometime, and that the memory of loss of nearest and dearest grows dim in time. The eventful character of all existences is no reason for consigning them to the realm of mere appearance any more than it is a reason for idealizing flux into a deity. The important thing is measure, relation, ratio, knowledge of the comparative tempos of change. In mathematics some variables are constants in some problems; so it is in nature and life. The rate of change of some things is so slow, or is so rhythmic, that these changes have all the advantages of stability in dealing with more transitory and irregular happenings—if we know enough. Indeed, if any one thing that concerns us is subject to change, it is fortunate that all other things change. A thing "absolutely" stable and unchangeable would be out of the range of the principle of action and reaction, of resistance and leverage as well as of friction. Here it would have no applicability, no potentiality of use as measure and control of other events. To designate the slower and the regular rhythmic events structure, and more rapid and irregular ones process, is sound practical sense. It expresses the function of one in respect to the other.

Value

Thomas Aquinas   18. THE NATURE OF GOOD

Certain logical aspects of reality have traditionally been distinguished under the title "transcendental attributes," or modes, of being. These are identified as unity, truth, goodness, and beauty. The latter three are often lumped together under the term "value." In this selection, St. Thomas addresses himself to an investigation of the character of these modes, particularly that of goodness.

Is goodness or value separate from being? Is it something added to being? St. Thomas answers such questions by distinguishing the manner in which additions can be made to a being. There are three ways, he says, in which this may be understood: (*a*) as the addition of a certain reality outside the essence of a thing (for example, a "white" paper); (*b*) as the addition of a determination of a being (thus, "man" adds to "animal" by limitation or contraction of "animal"); and (*c*) as the addition of a logical character to a real being ("blind" adds to "man" as a privation of the natural capacity of sight).

Now nothing can be added to being in the first way, St. Thomas points out, because what is outside reality cannot be added to reality. In the second sense, however, certain things can be added to a being in the form of the ten categories that limit it as "a determinate mode of existing which is rooted in the very essence of the thing." Goodness, however, does not add to being in this way, because it also is divisible into ten categories. Hence, the relation that goodness adds to being is one of reason only. The term "good" adds to the concept of being the aspect of perfectiveness, be-

From *An Introduction to the Metaphysics* of St. Thomas, edited by James F. Anderson. Copyright 1953. Reprinted by permission of the publisher, Henry Regnery Company, Chicago.

cause it shows that the thing "has the aspect of an end in respect to that which is perfected by it." Goodness is *in* the thing, and not other than the thing. The thing's goodness *is* its being, just as its unity, its truth, its beauty is each, and respectively, its being. Goodness thus indicates the dynamic teleological character of things in their pursuit of their end. Every being is good precisely because it has the act of existing, and the act of existing has itself the character of goodness. Good and being are therefore convertible terms, since there is no being that is not good, nor is there any good that is not in being.

. . . Something can add to another in three ways. *In one way,* so that it adds a certain reality which is outside the essence of the thing to which it is said to be added. In this manner white adds to body, because the essence of whiteness is extrinsic to the essence of body. *In a second way,* something is said to add to another by limiting and determining it. In this way man adds something to animal, not indeed in the sense that there is in man any reality altogether outside the essence of animal; otherwise it would have to be said that man as a whole is not animal, but that animal is only a part of man. On the contrary, animal is limited by man in the sense that what is contained determinately and actually in the concept of man, is contained implicitly and as it were potentially in the concept of animal. Thus, it is the essence of man that he have a rational soul, and of the essence of animal that it have a soul, though not necessarily a rational soul and not necessarily a non-rational one. However, this determination, by reason of which man is said to add to animal, is founded upon something real. *In a third way,* something is said to add to another only according to reason. This is the case when something is of the essence of one thing which is not of the essence of the other and this "something" has no being in the nature of things but only in reason, whether the thing it is said to be added to, be restricted by it, or not. Thus, *blind* adds something to *man,* namely, blindness, which is not a being existing in nature, but only a being of reason, in so far as "being" includes privations. And by this privation man is restricted, because not every man is blind. When, however, we speak of a mole as blind this addition effects no restriction.

Now nothing can be added to universal being in the first way—by addition of something real—although some addition to some particular being can be made in that mode. The reason is that there is no thing of nature which is outside the essence of universal being, although some thing does exist outside the essence of this particular being. However, in the second way—by contraction and determination—there are certain things that add to being, because being is limited by the ten categories, each of which adds something over and above being—not indeed an accident, nor a differentia lying outside the essence of being, but rather a determinate mode of existing which is rooted in the very essence of the thing. But it is not in this way that goodness adds to being. For the good is divided into the ten categories just as being is—a point made clear in the first book of the *Ethics.* Consequently, goodness either must add nothing to being, or if it adds something, this must be according to reason only. For if goodness added something real it would follow necessarily that being was limited, by the notion of goodness, to some special genus. However, since being is that which first falls in the conception of the mind, as Avicenna says, it follows of necessity that every name is either synonymous with being (which cannot be said in the term *good,* since it is not nugatory to predicate *good* of *being*), or adds something to being at least in idea. And so the good, by which being is not restricted, must add to being something pertaining to reason alone. But that which pertains to reason alone can be twofold only. For every absolute affirmation signifies something existing in the nature of things.

So, then, to being (which is the first conception of the intellect) *one* adds that which pertains only to reason, namely, a negation; for *one* signifies *undivided* being. True and good, however, are said affirmatively; so that they can add to being only a relation of reason. Now, according to the Philosopher in the fifth book of the *Metaphysics,* that relation is said to be one of reason alone, whereby what does not depend is said to be referred to its correlative; but when the relation itself is a certain dependency, it is real, as is evident in the case of the relation between knowledge and the knowable, or between sense and the sensible. For knowledge depends on the knowable and not conversely, so that the relation by which knowledge is referred to the knowable is real, while that by which the knowable is referred to knowledge is purely one of reason. Thus, according to the Philosopher, the knowable is said to be relative (or better, referable), not because it is itself referred to something else, but because something else is referred to it; and so it is with all other things that are related to each other as measure and measured, or as perfective and perfectible.

Necessarily, then, the terms *true* and *good* add to the concept of being the aspect of perfectiveness. Now, in any being two things are to be considered: its specific intelligible nature or form (*ipsam rationem speciei*), and the very act of being by which it subsists in that nature. And so it is that a being can be perfective in two ways. *In one way,* as regards specification only, and thus does being perfect the intellect according to the intelligible nature of being. Yet being is not present in the intellect according to its natural existence; and therefore this mode of perfecting adds the true to being. For truth is in the mind, as the Philosopher says in the sixth book of the *Metaphysics.* And every being is said to be true to the extent that it is conformed or is conformable to an intellect; so that all who define truth rightly place intellect in the definition of it.

In a second way, a being is perfective of another not only as regards intelligible specificity, but also as regards the actual existence (*esse*) which it has in the nature of things. And it is in this mode that goodness is perfective; for the good is in things, as the Philosopher says in the text just referred to. Now, so far as one being is by its very act of existing perfective and conservative of another, it has the aspect of an end in respect to that which is perfected by it. And for this reason all who rightly define the good place in its definition something pertaining to the character of final causality. Accordingly, the Philosopher states in the first book of the *Ethics* that those defining the good in the most correct way declare it to be that which all desire (or aim at).

Goodness, then, is primarily and principally predicated of being as perfective of another in the manner of an end. But a thing that is conducive to an end is said to be good derivatively—in the sense that the useful is said to be good. Or a thing is called good derivatively which is by its nature ordered to an end, as healthy is predicated not only of that which has health, but also of that which perfects and conserves and signifies health. . . .

Since the essence of goodness consists in this, that something be perfective of another in the manner of an end, every thing having the nature of an end, has also the nature of goodness. Two things, however, pertain to the nature of an end: 1) that it be sought after or desired by those things which have not yet attained it, and 2) that it be loved by, and as it were lovable to, those things which share in its posssession; for it pertains to the same nature to tend toward its end, and in some way to rest in it, just as it is by one and the same nature that the stone is moved toward the center and rests there. Now these two things [tendency and rest] belong to the very act of existing (*ipsum esse*). For those things which do not yet have this act, tend toward it by a certain natural appetite. Thus matter, as the Philosopher says, desires form. All things that presently have existence, however, naturally love that existence, and preserve it with all their power. So, in the third book of *The Consolation of Philosophy,* Boethius says: "The divine providence gave to the things created by Him this special reason for remaining in existence, that to the extent of their capacity they would naturally desire to preserve their being. Wherefore you can in no way doubt this fact, that all things naturally desire the continuance of their existence and naturally shun their own destruction." The very act of existing (*ipsum esse*) thus has the character of goodness. Hence, just as it is impossible that there be any being which does not have this act, so it is necessary that every being be good precisely because it has this act; although in certain entities many aspects of goodness are superadded to the act of being whereby they subsist.

Now, since goodness includes the notion of beings, as is clear from what has been said already, there could be no good which is not a being. It remains, therefore, that good and being are convertible.

D. J. B. Hawkins

19. VALUE AND
VALUE-JUDGMENTS

The refusal by many modern thinkers to accord value or goodness an objective status in being, says Father Hawkins, is destructive of both tradition and every rational analysis of being.

Opposing the notion that the term "good" is indicative of nothing more than a subjectivist response, Hawkins asserts that good is intrinsic to each being, as well as to being itself. Contemporary philosophy, he says, fails to understand that there is a real meaning in the phrase *good in itself,* because it looks upon value-judgments either as assertive of the emotive use of language, or merely as the object of liking or desire. While it is true, he points out, that value terms may lend themselves to emotive use, it does not follow that they always do. Nor does it follow that this is the reason for their character. It is also true that "good" indicates an object of desire, but this is not all; for in holding such a view, we still have not answered the question of why we differentiate desires—why we like *this* rather than *that.* We cannot say, furthermore, that the good is simply the "fitting," since such a term already presupposes the good. Nor should we confuse the assumption that good is unanalyzable into a higher "category" with the assumption that it is therefore unintelligible.

What marks out and distinguishes the good experientially, Hawkins maintains, is an intrinsic and objective character that resides in the development and fulfillment of the natural potentialities of a being. By "good," we mean actuality, and by actuality we mean good. When we speak of good we speak of being, and we cannot speak of it apart from being. Good thus accedes to the ontological demand of any being—the demand for its self-perfection. Hence, "the complete good of anything is the fullest possible development of its potentialities in harmony and proportion." Without the notion of finality, therefore, goodness can have no meaning.

THE ARISTOTELIAN conception of good or value as residing in the fulfilment of natural capacity arises at once from the discussion of substance, but, from the point of view of contemporary philosophy, some preliminaries are needed. Terms expressive of absolute value are a puzzle to the followers of Hume. The relative values of economics can be interpreted easily enough in terms of what people are ready to pay for things, but, when we say that things are good in themselves, as when we say that actions are right in themselves, the case is different. Ethical and aesthetic values are not observable qualities in the sense admitted by Hume; there is no distinctive impression or idea corresponding with the goodness of a man, the rightness of an action or the beauty of a work of art. Nor can these notions be reduced with any show of plausibility to the purely formal linguistic or symbolic status which has sometimes been assigned to logic and mathematics. Value-judgments appear to assert something about the real character of things. Yet, within the limits set by logical positivism, it is exceedingly difficult to say what they assert.

Hence it is sometimes alleged that value-judgments assert nothing at all but are instances of the emotive use of language. They do not even assert the existence of an emotion; they are direct expressions of it. That language has an emotive use which is other than assertoric is clear enough. "X is a liar" and "X is a rotten liar" are sentences which make the same assertion; the addition of "rotten" is merely an expression of your justifiable dislike of lying. It is also true that sentences which appear to assert something may turn out to make no easily discoverable assertion or even no assertion at all. This is familiar in poetry. Was Keats trying to assert anything when he said " 'Beauty is truth, truth beauty'—that is all ye know on earth, and all ye need to know"? It is certainly not easy to decide what he was intending to assert, for, if his words are taken literally, it is too obvious that beauty and truth are not identical and that, even if they were, this would not be the only available or necessary piece of information on earth. A reasonable person will interpret the passage rather as an expression of Keats' feelings about truth and beauty and nothing more. No literary critic, plainly, would waste his time considering the possible validity of the literal paraphrase which we have just made.

There can be no doubt that value-terms lend themselves to emotive use and that ostensible assertions about value are often no more than expressions of feeling. It does not follow that they are always such, and it must be remembered that to every expression of feeling corresponds a reflex statement asserting that someone has that feeling. Even if your cry of "Good shot!" is simply an expression of what you are feeling, the situation has to be described by the statement that you are feeling approval of the stroke made. Consequently the emotive interpretation is not fundamentally different from the theory that value-judgments are statements about emotional attitudes and mean that I or others have feelings of liking, desire and approval or of dislike, aversion and disapproval.

Again there can be no doubt that the good in a general sense is an object of liking, desire and approval and that the bad provokes dislike, aversion and disapproval. If, for example, it is said that someone likes an uncomfortable chair, it means either that he finds comfort in what other people would regard as uncomfortable or that he pursues an ascetic value in the absence of comfort. No one can like the bad precisely as bad or dislike the good precisely as good. But our present business is not to emphasize these truisms; it is to consider the kind of theory which goes no farther and is content with a definition of good as the object of such feelings as desire and approval and of evil as the object of such feelings as aversion and disapproval. Hobbes provides the classical example of a bald statement of this subjectivist view.

Whatsoever is the object of any man's appetite or desire, that is it which he for his part calleth *good:* and the object of his hate and aversion, *evil;* and of his contempt, *vile* and *inconsiderable.* For these words of good, evil, and contemptible, are ever used with relation to the person that useth them: there being nothing simply and absolutely so; nor any common rule of good and evil, to be taken from the nature of the objects themselves.

Subjectivist theories of value have been the object of vigorous refutation by contemporary philosophers such as Professor G. E. Moore and Dr. A. C. Ewing. The main points are that if, when I say that a thing is good or evil, I mean only that I have a certain attitude or feeling towards it, I can never be wrong except through a failure in introspection and can never be at odds with anyone else on the question. For if another man holds to be evil what I call good, all he means is that he has a different attitude or feeling towards it, which involves no contradiction. But people certainly discuss values as if they were doing something more than comparing notes about their feelings. Even in aesthetic matters it is not usually supposed to be adequate criticism to say that you do not know whether it is good art but you know what you like, and with moral values the claim to objectivity is even clearer. We do not merely dislike cruelty; we think that cruelty is objectively detestable and that, consequently, every one else should detest it also.

To meet this difficulty the subjectivist theory may be emended in the form that good means that of which the majority of men, or the majority of those of our age and civilization, are in favour, while evil means that to which they are opposed. The theory is now no longer purely individualistic but has acquired a measure of quasi-objectivity although value is still construed in terms of feeling. Correct valuation would thus become a matter of statistical inquiry. But that does not seem to correspond any better with what we think ourselves to be discussing when we are discussing values. On this theory aesthetic innovators and moral reformers would be, by definition, wrong, whereas we spontaneously suppose, not that they are always right, but that it is quite possible that they may be right.

The truth is that we cannot help asking why we like this and dislike that. We cannot help asking why other men judge values as they do and whether they are justified in doing so. What we are looking for is some objective character in what is judged to be good or evil. We could not linger in the subjectivist theory unless we gave up this objective quest as hopeless.

Dr. Ewing thinks that the necessary transition to objectivity can be made by introducing the notion of fittingness. He defines good as the fitting object of a pro-attitude. That this is a sound definition in the sense that it applies to all of the defined and only to the defined may be admitted, but it does not pass the test that the terms of a definition should be logically prior to what is defined. We should all naturally say that a pro-attitude is fitting because its object is good, not that a thing is good because a pro-attitude towards it is fitting. Hence we are still looking for an intrinsic character of value and are compelled to ask wherein it consists.

At this stage we meet G. E. Moore's celebrated doctrine that good is a simple unanalysable quality which we have only to recognize as attaching to certain things and situations. Moore's positive argument for this view is summed up in the sentence: "The most important sense of 'definition' is that in which a definition states what are the parts which invariably compose a certain whole; and in this sense 'good' has no definition because it is simple and has no parts." His supplementary negative argument is a painstaking demolition of the attempts made by various philosophers to define goodness.

While Moore may be right in thinking the meaning of goodness to be intrinsically simple, it does not follow that it cannot be defined in the sense of making it intelligible by exhibiting its necessary relations. The notion of moral obligation, for example, is *sui generis* and irreducible to anything else, but it is made intelligible by defining the kind of situation in which it arises. Individuality we found to be a simple and irreducible notion, but we tried to make it intelligible by discussing the conditions of individuality. The only kind of notion which is absolutely indefinable except in the somewhat Pickwickian sense of ostensive definition by being pointed out is a notion which is not only simple but logically primitive. You cannot define what yellow means except by showing an instance of it, because the notion of yellowness has no logical presuppositions.

Moore actually assimilated good to yellow as simple unanalysable notions, but he soon came to see that there was an important logical difference although he was unable to describe the difference clearly.

I can only vaguely express the kind of difference I feel there to be by saying that intrinsic properties [like yellow] seem to *describe* the intrinsic nature of what possesses them in a sense in which predicates of value never do. If you could enumerate *all* the intrinsic properties a given thing possessed, you would have given a *complete* description of it, and would not need to mention any predicates of value it possessed; whereas no description of a given thing could be *complete* which omitted any intrinsic property.

Sir David Ross makes the difference more precise by pointing out that value "seems quite definitely to be based on certain other qualities of its possessors, and not the other qualities on the value" and that it "follows from the *whole* intrinsic nature of its possessors" and may therefore be called "a toti-resultant property."

Hence we may conjecture, with Bosanquet, that goodness, however simple in itself, is complex in its conditions and that "definable, by properties and function, is just what it is, and indefinable—merely designable by pointing—is just what it is not."

Returning to Aristotle, we can now ask whether the kind of analysis of value suggested by him does justice to the various ways in which we talk about value. At a first glance his description of the springs of change looks immoderately anthropomorphic. Change is said to presuppose that something by its nature tends towards the possession of something "divine and good and desirable" which it lacks. In the light of Aristotle's doctrine of substance, however, we can see that he wants to draw a fairly close analogy between conscious tendency and desire, on the one hand, and on the other the unconscious tendency towards development and fulfilment which he attributes to every substantial nature. That his universal teleology did not turn out in the end to be an adequate tool of scientific investigation need not make us deny its rightful place in the metaphysicsl analysis of change. Change, from the point of view of its active source, is a tendency towards a natural end or fulfilment, and the end or final cause is "good or apparent good."

Good, then, is the object of desire and approval, and it is a fitting object of desire and approval, but this is because intrinsically it resides in the development and fulfilment of natural potentialities. Good is actuality and actuality is good; degrees of actualization are degrees of goodness or value. The complete good of anything is the fullest possible development of its potentialities in harmony and proportion. But, since everything must be actualized to some extent in order to exist at all, being has some degree of value: *omne ens est bonum*. Being and value are one in reality, but the notion of value adds to that of being the element of more or less, of degree of quantity in the widest sense.

Such is the primary notion of intrinsic value or good as an end, with which we must contrast instrumental value or good as a means. The distinction is familiar enough. A banknote is a piece of paper with a design which we may or may not regard as aesthetically attractive; the truth is that most of us have scarcely examined the design, for we are interested not in the note's intrinsic value, which is in any case small, but in its instrumental value as something which we can exchange for more solid satisfactions. Even the miser can hardly be supposed to have a passion for the intrinsic value of his coins or banknotes; his curious turn of mind lies in a preference for the power of obtaining satisfactions over their actual enjoyment. On the other hand the insistence of the craftsman on worthy design is a desire to invest what are primarily means or instruments with some of the characteristics of ends, so that man may not lose himself in an uncomely world of means and forget the significance of intrinsic value. Intrinsic value for man must lie in the fulfilment of his nature, of his intellectual powers in knowledge, of his intellectual and sensory powers combined in aesthetic experience, and of his affective nature in friendship and love.

A thinking being can envisage value both in the present and in the future, both in himself and in others. This is the basis of the discrimination, which is directly relevant to ethics, made by Aristotle when he says that "there are three motives of choice and three of avoidance, on the one hand the noble, the expedient and the pleasant and on the other the base, the harmful and the painful." Pleasure arises from the conscious possession of present value, and this is true not only of pleasures of which we approve but also of pleasures of which we disapprove, for we disapprove of the latter not precisely because of what makes them pleasant but on account of the much greater values which they exclude. Even the most perverse and odious of pleasures must be admitted by the philosopher to contain an element of genuine value in, for example, a certain intensity of experience; otherwise it would not be a source of temptation to anyone. Everything that is desired is desired *sub ratione boni*.

The expedient is what is good as a means to future intrinsic good. There may or may not be a conflict between pleasure and expediency; the puritan is the man who thinks that there is always such a conflict while the hedonist at least implicitly supposes that there cannot be. Neither extreme can be rationally upheld.

Finally the noble is the absolutely good, that which is good in the widest range of reference, not only for the individual but for everyone else as well. The word we render as "noble" is καλόν, which in other contexts means "beautiful" and always conveys the suggestion that moral and aesthetic value coincide at least in their fullest forms. Right action, says Aristotle repeatedly, is for the sake of the noble.

What becomes of evil in this account of value? The difficulty has often been raised that, if value consists in degree of being, we can speak of better and less good but never of evil, for this would mean less than nonentity. Since we have already repeated the adage that all being is good, we cannot baldly deny all that is said in this objection. It is true that nothing can be absolutely and completely evil, for everything has some measure of being and, therefore, of value. Nor, if actuality were alone to be considered, would there be anything in the notion of evil except that of a lesser good, but in accordance with the doctrine of substance, actuality has to be measured in proportion to potentiality. It is from this that evil acquires its force and poignancy. The doctrine of substance, therefore, is of fundamental moment in the theory of value.

A change may be in the direction either of greater or of lesser actualization. Moreover a reduction in actuality may be either a mere lessening of activity or a definite frustration of a natural tendency. On the sensory level pain is the evidence of a frustration or, in Aristotelian language, a privation (στέρησις) of natural activity. Pain has its positive biological function as a warning to the organism and a stimulus to readapt itself in the sequel, but at the moment it is evidence of a negation of natural potentiality. Thus anything whose potentialities are partially frustrated, even though it possesses value to the extent that it is actualized, is in another respect in a condition of disvalue or evil.

Intrinsic evil, therefore, resides not simply in a situation of lesser value but in a definite frustration of natural potentiality or tendency. Furthermore, just as we can speak of instrumental value, so we have to recognize instrumental disvalue. A thing, whatever its intrinsic actuality may be, can be predominantly evil in its effects. Although an earthquake may be a magnificent exhibition of the powers of nature, nevertheless, if it takes place at the site of a city like Lisbon or Messina, we naturally regard it from our human point of view on account of its effects as evil. Effective disvalue attaches typically to the evil will. While we are inclined to pity at least as much as we condemn a man who is his own worst enemy on account of his devotion, say, to Bacchus or to Venus in her more lascivious aspects, we reserve our utter condemnation for the man who spreads suffering and ruin around him and especially for the cruelty which rejoices in doing so.

The theory that evil resides in a negation of being does not, therefore, deserve the reproach that it reduces evil to nothing. A frustration of natural tendency is a significant negation. Equally the source of such frustrations is evil in a still more significant sense. Yet it remains true that no positive degree of being as such is evil.

The concept of importance suggests itself here, for it is related to value while covering both value and disvalue. The sources of great good and the sources of great evil are equally important. If we sometimes ask to be delivered from great men, we are thinking of the harm which one kind of great man does. The great conquerors of history, for example, have done immeasurably more harm than good. But it would be a petty revenge of less powerful personalities to deny their greatness when their day is over. That is a point on which Nietzsche is instructive. In our own day, whatever may have been the physical and psychological defects from which Adolf Hitler suffered, to overlook his demonic force is both a stupidity in itself and a dishonour to those who stood out against him and only just succeeded in defeating him and the evil that he so powerfully spread.

If value consists in degrees of being, it follows that some sort of comparison of values is possible. But not everything that has a quantitative aspect is precisely measurable, and we need not expect to be any more successful than Jeremy Bentham if we look for a calculus of value. Where the degrees of actualization of a substance are related as AB to A, we are entitled to say without hesitation that AB is more valuable than A. But between A and B, between two possible forms of life, for example, that the same person might adopt, it is by no means easy to decide which better corresponds with his potentialities. What is of practical importance is to make an honest choice in accordance with the probabilities and to abide honestly by the choice made unless it turns out to be intolerable. but that is a matter of ethics rather than of metaphysics.

An even rougher comparison is possible between different things than is possible between different actualizations of the same thing. Whether philosophers are more important than poets, and either more important than plumbers, are scarcely questions which call urgently for an answer. The philosopher, the poet and the plumber can appropriately get on with their respective jobs without struggling for precedence. But a hierarchy of types of being is both a feature of traditional philosophy and susceptible of general justification. A living thing has a specific kind of activity which exceeds inorganic nature; to be sentient is more than to be merely alive; to think is more than to be merely sentient. Apart from these comparatively clear degrees of being comparison is not very rewarding. It is scarcely reasonable to ask whether it is better to be a rose than to be a tulip or better to be a dog than to be a cat.

It is still more hazardous to ask what would be the best kind of world. Is it one in which no type of thing is admitted which could be a source of harm to others, supposing that this is a possible kind of world at all, or one in which the variety of possible things is more completely displayed in spite of rivalry and conflict? Is it one in which there is free choice with all its momentous consequences of good and evil or one in which all tendencies are overruled for good? Human reason does not seem capable of making any answer. Still more, it seems that such worlds represent alternative and incompatible kinds of value. Hence the questions, what is the best possible kind of world and whether this is the best possible world, are probably nonsensical.

It is more to the point to ask how value is manifested by the various kinds of thing which make up the world we know. Inorganic nature does not show any obvious variation of value and disvalue. The inorganic thing is what it is and occupies its place in the order of being, whatever may be the relationships into which it enters. While its activity must be in accordance with its nature, its alternatives of realization seem to be alternatives of equal value. Hence teleological considerations are irrelevant to physics and chemistry.

Biology, however, cannot dispense with teleological thinking. A plant, tree or vegetable is in a quite literal sense healthy or unhealthy and achieves a greater or a lesser development. Such differences in actualization or value are precisely what interests the biologist from both a theoretical and a practical point of view, and he would be foolish if he thought that his kind of science could eventually dispense with teleology. For an organism is a self-maintaining, self-developing and self-reproducing structure, and that is to be essentially a teleological unit.

An animal, a sentient organism, is also and evidently a teleological unit capable of more or less complete realization in accordance with its natural potentialities. A thinking mind, whether in association with an organism or not, is evidently capable of greater or lesser actualization or may be frustrated and deprived of its natural development. Here in the middle of the scale of being comes the full force of the alternatives of good and evil.

At the upper end of the scale absolute being is necessarily and timelessly all that being can be. Here is no alternative of intrinsic good or evil; the fullness of intrinsic value must belong without question to the fullness of being. Such a being, however, is beyond the world of ordinary human experience, and the question of its existence belongs not to general metaphysics but to natural or philosophical theology.

This whole doctrine of value as degree of being and fulfilment of nature commends itself as explaining why we use emotive language and why we experience desire and aversion. It does not deny that some ostensible value-judgments are merely expressions of emotion or that others merely state that we have this or that attitude of mind. It is only too clear that we often speak without thinking or without thinking sufficiently. But, when we do think, the test of the justification of our emotions or attitudes of mind is be found in an objective criterion, and that criterion when analysed turns out to be the recognition that value consists in degree of being and fulfilment of nature, while disvalue resides in frustration and privation of being.

Dietrich von Hildebrand

20. THE ROLE AND PRIMACY OF VALUE

That value is intrinsic to being, Professor von Hildebrand has no doubt. In this, he is, obviously, in full agreement with Father Hawkins. But that value is intrinsic *because* it signifies the fulfillment of a natural teleological trend in being, von Hildebrand denies. Teleology, he asserts, already presupposes value, and therefore cannot be ascribed as the *raison d'être* of value.

Von Hildebrand approaches the question of value through an analysis of the notion of "importance," which is first a category of motivation, and second, a category of being. Three categories of motivation, he says, may

From *Christian Ethics* by Dietrich von Hildebrand. Coypright, 1953, by Dietrich von Hildebrand. Courtesy of David McKay Company, Inc.

be distinguished: (*a*) the *subjectively satisfying,* by which a being is desired because it is deemed "agreeable"; (*b*) the *objective-good-for-the-person,* by which a being is legitimately desired and is placed before the person as a rightful good for him; and (*c*) the *important-in-itself,* or value. Under analysis, only the last two can claim to be both categories of motivation and of being—though, in fact, it is the last that gives full title to the second category. There are, then, no things that in themselves are only subjectively satisfying.

Value, therefore, is as fundamental as being. It is the face of being. Though the datum of value is universally presupposed, it is not a mere postulate or methodological presupposition. We have to suppose value only because it is *in experience of being*—indeed, it is the objective and valid title of being. Values are real—and not simply logical—properties of being, and can be found even after abstracting from any possible motivation. Value is not an empirical or contingent link, but is intuitively grasped as a necessary and intelligible presence.

For this reason, von Hildebrand claims, any attempt to reduce value to something other than itself is futile. To say that value is a mere "suitability" that appeases a natural appetite is erroneous. Values presuppose knowledge; whereas, urges and appetites arise spontaneously. Value has the role of a *principium;* whereas the satisfaction bestowed by a value has the role of *principiatum.* When one makes the value nothing but a means to appease an appetite or an urge, one simply reverses these ontological roles and makes the satisfaction the *principium,* and the value the *principiatum.*

ONCE WE GRASP the meaning of importance we become aware that this ultimate question exists independently of our motivation. In approaching a being the question of its importance presents itself not merely from the point of view of any possible motivation. The question of importance has as much an original and objective meaning as the question of truth and existence. It is clearly absurd to suppose that the question of being and existence presents itself only for our knowledge and from the point of view of satisfying our knowledge. The same applies to the question of importance. The contrast between the gray, insipid emptiness of the indifferent and the colorful, meaningful plenitude of the important discloses to us the ultimate import of this question. We could not sustain for one moment the fiction of an absolutely neutral and indifferent world. Importance is as *fundamental as being.* The supposition that there exists no importance, that everything is in reality neutral, that all importance is a mere relational aspect, would mean a complete collapse of the universe. We realize the fundamental—I would even say, *inevitable*—significance of the question: What is the meaning, the importance, of a being?

These are ultimate questions rooted in our very existence: *existential* in the truest sense of the term, but transcending the realm of our own being in referring to something which has its inner necessity independently of ourselves, and which touches the ultimate metaphysical stratum. Such is the question of the meaning and importance of a single being, but above all of the entire universe. If we know only that something *is,* or exists, we have not yet reached the full answer which objectively imposes itself and for which our mind essentially thirsts. The existence of something necessarily calls forth the question of its meaning, its importance. The metaphysical dissatisfaction which we experience, as long as we have no answer to this ultimate question concerning the universe, is a prelude in the realm of nature to the "unrest" which, according to St. Augustine, fills our heart until we find God.

Even in the concept of *raison d'être* the notion of importance is ultimately included. For with respect to any final cause which indicates the *raison d'être* of its means, the same question would arise, and only the importance of the object could give a satisfactory answer. Moreover, for many beings the question of their *raison d'être* leads in no way in the direction of a final cause. We must realize that this question of importance is constantly present for us: indeed, it is so self-evident that it often fails to become an object of our philosophical wonder.

But once we become fully aware of this question and its meaning, we grasp that this importance is synonymous with the important-in-itself, with the value. Any other importance could never give the ultimate answer. In stating that something is subjectively satisfying, or even that something is an objective good for the person, the basic question of its ultimate importance remains unanswered.

The real fulfillment of meaning and importance can only be given in terms of importance in itself. As the ultimate fulfillment of our quest for truth can only be offered by the autonomy of being (i.e., its precedence over consciousness and its independence from our mind), so equally, the inevitable metaphysical question of importance can only be answered by the autonomously important, the important-in-itself, the value.

There are problems in philosophy concerning which it suffices only to *pose* the question in order immediately to grasp the answer. In these cases then the main philosophical achievement is to pose the question, which is so obvious. Such is the question: Which is the true, valid importance? *It cannot but be the value. . . .*

The datum of value is presupposed everywhere. There is no need to stress how many predications imply the notion of value. Whether we praise a man as just, or as reliable; whether we want to persuade someone that science is important; whether in reading a poem, we find it beautiful; whether we praise a symphony as powerful and sublime; whether we rejoice about the blossoming trees in spring; whether we are moved by the generosity of another person; whether we strive for freedom; whether our conscience forbids us to profit by injuring another—there is always presupposed the notion of something important-in-itself. So soon as we try to abstract from the importance and view everything as completely neutral and merely factual, all these predications, all these responses, lose their meaning. As a matter of fact they become impossible. Whenever we deliberate an action from the moral point of view we presuppose the datum of value, of something important-in-itself. In all indignation at something mean and debased; in every exclamation that some event is a great misfortune; in all assertions that one philosopher ranks higher than another, that one painter is a greater genius than another, we always presuppose the datum of value.

If we try to imagine a world which is completely neutral—an essentially impossible fiction—we realize that everything would lose all significance: our life would be reduced to an absurd and vicious circle; it would even sink below the level of animal life. Even in a world where there existed no importance other than the subjectively satisfying, our life would collapse. Imprisoned in our self-centeredness without the "Archimedean point" of objective importance, true happiness as well as all self-donation would be banished: all love, all enthusiasm, and all admiration. It would be impossible even to say that wisdom was preferable to folly. There would be no objective reason for us to turn in one direction instead of another, save that we were impelled either by our instincts or our desires for the subjectively satisfying, or because the neutral laws of nature forced us to conform to them.

In stressing these facts we in no way introduce value as a *postulate*. So to interpret it would be completely to misunderstand our meaning: we *have* to suppose the notion of value to make our life bearable or meaningful. Our aim consists exclusively in drawing the consequences of a denial of the notion of value and in showing to what extent it is constantly presupposed. We wish to give the reader the opportunity for a *prise de conscience* of that of which in a deeper stratum he is always aware, to which he constantly refers, and on which he continuously counts *because* he is implicitly aware of it. Our aim at present is to remind everyone of what he possesses in a deeper stratum, to draw him to this deeper stratum in which the datum of value is grasped and which even constitutes the pivotal point of existence and life.

We want only to aid the reader to realize that, despite the screen which philosophical theories and explanations have placed between his immediate contact with being and his philosophical awareness, value is not something peculiar; that it is not some strange thing introduced by a new philosophical theory; on the contrary, that it is something of which he is constantly aware. We want to make him realize that value is so self-evident that in every moment we presuppose it. Once we free ourselves from all falsifying interpretations and theories, we see the reality of value in such overwhelming clarity that we can no longer understand how, even theoretically, it was possible for us to overlook it or fail fully to admit it. . . .

If value is an objective property of a being, it is *a fortiori* the valid title of this being. This should be clear after our previous analysis of the nature of value. In the case of the subjectively satisfying, however, the question of whether or not there are objects which possess the potentiality of bestowing pleasure on us as a property of their own, clearly differs from the question of whether their agreeability is part of their God-given meaning, i.e., what we might call their valid, objective title.

The exact formulation of our question should run as follows: What corresponds in beings as their objective, valid meaning to the three categories of importance which we distinguished in the realm of motivation; namely, the merely subjectively satisfying, the objective good for the person, and the value? We shall first analyze this problem with respect to the subjectively satisfying, then with respect to the objective good for the person, and finally with respect to the value.

If we look at those things of which we predicate the quality of agreeability (for instance, a warm bath or a cool, soft breeze during great heat), we easily see that the qualitative content of the agreeable is rooted in the pleasure which these things cause in our body. Nevertheless the term agreeable as such also implies a characteristic of an object. Although the source of this type of importance is the pleasure which we experience through certain goods, yet this capacity of bestowing pleasure on us is without doubt a real quality of these beings. It is *this* quality which we term "agreeable."

It is a true characteristic of certain things to be agreeable and of others to be disagreeable, a characteristic which of course loses every meaning if we abstract from any being which is able to experience pleasure. But the character of agreeability is not the entire objective reality so far as the importance of things is concerned. Let us recall that our love tends naturally to bestow agreeable things on the beloved, and to avert what is disagreeable from him. It belongs to the display of the *intentio benevolentiae* in every love for a creature that we also want to offer to him a good meal, to make everything comfortable for him, and to protect him from disagreeable things. This clearly shows that legitimately agreeable beings have the character of something beneficent, of a gift for the person. They are objective goods *because* of their being agreeable, and the "pro" embodied in the agreeable is here the basis of the character of an objective good for the person. Although it occupies the lowest rung in the hierarchy of the objective good for the person, this type nonetheless possesses the dignity that belongs to all members of that hierarchy. We should indeed thank God that there exist agreeable things, such as the fresh breeze or the restorative swim on a very hot day, the warmth in a room when it is very cold, an excellent wine, a delicious meal, a bed or a chair if one is tired. These things have, as such, the character of objective goods for the person.

But rarely is this importance of agreeable things seen when they are the object of our *own* desire. We are normally tempted to approach them from the point of view of the merely subjectively satisfying. In this case, the importance which an object has independently of our approach does not coincide with the importance usually motivating this approach.

Abstracting from their possible role in our motivation—though obviously including their relation to man's susceptibility—we can state that there exist agreeable and disagreeable things. Their being agreeable certainly implies that they are subjectively satisfying, but it is also the root of their being an ob-- jective good for the person, granted that the things are agreeable with respect to a legitimate center. Insofar as we look at their objective significance, which we see much more clearly when the agreeable good for another person is at stake, their real importance lies in their status as objective goods for the person. Strictly speaking then, there exist no things which in themselves are only subjectively satisfying. So soon as there are at stake things which have the character of agreeability (and we imply hereby that they are so with respect to a legitimate center), they are as such objective goods for the person, even if for higher reasons the person should abstain from them in a concrete situation. Insofar as the significance of a being as such and not the point of view under which we approach it is our concern, every legitimately agreeable being is not only subjectively satisfying, but also an objective good for the person. And this is its valid, objective character. Although to approach the merely agree- able things from the point of view of the merely subjectively satisfying is not a distortion, it is at least an incomplete vision of them. Their being agreeable obviously implies their subjectively satisfying character. But we remain on the first level of appreciation if we do not also grasp their valid, objective type of importance.

We must clearly distinguish the point of view of the merely subjectively satisfying as such from the objective quality of the agreeable. This point of view makes our subjective satisfaction, whether legitimate or not, the only measure of our motivation so that when confronted with each and every good we ask but one question: What possible satisfaction for our pride and con- cupiscence may we get out of it? Now this can never coincide with the im- portance which a being as such possesses. If we ask what objectively is a being's importance, what kind of importance does it possess, what is its ob- jective, valid title in this respect, we would find there is no being which would be merely subjectively satisfying.

Thus we find here a split between a category of importance which plays a great role in our motivation and the importance with which the object is en- dowed in its God-given meaning. Plainly enough, the misfortune of a neighbor which is a source of subjective satisfaction to the envious person is objectively and in itself an evil. Here the point of view is in radical contradiction to the objective character involved: a manifest evil is a source of satisfaction; it is considered as something positive. In other cases, there may not be such a radical contradiction but still a thorough distortion. A position of powerful influence granted to a man and implying great responsibility is as such an objective good for him. But the man who relishes his position because of his ambition and pride and who strives for it because of his lust for power, approaches it as something exclusively subjectively satisfying. With respect to any good possessing a value, the approach from the point of view of the merely subjectively satisfying necessarily implies at least a distortion which can assume very different degrees.

As soon as the *merely* subjectively satisfying becomes a general point of view of our approach to life and being, it is in manifest contrast to the innocent subjectively satisfying character which is immanent in the agreeable. The merely subjectively satisfying as a general point of view of our motivation is an egocentric outgrowth of pride and concupiscence; it implies a blindness to the important-in-itself and to the objective good for the person, a blindness to the significance which beings objectively possess. In a word, it implies a falsification of the universe.

There is, however a naive motivation by the subjectively satisfying which must be distinguished from the general approach toward life and being under the exclusive or predominant viewpoint of the merely subjectively satisfying The naive approach, for instance, of Sancho Panza, is an incomplete but not a distorted approach toward agreeable things. Confronted by a good which is merely agreeable, we rightly grasp that it imposes no obligation on us to take an interest in it, to respond to it. The response which we give is up to us and our subjective inclination, granted that no disvalue connected with its possession forbids a positive interest in it. Far from calling for a conforming to it, the agreeable is objectively a mere offer; it conforms, as it were, to our mood.

But notwithstanding the fact that the agreeable imposes no obligation on us to conform to it, a response to the "gift" character of the existence of agreeable things as such should be given. We should also recognize the bounty of God manifesting itself in the very existence of agreeable things. This does not at all imply that we must strive for them or even accept them in concrete situations. On the contrary, we may refrain from pursuing them because of the danger which they may imply for our concupiscence and pride. Again, this appreciation of agreeable things, insofar as they are objective goods for the person, does not do away with the fact that we are never obliged to enjoy a certain thing when instead we wish to abstain from its fruition. But the right vision of these goods nevertheless ordains that we understand them as such to be a specific type of objective good for the person; and indeed we always do this whenever in a loving attitude we are confronted with agreeable goods for *another* person.

Our present analysis of the subjectively satisfying has already revealed that the character of an objective good for the person is not only a category of our motivation, but also an objective characteristic of a being. There is no split here between the importance which is an objective property of a being, and the importance which is a point of view of our motivation, such as there is with respect to the merely subjectively satisfying. Certainly in predicating of health, for instance, that it is an objective good for the person, we refer to an importance which essentially implies a relation to the person. But independently of the possible motivation, the "pro" or the friendly character of this good toward the person, we understand that it is a gift in agreement with man's true interest, and that its significance is rooted in the nature of health and likewise in the nature of a human person. Again, in predicating of the fruition of beauty that it has the character of an objective good, we clearly grasp that this character is objectively rooted in the value of beauty and in the noble happiness which it is superabundantly able to bestow on man.

We have to state, however, that different instances must be distinguished and that one and the same thing may be at once an objective evil for the person in a first instance, and an objective good in a second higher instance, or vice versa. An operation or a painful cure are in the first instance objective evils, but insofar as they restore health or perhaps even save life, they are objective goods for the person. An injustice inflicted on us is as such an objective evil for the person, but it may be an objective good for our spiritual life.

With respect to this type of importance there exist, so to speak, different levels, one of which is superior to another. But this hierarchy of levels refers not only to different strata in man, but also to causal consequences. Thus it may happen that a former objective evil has the character of being a causal precondition for an objective good which by far surpasses in its rank the good which we lost before.

This dimension of the objective good for the person is not accessible to philosophical analysis; for we touch here the significance which events have in the light of Providence which is, as it were, the final word on them; and this only the entirety of a life can reveal. Even then, however, we could give little more than a vague interpretation since we should be ignorant of the most important and decisive part of human existence: the judgment of God on man's eternal life.

Two dimensions concerning these different levels must therefore be distinguished: In the first, a thing which as such has the character of an objective evil for a man, e.g., an illness, may in a given situation be an objective good for him; it may awaken him from his indifference and turn his mind to eternity. Or any great trial, undoubtedly in itself an objective evil, may be the instrument for purification and for moral and religious progress, and thus a presupposition for a high objective good for the person. As a matter of fact, in many ascetic practices one chooses as a wholesome means something which in itself would be an objective evil; to inflict this on another person without any pedagogical or other necessity would be against charity and perhaps even justice.

This change of sign, this turning into an objective good something which in itself is an objective evil for the person, is here conditioned by the different strata in man. A thing which as such is an objective evil for the person, inasmuch as it is disagreeable (or as we can say, an objective evil of the sphere wherein the lowest type of goods for the person is to be found), happens to be connected with an objective good for the person which is situated in a higher sphere of objective good. Thus the same thing may be an objective evil with reference to a lower stratum, but an objective good with repect to a higher one. A surgical operation is an evil because of the bodily ordeal which it entails, but it becomes an objective good when it saves a human life.

The final word here rests always with the higher ranking stratum. Nevertheless, such things have in the first instance really the character of an evil. This character is a mere appearance as in the case of a simple error. Taken in itself and isolated from any other context, it has as such the character of an objective evil, but it assumes the character of a benefit and objective good as soon as it is related to other higher ranking objective goods in such a way that it is instrumental for the possession of these higher goods. Therefore, in this concrete case, the valid significance of that which in the first instance appears as an evil is determined by its relation to the higher ranking stratum in the person.

The changing of sign, the turning of something evil for the person into something good for him, has a second dimension. Here more is involved than merely the differing strata in man to which the evil and the good respectively refer, namely, the course of events and their extension in time. A thing which is definitely an objective evil as such (for instance, being forced to flee a country, to give up great material goods, or to relinquish the presence of beloved persons, a beautiful house, and so on) may prove years later to have been the way to an even greater and higher ranking good: for example, it may provide the circumstances which prepare the way for a conversion.

In the sphere of the objective good for the person we are also confronted with the fact that one and the same event may be a good for one person and a misfortune to another. The outcome of a war which is victory for one side is defeat for the other. We could name innumerable examples of great events and also of trifles possessing objectively a different significance for different persons.

This fact may impose many difficult problems on man. It is one of the great ethical dilemmas which result from the divergent legitimate aspirations of different persons and the opposite significances which one and the same event possesses objectively for them. But it can only enter into our ethical consideration if an objective value turns the scale for one or another decision, provided, of course, that the divergence of aspirations and difference of events can be ascertained. Yet the intermingling of all things which are at once objective goods for one person and objective evils for another may definitely surpass the frame of human prevision; especially with respect to the significance which they may assume in the light of unpredictable future circumstances. This intermingling belongs to those things which must be left to Providence and to Providence alone.

This may suffice to explain the discrepancy between the aspects which one and the same thing may offer concerning the type of importance which we termed the objective good for the person. We can easily see that a possible and quite frequent discrepancy in no way contradicts the fact that this kind of importance really inheres in the object, although, to be sure, it implies reference to a human person.

The central problem, however, is the question whether the values are real properties of beings, properties which we can find in beings even after we have abstracted from any possible motivation. In saying of an act of contrition that it is morally good, or in praising a man as intelligent or as a genius, or in speaking of the dignity of a human person, we undoubtedly refer to excellences which are properties of the respective beings; we do not refer merely to points of view of possible motivation. The moral nobility of an act of contrition, its importance in itself, is, if we contemplate the nature of such an act, univocally given to us. In order to perceive the intrinsic goodness and moral beauty of contrition we need not approach it from a certain point of view; it suffices merely that our mind be unhampered by pride and concupiscence, that the eyes of our mind be not blinded by a perversion of our will.

And when we grasp this intrinsic goodness, this moral value, as actually inhering in contrition, it is not merely an apprehension similar to that which allows us to state that blood is red. Rather we understand and grasp that there exists an essential link between the value and the object. It is not only another and deeper relation than the one which exists between substance and accident, the typical inherent relation, but it is moreover a necessary intelligible link, not a mere factual and accidental one. We understand that contrition is morally good and that it must be so.

This does not, however, mean that we could prove the value of contrition by deducing its importance from something else. We saw before that the importance in itself can never be deduced from something neutral. Every value has to be grasped; if a person is blind to a value, all we can do to help him grasp it is to pave the way by removing the obstacles of his will and by trying to draw him under its spell.

But if it is true that the value of contrition cannot be deduced from the neutral sphere, from neutral laws, or from the immanent logic of a neutrally conceived being, it is also a fact that once we have grasped the value we understand that it is essentially rooted in the nature of contrition. The essential link between moral goodness and contrition is nonetheless univocally given.

In other words, the relation between a being and its value, insofar as a direct importance in itself is concerned, is not empirical and contingent but is rather necessary and intelligible. In contemplating charity, we grasp at once that it is necessarily good; we do not just bluntly state it, but we understand that it is so and must always be so. It is plainly nonsensical to say of acts of charity or justice that in speaking of their value we only refer to such a point of view of motivation; for evidently the value discloses itself as a property of these acts. In order to grasp that the moral goodness of justice, the beauty of a star-covered sky, the value of a human person, or his dignity as an *imago Dei* are in the fullest sense properties of these beings, we have only to compare the character of being endowed with an intrinsic value with the mere character of being commanded by a true authority.

In the case where the moral significance of an object results exclusively from the commandment of a true authority, the importance is obviously superimposed on the object. It is an importance which is located in the object, but is not rooted in its essence.

Someone may object: The value is only an ideal, rooted in the essence of something but not a property of a real concrete indivdual act. This objection is based on an error. If extension essentially belongs to the nature of matter, it is obvious that wherever a concrete corporeal being is be found, extension will also be found as a concrete real property of it. All those elements, marks and properties which are essentially rooted in the nature of some quiddity become real. Thus the question of whether the value is also to be found in a concrete individual act of a certain kind is as such already futile. If the value is necessarily rooted in the nature of an act, it must become real as soon as the act is actually accomplished.

But even apart from this, it is mostly in the awareness of a person's concrete real attitude that we perceive certain values for the first time. It is not only in abstract contemplation of the quiddity of certain acts or attitudes that we discover their value, but also and especially we discover the value in concrete real acts. The real concrete existence of a being endowed with a value is, however, in no way an essential condition for discovering its value; the moral value of a heroic deed may be grasped just as well in the action of the hero of a novel.

We see then that the important-in-itself or the value is objective in every sense of the word. It is objective insofar as it is a real property of the being of which we predicate a value; beings are endowed with values even if we abstract from any possible motivation. Values are so much proper to beings that they form the core of their significance. Values can in no way be interpreted as mere relational aspects of being which it possesses with respect to our desire or will. . . .

Many attempts have been made to reduce value to something other than itself. But these attempts are futile and vain because the notion of value refers to an ultimate datum, not only in the sense that it is grasped solely in an original intuition and is undeducible (this would also apply to the color red), but also in the sense that it is a fundamental datum which we necessarily always presuppose. Value is an ultimate datum in the same way as essence, existence, truth, knowledge—these we cannot deny without tacitly reintroducing them. We shall now discuss the main attempts to reduce value to something else; such an analysis will simultaneously further clarify the nature of value.

Many objects assume a character of importance because of their suitability to appease an urge or an appetite in us. Water becomes important for the thirsty person; though he looked with indifference at water so long as he was not thirsty, it suddenly assumes a character of importance because of his thirst.

Our life is pervaded by bodily urges and appetites of our soul, and the objects suitable to appease them thereby assume an importance. To drink becomes an attraction for the thirsty; to rest becomes important for the tired; to move and run about is a delight for the vital energies of a child; to remain silent is for the loquacious person painful, and so on. The object which is able to appease an urge or an appetite, so long as this urge or appetite is not appeased, presents itself to us either as something merely subjectively satisfying or as an objective good for the person.

Now any attempt to reduce value to mere suitability for appeasing an urge or an appetite is futile. The essential difference between value and the importance rooted in this suitability clearly manifests itself in the following marks: First, the relation between the object and our interests in it differs radically in each case. Urges and appetites are rooted in our nature. In order to arise, they do not presuppose a knowledge of the object or activity which is capable of appeasing them. Their arising in us is due to our nature and hence they may even precede the knowledge of the object. The inner movement which is proper to them is not engendered by the object; thus the urge or appetite has the role of the *principium,* and the importance, rooted in the suitability of an object or an activity to appease an urge or appetite, is the *principiatum.* The importance of the object is clearly something secondary; it is a means of appeasement. Its suitability is important only because the urge and appetite exist; as soon as the urge or appetite disappears, the object loses its importance and falls, so far as our experience is concerned, to the level of the indifferent.

Our admiration of a person's humility, on the contrary, is not something arising spontaneously in our nature without a knowledge of the humility of this person. Rather, such admiration essentially presupposes a knowledge of the object. It is an inner movement which depends entirely on the object, which is motivated by the object, and which essentially implies that we understand the importance in itself of the object. The importance of the object presents itself clearly as independent of my admiration; it is the *principium,* and my admiration is the *principiatum.*

There can be no question of any urge or appetite for which the existence of a moral value as such would be an appeasement. To pretend that there exists within the person an unconscious appetite to admire certain things (as, for instance, that an act of forgiveness is important only because it satisfies such an appetite) would obviously be a mere fiction suggested only to save the theory at any cost. In reality there is nothing which supports this supposition.

But even if there were such an urge to admire, to look up to things greater than ourselves, it would yet be impossible to reduce the value of the act of forgiving to a mere capability for appeasing this appetite. An appetite or urge to find an object which we can admire could be appeased only if an object presented itself as *admirandum;* that is to say, as being worthy of our admiration—but this again means being endowed with a value. Admiration essentially presupposes an awareness of the value of the object; thus to pretend that the value is nothing but a suitability to appease our urge to admire is to revolve in a circle. For in order to engender or motivate our admiration, the object must itself possess more than mere suitability; it must present itself precisely *as* important in itself.

S. Alexander   **21. VALUE AND STANDARD SATISFACTION**

In this essay, Samuel Alexander puts forward a blend of ideas already espoused by Father Hawkins and Professor von Hildebrand. He envisions value, with Hawkins, as a natural satisfaction; with von Hildebrand, as an objective character of realities. Yet his eventual conclusion terminates in a position that would be acceptable to neither.

Approaching the question of value without prepossession or bias, says Alexander, one must ask what in values *makes* their value. A value is, first, that which satisfies; but, second, it can be said to satisfy only because it is regarded for its own sake.

What, then, makes us regard a value for its own sake? It could be said that values engender our happiness, but this does not answer the question of why we are attracted to them. We desire good ends for their own sakes "because there is a controlling passion which does not allow us to satisfy any particular passion . . . as it arises, but subjects that particular passion to the control of another passion, that of sociality, or regard for the wishes of others.'

From *Philosophical and Literary Pieces* by S. Alexander. Reprinted by permission of Macmillan & Company Ltd., and the University of Manchester.

The same applies to that which gives things the value of truth: "It is that we seek to systematize our acquaintance with things." We are thus motivated toward truth by a passion for systematic inquiry. It is such a passion that turns our acquaintance with things "from practical knowledge into truth acquired for its own sake." Truth is truth because it satisfies curiosity in a refined human form, "and its value lies in the satisfaction it brings to us thus."

The clearest case for his view, Alexander believes, is to be found in the value of beauty, which is that which satisfies the impulse of constructiveness in a form that is both human and contemplative. "Human constructiveness is pursued for itself, Beauty or the beautiful is what satisfies this impulse."

Hence, at the root of our search for, and interest in, the values of good, truth, and beauty are three specific passions: the *social sentiment,* the *sentiment of disinterested curiosity,* and the *sentiment of constructiveness.* When we speak of the "objectivity of value," we simply mean the relation between these passions and what may be called a standard individual. We establish this criterion through trial and error, or "by finding out who are in agreement" with specifically denoted objects under the title "value."

THE IDEA OF VALUE has become the subject of so much loose usage and loose thinking, which does almost more harm than false thinking, that the very name has an ill odour in philosophy. At a recent conference of philosophers at Reading a remark made incidentally that the word was detestable was received with applause. The reason is that the name is used to suggest something admirably mysterious, to be received with reverent acceptance, and no questions asked of its authority. The highest values, the old triad of truth and goodness and beauty, stand for something precious in our lives and the word value has acquired an aroma rare and exquisite. But in science and knowledge we dare not allow our practical prepossessions to colour the ethical neutrality (I borrow a phrase of Bertrand Russell's) we have to observe in theoretical enquiry. We need to ask what value is without prepossession.

There is a general feeling in the air that value is an essential feature in the constitution of the universe. But till we know what value is, and what the word means, we may be fancying that the highest values themselves may be the most important features of the universe. Whereas it may turn out merely that there is something in the universe which at a higher stage is familiar to us under the form of the highest values, but is in itself something very simple and divested of emotional trappings. Mr. Laird has offered to find this simple and pervasive feature in what he calls "natural election," the fact that everything in the universe has something else which matters to it or to which it matters, like the magnet and the iron filings. Before him Mr. Perry of Harvard had extended the meaning of value to cover any kind of interest. Whatever is interesting to a conscious being is a value or valuable for that being. That would be making value something purely psychological, and the highest values would be (though we have yet to hear Mr. Perry on the subject in a new volume) particular cases of such interest. Mr. Laird goes further and extends the meaning beyond conscious beings to all beings, and I see no reason why we should stop at conscious beings. Now if Mr. Laird is right, and I think he is, value would be a very important feature in the universe, and would be another way of expressing the fact that everything directly or indirectly, closely or remotely, is connected with the whole of things, that as Mr. Whitehead puts it, everything in the world has all the rest of the world for its field. But at least we know here just how much and how little value means, and we are not tempted to loose talk about beauty and goodness. For in a simple and comprehensive notion like this we have got very far away from our own highest values. They may be instances of natural election or of interest. But there is nothing exciting or emotional about natural election, and that is its great merit. It is an attempt to show what value ultimately means, And I am persuaded that we must give up talking at large about value till we have found out what makes a thing valuable.

I propose to confine myself to the familar highest values and to ask what it is in them which makes their value. Now there are two things which strike us at once about these values of beauty and goodness and truth. The first is that they are relative to us humans and satisfy us in certain respects; and the second is that when we value anything as true or good or beautiful the objects we value under these terms are regarded for their own sakes. When we answer the question how such objects come to be regarded for their own sakes, we shall be answering also the question in what respects they satisfy or are satisfactory to us. I will deal with the first question, I mean how objects come to be regarded for their own sakes, first, because the need of answering it is often overlooked. It is so easy to say that a good act or a good character is regarded for its own sake, or contemplatively; or that a beautiful face or statue or picture is regarded for its own sake, that this contemplation of objects for their own sakes seems hardly to require accounting for. Yet when we have accounted for it we have in fact solved the question how such objects have value.

Take morals first. It is a commonplace of the unsophisticated mind that we tell the truth and pay our debts not for the sake of the consequences or to avoid the pains and penalties of the law or public opinion, but because the two objects in view are respectively telling the truth and paying debts. Then sophistication comes in with ethical theory. One kind of theory says we approve these actions because they bring with them happiness, and some even go so far as to hold that we desire not the paying of debts but the happiness that comes of it. Now it may very well be that good actions do bring happiness, and yet it need not be true that they are approved for that reason. This theory hardly concerns us, for it holds that it is only by force of habit that we desire good ends for their own sake. Moreover, all the time there may be a different answer: that we are temperate and pay our debts not because it pays us better (though on the whole it does pay us better), but because we prefer temperance and honesty.

There is a different form of sophistication possible. Because when we do good actions we do them for their own sakes, this may be taken to mean that we do right because it is right, and that there is a right or a good which is a fundamental character of goodness, quite distinct from all consideration of consequences or motives. Kant followed this line when he tried to show that the goodness of good action lay in its categorical character, its universality, and set up a barren criterion of goodness. Our latter-day moralists follow a different line, and declare that right action is something which only intuition of its rightness can settle. Here again possibly there is an alternative which has been overlooked. Utilitarian theories hardly account at all for why actions are desired for their own sakes. These other theories offer a theory but it goes beyond the necessities of the situation. For actions may be desired for their own sakes not because of some mysterious property of rightness they possess, which we learn by intuition or by rationality, but because they satisfy some desire different from the desire which leads to the action. I desire drink, but I desire temperance in drinking because I carry my fellows with me when I stop, and do not when I exceed. Or I respect your right to life because I and other people dislike murder, as the Bible illustrates when Cain, after killing Abel, is met by the wrath of God. Now this suggests that I come to regard actions for their own sake, not because of another passion which makes me sympathetic with the wishes of other persons in society.

Consequently we desire ends for their own sakes, as ordinary moral experience tells us we do, because there is a controlling passion which does not allow us to satisfy any particular passion, thirst or jealousy or what not, as it arises, but subjects that particular passion to the control of another passion, that of sociality or regard for the wishes of others. The social feeling, or the tribal self, confronts and limits the mere particular self. In this way any object when subjected to this control is lifted out of the mere class of objects which satisfy my individual or material passions, and becomes an object desired for its own sake. As I said before, by discovering how objects come to be desired for their own sake, we at the same time learn that such objects satisfy the social self or the social impulse. Goodness thus derives its value from its satisfying the social impulse in a man. The two questions have been answered together. We may add that the value of the good act or character is thus the relation between the act in question and the impulse it satisfies and that value is experienced by us as the pleasure of having our social passion gratified.

Consider, next, truth which may be described as acquaintance with the world of things, in so far as that acquaintance is pursued for its own sake. Our acquaintance with things is in the first instance practical: we know things in their uses for us. Indeed it might be maintained, were this the proper place to do so, that knowledge comes to us essentially through practice. We do not first know things and then act; we know things through acting upon them. The things which surround us excite us physically to response or, as we commonly say, to reaction. In that reaction upon them we become aware of them or know them. Light provokes us to turn our eyes to it and we then see it as light. All our knowledge is thus a revelation to us of things which first provoke us to repond to them. Differences in things provoke different responses, and difference in the response brings us face to face with the things as we know them. This relation begins with the data of sense, it is completed through the other responses of our so-called cognitive processes, and in the end the world as we know it is a vast system revealed to us through all the ways of sense, imagination, thought. But things which begin by being instruments of practice become emancipated from their practical uses and are observed and thought about for their own sakes. The connection with practice is never severed; just as right and goodness are never severed from their roots in passion and desire. But as in morals a new passion enters to emancipate us from the pressure of personal passions, so in knowing we leave the calls of utility and study things for themselves and create science. Science begins with practical uses, leaves them and enters the pure empyrean of theory and returns to practical uses again.

Now what makes acquaintance with things into truth and gives it the value of truth? It is that we seek to systematise our acquaintance with things, which gives us varying and often contradictory information about them. The data of the senses conflict with one another and with the other data supplied through memory. For man is a creature of ideas, and while the animal is content with the data of the moment, or is so for the most part, man brings, through his gift of imagination and memory and reflection, all the scattered fragments of his experience together and weaves them into an integral whole, makes theories and systems, invents hypotheses to unite his separate data, and, always under guidance from the world he is subject to, may construct systems which at first seem remote entirely from the sensible world, but in the end are verified by that sensible world, under pain or modification or rejection.

It is this passion for systematic enquiry which, with all the helps of his cognitive powers, turns his acquaintance with things from practical knowledge into truth acquired for its own sake. The impulse which leads him on is curiosity, not in the mere animal form which makes a dog sniff about in the interests of food or sex, but in the form of humanised and systematic curiosity sublimated as it were through the presence of ideas. Such curiosity is of its own nature systematic.

As before with goodness so with truth. Truth is truth because it satisfies curiosity in this refined and human form, and its value lies in the satisfaction it brings to us thus. Truth has no doubt many other characters which there is not space to describe, all flowing from this original character. But truth is a value or has value because it satisfies this human curiosity, always under guidance or control from things themselves. The passion of enlightened curiosity which we call enquiry makes knowledge desired for its own sake and at the same time makes that knowledge a value as the satisfaction of a human need.

When we come to beauty, the third of these highest values, the situation is still plainer, and I am myself more interested in beauty just because the study of it affords a readier approach to the essential nature of value. Here too the beautiful object is not merely seen or heard but contemplated for its own sake. The beautiful object, whether in nature or art, is a material thing; in art, where the fact is sometimes overlooked, it consists of tones or pigments or bronze or marble or, as in literature, of words. Now these objects, whether in nature or in art, convey practical pleasures or, as they may usefully be called, material pleasures. Partly the actual material pleases, as with tones or the texture of marble; partly the subject (when, as in representative art, there is a subject distinct from the materials themselves) pleases. These pleasures enter into the total effect of beauty but they are not themselves the pleasure of beauty and may even divert the mind from beauty itself. An erotic love song or an unskillful or inartistic painting of the nude may excite and please material passions, and when such pleasure is predominant the experience is not aesthetic. Even in a portrait the mere pleasure of recognition which accompanies a successful likeness to the subject is subsidiary to the aesthetic success which is different from mere likeness. In a beautiful love song, say, "My love is like a red, red rose"; or the charming conceit of Carew quoted by Edward Fitzgerald in one of the first in the collection of his letters,

> Ask me no more where Jove bestows,
> When June is past, the fading rose, etc.,

the material passion is indeed excited or suggested but in such subordination to the unity of the whole poem that it does not excite practically. The green field may give pleasure to a cow, but it is not appreciated by her, we may presume, as beautiful just because though seen it is not contemplated for itself.

How do sights and sounds as in a work of art or as in nature seen with an aesthetic eye come, then, to be thus contemplated? I have tried to give the answer in a paper of some years ago by pointing to the fact that a beautiful object is never seen as it actually is but the mind introduces into the object its own interpretations and imputes to the object characters which it does not really possess. I have to repeat myself. The marble which is dead looks alive or full of character; the words of a poem not only have their meanings in the sense that they stand for objects, but the meaning and the word are blended, the words as I have put it are charged with meaning. Even such simple beauty as that of a pure colour or a pure tone pleases aesthetically or is beautiful because the mind is aware of its purity, its freedom from admixture of other tones or colours; such purity has its basis in the material fact, but needs the presence of the mind to apprehend through contrast or comparison. There is the added interpretation by the mind itself. So much truth at least there is in the famous notion of "empathy," which has played so large a part in recent aesthetical theory. I need not stay to ask how we thus alter the actual material things so as to give them a meaning they do not themselves possess. The sculptor portrays a Hermes and he shapes the marble so that it means for the appreciative onlooker godhead and playfulness. The marble has this meaning in the same way as we see the ice cold. The marble takes a significant shape because the artist's choice of line and plane and volume embodies the ideas or images or thoughts the artist himself brings to the work.

Thus the work of art is according to the old phrase which C. E. Montague quotes *homo additus naturae*. Now it is this addition to the physical material of a "foreign" meaning from the side of the creative or appreciative mind which lifts the object out of its practical character and allows it to be contemplated for its own sake. Observe that this applies not only to art but to nature as well. For nature when it is seen beautiful and not merely pleasing to the sense is altered by our interference: we select those elements in the natural object which suit our mood. Nature when she is seen beautifully is subjected to our interference, according to the well-known lines of Coleridge,

> O Lady we receive but what we give
> And in our life alone does nature live;

which however, does not allow for nature's existence apart from our finding her beautiful. The addition from our mind of interfering elements which we attribute to the material, not only brings those elements themselves before our minds but it divests the actual material elements present of their purely material character. By being interfered with they are diverted from their normal practical function and become the subject of contemplation. I have quoted elsewhere Shakespeare's line,

> Do paint the meadows with delight.

Delight and painting are introduced plainly by the poet, but the meadows themselves are transfigured in the process.

It is not always so easy to see that this statement holds in a non-representative art like music or in architecture, which comes nearest to music. Nor am I able to deal with the difficulties as they deserve. I must refer you here, if you care to pursue the theme, to what I am about to say in a more systematic treatment of the whole subject of this lecture which I hope may shortly appear. Everywhere it will be found, I think, that where there is beauty, even in the most formal art, significance belongs to the work through the interference of the artist or the spectator. And the study of non-representative art forces upon us the conviction that the beauty of the beautiful does not belong as such to the material effects of the beautiful but to its formal character, which it owes to the active constructive operation of the mind, which, out of elements, some of them given in the material, gives unity and harmony to the whole according to the old Greek account of beauty as unity in variety.

In discovering how the beautiful object is contemplated for itself, we have discovered what beauty is and what makes it a value. Beauty is that which satisfies the impulse of constructiveness, that is, constructiveness of materials, not the mere construction which the man of science uses in thinking—when that constructiveness has become human and contemplative. For constructiveness is found also among certain animals, but their constructions, like the hive of the bee, or the beaver's dam, or the nightingale's song, are part of practical arrangements, storage of food, or care for the young, or courtship. Human constructiveness is pursued for itself. Beauty or the beautiful is what satisfies this impulse, and beauty is a value because of the particular pleasure it brings to this impulse. They are therefore right who say there is an aesthetic sentiment, and I add that it is the human representative of animal constructiveness.

The value of beauty is thus eminently a relation, as between the beautiful object and the mind which creates, or appreciates; for appreciation is but creation at the bidding of the creator, it is going over again the work of creation when that work has been already performed. How essentially beauty is relative is seen from the constitution of the beautiful object itself, part given, part added by the mind; so that the relation of beauty to the mind is implied in the very nature of beauty.

The situation then is a complex one. An object is created or discovered which satisfies the impulse of constructiveness, and is a value because it so satisfies. Beauty is referred to the object as belonging to it, but it is not a quality of the object like yellow or sweet, but is the relation which the object has to the constructive person. He experiences the pleasure of beauty in the satisfaction of the constructive or, let us say now, of the aesthetic sentiment. The pleasure belongs to the person who feels it, the beauty is referred as a quality to the object which so pleases. Strictly it is not a quality at all, but a value, that is, a relation of the object to the person of satisfying the aesthetic sentiment.

One feature has been, however, omitted in each of these three cases, namely, the objectivity of value. None of these values is such for the individual alone but for many individuals. Virtue satisfies the social sentiment, truth the sentiment of disinterested curiosity; beauty satisfies the sentiment of constructiveness when that sentiment is emancipated from practice and thereby becomes impersonal. Thus all three values have their value in relation not to a particular individual but in relation to what may be called a standard individual, in morals the wise or good man, in truth the knowing man, in art or beauty the aesthetic judge. The mere disinterestedness of these values is enough to indicate their being satisfactions, not of one but of many and in general of a society of people. It is this impersonal character which gives a meaning to the "absoluteness" of the highest values. Relative to individuals at any one time, they are at that time not relative to a particular but to a standard individual. And if you ask me how the standard is set up or discovered I answer, by trial, by finding out who are in agreement with it. The good and the knowing and the tasteful discover themselves and they exclude from those titles those who do not come up to the standard. The judges are discovered at the same time as the rule by which they judge. From one point of view the standard is set up by a piece of tyranny, but the tyranny is established in the effort to secure goodness and truth and beauty.

Now if, bearing in mind the standard or objective character of the highest values, we go down the scale and consider what corresponds to these values among the animals (including man as an animal) and lower down amongst plants, we see that what is valuable to them is what satisfies generic wants. Food is valuable to the animal because it maintains the life of the species. Merely as pleasant to him, it has not value but is pleasant; in as far as it is nutritious it secures life in the animal's kind. Thus even lower than beauty and goodness and truth, the feature of objectivity of value is retained. Only what is established amongst ourselves by trial or experiment is already fixed in the animal in the needs of his species.

Descending still lower than life, we find that there is value amongst material things in so far as one thing can satisfy another, as the chemists used to say long ago about the satisfaction of one atom by another within the molecule. Here, too, value remains objective. Only the distinction between the individual and the species has not yet emerged in the scale of existence, and all interest of one thing in another is objective: there is no room for that difference of individuals from one another which makes one man's interests differ from those of another, and may, if he cannot submit himself to the standardisation of value, make him the subject of purely personal values, called so merely because they satisfy him as true value satisfies the standard man. Such so-called values are miscalled value, omitting as they do the reference to the generic or standard which, as we have seen, lies at the basis of real value. In other words, it is only when the notion of value, that is, standard satisfaction, is familiar, that it becomes possible for the individual to claim that his satisfactions are "values" for himself. Thus standard or real value is not as it were a compromise between a multitude of personal values, but rather personal likings arrogate to themselves the title of value to which they have no claim. Personal value is a defect from real value, and value a growth from personal values.

Time and Space

J. A. McWilliams, S.J.

22. SPACE AS A
RECEPTACLE

Within human experience, each being is "encapsulated" in both space and time. In this selection, Father McWilliams attempts, on behalf of moderate realism, to portray the meaning and status of one of these factors.

Space, he says, is not a being or a type of being, because we always refer to material entities as being *in* space. We do not directly perceive space as such but speak of it as a context. It is, however, not merely a part of one's mental equipment or a categorizing power of the mind.

The perception of space involves at least three separate acts of the mind. Beginning with the perception of bodies extended in space—and this is all we directly "see"—the mind abstracts the characteristic of extension, and ultimately the note of space. Direct perception of bodies, therefore, does not, as Kant held, suppose the prior notion of space, since it is "two removes in advance of that notion."

By space, then, we mean *abstract extension that is considered a receptacle for bodies*. Space as such is consequently a product of the mind, but it has a foundation in extramental reality. The sum of *real* space—that is, space occupied by real bodies—and *possible* space—that is, unoccupied space—is called *absolute* space.

THE WORD "SPACE" is in daily usage among men, and every one readily understands what is meant by it. A printer will speak of space for an article, the captain of a ship will say there is space for so much cargo in the hold of the vessel, a taxicab driver can accurately judge the space needed for his car to slip between two vehicles or the amount of room required to park it at the curb. The vacationist seeks the great open spaces of the country, and the astronomer studies the heavenly bodies immersed in an illimitable sea of space. Even children understand what is meant by space. Still, very few people, if asked, could give an exact definition of the term. The space we speak of in the thesis is not different from that of everyday usage; and our purpose is simply to *defend the definition* there set down.

. . . Kant held that the notion of space is a part of the mental equipment with which we come into the world. But that conclusion of his was a result of self-deception. The error occurs in the following manner. I reflect that I always see bodies, and think of them, as *in space;* they occupy space, they are each contained in just so much space, they are surrounded by space, they are immersed in space, and if they move there must be ahead of them ready and waiting a space into which to move. But if the notion of space thus antecedes the most direct sense perception, that notion must be innate. The deception comes from supposing that we have *always,* even from our earliest infancy, perceived bodies as in space, and that we *cannot* perceive them, or think of them otherwise. A little analysis of the data of consciousness will reveal the fact that the notion of space is not the first item, as Kant supposed, but the third. The first perception is that of exended bodies, which we become aware of by their color, or their resistance, and by our own movement about or among them. The next mental act is to make an abstraction. We prescind from their hardness or softness, their smoothness or roughness, their color, and all such qualities, and concentrate our attention upon their extent. We now have arrived at the notion of abstract extension, but this is not as yet "space." We have achieved a representation of extension from which all existing and individual bodies are obliterated, of extension as something standing alone by itself and independent of all bodies. The third operation is to restore the bodies to the expanse from which they have been banished. It is only then that we think of bodies as *in space.* But the whole completed operation is so much a matter of habit in adult life that we are apt to overlook the fact that it contains three distinct mental acts instead of one. The seeing of bodies in space is so far from being a primitive fact of consciousness that it is really the last of the trio. The direct perception of bodies does not suppose the notion of space, but is two removes in advance of that notion.

. . . Our *definition* therefore is that *space is abstract extension considered as a receptacle for bodies.* The *phantasms* which one may form to attend this concept will, of course, be various. In order to imagine anything I must fancy it endowed with *some sensible property,* with color, smoothness, cold, etc. Thus I can picture the vast interstellar spaces as having the cerulean tint of the sky. Or I can liken space to an immense sea in which bodies near and far are immersed and move about. If I restrict my consideration to a single body, I can still consider the space which that body alone occupies, and can represent the space as a container, or box, with extremely thin sides; or, better, as some kind of absorbent entity, which instead of moving out of the way for bodies, swallows them up, so to speak, drinks them in and completely engrosses them. Different persons will form different material images, but the underlying notion is that space is a container or receptacle for bodies.

... Space is divided into *real* space, *possible* space and *absolute* space. Real space is that which is occupied by a body, or bodies. Possible space is unoccupied space. Absolute space is the sum of the two. Hence absolute space takes in all space. We form this notion by prescinding from whether the space be occupied or not, and consider it only as being capable of occupation; in absolute space we break down the barriers between real and possible space and view it all as one. And, whereas real space is limited by the confines of the bodies in existence, and possible space is excluded from the compass of those bodies, absolute space recognizes no limits whatever, and expands indefinitely in all directions. It corresponds to the "infinite" of mathematics. On the other hand, possible space may be very restricted; for if there are vacua within the universe, little volumes not occupied by any matter whatsoever—not even by the ether—these vacua are as truly possible space as that which begins at the outer rim of the universe and stretches from there on illimitably. Real space is always coterminous with the body concerned.

... In the science of geometry space is regarded somewhat differently from the way it is regarded in the present thesis. Firstly, in mathematics space is considered in one, two or three dimensions; in this thesis we consider it in three dimensions only. It is clear that a body cannot occupy any but three-dimensional space. Secondly, geometry does not regard even its three-dimensional space as being occupied at all; in fact it prescinds from the whole question of occupation by bodies. Nevertheless, this abstention from any reference to occupation does not make geometric space identical with absolute space; for absolute space has no divisions nor any boundaries within or without, whereas geometric space is divided and bounded at will. The explanation is simply this: to form the notion of *geometric space* we abstract the note of extension from the bodies around us, and consider that extension in itself; we stop short of the third mental act necessary to give us the concept of space with which we are concerned in this thesis. Geometric space is also called "pure space" because of its total disassociation from bodies.

... *Clarke,* in a controversy with Leibnitz, defended space as a real existent being, uncreated and divine, in short the immensity of God. *Fénelon* and *Bayma* (and even Newton at times) appear to lean toward the same opinion. *Gassendi* taught that space is an existing being, unique in its kind, halfway between body and spirit, and neither substance nor accident. *Kant* called space a sense-form, not derived from sensation but preceding it. *Descartes* maintained that there is no space apart from the actual extended body, and that extension constitutes corporeal substance.

... Space is abstract extension considered as a receptacle for bodies; hence space as such is a product of the mind, but with a foundation in external reality.

Part I (a) Space is abstract extension

Argument. Expansion in three dimensions is a note which is essential to the common concept of space, while other properties such as color, resistance, temperature, or forces of any kind, do not enter into the concept. But expanse represented without the other common and sensible properties of bodies is abstract extension. Therefore space is abstract extension.

Part I (b) This extension is considered as a receptacle for bodies

Argument. That which is considered as filled with bodies or void of bodies, that in which bodies are said to be contained and move about, is considered as a receptacle for bodies. But we so consider the expanse which we call space. Therefore space is abstract extension considered as a receptacle for bodies.

Part II (a) Space is a product of the mind

That is called a product of the mind which is represented as an existing being but which in itself cannot exist. But space as such is represented as if it were an existing being, whereas it cannot as such exist by itself. Therefore space as such is a product of the mind.

Part II (b) This mental product has a foundation in external reality

A mental representation is said to have a foundation in external reality when there actually exists in the concrete state something which corresponds to the representation, although it does not exist in the abstract condition in which it is represented by the mind. Now there exist bodies with the concrete attribute of extension, and it is this attribute which is represented in an abstract manner in the notion of space as such.

Therefore space as such is a product of the mind with a foundation in external reality.

John Wild   **23. TIME: THE MEASURE OF CHANGE**

The other side of the issue of space—that is, time—is discussed in this selection by realist John Wild.

From *Introduction to Realistic Philosophy* by John Wild. Copyright 1948 by Harper & Brothers. Used by permission of the publisher.

Wild identifies time as "a certain mode of existence really present in external changes so far as they provide a foundation for the measuring concept in the mind." Where Father McWilliams sees space as "abstract extension" having a foundation in external reality, Wild considers time, in similar terms, as "a mental measure with a foundation in extra-mental reality." Time is not change itself, but only the mental measure of change.

Since the basis of any discussion of time must be located in the fact of change, Wild undertakes his analysis of the problem in terms of the doctrine of potency and act.

Change, he says, is accomplished by intermediate stages, through which a being passes toward a terminating position. The changing thing "does not exist all at once but only successively, with further being constantly added to what has been." At the termination of change new being is added. Changing being, therefore, becomes actual only at an instantaneous *now,* "which is the term of a change already passed and the inauguration of a change about to be."

In the perception of time, the mind performs three operations. First, it abstracts "the terminus of a process from the continuous, material matrix with which it is confused in nature"; second, it remembers this abstraction "while it similarly fixes successive *nows* at regular intervals"; and finally, in the light of memory, it compares "the number of one motion with that of another," and thus establishes comparative relations "between the duration of different motions and changes." Time is sharply distinguished from spatial extension, he concludes, and, consequently, should not be confused with it

Time is a mode of being which permeates every mode of change and to which we refer in a great variety of ways. All the verbs of our language are divided into tenses which indicate different modes of time. Sometimes we use prepositions in referring to the time *at* which or *through* which something happened. We also have an elaborate series of nouns, such as seconds, minutes, hours, days, weeks, months, years, and so on to indicate periods of time. Like most phases of being which are important and ubiquitous, time is something extremely elusive and difficult to focus clearly by conceptual analysis. As we shall see, this is primarily due to a peculiar complexity in its structure.

This complexity becomes more apparent if we notice two different ways in which we refer to time. Sometimes, as when we are speaking about the dates of certain events, it is clear that we are thinking of something primarily mental and due to human enactment. The minute hand of the watch is really moving. The moon is revolving around the earth and the earth around the sun. But no one upon reflection really believes that seconds, months, and years actually exist in nature. Otherwise we could not explain the many different schemes for measuring time which have been invented by man. But sometimes, as when we say *the time is ripe* or *his time has come* or *time marches on,* we seem to be referring to a time which is inherent in the extra-mental change itself.

It is not surprising that this duality in our concept of time should be reflected in the views of two sharply opposed schools of philosophic thought. On the one hand there are those like Parmenides, Spinoza, and Bradley, who hold that time is a sheer, mental figment, or construction with no basis in reality. On the other, there are those like Bergson and his followers who hold that time is an extra-mental reality to which the mind contributes nothing save distortion and misunderstanding. The truth lies at neither of these extremes, but between them.

Time is the measure of change. As such it has something in it which is purely mental and not found outside the mind, as the piece of wood in front of me is not neatly divided into the inches and feet by which I measure it. But time is not a pure construction or fiction. It is founded upon something really existing in the extra-mental change, just as the correct measure of the stick is based upon an extension really in the wood. Time is a certain mode of existence really present in external changes so far as they provide a foundation for the measuring concept in the mind. In order to understand this more clearly we must once more examine the nature of change, but now from a slightly different point of view.

The process of change is continuous up to its extrinsic term, when the change is over. Thus the flight of the arrow proceeds without interruption until it hits the target, when it comes to rest. Of course the arrow goes through determinate, intermediate positions. But between these positions it is in a flight which passes away as soon as the intermediate term is reached. But even this term itself passes away as a new part of the flight begins. Both the intermediate and the terminating portions of a change are in constant transition. This is because the changing thing does not exist all at once but only successively, with further being constantly added to what has been.

This new being is added at the termination of the change. While changing, the being is not yet actual but only in potency. While freezing, the water is not yet frozen. *When* frozen, the change is over. The change reaches actuality only at an instantaneous term. A new process may take its origin *from* this term. But this new process, not yet being at its term, is as yet only in a state of potency and not actual.

We must conclude that changing being can become actual only at an instantaneous *now* which is the term of a change already passed and the inauguration of a change about to be. Hence outside the mind, past and future are non-actual. All that is in full existence is a *now,* which realizes a past change and initiates a future still in potency. Of course, as we have already pointed out, the *now* itself no sooner comes into existence than it too passes away.

Finally, in extra-mental nature there is not just one great process of change going on which includes all the other changes. Since there are many changing substances, there are many independent processes of change, each having its own intrinsic structure. It is true that certain ones coexist and others do not.

But they do not endure long enough to found any real relations. We cannot say that one actuality lasts *longer than* another, since outside the mind the past no longer exists. There is only a set of instantly actual entities which have already disappeared to be replaced by a new set. These successive actualities, existing at an instantaneous *now,* are the foundation for what we call time. But the mind must perform three operations before time can result, as the measure of change.

First of all, the mind must abstract the terminus of a process from the continuous, material matrix with which it is confused in nature.

Second, it must hold this in memory while it similarly fixes successive *nows* at regular intervals as it chooses—seconds, days, months, and so on. This series of remembered and projected *nows* is discontinuous and therefore unlike the actual processes of nature, which have successive termini, but always with a potential matrix in between. The dates of time have been freed from this matrix. They are not the motion itself but rather the number of the motion, and therefore able to measure it, or count off its emergent actualities.

Finally, the mind, making use of its capacity to remember the past and to anticipate the future (not actually in existence), can compare the number of one motion with that of another, and thus set up comparative relations (not existing outside the mind) between the duration of different motions and changes.

Hence time, the measure, is distinct from the change it measures in these three ways. Time consists of discontinuous *nows* which can be filled in with the continuous content of any actual process, whereas change consists of *nows* filled in with a continuous matrix peculiar to each actual process. Time includes both the number of an indefinite past and an indefinite future, whereas the extra-mental reality exists only at an instantaneous *now.* Time can bring any change of which we are aware under its measure, or, as we say, everything that occurs must happen in this single time. But such acts of comparison do not exist outside the mind. Here we have only a number of processes, each of which occurs only in itself, and not in any other.

If extra-mental reality consisted only of transient changes, the very limits of which were constantly passing away, it would have no permanent structure. So far, we have been examining such transient duration and its measure, which we call time. We must now note that permanent substance and accident terminate this transient change. This permanent structure also endures. *Transient being* endures by the addition of distinct existence. *Permanent being* endures by the conservation of one existence. Neither of these modes of being contains the whole of its existence all at once. Each involves a successive duration, either of one thing persisting or one thing succeeding another. Each is closely related to the other. Change may come to rest, and any resting thing may change. So both of these successive durations may be measured by time. We may count off the duration of a rest by the discontinuous dates of time, just as we can count off the duration of a process of change.

Bergson and others have justifiably called attention to a tendency to confuse time, the measure of duration, with space, the measure of quantitative extension. This confusion is manifest in the widespread habit of referring to time as a sort of "dimension" which can be counted off in regular intervals, like an indefinite geometric line. The pure measure of time, abstracted from the real duration which it measures, doubtless has this structure. It is thought of as an infinite line of time into which all events can be fitted and marked off by relations of before and after, just as a spatial dimension or space itself can be conceived as a great empty container with no end into which all the definite extensions of things can be fitted. But each of these, taken apart from the extra-mental things measured, and projected into the external world, is a sheer delusion. There is no such thing as a pure absolute time or a pure absolute space outside the mind. What really exists are different things each having a certain, individual duration and extension of its own.

When the measures of space and time are adequately conceived in relation to the real extensions and duration which they measure, there are important differences between them which cannot be ignored without grave confusion. Real extensions, in so far as they are stable and not in flux, coexist and endure. Hence they have real relations of distance between them and really contain one another. But real times do not coexist together in this way. Outside the mind time is divided into present, past, and future, which have no counterpart in spatial extension.

Furthermore in reality the past exists only so far as it is actualized in a present *now,* and the future exists only in so far as this present *now* is beginning it in potency. All that actually exists is a *present.* So there are no *real* relations between things existing at different times. There are only *mental* relations, which have a real foundation, so far as the mind accurately remembers what actually happened in a preceding *now,* no longer existent, or accurately anticipates what actually will be in a non-existent future.

Finally, each present *now* is ever passing, and except in the case of enduring entities which always change eventually, gives way to something different. Hence it is impossible for temporal events or enduring states to be *in contact* with one another, as spatial lines and planes. A change is terminated by a rest, but as we have noted . . . the first instant is *extrinsic* to the change. By the time the change is finished there is no change. There is a last instant of rest, but at this instant the thing is not yet changing. Change occurs only beyond this instant. Furthermore one state of rest cannot be in contact with another, for a process of change must intervene between the two. Temporal states of rest and change succeed each other. Time cannot wait long enough for a contact to be established.

We must conclude that the category of time is sharply to be distinguished from spatial extension. Time is the measure of change, not the measure of extension. It is founded on the fact that natural entities do coexist and succeed one another in a certain order. But the mind, with the aid of memory and anticipation, chooses some standard process and marks it off in regular intervals, disregarding what occurs between the discontinuous numbers. Then it uses this series of numbers as a means of comparing and measuring the duration of other changes and periods of rest. Time, therefore, is a mental measure with a foundation in extra-mental reality.

Alfred North Whitehead   **24. TIME IS INTRINSIC**

To Alfred North Whitehead and what is generally called "the new physics," an absolute cleavage between space and time is deemed unthinkable. This is not to say that in the new physics space and time are considered identical. The difference between them, however, is less sharp than that which pre-Einsteinian mechanics makes provision for. Space and time are considered co-ordinates of events. Just as in co-ordinate geometry where the *x-axis* and *y-axis* are distinct yet inseparable, so too (the new physics contends), space and time, though distinct, are inseparably partnered.

In the selection that follows, Whitehead attempts to establish the relation existing between "events" and time. What is perceived in nature, which is a "field," is neither time nor space (these are abstractions), but events (some of which are objects) manifesting space and time. Nature is, in fact, a complex of passing events. And in the complex can be discerned definite mutual and internal relations between component events. These are their relative positions, which are, in turn, expressed partly in space-terms and partly in time-terms. Events cannot be torn apart from their relation to space-terms and time-terms, since space and time are "constitutive of the entity." Consequently, we cannot say that space is merely a receptacle, or tub, for events, or that time is merely the measure of change. There is no such thing as "nature at an instant" or the "simple location" of a body *in* space. Neither time nor space is absolute; they are relative to specific events. As relationships of an event, each "enters into the essence of an event."

Whitehead thus flatly denies that space and time are external relationships, since neither can be extruded from the event. "The event is part of the duration; i.e., is part of what is exhibited in the aspects inherent in itself; and conversely, the duration is the whole of nature simultaneous with the event, in that sense of simultaneity." As a relation to an event, space is an intimate of time: "a duration is spatialized; and by 'spatialized' is meant that the duration is the field for the realized pattern constituting the character of an event."

AN EVENT is the grasping into unity of a pattern of aspects. The effectiveness of an event beyond itself arises from the aspects of itself which go to form the prehended unities of other events. Except for the systematic aspects of geometrical shape, this effectiveness is trivial, if the mirrored pattern attaches merely to the event as one whole. If the pattern endures throughout the successive parts of the event, and also exhibits itself in the whole, so that the event is the life-history of the pattern, then in virtue of that enduring pattern the event gains in external effectiveness. For its own effectiveness is re-enforced by the analogous aspects of all its successive parts. The event constitutes a patterned value with a permanence inherent throughout its own parts; and by reason of this inherent endurance the event is important for the modification of its environment.

It is in this endurance of pattern that time differentiates itself from space. The pattern is spatially *now;* and this temporal determination constitutes its relation to each partial event. For it is reproduced in this temporal succession of these spatial parts of its own life. I mean that this particular rule of temporal order allows the pattern to be reproduced in each temporal slice of its history. So to speak, each enduring object discovers in nature and requires from nature a principle discriminating space from time. Apart from the fact of an enduring pattern this principle might be there, but it would be latent and trivial. Thus the importance of space as against time, and of time as against space, has developed with the development of enduring organisms. Enduring objects are significant of a differentiation of space from time in respect to the patterns ingredient within events; and conversely the differentiation of space from time in the patterns ingredient within events expresses the patience of the community of events for enduring objects. There might be the community without objects, but there could not be the enduring objects without the community with its peculiar patience for them.

It is very necessary that this point should not be misunderstood. Endurance means that a pattern which is exhibited in the prehension of one event is also exhibited in the prehension of those of its parts which are discriminated by a certain rule. It is not true that any part of the whole event will yield the same pattern as does the whole. For example, consider the total bodily pattern exhibited in the life of a human body during one minute. One of the thumbs during the same minute is part of the whole bodily event. But the pattern of this part is the pattern of the thumb, and is not the pattern of the whole body. Thus endurance requires a definite rule for obtaining the parts. In the above example, we know at once what the rule is: You must take the life of the whole body during any portion of that same minute; for example, during a second or a tenth of a second: In other words, the meaning of endurance presupposes a meaning for the lapse of time within the spatio-temporal continuum.

The question now arises whether all enduring objects discover the same principle of differentiation of space from time; or even whether at different stages of its own life-history one object may not vary in its spatio-temporal discrimination. Up till a few years ago, everyone unhesitatingly assumed that there was only one such principle to be discovered. Accordingly, in dealing with one object, time would have exactly the same meaning in reference to endurance as in dealing with the endurance of another object. It would also follow then that spatial relations would have one unique meaning. But now it seems that the observed effectiveness of objects can only be explained by assuming that objects in a state of motion relatively to each other are utilising, for their endurance, meanings of space and of time which are not identical from one object to another. Every enduring object is to be conceived as at rest in its own proper space, and in motion throughout any space defined in a way which is not that inherent in its peculiar endurance. If two objects are mutually at rest, they are utilising the same meanings of space and of time for the purposes of expressing their endurance; if in relative motion, the spaces and times differ. It follows that, if we can conceive a body at one stage of its life-history as in motion relatively to itself at another stage, then the body at these two stages is utilising diverse meanings of space, and correlatively diverse meanings of time.

In an organic philosophy of nature there is nothing to decide between the old hypothesis of the uniqueness of the time discrimination and the new hypothesis of its multiplicity. It is purely a matter for evidence drawn from observations.

In an earlier lecture, I said that an event had contemporaries. It is an interesting question whether, on the new hypothesis, such a statement can be made without the qualification of a reference to a definite space-time system. It is possible to do so, in the sense that in *some* time-system or other the two events are simultaneous. In other time-systems the two contemporary events will not be simultaneous, though they may overlap. Analogously one event will precede another without qualification, if in *every* time-system this precedence occurs. It is evident that if we start from a given event *A,* other events in general are divided into two sets, namely, those which without qualification are contemporaneous with *A* and those which either precede or succeed *A.* But there will be a set left over, namely, those events which bound the two sets. There we have a critical case. You will remember that we have a critical velocity to account for, namely the theoretical velocity of light *in vacuo.* Also you will remember that the utilisation of different spatio-temporal systems means the relative motion of objects. When we analyse this critical relation of a special set of events to any given event A, we find the explanation of the critical velocity which we require. I am suppressing all details. It is evident that exactness of statement must be introduced by the introduction of points, and lines, and instants. Also that the origin of geometry requires discussion; for example, the measurement of lengths, the straightness of lines, and the flatness of planes, and perpendicularity. I have endeavoured to carry out these investigations in some earlier books, under the heading of the theory of extensive abstraction; but they are too technical for the present occasion.

If there be no one definite meaning to the geometrical relations of distance, it is evident that the law of gravitation needs restatement. For the formula expressing that law is that two particles attract each other in proportion to the product of their masses and the inverse square of their distances. This enunciation tacitly assumes that there is one definite meaning to be ascribed to the instant at which the attraction is considered, and also one definite meaning to be ascribed to *distance*. But distance is a purely spatial notion, so that in the new doctrine, there are an indefinite number of such meanings according to the space-time system which you adopt. If the two particles are relatively at rest, then we might be content with the space-time systems which they are both utilising. Unfortunately this suggestion gives no hint as to procedure when they are not mutually at rest. It is, therefore necessary to reformulate the law in a way which does not presuppose any particular space-time system. Einstein has done this. Naturally the result is more complicated. He introduced into mathematical physics certain methods of pure mathematics which render the formulae independent of the particular systems of measurement adopted. The new formula introduces various small effects which are absent in Newton's law. But for the major effects Newton's law and Einstein's law agree. Now these extra effects of Einstein's law serve to explain irregularities of the planet Mercury's orbit which by Newton's law were inexplicable. This is a strong confirmation of the new theory. Curiously enough, there is more than one alternative formula, based on the new theory of multiple space-time systems, having the property of embodying Newton's law and in addition of explaining the peculiarities of Mercury's motion. The only method of selection between them is to wait for experimental evidence respecting those effects on which the formulae differ. Nature is probably quite indifferent to the aesthetic preferences of mathematicians.

It only remains to add that Einstein would probably reject the theory of multiple space-time systems which I have been expounding to you. He would interpret his formula in terms of contortions in space-time which alter the invariance theory for measure properties, and of the proper times of each historical route. His mode of statement has the greater mathematical simplicity, and only allows of one law of gravitation, excluding the alternatives.

But, for myself, I cannot reconcile it with the given facts of our experience as to simultaneity, and spatial arrangement. There are also other difficulties of a more abstract character.

The theory of the relationship between events at which we have now arrived is based first upon the doctrine that the relatednesses of an event are all internal relations, so far as concerns that event, though not necessarily so far as concerns the other relata. For example, the eternal objects, thus involved, are externally related to events. This internal relatedness is the reason why an event can be found only just where it is and how it is,—that is to say, in just one definite set of relationships. For each relationship enters into the essence of the event; so that, apart from the relationship, the event would not be itself. This is what is meant by the very notion of internal relations. It has been usual, indeed, universal, to hold that spatio-temporal relationships are external. This doctrine is what is here denied.

The conception of internal relatedness involves the analysis of the event into two factors, one the underlying substantial activity of individualisation, and the other the complex of aspects—that is to say, the complex of relatednesses as entering into the essence of the given event—which are unified by this individualised activity. In other words, the concept of internal relations requires the concept of substance as the activity synthesising the relationships into its emergent character. The event is what it is, by reason of the unification in itself of a multiplicity of relationships. The general scheme of these mutual relationships is an abstraction which presupposes each event as an independent entity, which it is not, and asks what remnant of these formative relationships is then left in the guise of external relationships. The scheme of relationships as thus impartially expressed becomes the scheme of a complex of events variously related as wholes to parts and as joint parts within some one whole. Even here, the internal relationship forces itself on our attention; for the part evidently is constitutive of the whole. Also an isolated event which has lost its status in any complex of events is equally excluded by the very nature of an event. So the whole is evidently constitutive of the part. Thus the internal character of the relationship really shows through this impartial scheme of abstract external relations.

But this exhibition of the actual universe as extensive and divisible has left out the distinction between space and time. It has in fact left out the process of realisation, which is the adjustment of the synthetic activities by virtue of which the various events become their realised selves. This adjustment is thus the adjustment of the underlying active substances whereby these substances exhibit themselves as the individualisations or modes of Spinoza's one substance. This adjustment is what introduces temporal process.

Thus, in some sense, time, in its character of the adjustment of the process of synthetic realisation, extends beyond the spatio-temporal continuum of nature. There is no necessity that temporal process, in this sense, should be constituted by one single series of linear succession. Accordingly, in order to satisfy the present demands of scientific hypothesis, we introduce the metaphysical hypothesis that this is not the case. We do assume (basing ourselves upon direct observation), however, that temporal process of realisation can be analysed into a group of linear serial processes. Each of these linear series is a space-time system. In support of this assumption of definite serial processes, we appeal: (1) to the immediate presentation through the senses of an extended universe beyond ourselves and *simultaneous* with ourselves, (2) to the intellectual apprehension of a meaning to the question which asks what is *now immediately happening* in regions beyond the cognisance of our senses, (3) to the analysis of what is involved in the *endurance* of emergent objects. This endurance of objects involves the display of a pattern as now realised. This display is the display of a pattern as inherent in an event, but also as exhibiting a temporal slice of nature as lending aspects to eternal objects (or, equally, of eternal objects as lending aspects to events). The pattern is spatialised in a whole duration for the benefits of the event into whose essence the pattern enters. The event is part of the duration, *i.e.,* is part of what is exhibited in the aspects inherent in itself; and conversely the duration is the whole of nature simultaneous with the event, in that sense of simultaneity. Thus an event in realising itself displays a pattern, and this pattern requires duration determined by a definite meaning of simultaneity. Each such meaning of simultaneity relates the pattern as thus displayed to one definite space-time system. The actuality of the space-time systems is constituted by the realisation of pattern; but it is inherent in the general scheme of events as constituting its patience for the temporal process of realisation.

Notice that the pattern requires a duration involving a definite lapse of time, and not merely an instantaneous moment. Such a moment is more abstract, in that it merely denotes a certain relation of contiguity between the concrete events. Thus a duration is spatialised; and by "spatialised" is meant that the duration is the field for the realised pattern constituting the character of the event. A duration, as the field of the pattern realised in the actualisation of one of its contained events, is an epoch, *i.e.,* an arrest. Endurance is the repetition of the pattern in successive events. Thus endurance requires a succession of durations, each exhibiting the pattern. In this account "time" has been separated from "extension" and from the "divisibility" which arises from the character of spatio-temporal of extension. Accordingly we must not proceed to conceive time as another form of extensiveness. Time is sheer succession of epochal durations. But the entities which succeed each other in this account are durations. The duration is that which is required for the realisation of a pattern in the given event. Thus the divisibility and extensiveness is within the given duration. The epochal duration is not realised *via* its *successive* divisible parts, but is given *with* its parts. In this way, the objection which Zeno might make to the joint validity of two messages from Kant's *Critique of*

Pure Reason is met by abandoning the earlier of the two passages. I refer to passages from the section "Of the Axioms of Intuition"; the earlier from the subsection on *Extensive Quantity,* and the latter from the subsection on *Intensive Quantity,* where considerations respecting quantity in general, extensive and intensive, are summed up. The earlier passage runs thus:

> I call an extensive quantity that in which the representation of the whole is rendered possible by the representation of its parts, *and therefore necessarily preceded by it.* I cannot represent to myself any line, however small it may be, without drawing it in thought, that is, without producing all its parts one after the other, starting from a given point, and thus, first of all, drawing its intuition. The same applies to every, even the smallest, portion of time. I can only think in it the successive progress from one moment to another, thus producing in the end, by all the portions of time, and their addition, a definite quantity of time.

The second passage runs thus:

> This peculiar property of quantities that no part of them is the smallest possible part (no part indivisible) is called continuity. Time and space are quanta continua, because there is no part of them that is not enclosed between limits (points and moments), *no part that is not itself again a space or a time. Space consists of spaces only, time of times. Points and moments are only limits,* mere places of limitation, and as places *presupposing always* those intuitions which they are meant to limit or to determine. Mere places or parts that might be given before space or time, could never be compounded into space or time.

I am in complete agreement with the second extract if "time and space" is the extensive continuum; but it is inconsistent with its predecessor. For Zeno would object that a vicious infinite regress is involved. Every part of time involves some smaller part of itself, and so on. Also this series regresses backwards ultimately to nothing; since the initial moment is without duration and merely marks the relation of contiguity to an earlier time. Thus time is impossible, if the two extracts are both adhered to. I accept the later, and reject the earlier, passage. Realisation is the becoming of time in the field of extension. Extension is the complex of events, *qua* their potentialities. In realisation the potentiality becomes actuality. But the potential pattern requires a duration; and the duration must be exhibited as an epochal whole, by the realisation of the pattern. Thus time is the succession of elements in themselves divisible and contiguous. A duration, in becoming temporal, thereby incurs realisation in respect to some enduring object. Temporalisation is realisation. Temporalisation is not another continuous process. It is an atomic success. Thus time is atomic (*i.e.,* epochal), though what is temporalised is divisible. This doctrine follows from the doctrine of events, and of the nature of enduring objects. In the next chapter we must consider its relevance to the quantum theory of recent science.

It is to be noted that this doctrine of the epochal character of time does not depend on the modern doctrine of relativity, and holds equally—and indeed, more simply—if this doctrine be abandoned. It does depend on the analysis of the intrinsic character of an event, considered as the most concrete finite entity.

In reviewing this argument, note first that the second quotation from Kant, on which it is based, does not depend on any peculiar Kantian doctrine. The latter of the two is in agreement with Plato as against Aristotle. In the second place, the argument assumes that Zeno understated his argument. He should have urged it against the current notion of time in itself, and not against motion which involves relations between time and space. For, what becomes has duration. But no duration can become until a smaller duration (part of the former) has antecedently come into being [Kant's earlier statement]. The same argument applies to this smaller duration, and so on. Also the infinite regress of these durations converges to nothing—and even to the Aristotelian view there is no first moment. Accordingly time would be an irrational notion. Thirdly, in the epochal theory Zeno's difficulty is met by conceiving temporalisation as the realisation of a complete organism. This organism is an event holding in its essence its spatio-temporal relationships (both within itself, and beyond itself) throughout the spatio-temporal continuum.

Bruno de Solages

25. CYCLIC AND EVOLUTIONARY TIME

With the inception of modern ideas about space and time, a dramatic challenge is clearly placed before traditional philosophy. In this essay, Monsignor de Solages makes a plea for a realistic assessment of this challenge.

Contrasting the ancient cyclic time with the contemporary belief in cosmic process, de Solages suggests that a failure by traditional thought to make provision for these differences will tend to weaken its effect before posterity. To pretend that nothing has altered in man's view of nature since the time of Aristotle is to expose the truths of traditional philosophy to ridicule.

In place of the clock as the image of time, the modern world puts forward the image of a living cell. In terms of a living cell, history is intrinsic to life and is another name for life. So, too, in macrocosmic terms, history is not external to reality, but becomes intrinsic to it. Duration can thus no

Originally entitled "The Concepts of Cyclic and Evolutionary Time" by Bruno de Solages, in *The Human Person and the World of Values,* edited by Balduin V. Schwarz (New York: Fordham University Press, 1960), pages 49–56. Reprinted by permission of the publisher.

longer be looked upon as an external framework in which substances are deposited, but must be understood "as a constituent element of the substances." History, furthermore, exposes the inner core of experiential reality as typically contingent: "contingence now takes its place at the very heart of evolutionary time," and gives real meaning to the notions of innovation and unpredictability.

The implications of this view are enormous, says de Solages, and all those who wish to follow in the spirit of Aristotle and St. Thomas must now take these facts seriously. Furthermore, the acceptance of this new image of time cannot be passive and grudging, but must be active and reflective—for "we must rethink every philosophical problem that has been more or less secretly allied to the ancient concept of the Universe."

WHENEVER THINKERS who have been trained to a Thomistic view of reality have endeavored to bridge the gap between traditional philosophy and modern thought, they have been halted by the objection: "You live in the category of being whereas we are in that of becoming."

To this reproach of philosophic staticism, a reproach which to them seems a radical misunderstanding of their philosophic positions, they usually reply with a touch of indignation: "How can such an objection be raised against a system whose Aristotelian foundation is precisely the analysis of becoming? Are not the keystones of the edifice—matter and form, act and potency—fashioned from this analysis?" And yet the opposition remains real and clear, for there has been a misunderstanding: the modern mind looks upon the Aristotelian concept of becoming as nothing less than a species of this philosophic staticism. Becoming and the analysis of time to which it gives birth are dominated by the idea of the prime mover of the first sphere. Nothing new really becomes; the Universe is like the revolving mechanism of a huge clock.

For our contemporaries, on the contrary, there is in fact something new in the Universe, something which becomes. To describe the Universe, they would substitute for the image of the revolving mechanism of a clock that of a living organism which undergoes a true development. Becoming and cyclic time versus becoming and evolutionary time: this is the key opposition which I should like to emphasize and from which I should like to draw several conclusions.

The Aristotelian Concept of Cyclic Time

The cyclic time of the ancients took its technical form in the physics of Aristotle, a form which was to impose itself on the thought of the West for two thousand years. In a penetrating axiom, the philosopher first pointed out the fundamental connection between time and becoming: "time is the measure of motion." This he followed up with analysis and classification of the types of motion: local motion (κατὰ τόπον), motion according to quality (ἀλλοίωσις), motion according to quantity (αὔξησις), and finally motion which reached the heart of substance itself, namely generation and corruption (γένεσις καὶ φθόρα). One might have expected that in the hierarchy of Aristotelian categories (relation, mode, substance) the primacy would be given to substantial change, and local motion, which touches only relations, would be relegated to the lowest place. But here the cosmographic conceptions of the Hellenic world interfered with the Aristotelian cosmology and upset the scale of values. The spherical Universe turning around the earth had been essentially divided into two zones: the higher or heavenly zone and the inferior or earthly zone. Now only the inferior zone, ours, was subject to this change of substance and to the substantial movement which the philosopher had analyzed. No corruption entered to change the heavenly eternal world which was composed of an essence different from that of human experience. Local motion alone reigned in these sovereign heights and this movement was of one particular type, namely, that uniform circular movement to which the aesthetic soul of the Greeks responded so eagerly, a movement which came as close as possible to the dignity of immobility, a motion which from eternity regulated the calendar of men. Furthermore, it is this motion which begins the movement from the first sphere down to the sublunary world. Thus this particular type of movement was promoted to the supreme place of honor. It will control earthly time. Cosmography has now in some way assumed ontological value. Absolute value has been given to cyclic time. Consequently nothing can come into being except within its regulating frame.

This conception was freighted with metaphysical implications. Necessity, an eternal necessity, regulated this clocklike Universe. The eternal return with its great year which puts into place all the pieces of the huge mechanism was included in this necessity, as were human events—at least in the opinion of certain disciples of Aristotle, such as Averroes.

The Medieval Adaptation

We shall now try to see how this conception of the clocklike Universe and of cyclic time fitted into the system of Christian thought. As a matter of fact, it continued as the general framework in which was placed the Christian *economy* and the *history* of humanity which that economy included. Only two important, though extrinsic, correctives were added to the original conception. First, the huge clocklike Universe is no longer considered the first reality. Secondly, the Universe is not eternal, but has been created by God, in time, or, to be more exact, with time, four or five thousand years ago, and it will come to an end. and be transformed at the return of Christ in the Last Judgment.

But these correctives placed on the eternity of the Universe in no way affected the nature of the mechanism of the Universe nor of cyclic time which is joined to it. The most suggestive proof of this rests in the fact that the most powerful of these medieval thinkers, St. Thomas Aquinas, was never willing to admit the possibility of demonstrating from reason alone that this Universe and its movement were not eternal. It was in the cyclic time of the ancients that his theological thought placed the essentially singular, contingent and historical events of the Biblical narratives. Here was a glaring contrast indeed —though not necessarily a contradiction—yet one which medieval thought seems never to have recognized: on the one hand, the historic time of the Christian economy is essentially characterized by an origin, an orientation and an end; while, on the other, the cyclic time of Aristotle which serves as a framework for that economy, is indifferent to it. Of itself, cyclic time has neither origin nor end, and consequently, no true orientation.

The Growth of the Concept of Evolution

In modern thought, little by little, we can watch the growth of the view that the entire Universe is alive. The image of a clocklike Universe fades away and is replaced by that of a living Universe, one which has acquired an historical character. Time, as a category, joins that of human history. However, it is no longer cyclic time but evolutionary time.

This change of view was not a sudden one. Though the deciding factors in the change of perspective were the discoveries in the field of paleontology and the nineteenth-century theory of the evolution of species to which these discoveries gave birth, nevertheless, the change had been foreshadowed from the beginnings of modern science. The Copernican revolution broke to bits the crystalline spheres of the Aristotelian world, while at the same time it unintentionally shattered the static character of the Universe. Nothing is more characteristic of this change of perspective than the quiet insinuations of Descartes in the Fifth Part of the *Discourse on Method*. He is perfectly aware that he is substituting a genetic for static representation of the Universe, for example, when he says: "And it is much easier to grasp their nature (i.e. material things) when one sees them developing little by little in this way than when one considers them only as completely formed."

This conception stands out more sharply in Buffon's *Epochs of Nature*. Thereafter all the general theories of the Universe were evolutionary in character, insofar as they endeavored to explain how the Universe was made rather than to define what it is. Such, in the nineteenth-century, was the character of the celebrated theory of Laplace on the formation of the solar system through the condensation of an original nebula. Such too, in the twentieth century, was the theory of Canon Lemâitre on the Universe in expansion after the disintegration of the first atom.

Meanwhile, during the entire course of the nineteenth century, the very concept of evolution was taking shape in modern thought. It was born when the theory of evolution of species, suggested by Lamarck and by Darwin, because of paleontological discoveries was wed to Hegel's philosophic speculations on history. But Hegel, curiously enough, did not believe in the evolution of species!

From that period on, all the branches of modern science are drawn one by one into the orbit of the evolutionary perspective, that is, general evolution in which the evolution of the species becomes but a particular type. Scientific research, for example, takes on a progressively historic character, while the study of origins takes precedence over that of natures. All the elements of the Universe from the disintegrating atom to the stars passing through different phases are all viewed in a process of constructing their own history.

Evolutionary Time

This change in perspective was accompanied by a corresponding change in the concept of time. From a thing which is somehow extrinsic to reality, it now becomes intrinsic to reality. Beings in cyclic time bear upon themselves no mark of their age. Examining the movement of the Universe is like examining that of a clock: there is no indication of the number of completed revolutions that have been made, since by hypothesis at the end of twelve hours or of a great year, a return has been made to the original starting point; nothing has changed. Living beings, on the contrary, bear in their very make-up the stamp of their age. Cut down a tree, examine its rings and you have its age. It reveals the evolutionary time which has become that of all the elements of the Universe. By examining the ore bearing uranium, the geophysicist can date the geological age of its formation, according to the statistical laws of disintegration. Duration is no longer looked upon as an external framework in which substances are placed as they are in space, but rather as a constituent element of these substances. Consequently, the Bergsonian analyses lead us to take as the type of becoming, not local motion, but rather living movement, and from that, conscious movement.

This view of the Universe implies deep metaphysical differences. For example, cyclic time showed a marked affinity to determinism, whereas contingence now takes its place at the very heart of evolutionary time. Again, in the cyclic view of the Universe the eternal return was the spontaneously conceived form of the world. Innovation and unpredictability, on the other hand, are essential characteristics of evolutionary time. The resulting change of perspective in our conception of the Universe can hardly be exaggerated.

The Necessity for the Integration of the Evolutionary Perspective with Traditional Philosophy

Now this shift of perspective is imposed upon all except those who systematically ignore the progress of human knowledge. In fact, there is no question here of some particular theory whose abandonment might be expected in time, but rather of a general way of conceiving the different domains of reality. This point of view tends more and more to identify itself with the very method of science—an investigation into the genesis of things.

Refusal to adopt this viewpoint because of Aristotelianism is an especially paradoxical attitude since this means simply to betray Aristotle's spirit while retaining the letter of Aristotelianism. The fundamental procedure of Aristotle is always characterized by observation of what is, and his metaphysical theories themselves are inspired by what he believed he drew from nature. The easiest way to falsify rational empiricism is by refusing to recognize the converging testimony of different sciences. That is why it is time today for all those who wish to continue in the spirit of Aristotle and St. Thomas to bow to evidence and integrate this perspective into their basic philosophy of nature. It will not be enough to abandon Aristotelian cosmography with its geocentric universe and crystalline spheres; we must re-think every philosophical problem that has been more or less secretly allied to the ancient concept of the Universe. Becoming and cyclic time are two such problems.

Does it follow that every detail of the Aristotelian analysis of becoming is to be rejected? Evidently not. His theory of act and potency was suggested less by local motion—it is even difficult to apply it here—than by substantial change, *vital* becoming. Consequently, it does not appear to be necessarily bound up with a cyclic conception of becoming and of time. The living being is born, develops, acts. Aristotelianism accounts for this quite well, but it does not appear to have taken into account with sufficient explicitness the finalized, orientated, irreversible and partly contingent character of the living being's becoming; moreover, it ignores the global evolutionary becoming of the Universe, which also manifests this orientated, irreversible and partially contingent character.

In this new perspective, the Prime Mover, first conceived by Aristotle in order to explain the movement of the spheres, will become the first origin of quite another movement—the movement which constitutes the general evolution of the Universe and of life. His task is no longer to put the wheels in motion but to cause the evolution of the world he has created.

It would be vain to attempt to conceal the fact that such a perspective, introduced at the basis of traditional philosophy, will raise several problems. First of all there will be the problem of the meaning which the motion of the *nature* of things will retain when this nature is in the process of becoming.

Beyond any doubt the concept of nature will have to be transformed: from static it will become dynamic. It will no longer be conceived as an unvarying form, but rather, within certain limits, as a law of development, for evolution itself has its laws and its stages.

Since the generalized evolution of reality cannot fail to touch ideas, even values, the problem will then be posed as to how to maintain the transcendence of values within an evolutionary framework.

The efforts of traditional philosophy to integrate the results of modern thought and investigation into its own synthesis should not stop with this one case, important though it is. This is merely one example of the task set before those who belong to a philosophic tradition that has reigned so gloriously in Christian thought ever since the thirteenth century. It is a task which renews, yet remains faithful to the great synthesis, for true fidelity attaches itself less to literal conformity than to the animating spirit.

Robert O. Johann, S.J.   **26. CHARITY AND TIME**

The contemporary view of time, Father Johann points out in this essay, is not anti-pathetic to Christian tradition. If viewed rightly, it is, in fact, completely indigenous to tradition. This assertion is brought out more fully when the meaning of time is placed in the context of charity, for charity enables us to unfold the inner fiber of the present moment. Where faith and hope are virtues of the future—the one concerned with the *still-unseen,* the other with the *not-yet-possessed*—charity unites the realm of the still-unseen and the not-yet-possessed with the *now.* The union involved in charity transcends the whole order of becoming, for "charity already is communion with the Absolute," and is founded wholly on actuality.

Rooting man in the present, charity deepens the meaning of now, by showing how rich it is with the presence of God. Indeed, we cannot speak of any now except in relation to a presence. Nor can we speak of a presence except in relation to "attention." It is preoccupation or attention, together with an actual presence that engenders the now. Hence, "on the nature of my preoccupation will depend the nature of my *now,*" while a difference in the character of the attention I devote to experience will imply a difference in the kind of *moment* I am actually living.

Now charity indicates a specific kind of attention. It is an attention to the eternal, the meta-historical, insofar as the eternal penetrates the history of

This selection is excerpted from *Cross Currents* Vol. 9, No. 2 (1959), and is reprinted through the courtesy of the author and the publisher.

my daily life. This means that without deepening my sense of the daily-historical by a sense of God and the meta-historical fulfillment of history, I cannot understand the meaning of time. God ceases to be a presence for me (despite his ontological nearness) precisely in proportion to my lack of charity. It is, therefore, only by the preoccupation of charity that I am able to engender a now that is constituted by God's presence. Charity renders me present to God, and "the *now* which is defined by His presence is in a real sense the *now* of eternity."

. . . WHAT IS THE ontological significance of time? What is its ultimate finality? What orientation must temporalized consciousness assume if it is to live this significance vitally and achieve this finality? These are the questions that trouble the modern mind. And to propose a tentative and Christian solution to them is the purpose of this paper.

First of all, what has contemporary thought to say about time? The answer may be briefly put. For modern man, the basic fact of time is that it is linear. In place of the cyclic notion of the Greeks the modern substitutes the image of a straight line. Time is an irreversible "becoming" that arises out of the past and proceeds in a straight line towards the future goal. Any given moment is simply a point on that line. Its significance is dependent on its ordination to a future terminus. For Marxist and secularist thought in general, this terminus is to be achieved in this world. It is the Kingdom of Man. For religious thought it is the Kingdom of God. But in either case the meaning of time, as in all becoming, derives from the term of the process. Man, situated at a particular point in time, can look only to the future. Either he plunges into the stream and is swept along by it with those who are striving for a dream—this holds true for Marxist and Incarnationalist alike; or he stands aside with his eyes fixed on the horizon and waits for the coming of the Kingdom of Saints—here we have the Eschatologist. For all alike, today is a fragment whose meaning depends on tomorrow. The present lacks ultimate depth. Fulfilment belongs to the future. Not where we are, but where we are going; not what is, but what is to be. Thus the psychological orientation is basically one of expectancy.

The Meaning of Work

This attitude of expectancy, characteristic of modern man's temporal orientation, is manifest in his outlook on the value of work. Here his radical absorption with the finality of becoming is clearly in evidence. What is the significance of work? For the modern man, work is important only for what it accomplishes. Its whole value is to be measured in terms of results, of output. Its total significance lies in the contribution it makes towards a better world—

for the individual himself or for mankind generally. Thus the fragments of the present are seen merely as building blocks for the brave, new future. There one's attention must be directed. Work therefore is coterminous with effort—the effort to give some sort of direction to the current of life, to point the horizontal line of becoming towards the elusive peace and happiness that man craves. For modern man, work and life are an uninterrupted anticipation of tomorrow. He is forever expecting, looking forward to, a better day.

What is the result? For one thing, modern man has lost his "feel" for the present and with it his capacity for leisure. He is forever in a state of tension. Divided between what is and what will be, he lacks a sense of wholeness. Life for him means simply being further down the road tomorrow than today, and the consequence has been to chain him to the wheel of "progress." As Pieper observes, it is precisely this conception of work that has resulted in proletarianizing man. Man has been subordinated to the process of betterment. Living always in expectation, he lives without fulfilment. Distracted from the present, he misses the reality about him and his life becomes a sort of anxious vigil. Indeed, like the pathetic Marcher in James' *Beast in the Jungle,* he too often comes to the end of his life without ever having lived at all.

Time and Becoming

To a certain extent this attitude of expectancy is inevitable. It is, indeed, nothing more than a psychological translation of the process of "becoming." To the extent therefore that time is a becoming, an evolution, a movement towards a term, temporalized consciousness is necessarily wrapped up with the future. Discontent with the present and unceasing restlessness are the inevitable consequence; they become the inseparable characteristics of being in time.

But does this orientation translate the whole significance of time? Is it man's fate always to be dissatisfied with now? Is the wholeness he craves only to be looked for in tomorrow? Must he consider the present simply a springboard for action, a mere foothold in reality where he cannot rest, but whence he must project himself towards what is not? The whole question, indeed, reduces itself to the meaning of the *now.* For, as St. Thomas observes, the *now* is the only point of time that exists. If, therefore, the *now* is merely a point of transition, a dot on the horizontal line of becoming, if it is simply a scene glimpsed from the window of a rushing train so that its only meaning for man is to mark the stages of his journey, then resignation to the torment of Tantalus is his only course. If, however, the *now* is something more than a moment in a process, a point of passage situated between before and after; if, though enveloped by change, it transcends change and is endowed with the quality of permanence, then perhaps restlessness for man need be no more than a temptation, and tranquillity instead his proper state.

To investigate the possibility of the *now* being more than a passing phenomenon, we will look into the significance of charity. For if time is seen as pure transition, it is because man is seen as pure "becoming." This, however, is a one-dimensional view, and an analysis of charity will show it to be such. Adding another and more profound dimension to the life of man, charity by that very fact reveals another and more profound dimension to the meaning of time. Let us see how this is so.

The Permanence of Charity

In extolling the merits of charity, Saint Paul makes much of its permanence. The time will come, he writes, when we shall outgrow prophecy, when speaking with tongues will come to an end, when knowledge will be swept away; but we shall *never* have finished with charity (1 Cor. 13:8). Somehow, though a part of our temporal scheme of things, an orientation to be assumed by man while still on the road towards fulfilment, charity nevertheless participates in that fulfilment and transcends the imperfections of those things that belong to the world of time. It has a completeness about it, and therefore a permanence, that belong to the order of the eternal. In this it is distinguished even from the other theological virtues. For that "conviction of things we cannot see," which is faith, will one day give way to vision, to a sight of God "face to face." And what we now only hope for, we will one day hold in our hands; hope will yield to possession. But "caritas numquam excidit." It already manifests the fulness, the perfection, the finality of the life of God who is Love.

The reason for this special excellence of charity is not difficult to trace. St. Thomas, indeed, presents it in a few sentences. Asking himself whether or not charity is the greatest of the theological virtues, he replies that the importance of a particular virtue can generally be determined from its object. In this case, however, since all three theological virtues look to God as their proper object, one cannot be said to be superior to the others because its object is higher. Here, rather, we must examine the *nearness* of each one to its object: and it is its special *nearness* that constitutes the distinctive perfection of charity. For faith and hope each imply a certain distance from their term: faith concerns itself with the still-unseen, hope with the not-yet-possessed. But the love of charity is already united to its term. For by charity the beloved is somehow already in the lover and the lover is drawn into communion with the beloved. As St. John observes, "God is love; he who dwells in love, dwells in God and God in him." (1 Jo. 4:16)

Charity and Union

Hence the completeness and abiding character of charity. Through charity man is already in union with the infinite, unchanging God. But this union, it must be understood, is not a mere passive union of potency and act. Charity is not simply another form of becoming that has somehow reached its term. It is not merely the satisfaction of a particular desire, or the actuation of a particular potency, a sort of partial fulfilment of man that leaves his total fulfilment to a future date. No, charity is an active union. It is a union of mutual presence and communion, a dialogue between lovers. For, as St. Thomas indicates elsewhere, charity is friendship with God. But the dynamism of friendship, *amor amicitiae,* is not the dynamism of the potential. It is not the thirst or appetite of potency for act, the drive which is the metaphysical basis of all change and becoming, and which is technically known as *amor concupiscentiae.* "Love of friendship" is radically distinct from this. It is founded instead on actuality. Its dynamism is not that of a nature in need, but of a person in love, a "self" enchanted with the presence of his beloved and making a gift of himself. As St. Thomas pregnantly observes, faith and hope are in a sense possessive. They look to God for what we get out of Him, in one case the knowledge of truth, in the other the possession of good. But charity looks to God Himself, not for anything that may come to us from Him, but solely in order to rest in Him alone.

The reason, therefore, for the permanence and completeness of charity and its superiority to the other theological virtues is that the union it involves completely transcends the whole order of becoming. While faith and hope look to a future acquisition which will mean their own disappearance, charity already is communion with the Absolute. Founded wholly on actuality, it is a participation in the pure and eternal love that God has for Himself. And just as human love is able to survive the wasting of bodies and the wreckage of time and, itself unchanged, still shine forth brightly from dimming eyes, so and infinitely more is divine charity above the rush of the temporal. Born in time, it belongs to the forever. Born on earth, it is the beginning of heaven. Charity, writes St. Thomas echoing St. Paul, is not swept away even by the consummation of glory but remains forever the same—"eadem numero manet."

Charity and Time

Now the purpose of these reflections on charity was to see what light they might throw on the meaning of time. How does charity, which belongs to the essence of his life as a Christian affect man's life as a being existing in time? One part of the answer to this question is immediately evident—that, namely, which concerns man's temporal orientation. For charity by its very nature roots man in the present. Insofar as it is already active communion and not therefore ordered to future acquisition it is concerned with what is at hand. In place of an ever-fleeing tomorrow, the *now* becomes the center of preoccupation. In place of anxious expectancy, there is substituted loving attention. *Ubi amor, ibi oculus.*

But if charity recalls man's attention to the *now* as to a sort of privileged moment, the moment of communion, it does by the same token deepen the meaning of the *now*. Where in the linear conception of time, the *now* was simply a point of transition, a moment in a process whose whole significance depended on a future term, the *now* of charity is rich with the presence of God. Indeed, for charity this all-pervading Presence, or more precisely our attention to it, may be said to constitute the *now*. Since this is the central point of our thesis, let us examine it more closely.

The Meaning of the Present

If we ask ourselves the meaning of the present as opposed to the past or future, our first answer might be that the present is the actual—that which actually exists as opposed to what did exist or may yet come to exist. But while the actual, thus understood objectively, can be said to be the ontological or material foundation of the present, it does not formally constitute it. For the present or the *now* is always understood in opposition to past and future, and by its very nature occupies an intermediary position between the two. For this to be possible, however, the two must in a sense co-exist with the present; and since they do not do so in the objective order (where what alone is had is the actual), but only in the mind, we come to the conclusion that mind or consciousness has an essential role in the constitution of the present. It is not therefore the actual by itself but the presence of the actual to one's consciousness—where indeed there also abides a recollection of a past presence and the expectation of a future presence—that formally constitutes the present or *now*.

These ideas are, of course, familiar enough. They are indeed hardly more than a re-phrasing of Augustine's position that time is spiritual extension—*distentio animae:* the past is the soul's remembrance, the future its expectation, and the present its attention. Two points, however, must be noted, and it is Heidegger who has brought them out.

The Present and Presence

First of all, if it is not the actual itself by my attention to it—or conversely, its presence to me—that constitutes the *now,* then we must say that any given *now* is correlative to the presence of some object or other. To speak of *now* is to affirm a *presence*. For instance, at this moment my *now* consists in the presence of this desk at which I sit, the books that clutter it, the pencil in my hand and the paper spread before me. These are the objects on which my attention is focused. They form my present world. Their presence defines my *now*. When a little while ago I was walking with a friend, then it was his presence and the presence of the path and the objects along the way that defined my *now*. In a little while, the presence of a classroom, of forms, a blackboard, a multitude of nodding heads and a teacher expounding a thesis will engender a new *now*. In every case the *now* is defined by presence. If the presence is merely remembered, the moment (that "now") belongs to the past; as anticipated, it is part of the future. But the presence of those things that actually hold my attention is what makes up the moment in which I live; their actual presence to me constitute my *now*.

Presence and Preoccupation

Second and even more important is the element of preoccupation. For if it is a presence that constitutes my *now,* it is my preoccupation, the focus, that engenders the particular presence. True enough, my attention does not make the thing actual. This desk exists quite independently of me. But only to the extent that I *pay attention* to it, am in a sense *preoccupied* with it, is it present to me. By my preoccupation—in this case the writing of this article—I actively render myself present to the desk and so make it a presence constitutive of my present. Should I interrupt my writing to look out the window at the boys throwing snowballs, my desk, though still in the room with me, would no longer be present to me nor a part of my present. It is thus *preoccupation* or the particular focus of one's attention which, together with the actual, engenders the *now*.

This is extremely significant. For it means that on the nature of my preoccupation will depend the nature of my *now*. A difference in my attention will mean a difference in the moment I am living. If, for example, I am preoccupied with the past and so engender a present that consists of remembered presences; or if, on the other hand, I occupy myself with the future by rendering my self present to expected presences, in either case my *now* is lacking in actuality. The only thing actual about it is the act itself of remembering or expecting. I am truly lost in a world of non-being. In short, I am a dreamer. But even if I am preoccupied with the actual and actively render myself present to it, the now which I engender is still capable of varying degrees of richness and density according to the degree of actuality in that to which I direct my attention.

. Preoccupation with Becoming

I may, for instance—and this is unfortunately too often the level of our lives—allow myself to become absorbed with the order of becoming. My attention is fixed on the surface of this changing world. It is the realm of rushing confusion, the paper I have to write, the examination I have to study for, my part in the play which I must rehearse, all the endless tasks I have to perform. My preoccupation is split in a hundred ways and consequently so is my life. My life becomes divided into a multitude of disconnected *nows* with its only unity a unity of succession. And not only is it divided; it is impoverished. For look at the *nows* which make it up. Not only are they constituted by the presence of objects that are purely transitory, so that my present is always slipping through my fingers. These objects themselves, these endless tasks to be performed, are also by the very dynamism which is proper to them constantly drawing my attention into the future, to the countless deadlines that must be met. Thus I abandon even the minimal actuality they offer me for the nothingness of tomorrow. My already piecemeal life hovers perpetually between realities that are shallow and gone as soon as they appear and a "reality" (the future) that is not at all.

But this is not the only possibility. It has been the purpose of this paper to point out another—and with that we get back to the effect of charity on time, which we were discussing a few paragraphs back. We had said that charity, precisely because it is active communion, firmly plants us in the present. As a preoccupation with the actual it engenders a present. But we were remarking when we broke off that this present, this *now* of charity, is different from the *now* of linear time. This *now,* we said, is rich with the presence of God. What we meant by that can at the present juncture be readily understood.

Preoccupation with God

For charity is a special form of attention. It is a preoccupation with the eternal, not indeed as with a presence to be achieved at the end of our earthly life—an expected presence, therefore, a future—but precisely insofar as the eternal penetrates our every day. In this connection it is well to remember a remark of St. Thomas. It is in answer to an objection that friendship, and consequently charity, is not possible between God and man, since friendship implies intimate union and conversation between the friends, whereas God is infinitely distant from His creatures. To this he replies that although it is true that God, on the scale of ontological perfection, is infinitely above what He has made, still, precisely because of that perfection, He is in reality nearer to each thing than that thing is to itself. Precisely because He is the Creator, the absolute source of all that is, He is operative with the greatest intimacy in everything and is present in everything; and therefore, St. Thomas concludes, "potest salvari etiam ratio amicitiae." As Augustine observes: "God . . . who abideth forever, for whose presence no one has to wait, whose absence no one has to fear, for the very reason that He truly *is,* is ever present." And if we add to this universal nearness of God to all things by reason of His absolute being, the special nearness He has through grace to the souls of the just— for charity, as supernatural, is built on this special presence—then we see that there is no question of absence as an obstacle to communion with God.

If there is an obstacle it is in ourselves—in our lack of attention. "Thy God is whole everywhere," writes Augustine; "if thou fall not off from Him, He will never fall away from thee." We fall away from Him precisely to the extent that we lack charity, that we become absorbed and preoccupied with other things. For despite His ontological nearness, God is not a *presence* for us except insofar as we focus our attention on Him. It is only by the preoccupation of love, of charity, that we engender a *now* that is constituted by *His* presence. Through charity we render ourselves present to Him and the *now* which is defined by His presence is in a real sense the *now* of eternity.

The Now of Charity

Let us, therefore, examine briefly the characteristics of this present engendered by the preoccupation of charity. We saw before that the life of one who is preoccupied with the endless tasks in the order of becoming is split up into an infinity of distinct *nows* whose only unity is one of succession. To this condition the *now* of charity opposes a radical wholeness. For the presence of God which constitutes it is absolute and total; it does not therefore define a *now* which is one in a series, a *now* situated alongside other *nows* constituted and defined by finite presences. Rather is it a *now* which dominates the whole flow of "becoming," a Presence which embraces all presences.

For consider the parallel to be found in human friendship. A conversation with my friend is made up of a whole series of words and gestures, an amalgam of ideas, banter and repartee. Were I to become preoccupied with these disparate elements so that, in place of my friend, these separate items dominated my attention, I would by that change of focus destroy the conversation. The *now* of active communion, constituted by the presence of my friend, would give way to a series of distinct *nows,* each one defined by the presence of the particular item that was at the moment absorbing my attention. And, indeed, we all know too many people who, when talking to one, get so wrapped up in their own train of thought that one might just as well not be there. So long, however, as the conversation remains a conversation, my *now* is radically defined by the presence of my friend. All the items of the conversation serve only to mediate that presence. Hence the presence of my friend and the *now* constituted by that presence envelop with a unity and a wholeness what would otherwise be a mere series of fragments.

So also with the *now* of charity. Charity, as active, is continual communion with God, a preoccupation that engenders His Presence. The *now* defined by His presence, since it belongs to a different and superior order to those engendered by the world of becoming, is able to embrace in its radical unity all the fragments of our lives. To the extent, therefore, that I am preoccupied with the loving God and refuse to let myself become *absorbed* in the welter of disparate tasks that make up everyday life, then all these various activities, like the elements in a conversation, will be gathered together into wholeness and, instead of splitting up my life, serve only to mediate God's unifying presence. And since, moreover, the presence engendered by charity is the presence of God, the *now* of charity is rooted in the Absolute. It has maximal density and maximal consistency. It is indeed a *now* which does not pass away but of which heaven itself will be only the continuation. For it is already a participation in the eternal presence of God to Himself, the eternal *Now* of God Himself.

The Personal Center

Jacques Maritain

27. SUBJECT AND *SUPPOSITUM*

The dominant character of the reality that we call a human person, says Maritain in this essay, is that it is a *suppositum*—a substance, or subsistent real, which has an essence, and exercises existence and action.

The person's knowledge of other persons differs essentially from the knowledge he has of himself. Others, he knows as objects rather than as subjects; but himself, he knows as a subject, not as an object. In both cases, however, the knowledge of the substance of personality is obscured, either totally or relatively. The knowledge of one's self, or subjectivity, is achieved in an existential intuition "which surrenders no essence to us." One's own self *is*

From *Existence and the Existent* by Jacques Maritain. Reprinted by permission of the publishers, Pantheon Books, Inc., New York, and Editions Paul Hartmann, Paris, 1948.

known or felt, first, "in virtue of a formless and diffuse knowledge which, in relation to reflective consciousness, we may call unconscious or pre-conscious knowledge." Such consciousness Maritain also calls *concomitant* or *spontaneous*. Secondly, there is a "knowledge" of subjectivity given by *mode of inclination,* or connaturality, rather than *by mode of knowledge*— that is, by "conceptual objectisation."

There is no reason to believe, Maritain contends, that the person is in any way demeaned in being made into an "object of the intellect," for "the ob-jectisation which universalizes it and discerns in it intelligible natures, makes it known by a knowledge destined doubtless to continue to deepen." This is because the person has an essential structure. It is a substance "equipped with properties," and "is acted upon and acts by the instrumentality of its potencies." Ontological self-knowledge (as opposed to merely phenomenal reflection) brings out the fact that the person, far from being imprisoned, opens out on *being*.

W HAT WE CALL *subject* St. Thomas called *suppositum*. Essence is *that which* a thing is; suppositum is *that which* has an essence, *that which* exercises exist-ence and action—*actiones sunt suppositorum*—*that which* subsists. Here we meet the metaphysical notion which has given students so many headaches and baffles everyone who has not grasped the true—the existential—founda-tion of Thomist metaphysics, the notion of *subsistence*.

We are bound to speak of this notion of subsistence with great respect, not only because of the transcendent applications made of it in theology, but because, in the philosophical order itself, it bears witness to the supreme tension of an articulated thought bent on seizing intellectually something which seems to escape from the world of notions or ideas of the intellect, namely, the typical reality of the subject. The existential subject has this in common with the act of existing, that both transcend the concept or the idea considered as the terminus of the first operation of mind or simple ap-prehension. I have tried to show in an earlier section how the intellect (be-cause it envelops itself) grasps in an idea which is the first of its ideas, that very thing, the act of existing, which is the intelligible (or rather the super-intelligible) proper to the judgment, and not to simple apprehension. Now we are no longer dealing with the act of existing but with that which exercises that act. Just as there is nothing more commonplace in language than the word being (and this is the greatest mystery of philosophy) so there is nothing more commonplace than the "subject" to which in all our propositions we attribute a predicate. And when we undertake a metaphysical analysis of the reality of this subject, this individual thing which maintains itself in exist-ence, this supremely concrete reality, and undertake to do justice to its irre-ducible originality, we are forced to appeal to that which is most abstract and most elaborate in our lexicon of notions. How can we be astonished that minds which are fond of facility should regard as so many vain scholastic refinements and Chinese puzzles the elucidations in which Cajetan and John of St. Thomas show us that subexistence is distinct both from essence and from existence, and describe it as a substantial mode? I concede that the style of their dissertations seems to carry us very far from experience into the third heaven of abstraction. And yet, in reality their aim was to form an *objective notion* of the *subject* itself or the suppositum, to reach objectively, within the ontological analysis of the structure of reality, the property which makes the subject to be subject and not object, and to transcend, or rather exceed in depth, the whole universe of objects.

When they explain that an essence or a nature, considered strictly, cannot exist outside the mind as an object of thought, and that nevertheless individual natures do exist, and that, consequently, in order to exist, a given nature or essence must be other than it has to be in order to be an object of thought, that is to say, it must bear in itself a supreme achievement which adds nothing to it in the line of its essence (and consequently does not enrich our understanding by any new note which qualifies it), but which *terminates* it in that line of essence (closes or situates it, constitutes it as an *in-itself* or an inwardness face to face with existence) in order that it may take possession of this act of existing for which it is created and which transcends it; when they explain in this fashion *that by which,* on the plane of reality, the *quod* which exists and acts is other than the *quid* which we conceive, they attest the existential character of metaphysics, they shatter the Platonic world of pure objects, they justify the passage into the world of subjects or supposita, they rescue for the metaphysical intellect the value and reality of subjects.

God does not create essences to which He can be imagined as giving a last rub of sandpaper of subsistence before sending them forth into existence! God creates existent subjects or supposita which subsist in the individual nature that constitutes them and which receive from the creative influx their nature as well as their subsistence, their existence, and their activity. Each of them possesses an essence and pours itself out in action. Each is, for us, in its individual existing reality, an inexhaustible well of knowability. We shall never know everything there is to know about the tiniest blade of grass or the least ripple in a stream. In the world of existence there are only subjects or supposita, and that which emanates from them into being. This is why ours is a world of nature and adventure, filled with events, contingency, chance, and where the course of events is flexible and mutable whereas the laws of essence are necessary. We know those subjects, we shall never get through knowing them. We do not know them as subjects, we know them by objectising them, by achieving objective insights of them and making them our objects; for the object is nothing other than something of the subject transferred into the state of immaterial existence of intellection in act. We know subjects not as subjects, but as objects, and therefore only in such-and-such of the intelligible aspects, or rather *inspects,* and perspectives in which they are rendered present to the mind and which we shall never get through discovering in them.

As we pass progressively to higher degrees in the scale of beings we deal with subjects of existence or supposita more and more rich in inner complexity, whose individuality is more and more concentrated and integrated, whose action manifests a more and more perfect spontaneity, from the merely transitive activity of inanimate bodies to the occultly immanent activity of vegetable life, the definitely immanent activity of sentient life, and the perfectly immanent activity of the life of the intellect. At this last degree the threshold of free choice is crossed, and therewith the threshold of independence properly so-called (however imperfect it be) and of personality. With man, liberty of spontaneity becomes liberty of autonomy, the suppositum becomes *persona,* that is, a whole which subsists and exists in virtue of the very subsistence and existence of its spiritual soul, and acts by setting itself its own ends; a universe in itself; a microcosm which, though its existence at the heart of the material universe is ceaselessly threatened, nevertheless possesses a higher ontological density than that whole universe. Only the person is free; only the person possesses, in the full sense of these words, inwardness and subjectivity—because it contains itself and moves about within itself. The person, St. Thomas, says, is that which is noblest and highest in all nature.

Subjectivity as Subjectivity

By sense or experience, science or philosophy, each of us, as I said a moment ago, knows the environing world of subjects, supposita, and persons in their role as objects. The paradox of consciousness and personality is that each of us is situated precisely *at the centre* of this world. Each is at the centre of infinity. And this privileged subject, the thinking self, is to itself not object but subject; in the midst of all the subjects which it knows only as objects, it alone is subject as subject. We are thus confronted by subjectivity as subjectivity.

I know myself as subject by consciousness and reflexivity, but my substance is obscure to me. St. Thomas explains that in spontaneous reflection, which is a prerogative of the life of the intellect, each of us knows (by a kind of knowledge that is not scientific but experimental and incommunicable) that his soul exists, knows the singular existence of this subjectivity that perceives, suffers, loves, thinks. When a man is awake to the intuition of being he is awake at the same time to the intuition of subjectivity; he grasps, in a flash that will never be dimmed, the fact that *he is a self,* as Jean-Paul* said. The

---

* The reference is to Jean-Paul Richter; see above, page 205. It also suggests remarks quoted earlier in *Existence and the Existent* in a discussion of Sartre's *L'Être et le Néant* [Paris, 1943], especially the passage on the "profound self," pages 78–81—ED. NOTE.

force of such a perception may be so great as to sweep him along to that heroic asceticism of the void and of annihilation in which he will achieve ecstasy in the substantial existence of the self and the "presence of immensity" of the divine Self at one and the same time—which in my view characterises the natural mysticism of India.

But the intuition of subjectivity is an existential intuition which surrenders no essence to us. We know *that which* we are by our phenomena, our operations, our flow of consciousness. The more we grow accustomed to the inner life, the better we decipher the astonishing and fluid multiplicity which is thus delivered to us; the more, also, we feel that it leaves us ignorant of the essence of our self. Subjectivity as subjectivity is inconceptualisable; is an unknowable abyss. It is unknowable by the mode of notion, concept, or representation, or by any mode of any science whatsoever—introspection, psychology, or philosophy. How could it be otherwise, seeing that every reality known through a concept, a notion, or a representation is known as object and not as subject? Subjectivity as such escapes by definition from that which we know about ourselves by means of notions.

Yet it is known in a way, or rather in certain ways, which I should like briefly to enumerate. At the very beginning and above all, subjectivity is known or rather felt in virtue of a formless and diffuse knowledge which, in relation to reflective consciousness, we may call unconscious or pre-conscious knowledge. This is knowledge of the "concomitant" or spontaneous consciousness, which, without giving rise to a distinct act of thought, envelops in fact, *in actu exercito,* our inner world in so far as it is integrated into the vital activity of our spiritual faculties. Even for the most superficial persons, it is true that from the moment when they say *I,* the whole unfolding of their states of consciousness and their operations, their musings, memories, and acts, is subsumed by a virtual and ineffable knowledge, a vital and existential knowledge of the totality immanent in each of its parts, and immersed, without their troubling to become aware of it, in the diffuse glow, the unique freshness, the maternal connivance as it were, which emanates from subjectivity. Subjectivity is not known, it is felt as a propitious and enveloping night.

There is, secondly, a knowledge of subjectivity as such, imperfect and fragmentary of course, but in this instance formed and actually given to the mind, and which is thrown into relief by what St. Thomas calls knowledge by mode of inclination, sympathy, or connaturality, not by mode of knowledge. It appears before us under three specifically distinct forms: (1) practical knowledge, which judges both moral matters and the subject itself, by the inner inclinations of the subject (2) poetic knowledge, in which subjectivity and the things of this world are known together in creative intuition-emotion and are revealed and expressed together, not in a word or concept but in a created work; (3) mystical knowledge, which is not directed towards the subject but towards things divine, and does not of itself issue in any expression, but in which God is known by union and by connaturality of love, and in which this very love that becomes the formal means of knowledge of the divine Self, simultaneously renders the human self transparent in its spiritual depths. Let the mystic reflect an instant upon himself, and a St. Theresa or a St. John of the Cross will show us to what extent the divine light gives him a lucid and inexhaustible knowledge of his own subjectivity.

But in none of these instances is the knowledge of subjectivity as subjectivity, however real it be, a knowledge by mode of knowledge, which is to say, by mode of conceptual objectisation.

In none of these instances is it philosophical knowledge. It would be a contradiction in terms to seek to make a philosophy of that sort of knowledge, since every philosophy—like it or not—proceeds by concepts. This is the first point to which the consideration of subjectivity draws our attention; and it is a point of capital importance. Subjectivity marks the frontier which separates the world of philosophy from the world of religion. This is what Kierkegaard felt so deeply in his polemic against Hegel. Philosophy runs against an insurmountable barrier in attempting to deal with subjectivity, because while philosophy of course knows subjects, it knows them only as objects. Philosophy is registered whole and entire in the relation of intelligence to object; whereas religion enters into the relation of subject to subject. For this reason, every philosophical religion, or every philosophy which, like Hegel's, claims to assume and integrate religion into itself, is in the last analysis a mystification.

When philosophy, taking its start in the being of things, attains to God as the cause of being, it has then, thanks to ana-noetic knowledge, rendered the divine Self an object of philosophical knowledge expressed in concepts. These concepts do not circumscribe the supreme reality presented by them. On the contrary, that divine reality infinitely overflows the banks of conceptual knowledge. But philosophy knows thereby, or ought to know, that the reality thus objectised "through a glass, darkly," is the reality of a transcendent Self inscrutable in its being and its goodness, in its liberty and its glory. And all the other intelligent *selves* who know it, from the instant that they do know it, owe to it, as their first duty, obedience and adoration. St. Paul blamed pagan wisdom for not recognising that glory of God of which it was in fact aware. But in fact, to recognise that glory is already to adore it. It is something to know that God is a transcendent and sovereign Self; but it is something else again to enter oneself and with all one's baggage—one's own existence and flesh and blood—into the vital relationship in which created subjectivity is brought face to face with this transcendent subjectivity and, trembling and loving, looks to it for salvation. This is the business of religion.

Religion is essentially that which no philosophy can be: a relation of person to person with all the risk, the mystery, the dread, the confidence, the delight, and the torment that lie in such a relationship. And this very relation-

ship of subject to subject demands that into the knowledge of uncreated subjectivity which the created subjectivity possesses there shall be transferred
something of that which the latter is as *subjectivity,* i.e. as that uncreated
subjectivity is in the mystery of its personal life. Whence all religion comports
an element of revelation. Therefore in the true faith it is the First Truth in
Person which makes known to man the mystery of the divine subjectivity:
unigenitus filius, qui est in sinu patris, ipse enarravit. This knowledge is still
"through a glass, darkly," and therein the divine subjectivity is still objectised
in order to be grasped by us. But this time it is in the glass of the super-analogy
of faith, in concepts which God Himself has chosen as His means of speaking
to us about Himself—until at the last every glass falls away and then we know
truly as we are known. Then we shall truly know the divine subjectivity as subjectivity in the vision in which the divine essence itself actuates our intellect
and transports us in ecstasy within itself. While awaiting this state, the connaturality of love gives us in apophatic contemplation, a dim sort of substitute
and obscure foretaste of such a union.

Generally speaking, to *situate* the privileged subject which knows itself as
subject in respect of all other subjects, which it knows as objects; to situate
the self, that thinking reed in the crowd of thinking reeds, sets a singular
problem. Each of us is able to say with Mr. Somerset Maugham: "To myself I
am the most important person in the world; though I do not forget that, not
even taking into consideration so grand a conception as the Absolute, but
from the standpoint of common sense, I am of no consequence whatever. It
would have made small difference to the universe if I had never existed." This
is a simple remark; but its implications are very wide.

Being the only subject which is a subject for me in the midst of a world of
subjects which my senses and my intelligence can know only as objects, I am
at the centre of the world, as we observed a moment ago. With regard to my
subjectivity in act, I am the centre of the world ("the most important person
in the world"). My destiny is the most important of all destinies. Worthless as
I know myself to be, I am more interesting than all the saints. There is me, and
there are all the others. Whatever happens to the others is a mere incident in
the picture; but what happens to me, what I myself have to do, is of absolute
importance.

And yet, as regards the world itself, from the most obvious "standpoint of
common sense," I know perfectly well that "I am of no consequence whatever" and that "it would have made small difference to the universe if I had
never existed." I know that I am one of the herd, not better than the rest,
worth no more than the rest. I shall have been a tiny crest of foam, here one
moment, gone in the twinkling of one eye, on the ocean of nature and humanity.

These two images—of myself and of my situation in respect of other subjects—can positively not be superposed. These two perspectives cannot be

made to coincide. I oscillate rather miserably between them. If I abandon myself to the perspective of subjectivity, I absorb everything into myself, and, sacrificing everything to my uniqueness, I am riveted to the absolute of selfishness and pride. If I abandon myself to the perspective of objectivity, I am absorbed into everything, and, dissolving into the world, I am false to my uniqueness and resign my destiny. It is only from above that the antinomy can be resolved. If God exists, then not I, but He is the centre; and this time not in relation to a certain particular perspective, like that in which each created subjectivity is the centre of the universe it knows, but speaking absolutely, and as transcendent subjectivity to which all subjectivities are referred. At such time I can know both that I am without importance and that my destiny is of the highest importance. I can know this without falling into pride, I know it without being false to my uniqueness. Because, loving the divine Subject more than myself, it is for Him that I love myself, it is to do as He wishes that I wish above all else to accomplish my destiny; and because, unimportant as I am in the world, I am important to Him; not only I, but all the other subjectivities whose lovableness is revealed in Him and for Him and which are henceforward, together with me, a *we,* called to rejoice in His life.

I am known to other men. They know me as object, not as subject. They are unaware of my subjectivity as such; unaware not merely of its inexhaustible depth, but also of that presence of the whole in each of its operations, that existential complexity of inner circumstances, data of nature, free choice, attractions, weaknesses, virtues perhaps, loves and pains; that atmosphere of immanent vitality which alone lends meaning to each of my acts. To be known as object, to be known to others, to see oneself in the eyes of one's neighbour (here M. Sartre is right) is to be severed from oneself and wounded in one's identity. It is to be always unjustly known—whether the "he" whom they see condemns the "I," or whether, as occurs more rarely, the "he" does honour to the "I." A tribunal is a masquerade where the accused stands accoutered in a travesty of himself, and it delivers his acts to be weighed in the balance. The more the judges stray from the crude outward criteria with which formerly they contented themselves, and strive to take account of degrees of inner responsibility, the more they reveal that the truth of him whom they judge remains unknowable to human justice. Interrogated by such a tribunal, Jesus owed it to Himself to remain silent.

I am known to God. He knows all of me, me as subject. I am present to Him in my subjectivity itself; He has no need to objectise me in order to know me. Then, and in this unique instance, man is known not as object but as subject in all the depth and all the recesses of subjectivity. Only God knows me in this wise; to Him alone am I uncovered. I am not uncovered to myself. The more I know of my subjectivity, the more it remains obscure to me. If I were not known to God, no one would know me. No one would know me in my truth, in my own existence. No one would know me—*me*—as subject.

What this comes to is that no one would render justice to my being. There could be no justice for me anywhere. My existence would be immersed in the injustice of the knowledge of me possessed by all the others and by the world itself; and in my own ignorance of myself. But if there is no justice possible with regard to my being, then there is no possible hope for me. If man is not known to God, and if he has the profound experience of his personal existence and his subjectivity, then he has also the experience of his desperate solitude; and the longing for death—more than this, the aspiration to total annihilation, is the sole spring that can gush forth within him.

Finally, to know that I am known as subject in all the dimensions of my being is not only to know that my truth is known, and that in this knowledge justice is done me; it is also to know that I am *understood*. Even though God condemn me, I know that He understands me. The idea that we are known to Him who scrutinises the loins and the heart dissolves us at first in fear and trembling because of the evil that is within us. But on deeper reflection, how can we keep from thinking that God Who knows us and knows all those poor beings who jostle us and whom we know as objects, whose wretchedness we mostly perceive—how can we keep from thinking that God Who knows all these in their subjectivity, in the nakedness of their wounds and their secret evil, must know also the secret beauty of that nature which He has bestowed upon them, the slightest sparks of good and liberty they give forth, all the travail and the impulses of good-will that they drag from the womb to the grave, the recesses of goodness of which they themselves have no notion? The exhaustive knowledge possessed by God is a loving knowledge. To know that we are known to God is not merely to experience justice, it is also to experience mercy.

In any case, what I should like to say is that our acts are tolerable to ourselves only because our consciousness of them is immersed in the obscure experience of subjectivity. Our acts are hatched in it as in a nest where everything, even the worst rendings and the worst shames, connives with us to emanate from us in the unique freshness of the present instant that we are living. They bathe in that maternal atmosphere emanating from subjectivity, of which I spoke earlier. There is nothing which crushes us so much as our own acts when, forgotten and then one day evoked by some relic of past time, they pass to the state of objects, separated from the living waters of subjectivity. Even if they were not specifically evil, we are no longer sure that they were good and that some unknown illusion or hidden impurity had not tainted them —those strangers who fling themselves upon us like the dead come forth from within to bring doubt and death to us.

It must be one of the natural features of the state of damnation that the subject, not seeing himself in God, and therefore not seeing his whole life in the eternal instant to which everything is present, all his good and evil acts come back upon him in the sterile endlessly questioning light of the memory of the dead, like enemy objects wholly detached from the actual existence in which subjectivity is definitively set, in the solitude of its ill-will which renders its own past a separate thing for it.

But when the subject reaches his end and sees himself in God and in divine eternity, all the moments of his past life are known to him in the actuality and the presentness of the instant in which they were lived, and all his acts (even the evil, now not only forgiven but leaving no spot nor shadow) are known as emanating presently out of the freshness of subjectivity, now itself becomes trans-luminous. And in the virtue of the vision in which his intelligence possesses the *Ipsum esse subsistens* he knows not only himself and all his life in a sovereignly existential manner, but also the other creatures whom in God he knows at last as subjects in the unveiled depth of their being.

The Structure of the Subject

To objectise is to universalise. The intelligibles in which a subject objectises itself for our mind are universal natures. It is in relation to the individuality itself of the subject (which the intelligence is not capable of grasping directly); in relation to its subjectivity as subjectivity, as something unique and singular, incommunicable and unconceptualisable, and in relation also to the subject's own experience of its own subjectivity, that objectisation is false to the subject and that, known as object, it is unjustly known, as we have already observed. On the other hand, in relation to its essential structures, the subject is in no wise betrayed when it is made object. The objectisation which universalises it and discerns in it intelligible natures, makes it known by a knowledge destined doubtless to continue to deepen, but not one that is in any sense unjust. Such a knowledge does no violence to the truth of the subject, but renders that truth present to the mind.

The subject, or suppositum, or person has an essence, an essential structure. It is a substance equipped with properties and which is acted upon and acts by the instrumentality of its potencies. The person is a substance whose substantial form is a spiritual soul; a substance which lives a life that is not merely biological and instinctive, but is also a life of intellect and will. It is a very simple-minded error to believe that subjectivity possesses no intelligible structure, on the ground that it is an inexhaustible depth; and to conceive of it as without any nature whatsoever for the purpose of making it an absurd abyss of pure and formless liberty.

These observations allow us to understand why many contemporary philosophers, while they talk of nothing but person and subjectivity, nevertheless radically misunderstand those words. They remain lightheartedly ignorant of the metaphysical problem of that *subsistence* concerning which something was said in a preceding section. They do not see that personality,

metaphysically considered, being the subsistence of the spiritual soul communicated to the human composite, and enabling the latter to possess its existence, to perfect itself and to give itself freely, bears witness in us to the
generosity or expansivity of being which, in an incarnate spirit, proceeds from
the spirit and which constitutes, in the secret springs of our ontological structure, a source of dynamic unity and unification from within.

Because analysis wearies them, they are ignorant of what the proper life
of the intelligence consists in, and in what the proper life of the will consists.
They do not see that, because his *spirit* makes man cross the threshold of independence properly so-called, and of self-inwardness, the subjectivity of the
person demands as its most intimate privilege communications proper to love
and intelligence. They do not see that, even before the exercise of free choice,
and in order to make free choice possible, the most deeply rooted need of the
person is to communicate with *the other* by the union of the intelligence, and
with *others* by the affective union. Their subjectivity is not a *self*, because it is
wholly phenomenal.

I have already cited St. Thomas's aphorism, that the whole root of liberty
is established in the reason. What reveals subjectivity to itself is not an irrational break (however profound and gratuitous it may be) in an irrational
flow of moral and psychological phenomena, of dreams, automatisms, urges,
and images surging upwards from the unconscious. Neither is it the anguish of
forced choice. It is self-mastery for the purpose of self-giving. When a man
has the obscure intuition of subjectivity, the reality, whose sudden invasion of
his consciousness he experiences, is that of a secret totality, which contains both
itself and its upsurge, and which superabounds in knowledge and in love. Only
by love does it attain to its supreme level of existence—existence as self-giving.

This is what I mean: Self-knowledge as a mere psychological analysis of
phenomena more or less superficial, a wandering through images and memories, is but an egotistic awareness, however valuable it may be. But when it
becomes ontological, then knowledge of the Self is transfigured, implying intuition of Being and the discovery of the actual abyss of subjectivity. At the
same time, it is the discovery of the basic generosity of existence. Subjectivity,
this essentially dynamic, living and open centre, both receives and gives. It
receives through the intellect, by superexisting in knowledge. It gives through
the will, by superexisting in love; that is, by having within itself other beings
as inner attractions directed towards them and giving oneself to them, and by
spiritually existing in the manner of a gift. And "it is better to give than to receive." The spiritual existence of love is the supreme revelation of existence
for the Self. The Self, being not only a material individual but also a spiritual
personality, possesses itself and holds itself in hand in so far as it is spiritual
and in so far as it is free. And to what purpose does it possess itself and dispose of itself, if not for what *is better,* in actual existence and absolutely

speaking, or to give of itself? Thus it is that when a man has been really awakened to the sense of being or existence, and grasps intuitively the obscure, living depth of the Self and subjectivity, he discovers by the same token the basic generosity of existence and realises, by virtue of the inner dynamism of this intuition, that love is not a passing pleasure or emotion, but the very meaning of his being alive.

By love, finally, is shattered the impossibility of knowing another except as object. I have emphasised this impossibility above at length and noted that it directly concerns the senses and the intellect. To say that union in love makes the being we love another *ourself* for us is to say that it makes that being another subjectivity for us, another subjectivity that is ours. To the degree that we truly love (which is to say, not for ourselves but for the beloved; and when—which is not always the case—the intellect within us becomes passive as regards love, and, allowing its concepts to slumber, thereby renders love a formal means of knowledge), to this degree we acquire an obscure knowledge of the being we love, similar to that which we possess of ourselves; we know that being in his very subjectivity (at least in a certain measure) by this experience of union. Then he himself is, in a certain degree, cured of his solitude; he can, though still disquieted, rest for a moment in the nest of the knowledge that we possess of him as subject.

Joseph de Finance, S.J. **28. BEING AND SUBJECTIVITY**

A person cannot be for us an "object" of the understanding, says Father de Finance, unless we wish to imply that the person is a "thing." Thus, if Thomism uses the term "object of the understanding" to indicate the being of personality as a mere thing, it could be rightfully reproached.

The question of being, he asserts, is, in the first place, unnecessarily confused by the introduction of the terms "subject" and "object." The idea of being must envelop within itself the value, not only of every object, but even of the most intimate subjectivity; for "The 'I' which thinks being, the act by which I think it, the liberty which takes sides with respect to it, all that is most interior and most singular in my personal attitude—all this is being." It follows, then, that the idea of being cannot be totally objectified, since no subject can exclude itself from it.

This selection appeared in *Cross Currents* Vol. 6, No. 2 (1956), and is reprinted by permission of the translator, W. Norris Clarke, S.J.

By genuine being, says de Finance, we mean existence, which itself can never be the object of a concept. From the point of view of the subject, the apprehension of being cannot be cut away from its affirmation. In the apprehension of being, the mind posseses it not by a form superimposed but by means of an act "in which it relives according to its own mode of being the very act itself." It is misleading, therefore, to look upon being in terms of subject-object, because being itself is neither subject nor object, since both by definition share *in* being.

Our primary personal affirmation of being is given in terms of the statement "The existent exists," or simply "It is." Such a statement, de Finance maintains, affirms two things: it affirms both being in myself and myself within being. But it is only through the medium of subjective reflection that being appears as existent in the fullest sense of the term. "I know being only because I am myself a sharer in being."

The affirmation of being opening onto this double consequent—that is, of "myself-within-being" as well as of "myself-and-others-and-objects-within-being"—indicates specific degrees of qualification. Plainly, subject and object, a "that is," is clearly distinguishable from my own existence as an "I am." In contrast to the difference between subject and object, the affirmation of being without qualification (which is nonetheless included in every existential affirmation) opens out onto the affirmation of God. This becomes unmistakably clear in the affirmation of one's own unique personhood—in one's "ipseity"—because one exists more intensely in proportion to the degree to which one is committed to the higher values implied in unqualified Existence.

. . . THE TERM "OBJECTIVE" carries with it a pejorative connotation today. This is due in good part, we feel, to the accepted meaning this word has taken on in ordinary language. It calls up at once the notion of *thing,* in the most opaque sense of the term, as a reality which I can get hold of and handle because it is entirely in front of me and outside of me. Since I am not involved in it, its intelligibity is independent of me, and anyone else in my place would see it just as I do. But this very universality, which seems to guarantee the truth of our knowledge, is, on the contrary, just what constitutes its limitation and its incurable superficiality; for it proves that all I penetrate to in the being in question is what it yields up to all comers and not the precious core of its intimate singularity. No doubt, when it is a question of things, this is of no great moment. A mere thing as such has no depth, no interiority. To know it according to the mode of an object is to know it truly, or, at least, to know it insofar as the knowledge of it interests us. But it is quite otherwise when we are dealing with *persons,* with *subjects.* To understand them in the manner of an object is in reality to misunderstand them.

If Thomism, therefore, when it affirms that being is the *object* of the intellect, were to interpret the word object in this narrow sense, it could not escape the reproach of depriving being of its existential dimension, of turning it purely and simply into an essence. . . . It is impossible to refuse the value of being to the subjective distinctiveness of each one of us. My consciousness of myself—not as the knowledge of a particular object which happens to be me, but as the absolutely incommunicable presence of the "I"— is not nothing. In a sense even, it is everything, since the universe of objects exists for me only through it. Thus the idea of being must envelop within itself the value even of the most intimate subjectivity. The "I" which thinks being, the act by which *I* think it, the liberty which takes sides with respect to it, all that is most interior and most singular in my personal attitude—all this is being.

It follows evidently that the idea of being cannot be totally *objectified*. Not only can I not isolate it completely from the particular determinations of the beings which confront me, but I cannot even disengage it fully from the atmosphere, as it were, in which it is enveloped by the very act in which I think it. Neither can I exclude my own self from the domain of being to consider it as something alien. In other words, according to the remark and the terminology of M. Gabriel Marcel, being is a mystery, that is to say, "a question which encroaches on its own data." It is in those doctrines, on the contrary, where the idea of being is presented as capable of being isolated from its differences that being appears far more as a mere *object*. There I can stand back at a distance from it. It turns into a *problem,* the same author would say. Reason is more at ease here, for being thus conceived is so much clearer and easier to handle. But we know well enough what difficulties arise when we try to apply this strictly objectified and univocal notion to reality itself.

If the idea of being is for us a "mystery," there can be no question of making it perfectly clear. At the same time we should go as far as we can in laying bare its structure. But to say, as we have so far, that it includes its own differentiating notes, that it envelops the very act which thinks it, is to surround it with a question mark rather than to shed light on it. We must take up at a deeper level the problem of the relations between the subject and being.

Being, says St. Thomas, is the first object which falls under the apprehension of the intellect. But being is not an essence abstracted from existence. Genuine being, *ens,* is the *existent,* and only in function of it can the possible be conceived; for the possible is *that which can exist.* The idea of being implies, therefore, the apprehension of existence, and by this I mean existence as *actually exercised,* since, without reference to the latter, existence as *signified* (i.e., as merely thought about without being affirmed) would be nothing but an empty form. But the apprehension of existence in the concrete cannot be separated from its affirmation. If we are using terms in their full rigor, existence cannot be the object of a concept. The mind does not possess it by a form impressed upon it, but by means of an act in which it relives according to its own mode of being the very act itself of the other. The idea of being implies, therefore, its own affirmation, and, up to this point, the ontological argument is valid (that is to say, in this one case, at least, the idea necessarily implies the existence of its object).

But just what is this "being" whose affirmation conditions all our intellectual activity? It can be neither subject nor object for both subject and object are grasped within being. They share *in* being, hence their affirmation logically presupposes the affirmation of being itself. The primary affirmation—primary not in this sense that it precedes all others chronologically, but in the sense that it expresses the fundamental reaction of the mind towards the empirical variety of whatever it affirms—the primary affirmation is the following: "There is an existent," or, if you wish, "The existent exists" (but not in the same sense in which one would say, "The square is square," there is no question here of the logical inclusion of the predicate within the subject; we are at the roots of the logical order itself). Being at this stage is posited neither as exterior nor as interior to the intelligence. *It is,* purely and simply.

This primary evidence, constitutive of the very structure of the mind, alone permits the surmounting of rationalistic idealism, while making use of it up to a certain point in order to transcend the empiricism of the immediately given. But, in addition to the fact that this evidence is never present in a pure state (I affirm being only in affirming some being, this particular being), the mind, at the very moment when it brings it into focus by reflection, cannot go on to clarify it without seeing it open out into multiple affirmations. I cannot affirm being without affirming myself within being. The affirmer, submerged at first in his own affirmation, emerges under the light of reflection. I am in being and being is in me. Or, if one prefers, being presents itself to me at once as the object of my thought and as constitutive of my subjectivity itself. If the idea of being came to me from consciousness and the *Cogito* alone, I would be in danger of remaining locked up within my ego. Descartes escapes subjectivism only by discerning, in the most intimate depths of his consciousness, the liberating presence of the Idea of God. But in reality there is no innate idea of God other than the movement of the mind itself towards the Absolute, which gives our affirmations their firmness and our idea of being its transcendence.

By this presence of the Absolute within me, my consciousness acquires a firm foundation and a universal validity: a validity and a truth for all. My toothache cannot be communicated, but the knowledge that I have of it, objectively considered, can be. At the same time the "I" inserts itself in an order wider than itself: I *am not* being; I am *within* being, I *share in* being. Solipsism is radically excluded. The *objective* presence of being, the sign of the presence of the Absolute within us, is indispensable in order to save our thought from the asphyxiation of subjectivism.

Logically even, this objective presence is prior. But must it be dissociated from the other mode of presence, the subjective? Must it be taken as sufficient by itself to open up all the depths of being? We do not think so. It is only through the medium of subjective reflection that being reveals its dimension of interiority. In this light, and in this light only, does it appear as *existent* in the full sense of the word. Without the immediate grasp of the ego the idea of being would remain as empty as the Kantian categories deprived of intuition. The ego in its relation to the Absolute and the universal thus manifests itself as the datum which underlies the entire activity of the mind. We must not, however, distinguish the ego and its relation to the Absolute as two elements which can be isolated. The ego is nothing without this relation, which enters into its intimate constitution precisely as ego (a more detailed analysis would bring this out without difficulty), and this relation, on its part, is immediately given to me only in the ego, in the experience of my own spiritual activity.

But, it may be said, does not the objective presence of being imply of itself the existence of being in general? Undoubtedly it does, since, as we have shown, it is impossible to think being without referring to some existent in act. But the point is that it is also impossible for me to think an existent otherwise than in its relation to the ego.

Objectively, being presents itself to me as that which imposes itself on my affirmation, that which I cannot avoid, that which is not relative to my caprice or to my contingent peculiarities, in a word, that which exists for every mind, for Thought in its absoluteness. It should be noted that these latter characteristics, which seem to eliminate the point of view of the ego, actually include it by that very fact. To say that being, objectively considered, is that which does not depend on my ego is to introduce the ego itself into the notion of the objective. Besides, what experience can I have of Thought outside of the experience of *my* thought? But it remains that being, apprehended solely as object, as correlative to the ego, is lacking in depth. I cannot endow it with a "third dimension," so to speak, except by affirming an act which corresponds to my own act of affirmation and which the latter takes up and makes interior to itself. It is in the act of the mind that I truly grasp the act of being.

Now the affirmation can be envisaged from two points of view: in its subjective reality, as determination of the ego and, in the last analysis, as a modality of existence; or in its intentional content, its "objective being." Under the latter aspect the act of existing is present in the affirmation in somewhat the same way as the term of motion is present in the motion itself. The analysis of judgment and of its objective implications could, indeed, lead us to posit an Absolute in the order of existence, which grounds the validity of our partial affirmations. But this Absolute and the existences which depend upon it would remain deprived of true interiority for us, if the ego did not make manifest a new order of value that objective thought, as such, is unable to perceive. In other words, not only is being, properly speaking, incapable of being represented, of becoming an *object,* but our reflection of the affirmation, if it stopped short at the intentional content of the latter, that is, if it attained to thought *exclusively as thought,* would deliver to us only an existence without depth and, in the last analysis, a non-existing existence.

The latter hypothesis, of course, is unthinkable and, ultimately, self-contradictory. First of all, the ego (despite what some may hold) is not absent from any of its acts, and especially not from the judgment, which of its very essence involves a reflection on the subject. Secondly, since the relation to the absolute is, as we have said, constitutive of the ego, it is impossible to grasp it in all its truth and depth independently of the latter. It is only by losing myself in the Absolute and the Universal that I find myself and discover my true self in its most intimate privacy. But, conversely, it is only by descending to the deepest level of myself, to what constitutes me as *I,* to this irreducible core of my personality, the shrine of what is most serious and authentic in me, and the theater of my eternal commitments, that I meet the Universal and the Absolute.

It is, therefore, precisely insofar as it is a modality of my own existence that the act of affirmation enriches my notion of being with the dimension of interiority. In other words, if the affirmation is in fact capable of seizing within its grasp the existence of the object, it is only because, as activity, it is rooted in the existence of the subject. I know being only because I am myself a sharer in being. Identity in the intentional order presupposes connaturality in the real order. I know the being that I am thinking about, not merely as there before me, as one with me in the act of thought, but, more profoundly, as communing with me in existence as participating in its own way in this same standing-out-from-nothing which makes me here and now present. Subjective thought and objective thought, consciousness and knowledge mutually include each other and can be isolated only by attraction. The idea of being includes at once being as present to the mind in its role as object and being grasped immediately as constituting the very reality of the ego. It involves a relation and a tension, as it were, between my *consciousness of self* and my *tendency towards the absolute.*

But that is not all. If I do not affirm being without affirming myself, neither do I affirm myself without affirming opposite me an object, in the narrowest sense of the term. The shock of some sense object, whatever it may be, is, for the human mind, the necessary condition for every affirmation of existence. Thus the affirmation of being in us involves essentially (and not merely in virtue of contingent circumstances) the affirmation both of subject and of object, both of the ego and of the thing. A further analysis would be required to ascertain that, if the ego cannot affirm being without affirming itself and the object, this necessity is due to the fact that it is I, a human subject, who am making the affirmation. It is not due to being as such.

Furthermore, it would perhaps be more exact to say, in company with a good number of our contemporaries, that the first distinct datum, known either after or together with the ego itself, is another ego, a *thou*. Experience seems to confirm this view of things, for the child does indeed seem to be interested in and to recognize persons before recognizing things. But, in any event, this communication with persons, this affirmation of a *thou* confronting an *I,* is made possible only through the mediation of a thing, an object. At the very least, the ego must objectify itself in a sign.

Thus the affirmation of being opens out into the affirmation of myself-within-being, then into the affirmation of myself-and-others-and-objects-within-being. It is in this way that the notion of plurality enters in. By this we do not mean a plurality that is merely superficial, a plurality of mere aspects or modalities which would remain on the surface of the compact mass of otherwise undifferentiated being. That this multiplicity affects being radically and in depth is assured me by the presence within being of the personal value of my own ego, which, by its very act of affirmation, takes its stand in the presence of being, commits itself, and so manifests its irreducible singularity. Monism is thus ruled out at once. It is essential to being that it be open to participation by different subjects. To ask the why of this, to seek the means of passing from the idea of pure Being, subsisting in itself, to that of participation, would imply that the idea of being could be given to us outside of participation. This would come back to admitting the totally objectified notion of being, scraped clean of all its differentiating notes, which we have already rejected. Creation, certainly, remains a mystery, a profound mystery. But it is none other than the mystery of being itself.

The totality of other egos and things makes up the *world.* Thus we end up with the formula: myself-in-the-world-within-being. The relationship between these expressions, myself-within-being and myself-in-the world, is exactly the same as that acknowledged by Thomists between the *formal* object of the human intellect, being, and its *proper* object, being with its intelligibility immersed in the sensible (*quidditas seu natura in materia corporali existens— Sum. Theol.,* I. q. 84, a. 7). Nothing obliges us to restrict the meaning of the latter expression to that of inert things. Let us not forget that man, for the Scholastics as well as for Aristotle, is a *res sensibilis* (a thing belonging to the sensible order), although *sui generis,* and that the treatise *On the Soul* remains a branch of Physics. The traditional formula excludes by right only the disincarnated spiritual from the proper object of human knowledge. If we were to set off, therefore, within the scope of this *proper object, human reality* as the *most proper object* of our knowledge, we would no doubt be giving an unforeseen extension to the classic thesis, but would by no means be distorting it. One could even hold that such a position is more in harmony with the principle invoked by St. Thomas himself: "The potency of a cognitive agent is proportioned to the object of its knowledge"—on condition, of course, that it be expanded a little.

Subject and object, ego and thing, evidently constitute two very different types of being. I exist *for myself;* the object, as such, exists *in itself.* But not only is it a phenomenon relative to my knowledge of it; it does not truly exist *for itself.* I appear to myself, precisely insofar as I am an *I,* as possessing a value incommensurable with that of mere things, by my thought I introduce a kind of new dimension into the world; by my liberty I am in some manner cause of myself. It is quite evident that this is a way of existing quite different from that of a mere thing. (It would not be to the point to object here that liberty and thought are on the level of accidental operation, not of substantial being. For operation, too, is in the order of being. And if the ego were not radically different from a mere thing in its profoundest being, how could it be so in its activity?)

The word being, therefore, does not mean exactly the same when applied to the ego and to a thing. Subject and thing differ in the mode of their existing (*in ratione essendi*). In the propositions "I am" and "That is," the verb undergoes a shift in value; it is colored by its subject. For the same reason, I cannot affirm being univocally of myself and of others. For each subject the verb in the "I am" has an incommensurable value. To attribute existence to them in a univocal sense would be to neglect this originality which forms one with their existence, which is their very existence; for to exist, both for myself and for others, is to be an *I.* A perfect knowledge, one which would match with complete fidelity the consciousness that each subject has of himself, would see the being in each one as differentiated from within.

Our analysis of the idea of being can be pushed still further. Further reflection would show—this is not the place to detail how—that the affirmation of myself-in-the-world is not the adequate equivalent of myself-within-being. The being posited in the latter, more basic affirmation transcends that of the universe and of society. Only an infinite and absolute reality can exhaust its virtualities. The affirmation of being without qualification, included in every existential affirmation, thus opens out, at a deeper level of reflexive analysis, onto the affirmation of Being, the affirmation of God. (It is without doubt the dim perception of this truth which was responsible, a century ago, for the success of ontologism. Its error was to mistake for a vision, even obscure, what was only an implicit affirmation, or, better still perhaps, a transcendental condition of every affirmation. Today, when the controversies have died down and the problems been more carefully sifted out, we can afford to be more equitable in our estimate: "It dared too much, but it was noble in its excess.")

It is evident that the term being as used in the last named affirmation involves yet another shift in meaning. The Being in relation to which both subject and object are affirmed cannot exist in the same way as they do. In reality, if subject and object are included within being, God is beyond it. It is only from an incomplete and provisory point of view that God can be regarded as an "inferior" of being. We know that there is nothing superior to Him. The idea of being appears rather as a kind of perspective on the order of finite beings. It is turned entirely towards them, and designates God only indirectly, as the mysterious source from whence they emanate. It has God behind it, so to speak.

My self, other selves, things, the Absolute—all these appear as so many different types of being which have been revealed to us by the analysis of the idea of being, and so many diverse affirmations into which the basic affirmation unfolds as it passes to full explicitness. Still other types could be brought out without difficulty, and this could serve as a basis for a truly rational theory of categories. But what has so far been said is enough to show that the idea of being is far from enjoying a perfect unity; rather it is pregnant with a prodigious diversity. Its unity was due only, it seems, to its extreme indistinctness. A truly distinct idea of being would involve nothing less than the exhaustive knowledge of all beings in their unity as well as in their distinction, a knowledge in which the most minute details, the most individual particularities, and the most intimate secrets would be exposed in full light and grasped in a single look. Now such an adequate and concrete idea of being does indeed exist. But it is the Word of God. And all the progress of human thought tends but to one goal: to imitate in the least imperfect way possible this inaccessible ideal. . . . The act of existing imitates, on the level of the creature, that self-sufficiency, that completeness, that exclusiveness, which are proper to the subsisting *Act of Existence*. In the abyss of its irreplaceable subjectivity each "only one" imitates Him who admits no peer.

Yet it is in this same abyss that it meets all other singulars. For this absolute subjectivity in which mine participates is also that in which all other subjects participate. And the more each one strives to be itself and to advance towards perfect authenticity, the more also it enters into profound communion with all the others, since it is the same Act which is acting in all and communicating itself to all. It is not, therefore, by some illusory renunciation of being oneself that we bring about the meeting with another, but in a deepening of one's own self. Nevertheless we must distinguish here between simple individuality, which belongs to the order of nature or essence, and "ipseity" or selfhood, which belongs to the order of act, of existing, while at the same time being conditioned by the former. To cling stubbornly to the former is to imprison oneself in one's poverty. To descend more deeply into the latter is to make oneself ever more open to others. One becomes truly himself not by cultivating originality for its own sake but by existing more intensely, that is, by committing one's life to higher and higher values. This must not be understood as the effacing of my ego before some impersonal ideal. It involves, on the contrary, an eminently personal adhesion to the source of all personality. I root myself more firmly in existence in the measure in which I turn towards God, so that I find my proper place under His eye. But this divine look which consolidates my being is also that which permits me to see others as true beings, as *subjects*. Essential as is the presence of others for us, nothing is more difficult for us to admit than that they really and truly *exist*. I learn to go out of myself, to love others with a sincerely disinterested love, only when I see in them the image of God, posited in being by the same Good Will.

Thus the deepening in subjectivity, the becoming conscious of what makes us ourselves, far from closing us in and isolating us, is on the contrary, the condition without which our relations with others would never go beyond the stage of an objective and superficial community. The reason, once again, is that the act of existing is at one and the same time the principle both of incommunicability and of communion.

Inversely, essence—we are speaking here evidently of the *singular* essence—at the same time that it limits being to this particular being and so distinguishes it from all others, presents itself to us, basically, as *that which, within a being, can be communicated:* "Every form, precisely as form, is communicable" (St. Thomas, *In I Sent.,* d. 4, q. 1, a. 1). Even a pure form, which, according to St. Thomas, is not multipliable according to its "natural" being, can be multiplied and communicated according to its "intentional" being. "Michaelity" subsists only in Michael; but it can be present in the order of ideas to an infinity of minds. There is indeed a difference in the mode of being. Michaelity in Michael is the law of the *act of existing;* in Gabriel, in Raphael, etc., it is the law of the *act of thinking*. But in the formal line of quiddity the identity is absolute. And it needs must be; otherwise it would not be Michael that Gabriel and Raphael would know (cf. the celebrated passage of Kant on the hundred thalers in his pocket and in his idea). In short, the essence is representable, objectifiable, and thus communicable, precisely because it is of itself impersonal and becomes a person only by the incommunicable act of existence.

Perhaps, rather than distinguish communicability and incommunicability, it would be better to distinguish two kinds of communication. There is the communication of which we have just spoken, that of essence or of form, which is susceptible of being represented. And there is another, quite different, which is proper to act, to existing. (We are here taking the term act in the very strict and formal sense of terminal act, which excludes from its own proper line all potentiality. In a wiser sense form and essence are also acts.) As St. Thomas puts it: "It is of the nature of every act to communicate itself" (*De Pot.,* q. 2, a. 1). We would not go so far as to affirm that the opposition between the passive form, "communicable," in the text cited further back, and the active form, "to communicate itself," in the text just cited, was intentional on the part of St. Thomas. But it is at least suggestive.

In the communication of which we are now speaking it is not a question of a form which is repeated, either identically or imperfectly, according to its in-

telligible structure, but of an act, of an existence which calls up another existence, of a subject which posits opposite itself another subject. The Absolute
does not communicate itself after the manner of a model, of which the various
finite beings would be a more or less faithful reproduction, or after the manner of a musical theme, which would be repeated more or less diminished in intensity. At least that is only a partial and secondary point of view. If we
wished to find an apt comparison, we should look rather to the order of love
and will. Love directs itself towards the other according to the latter's own
proper existence; it takes up on its own account and prolongs within itself the
act by which the other inserts itself in the order of existence. Let us now suppose a love which would not be a spiritual participation in the existence of
another, but of which this existence would rather be the expression. This is
what we mean by that communication of act, raised to its highest degree, which
is *Creation*. (At least this is the highest degree which is rationally accessible to
us. The mysteries of the Trinity and the Incarnation present us with incomparably higher forms of communication which the mind of man, left to itself,
would never have been able to suspect.)

The deepest relationship between being and God is not one of resemblance or of difference (for all that is of the order of essence, and it is the act
of existing which is central in any being; it is this which is the formal term of
the creative act). It is rather an "existential" relationship, and therefore one
that is strictly speaking impossible to define. One can do no more than evoke
it by suggestion, as that act by which beings are both made present and present themselves before God, and thus at once are distinguished from Him and
turn towards Him, adhering to Him as to the Source on which they depend.
This relationship, once grasped by the spiritual subject, can follow out two
divergent paths within him, that of love or of hate, that of confident adoration
or of rebellious pride.

What is more, if the divine Act communicates itself by calling forth
other acts into existence in its presence, then without doubt the latter must pre-
exist within it in some manner. But it would not be adequate to conceive this in
terms of the pre-existence of the image in the model. For the model contains
the image only insofar as the latter resembles it, whereas the divine Act, as
the total cause of creatures, must contain them according to all that they are,
hence according to their very subjectivity, i.e., according to the very aspect
which opposes them irreducibly to Himself. What else can this mean save that
they are present to Him in the only manner in which it is possible for another,
as other, to be present, namely according to the mode of thought and of love?
This does not mean by a love somehow added on to the divine Being, but by
a love which is this very Being itself; for, if there were any distinction between
Love and Being, it would be necessary to put first of all into the latter all that
had to be present in the former. The absolute Act of Existing, precisely be-

cause it precontains within itself all other acts of existence according to all
their subjective depth, cannot be conceived save as an absolute Love. "God is
Love." The metaphysics of existence thus rejoins in its own way the spiritual
intuition of the apostle of love.

Robert O. Johann, S.J.   **29. THE MEANING**

OF LOVE

The meaning of one's own *ipseity,* or unique being, as suggested by Father de
    Finance in the previous selection, is subjected to further analysis in this
    statement by Father Johann.

    The recognition of one's unique ontological value, or ipseity, he says,
is the precondition of love. Unless one cherishes one's own self, one cannot
cherish another's. What one grasps in loving another is not just an assemblage of "personality traits," but "the presence of a living and original
intention," the profundity of personal consciousness. Love involves a relation of an "I" specifically vis-à-vis a "thou". The context of this relationship, however, is to be found in something other than either the "I" or
"thou"—it is to be found in the community of beings within Being Itself.
For this reason, love implies a metaphysics of participation, since direct love
is fundamentally "an encounter with the absolute, an encounter with being."
I, as a person, establish myself in existence only according to the degree in
which I turn to God. I am able to love another only insofar as I perceive
that "I am present to a new and transcendent revelation of that value I love
in myself."

    The communion sought in the love of one person for another thus takes
on cosmic and ontological dimensions, since its significance is that "it
achieves and consummates that participation of the multiple in the plenitude
of Being which is its foundation."

I⟍T IS CLEAR, at the outset, that if a being is to find his own good in the
proper and incommunicable subsistence of another, his own ipseity must first
of all be a value to himself. He must be conscious of himself, apprehend himself in his uniqueness and cherish himself, if he is to be present to and cherish
the "self" in another. A being that is absorbed, as it were, in a material nature,
never really conscious of its own proper subsistence, unable to utter the simple

    From *The Meaning of Love* by Robert O. Johann, S.J. Reprinted by permission of the
publisher, The Newman Press, Westminster, Maryland, 1956.

but electrifying "I am," is equally and strictly incapable of really loving itself. It may subsist in its own right. It may even have certain operations by which it is perfected. But its existence is imprisoned in its nature and its operations are wholly necessitated. They follow a pattern of rigorous determinism; their real initiative is elsewhere. The animal that seemingly loves itself in seeking its proper perfection is in reality moved and directed by Another. If the animal is a value, it is not such to itself. And though indeed it is loved, it is not loved for itself. Direct love for a "second self," therefore, is in this order without meaning.

We must ascend, then, to the level of personality. There for the first time the "self" is seized and held in hand, is present to itself and a value to itself. There, consequently, for the first time self-love has real meaning. Let us, therefore, examine briefly the subject's original recognition of himself as a value. A description of this experience will help us grasp the significance of the presence of the other as a "second self."

The subject is present to himself as the secret and profound source of his activity. This is to say he knows himself precisely as *subject*. He experiences himself concretely from within as really existing, as exercising a true initiative. He has a living and experimental consciousness of himself as an "I." This *self* to which the subject is present is thus ineffable and incommunicable. It is not an abstract concept. The concept of the self remains exterior to that which it would signify and of which consciousness affirms the presence. Abstractly, the self is a characteristic common to all men. But the self of which there is here question poses itself in its unique exercise of existence, manifests in its singularity its responsible causality, renews itself incessantly in its identity in an act that is concrete and lived. It is a subsistent plenitude revealed to itself in its own immanent activity; a generous abundance of being open to itself, not indeed as a pure datum of introspection, capable of being isolated and determined by a collection of attributes, but as affirmed and attained in the act by which it poses itself. This profound source is, therefore, unequaled by the knowledge had of it. It is a wealth, a richness, an expansive power of action, present indeed, but never wholly rejoined, never exhausted, always experienced as capable of new manifestations, new revelations. And it is this original and subsistent value, seized in the existential act of giving itself to itself, that I love when I love myself. Willing good to myself, I give and devote myself explicitly to the full unfolding in being of this intimate value, this unique subjectivity to which I am present in myself, and which as in me is myself.

The apprehension of the other as a "second self" is, in this light, full of significance. Since it is the basis of my loving him directly as myself, it cannot consist simply in seizing him as an existing nature, a being with such and such specific determination, a *taleity*. I am not present to the *self* in the other if I see in him merely a variety of impersonal qualities and attributes that might equally well be found in others. Rather must I somehow grasp the presence of a living and original intention, the profundity of personal consciousness. It is precisely because these would be lacking that I could not love directly an automaton, however perfect it might be and however capable I fashioned it to lavish me with the attentions and marks of friendship. To love the other directly, I must somehow be present to that unique principle of action which he is in himself, to the veritable subject with all his depth and mystery. It is to this inexhaustible source that my love looks, to this subsistent plenitude whose "very presence enchants me" and to whom I would supply whatever is needed for his complete development.

Hence also the insufficiency, for direct love, of a merely abstract recognition of another's subjectivity. Considering, for example, the sad plight of peoples in another land, the horrors faced by soldiers in a war, I may be stirred by a sentiment of pity and wish them well—*bonum alteri volens*. St. Thomas uses the example of a person watching two pugilists in a ring and wishing victory to one or the other. There is a sort of benevolence here. But it is not really love. Besides this simple act of the will, says St. Thomas, love implies a certain affective union of lover and beloved. Two unique existents are somehow mysteriously united, and the one, esteeming as his own good the full unfolding of the other in being, tends to and cherishes him in his very uniqueness. . . .

How then must the other be present to me if I am to love him directly? From what we have seen thus far, we can say that the answer to this question must meet and reconcile two apparently divergent exigencies. First af all, the presence of the other must be such that his uniqueness as a being and a value is fully recognized. Whatever be the union effected by love, it cannot be one of fusion or identification, where the originality (in the line of value) of each of the terms is absorbed and lost in some common denominator. Loving the self in the other, I cherish his proper initiative, that by which he is radically distinct from me. Instead of eliminating this distinction, direct love will, if anything, maintain and intensify it. Necessarily inherent in communion is the element of otherness. This, however, brings us up against the second exigency. The otherness implied in communion cannot be one of exclusiveness. It cannot be that of mere individuals whose distinction is spatial and rooted in matter and whose only contact with one another is exterior, a touching of surfaces, a contact by juxtaposition. For, to love another directly, I must somehow attain that secret abundance, the intimate self of the other. He cannot be present to me merely as an inert thing, nor even as a rational nature, if this is seen simply as a concrete aggregate of specifications and recognized only from the outside as endowed with the prerogatives of personality. He must be present precisely as a unique and free initiative who in his uniqueness is turned towards me and, through the nature in which he subsists, reveals somehow that hidden treasure which is himself.

Now the only *presence* that meets these exigencies, that preserves distinction while at the same time allowing for intimacy, is that of the *thou*. This is nothing more or less than to say that direct love implies between two persons a state of reciprocal consciousness. The presence of the other as really a "second self" is necessarily that of a subject open to me in some sense as I am to myself—it must be a presence which permits exchange and dialogue. As M. Marcel observes, I address in the second person only what I regard as able to answer me, in whatever fashion that may be—even if that response is an "intelligent silence." Where no response is possible there is only place for the *he*. Thus only when the other is present as a *thou,* do I contact concretely that unique value which is himself. It is not the essence as nature, according to M. Marcel in another place, that I attain in the *thou*. On the contrary, in treating the other as *thou,* I treat him, I seize him as liberty; I seize him as liberty for he is also liberty and not simply nature. And by love, I aid him in a certain way to be free, I collaborate with his liberty.

This need for mutual consciousness as the basis of direct love has been well analyzed by M. Nédoncelle. And in answer to an objection that this notion immediately suggests, I can do no better than cite him directly.

The basis of the objection is precisely the doctrine we have presented. There is, notes M. Nédoncelle, a *minimum of reciprocity* in the fact that love has for its origin the perception of something lovable in the beloved. If it is truly the other that I love and not an impersonal quality pinned on him, it is he who in a sense has begun to love me. He has promoted and enriched me by the very fact of his presence open to my perception. My love for him should begin with a sort of thanksgiving. The objection is then put: This person does not even know that a virtue has gone out from himself; perhaps he even ignores that I exist. What do you mean then by saying that he is my benefactor? More pointedly even: How can two persons be in a relation of reciprocity unless each is conscious of and open to the other? And yet it is all too evident that such a relation does not always exist at the beginning of one's love for another.

M. Nédoncelle replies that, although this person has not expressly willed me nor turned himself towards me by any particular decision, he has, nevertheless, given himself to the world. He has willed it in willing to expend his energies there and there let his personality shine through. It is true that he causes his being to radiate into my own, and this radiance is inseparable from any personal existence. To be in the world, therefore, is to be at least a minimum of goodness offered in public. Human consciousness is hidden in many respects by the cosmic masquerade. But there is an aspect under which it cannot do otherwise than give itself as a spectacle, communicate its part of excellence to those who contemplate it. A face that comes into sight is a reality that surrenders itself, a secret that furtively unveils itself, a value that diffuses itself and does not take itself back. It is always for this initial moment that love lies in wait and that is why it is born in reciprocity, although often it has to bury itself in solitude. But it has not the vocation of hermit; it wishes always the *maximum of reciprocity*.

It is in the light of these last remarks that one must understand the distinction which St. Thomas, following Aristotle, makes between love of benevolence and friendship. For friendship, it is not sufficient that I love another directly as myself; to be friendship, my love of benevolence must be *explictly* reciprocated. Friendship exists only between those who love one another. Thus, it is conceived as *adding* to a one-sided love of benevolence a certain society of lover and beloved in their love. However, this does not mean that direct love which is not yet friendship, can exist without any reciprocity whatever. It does not deny the necessity of that initial reciprocity which we have described as demanded by the very realism of direct love. It merely affirms, what all the world knows, that there is no real friendship until the love of the subject is consciously reciprocated by the beloved. Furthermore, that direct love anticipates and seeks a response, that to love is to will also to be loved, neither Aristotle nor St. Thomas would deny. For the unique subsistence of another person, which, resisting appropriation, demands to be loved for itself, can at the same time be considered a value to the subject only if that plenitude is turned towards the subject and that person freely surrenders the treasure which is himself to the subject in friendship.

Thus, reducing the question to basic principles, we may say that love requires a certain apprehension of the good that is loved, and that the more fully a good is known, so much the more lovable it becomes to us. But the good in another which is the object of direct love, that unique core of personality which is himself, can never be known at all and so never beloved unless it is somehow present to me in its uniqueness as a free initiative ready to engage in a dialogue. Only as a *thou* is the other open to me as an absolute value, and the love by which I constitute myself a friend to the other then alone attains the term it really seeks when it attains friend. *Amicus est amico amicus. . . .*

. . . For an understanding of the extension of direct love to another, we have already insisted that a profound metaphysics of participation is required. St. Thomas presents such a metaphysics and we have indicated its main lines insofar as they pertain to our problem. Only the community of beings in Being provides the basis upon which to build a theory of love. But it is clear by now that this community alone is insufficient to explain the total structure. What then must be added?

The first point has already been indicated. Both the subject and term of direct love must not only exist, but exist in an eminent way. They must exist spiritually, present to themselves and with dominion over themselves, if each is to be able to offer himself to the other and find his own good in the self of the other. Direct love in this world, then, can be found only between beings that share, besides existence, a rational nature—*subsistentes in natura rationali*. And we have thus the first qualification, a qualification derived from the side of essence and nature, of that community in being which founds the extension of direct love.

This first addition, however, immediately entails a second. For insofar as the *I* and *thou* of human love are, as it were, "incarnate spirits," they are in a real sense separated from each other by the natures in which they subsist. Unlike myself, present to myself in my own immanent activity, the *thou* is present to me only through the mediation of sign and gesture, only through the mechanism of the material world. Correspondingly, my love can attain another and promote him in his own personal existence only insofar as it too plunges itself into the world of things, vivifies them with a living intention, and uses them as instruments in its service. Hence the inevitable association of *gifts* and *sacrifice* with the act of love. Material things are assumed into an order which surpasses them, they become the vehicles of a love that goes from person to person, the sign and expression of their union. In addition, then, to community in existence, in addition also to similitude in rational nature—even to a similitude that extends to the ultimate accidents of being, where two beings are alike not only in their essential form but also in peculiarities of taste and development—there is need for a community in situation, interests, and aims. As Père Gillon observes, it is hardly necessary to indicate how much the idea of similitude is surpassed by the notions of common possession (*l'avoir commun*) and of common good. Two hoplites, one in Sparta, the other in Athens, are alike by reason of the occupations, the profession they practice. They do not however share the same κοινωνία; they do not pursue the same common good. Human love, therefore, requires a concrete association in exterior goods and in ends pursued. Only such a community provides the proximate basis for the spiritual encounter of two embodied persons. Only in their common enterprise, in the sharing of their efforts and their ambitions, can the communion of one with the other find its expression and realization. As St. Thomas remarks, friendship requires that a person wish another the good he wishes for himself, so that he desires to converse with him and share with him those aspects of his life that he especially values.

But if these qualifications must be added to that fundamental community in being, to that participation in the plenitude and sufficiency of Subsistent Existence, it must be remembered, nevertheless, that they are secondary and merely conditions for the realization of that communion which the creative presence in the multitude of Absolute Ipseity alone can found. As Père de Finance observes:

> In the abyss of its own irreplaceable subjectivity, each "unique" reflects Him who leaves no room for a second. But it is in this same abyss that he encounters the other uniques. For the Absolute Subjectivity in which my own participates is that

also in which participate the other subjects. And the more each one strives to be himself, the more he advances towards perfect authenticity, the more also he enters with the others into a profound communion, since it is the same Act which acts in all and communicates itself to all.

Direct love is thus an encounter with the absolute, an encounter with being—and hence it is only on the level of being that the communion it establishes and the absolute value which is its wellspring and its term, can be seized in their real significance. . . .

We have shown how direct love of another implies the reciprocity of two *selves, I* and *thou;* how it is the presence to me in the *thou* of the same value I love in myself—the value of being as subjectivity, ipseity, subsistent plenitude, in which we each participate and which unites us at the very moment it distinguishes us irreducibly—that permits me to love him as I love myself. However, to understand properly the communion of *I* and *thou* in love, we must realize that it is not simply a question of being able to love another as myself but rather that only insofar as I love another do I really love myself. And this second truth has exactly the same foundation as the first—the metaphysics of participation.

What indeed do I love in myself but a value that transcends me on every side? M. Lavelle remarks that my love always goes beyond myself because I can love in myself only what is the source itself of being and life. And St. Thomas himself is no less vigorous:

The good, he writes, that we especially wish to safeguard is the good we especially value; . . . and this for each one of us is his own good. Whence it happens that according as the goodness of a particular thing is or is thought to be more pertinent to the good of the lover, so much the more does the lover wish to safeguard this in what he loves. The good of the lover, however, is found more completely where it exists more perfectly. . . . Since, therefore, our good is perfect in God, as in the first, universal and perfect cause of all good, so it is that the good in Him is naturally of greater value to us than the good in ourselves. And so it is too that man naturally loves God with a love of friendship (i.e. direct love) more than he loves himself.

This is obviously true first of all on the level of metaphysical structure rather than on that of conscious life. Man is not (consciously) placed at the outset in his natural attitude regarding the Supreme Good; he must rather by his free effort acquire and constitute it. However, the fact that what draws us on, even when we are not conscious of it, is a direct love of God, indicates that the most profound and original orientation of our spirit is, not towards the self confined within the limits of our proper nature, but towards a *Thou.* That is why a man becomes himself only in existing more intensely, only in suspending his life from values that surpass the narrow limits of his own existence—and this does not mean the effacement of the I before an impersonal ideal, but on the contrary an adhesion that is eminently personal to the Source of all personality. I establish myself in existence only in the measure that I turn myself towards God and situate myself before his eyes. The original call to love is made by God, present in us by participation. It is a call to generosity, to the direct love of value in all its plenitude. And a love that restricts its horizons to the narrow limits of the *I*, that loves one finite self to the exclusion of other *selves,* is a love that never attains this plenitude. In the words of M. Lavelle, self-love (in this exclusive sense) is a love that fails.

Since then the fundamental drive of our being goes beyond ourselves, even at the outset, towards an infinite Good, and invites us to constitute ourselves by love for beings other than ourselves, we can begin to understand what the communion in love of *I* and *thou* really means. It is not simply a luxury. On the contrary, if we would begin to realize in our conscious life the highest and most secret aspirations of our being, it is strictly an exigency.

If the metaphysical law of being is, as it were, the envelopment of the multiplicity in the one, friendship is the access to a life that is actually the expression of that truth. It resolves the problem which the constitution of being leaves in a certain sense open: how can we realize in our life that which is the very law of reality, how can we bring ourselves into harmony with that which is constitutive of all existence? That is why, it seems to us, friendship is so moving; . . . it makes us enter into that profound law of reality where all is in communion and nothing is absorbed. [Aimé Forest.]

When I love another directly, I break the little circle I form with myself where I would lodge the other simply as an idea. I discover a new existence, I am present to a new and transcendent revelation of that value I love in myself. And by that very fact, I cure myself of the exclusiveness, the poverty, the solitude that are my lot and my curse when, through egoism, I constitute myself the center of the universe and the absolute. Here for the first time I am open to Value in all its infinity and mystery. So long as I love myself exclusively, I fail to realize the transcendent and absolute character of the value present in myself; it is loved precisely where its participation in plenitude is interrupted, precisely as detached and alone. The only way to fathom the depths of the value which I am in myself is to turn towards and be open to that same value where it exceeds the bounds of my proper subjectivity. I cannot really love myself without loving other selves. Only when drawn into communion with other selves is my own person confirmed in being and my own love equal to the perfection to which it secretly aspires.

But if, on the one hand, the presence of a thou brings to me such an enrichment, I by my love for the thou would bring him no less. Willing his good as a subject, his complete unfolding and expansion in being, the full development of that power to love which he is, I constitute myself by my love a gift to him. I in my turn become a thou to him. In my presence to him, he too can escape over the frontiers of his own solitude, discover in me a "second self," and in his love for me be drawn towards that complete communion in being for which as a person he longs. The significance then of communion in love is that it achieves and consummates that participation of the multiple in the plenitude of Being which is its foundation; it is the living realization of that union to which our participation in the One is the call.

Nikolai Berdyaev

30. DIFFERENTIATIONS OF
THE PERSON

The being of personality is to be sharply distinguished, says Berdyaev, from that of all inferior realities. It must also be distinguished as a category of *action* attainable by a human being.

A human being does not become a "person," does not have "personality," simply because he *is* a human being. The category of personality is set apart from that of the "individual" (which all realities occupy), as well as from that of the "ego" (or human individuality). Personality is attained only through conflict and an ascension into the realm of spirit. In the presence of a personality, I face a true "thou," which "concentrates in itself the whole mystery of Being, of Creation."

The characteristics of personality are, for Berdyaev, evident in the fact that it is capable of both joy and suffering—which is to say, that it is capable of tragic experience. Apart from tragedy, joy and suffering are meaningless. The mere *ego* of the egocentric man is incapable of "declaring for" personality, because it is devoid of "all sense of reality." The personality, in contrast, achieves a sense of reality in opening itself to "community" and to love. The person is not confined within himself, as is the egocentric man.

By being a personality, one subjects oneself, however, to tragic conflict. One is threatened, in the first place, by false "solitude" or "self-confinement"; secondly, one is threatened by "society" as an objectivization.

An existential harmony must be worked out by personality, therefore, by which it emerges from self-confinement into communion with other personality, but does not become objectivized in a dehumanized society. The tragic factors in this process from solitude to society is that one must choose between true "solitude," or interiority, and the false "solitude" of confinement; so, too, one must distinguish between the "society" of communitive love and that of spiritless thingdom.

From *Solitude and Society* by Nicholas Berdyaev. Reprinted by permission of the publisher, Messrs. Geoffrey Bles, London.

THE FUNDAMENTAL PROBLEM of Existential philosophy is that of the personality. I am an Ego before I become a personality. The Ego is primary and undifferentiated; it does not postulate a doctrine of the personality. The Ego is postulated *ab initio;* the personality is propounded. The Ego's purpose is to realize its personality; and this involves it in an incessant struggle. The consciousness of the personality and the endeavor to realize it are fraught with pain. Many would rather renounce their personality than endure the suffering which its realization involves. The idea of Hell—impersonal Being has no notion of it—is connected with this human endeavor to preserve and develop the personality. The personality is not the same thing as the individual, which is a natural biological category comprehending not only the animal and the plant, but also the stone, the glass, the pencil.

The personality is a spiritual category; it is the spirit manifesting itself in nature. The personality is the direct expression of the impact of the spirit on man's physical and psychical nature. A brilliant individual may have no personality. Men of great talent and individuality may be impersonal and unable to furnish the effort required to realize their personality. We may say of a man that he lacks personality, but we cannot deny him individuality. Maine de Biran and Ravaisson both maintained that the personality was intimately connected with human endeavor, which, in its turn, is inseparable from suffering. This endeavor is free from any exterior determination. The personality, like God, is extra-natural; and since it is the image and likeness of God, it is intimately related to Him. It postulates the supra-personal: it could not exist but for a Higher Power, a supra-personal content. The personality is above all an "axiological" category: it is the manifestation of an existential purpose. The individual, on the other hand, does not necessarily postulate such a purpose or contribute any value to life.

The personality is not in any sense substantial. To conceive it as such would be to adopt a naturalist, non-existential position. Max Scheler defines the personality more correctly as the union of our acts and their potentialities. The personality may also be defined as a complex unity, made up of the spirit, the soul, and the body. An abstract spiritual unity, lacking in diversity and complexity, does not constitute a personality. The personality is totalitarian, for it integrates the spirit, the soul and the body. The body is an integral part of the personality; it has its place not only in the material, but also in the cognitive sphere.

The personality is also the symbol of human integrity, of permanent values, of a constant and unique form created in the midst of incessant flux. In this way, the individual identity of the body is preserved despite the total renewal and change in its material composition. The personality postulates further the existence of a dark, violent, and irrational principle, the soul's capacity to experience powerful emotions; it also postulates the soul's ultimate and everlasting triumph over this irrational principle. But although it is rooted in the unconscious, the personality implies an acute self-consciousness, a consciousness of its unity in the midst of change. It is sensitive to all the currents of social and cosmic life and open to a variety of experience, but it takes care not to lose its identity in society or in the cosmos. Personalism is opposed to either social or cosmic pantheism. The human personality has nevertheless a material content and foundation. It cannot be a part of any social or cosmic whole; it has an autonomous validity which prevents its being converted into a means. It is an axiom of an ethical kind—the sort of axiom that enabled Kant to express an eternal truth in a purely formal manner. From the Naturalist standpoint, the personality is only a minute part of nature; from the Sociological standpoint, it is only a minute part of society. But from the Existential standpoint, from the standpoint of Spiritual philosophy, the personality cannot be conceived as anything particular and individual as opposed to anything general and universal. This opposition, so characteristic of the natural and the social life, is no longer applicable to the human personality. The suprapersonal helps to build up the personality, while the general constitutes the foundation of the particular without transforming the personality into a means. Therein lies the mystery of the personality—a mystery based on the co-existence of contraries. The error of universalism, which would make the personality an organic part of the world, lies in its inorganic conception of the personality. Parallel theories of society are all equally impersonalist, and attribute to the personality a merely organic function. To understand the personality, we must approach the relationship between the part and the whole not from the naturalist, but from the axiological standpoint. The personality is never a part but always a whole, never a datum of the external world but always a datum of the inner world of existence. It is not an object, and has no place in the abstract objective world. It is not of this world: when confronted with the personality, I am in the presence of a *Thou.* It is not an object, a thing, or a substance; nor is it an objectified form of psychic life—the object of psychology. Thus, the triumph of the personality will mean the annihilation of the objective world. The personality has an "image," a concrete form; but that image is the expression of a whole, never of a part. The personality is the realization within the natural individual of his idea, of the divine purpose concerning him. It therefore supposes creative action and the conquest of self. The personality is spirit and, as such, it is opposed to the thing, to the world of things, to the world of natural phenomena. It reveals the world of men, the world of living beings, who are concrete by virtue of their relationship and of their existential communion. The personality postulates discontinuity and thus excludes monism. Being a conscience, it is not determined by any psychophysical structure; it has its roots in another order. The personality is a biography, one and unique, an "history." Existence is invariably "historical."

... Another most important property distinguishes the personality from the thing, that of being able to experience joy and suffering. It is endowed with a sensibility wanting in the supra-personal realities: the sense of a unique and indivisible destiny is its essential constituent. That is the absolutely irrational aspect of the personality's existence, whereas the freedom of choice constitutes its rational aspect. The essential character of the personality lies not so much in its teleology, as in its power to achieve an antinomian blend of freedom with predestination when working out a troubled destiny.

As a matter of curiosity, we may note that the Latin word "persona" signifies a "mask" and has theatrical associations. The personality is essentially a mask. Man employs it not only to disclose himself to the world, but also to defend himself from its importunity. Thus acting and "representation" symbolize not only man's desire to play a part in life, but also his need to protect himself from the surrounding world, to preserve his identity in the depths of this Being. The theatrical instinct has a dual significance. On the one hand, it is the result of man's social condition, of his life in the midst of a multitude of fellow-men among whom he aspires to act a part, to occupy a position. The theatrical instinct is fundamentally a social one. On the other hand, it symbolizes the Ego's identification with another Ego, its reincarnation, the personality's masquerade. This is invariably a sign that the personality has failed to overcome its solitude in society, in the natural intercourse between men; that man is everlastingly solitary beneath his disguise. The Dionysiac orgies endeavored to overcome solitude by annihilating the personality. Solitude, indeed, can be overcome only in communion, only in the knowledge of the spiritual world, and not in the world of social frequentation, of the multitude and its objective relationships. When authentic community is achieved, the personality is strictly itself, and obeys the dictates of its own nature; instead of reincarnating itself in another Ego, it unites with the Thou while at the same time preserving its own identity. But when the personality is plunged into the midst of the multitude, into the midst of the objective world, it invariably aspires to play an assumed role, to reincarnate itself in others, and thereby ceases to be a personality, becoming merely a person or an individual. A social position generally involves acting a part, assuming a mask, incarnating a personage imposed from without. But on the existential plane, on the extra-natural and extra-social plane, the personality insists on being itself; and man seeks to find his own reflection in another human countenance, in the Thou. This longing to be truly reflected is inherent in the personality and its "image." This latter seeks a faithful mirror. In a certain sense it implies narcissism. Love, the lover's image, is such a faithful mirror, the desired communion. There is something distressing about photography, which does not mirror the loving countenance, but only objectifies it and thus robs it of its true expression.

Nothing is more significant, nothing reflects more the mystery of existence, than the human image. It is intimately related to the problem of the personality. Like a beam of light from the mysterious world of human existence, which reflects also the divine world, it invariably breaks the spell of the objective world. Thanks to it, the personality can enter into communion with other personalities. There can be no comparison between the perception of a countenance and that of a physical phenomenon; it is a communion with the soul and the spirit. It is evidence that man is an integral being, as opposed to one divided in flesh and spirit, in body and soul. It symbolizes the victory of the spirit over the resistance of matter. That is, indeed, Bergson's definition of the body. But it applies above all to the human image. The expression of the eyes is not an object, a physical phenomenon; it is the pure manifestation of existence, the apparition of the spirit in a concrete form. An object only serves human ends: the human image exists only for communion. As Stern has very rightly observed, the personality's Being is "meta-psychophysical."

The Ego may be able to realize itself, to become a personality. But this realization is invariably accompanied by a self-limitation, a free subordination of the self to the supra-personal, the creation of supra-personal values, the escape from self and the penetration of other selves. The Ego may also remain egocentric, absorbed in itself, incapable of identifying itself with others. But egocentrism is fatal to the development of the personality; it is the greatest obstacle in the way of its realization. The free development of the personality precludes self-interest, and must be based entirely on its aspiration to commune with the Thou and the We. The egocentric man is completely devoid of personality, of all sense of reality; his world is one of phantasms, illusions and mirages. The personality, on the other hand, supposes a sense of realities and the ability to comprehend them. Extreme individualism leads to the negation of the personality. From the metaphysical standpoint, the personality is social because it feels the need of communicating with others. Personalist ethics are likewise directed against egocentricity, which endangers the preservation of man's identity, unity and personality. Egocentricity may, indeed, bring about the destruction of that identity, and may disaggregate it into distinct instants unconnected by any thread of memory. The egocentric man may have no memory, he may lack the very essence of the personality's identity and unity. Memory is a spiritual phenomenon, it is a spiritual endeavour to preserve man's being from the disintegrating influence of time. Time's evil effect is to disintegrate the personality's unity into independent fractions. But this evil has no power to create an integral personality in its own image. Thus an element of goodness is always preserved. The struggle to preserve the personality is also one directed against megalomania and madness. To abandon this struggle may lead to mental derangement and the loss of all sense of reality. Hysterical women are generally unbalanced and obsessed by their Ego—a state of mind most destructive to their personality. A divided personality is the outcome of egocentricity. Solipsism, although no more than an intellectual exercise in philosophy, is synonymous, in psychology, with the negation of the personality. If the Ego is self-sufficient, the question of the personality does not arise. There are various forms of egotism; some are commonplace and trivial, others exalted and idealist. Egoistic idealism is not at all propitious to the development of the personality. Philosophical idealism, as expressed in early nineteenth-century German philosophy, leads directly to impersonalism. That is especially evident in Fichte's theory of the Ego, stripped of all human attributes. The pernicious effects of this impersonalism are particularly manifest in the Hegelian doctrine of the State.

Monism in any form is incompatible with personalism. The very idea of the personality implies a dualism. The monist doctrine of the universal Ego has nothing in common with the doctrine of the personality. Personalism, however, is to be met with but rarely in philosophy; rationalistic systems of thought have invariably been monistic. The enigma of the personality has proved most baffling for philosophical thought as the enigma most dependent upon Revelation for its solution. Unlike the individual, the personality is not a natural phenomenon; nor is it a datum of the natural or the objective world. The personality is the image and likeness of God, and that is its sole claim to existence; it appertains to the spiritual order and reveals itself in the destiny of existence. The anthropomorphic aspects of knowledge are, in spite of their frequent deformation, intimately bound up with the destiny of the personality, with the immediate semblance of the divine and human images. And that is the strongest evidence of the real distinction between the personality and egocentricity.

According to Christianity, the ontological kernel of the human personality is situated in the heart, which represents not a differentiated element of human nature, but an integral whole. It also represents the essence of man's philosophical knowledge. Intelligence alone cannot constitute such a kernel of the human personality. Moreover, both contemporary psychology and anthropology reject the classical division of human nature into the intellectual, the volitional, and the affective elements. The heart is not any of these distinct elements; it is the seat of wisdom and the organ of the moral conscience, which is the supreme organ of all evaluation.

It is essential to distinguish between the two senses in which the notion of the personality may be interpreted. The Being of the personality is distinct and original, and has no affinity to any other Being. The idea underlying the personality is aristocratic in the sense that it suffers no promiscuity, and that it implies selection and a qualitative standard. Thus the problem of the personality in general becomes that of the personality endowed with a particular vocation, with a goal in life, and with creative power to achieve it. The propagation of democratic forms in a given society may help to undermine the personality, to bring about a general levelling, to reduce all men to an average standard, and, finally, to produce "impersonal" personalities. On the basis of this affirmation, we might be tempted to conclude that the whole *raison d'être* of history and culture lies in the elaboration of a small number of exceptional personalities, original in quality and endowed with remarkable creative gifts; it would follow that the bulk of mankind was destined to be swallowed up in an impersonal and anonymous life. From the naturalist standpoint, this would be a very feasible solution, but it would not be a Christian one. Christianity affirms that every man has in his power to become a personality, and that he must be afforded every opportunity of achieving this end. Every human personality has an intrinsic value, and cannot be reduced to a common denominator. All men are equal before God, and are called upon to share in the Eternal Life and the Kingdom of God. The deep-rooted inequality of men's gifts and qualities, vocations and merits, in no wise contradicts this assumption. In the case of the personality, this equality is founded upon a hierarchical order of original and diverse qualities. The ontological inequality between men is not determined by their social position, which is but a perversion of the true hierarchical order, but by their real qualities, gifts and merits. Thus the doctrines of the personality combines the aristocratic and democratic principles. A metaphysical system based on purely democratic principles is bound to misunderstand the problem of the personality; and such a misunderstanding is the result of a spiritual rather than a political error. . . .

The problem of the personality is also related to the traditional problem of the general and the particular propounded by the Realist and Nominalist philosophies. It is commonly admitted that nominalism is more favourable to the personality than realism. The individualistic currents of European thought have always tended to be nominalist. The problem of the personality or of the individual plays no part in Greek philosophy. Platonism was apparently unable to conceive the possibility of a passage from non-Being to Being; it maintained that Being was individual only when added on to non-Being, and that it was general when non-Being was subtracted. But for the most part, the problem of the "general" has been misstated because its social and objective origin has usually been overlooked. The "general" is not an existential, but a purely sociological category. The "general," as opposed to the individual, is real only when it is itself individual and unique. The non-individual "general" is a logical rather than an ontological category; and its logical significance is determined by the degree of community existing between consciousnesses that have no bond of communion; in other words, since the terms objective and social are synonymous, its nature is fundamentally sociological. The concept of the "general" is a product of social conditions which have nothing in common with communion. This concept serves to establish an identity, to make communication possible; but it does not make for "familiarity" or inner communion. That is, indeed, the determining factor in the problem of the personality. Objective and social processes give rise to number, which becomes the measure of all things in the sphere of the general. Society is governed by the law of number, whose sway also extends over knowledge in its social form. Where the law of number reigns supreme, where the part and the whole co-exist, there we are confronted with the object as an obstacle to authentic existence or the spiritual life. Spiritual life takes no account of number, its symbol is unity; it is not concerned with the categories of a divided world, the whole and the part, the general and the individual. Kierkegaard maintains that, from the religious standpoint, the individual has priority over the species. I am fully prepared to endorse this view on condition that the term "personality" is substituted for that of the "individual," which belongs to the same category as the notion of species. In defining the personality, it is important to conceive it as a whole and not as a part, as something that can never be a part. The personality is never anything particular as opposed to anything general. It can become a part either of society or of some other general whole only when it has been objectified. But intrinsically, the personality can never be a part of any genus, such as nature or society. The personality is spirit; and it belongs to the spiritual world which completely ignores any correlation of the part and the whole, of the individual and the general.

Solitude is the direct outcome of the pressure exerted on the personality by the natural and social worlds, of its conversion into object. But the personality has a creative function to perform in social and cosmic life. Spiritually, the personality is never isolated, for it postulates the existence of others, of the Thou and the We, without at the same time ever becoming a part or a means. The Ego's solitude is born of its objective existence; it occurs only in the natural world. That the category of number is inapplicable to the personality is best exemplified in the fact that one human personality may be worth more than two men, than a considerable number of men, or even a whole society of men. Ten men are not twice five men, nor a hundred men ten times ten men.

The personality is the principal category of existential knowledge. Both particularism and universalism are equally erroneous as the products of strictly rationalist thought obedient to the law of an objective world. The antithesis of the universal and the particular is a peculiarly objective one. The personality is not anything partial or particular. That is already manifest in the fact that it never constitutes a part of anything. The particular does not comprehend the universal, and the error of particularism lies in its attempt to endow the particular with a universal character. That is, indeed, a grave temptation. The fact that the personality has a universal content is what distinguishes it from the particular and the partial. It can do what no mere part can aspire to do—it can realize itself in the process of making its content universal. It is a unity in the midst of plurality, and can thus comprehend the universe. From the standpoint of the objective world, however, the existence of the personality constitutes a paradox: the personality is the incarnated antinomy of the individual and the social, of form and matter, of the infinite and the finite, of freedom and destiny. For this reason, the personality cannot be a complete whole; it is not an objective datum; it fashions and creates itself, it is dynamic. It is essentially the union of the finite and the infinite. It would dissolve into nothing as soon as it discarded its limitations and supports, as soon as it merged in cosmic infinity. But the personality would not be the image and likeness of God, if it were not endowed with infinite capacity. No partial thing could comprehend this infinite content: the personality alone fulfills this role because it is indivisible. In that consists its essential mystery. The human personality alone represents the intersection point of several worlds, none of which completely contains it; in this way, it belongs only partially to any society, State, confession, or even the universe. The personality thus exists on several planes. The uni-plane existence advocated by monism can only undermine and destroy the basis of the personality; since the personality is all-comprehensive; it is not confined to any particular plane or system, although it always postulates a reality beyond that of its immediate awareness. A logically expounded nominalism is incapable of laying the foundations of a doctrine of the personality, because it tends to subdivide reality and to disintegrate the personality; it is quite incapable of grasping the personality as a whole.

Platonism is not a personalist philosophy but one of general principles. The Christian Revelation, in so far as it involved the idea of the personality and thereby could never adequately express itself through the medium of the Greek philosophical categories, contributed an absolutely new content. Nor is the doctrine of the personality expounded in the often profound Hindoo philosophy, although monism is not its exclusive characteristic when we consider the diversity of the Hindoo philosophical system. The Atman is the very foundation of the Ego, the kernel of the personality; the Brahman is the impersonal divinity. The doctrine of Atman may, indeed, be interpreted in the personalist sense. Throughout the history of philosophical thought, monism and pluralism have been constantly opposed, and have proved most difficult to reconcile. The fundamental problem is how to reconcile the doctrine of the unity of the Divine Personality with the plurality of human personalities. Christianity alone holds the key to this problem and thus helps to enrich our philosophical knowledge. Dilthey very rightly maintains that metaphysical science is an historically limited fact, whereas the metaphysical consciousness of the personality is external. No rationalist theory of metaphysics has known how to give expression to this consciousness. Existential philosophy alone is able to propound the problem of the personality.

There are various categories of the individuality in the objective, natural and social worlds. The "nation" is one such category. Humanity is inconceivable in terms of an abstract, non-qualitative unity; it is a concrete, qualitative unity comprehending all the categories of individuality. An exception must be made in the case of the State, which is only a simple function without any ontological value. But there is this difference between real values such as humanity, society, and nationality, which we encounter in the objective world, and the human personality, that the former are unable to experience any sense of joy and pain, while the latter is a living and concrete manifestation. From the standpoint of man's inner existence and destiny, these real values, although they appear to be supra-human, are the attributes of the qualities inherent in the human personality. The personality realizes itself concretely, through the qualitative values expressed in the relations of one or another group, of society, of the nation, of humanity. But as the image and likeness of God, it has a far greater ontological reality than the supra-personal realities dominating the objective world.

These propositions can be applied equally well to the problem of the relationship between the personality and the Idea. The *raison d'être* of the personality may lie in its allegiance to an idea for which it may, and sometimes must, sacrifice itself. But it must never be regarded merely as a means, as an instrument in the service of some idea. The idea should, on the contrary, be the means and instrument by which the personality can realize itself, grow, and achieve qualitative ascension. By its devotion to, and, if necessary, sacrifice and death for an idea, the personality will affirm its higher validity and, ultimately, acquire the symbolic expression of eternity. It concentrates in itself the whole mystery of Being, of Creation. The personality holds the supreme place in the scale of values. But its supreme value supposes an inherent content surpassing it, a supra-personal element for which it is more than a mere instrument. God, Who is the source of all value, could never employ the personality as a means. If the contrary is true of society, of the nation, or of the State, their potentially dark and demoniac power is responsible. The personality alone can reveal the pure and original conscience, free from objectification, and sovereign in all matters.

Knowledge

Plato

31. GRADATIONS OF HUMAN KNOWLEDGE

The theme of reality "knowingly grasped" ranks high in the work of Plato. Two realms of "knowing," he says in this classic passage from the *Republic*, are to be distinguished: the realm of opinion and the realm of knowledge.

This selection from Books VI and VII of the *Republic* appears in the translation by Benjamin Jowett, and is reprinted with the kind permission of Oxford University Press.

Each of these is, in turn, indicative of types of reality: the visible or sensible, and the invisible or intelligible. To make his meaning clearer, he employs two myths or parables, which have become known as the myth of the "line" and the "cave myth."

Imagine a line, he suggests, divided into the two unequal parts, A and B, and each part subdivided proportionately to the first division—A¹, A², and B¹, B². Let A represent the realm of the visible or sensible; B, the realm of the intelligible and, therefore, of knowledge. The first subdivision then represents conjecture and unguided sense experience (images); the second, belief and "shrewd" sense experience (objects); the third, mental activity and mathematical or other logical reals (figures); the fourth, understanding and the principles of reality (forms).

Thus, A¹ and B¹ are isomorphic, the one being the lower grade of object-perception, the other, of intelligible-perception. Similarly, A² and B² represent the higher levels of each main division. Hence, the ratio A is to B as A¹ is to B¹, and A² is to B².

Against this myth of the "line" Plato sets forth a complementary parable to show how both things and the knowledge of things approach nearer and nearer true reality.

Imagine a cave where slaves are bound hand and foot, facing a wall on which shadows are cast from a fire above and behind them. If a slave were to free himself, he would be able to move from experiencing nothing but shadows cast on a wall, and look at the objects casting those shadows; he could see them also in the clearer light of the sun; and, finally, he could look upon the sun itself, the source of all light. Plato, apparently, meant us to compare each of the stages of the slave's journey to each of the divisions in the "line" myth.

[In the following selection Socrates, the narrator in the dialogue, addresses his remarks to Glaucon.]

YOU HAVE TO IMAGINE, then, that there are two ruling powers, and that one of them is set over the intellectual world, the other over the visible. I do not say heaven, lest you should fancy that I am playing upon the name (οὐρανός, ὁρατός), May I suppose that you have this distinction of the visible and intelligible fixed in your mind?

I have.

Now take a line which has been cut into two unequal parts, and divide each of them again in the same proportion, and suppose the two main divisions to answer, one to the visible and the other to the intelligible, and then compare the subdivisions in respect of their clearness and want of clearness, and you will find that the first section in the sphere of the visible consists of images. And by images I mean, in the first place, shadows, and in the second place, reflections in water and in solid, smooth and polished bodies and the like: Do you understand?

Yes, I understand.

Imagine, now, the other section, of which this is only the resemblance, to include the animals which we see, and everything that grows or is made.

Very good.

Would you not admit that both the sections of this division have different degrees of truth, and that the copy is to the original as the sphere of opinions is to the sphere of knowledge?

Most undoubtedly.

Next proceed to consider the manner in which the sphere of the intellectual is to be divided.

In what manner?

Thus:—There are two subdivisions, in the lower of which the soul uses the figures given by the former division as images; the enquiry can only be hypothetical, and instead of going upwards to a principle descends to the other end; in the higher of the two, the soul passes out of hypotheses, and goes up to a principle which is above hypotheses, making no use of images as in the former case, but proceeding only in and through the ideas themselves.

I do not quite understand your meaning, he said.

Then I will try again; you will understand me better when I have made some preliminary remarks. You are aware that students of geometry, arithmetic, and the kindred sciences assume the odd and the even and the figures and three kinds of angles and the like in their several branches of science; these are their hypotheses, which they and every body are supposed to know, and therefore they do not deign to give any account of them either to themselves or others; but they begin with them, and go on until they arrive at last, and in a consistent manner, at their conclusion?

Yes, he said, I know.

And do you not know also that although they make use of the visible forms and reason about them, they are thinking not of these, but of the ideals which they resemble; not of the figures which they draw, but of the absolute square and the absolute diameter, and so on—the forms which they draw or make, and which have shadows and reflections in water of their own, are converted by them into images, but they are really seeking to behold the things themselves, which can only be seen with the eye of the mind?

That is true.

And of this kind I spoke as the intelligible, although in the search after it the soul is compelled to use hypotheses; not ascending to a first principle, because she is unable to rise above the region of hypothesis, but employing the objects of which the shadows below are resemblances in their turn as images, they having in relation to the shadows and reflections of them a greater distinctness, and therefore a higher value.

I understand, he said, that you are speaking of the province of geometry and the sister arts.

And when I speak of the other division of the intelligible, you will understand me to speak of that other sort of knowledge which reason herself attains by the power of dialectic, using the hypotheses not as first principles, but only as hypotheses—that is to say, as steps and points of departure into a world which is above hypotheses, in order that she may soar beyond them to the first principle of the whole; and clinging to this and then to that which depends on this, by successive steps she descends again without the aid of any sensible object, from ideas, through ideas, and in ideas she ends.

I understand you, he replied; not perfectly, for you seem to me to be describing a task which is really tremendous; but, at any rate, I understand you to say that knowledge and being, which the science of dialectic contemplates, are clearer than the notions of the arts, as they are termed, which proceed from hypotheses only: these are also contemplated by the understanding, and not by the senses: yet, because they start from hypotheses and do not ascend to a principle, those who contemplate them appear to you not to exercise the higher reason upon them, although when a first principle is added to them they are cognizable by the higher reason. And the habit which is concerned with geometry and the cognate sciences I suppose that you would term understanding and not reason, as being intermediate between opinion and reason.

You have quite conceived my meaning, I said; and now, corresponding to these four divisions, let there be four faculties in the soul—reason answering to the highest, understanding to the second, faith (or conviction) to the third, and perception of shadows to the last—and let there be a scale of them, and let us suppose that the several faculties have clearness in the same degree that their objects have truth.

I understand, he replied, and give my assent, and accept your arrangement.

And now, I said, let me show in a figure how far our nature is enlightened or unenlightened:—Behold! human beings living in an underground den, which has a mouth open towards the light and reaching all along the den; here they have been from their childhood, and have their legs and necks chained so that they cannot move, and can only see before them, being prevented by the chains from turning round their heads. Above and behind them a fire is blazing at a distance, and between the fire and the prisoners there is a raised way; and you will see, if you look, a low wall built along the way, like the screen which marionette players have in front of them, over which they show the puppets.

I see.

And do you see, I said, men passing along the wall carrying all sorts of vessels, and statues and figures of animals made of wood and stone and various materials, which appear over the wall? Some of them are talking, others silent.

You have shown me a strange image, and they are strange prisoners.

Like ourselves, I replied; and they see only their own shadows, or the shadows of one another, which the fire throws on the opposite wall of the cave?

True, he said; how could they see anything but the shadows if they were never allowed to move their heads?

And of the objects which are being carried in like manner they would only see the shadows?

Yes, he said.

And if they were able to converse with one another, would they not suppose that they were naming what was actually before them?

Very true.

And suppose further that the prison had an echo which came from the other side, would they not be sure to fancy when one of the passers-by spoke that the voice which they heard came from the passing shadow?

No question, he replied.

To them, I said, the truth would be literally nothing but the shadows of the images.

That is certain.

And now look again, and see what will naturally follow if the prisoners are released and disabused of their error. At first, when any of them is liberated and compelled suddenly to stand up and turn his neck round and walk and look towards the light, he will suffer sharp pains; the glare will distress him, and he will be unable to see the realities of which in his former state he had seen the shadows; and then conceive some one saying to him, that what he saw before was an illusion, but that now, when he is approaching nearer to being and his eye is turned towards more real existence, he has a clearer vision,—what will be his reply? And you may further imagine that his instructor is pointing to the objects as they pass and requiring him to name them,— will he not be perplexed? Will he not fancy that the shadows which he formerly saw are truer than the objects which are now shown to him?

Far truer.

And if he is compelled to look straight at the light, will he not have a pain in his eyes which will make him turn away to take refuge in the objects of vision which he can see, and which he will conceive to be in reality clearer than the things which are now being shown to him?

True, he said.

And suppose once more, that he is reluctantly dragged up a steep and rugged ascent, and held fast until he is forced into the presence of the sun himself, is he not likely to be pained and irritated? When he approaches the light his eyes will be dazzled, and he will not be able to see anything at all of what are now called realities.

Not all in a moment, he said.

He will require to grow accustomed to the sight of the upper world. And first he will see the shadows best, next the reflections of men and other objects in the water, and then the objects themselves; then he will gaze upon the light of the moon and the stars and the spangled heaven; and he will see the sky and the stars by night better than the sun or the light of the sun by day?

Certainly.

Last of all he will be able to see the sun, and not mere reflections of him in the water, but he will see him in his own proper place, and not in another; and he will contemplate him as he is.

Certainly.

He will then proceed to argue that this is he who gives the season and the years, and is the guardian of all that is in the visible world, and in a certain way the cause of all things which he and his fellows have been accustomed to behold?

Clearly, he said, he would first see the sun and then reason about him.

And when he remembered his old habitation, and the wisdom of the den and his fellow-prisoners, do you not suppose that he would felicitate himself on the change, and pity them?

Certainly, he would.

And if they were in the habit of conferring honours among themselves on those who were quickest to observe the passing shadows and to remark which of them went before, and which followed after, and which were together; and who were therefore best able to draw conclusions as to the future, do you think that he would care for such honours and glories, or envy the possessors of them? Would he not say with Homer,

"Better to be the poor servant of a poor master,"

and to endure anything, rather than think as they do and live after their manner?

Yes, he said, I think that he would rather suffer anything than entertain these false notions and live in this miserable manner.

Imagine once more, I said, such an one coming suddenly out of the sun to be replaced in his old situation; would he not be certain to have his eyes full of darkness?

To be sure, he said.

And if there were a contest, and he had to compete in measuring the shadows with the prisoners who had never moved out of the den, while his sight was still weak, and before his eyes had become steady (and the time which would be needed to acquire this new habit of sight might be very considerable), would he not be ridiculous? Men would say of him that up he went and down he came without his eyes; and that it was better not even to think of ascending; and if any one tried to loose another and lead him up to the light, let them only catch the offender, and they would put him to death.

No question, he said.

This entire allegory, I said, you may now append, dear Glaucon, to the previous argument; the prisonhouse is the world of sight, the light of the fire is the sun, and you will not misapprehend me if you interpret the journey upwards to be the ascent of the soul into the intellectual world according to my poor belief, which at your desire, I have expressed—whether rightly or wrongly God knows. But, whether true or false, my opinion is that in the world of knowledge the idea of good appears last of all, and is seen only with an effort; and, when seen, is also inferred to be the universal author of all things beautiful and right, parent of light and of the lord of light in this visible world, and the immediate source of reason and truth in the intellectual; and that this is the power upon which he who would act rationally either in public or private life must have his eye fixed.

Wm. Oliver Martin   # 32. KINDS OF KNOWLEDGE

A realist version of Plato's contention that kinds of "knowing" are governed by kinds of realities is given here by Professor Martin. Knowing, says Martin, can be understood only if it is hierarchically distinguished according to its various subject matters. Although "the order of knowledge and the order of being should not be confused," it is still true that "kinds of knowledge should have something to do with kinds of being." At the top of this hierarchy is metaphysics, which is the highest kind of natural knowledge, and is not only a type of knowledge but the criterion of all other knowledges.

The proper objects of various kinds of knowledges are to be distinguished as either theoretical or practical, and autonomous or synthetic. A synthetic knowledge is the product of the integration of two or more kinds of autonomous knowledge. Theoretical knowledge is concerned primarily with knowing; whereas, practical knowledge is concerned with doing. Knowledges that are both theoretical and autonomous may be further distinguished as positive—that is, nonontological—and nonpositive. For instance, mathematics is a nonontological knowledge (meaning, it is positive) that is both theoretical and autonomous; but the philosophy of mathematics, which is the integration of nonontological and ontological knowledges, is theoretical-synthetic and nonpositive.

Now metaphysics is an ultimately autonomous and nonpositive science arising directly and intuitively from experience, without the constitutive mediation of any other kind of knowledge. As such, it is the only knowledge capable of assigning meaning to all other kinds of knowledge. For it is in *its* terms "that the subject matter of the elemental and fundamental disciplines must be determined."

This is made clearer, Martin suggests, if one distinguishes between knowledges that are "regulative of," "constitutive of," and "instrumental to" other knowledges. Metaphysics is the only knowledge that is "regulative of" other knowledges; historical and experimental propositions are "constitutive of" other knowledges; while logic is "instrumental to" other knowledges. Metaphysics is the only science by which all other sciences can be integrated. Therefore, any attempt to confuse the knowledge given by metaphysics with that given by any other science is, in the long run, destructive of knowledge itself.

A KIND OF KNOWLEDGE is to be understood through natural, not artificial, classification. That is, a kind of knowledge is to be understood in terms of its subject matter. The use that is made of knowledge is altogether another matter. Unless a kind of knowledge had a *nature* independent of its use, it could not be used. There is a place for "utility," and there is the "practical" and a "pragmatic" element in knowledge. But the modern pragmatic naturalist, for the most part, has not been concerned with "knowing" but with acting or doing. With but few exceptions, equipped but with an "attitude" (naturalistic and anti-theistic) and a "method" (something called "scientific"), he sallies forth to conquer nature, i.e., adjust to the environment; and conversely. Fundamental kinds of subject matter are concerned with fundamental kinds of being, or with its modes or aspects. In this respect metaphysics is in a peculiar position relative to other kinds of knowledge. Yet, not only is this as it should be, but it could not be otherwise, for that knowledge which is *about* the nature of knowledge is itself one kind of knowledge among others.

We have given reasons for believing that moderate realism is the most *adequate* metaphysical position to account for the nature and kinds of knowledge. This adequacy, in itself, is not sufficient for demonstrating the truth of realism. Rather it is one *sign,* among others, of its truth. But unless the truth of realism could be demonstrated independently, it could not serve its purpose in the classification of knowledge. Kinds of knowledge should have something to do with kinds of being. Hence, we have spoken of "contexts" and "domains" of knowledge. Of course, these are mental, not real, entities. But they do have a "foundation in things." If they did not, then they would be *nothing but* mental fictions, and would represent nothing real but only human purposes willed in abstraction from the rational.

There is theoretical and practical knowledge. The practical is synthetic, i.e., composed of kinds of knowledge, integrated. The theoretical may be either autonomous or synthetic. An autonomous kind of knowledge is that which is not the product of the integration of two or more kinds of knowledge. Synthetic knowledge is constituted by kinds of autonomous knowledge. Since in common speech an autonomous kind of knowledge more often than not is called by the same name as a synthetic kind of knowledge, . . . the . . . following considerations are to be kept in mind.

(1) The order of knowledge and the order of being should not be confused, and it is our hope that we shall not do so. Sometimes the same term will refer, at different times, to each. For example, the "ontological" may refer to a context of knowledge or to the aspect of being which is the foundation. In any given case the specific meaning should be disclosed by the universe of discourse.

(2) When a kind of knowledge is thought of in and for itself, and hence in abstraction from the ontological, then the knowledge is considered as "positive." It is in this sense that a nonontological kind of knowledge is autonomous.

(3) When a nonontological kind of knowledge is integrated with the ontological we have a synthetic kind of knowledge. Historically an autonomous and a synthetic kind of knowledge have often been called by the same name. The term "mathematics" may be the name for the study of quantity *qua* quantity or of quantitative being. The first is mathematics in its positive and autonomous sense; the second is synthetic and is the philosophy of mathematics. Again, the specific meaning will often be determined by the context of the discourse.

How may the various contexts be determined? And why is a context *what* it is? It may seem that the most obvious way to find the answer is to make an empirical or phenomenological description of what men are doing when they are working in their special fields of knowledge. We can observe, for example, experimental scientists and theologians at work and discover what kinds of "things" they are talking about. Presumably we would then know what experimental science and theology are. In the same manner it would seem that we could find out what home economics, civil engineering, etc., are. The Christian theologian is concerned, for example, with such propositions and their implications as are to be found in the Apostles' Creed. On examination it will be observed that the propositions are not generalizations. And although descriptive of uniqueness they seem to be different from the kinds of propositions the historian seeks. On the other hand, the experimental scientist never seems to be interested in any particular thing except as a member of a class.

And so on. One could go to some length with such observations. And yet a little thought will reveal that, however helpful and necessary such descriptions are, in themselves they can never give us the answer we wish. We cannot observe a scientist at work and know what science is, as we might observe the behavior of a wasp in order to know what it is. And the reason is this, that we have first to know what experimental science is in order to know when the scientist is working as a scientist, and when he is not; when he is talking science and when he is not. Presumably the wasp always works as a wasp. Otherwise the question is begged, or we fall into the sophistry of saying that experimental science is simply that which the experimental scientist does.

A biologist may talk about living matter, the scientific method, and biology. The first is the subject matter of biology; the second is about a method used in studying the subject matter. One and the same man talks about living matter and a method, but the subject matter is quite different in the two cases. He may be an authority on the first, and not on the second. For it does not follow at all from the fact that he uses a method that he knows the method quite as well as the subject matter which is studied by the method. Of course, he may. But if so, it is because he knows logic as well as biology. On the other hand, in the third case he is talking about a kind of knowledge called biology. He is not talking as a biologist primarily, but perhaps as a philosopher. But one could not know all this, in fact one could not even make these distinctions, if kinds of knowledge could not be distinguished independent of the oral and social behavior of a person. And to confuse a proposition about living matter with one about biology as a kind of knowledge, as if the evidence were the same, or as if an authority on the first was *by that fact* an authority on the second, would be simply to confuse first and second intentions, or in positivist terminology, an object language with a meta-language.

It is in terms of a metaphysics that the subject matter of the elemental and fundamental disciplines must be determined. A factual description of what the practitioner of a discipline does has two functions. First, it is instrumental to the metaphysical problem. Historically man did not begin with clearly defined subject matters. The latter emerged from a confused whole. And even today were it not for the fact that in some manner or other such emergent disciplines exist there would be no problem of the metaphysics of knowledge. However, a factual description of these existing disciplines, so far from solving the problem of the order of knowledge, really presents or creates a problem.

Second, a factual description based upon observation of what the various practitioners of fields of knowledge do provides a check upon any metaphysical analysis. For example, it would be a sign of metaphysical inadequacy, and an unfortunate kind of *apriorism,* if one were to insist that experimental science is not concerned with quantive measurement or with moving things. Not only would there be an irresponsible use of "names," but if a metaphysical analysis literally has nothing to do with what a practitioner of a kind of knowledge does, then so much the worse for the metaphysics in question.

The Phenomenological Context

Man is a creature who knows, acts, and makes, as well as experiences. He wishes to know "things"; what he makes are artifacts. Artifacts and things are

both phenomenological. They appear, have space and/or time characteristics. But an artifact lacks a private nature independent of the knower and maker. Things have this private nature, and we may speak of it as the ontological aspect of things in contradistinction to the phenomenological. These are two contexts with which we are already familiar. There is also a "mathematical" context.

Within the phenomenological context there are two domains, history and experimental science. Both are positive disciplines, since they are considered in themselves and as autonomous. The first seeks the singular proposition; the second, the generalization. It is "signate matter" that defines the possibility of history. Since there can be no science of particulars or individuals as such, history is not a science in the sense in which other kinds of knowledge are. It is "common sensible matter" which makes possible generalizations and experimental science. Since neither signate nor common sensible matter can exist without the other, the context of history and exprimental science is the same. As domains they are distinguished by the type of proposition sought. In historical knowledge generalizations function as means to the end of discovering true historical propositions. In experimental science historical propositions function as means to the end of arriving at true generalizations.

The Mathematical Context

It is "intelligible matter" that makes possible mathematical knowledge, and hence distinguishes another context. Why should signate and common matter distinguish domains, and intelligible matter a context? The reason is that intelligible matter can have a mental existence in abstraction from signate and common matter. The range of possible mathematical forms in man's imagination is much wider than the actual forms which exist in common and signate matter. The latter are limitations upon the former. The mathematical context has only one domain, the general, and which is identical with the context itself. For this reason the context may be called "formal," provided of course that one understands that the kind of forms considered are only those ordered to intelligible matter.

The Ontological Context

The ontological context is composed of two domains, the metaphysical and the theological, depending upon whether the general (universal) or the singular and unique is sought. Whether or not there are theological truths is not in question here. Even if one were to deny that there are any such truths, it would be necessary to be clear about the kind of proposition and the kind of

"knowledge" that is being denied. There is a difference between saying that "quality is a function of quantity" and "the Father and the Son are of one substance." The first is general; the second is singular, which we shall speak of as "descriptive of uniqueness." But the content of such singularity is quite different from that of an historical proposition, for God is not one thing among others. If the theological is denied, then particularity is confined to the spatial-temporal. And conversely.

Attention is to be called again to the kind of propositions composing the Apostles' Creed, which is a good example of what some theologians do when they are working as theologians. They are not primarily value judgments, historical propositions, generalizations, or even general or universal propositions about being—except in the sense that for certain purposes a singular can be taken as universal. The term "God" is equivocal, sometimes being the subject of a metaphysical proposition, sometimes of a theological proposition. In the first case are included all propositions derived through reasoning upon evidence given naturally in human experience. In the second case are included all of those propositions for which the evidence is divine revelation. The Christian would prefer to speak of these as truths of revelation rather than revealed truths. A theological proposition is, then, strictly speaking, a truth of revelation. "Natural theology," is really metaphysics; it is not theology based upon revelation.

Whether the domain of a proposition is metaphysical or theological in any given case is sometimes difficult to determine. Nevertheless the distinction remains and clear-cut cases of each can be given. To speak of God as the cause of the world is metaphysics, for "God" is taken merely conceptually. The evidence for God's existence must be independent of revelation. On the other hand, to speak of God as one member of the Trinity is strictly theological. Such uniqueness could not be known except through divine revelation. The being of God is the same, but the source of knowledge is different. If there is some evidence metaphysically for the existence of God, then there is some ground (not sufficient evidence) for faith in a truth of revelation such as the doctrine of the Trinity. But there is no reason why one should have faith in a doctrine *about* God if there is no reason at all to believe *that* he exists. From the standpoint of the order of being the theological has priority over the metaphysical, i.e. the God who is the cause of the world is first the God of the Trinity. From the standpoint of the order of knowledge the converse is true. The modern world may be said to have begun with a denial of this, and with the assumption that one can have the theological without the metaphysical. This soon turned into its opposite, and so by the eighteenth century we have metaphysics without theology. The twentieth century is witness to the logical conclusion of the process—neither metaphysics nor theology, but the triumph of positivism and subjectivism.

Because the strictly theological proposition is singular and ontological, it does not necessarily follow that an extreme Platonic interpretation is correct. That is, a theological proposition may have a phenomenological reference, and a historical proposition may have an ontological (theological) reference. For example, a miracle may take place in space and time, the uniqueness of which may be described in terms of a historical proposition. If it is true that through supernatural power Christ healed a certain person—and whether it is true or not is irrelevant for the present—then this is at least a historical fact, expressible in a historical proposition. But it is also a theological proposition, for it is a historical proposition with an ontological reference. Metaphysically we would say that the primary cause is referred to directly, not secondary causes. From the standpoint of knowledge the evidence sufficient to prove or make plausible the historical proposition would be necessary although not sufficient to prove the theological proposition, i.e., the same historical proposition with an ontological reference.

The Synthetic Context

An autonomous, theoretical science is obtained by abstracting a mode or kind of being from being. The autonomy exists only in the order of knowledge. In the order of being a mode is completely dependent. When history, experimental science, and mathematics are thus autonomous they are "positive" disciplines. When the contents of these disciplines are considered as they *really* are, i.e., in relation to being, then we have the "philosophy" of these subjects—the philosophy of history, the philosophy of nature (which is *natural* science), the philosophy of mathematics. As has been pointed out, the name of a discipline is often used equivocally, e.g. "natural science" sometimes meaning the "philosophy of nature," and other times meaning "experimental science." . . .

The "philosophy" of a discipline defines a theoretical, synthetic context. This means that the mathematical and the phenomenological domains are integrated with the ontological. The ontological is not only that *with which* the positive disciplines are integrated, but also is that *by which* they are integrated. The last fact is important. First, if it were not so, then an infinite number of kinds of knowledge would be necessary; $n + 1$ to integrate n kinds of knowledge, $n + 2$ to integrate $n + 1$, etc. But this would be equivalent to the impossibility of any integration. A corollary would be that the impossibility of metaphysics is equivalent to the impossibility of integration of knowledge, or any order of knowledge at all. Second, the ontological domains are not positive sciences, and hence nothing could integrate them.

There is nothing mysterious about the notion of integrated knowledge, or that of a synthetic context. All that one must understand is how one obtains the autonomous, positive science. Chronologically, and psychologically, the synthetic contexts are prior. Inquiries are made about *nature, natural things,* the *natures* of things; in other words, about *changing* being. The emphasis may be on change or on being. Historically, as well as psychologically, it has been on the latter. However, a division of labor allows the mode to be mentally abstracted in order that the details may be explored. It was then that "experimental science" emerged. Experimental science is theoretical and autonomous because the details are just what they are. But what has been separated for a purpose must be put together. This is a synthesis of the ontological with the phenomenological, of metaphysics with experimental science. And now we understand not merely change *qua* change, or being *qua* being, but changing being—in short, *natural things.* We now have natural science. We begin with and end with questions of natural science. Experimental science is that which emerges in the process.

And so with mathematics. We begin with an inquiry into quantitative being, through analysis consider quantity *qua* quantity, and through integration with metaphysics (being) return to quantitative being. As autonomous and independent of the metaphysical, mathematics is "positive" and concerned with quantity *qua* quantity. Mathematics means the "philosophy of mathematics" when reference is to the synthetic context, that of quantitative being.

Wherein lies the autonomy of a science? A science is autonomous if it arises directly from experience without the *constitutive* mediation of any other kind of knowledge. The term "constitutive" is important, for another kind of knowledge may be "regulative of" or "instrumental to" an autonomous science.

For human beings there are only two sources of experience, sense and divine revelation. The latter is the source of theological propositions, if it is admitted that they are possible. Sense experience is the basis of all historical propositions, whether they be derived from immediate experience as in experimental science or by witness as in history. Of course, generalizations are not sensed, but they are, as we shall see, wholly constituted by propositions (historical) that are based on sense. The autonomy of both mathematics and metaphysics lies in the fact that they are obtained through abstraction from sense experience. The denial of this makes an unintelligible mystery of the problem of how sense and intellect can ever get together. The mystery is only deepened by appeal to such a notion as "isomorphism," which is of course a perfectly valid concept in any special science concerned with instrumental signs. It is wise to relegate mystery to the theological where it belongs. When this is not done its locus is simply shifted elsewhere, thus creating the modern alternatives either of an anti-intellectualistic, formalistic *apriorism* or of a doctrine of "created Truth," thus confusing knowing with making and fact with artifact.

The Synthetic Context of Logic

Is logic a theoretical or a practical synthetic knowledge: The answer depends partly upon how the term "practical" is to be used. For historical reasons the term as here used is confined to knowledge of acting and making. Of course logic is an instrument in knowing, but knowing logic is still knowing and not acting or making. It is true that logic may be said to be practical, to be useful, in knowing. But when the term acquires such a broad meaning its distinction from the theoretical breaks down. Mathematics is practical and useful in knowing about the physical world, but it is not for that reason a practical, as opposed to a theoretical, science.

As synthetic the object of logic is intentional being; and "logic" means "material logic" as well as "formal logic." What is it that is integrated? It is metaphysics and strictly "formal" logic. It is possible, for a limited purpose, to abstract intentionality from being and consider intentionality *qua* intentionality. This is logic in a positive sense, and is usually what is called "formal logic," that which is studied somewhat mechanically and in abstraction from what is intended, and from all metaphysical considerations. When *what* is intended is considered, i.e., the kind or mode of being, the "matter" referred to, then we have what is called "material logic."

One may have a questioning feeling about this analysis. If there is a positive side to logic, why has it not developed in its autonomy as has mathematics and experimental science? Insofar as logic has some semblance of identity over a period of two thousand years, it seems to be directly based upon metaphysics, and hence to have no autonomy. Insofar as it seems to have acquired autonomy and become a positive science, it seems to have little to do with traditional logic—and this in spite of the fact that recent logic is said to include, and not repudiate, whatever contribution Aristotle made. Is there not a difference between the periods from Aristotle to Leibnitz and that from Leibnitz to Carnap and Quine? Furthermore, if logic as positive is concerned with intentionality *qua* intentionality, then why is it that recent logic seems to pay little if any attention to it? In short, mathematics as positive still seems to be concerned with quantity, and experimental science with motion; but logic as positive is no longer concerned with intentionality. Is there not something wrong with our analysis of the nature of logic?

Part of the answer perhaps lies in the proper use of a name. Because of the chaos that has existed in the order of knowledge there has been unclarity about the nature and limits of subject matters, and what name should go with what subject matter. Sometimes "logic" is a name given to what is really the "philosophy of mathematics." At other times it is identified with "inductive techniques," "system construction involving real relations," "grammar," or "linguistic analysis." The confusion has been concomitant with the decline of

metaphysics and the rise of positivism. In the absence of an order of knowledge about all one can do is arbitrarily take one's pick among the lot. Otherwise logic must be delimited and defined, as we have attempted to do, so that
it has a nature of its own. It has already been pointed out that to identify logic
with general system structure or construction in terms of real relations is
simply to misuse a term in addition to denying the existence of logic as knowledge.

However, logic as positive does present a peculiar problem, but one which
may be understood if we realize that "positive" is a matter of degree. Or, we
might say that not every positive science is equally positive. This may be seen
by examining metaphysics and each synthetic science. Metaphysics is autonomous but not positive, for it is concerned with being, not anything in abstraction from being. It is not an integrated science, but rather is that by which
another science is integrated. The other synthetic sciences all have a metaphysical part, but they are more or less metaphysical—not of course in the
order of being, but in the order of knowledge. The order of more or less should
be represented by logic, natural science (or the philosophy of nature), and
the philosophy of mathematics. Logic is chiefly metaphysical; its autonomous
side is not very important. The philosophy of nature, on the contrary, is composed essentially of equal mixtures of metaphysics and experimental science.
On the other hand, what appears to be of chief importance in the philosophy
of mathematics is the mathematics itself. It is for these reasons that historically logic has always been "close" to metaphysics, while mathematics has
always *seemed* to be so independent of metaphysics.

When logic is taken as positive there is little of importance that can be
said, and this is in contrast to something like, say, mathematics. The principle
of contradiction, for example, can be abstracted from its metaphysical foundation; and as such it becomes just a principle which seems, strangely enough, to
be necessary to intelligible discourse. All of which is true, of course. To understand why it is so, one must turn to metaphysics. Otherwise, it becomes a
mystery why what *is* so *must* be so. At this point, without metaphysics, there
is the temptation to "speculate." The consequence is that it will occur to one
person that perhaps the principle is not necessary at all, and that there are
"alternative logics" to be chosen according to convenience; to another person
that the principle is a "law of thought," that by its "structure" the mind
must think with it; etc. In the latter case "speculation" is simply the unfruitful exercise of making a metaphysics out of logic as positive. This is Hegelianism. After Hegelianism comes cynicism and despair. The end result is the contemporary scene in which logic as intentional, i.e., logic in the sense in which
it has a *nature,* has practically vanished, not only in the professional journals
but also in the educational system.

Other illustrations can be given of the positive side of logic. The form of
the syllogism *can* be—whether it ought to be or not—interpreted as a transi-

tive relation. The mechanics of the syllogism as taught in the classroom is also representative of the positive side of logic, . . . and as every teacher knows, a good deal can be learned without the necessity of introducing the metaphysical.

But therein lies the danger, that of reducing logic to a formal science such as mathematics. The peculiar nature of logic lies in the fact that it is concerned with knowing about knowing itself. Hence its formal nature lies in the fact that it is concerned with formal signs, not instrumental signs. Now an instrumental sign has a nature over and above its intending, while the whole nature of a formal sign lies in its intending. For this reason the formal nature of intentional signs is quite different from the formal nature of nonintentional signs. Since in mathematics the forms are nonintentional, the positive aspect of mathematics becomes very important and useful. On the other hand, in logic, since the whole being of intentional forms lies in the intending, consideration of them in-and-for-themselves is of little importance and not very useful, although, of course, it can be done. But, once again, in so doing there is the danger that logical relations are reduced to real relations, second intentions to first intentions. But is there not a contradiction? Have we not said that logic as a synthetic science is concerned with intentional being, whereas logic as positive is concerned with intentionality *qua* intentionality (in abstraction from being), and at the same time that logic as merely positive tends to lose its intentional character? No, there is no contradiction; rather a paradox, the kind attending any positive science. In metaphysics there is abstraction in order to obtain being, and in positive science to obtain a mode or kind. Since being must be interpreted analogically, that which is abstracted from being is also being. And yet to the extent that anything is conceived as other than being, it becomes (in knowledge) nonbeing. And so intentionality remains such only in intentional *being*. The moment one attempts to grasp it in and for itself, intentionality *qua* intentionality, then one loses it; one grasps only the nonintentional.

The paradox is not peculiar to logic, but characterizes all positive science. In natural science one abstracts the mobile from mobile being in order to understand the mobile *qua* mobile, which is experimental science. Yet in the very process of grasping motion in this manner one tends to lose it, recapturing it only by a return to metaphysics. When the return is not made, but rather a metaphysics is created out of the positive science, then the science becomes art. The "motion" of making the world in idea is confused with the motion of the world.

In mathematics as a synthetic science, i.e., the philosophy of mathematics, the same thing occurs. When one attempts to grasp quantity *qua* quantity, and the relation of quantity to being is forgotton, then what one obtains are "relational structures," and mathematics ceases to be concerned with understanding intelligible matter and becomes identified with the art of "system construction."

The Synthetic Context of Value

The context of value is concerned with knowledge about acting and making, together with the experiences ordered to them. Such knowledge is "practical." Aesthetics has to do with making, and hence with the arts. The moral and religious sciences are concerned with acting. Since the religious implies a theological factor, and theology is to be left to a subsequent study, the analysis will be confined to the moral and the arts.

It has been pointed out that there is (1) theoretical, autonomous knowledge; (2) theoretical, synthetic knowledge; (3) practical, synthetic knowledge. The context of the latter is that of "value." The "practical" cannot be "autonomous." The denial of this reduces evaluations either to generalizations or to ontological propositions. Practical propositions are neither.

Evaluations may be singular or general, depending upon the nature of the minor premise in the "practical syllogism." Examples of such propositions are: "Beethoven's Eighth Symphony is more beautiful than Berlioz's *Symphonie Fantastique*"; "The American youth of today are morally better than the youth of twenty years ago." These propositions are of a type different from such propositions as, "Sheep are cloven-footed," "This is a red book," or "Caesar crossed the Rubicon," which are phenomenological propositions. (While a sentence in which "this" is indeterminate is literally an incomplete proposition, for the purpose of economy it may so remain with the understanding that some definite reference is always assumed.) For the understanding of evaluations an ontological reference is necessary. On the other hand, for the understanding of the proposition "This is a book," the ontological does not seem to be necessary. There is certainly a great deal of difference between the proposition stated about American youth and a similar proposition with a couple of words changed, namely, "The American youth of today are taller than the youth of twenty years ago." Not only is the nature of the evidence to which appeal is made quite different in the two propositions, but also the manner in which the truth or falsity of two propositions is discovered is quite different.

Knowing, doing (acting), and making are human activities, but they are not the same. The practical disciplines—religious, moral and artistic—are concerned with the latter two. Yet knowing about acting is knowing, and not acting; and knowing about making is knowing and not making. The distinction between acting and making arises because there are only two things one can perfect: one's own nature (or another's) or the nature of a "thing." The one is a "fact," the other is an "artifact." In the former, one "acts"; in the latter, one "makes." In acting the good of the self is ultimate; in making it is the good of the work or object. In the latter we have art; in the former we have the moral and religious sciences as practical disciplines. If the theological is not admitted, then the moral is absolute. For illustrative purposes only we shall limit ourselves to art and the moral sciences.

Although acting and making are both practical, in contrast to knowing, they are not the same for the reasons that have been given. To break down the distinction is to destroy both art and morality. The phrase "making or re-making human nature" can be misleading. A child is potentially a man in-dependently of anyone's purpose. On the other hand, a piece of marble is po-tentially—what? As an art object it is potentially a statue or wall-paneling. Independent of the mind of the artist it is either or both or neither. In perfect-ing human nature the end is given; in perfecting a work of art the end is hu-manly determined.

Don Luigi Sturzo **33. KNOWLEDGE IN THE CONCRETE**

Don Luigi Sturzo's command of the relation between sociological and metaphysical knowledges is given generous play in the following essay, written in America during his exile by the Fascist government.

Knowledge, he asserts, is characterized by both individual and social as-pects, inseparable one from the other, since "the social aspect of human experience affects the genesis of knowledge, its character, and its finality." Knowledge is carried on within society. It bears the weight of the cultural inheritance of man, and is "ordered to the lives we live." As a social reality, knowledge implies the co-existence of other beings "which, taken together with the knowing subject, can be considered as a totality." It is this "totality" which provides the true context of knowledge. But this same totality, which the knower comprehends in the knowledge of any reality, presents itself not in a definite, but only in a confused, form: "at first sight it seems only a *cognitive situation*."

This cognitive situation is "related to an indefinite whole which comprises in various ways the subject and the object"; it is neither prior to, nor consequent upon, experience, but is "a direct and obscure intuition present in every act of knowledge." The relation that knowledge has to every exist-

From "The Problem of Knowledge and the Intuition of God," which originally appeared in *Thought*, Vol. 16 (1941), No. 61. Reprinted by permission of the publisher.

ent is founded upon the fact that it *is* a concrete existent, since "the relation with all reality can be predicated of every existent thing." In every act of knowledge this obscure intuition of reality is present. It is a precognition "which the subject affirms inasmuch as the subject is part of this whole, lives in it, could not exist apart from it, intuits it as existent reality, but does not define it." We are conscious of this undifferentiated and total reality in the same manner that we are conscious of ourselves.

This "whole" that we are conscious of is neither idealistic nor phenomenalistic. It is, first, the existential whole of space and time of which we are a part. It is also the abstract whole of intellectualized universals, which, through experience and reflection, we come to envision as a logical-metaphysical image. Finally, in the intuition of the whole there is a "movement of interior necessity towards the absolute," and an obscure intuition of God.

THIS WORLD OF EXPERIENCES and system of knowledge is never individual or singular. If it were, it would be isolated, sterile, self exhaustive. Although each one has a particular measure of interior life (that forms the richness or poverty of one's own spirit) the system is related to, and has much in common with, the environment in which one lives. In this way the experiences of others, whether past or present, become in various ways common experiences. Human knowledge is individual-social; even when it is most individual it is always inter-communicated; otherwise, it would not be true knowledge but would be lost in the depths of vain and unrealized thoughts.

The social aspect of human experience affects the genesis of knowledge, its character, and its finality. It affects the genesis of knowledge, because in most cases the object is not received by the subject in its existential presence, but through the experience of others and in the terms of social life. It affects the character of knowledge, because the systems which we must construct in order to give it value and perspective depend in great part upon our cultural heritage and surroundings. Lastly, it affects the finality of knowledge, which, being ordered to the lives we live, is eminently practical and tends both to assimilate and enrich the social background, by whatever means nature and art have given us. There is no science however speculative—not even metaphysics, mathematics, or astronomy—which is not ordered to practical ends, whether individual or general, subjective or objective. This movement to an end can never exhaust itself because it has an exigency for an absolute terminus.

In philosophy, we are accustomed to consider the critique of knowledge as a critique of subject and object, individually and abstractly, because everything that can be referred to social factors and to environment is left to the pedagogue, the psychologist, and the sociologist. It is my suggestion that we ought to reconsider the problem of knowledge in its entirety, before making it a matter of speculative analysis.

In the concrete, there is never any knowledge of reality which does not, at the same time, imply the coexistence of other beings which, taken together with the knowing subject, can be considered as a totality. The subject, at one time, feels himself to be the center to which the objects that interest him are directed, but at other times he feels the need to seek for some center of orientation and unification. The elements of his knowledge crowd together within the circle of some whole, which for the moment is ill-defined, but which reflects the two states of mind described above. The origin, character and social finality of knowledge play a part in such a vision. And since human knowledge is either systematic or not true knowledge, there cannot be in fact any cognitive systematization without reference to a whole.

But to what whole? Certainly not to that which fall under our senses. We cannot look at the horizon without knowing that beyond the mountains there are other lands and other beings; or gaze at the stars without thinking of others which we do not see. And just as space widens out indefinitely, so does time stretch out in the past and in the future. In thousands of forms the knowledge of facts, theoretical ideas and hypotheses themselves become part of the whole whose limits we do not know, but within which our being, and all other beings are plunged without being submerged.

That which the subject comprehends as a whole in the knowledge of reality is not something definite; it is only an indefinite something, so that at first sight it is presented merely as a *cognitive situation*. The subject can consider the indefinite whole as the object of his experience, something outside himself, even though there can be no totality once the subject is taken away from it. The subject can also consider himself as within an indefinite whole while, of course, remaining definite as the thinking subject. It is this datum which is the starting point of the present discussion.

Our *first question* is this: Is this "whole," at first sight indefinite and presenting itself merely as a cognitive situation, antecedent to all thought or is it a product of experience?

The inquiry may not seem new; it may even be confused with questions of another age, whether the idea of being is prior to every actual cognition? From this point of view it is possible to reach one of two extremes: either the idea of being is conceived as a logical antecedent, as a means of knowing the object (ontologism): or it is presented as the idea of reality affirmed *a priori,* in axiomatic form and not by experience (dogmatic realism).

Ever since the Cartesian *Cogito*—whether it be understood in an idealistic manner, or merely as a critical instrument, or even (as some French Catholics are accustomed to do) in a realistic sense—it has been customary to start with the experience of the *ego* in order to arrive at the experience of the *non-ego* or "the other." The experience of the "I" might be taken as a sort of logico-critical antecedent.

The Italian Neo-Scholastics, in their struggles with the idealism of Croce and even more so with the "actualism" of Gentile and his disciples, insist upon two essential principles of Thomism: 1) that "our intellect is meant to know primarily the external world and by reflection its own cognitive act"; and 2) that "directly and immediately our intellect grasps an essence in every existent being and in every essence the existence." For them the existent objective reality is prior to cognition, but in the act of knowing it is concomitant with the abstractive power of the intellect and is apprehended simultaneously in every essence abstracted from the object. In the above four theories (ontologism, dogmatic realism, Cartesianism in all its interpretations, Thomistic realism) the problem of an indefinite whole as a cognition has no place.

Nevertheless every individual, in order to know, must feel himself a participant in the whole of reality to which he has affinities and natural attractions; so that knowing it and realizing it he may find himself in the common reality, with all his faculties fully satisfied.

This would be impossible, if our knowledge lacked the sense of the whole, or if the indefinite whole (besides being the object of experience and particular definitions) did not appear as a general mental outlook. The two cognitive situations which were indicated above as our factual datum present themselves as an epistemological exigency. In the first situation (the whole as object), we prescind from our existence as the knowing subject; in the second, the whole is one with us, the subject, and we are one with the whole, as the object; and according to our different philosophical systems, either we try to submerge our personality in the whole or we include the whole in our personality.

Starting as we did from a provisional hypothesis we have been led to this *first affirmation:* In every act of knowledge there is implicit a cognitive situation related to an indefinite whole which comprises in various ways the subject and the object.

It is possible for us not to be conscious of this implicit datum in the cognitive act; it is possible not to have reflected on it; but once we have become aware of it, it seems evident that the fact is so; the reference to an indefinite whole is found in every act of knowledge.

Let us analyze a little more closely what we have been calling, provisionally, a cognitive situation. Is this, perhaps an unknown category; or a neglected aspect of the category of relation?

The relation with all of reality can be predicated of every existent thing. From this point of view, it might be said that the category of relation can indicate the simultaneous and total coexistence of beings which cannot be thought of except in correlation.

The categories, however, although founded on reality are only logical modes of knowing. The real may be considered abstractively, outside of every category and under a universal aspect, as entity; or the categories can be considered as apart from all reality, as happens with the ideas of time and space.

Reality can also be regarded under a single category, abstracting from the others, as for example under the category of substance. In these analytic acts, although we are considering abstract reality we find there implicitly the cognitive situation of the indefinite whole, but we do not find the category of relation. The ideas of entity, space, time, substance, would be inconceivable without the substratum of an indefinite whole. Even though not thought of in actual and reflex form, it gives a tone (to use a musical or medical word) to the meaning of the various aspects under which we grasp the existent real.

However, it seems to us to be nearer the truth to describe the whole of which we are speaking as *an obscure but direct intuition of reality in its undifferentiated entirety, that accompanies every cognitive act.*

Let us try to make this clearer. Intellectual knowledge proceeds by abstraction from the sensible and is achieved by means of the intelligible species; it is therefore a universalizing and a categorizing process. The intuition of this stage is nothing but a rapid surpassing of the intellective process in the apprehension of existent reality and in the inductive experience. Baron Fatta . . . writes: "We could not say: 'This being has existence,' if the indescribable and self-luminous actuality of existing were not already intuited by us before being affirmed in the form of a judgment."

But this intuition and others like it are clear, they specify the object or the qualities and relations of the known object whether it be a physical fact or a principle of metaphyics or ethics. When we say that the intuition of the undifferentiated whole is obscure, we mean that there is lacking in it either the implied judgment or the inductive experience or what Fatta calls the "self-luminous actuality," to give clearness to the intuition. The obscurity is due to the fact that the object, the whole, is not definite, nor differentiated; the intellect receives no light from it and makes no judgment on it. Nevertheless it is a direct intuition without the mediation of species, since there could be no occasion for their formation; it may be called a "precognition," which the subject attains inasmuch as the subject is part of this whole, lives in it, could not exist apart from it, intuits it as existent reality but does not define it because, as the whole, he cannot define it.

If this were not so, before knowing we ought to feel ourselves in complete isolation; in every act of knowing, we ought to feel ourselves in exclusive contact with the perceived object; cognitive synthesis would be impossible because of the discontinuity of the objects known and the lack of any synthetic correlativity. Moreover, each individual would have his own not wholly coherent group of cognitions, and this would render impossible vital communication in regard to a common reality.

It should not be thought that these are arbitrary deductions as in an utterly imaginary process *per absurdum.* The world of experience is partial, limited, discontinuous; the world of coherent reasoning is an effect of tradition, study, actualization. Taken together, they give us the common individualized reality. It is only the direct intuition of the whole that gives us the common undifferentiated reality. For that reason we call it obscure (as opposed to clear and definite) but at the same time direct, that is, concrete (opposed to abstract).

We are conscious of this contact with the undifferentiated and total reality as we are conscious of ourselves. We are not aware of this except in the act of understanding and in all the acts in which understanding is correlated with willing and acting. There is, in fact, never a pure intellection unassociated with either willing or action; but in the way in which we analyze our acts we can very well say that the intuition of the undifferentiated whole is an act of the intellect that has repercussions in willing and action. Willing and acting complete our knowledge, for they give it its full reality in fact; there is always present in it the obscure and direct intuition of the whole.

We are now in a position to answer the question we proposed to ourselves, whether the whole, as a cognitive situation, is antecedent to all thought or rather a product of experience. We may say that it is neither one nor the other. It is not a logical antecedent, in the sense of a means to knowing, like the idea of being for the ontologist; nor is it a real antecedent, in the sense that there is an intuition of the whole apart from and antecedent to every other act of knowing. Nor is it a product of experience, which as such is never obscure, is only occasionally direct, and is never the undifferentiated whole but a definite particular.

The *factual datum* from which we started, described as a *cognitive situation* in regard to an undifferentiated whole, *may now be defined more precisely as a direct and obscure intuition present in every act of knowledge.*

We have still to examine what this "whole" is which is intuited directly but obscurely. Many times in the course of this analysis we have spoken of it as of a reality. What we had in mind to exclude was either an "idealistic" whole or a pretended "phenomenalistic" whole.

That we are dealing with a real whole may be proved in two ways. One proof is derived from the realist interpretation of the apprehension of truth, which traditional philosophy affirms—and on this I have no need to dwell. The other proof is by the direct knowledge of the self. In both experiences, the objective reality bursts upon us with evidence; the first is the royal road of abstraction from the sensible; the other, the knowledge of ourselves, has an interior existence; if it offered no testimony of our reality we would be condemned to solipsism.

From the viewpoint then of the validity of our knowledge there would be, *a priori*, no objections to a direct intuition (however obscure) of the whole being able to attain objective reality. But two questions must be asked: 1) does it *de facto* attain this reality; 2) does it really attain a totality?

We are led to answer the first question affirmatively for three reasons: 1) because there is no doubt that such an intuition includes in the whole the personality of the subject as a reality; 2) because, when we isolate the subject from the whole, we are aware that such a situation is mental and not real, analytic and not synthetic, notwithstanding that the intuition of the whole remains as the realistic foundation of our mental operation; 3) because, if the whole were a subjective fact, it would be either a pure fancy which experience would destroy (and that is contradicted by our analysis) or it would be simply a logical situation and, therefore, by its very nature abstract and clear, while we assume that the intuition is obscure and direct. Finally, the answer we shall give to the second question will serve as further proof for the affirmative answer we have given to the first.

We can look at this whole, of which we have an intuition, under various aspects. It is, first of all, the existential whole of which we are part; we may call it the spatial-temporal whole. Our personal existence is in space and time. We cannot conceive of it as otherwise, because space is the same continuous reality of which we are part, and time is the same continuous reality in whose movement we move. Just as there is no spatial reality which is not temporal, so there is no temporal reality which is not spatial. Time is the rhythm (movement) of coexisting substance, just as space is the coexistence of rhythmic (moving) substance. With experience and science we can form some approximate ideas of this coexistent and moving world and of its various continuous and rhythmic systems, up to the limits of the known. However variously it is conceived in different ages and cultures, we have the intuition of it as an indefinite reality. Before having experience, we are aware that we share (with our own position and rhythm) in the cosmic reality, as a unit in its multiplicity. Analytic ideas illumine our obscure and direct intuition.

The other whole—that of abstract thought, the universals derived from concrete reality and signifying noumenal reality—is a product of our logical thought, the fruit of experience and scientific endeavor. It has as its foundation cosmic reality, not only in the individuals which compose it but also in its existential totality. It is the intellect which discovers, from a limited knowledge of a certain number of individuals, genera and species, and which defines, categorizes, universalizes; meanwhile the intuition of the whole accompanies such intellectual activity in all its forms.

Moreover, the necessity of unification draws us towards two opposite poles: the self and the whole. This whole cannot be incoherent, an aggregate of individual realities or an accumulation of disconnected ideas; the whole is either unified or it is not, both in reality and in the construction of the mind. When we reach the concept of entity, we have found the most abstract and at the same time the most concrete expression of reality, its central point of systematic unification. Logic and metaphysics have the same point of destination, they represent for us, in being, the psychic cosmic whole as a coherent system of ideas and of reality. Thus we come to have, through experience and reflection, a logical-metaphysical image of that reality which presents itself to us in every act of knowledge as an undifferentiated whole obscurely intuited.

Is this the whole? The cosmos is presented to us as concrete, but caused and contingent; being confronts us as universal, but abstract and indeterminate. We reason to the First Cause and the Concrete and Infinite Universal. All this is accepted, and we presuppose it as demonstrated along the lines of traditional philosophy. What still urges us to a further point in our investigation is the desire to verify the hypothesis . . . . Seeing the problem of the intuition of God in a new light, we are led to ask the question: Is there also, in the direct and obscure intuition of the whole—the world of real concreteness and universalized abstraction—an intuition of the First Cause, of Being, Infinite, universal and concrete?

Theologians and philosophers agree that God is in all things *per essentiam, per potentiam et per presentiam.* St. Paul said to the Athenians: "In Him we live and move and have our being." In all creatures the divine archetypes are realized, and man especially was made "in our image and likeness." Hence Tertullian could well speak of a soul *naturaliter christiana,* and St. Augustine could direct to God his powerful *fescisti nos ad te.* This, though, does not prove that, in the intuition we have been studying, Divinity is attained as the Infinite Being or First Cause or as any of the other ideas we formulate by means of inductive or deductive reasoning. We can say only that the whole of intuited reality is neither apart from God, nor is it conceivable by itself as a true whole. These explicit affirmations, which become clear when we define reality, are found implicit in the apprehension of the undifferentiated whole. For this reason it seems to us that the French philosopher Lavelle in his interesting work, *La Présence totale* (1934) failed to point out this difference, and so gives the impression of inclining towards a pantheism which might be called "pre-logical," and which is not devoid of dangers.

The experience of individuated reality makes us notice the intuition of the undifferentiated whole as concomitant with every cognitive act. There is no "prelogism," therefore, and no confusion of the cosmic whole with the Infinite Whole. If, on the one hand by our obscure and direct intuition of reality, we attain undifferentiated reality, we are able, on the other hand, to distinguish and pick out its meaning gradually while at the same time apprehending the distinct reality. Now one of the implications inherent in our knowledge is its essential relation to the Absolute. "Au sein de toute intellection humaine *l'élément de signification* objective enveloppe une relation ontologique à l' Absolu" [J. Maréchal, S.J.]. This ontological relation could not be explained if it were a simple consequence of knowledge. Instead, it is intrinsic to the very nature of the knowing subject and to the nature of the objects both knowable and known. It is an essential fact which affects knowledge and gives it an inexhaustible dynamism; the will and human action are permeated with it; that which is the absolute for the intellect is the good for the will.

Maréchal also states:

Si la relation des données à la Fin dernière de l'intelligence est un condition a priori intrinsèquement *constitutive* de tout objet de notre pensée, la connaissance analogique de l'Etre absolu, comme terme supérieure et ineffable de cette relation, entre *implicitement* dans notre conscience immédiate de tout objet en tant qu'objet;

and a little further on he says: "nous trouvons celui-ci [l'Etre absolu] implicitement affirmé comme *noumène* positif dans tout jugement."

It must be noted immediately that Père J. Maréchal excludes every kind of intuitive thought. That which is for us the intuition of the whole is for him only "besoin rationnel de totaliser." We quote him because his statement concerning the intrinsic objective relation of cosmic reality to the absolute is of interest to us for our conclusion.

The intrinsic relation is connatural to the thinking subject in such a way that it must be attained in some manner or other by every subject in its intuition (or awareness) of itself. In such an act, the subject forms a distinct idea neither of the absolute nor of the contingent, nor of their connection; but it understands the necessity of a stable reality to which it is related and in which in a certain manner it participates. The intuition of the "whole" as we have explained and discussed it is a movement of interior necessity towards the absolute.

This absolute, not clearly defined in its outlines, is the mysterious and solid foundation of the undifferentiated whole; it reveals itself to us gradually as the intellect understands particular reality in its essences and individualizations, in its systematizations and in its relations; it reveals itself gradually as the will and human action realize, in fact, the truths which are known.

We can conclude, therefore, that we have "naturally" an obscure intuition of God as the Absolute in our obscure and direct intuition of the undifferentiated whole, and consequently in every cognitive act.

Freedom

Aurelius Augustine   ## 34. FREEDOM OF THE WILL

That freedom is both a blessing and a burden, St. Augustine well knew—indeed, this fact became the theme of many of his writings, including these passages from *De Libero Arbitrio*.

This selection consists of the first, second and thirteenth chapters from Book II of *De Libero Arbitrio*, and is reprinted through the courtesy of Charles Scribner's Sons from *Medieval Philosophers*, edited and translated by Richard McKeon; copyright 1929, Charles Scribner's Sons; renewal copyright © 1957.

Why did God give man free will, Evodius is made to ask, if man can sin by it? Because, answers Augustine, man also acts rightly by it, and without it there could be no "right" action for man because there would be no "wrong" action. Without free will, how could we honor just acts and condemn unjust acts? In punishing a sinner, Augustine suggests, God seems to ask why the free will He had given is not used for what it *was* given; namely, right action. Yet the will is susceptible to sin, Evodius observes. Why should this be so?

Augustine answers this question in the same spirit that characterizes the entire dialogue. The purpose of the dialogue is to deepen understanding of the content of faith, or of what one already believes, rather than to arrive at what one *may* believe. What has been established by God, Augustine points out, cannot be reprehensible. It is true that free will is divinely ordained; hence, it cannot be reprehensible—even though it can be wrongly used.

The central point Augustine makes, however, is based on a distinction between *free action* and *freedom*. The true meaning of freedom is to be found in subjection to the truth. That is, man is most truly free when he acts rightly. He is not at all free (although he still has free will) when he acts wrongly. Hence, the distinction between freedom and free will. Freedom is attained in the right use of free will, and slavery, in its wrong use. The reason man has been given free will is to enable him to choose God freely. God thus has a cosmic stake in the issue of free will, since He gave it to enable man to enter into the realm of freedom, which is also the realm of the divine.

1. *Evodius.* Now explain to me, if you can, why God gave man free judgment of will, for obviously, if man had not received free will, he would not be able to sin.

Augustine. Is it certain and known to you then that God gave man this which you do not think should have been given?

E. So far as the preceding book is concerned I seem to have understood both that we have free judgment of will and that we sin only by it.

A. I too recall that that has already been made clear to us. But I have just asked whether you know that God gave us this which we clearly have and by which clearly we sin.

E. I think no other than God. For we are from him; and whether we sin or act rightly, we merit punishment or reward from him.

A. I want to know also whether you know this clearly or whether you are moved, not unwillingly, to believe it by authority even though you do not know it.

E. I answer that in what concerns this thing I first believed by authority. But what is more true than that every good is from God and that every just act is good, and that the punishment of sinners and the reward of those who act rightly are just? From this it comes about both that sinners are afflicted by God with misery and that those who act rightly are visited with felicity.

2. *A.* To that I have no objection, but I raise this other question: how do you know that we are from him? For this you have not yet explained, but you have explained that we merit from him either punishment or reward.

E. That, too, I see is clear no otherwise than because we know already that God judges sins. Certainly, all justice is from him. For as it is not characteristic of any goodness to show its benefits in what is alien to it, so it is not of justice to judge in what is alien to it. Wherefore, it is clear that we pertain to him, not only because he is most benign in showing his benefits in us but also most just in judging. Finally, from what I have stated and from what you have conceded, every good, including man, can be understood to be from God. For man himself in so far as he is man is something good, because he can, when he so wishes, live rightly.

3. *A.* Clearly if these things are so, the question which you proposed has been solved. For if man is something good and can not act rightly except when he wishes, he ought to have a free will without which he could not act rightly. For it is not to be believed that, because sin is committed by it too, God gave free will for sin. Therefore, since without it man can not live rightly, there is cause enough why it should have been given. It can, moreover, be understood to have been given for this and on this account, because if anyone shall have used it for sinning, it is condemned in him by God. But this would be done unjustly if free will had been given, not only that one might live rightly, but also that one might sin. For how could he be punished justly who had used his will for that purpose for which it has been given? But then, when God punishes the sinner, what else does he seem to you to say except, Why have you not used your free will for the purpose for which I gave it to you, that is, for doing rightly? Further, if man lacked free judgment of will, how would that be good, for which justice itself is commended when it condemns sins and honors deeds rightly done? For that which was not done by the will would be neither sinfully nor rightly done. And according to this if man did not have free will, both punishment and reward would be unjust. However, there must have been justice in both punishment and reward, since it is one of the goods which are from God. Therefore, God must have given man free will.

4. *E.* I concede now that God gave it. But I ask you, does it not seem to you that, if it has been given for acting rightly, it should not be susceptible of being turned to sinning? As in the case of justice itself, which was given to man that he might live well: for can anyone live evilly by his justice? So too, no one would be able by will to sin, if the will had been given for acting rightly.

A. God will grant, I hope, that I shall be able to answer you, or rather that you reply to yourself by the same truth, teaching within, which is the supreme mistress of all. But I want you to tell me briefly, if you hold as certain and known that of which I have asked you, that God has given us free will, whether or not it be necessary to say that that should not have been given which we acknowledge God to have given. For if it is uncertain whether or not he gave it, we inquire rightly whether it was well given, that it may be discovered also, when we shall have found it was well given, that he gave it by whom all goods have been given to man; if however we should find that it was not well given, we may understand that he did not give it, whom to blame is sinful. But if it is certain that he himself gave it we must acknowledge that, in whatsoever manner it has been given, it should neither not be given nor be given otherwise than it was given. For he gave it whose deed can not rightly be reprehended in any stipulation.

5. *E.* Although I hold these things with unshaken faith, still, since I do not hold them in knowledge; let us inquire as if all things were uncertain. For I see, since it is uncertain whether free will was given for doing rightly (since we can also sin by it) that it becomes uncertain too whether it should have been given. For if it is uncertain that it was given for doing rightly, it is also uncertain that it should have been given, and by that it will also be uncertain whether God gave it; because if it is uncertain that it should have been given, it is uncertain that it has been given by him, of whom it is sinful to believe that he has given anything which should not have been given.

A. At all events you are certain that God is.

E. That too I hold unshakable, not by contemplation, but by belief.

A. If, then, any of those fools of whom it is written, *The fool hath said in in his heart, There is no God,* should say that to you, and should not wish to believe with you what you believe, but wished to know whether you believed the truth; would you leave the man, or would you judge that he was to be persuaded in some way of what you hold unshakable, particularly if he wished, not to oppose it obstinately, but seriously to learn it?

E. That which you stated last warns me sufficiently what I should answer him. For, of course, even if he were extremely stupid, he would grant me that one must not argue deceitfully and obstinately about anything whatever, and particularly not about so great a thing. After he had conceded that, it would first be important to me that I should believe he inquired this in good faith and did not conceal within himself any obstinacy and deceit in what pertains to this question. Then I should demonstrate (which I think would be extremely easy for any one), how much more reasonable it would be (since he was willing to believe another who was not acquainted with them in respect to hidden matters of his own mind, which he himself knew) to believe also from the Books of so many men who left testimony in letters that they lived with the Son of God, that God is; for they have written that they saw deeds which could never have been done if there were no God; and he would be very stupid, if he, who for himself wanted me to believe these things, should reprove me for believing them. Moreover, since he would not be able to reprove me rightly, he would in no wise find a reason why he too should not imitate me.

A. If, then, you think it sufficient in the question of the existence of God for us to have judged that so many men could not have believed thoughtlessly, why, I ask you, do you not think similarly that the authority of those same men is to be credited in those matters too, which, uncertain and obviously unknown, we have undertaken to examine, and so spare us the labor of further investigation of them?

E. But we wish to know and to understand that which we believe.

6. *A.* You remember correctly what we undeniably asserted at the beginning of our previous discussion. For if to believe were not one thing and to understand another and if we did not have to believe first whatever great and divine truths we wished to understand, the prophet would have said in vain, *If ye will not believe, ye shall not understand.* Our Lord himself also urged by both his words and his deeds that they whom he called to salvation should first believe. But later when he spoke of the very gift which was to be given those who believe he did not say, And this is life eternal, that they should believe; but he said, *And this is life eternal that they should know thee the only true God and him whom thou didst send, Jesus Christ.* Then again he says to believers, *Seek and ye shall find;* for neither can that be said to have been found which is believed while unknown, nor is any one made suitable to find God unless he shall first believe what later he is to know. Wherefore, obedient to the precepts of God, let us seek earnestly. For what we seek when he urges us, we shall find by his pointing the way, so far as these things can be found in this life and by such as we: for it is to be believed that they can be distinguished and known very evidently and very perfectly by better men even while they inhabit this earth, and certainly by all good and pious men after this life; and it is to be hoped that it will be so with us. Once earthly and human things have been despised, these things are in every manner to be desired and loved. . . .

35. However, I had promised, if you remember, that I should demonstrate to you that there is something which is more sublime than our mind and reason. Behold it is truth itself: embrace it if you can, and enjoy it, and delight in the Lord, and he will give you the desires of your heart. What more, indeed, do you seek than that you be happy? And who is more happy than he who enjoys the unshaken and immutable and most excellent truth? But do men cry forth that they are happy when they embrace the beautiful bodies, of wives or even of prostitutes, for which they have lusted with great desire: and do we doubt that we are happy in the embrace of truth? Do men cry that they are happy when, their jaws arid with heat, they come upon an abundant and healthgiving fountain, or when, hungry, they find a meal or dinner splendidly furnished and plentiful: and will we deny that we are happy when we slacken

our thirst and feed on truth? We are used to hear voices of those crying out that they are happy if they lie down in roses or other flowers or even if they enjoy very sweet smelling unguents: what is more fragrant and what more pleasing than the inspiration of truth? And do we hesitate to call ourselves happy when we are inspired by it? Many make for themselves a happy life in the song of voices and of strings and of flutes, and when these are taken from them, they judge themselves miserable; but when they are present they are carried away with joy: and shall we seek some other happy life when, with no crashing, so to speak, of songs, a kind of eloquent silence of truth flows into our minds, and shall we not enjoy the happiness so certain and so present? Men who are delighted in the light of gold and silver, in the lustre of gems and of other colors, or in the clearness and the joy of the very light which is proper to the eyes, whether in terrestrial fires or in stars or the moon or the sun, seem to themselves happy when they are not recalled from this pleasure by any vexation or by any need, and they wish to live always for these: and have we feared to place the happy life in the light of truth?

36. By all means, since the supreme good is known and secured in truth, and since that truth is wisdom, let us see the supreme good in truth, and let us secure and enjoy it. He is surely happy who enjoys the supreme good. For this truth reveals all goods which are true, which men of understanding, each according to his capacity, choose singly or together to enjoy. But just as they who choose in the light of the sun that which they look at willingly and are rejoiced by that sight; whereas if perchance there were any among them endowed with very vigorous and healthy and very strong eyes, they would look upon nothing more willingly than the sun itself, which likewise lights up other things by which weaker eyes are pleased: so the keen and vigorous perception of the mind when it has gazed with sure reason on many true and immutable things, directs itself to that truth itself by which all things are shown forth, and inhering in it, as it were, forgets other things, and at once in it enjoys them all. For whatsoever is pleasant in other truths, is pleasant assuredly in the truth itself.

37. This is our freedom when we are subjected to this truth: and it itself is our God, who frees us from death, that is, from the condition of sin. For Truth itself speaking as man with men, says to those who believe in him: *If you have abided by my word, then truly you are my disciples and you will know the truth and the truth will make you free.* For the soul enjoys no thing with freedom except that which it enjoys with security.

Thomas Aquinas   **35. FREEDOM OF CHOICE**

Free choice, St. Thomas points out, is undeniably present in human experience,
since man shows in many ways that he is capable of action through free
judgment. Free choice is neither a habit nor a determination from without,
but the power to act. Its proper act is election, that is, a commitment to
this rather than to *that*. Although strictly speaking an act, it is commonly
thought of as the principle by which man judges freely.

Election implies two elements, one of which is cognitive, or intellective,
the other appetitive. The cognitive power provides the necessary counsel
required by election, whereas the appetitive power brings it about that the
judgment of counsel is accepted. Consequently, election is an intellectual
appetite.

When we speak of free choice and will, St. Thomas observes, we do not
mean two powers, but one. Likewise, when we speak of intellect and
reason, we imply not two powers, but one. Hence, free choice is related to
will, as reason is related to intellect.

M AN HAS FREE CHOICE, or otherwise counsels, exhortations, commands,
prohibitions, rewards and punishments would be in vain. In order to make
this evident, we must observe that some things act without judgment, as a
stone moves downward; and in like manner all things which lack knowledge.
And some act from judgment, but not a free judgment; as brute animals. For
the sheep, seeing the wolf, judges it a thing to be shunned, from a natural and
not a free judgment; because it judges, not from deliberation, but from natural
instinct. And the same thing is to be said of any judgment in brute animals.
But man acts from judgment, because by his apprehensive power he judges
that something should be avoided or sought. But because this judgment, in the
case of some particular act, is not from a natural instinct, but from some act
of comparison in the reason, therefore he acts from free judgment and retains
the power of being inclined to various things. For reason in contingent matters
may follow opposite courses, as we see in dialectical syllogisms and rhetorical
arguments. Now particular operations are contingent, and therefore in such
matters the judgment of reason may follow opposite courses, and is not
determinate to one. And in that man is rational, it is necessary that he have
free choice. . . .

Excerpted from *Summa Theologiae*, I, q. 83 (aa. 1–4), this selection is from *Basic Writings
of St. Thomas Aquinas*, edited by Anton C. Pegis. Copyright 1945 by Random House, Inc.
Reprinted by permission of Random House, Inc., New York, and Burns & Oates Ltd., London.

Although *free choice,* in its strict sense, denotes an act, in the common manner of speaking we call free choice that which is the principle of the act by which man judges freely. Now in us the principle of an act is both power and habit; for we say that we know something both by science and by the intellectual power. Therefore free choice must be either a power, or a habit, or a power with a habit. That it is neither a habit nor a power together with a habit can be clearly proved in two ways. First of all, because if it is a habit, it must be a natural habit; for it is natural to man to have free choice. But there is no natural habit in us with respect to those things which come under free choice, for we are naturally inclined to those things of which we have natural habits, for instance, to assent to first principles. Now those things to which we are naturally inclined are not subject to free choice, as we have said in the case of the desire of happiness. Therefore it is against the very notion of free choice that it should be a natural habit; and that it should be a non-natural habit is against its nature. Therefore in no sense is it a habit.

Secondly, this is clear because habits are defined as that *by reason of which we are well- or ill-disposed with regard to actions and passions.* For by temperance we are well-disposed as regards concupiscences, and by intemperance ill-disposed; and by science we are well-disposed to the act of the intellect when we know the truth, and by the contrary habit ill-disposed. But free choice is indifferent to choosing well or ill, and therefore it is impossible that it be a habit. Therefore it is a power. . . .

The proper act of free choice is election, for we say that we have a free choice because we can take one thing while refusing another; and this is to elect. Therefore we must consider the nature of free choice by considering the nature of election. Now two things concur in election: one on the part of the cognitive power, the other on the part of the appetitive power. On the part of the cognitive power, counsel is required, by which we judge one thing to be preferred to another; on the part of the appetitive power, it is required that the appetite should accept the judgment of counsel. Therefore Aristotle leaves it in doubt whether election belongs principally to the appetitive or the cognitive power: since he says that election is either *an appetitive intellect or an intellectual appetite.* But he inclines to its being an intellectual appetite when he describes election as *a desire proceeding from counsel.* And the reason of this is because the proper object of election is the means to the end. Now the means, as such, has the nature of that good which is called useful; and since the good, as such, is the object of the appetite, it follows that election is principally an act of an appetitive power. And thus free choice is an appetitive power. . . .

The appetitive powers must be proportionate to the apprehensive powers, as we have said above. Now, as on the part of intellectual apprehension we have intellect and reason, so on the part of the intellectual appetite we have will and free choice, which is nothing else but the power of election. And this is clear from their relations to their respective objects and acts. For the act of *understanding* implies the simple acceptation of something, and hence we say that we understand first principles, which are known of themselves without any comparison. But to *reason,* properly speaking, is to come from one thing to the knowledge of another, and so, properly speaking, we reason about conclusions, which are known from the principles. In like manner, on the part of the appetite, to *will* implies the simple appetite for something, and so the will is said to regard the end, which is desired for itself. But to *elect* is to desire something for the sake of obtaining something else, and so, properly speaking, it regards the means to the end. Now in appetitive matters, the end is related to the means, which is desired for the end, in the same way as, in knowledge, principles are related to the conclusion to which we assent because of the principles. Therefore it is evident that as *intellect* is to *reason,* so *will* is to the *elective power,* which is free choice. But it has been shown above that it belongs to the same power both to understand and to reason, even as it belongs to the same power to be at rest and to be in movement. Hence it belongs also to the same power to will and to elect. And on this account will and the free choice are not two powers, but one.

William James   **36. THE DILEMMA OF**

DETERMINISM

The threat to the notions of freedom and free will, created by the spirit of nine-teenth-century scientism, often provided William James the opportunity to reaffirm the traditional view of free will—in untraditional language. The belief in universal and unyielding laws of nature determining every possible result of fact and action, and consequently denying the actuality of freedom, impressed James as not only thoughtless but vicious.

Let us, he says in this essay, avoid any ambiguities that might result from using eulogistic or "sentimental" terms, such as "freedom." Let us, rather, translate the question into one between determinism and chance, for these terms are utterly antithetic and enjoin a quarrel that is "altogether meta-physical."

This selection first appeared in the Unitarian Review (1884), and was reprinted in the volume of James's essays, *The Will to Believe,* New York, Dover Publications, 1956.

The doctrine of determinism professes that there are no ambiguous possibilities hidden in nature. What exists is a totality, fixed from eternity. Indeterminism or chance, on the other hand, professes belief in a certain amount of "loose play" among the parts of the universe and asserts that possibilities may outnumber actualities. Loyal to the notion of pluralism, indeterminism "denies the world to be one unbending unit of fact," because "actualities seem to float in a wider sea of possibilities from out of which they are chosen; and *somewhere* . . . such possibilities exist, and form a part of truth."

What divides us into "possibility men" and "anti-possibility men," except our devotion to different faiths and different postulates? Those who believe in the possibilities inherent in the universe look upon chance for what it is: a "free gift," unguaranteed and unsecured—for the idea of chance is "at bottom, exactly the same thing as the idea of gift." Determinism fails to make provision for the fact of unique contributions—that there is something in the world really "of its own, something that is not the unconditional property of the whole."

Applying his argument to the question of human action, James asserts that it becomes clear that if we are determined to do *this* rather than *that*, and if there are no other possibilities than what we actually end up by doing, then all moral condemnation and approval are senseless. What sense can there be "in condemning ourselves for taking the wrong way unless we need have done nothing of the sort, unless the right way was open to us as well?" In man, and in all other world realities, there is *risk*. We risk action in a world of risks. Furthermore, it cannot be said that free will and freedom are incompatible with Providence—unless, however, one makes Providence nothing but another name for universal determinism; or in James's words, "provided you do not restrict Providence to fulminating nothing but fatal decrees."

. . . THE ARGUMENTS I am about to urge all proceed on two suppositions: first, when we make theories about the world and discuss them with one another, we do so in order to attain a conception of things which shall give us subjective satisfaction; and, second, if there be two conceptions, and the one seems to us, on the whole, more rational than the other, we are entitled to suppose that the more rational one is the truer of the two. I hope that you are all willing to make these suppositions with me; for I am afraid that if there be any of you here who are not, they will find little edification in the rest of what I have to say. I cannot stop to argue the point; but I myself believe that all the magnificent achievements of mathematical and physical science—our doctrines of evolution, of uniformity of law, and the rest—proceed from our indomitable desire to cast the world into a more rational shape in our minds than the shape into which it is thrown there by the crude order of our experience. The world has shown itself, to a great extent, plastic to this demand of ours for rationality. How much farther it will show itself plastic no one can say. Our only means of finding out is to try; and I, for one, feel as free to try conceptions of moral as of mechanical or of logical rationality. If a certain formula for expressing the nature of the world violates my moral demand, I shall feel as free to throw it overboard, or at least to doubt it, as if it disappointed my demand for uniformity of sequence, for example; the one demand being, so far as I can see, quite as subjective and emotional as the other is. The principle of causality, for example—what is it but a postulate, an empty name covering simply a demand that the sequence of events shall some day manifest a deeper kind of belonging of one thing with another than the mere arbitrary juxtaposition which now phenomenally appears? It is as much an altar to an unknown god as the one that Saint Paul found at Athens. All our scientific and philosophic ideals are altars to unknown gods. Uniformity is as much so as is free-will. If this be admitted, we can debate on even terms. But if any one pretends that while freedom and variety are, in the first instance, subjective demands, necessity and uniformity are something altogether different, I do not see how we can debate at all.

To begin, then, I must suppose you acquainted with all the usual arguments on the subject. I cannot stop to take up the old proofs from causation, from statistics, from the certainty with which we can foretell one another's conduct, from the fixity of character, and all the rest. But there are two *words* which usually encumber these classical arguments, and which we must immediately dispose of if we are to make any progress. One is the eulogistic word *freedom,* and the other is the opprobrious word *chance.* The word "chance" I wish to keep, but I wish to get rid of the word "freedom." Its eulogistic associations have so far overshadowed all the rest of its meaning that both parties claim the sole right to use it, and determinists to-day insist that they alone are freedom's champions. Old-fashioned determinism was what we may call *hard* determinism. It did not shrink from such words as fatality, bondage of the will, necessitation, and the like. Nowadays, we have a *soft* determinism which abhors harsh words, and, repudiating fatality, necessity, and even predetermination, says that its real name is freedom; for freedom is only necessity understood, and bondage to the highest is identical with true freedom. Even a writer as little used to making capital out of soft words as Mr. Hodgson hesitates not to call himself a "free-will determinist."

Now, all this is a quagmire of evasion under which the real issue of fact has been entirely smothered. Freedom in all these senses presents simply no problem at all. No matter what the soft determinist mean by it—whether he mean the acting without external constraint; whether he mean the acting rightly, or whether he mean the acquiescing in the law of the whole,—who cannot answer him that sometimes we are free and sometimes we are not? But there *is* a problem, an issue of fact and not of words, an issue of the most momentous importance, which is often decided without discussion in one sentence—nay, in one clause of a sentence—by those very writers who spin out whole chapters in their efforts to show what "true" freedom is; and that is the question of determinism, about which we are to talk to-night.

Fortunately, no ambiguities hang about this word or about its opposite, indeterminism. Both designate an outward way in which things may happen, and their cold and mathematical sound has no sentimental associations that can bribe our partiality either way in advance. Now, evidence of an external kind to decide between determinism and indeterminism is, as I intimated a while back, strictly impossible to find. Let us look at the difference between them and see for ourselves. What does determinism profess?

It professes that those parts of the universe already laid down absolutely appoint and decree what the other parts shall be. The future has no ambiguous possibilities hidden in its womb: the part we call the present is compatible with only one totality. Any other future complement than the one fixed from eternity is impossible. The whole is in each and every part, and welds it with the rest into an absolute unity, an iron block, in which there can be no equivocation or shadow of turning. . . .

Indeterminism, on the contrary, says that the parts have a certain amount of loose play on one another, so that the laying down of one of them does not necessarily determine what the others shall be. It admits that possibilities may be in excess of actualities, and that things not yet revealed to our knowledge may really in themselves be ambiguous. Of two alternative futures which we conceive, both may now be really possible; and the one become impossible only at the very moment when the other excludes it by becoming real itself. Indeterminism thus denies the world to be one unbending unit of fact. It says there is a certain ultimate pluralism in it; and, so saying, it corroborates our ordinary unsophisticated view of things. To that view, actualities seem to float in a wider sea of possibilities from out of which they are chosen; and, *somewhere,* indeterminism says, such possibilities exist, and form a part of truth.

Determinism, on the contrary, says they exist *nowhere,* and that necessity on the one hand and impossibility on the other are the sole categories of the real. Possibilities that fail to get realized are, for determinism, pure illusions: they never were possibilities at all. There is nothing inchoate, it says, about this universe of ours, all that was or is or shall be actual in it having been from eternity virtually there. The cloud of alternatives our minds escort this mass of actuality withal is a cloud of sheer deceptions, to which "impossibilities" is the only name that rightfully belongs.

The issue, it will be seen, is a perfectly sharp one, which no eulogistic terminology can smear over or wipe out. The truth *must* lie with one side or the other, and its lying with one side makes the other false.

The question relates solely to the existence of possibilities, in the strict sense of the term, as things that may, but need not, be. Both sides admit that a volition, for instance, has occurred. The indeterminists say another volition might have occurred in its place: the determinists swear that nothing could possibly have occurred in its place. Now, can science be called in to tell us which of these two point-blank contradicters of each other is right? Science professes to draw no conclusions but such as are based on matters of fact, things that have actually happened; but how can any amount of assurance that something actually happened give us the least grain of information as to whether another thing might or might not have happened in its place? Only facts can be proved by other facts. With things that are possibilities and not facts, facts have no concern. If we have no other evidence then the evidence of existing facts, the possibility-question must remain a mystery never to be cleared up.

And the truth is that facts practically have hardly anything to do with making us either determinists or indeterminists. Sure enough, we make a flourish of quoting facts this way or that; and if we are determinists, we talk about the infallibility with which we can predict one another's conduct; while if we are indeterminists, we lay great stress on the fact that it is just because we cannot foretell one another's conduct, either in war or statecraft or in any of the great and small intrigues and businesses of men, that life is so intensely anxious and hazardous a game. But who does not see the wretched insufficiency of this so-called objective testimony on both sides? What fills up the gaps in our minds is something not objective, not external. What divides us into possibility men and anti-possibility men is different faiths or postulates— postulates of rationality. To this man the world seems more rational with possibilities in it—to that man more rational with possibilities excluded; and talk as we will about having to yield to evidence, what makes us monists or pluralists, determinists or indeterminists, is at bottom always some sentiment like this.

The stronghold of the deterministic sentiment is the antipathy to the idea of chance. As soon as we begin to talk indeterminism to our friends, we find a number of them shaking their heads. This notion of alternative possibility, they say, this admission that any one of several things may come to pass, is, after all, only a roundabout name for chance; and chance is something the notion of which no sane mind can for an instant tolerate in the world. What is it, they ask, but barefaced crazy unreason, the negation of intelligibility and law? And if the slightest particle of it exist anywhere, what is to prevent the whole fabric from falling together, the stars from going out, and chaos from recommencing her topsy-turvy reign?

Remarks of this sort about chance will put an end to discussion as quickly as anything one can find. I have already told you that "chance" was a word I wished to keep and use. Let us then examine exactly what it means, and see whether it ought to be such a terrible bugbear to us. I fancy that squeezing the thistle boldly will rob it of its sting.

The sting of the word "chance" seems to lie in the assumption that it means something positive, and that if anything happens by chance, it must needs be something of an intrinsically irrational and preposterous sort. Now, chance means nothing of the kind. It is a purely negative and relative term,* giving us no information about that of which it is predicated, except that it happens to be disconnected with something else—not controlled, secured, or necessitated by other things in advance of its own actual presence. As this point is the most subtile one of the whole lecture, and at the same time the point on which all the rest hinges, I beg you to pay particular attention to it. What I say is that it tells us nothing about what a thing may be in itself to call it "chance." It may be a bad thing, it may be a good thing. It may be lucidity, transparency, fitness incarnate, matching the whole system of other things, when it has once befallen, in an unimaginably perfect way. All you mean by calling it "chance" is that this is not guaranteed, that it may also fall out otherwise. For the system of other things has no positive hold on the chance-thing. Its origin is in a certain fashion negative: it escapes, and says, Hands off! coming, when it comes, as a free gift, or not at all.

This negativeness, however, and this opacity of the chance-thing when thus considered *ab extra,* or from the point of view of previous things or distant things, do not preclude its having any amount of positiveness and luminosity from within, and at its own place and moment. All that its chance-character asserts about it is that there is something in it really of its own, something that is not the unconditional property of the whole. If the whole wants this property, the whole must wait till it can get it, if it be a matter of chance. That the universe may actually be a sort of joint-stock society of this sort, in which the sharers have both limited liabilities and limited powers, is of course a simple and conceivable notion.

Nevertheless, many persons talk as if the minutest dose of disconnectedness of one part with another, the smallest modicum of independence, the faintest tremor of ambiguity about the future, for example, would ruin everything, and turn this goodly universe into a sort of insane sand-heap or nulliverse, no universe at all. Since future human volitions are as a matter of fact the only ambiguous things we are tempted to believe in, let us stop for a moment to make ourselves sure whether their independent and accidental character need be fraught with such direful consequences to the universe as these.

What is meant by saying that my choice of which way to walk home after the lecture is ambiguous and matter of chance as far as the present moment is concerned? It means that both Divinity Avenue and Oxford Street are called; but that only one, and that one *either* one, shall be chosen. Now, I ask you seri-

---

* Speaking technically, it is a word with a positive denotation, but a connotation that is negative. Other things must be silent about *what* it is: it alone can decide that point at the moment in which it reveals itself.

ously to suppose that this ambiguity of my choice is real; and then to make the impossible hypothesis that the choice is made twice over, and each time falls on a different street. In other words, imagine that I first walk through Divinity Avenue, and then imagine that the powers governing the universe annihilate ten minutes of time with all that it contained, and set me back at the door of this hall just as I was before the choice was made. Imagine then that, everything else being the same, I now make a different choice and traverse Oxford Street. You, as passive spectators, look on and see the two alternative universes—one of them with me walking through Divinity Avenue in it, the other with the same me walking through Oxford Street. Now, if you are determinists you believe one of these universes to have been from eternity impossible: you believe it to have been impossible because of the intrinsic irrationality or accidentality somewhere involved in it. But looking outwardly at these universes, can you say which is the impossible and accidental one, and which the rational and necessary one? I doubt if the most iron-clad determinist among you could have the slightest glimmer of light on this point. In other words, either universe *after the fact* and once there would, to our means of observation and understanding, appear just as rational as the other. There would be absolutely no criterion by which we might judge one necessary and the other matter of chance. Suppose now we relieve the gods of their hypothetical task and assume my choice, once made, to be made forever. I go through Divinity Avenue for good and all. If, as good determinists, you now begin to affirm, what all good determinists punctually do affirm, that in the nature of things I *couldn't* have gone through Oxford Street—had I done so it would have been chance, irrationality, insanity, a horrid gap in nature—I simply call your attention to this, that your affirmation is what the Germans call a *Machtspruch,* a mere conception fulminated as a dogma and based on no insight into details. Before my choice, either street seemed as natural to you as to me. Had I happened to take Oxford Street, Divinity Avenue would have figured in your philosophy as the gap in nature; and you would have so proclaimed it with the best deterministic conscience in the world.

But what a hollow outcry, then, is this against a chance which, if it were present to us, we could by no character whatever distinguish from a rational necessity! I have taken the most trivial of examples, but no possible example could lead to any different result. For what are the alternatives which, in point of fact, offer themselves to human volition? What are those futures that now seem matters of chance? Are they not one and all like the Divinity Avenue and Oxford Street of our example? Are they not all of them *kinds* of things already here and based in the existing frame of nature? Is any one ever tempted to produce an *absolute* accident, something utterly irrelevant to the rest of the world? Do not all the motives that assail us, all the futures that offer themselves to our choice, spring equally from the soil of the past; and would not either one of them, whether realized through chance or through necessity, the moment it was realized seem to us to fit that past and in the completest and most continuous manner to interdigitate with the phenomena already there?*

The more one thinks of the matter, the more one wonders that so empty and gratuitous a hubbub as this outcry against chance should have found so great an echo in the hearts of men. It is a word which tells us absolutely nothing about what chances, or about the *modus operandi* of the chancing; and the use of it as a war-cry shows only a temper of intellectual absolutism, a demand that the world shall be a solid block, subject to one control—which temper, which demand, the world may not be bound to gratify at all. In every outwardly verifiable and practical respect, a world in which the alternatives that now actually distract *your* choice were decided by pure chance would be by *me* absolutely undistinguished from the world in which I now live. I am, therefore, entirely willing to call it, so far as your choices go, a world of chance for me. To *yourselves,* it is true, those very acts of choice, which to me are so blind, opaque, and external, are the opposites of this, for you are within them and effect them. To you they appear as decisions; and decisions, for him who makes them, are altogether peculiar psychic facts. Self-luminous and self-justifying at the living moment at which they occur, they appeal to no outside moment to put its stamp upon them or make them continuous with the rest of nature. Themselves it is rather who seem to make nature continuous; and in their strange and intense function of granting consent to one possibility and withholding it from another, to transform an equivocal and double future into an inalterable and simple past.

But with the psychology of the matter we have no concern this evening. The quarrel which determinism has with chance fortunately has nothing to do with this or that psychological detail. It is a quarrel altogether metaphysical. Determinism denies the ambiguity of future volitions, because it affirms that nothing future can be ambiguous. But we have said enough to meet the issue. Indeterminate future volitions *do* mean chance. Let us not fear to shout it from the house-tops if need be; for we now know that the idea of chance is, at bottom, exactly the same thing as the idea of gift—the one simply being a disparaging, and the other a eulogistic, name for anything on which we have no effective *claim.* And whether the world be the better or the worse for having either chances or gifts in it will depend altogether on *what* these uncertain and unclaimable things turn out to be. . . .

---

* A favorite argument against free will is that if it be true, a man's murderer may as probably be his best friend as his worst enemy, a mother be as likely to strangle as to suckle her first-born, and all of us be as ready to jump from fourth-story windows as to go out of front doors, etc. Users of this argument should properly be excluded from debate till they learn what the real question is. "Free-will" does not say that everything that is physically conceivable is also morally possible. It merely says that of alternatives that really *tempt* our will more than one is really possible. Of course, the alternatives that do thus tempt our will are vastly fewer than the physical possibilities we can coldly fancy. Persons really tempted often do murder their best friends, mothers do strangle their first-born, people do jump out of fourth story windows, etc.

. . . What interest, zest, or excitement can there be in achieving the right way, unless we are enabled to feel that the wrong way is also a possible and a natural way—nay, more, a menacing and an imminent way? And what sense can there be in condemning ourselves for taking the wrong way, unless we need have done nothing of the sort, unless the right way was open to us as well? I cannot understand the willingness to act, no matter how we feel, without the belief that acts are really good and bad. I cannot understand the belief that an act is bad, without regret at its happening. I cannot understand regret without the admission of real, genuine possibilities in the world. Only *then* is it other than a mockery to feel, after we have failed to do our best, that an irreparable opportunity is gone from the universe, the loss of which it must forever after mourn. . . .

But now you will bring up your final doubt. Does not the admission of such an unguaranteed chance or freedom preclude utterly the notion of a Providence governing the world? Does it not leave the fate of the universe at the mercy of the chance-possibilities, and so far insecure? Does it not, in short, deny the craving of our nature for an ultimate peace behind all tempests, for a blue zenith above all clouds?

To this my answer must be very brief. The belief in free-will is not in the least incompatible with the belief in Providence, provided you do not restrict the Providence to fulminating nothing but *fatal* decrees. If you allow him to provide possibilities as well as actualities to the universe, and to carry on his own thinking in those two categories just as we do ours, chances may be there, uncontrolled even by him, and the course of the universe be really ambiguous; and yet the end of all things may be just what he intended it to be from all eternity.

An analogy will make the meaning of this clear. Suppose two men before a chessboard—the one a novice, the other an expert player of the game. The expert intends to beat. But he cannot foresee exactly what any one actual move of his adversary may be. He knows, however, all the *possible* moves of the latter; and he knows in advance how to meet each of them by a move of his own which leads in the direction of victory. And the victory infallibly arrives, after no matter how devious a course, in the one predestined form of check-mate to the novice's king.

Let now the novice stand for us finite free agents, and the expert for the infinite mind in which the universe lies. Suppose the latter to be thinking out his universe before he actually creates it. Suppose him to say, I will lead things to a certain end, but I will not *now* decide on all the steps thereto. At various points, ambiguous possibilities shall be left open, *either* of which, at a given instant, may become actual. But whichever branch of these bifurcations become real, I know what I shall do at the *next* bifurcation to keep things from drifting away from the final result I intend.

The creator's plan of the universe would thus be left blank as to many of its actual details, but all possibilities would be marked down. The realization of some of these would be left absolutely to chance; that is, would only be determined when the moment of realization came. Other possibilities would be *contingently* determined; that is, their decision would have to wait till it was seen how the matters of absolute chance fell out. But the rest of the plan, including its final upshot, would be rigorously determined once for all. So the creator himself would not need to know *all* the details of actuality until they came; and at any time his own view of the world would be a view partly of facts and partly of possibilities, exactly as ours is now. Of one thing, however, he might be certain; and that is that his world was safe, and that no matter how much it might zigzag he could surely bring it home at last.

Now, it is entirely immaterial, in this scheme, whether the creator leave the absolute chance-possibilities to be decided by himself, each when its proper moment arrives, or whether, on the contrary, he alienate this power from himself, and leave the decision out and out to finite creatures such as we men are. The great point is that the possibilities are really *here*. Whether it be we who solve them, or he working through us, at those soul-trying moments when fate's scales seem to quiver, and good snatches the victory from evil or shrinks nerveless from the fight, is of small account, so long as we admit that the issue is decided nowhere else than *here* and *now*. *That* is what gives the palpitating reality to our moral life and makes it tingle, as Mr. Mallock says, with so strange and elaborate an excitement. This reality, this excitement, are what the determinisms, hard and soft alike, suppress by their denial that *anything* is decided here and now, and their dogma that all things were foredoomed and settled long ago. If it be so, may you and I then have been foredoomed to the error of continuing to believe in liberty. It is fortunate for the winding up of controversy that in every discussion with determinism this *argumentum ad hominem* can be its adversary's last word.

Karl Jaspers   # 37. FREEDOM AND TRANSCENDENCE

Man's freedom, Karl Jaspers contends, is signified in the belief that he opens out on infinite possibilities, and is not simply derived from the world. Any in-

This selection is excerpted from a chapter in Jaspers's *The Perennial Scope of Philosophy* (New York, 1949) and appears here with the kind permission of the publisher, Philosophical Library, Inc.

sight into man that absolutizes him and makes him a "nothing but" (for instance, Marxism, psychoanalysis, or race theory), destroys this awareness of freedom, because man "is always more than he knows about himself." He "cannot adequately account for his sojourn in the world by the laws immanent to the world."

Man's awareness of his freedom is at one with his awareness of his finite nature. He understands that it is not "through himself that he is originally himself," and he thereby becomes conscious of the fact that his transcendence of death and dependence is brought about by transcendent help: "It is only through freedom that I become certain of transcendence."

As a finite reality, man understands that he is not completely self-contained, as other creatures are, because his very sense of "openness" has become a sign of his relation to another order. Though man is in bondage to "self-contained" finitude, it is his freedom that breaks through this bondage. Freedom is therefore at the heart of man's sense of his potentialities. And these potentialities are infinite.

In the freedom of subjective conviction, says Jaspers, "God's voice becomes audible . . . and this is the only organ by which it can impart itself to man." This is not without its risk, however, since subjective convictions are not fully warranted and secured, like so many investment loans. The fact is, there can be no subjective security. It is risk, then, and the consciousness of risk, that "remains the condition for increasing freedom." It is risk that "excludes complete reliance on subjective certainty, forbids the generalization of the subjective commandment into a universal law, and bars fanaticism."

M AN CANNOT BE DERIVED from something else, but is immediately at the base of all things. To be aware of this signifies man's freedom, which is lost in every other total determination of his being, and comes entirely into its own only in this one total determination. All empirical causalities and biological processes of development would seem to apply to man's material substratum, not to himself. No one can tell how far science will advance in the knowledge of the development of this human substratum. And scarcely any field of research is more exciting and captivating.

Every insight into man, if it is absolutized into a supposed knowledge of man as a whole, destroys his freedom. And this is the case with such theories of man, meaningful for limited perspectives, as have been propounded by psychoanalysis, Marxism, racial theory. They veil man himself as soon as they attempt to investigate anything more than aspects of his nature.

Science, it is true, shows us remarkable and highly surprising things about man, but as it attains greater clarity, the more evident it becomes that man as a whole can never become the object of scientific investigation. Man is always more than he knows about himself. This is true both of man in general and of the individual man. We can never draw up a balance sheet and know the answer, either concerning man in general, or concerning any individual man.

To absolutize knowledge that is always particular into a whole knowledge of man leads to the utter neglect of the human image of man. And a neglect of the image of man leads to a neglect of man himself. For the image of man that we hold to be true is itself a factor in our life. It influences our behavior toward ourselves and others, our vital attitude, and our choice of tasks.

Each of us for himself is certain of what man is, in a way that precedes scientific research and also comes after it. This is the prerogative of our freedom, which knows itself bound up with cogent knowledge, but is not included in it as an object of cognition. For in so far as we make ourselves the object of scientific inquiry, we see no freedom, but factuality, finiteness, form, relation, causal necessity. But it is by our freedom that we have awareness of our humanity.

Let me sum up once again in order to gain a more secure foundation for our consciousness of freedom.

Man cannot be understood on the basis of evolution from the animals.

In opposition to this we have the thesis: Without such evolution it is impossible to explain his origin. Since this is the only intelligible explanation and since everything in the world takes place in accordance with intelligible laws, man must have come into being through such an evolution.

The answer: True, for our cognition, everything is intelligible, for only where there is intelligibility is there cognition; beyond cognition, nothing exists for cognition. But the whole of being does not by any means resolve into intelligibility, if by cognition we mean scientifically cogent knowledge capable of being communicated unchanged. This knowledge itself is always particular, it refers always to definite, finite objects—whenever it approaches the whole as such, it slides into fundamental fallacies.

The world as a whole cannot be apprehended on the basis of one or several or many intelligible principles. Cognition breaks it into fragments—after the first erroneous and vain thrust toward the whole. Cognition is in the world and does not comprehend the world. Universal knowledge—as in mathematics and in the natural sciences—does indeed encompass something universal, but never reality as a whole.

But it would be a new fallacy to effect a leap within knowledge to other knowledge. To imagine, for instance, that at the limit of the knowable there is a creator of the world, and to suppose that this creator intervenes in the course of the world. As far as knowledge is concerned, these are merely metaphoric tautologies for nonknowledge.

The world is disclosed as having no foundation in itself. But in himself man finds what he finds nowhere else in the world: something unknowable, undemonstrable, something that is never object, that evades all scientific inquiry: he finds freedom and what goes with it. In this sphere I have experience not through knowledge of something, but through action. Here the road leads through the world and ourselves to transcendence.

To those who deny it freedom cannot be proved like things that occur in the world. But since the primal source of our action and our consciousness of being lies in freedom, what man is, is not merely the object of knowledge, but also of *faith*. Man's certainty as to his humanity is one of the basic elements of philosophical faith.

But man's freedom is inseparable from his *consciousness of his finite nature*.

Let us briefly outline the main points: Man's finiteness is first of all the finiteness of all living things. He is dependent upon his environment, upon nourishment and sensory contents; he is inexorably exposed to the mute and blind natural process; he must die.

Man's finiteness is secondly his dependence on other men, and on the historical world produced by the human collectivity. He can rely on nothing in this world. The fruits of fortune come and go. The human order is ruled not only by justice, but also by the power of the moment, that declares its arbitrary will to be the organ of justice, and hence is always based partly upon untruth. State and national community can destroy men who work only on the loyalty of man in existential communication, but this cannot be calculated. For what one relies on here is not an objective, demonstrable reality. And the man closest to one can at any time fall sick, go mad, die.

Man's finiteness lies thirdly in the nature of his cognition, in his dependence on the experience that is given him, especially on direct perception. My intellect can apprehend nothing but the matter of direct perception that fills in my concept.

Man becomes conscious of his finiteness by comparison with something that is not finite, with the absolute and the infinite:

The *absolute* becomes actual for him in his decision, the fulfillment of which directs him to an origin other than that which science makes intelligible to him in his finite existence.

The *infinite* is touched, though not apprehended, first in the idea of infinity, then in the conception of a divine knowledge essentially different from man's finite knowledge, finally in thoughts of immortality. The infinite which though unfathomable does enter into man's consciousness, causes man to transcend his finiteness by becoming aware of it.

Through the presence of the absolute and the infinite, man's finiteness does not remain merely the unconscious datum of his empirical existence; but through the light of transcendence it becomes the basic trait in his consciousness of his created nature. Thus though man cannot annul his finiteness, he does break through it.

But if in the absoluteness of his decision in the face of everything finite in the world, he becomes through his independence, certain of his infinity as his authentic selfhood, this infinity also reveals a new mode of his finiteness. This finiteness as existence means that even as himself man cannot ascribe himself to himself. It is not through himself that he is originally himself. And just as he does not owe his empirical existence in the world to his own will, his self is a free gift to him by transcendence. He must be given to himself over and over again, if he is not to lose himself. If man maintains his inner integrity in the face of fate and even of death, he cannot do so by himself alone. What helps him here is of a different kind than any help in the world. Transcendent help reveals itself to him solely in the fact that he can be himself. That he can stand by himself, he owes to an intangible hand, extended to him from transcendence, a hand whose presence he can feel only in his freedom.

Man as object of investigation and man as freedom are known to us from radically different sources. The former is a content of knowledge, the latter a fundamental trait of our faith. But if freedom for its part becomes a content of knowledge and an object of investigation, a special form of superstition arises:

Faith stands on the road to freedom that is not an absolute and not an empty freedom, but that is experienced as the possibility of being given or not given to oneself. It is only through freedom that I become certain of transcendence. By freedom, to be sure, I attain to a point of independence from the world, but precisely through the consciousness of my radical attachment to transcendence. For it is not through myself that I am.

Superstition on the other hand arises by way of a something that is the express content of faith, and thus also through a supposed knowledge of freedom. A modern form of superstition, for example, is psychoanalysis taken as a philosophy, and the pseudo-medicine that makes man's freedom a supposed object of scientific research.

As I conceive of the nature of my humanity, so I conceive of transcendence—i.e. I conceive of it either as something that limits me or as something that enables me to soar, it is superstition steeped in the object (hence associated with scientific aberration), or faith, inner experience of the Comprehensive (hence associated with the consummation of nonknowledge).

Man, in common with everything he sees around him, in common with the beasts, is branded as a finite creature. But his human finiteness *cannot become self-contained,* in the same sense as the animal.

Every animal is perfect in its own way, in its limitation it fulfills itself within a continually repeated life cycle. It is exposed only to the natural process in which all things merge and are brought forth. Only man cannot fulfill himself in his finiteness. It is only man whose finiteness involves him in history, in which he strives to realize his potentialities. His openness is a sign of his freedom.

Because man cannot fulfill himself in his finite existence, because he must forever search and strive (rather than live unconsciously in the unchanging rut of recurrent cycles), he, alone of all living creatures, knows that he is finite. Because of his incapacity for perfection, his finiteness becomes more to him than is revealed in the mere knowledge of the end. Man feels lost in it, and as a result becomes aware of his task and potentialities. He finds himself in the most desperate situation, but in such a way, that from it issues the strongest appeals to raise himself up through his freedom. And that is why man has again and again been represented as the most astoundingly contradictory of creatures, the most wretched and the most magnificent.

The proposition that man is finite and unfulfillable has an ambivalent character. It is an insight, it derives from demonstrable knowledge of the finite. But in its universality it points to a faith content, in which the freedom of human tasks is generated. In the fundamental experience of his nature, transcending the plane of knowledge, he is aware of both his unfulfillment and his infinite potentiality, his bondage and his freedom that breaks through this bondage.

Conscious of his freedom, man desires to become what he can and should be. He conceives an *ideal* of his nature. As on the plane of cognition, the idea of man as an object of scientific inquiry may lead to a falsely definitive image of him, so on the plane of freedom he may falsely choose a path leading to an absolute ideal. From helpless questioning and bewilderment, he thus aspires to take refuge in a universal that he can imitate in its concrete forms.

There are numerous images of man that have served as ideals with which we wished to identify ourselves. There is no doubt that such ideals have been effective, and that social types actually influence our behavior. The ideal can be magnified to a vague conception of man's "greatness," of something in man that is in a sense more than human, that is superhuman or inhuman.

For our philosophical consciousness it is crucial that we convince ourselves of the untruth and impossibility of such paths. Kant has given us the purest expression of this. "To attempt to realize the ideal in an example, that is, as a real phenomenon, as we might represent a perfectly wise man in a novel, is impossible, nay, absurd, and but little encouraging, because the natural limits, which are constantly interfering with the perfection in the idea, make all illusion in such an experiment impossible, and thus render the good itself in the idea suspicious and unreal."

Just as we lose sight of man when he becomes an object of scientific inquiry in racial theory, psychoanalysis, or Marxism and is represented as fully understandable, so we lose sight of the human task when he becomes an ideal.

The ideal is something fundamentally different from the idea. There is no ideal of man, but there is an idea of man. Ideals of man collapse, the idea of man serves as a goal to his march forward. Ideals can in a sense be schemata of ideas, road signs. That is the truth in the great philosophical conceptions of the Noble Man in China, or of the Stoic Wise Man. They are not images of fulfillment, they only stimulate man's desire to rise above himself.

Something else again is orientation by the honored and beloved historical figure. We may ask: What would he say in this case, how would he act? And we enter into a living discussion with him, though without regarding him as the absolutely true model to be imitated unconditionally. For each man is a man, and therefore lives in finiteness and imperfection, and also in error.

All ideals of man are impossible, because man's potentialities are infinite. There can be no perfect man. This has important philosophical consequences.

1. The true value of man lies not in the species or type that he approximates, but in the historical individual, for whom no substitution or replacement is possible. The value of each individual man can be regarded as unassailable only when men cease to be regarded as expendable material, to be stamped by a universal. The social and professional types that we approximate have bearing only on our role in the world.

2. The idea that all men are equal is obviously false, in so far as psychological aptitudes and talents are concerned,—it is also untrue considered as the reality of a social order, in which at best there can be equal opportunities and equity before the law.

The essential equality of all men lies alone in those depths, where to each man the road is opened by freedom to attain to God by leading an ethical life. It is the equality of a value that no human knowledge can ascertain or objectify, of the individual as an eternal soul. It is the equality of rights, and of the eternal judgment according to which a man merits a place in heaven or hell. This equality means: a respect for every man which forbids that any man should be treated only as a means and not at the same time as an end in himself.

The danger facing man is the self-assurance which tells him that he already is what he is capable of becoming. The faith by which he finds the road of his potentialities, becomes then a possession that concludes his road, whether it take the form of moral self-complacency or of pride in his innate gifts.

From the Stoic view that man should live so as to be pleasing to himself, to the harmony with himself that Kant ascribes to the man who acts in an ethical way, there has prevailed an arbitrary self-complacency, to which St. Paul and St. Augustine, indeed Kant himself opposed the idea of man corrupted in the root.

The essential is that man as existence in his freedom should experience the fact of being given to himself by transcendence. Then human freedom is at the heart of all his potentialities and through transcendence, through the one, man is guided to his own inner unity.

This *guidance* is radically different from any guidance in the world; for it offers no objective certainty; it coincides with man's complete attainment of freedom. For it operates only by way of the freedom of subjective certainty. God's voice resides in the light that comes as his own conviction to the individual open to tradition and his environment. God's voice becomes audible in the freedom of subjective conviction, and this is the only organ by which it can impart itself to man. Where man's resolve arises out of his depths, he believes that he is obeying God, though he has no objective guaranty for his knowledge of God's will.

Guidance operates through man's judgment concerning his own acts. This judgment checks him and spurs him on, corrects and confirms. But in fact, man can never wholly and definitively base his judgment concerning himself upon himself. He desires to hear the judgment of his fellow men, in order to attain clarity through communication. But the crucial judgment is not in the last analysis that of the people he esteems, although this is the only judgment that is accessible to him in practice. The decisive judgment would be that of God.

Thus in time the truth of judgment is ultimately attained only by way of subjective conviction, whether the moral law claims universal or only historical validity.

Inward obedience to the freely accepted, universal ethical law—to the ten commandments—is bound up with the realization that transcendence is present in this very freedom.

But since specific action cannot logically be deduced from the universal law, God's guiding voice can be heard more directly in the primal source of the historically concrete law than in the universal. But for all the subjective certainty this voice gives, its meaning remains uncertain. Obedience to God's voice always involves the risk of error. For its message is susceptible to many interpretations, the freedom that would consist in the clear and unmistakable knowledge of the necessary, is never complete. The risk implied in the question of whether in this matter I am really myself, whether I have truly heard the guiding voice from the primal spring of being, never ceases.

In time, this consciousness of risk remains the condition for increasing freedom. It excludes complete reliance on subjective certainty, forbids the generalization of the subjective commandment into a universal law, and bars fanaticism. Even in the certainty of the resolve, there must, in so far as it is translated into practical action, remain a certain margin of indetermination. There can be no subjective security. The pride of the absolute truth destroys truth in the world. The humility of the permanent question is inherent in subjective certainty. For it is always possible that things will subsequently look quite different. Even the clear, but never adequately clear conscience, can embark on error.

Only in retrospect are we justified in admiring the unfathomable wisdom of God's guidance. But even then it is never certain, God's unfathomable guidance can never become a possession.

From the psychological point of view, God's voice has no other expression in time than man's judgment of himself. This judgment may come upon man with a sudden certainty, after man has honestly and carefully striven for it, weighing all the contradictory possibilities; and then he discovers in it God's judgment, though it is never definitive and always equivocal. But only in exalted moments is it audible. It is by such moments and for such moments that we live.

The road of the thinking man is a philosophical life. Philosophizing is a specifically human pursuit. Man is the only being in the world to whom being is manifested through his empirical existence. He cannot fulfill himself in empirical existence as such, he cannot content himself with the enjoyment of empirical existence. He breaks through all the empirical realities that find their seeming fulfillment in the world. As a man he only attains to real knowledge of himself when, open to being as a whole, he relates his life in the world to transcendence. In the very effort to master his empirical existence, he strives toward being. For he cannot adequately account for his sojourn in the world by the laws immanent to the world. Accordingly, he goes beyond his empirical existence, beyond the world, to the ground of existence and the world, where he attains awareness of his primal source. Here, though in a sense he is in communion with creation, he does not find a secure refuge, nor is he at his goal. He must seek eternity in his life, which mediates between the primal source and the goal.

In unfaith the human condition becomes a biological fact among other biological facts; man surrenders to what his finite knowledge determines as necessities and inevitabilities, he gives in to a sense of futility, the energy of his mind declines. He stifles in his supposed factuality.

Philosophical faith, on the other hand, is the faith of man in his potentialities. In it breathes his freedom.

God

Thomas Aquinas   ## 38. GOD: THE END OF ALL

The relation between God and all other realities is described by St. Thomas, in the following passage, in the Aristotelian terms of final causality. In distinction to the purely Aristotelian version, however, with its stress on

This selection is excerpted from chapters xvi–xx of the *Summa Contra Gentiles*.

immanent self-perfection, St. Thomas explains this relation by means of both immanent and transcendent elements.

Among all the causes, he says, that of finality is the chief and primary cause because it denotes both the goal of any entity and the reason for the initiation of that entity. God is both the *reason for which* everything comes to be and the *goal toward which* everything is ultimately drawn.

The immanent element in his explanation consists in the fact that everything "naturally" desires and seeks its own self-perfection and goodness; the transcendent element, in the fact that God is Himself the seat of goodness, and "the end of things as something to be obtained by each thing in its own way." Thus, all things tend to God as their last end "so as to acquire His Goodness." The only way in which a thing can be said to be good is by its participation in Goodness, just as the only way in which a thing can be said to be a being is by participating in being.

Creatures achieve being and goodness according to their rank in reality: "To be and to be good are not the same absolutely, although each one is good inasmuch as it exists." In creatures, "other things" besides being are required for their perfection. In God, by contrast, *to be* and *to be good* are absolutely one. Thus, all things tend toward God in proportion to their status in reality and seek to imitate Him so far as they are able.

. . . THE END HOLDS the primary place among causes, and it is from it that all other causes derive their actual causality; since the agent does not act except for the end, as was proved. Now it is due to the agent that the matter is made actually the matter, and the form is made the form, of this particular thing, through the agent's action, and consequently through the end. The later end also is the cause that the preceding end is intended as an end; for a thing is not moved towards a proximate end except for the sake of the last end. Therefore the last end is the first cause of all. Now it must necessarily befit the First Being, namely God, to be the first cause of all, as we proved above. Therefore God is the last end of all.

Hence it is written (*Prov.* xvi. 4): *The Lord hath made all things for himself;* and (*Apoc.* xxii. 13.), *I am Alpha and Omega, the first and the last.*

How God Is the End of Things

It remains to ask how God is the end of all things. This will be made clear from what has been said.

For He is the end of all things, yet so as to precede all in being. Now there is an end which, though it holds the first place in causing in so far as it is in the intention, is nevertheless last in execution. This applies to any end which the agent establishes by his action. Thus the physician by his action establishes health in the sick man, which is nevertheless his end. There is also an end which, just as it precedes in causing, so also does it precede in being. Thus, that which one intends to acquire by one's motion or action is said to be one's end. For instance, fire seeks to reach a higher place by its movement, and the king seeks to take a city by fighting. Accordingly, God is the end of things as something to be obtained by each thing in its own way.

Again. God is at once the last end of things and the first agent, as we have shown. Now the end effected by the agent's action cannot be the first agent, but rather is it the agent's effect. God, therefore, cannot be the end of things as though He were something effected, but only as something already existing and to be acquired.

Further. If a thing act for the sake of something already in existence, and if by its action some result ensue, then something through the agent's action must accrue to the thing for the sake of which it acts; and thus soldiers fight for the cause of the captain, to whom victory accrues, which the soldiers bring about by their actions. Now nothing can accrue to God from the action of anything whatever, since His goodness is perfect in every way, as we proved in the First Book. It follows, then, that God is the end of things, not as something made or effected by them, nor as though He obtained something from things, but in this way alone, that He is obtained by them.

Moreover. The effect must tend to the end in the same way as the agent acts for the end. Now God, who is the first agent of all things, does not act as though He gained something by His action, but as bestowing something thereby; since He is not in potentiality so that He can acquire something, but solely in perfect actuality, whereby He is able to bestow. Things therefore are not ordered to God as to an end to which something will be added; they are ordered to Him to obtain God Himself from Him according to their measure, since He is their end.

That All Things Tend to Be Like unto God

From the fact that they acquire the divine goodness, creatures are made like unto God. Therefore, if all things tend to God as their last end, so as to acquire His goodness, it follows that the last end of things is to become like unto God.

Moreover. The agent is said to be the end of the effect in so far as the effect tends to be like the agent; and hence it is that *the form of the generator is the end of the act of generation*. Now God is the end of things in such wise as to be also their first producing cause. Therefore all things tend to a likeness to God, as their last end.

Again. Things give evidence that *they naturally desire to be;* so that if any are corruptible, they naturally resist corruptives, and tend to where they can be safeguarded, as the fire tends upwards and earth downwards. Now all things have being in so far as they are like God, Who is self-subsistent being, since they are all beings only by participation. Therefore all things desire as their last end to be like God.

Further. All creatures are images of the first agent, namely God, since *the agent produces its like*. Now the perfection of an image consists in representing the original by a likeness to it, for this is why an image is made. Therefore all things exist for the purpose of acquiring a likeness to God, as for their last end.

Again. Each thing by its movement or action tends to some good as its end, as was proved above. Now a thing partakes of good in so far as it is like to the first goodness, which is God. Therefore all things, by their movements and action, tend to a likeness to God as to their last end.

How Things Imitate the Divine Goodness

From what has been said it is clear that the last end of all things is to become like God. Now, that which has properly the nature of an end is the good. Therefore, properly speaking, things tend to become like to God inasmuch as He is good.

Now, creatures do not acquire goodness in the way in which it is in God, even though each thing imitates the divine goodness according to its own manner. For the divine goodness is simple, being, as it were, all in one. For the divine being contains the whole fullness of perfection, as we proved in the First Book. Therefore, since a thing is good so far as it is perfect, God's being is His perfect goodness; for in God, to be, to live, to be wise, to be happy, and whatever else is seen to pertain to perfection and goodness, are one and the same in God, as though the sum total of His goodness were God's very being. Again, the divine being is the substance of the existing God. But this cannot be so in other things. For it was proved in the Second Book that no created substance is its own being. Therefore, if a thing is good so far as it is, and if no creature is its own being, none is its own goodness, but each one is good by participating in goodness, even as by participating in being it is a being.

Also. All creatures are not placed on the same level of goodness. For in some the substance is both form and actuality: such, namely, as are competent, by the mere fact that they exist, to be actually and to be good. But in others, the substance is composed of matter and form, and such are competent to be actually and to be good, though it is by some part of their being, namely, their form. Accordingly, God's substance is His goodness, whereas a simple substance participates in goodness by the very fact that it exists, and a composite substance participates in goodness by some part of itself.

In this third degree of substances, diversity is to be found again in respect of being. For in some substances composed of matter and form, the form fills the entire potentiality of matter, in such a way that the matter retains no potentiality to another form, and consequently neither is there in any other matter a potentiality to this same form. Such are the heavenly bodies, which exhaust their entire matter.—In others, the form does not fill the whole potentiality of matter, so that the matter retains a potentiality to another form, and in another part of matter there remains potentiality to this form; for instance in the elements and their compounds. Since, then, privation is the absence in substance of what can be in substance, it is clear that, together with this form which does not fill the whole potentiality of matter, there is associated the privation of a form, which privation cannot be associated with a substance whose form fills the whole potentiality of matter, nor with that which is a form essentially, and much less with that one whose essence is its very being. And seeing that it is clear that there can be no movement where there is no potentiality to something else, for movement is *the act of that which is in potentiality,* and since evil is the privation of good, it is clear that in this last order of substances, good is changeable, and has an admixture of the opposite evil; which cannot occur in the higher orders of substances. Therefore the substance answering to this last description stands lowest both in being and in goodness.

We find degrees of goodness also among the parts of the substance composed of matter and form. For since matter considered in itself is being in potentiality, and since form is its act; and, again, since a composite substance has actual existence through its form, it follows that the form is, in itself, good, the composite substance is good as having its form actually, and the matter is good as being in potentiality to the form. And although a thing is good in so far as it is a being, it does not follow that matter, which is being only potentially, is only a potential good. For being is predicated absolutely, while good is founded on order, for a thing is said to be good, not merely because it is an end, or possesses the end; but even though it has not attained the end, so long as it is directed to the end, for this very reason it is said to be good. Accordingly, matter cannot be called a being absolutely, in so far as it is a potential being, whereby it is shown to have an order towards being; but this suffices for it to be called a good absolutely, because of this very order. This shows that the good, in a sense, extends further than being; for which reason Dionysius says that *the good includes both existing and non-existing things.* For even non-existent things (namely, matter, considered as subject to privation) seek a good, namely, to exist. Hence it follows that matter is also good, for nothing but the good seeks the good.

In yet another way the creature's goodness falls short of that of God. For, as we have stated, God, in His very being, contains the supreme perfection of goodness. But the creature has its perfection, not in one thing but in many, because what is united in the highest is manifold in the lowest. Therefore, in respect of one and the same thing, virtue, wisdom and operation are predicated of God; but of creatures, they are predicated in respect of different things, and the further a creature is from the first goodness, the more does the perfection of its goodness require to be manifold. And if it be unable to attain to perfect goodness, it will reach to imperfect goodness in a few respects. Hence it is that, although the first and highest good is utterly simple, and although the substances nearest to it in goodness approach likewise thereto in simplicity, yet the lowest substances are found to be more simple than some that are higher. Elements, for instance, are simpler than animals and men, because they are unable to reach the perfection of knowledge and understanding, to which animals and men attain.

From what has been said, it is evident that, although God possess His perfect and entire goodness according to the manner of His simple being, creatures nevertheless do not attain to the perfection of their goodness through their being alone, but through many things. Therefore, although each one is good inasmuch as it exists, it cannot be called good absolutely if it lack other things that are required for its goodness. Thus a man who, being despoiled of virtue, is addicted to vice, is said indeed to be good in a restricted sense, namely, as a being, and as a man; but he is not said to be good absolutely, but rather evil. Accordingly, in every creature to be and to be good are not the same absolutely, although each one is good inasmuch as it exists; whereas in God to be and to be good are absolutely one and the same.

If, then, each thing tends to a likeness to God's goodness as its end; and if a thing is like God's goodness in respect of whatever belongs to its goodness; and if furthermore the goodness of a thing consists not merely in its being, but in whatever is required for its perfection, as we have proved: it is clear that things are directed to God as their end, not only in respect of their substantial being, but also in respect of such things as are accidental thereto and belong to its perfection, as well as in respect of their proper operation, which also belongs to a thing's perfection.

Etienne Gilson   ## 39. GOD: EXISTENTIAL ACT

St. Thomas's approach to the meaning and fact of God's existence, Etienne Gilson
    says, was formulated not merely according to the canon of Aristotle but
    according to the canon of the scriptural words in Exodus, Chapter 3, verse
    14, "I Am Who Am."

From *History of Christian Philosophy in the Middle Ages* by Etienne Gilson. Copyright © 1955 by Etienne Gilson. Reprinted by permission of Random House, Inc.

What did this scriptural text actually mean to St. Thomas? It meant, first of all, that God is Being; which is to say, the act pointed out by the verb "to be." Only in Thomas Aquinas, Gilson says, has Being received "the fullness of its existential meaning." Thus for St. Thomas, God is the Being whose whole nature is to be existential act, whose essence is *esse:* "This is the reason why his most proper name is, HE IS."

The comparison between our knowledge of the being of creatures and the being of God makes this distinction quite evident. A creature is "something that is;" whereas, though we know *that* God is, we do not know *what* He is, "because, in him, there is no what; and since our whole experience is about beings that *have* existence, we cannot figure out what it is to be a being whose only essence is 'to be.'" This is not to say that our knowledge of God is meaningless or irrational; rather, it is "analogical." For "we know that God is, with respect to the universe, in a relation similar to that which obtains . . . between causes and their effects."

The notion that God is the Absolute Act of Being flows from the five Thomistic demonstrations of His existence, which are "both possible and necessary." These five proofs or "ways" argue from the need to explain motion, efficient causality, necessity, the degrees of perfection and order in the world. They share two essential features: the existence of sensible reality, whose existence requires a cause, and the existence of a finite series of causes, which implies the existence of a Prime Cause.

LIKE ALL THEOLOGIES the doctrine of Saint Thomas is dominated by his own notion of God. Like all Christian theologians, he knew that the proper name of God was I AM WHO AM, or HE WHO IS (Exod. 3, 14), but even for men who agreed on the truth of this divine name, there remained a problem of interpretation. Modern philology has a right to investigate the question; naturally, it will find in this text what can be found in any text by means of grammars and dictionaries alone. This is not negligible but, philosophically speaking, it seldom amounts to much. Even with such a limited aim in mind, the grammarians have already achieved amazingly different results. What we are concerned with is very different. Our own problem is to know what meaning the Christian masters have attributed to this famous text. Most of them agreed that it meant: I am Being. But what is being? To Augustine, "who was imbued with the doctrines of the Platonists," being was eternal immutability. To John Damascene, absolute being was an "infinite ocean of entity." To Saint Anselm, it was that whose very nature it is to be: *natura essendi.* In all these cases, the dominating notion was that of "entity" (*essentia*). In the mind of Thomas Aquinas, the notion of being underwent a remarkable transformation; from now on, and so long as we will be dealing with Thomas Aquinas, the deepest meaning of the word "being" will be the act pointed out by the verb "to be." Since, in common human experience, to be is to exist, it can be said that, in the doctrine of Thomas Aquinas, being has received the fullness of its meaning.

In order to avoid all possible confusions with some modern uses of the word "existence," let us add that, in every being, "to be," or *esse,* is not to become; it is not any kind of projection from the present into the future. On the contrary, because it is act, "to be" is something fixed and at rest in being: *esse est aliquid fixum et quietum in ente.* In short, this act is the very core of all that is, inasmuch precisely as what is, is a being.

As Thomas Aquinas understands him, God is the being whose whole nature it is to be such an existential act. This is the reason why his most proper name is, HE IS. After saying this, any addition would be a subtraction. To say that God "is this," or that he "is that," would be to restrict his being to the essences of what "this" and "that" are. God "is," absolutely. Because "what" a thing is usually receives the name of "essence," or of "quiddity" (its "whatness"), some say that since he is "being only" (*esse tantum*), God has no essence or quiddity. Thomas Aquinas does not seem to have favored this way of expressing the purity of the divine act of being. He prefers to say that the essence of God is his *esse.* In other words, God is the being of which it can be said that, what in other beings is their essence, is in it what we call "to be." All the attributes of God are either deducible from this true meaning of his name, or qualified by it.

In our human experience, "being" is "something that is," or exists. Since, in God, there is no something to which existence could be attributed, his own *esse* is precisely that which God is. To us, such a being is strictly beyond all possible representation. We can establish *that* God is, we cannot know *what* he is because, in him, there is no what; and since our whole experience is about things that *have* existence, we cannot figure out what it is to be a being whose only essence is "to be." For this reason, we can prove the truth of the proposition "God is," but, in this unique case, we cannot know the meaning of the verb "is." Such is the Thomistic meaning of the classical doctrine of the ineffability of God.

Unknowable in himself, at least to us and in this life, God can be known by man imperfectly, from the consideration of his creatures. Two things at least are known of him in this way: first, that he is entirely unlike one of his creatures; secondly, that he is in himself at least what he has to be in order to be their cause. For this reason, our knowledge of God is said to be "analogical"; we know that God is, with respect to the universe, in a relation similar to that which obtains, in our human experience, between causes and effects. Such a cognition is not purely negative, since it enables us to say something true about God; it is not wholly positive, and far from it, since not a single one of our concepts, not even that of existence, properly applies to God; we call it "analogical" precisely because it bears upon resemblances between relations, that is, upon proportions.

This notion of God as the absolute act of being flows from the demonstrations of his existence. To demonstrate it is both possible and necessary. It is necessary because the existence of God is not immediately evident; self-evidence would only be possible in this matter if we had an adequate notion of the divine essence; the essence of God would then appear to be one with his existence. But God is an infinite being and, as it has no concept of him, our finite mind cannot see existence as necessarily implied in his infinity; we therefore have to conclude, by way of reasoning, that existence which we cannot intuit. Thus the direct way apparently opened by Saint Anselm's ontological argument is closed to us; but the indirect way which Aristotle has pointed out remains open. Let us therefore seek in sensible things, whose nature is proportioned to our intellect, the starting point of our way to God.

All the Thomistic proofs bring two distinct elements into play: 1) the existence of a sensible reality whose existence requires a cause; 2) the demonstration of the fact that its existence requires a finite series of causes, and consequently a Prime Cause, which is what we call God. Because movement is immediately perceptible to sense knowledge, let us start from the fact that movement exists. The only superiority of this "way" with respect to the other ones, is that its point of departure is the easiest to grasp. All movement has a cause, and that cause must be other than the very being that is in motion; when a thing seems to be self-moving, a certain part of it is moving the rest. Now, whatever it is, the mover itself must be moved by another, and that other by still another. It must therefore be admitted, either that the series of causes is infinite and has no origin, but then nothing explains that there is movement, or else that the series is finite and that there is a primary cause, and this primary cause is precisely what everyone understands to be God.

Just as there is motion in sensible things, there are causes and effects. Now what has just been said of the causes of movement can also be said of causes in general. Nothing can be its own efficient cause, for in order to produce itself, it would have to be anterior, as cause, to itself as effect. Every efficient cause therefore presupposes another, which in turn presupposes another. Now, in this order of causes, in which each higher one is the cause of the lower, it is impossible to go on to infinity, otherwise, there would be neither a first efficient cause, nor intermediate causes, and the effects whose existence we perceive could not possibly exist. There must therefore be a first efficient cause of the series, in order that there may be a middle and a last one, and that first efficient cause is what everyone calls God.

Now let us consider beings themselves. As we know them, they are ceaselessly becoming. Since some of them are being generated, while others are passing away, it is possible for them to be or not to be. Their existence then is not necessary. Now the necessary needs no cause in order to exist; precisely because it is necessary, it exists of itself. But the possible cannot account for its own existence, and if there were absolutely nothing but possibility in things, there would be nothing. This is to say that, since there is something, there must be some being whose existence is necessary. If there are several necessary beings, their series must be finite for the same reason as above. There is therefore a first necessary being, to whose necessity all possible beings owe their existence, and this is what all men call God.

A fourth way goes through the hierarchical degrees of perfection observed in things. There are degrees in goodness, truth, nobility and other perfections of being. Now, more or less are always said with reference to a term of comparison which is absolute. There is therefore a true and a good in itself, that is to say, in the last resort, a being in itself which is the cause of all the other beings and this we call God.

The fifth way rests upon the order of things. All natural bodies, even those which lack knowledge, act for an end. The regularity with which, by and large, they achieve their end, is a safe indication that they do not arrive at it by chance and that this regularity can only be intentional and willed. Since they themselves are without knowledge, someone has to know for them. This primary Intelligent Being, cause of the purpose there is in natural things, is the being we call God.

Since God is first from all points of view and with respect to all the rest, he cannot enter into composition with anything else. The cause of all other beings can enter into composition with none of them. Consequently, God is simple. His simplicity itself has many consequences. Because corporeal bodies are in potency with respect to both motion and being, they are not simple; hence God cannot be corporeal. For the same reason, since he is pure act, God is not composed of matter and form. He is not even a subject endowed with its own form, essence or nature. Divinity is something that God *is,* not that he *has.* But what is such a being which *is* all that he can be said to be, and *has* nothing? He is WHO IS. Since God *is* what other beings only *have,* there is in him no distinct essence to unite with the act of being. This unique being, the only one whose whole essence it is "to be," is so perfectly simple that it is its own being.

If this direct argument seems too abstract to satisfy the intellect, let us remember the conclusions of each one of the five "ways." All particular beings owe their existence to the Prime Cause. Consequently, they receive existence. In other words, what they are (i.e., their essence) receives from God the existence which it has. On the contrary, since the Prime Efficient Cause does not receive its own existence (otherwise it would not be prime) there is no sense in which it can be said to be distinct from it. If there were such a thing as a pure and absolute "fire," it would not *have* the nature of fire, it would *be* it. Similarly, God is not really "being"; he is the very act of what we call "to be." He does not share in it, he is it. Naturally, since we have no experience of this unique being, our mind is unable to conceive it and our language has no perfectly fitting words to express it. From the very first moment we attempt to say what God is, we must content ourselves with saying that he is not in the same way as other things are. As has already been said, we do not know what it is for God "to be"; we only know that it is true to say that God is.

The metaphysician thus joins, by reason alone, the philosophical truth hidden in the name that God himself has revealed to man: I AM WHO AM (Exod. 3, 14). God is the pure act of existing, that is, not some essence or other, such as the One, or the Good, or Thought, to which might be attributed existence in addition; not even a certain eminent way of existing, like Eternity, Immutability or Necessity, that could be attributed to his being as characteristic of the divine reality; but Existing itself (*ipsum esse*) in itself and without any addition whatever, since all that could be added to it would limit it in determining it. If he is pure Existing, God is by that very fact the absolute Plenitude of being; he is therefore infinite. If he is infinite Being, he can lack nothing that he should acquire; no change is conceivable in him; he is therefore sovereignly immutable and eternal, and so with other perfections that can be fittingly attributed to him. Now, it is fitting to attribute all of them to him, for, if absolute act of existing is infinite, it is so in the order of being; it is therefore perfect.

Such is the cause of the many deficiencies of the language in which we express him. This God whose existence we affirm, does not allow us to fathom what he is; he is infinite, and our minds are finite; we must therefore take as many exterior views of him as we can, without ever claiming to exhaust the subject. A first way of proceeding consists in denying everything about the divine essence that could not belong to it. By successively removing from the idea of God movement, change, passivity, composition, we end by positing him as an immobile, immovable being, perfectly in act and absolutely simple; this is the way of negation. But one can take a second way and try to name God according to the analogies obtaining between him and things. There is necessarily a connection and consequently a resemblance between cause and effect. When the cause is infinite and the effect finite, it obviously cannot be said that the properties of the effect are found in it such as they are in the cause, but what exists in effects must also be pre-existent in their cause, whatever its manner of existing. In this sense, we attribute to God all the perfections of which we have found some shadow in the creature, but we carry them to the infinite. Thus we say that God is perfect, supremely good, unique, intelligent, omniscient, voluntary, free and all-powerful, each of these attributes being reduced in the last analysis, to an aspect of the infinite and perfectly single perfection of the pure act that God is.

W. T. Stace   40. THE UNPROVABILITY

OF GOD

Attempts to demonstrate, by necessary reasons, the existence of God are both
foolhardy and illogical, Professor Stace flatly asserts. That God exists and
is not without witness, is not questioned. But His existence cannot be
"proved," and His witness is not logic and inference but intuitive revelation.
The reason that logic fails to betray the divine existence, Stace contends,
is that logic is incapable of transcending its own proper realm. Man and
his logic are inhabitants of the natural order of things, whereas God persists
in the eternal order. No logical transit can therefore be made from one
order to the other. All arguments from causality and purpose in the universe
fail to meet the requirements of the issue, since these remain within the
natural order. Arguments from the fact of miracle, which by definition
emanates from the divine order, also fail to meet the requirements of the
issue. Miracle remains within the divine order and cannot be demonstrated
in the natural order. In each case, a leap over and beyond logic is required.

Now inference cannot make such a leap from one order to the other and
still remain inference. When we speak of inference, we speak of the relation
between "premise" facts and "consequence" facts. The only result from
premise facts of the natural order are consequence facts of the natural
order. For "if I start from a natural fact, my inferential process, however
long, can end only in another natural fact." Nor can it be said that the end
of a finite series of facts must lead me to a divine First Cause, since
"a first cause *would not be God*." To argue in such fashion is to
make God one among other things in the world and, consequently, finite.

All of this simply means, Stace argues, that in order to arrive at a knowledge of God, who exists in the divine order, one must begin *with* God and
with the divine order. One cannot conceptualize one's way there. Indeed,
were one to argue from the existence of grades of perfection and order
in the world as an indication of God's existence, one would have to face
up to the classic rejoinder of scepticism, that there are just as many dis-
orders and imperfections in the world and, behind every blessing, there is
a plague.

The fact is, Stace concludes, the so-called traditional proofs of God's
existence mistake *symbolic,* for *literal,* truths. Their effect "is to drag down
the divine and the eternal from their own sphere into the sphere of the
natural and the temporal." Consequently, there can be no such valid
knowledge as that alleged to be given by any natural theology.

THE PURE RELIGIOUS CONSCIOUSNESS lies in a region which is forever beyond all proof or disproof.

This is a necessary consequence of the "utterly other" character of God from the world, and of the "utterly other" character of the world from God. The eternal order is not the natural order, and the natural order is not the eternal order. The two orders intersect, but in the intersection each remains what it is. Each is wholly self-contained. Therefore it is impossible to pass, by any logical inference, from one to the other. This at once precludes as impossible any talk either of the proof or disproof of religion.

When philosophers and theologians speak of the "proofs of the existence of God," or "evidences of Christianity," what they have in mind is always a logical passage from the natural order, or some fact in the natural order, to the divine order. They may, for instance, argue in the following way. Here is the world. That is a natural fact. It must have had a cause. Other natural facts are then pointed out which are supposed to show adaptations of means to ends in nature. Bees pollinate flowers. Surely not by chance, nor following any purpose of their own. Or the heart has the function—which is interpreted as meaning the purpose—of pumping the blood. This teleological mechanism was not made by us, and the purpose evident in it is not our purpose. Therefore the cause of the world must have been an intelligent and designing mind. Doubtless I have much over-simplified the argument, and this version of it might not be accepted by the theologian as a statement of it which is to his liking. Certainly it is not a full statement. That, however, is not the point. The point is that, however the argument is stated, it necessarily starts from the natural order, and ends with a conclusion about the divine reality.

In other cases the natural fact from which the argument starts may be some very astonishing occurrence, which we do not yet know how to explain, and which we therefore call a miracle. This is evidence, it is believed, of a divine intervention.

In all cases we use some fact or facts of the natural order as premises for our argument, then leap, by an apparently logical inference, clear out of the natural order into the divine order, which thus appears as the conclusion of the argument. The point is that the premise is in the natural world, the conclusion in the divine world.

But an examination of the nature of inference shows that this is an impossible procedure. For inference proceeds always along the thread of some relation. We start with one fact, which is observed. This bears some relation to another fact, which is not observed. We pass along this relation to the second fact. The first fact is our premise, the second fact our conclusion. The relation, in the case of the deductive inference, is that of logical entailment. In nondeductive inferences other relations are used, of which the most common is that of causality. Thus, although the sun is now shining, and the sky is cloudless, I see that the ground is wet, and the trees are dripping with water. I infer that an April shower has passed over, and that it rained a few minutes ago. My inference has passed along the thread of a causal relation from an effect as premise to a cause as conclusion. To pass in this way from facts which are before my eyes, along a relational link, to other facts which are not before my eyes—which are inferred, not seen—is the universal character of inference.

But the natural order is the totality of all things which stand to each other in the one systematic network of relationships which is the universe. Therefore no inference can ever carry me from anything in the natural order to anything outside it. If I start from a natural fact, my inferential process, however long, can end only in another natural fact. A "first cause," simply by virtue of being a cause, would be a fact in the natural order. It is not denied that it might conceivably be possible to argue back from the present state of the world to an intelligent cause of some of its present characteristics—although I do not believe that any such argument is in fact valid. The point is that an intelligent cause of the material world, reached by any such inference, would be only another natural being, a part of the natural order. The point is that such a first cause *would not be God.* It would be at the most a demi-urge. I shall return to this point later.

If God does not lie at the end of any telescope, neither does He lie at the end of any syllogism. I can never, starting from the natural order, prove the divine order. The proof of the divine order must lie, somehow, within itself. It must be its own witness. For it, like the natural order, is complete in itself, self-contained.

But if, for these reasons, God can never be proved by arguments which take natural facts for their premises, for the very same reason He can never be disproved by such arguments. For instance, He cannot be disproved by pointing to the evil and pain in the world.

But if, by arguments of the kind we are considering, the divine order can never be proved, nevertheless God is not without witness. Nor is His being any the less a certainty. But the argument for anything within the divine order must start from within the divine order. The divine order, however, is not far off. It is not beyond the stars. It is within us—as also within all other things. God exists in the eternal moment which is in every man, either self-consciously present and fully revealed, or buried, more or less deeply, in the unconscious. We express this in poetic language if we say that God is "in the heart." It is in the heart, then, that the witness of Him, the proof of Him, must lie and not in any external circumstance of the natural order. So far as theology is concerned we had better leave the bees and their pollination of flowers alone.

That the divine cannot be made the subject of proof is merely another aspect of the truth that the mystical illumination is incapable of conceptualization. For this means that God is inaccessible to the logical intellect. The attempt to prove His existence is an attempt to reach Him through concepts, and is therefore foredoomed to failure. The doctrine of the negative divine implies the same conclusion. For its meaning is that the door to an understanding of God is barred against the concept, and therefore against logical argument. And all this comes to the same as saying that God is known only by intuition, not by the logical intellect.

The great error of the traditional proofs of the existence of God is that they take a symbolic truth for a literal truth, a truth of fact, and then try to prove that it is a fact. The religious doctrine speaks of God as a mind or person, purposively controlling the world for good ends, and filled with love for men and all creatures. This symbolic language is taken as stating literal facts, and then "evidences" of these facts are sought. The results are invariably disastrous for religion. The evidences are torn to shreds by the sceptic without difficulty, and it then seems to all the world as if religion has been destroyed, although, if religion were truly understood, it would be seen that it emerges entirely unscathed from these sceptical attacks.

For instance, it is desired to prove that God is good and loves His creatures. The only possible "evidences" for this, to be found in the natural order, will consist in the various "blessings" which men undoubtedly enjoy—in other words, the various good things which the world contains and the happiness which men often experience. But if these are pointed out, all the sceptic has to do is to point to the evil and misery in the world, most of which cannot by any conceivable stretch of imagination be attributed to man's own fault, although some can. (Presumably none of the agony suffered by animals can be thought of as due to their fault.) This is evidence on the other side, and entirely destroys the religious argument. For the conclusion which that argument seeks to reach is not that God is partly good, and partly evil, which is what would follow from an impartial balancing of the good and evil things in the world, but that God is wholly good. The only refuge of the religious man will consist in saying that, while the good in the world is evidence for God's goodness, the evil in the world is not evidence of His badness, but only of the fact that the existence of evil is for man a mystery and an insoluble problem. But obviously, from the point of view of logical argument, to which the religious man has foolishly committed himself, he cannot be allowed thus to quote the evidence which is in his favor, while refusing to take any account of the evidence against him, under the pretext that it is a mystery.

These defects come upon religious men because they take their doctrines to be literal statements of fact, and therefore amenable to proof by argument. It must now be added that these attempts at proof not only fail of their purpose, and so do no good to religion, but that they positively degrade it. For their effect is to drag down the divine and the eternal from their own sphere into the sphere of the natural and temporal. As has already been pointed out many times, if we argue back along the chain of causes to a first cause, and call this first cause God, we thereby make Him merely one among other things in the world, that is, in the natural order. All the other alleged proofs have the same effect. They thus make God finite. For the natural order is the order of finite things. If God is related to other things as their cause, then He is finite, since the otherness of these other things limits His being. This is the result of taking God's causality in a literal sense—in the sense, that is, in which we say that heat is the cause of the boiling of water. This also places God in time, because the causal relation is a time relation. But if the causality of God is taken symbolically, then it plainly cannot be proved by going backwards along the causal chain, since this procedure implies the literal understanding of the causal concept.

It is a logical impossibility to pass by inference from the natural order to the divine order. But it is not, of course, a logical impossibility to pass from one thing in the natural order to another. Therefore it is not a logical impossibility that there should be evidences of a vast mind running the affairs of nature. All sorts of purely naturalistic suggestions of this kind are possible. We cannot be sure that the human mind is the largest in the universe. Nor are disembodied minds a logical impossibility. The earth might therefore be presided over by a great invisible mind, who might take orders from a still greater mind in charge of the solar system. This spirit might in turn be subordinate to another spirit which supervises the galaxy. The solar system might be a single atom—the earth a single electron spinning round the nucleus —in the blood stream of some vast animal, whose body is the entire material universe. Such fantasies could conceivably be true. But they are superstitions nonetheless, because they are groundless, gratuitous, and lacking in any foundation of evidence. The point, however, is that no such vast mind running the universe, or a part of the universe, however enormous, magnificent, powerful, intelligent, good, it might be, could be God. For it would be merely another natural being, a part of the natural order, or perhaps the whole of it. God so thought of is a superstition, a gigantic and perhaps benevolent ghost, an immense, disembodied, and super-earthly clergyman. And some such superstition is what is implied by all the supposed proofs of His existence.

We return to our position that there is no logical reasoning which will carry us from the natural order to the divine order. There is no such thing as natural theology. God is either known by revelation—that is to say, by intuition—or not at all. And revelation is not something which took place in the past. It takes place in every moment of time, and in every heart—although it reaches a climactic moment in the illumination of the great mystic.

James Collins   41. GOD AND MODERN
                               PHILOSOPHY

A realist philosophy must admit that God is both known and unknown, for there
are ways we can, and ways we cannot, know God. In this essay Professor
Collins shows how this is possible.

In the first place, he points out, we must qualify what we mean by
"demonstrations for the existence of God." We certainly cannot mean any
a priori proof that proceeds from the *idea* of God to His existence. Nor
can we mean that we prove that existence. What we can prove, however,
is the truth of our proposition affirming that existence. This proof we can
base formally, through the use of analogical predication, "upon the
evidence available to our natural intelligence."

In the second place, we must observe that by the use of analogical
predication we verify propositions about God not in a purely experiential,
nor in a purely inferential, process but in "an experiential-and-inferential
manner—that is, both by making direct acquaintance with some finite
things (by analyzing them in their composing principles of being) and by
carrying out the causal inference on this basis."

Existent things provide two principal ways to enable us to frame propositions about God. First, "they furnish the experiential warrent for the
validity of our causal inference leading to the proposition that God exists";
but second, they evidence the essential limitation of our knowledge,
indicating that the full mystery of the divine is not exposed to our intellectual penetration.

Any proof of God's existence that puts the question on an "all or nothing"
basis—that is, either that we have an essential insight, and clear intuition,
into God, or else that we know nothing of Him—errs in emphasis, if not
in logic. There is a third alternative, and this is that we can rationally and
validly be aware of the truth of the proposition affirming the divine
existence, but, at the same time, that we are rationally limited in proceeding
beyond this proposition. The known God and the unknown God are thus
not mutually contradictory.

LIKE THINKERS in any other age, modern philosophers have felt the attraction of making flat statements that either we have essential insight into the

divine being or we know nothing at all about God. Invariably, the function of critical intelligence has been to force qualifications to be placed upon these extreme statements. It is not primarily a question of degree: we can know a little about God, but not everything; rather, it is a question of kind: there are ways in which we can know God and ways in which we cannot know Him.

One way to achieve balance on this question is to clarify the meaning of the elusive words "proof of God's existence." They can mean either that the outcome of the inference is God's own act of existing or that it is the truth of our proposition concerning His act of existing. In order to sustain the former interpretation, the philosopher must proportion his mind to the divine existence itself, either through an immediate intuition of it or through seeing it flow from the divine essence or some attribute. This is the a priori path leading to the ontological argument, whose chief inconvenience for theists is (as Vico once noted) that it makes us gods of God. His existence is treated as the outcome of our process of reasoning, which proves His existence from a plane of metaphysical equality as we might solve an equation, discover an island, or produce a new compound. When this rationalist meaning for a proof of God's existence is also applied to a study of the divine essence, it has similarly disconcerting consequences. Sometimes even those who use the a posteriori proof of God's existence nevertheless approach His essence by way of a deduction from some privileged divine attribute or name. To do so in any fashion except verbally, however, would require a direct ordination of the human mind to some aspect of the divine essence instead of to finite beings.

The results of this kind of discourse about God are bound to be pretentious, despite personal disclaimers, since the method itself supposes a mode of knowing which surpasses our human state. From the older Samuel Butler and Voltaire onward, there has been a steady stream of satire directed against what William James once dubbed "the closet-naturalists of the deity," those who are methodologically forced to claim some familiarity with the divine essence. It is well to let Butler's acid portrait of the all too knowlegeable systematist sink home.

> He could raise Scruples dark and nice,
> And after solve 'em in a trice:
> As if Divinity had catch'd
> The Itch, of purpose to be scratch'd.

It is just such an attitude toward the study of God which has led the contemporary Calvinist theologian, Karl Barth, to regard any independent, philosophical doctrine on God as blasphemous and destructive of our sense of the divine majesty. And it has led Paul Tillich to seek God as the ground or power of being, lying beyond the idolatrous God of this finitizing and thingifying conception of theism, and to balance off every theistic statement with its atheistic counterpart. Yet the outstanding question which remains is whether there is a kind of philosophical theism that avoids the rationalist position and yet bases assent to its propositions about God formally upon the evidence available to our natural intelligence, even when suggestions from revelation are considered.

To open the trail toward the realist philosophy of God, the other meaning for "proof of God's existence" must be examined. What is proved is not the divine act of existing but the truth of our human proposition affirming that God or the purely actual being exists. The demonstrative work in philosophy of God does not proceed by placing the divine act of existing under the microscope or bringing it within range of some metaphysical telescope but by testing the evidence for or against the validity of our proposition that God exists. This evidence does not come from any direct sight of God's existential act and essential nature. A humanly developed philosophy of God must examine the structure of the existing sensible thing of our experience, discover its intrinsic composition and causal dependence in being for its concrete act of existing, and in this way infer the truth of the proposition that there exists a first, purely actual cause of this being. The causal inference terminates not in a view of the divine act of existing itself but in the humanly concluded knowledge that the proposition "The purely actual being and first cause, God, exists" is well founded and true. The realistic proof gives knowledge about the existing God, but not by using the divine act of existing as the conclusion of the inference itself. This is the most radical level at which one can see the nonfunctional approach of realistic theism to God.

With the help of the basic inferential proposition about the existing God and a further inspection of the concrete finite existents of our experience, we can discover compelling grounds for inferring the truth of some future propositions about God by way of causal source, negation of imperfect ways of existing and thinking, and the transcendent actuality proper to the infinite existent. But in none of these efforts at obtaining further warranted statements about God does a realistic theism proceed on the basis of making the divine act of existing serve our purposes or by using a claim to direct insight into the divine essence or some special attribute as a middle term of proof. Philosophy of God remains a thoroughly human science in its method, source of evidence, and order of inference. Its propositions about God must base their claim to our assent upon the findings of causal analysis of finite sensible beings and upon the causal analogy and other analogical inferences required both by these things and by the truth of the fundamental proposition that the infinitely actual being and first cause exists.

An integral part of realistic theism is a methodology of how its propositions are meant and what limits they must respect. This is the task of the theory of analogical predication, which requires that our propositions about God respect the difference, as well as the similarity, in respect to the ways in which the infinite being and composed, finite beings exist and have their actuality. The purpose of a doctrine on analogy is not to achieve a studied ambiguity concerning the perfections predicated about God but to render the propositions stating such predications as precise as possible. It is regulated by the analysis of our human condition of inference and discourse about God when the human inquirer is seeking to ascertain the truth or falsity of his propositions about the infinitely actual being through a causal inference from finite existents within his range of experience.

By the very situation and direction of such an inquiry, the underlying sort of analogy must be of a causal sort. Our propositions about God can be determined as true by showing their connection of causal implication with what we know about composed finite beings in our world. The verification of propositions about God is neither purely experiential nor purely inferential. If it were experiential alone, then it would either concern only the finite things of our acquaintance or it would suppose an intuition of the divine actuality. If it were inferential alone, it would proceed from some deductive premise grounded in an intuition of God or it would be purely formal and definitional, thus lacking in existential import. The truth of our propositions about God is determined, on the contrary, in an unavoidably compound way or through a joint process of experience and inference. The verification proceeds in an experiential-and-inferential manner, that is, both by making direct acquaintance with some finite things (by analyzing them in their composing principles of being) and by carrying out the causal inference on this basis. Hence in the order of human inquiry about God, the causal analogy is the fundamental approach for a realistic mode of establishing the truth of our propositions bearing on God. There are other kinds of analogy which can be brought into play once the claim of our proposition that God exists is shown to be an evidenced one. These additional analogical significations are required both because of the complexity and diversity of finite things and because of the truth about the purely actual being of God. In the philosophical order, however, their demonstrative force is owed to these controlling sources in experience and in the primary existential inference about God rather than to any autonomous validity. Precisely because of their intrinsic dependence on the causal inference, they differ from what we ordinarily call loose analogies, comparisons, and metaphors. The kind of analogy considered by Hume and Kant is a comparison which is not grounded in and controlled by a more basic causal inference, whereas in a realistic philosophy of God, the condition for valid employment of every proposed analogical predication is its relation with the true proposition that God exists, as established from intrinsic analysis of, and causal inference from, sensible existing beings.

Just as the philosophy of God must include a theory of analogy, so must it make explicit reference to the limits under which it develops. St. Augustine culminates his quest of God with a *pia confessio ignorantiae*, a humble acknowledgment that God is above everything he can say and think about Him, and, indeed, that God is best known by us on earth as being unknown. Similarly, St. Thomas holds that the summit of man's knowledge of God is to know that he does not know God. This is not the same as saying that man knows that God does not exist, or that he knows nothing about God, or that he must remain silent about Him. It means that once a man becomes fully aware of the natural source and mode of his inferences about God, he also recognizes that God, in His infinite actuality, always surpasses anything we can say about Him. To know in a human and philosophical way the truth of our propositions about God includes knowing the truth that the infinite actuality is really other than, and transcendent of, the finite beings which nevertheless constitute our sole philosophical routes to God. These existent things serve faithfully as *viae,* or ways, of knowing about God and do so in a twofold sense. For one thing, they furnish the experiential warrant for the validity of our causal inference leading to the proposition that God exists. Hence acceptance of this proposition as true is the outcome of an inference rather than an intuitive leap from nature to the beyond. Yet precisely in supplying the demonstrative ground for the theistic assent, the composed existents of our experience also yield the truth that God is not submitted in His own unlimited act of existing to our thought, since our philosophical approach to Him never ceases to be causally inferential or dependent upon the finite beings which are under analysis. This guards against the inclination to exploit the very being of God for the human purposes of either a speculative or a practical functionalism.

The theme of the unknown God runs contrapuntally throughout modern philosophy, especially since it is responsive to the Judaeo-Christian tradition. The wide variations in its interpretations indicate, however, that the individual minds have been rethinking and assessing it in keeping with their other philosophical and theological positions. Within the realistic context, it must be correlated with the meaning suggested for "proof of God's existence." God is both known and unknown by us. He is known in that we can determine the truth of certain propositions about Him in an experiential-inferential way; this removes the extreme claim of agnosticism and of atheism, whether of the emphatic or the unemphatic variety. God is unknown in that none of the finite things from which we draw our knowledge gives us a vision of His divine being in its own infinite actuality; this removes the extreme claim of the functionalists and dialectical monists, the ontologists and theosophists.

This conception of the philosophy of God avoids Barth's stricture against a blasphemous and idolatrous approach. In the strict sense, it does not permit us to speak about treating God or proving God but only of proving the truth of certain human propositions about God. To use the language of Gabriel Marcel in a different signification, there is a problem of our propositional knowledge about God, and yet this enables us to appreciate the mystery of God in His own being. This combination of problem and mystery conforms to our human condition, just as does the combination of notional and real assent. The problem of our propositions about God leads eventually to a verified notional assent (founded upon a speculative, experiential-causal inference) to their truth, thus encouraging us to give our real assent to the mystery of God's own infinite act of being or personal identity.

The realistic philosophy of the known and unknown God explores finite existents as far as they can lead men toward a knowledge of God, but it does not confuse the resultant human propositions about God with the infinite God in His own act of being. It agrees with Augustine in distinguishing between discovery and judgment in matters concerning God. Our minds "may rightly know the eternal law but may not judge it." Man can discover the truth that God exists and is eternal, but this knowledge does not make the eternal being of God dependent upon the human mind. Hence our inquiry about God does not submit God Himself to our superior judgment but conforms our mind to the truth concerning His infinite being. The philosophical inference to God enables us to know certain true propositions about Him, including the affirmation of His perfect independence in being.

There is no need to seek, with Tillich, for a God beyond the God of theism but only for a philosophical theism for which God is known to be other than all finite existents and conceptions. Apart from reference to the controlling principles of some particular philosophy of God, it is impossible to determine a priori whether God will be finitized and thingified through the predication of actuality and cause to Him or whether this result will follow from regarding Him as being-itself or as the ground and power of being. There can be no wholesale elimination of certain divine names, since each instance has to be considered on its merits and within some definite context of principles of inference and predication, where it will receive its determinate meaning and usage. Since realistic theism includes a definite theory of the analogical predication and limitation of human propositions about God among the dominant principles regulating its use of existence, act, and cause, it has its own safeguards for respecting the divine transcendence and uniqueness as being-itself and as the power of being, since the tradition of Boehme and Schelling carries its own problems about whether God is made functional to a special conception of human experience and history. To show the philosophical validity of his primary naming of God, he must make use of the common standard of relevance to finite things. But this opens the way for a nonsymbolical basis of causal analogy and hence for a procedure that safeguards the being of God otherwise than by a dialectical counterbalancing of symbolic terms.

The Nature of the Philosophy of God

There are four widely prevalent views today about the nature of a philosophy of God. The first two are that it is only a memorial surviving from the past, without any footing in the living tendencies of thought, and that it is indeed vital but only as a reflection on the Christian faith and its language. The other two views are that it deals with genuinely philosophical evidence, but only as an integral part of sacred doctrine, and that it is the equivalent of the philosophy of religion. The notion of the philosophy of God which has developed out of the present investigation does not conform exactly with any of these positions. It is only at the end of our study, however, that there is a sufficient inductive basis for showing the differences and thus specifying our historically relevant meaning for a realistic theism.

Those who regard the philosophy of God as a relic of the philosophical and theological past are themselves the heirs of one definite, historical tradition concerning God. Their view is the latest expression of what may be called the archaicizing argument, which was forged during the struggle against Hegel and the general recession from the theory of absolute spirit. Although useful for the original polemical purpose, this argument cannot be taken as a definitive judgment about the philosophy of God. For it rests on the assumption that all philosophical approaches to God can be narrowed down historically to the debate between Hegel and naturalism and that every present-day consideration of evidence must find its interpretative principles in the naturalistic explanation of the logic of inquiry. Since the historical part of this premise oversimplifies the data and since the theoretical part is the point at issue in the realist interpretation of existence, the archaicizing argument cannot stand permanently in the path of a renewed inquiry into the foundations of human knowledge of God.

The fideistic interpretation is sometimes theologically motivated, sometimes the result of philosophical scepticism, and sometimes the conclusion drawn from the phenomenalistic character of the sciences. The philosopher as such cannot deal with the theological grounds in a particular theory of man's Fall, but he can make a critical examination of the claim that all philosophical theories of God must terminate in some kind of idolatry and confusion of the human and the divine. Furthermore, analysis can be made of the contention that all proofs of the truth about God's existence are reducible to the ontological argument, which, in turn, is only a reasoned explication of faith. Both of these consequences of theological fideism clash with the realistic conception of how the human intellect comes to know something about God. Such knowledge does not rest upon analysis of our idea of God and does not confuse this idea with God's own being. When fideism appeals to the phenomenalism of modern scientific knowledge, it joins company with the empiricist and analytic tendency to limit philosophical inquiry to a study of the ordinary and scientific language, apart from any distinctive metaphysical inference. This significant convergence of fideistic and phenomenalistic positions underlines the twofold need of showing that the philosophical study of God is an aspect of the metaphysics of existent being and of making a careful examination of the meaning and limits of scientific methods and the techniques of analysis.

Some of the fundamental metaphysical aspects of a realistic theism are found in St. Thomas, who did his philosophizing within the context of his theology. While this theological orientation is recognized, there remains the question of whether thinkers in our day can develop, in a Thomistic spirit, their own philosophy of God, which is not formally integrated with, and ordered by, sacred doctrine. This can be done as long as one does not claim to be giving a purely historical presentation of the mind of Aquinas or to be doing the work of a theologian. Both the historical and the theological treatments are indispensable, but they do not exhaust the thought of Aquinas in the area of human inquiry about God, many aspects of which he establishes in terms of the philosophical evidence and with a basic respect for the order entailed by that evidence. Today there is a clear need to proceed deliberately and reflectively in developing this tendency into a doctrine on God that is formally and explicitly philosophical, both in its source of data and in its corresponding order of inference.

The same exigency is found when one's main intention is to establish some speculatively certain truths about God for their own sake and to do so within the intellectual setting provided by the modern history of the problem of God and its contemporary status. Such issues as the possibility of any metaphysical knowledge, the warrant in experience for the analysis of finite beings with respect to their essential nature and existential act, the validity of the causal inference and the causal analogy which reach beyond the finite order to the infinite actuality of God, the functional or nonfunctional significance of knowledge of God for one's whole philosophy and the conduct of life, the relations between a doctrine on the transcendent God and the various forms of pantheistic and atheistic monism, the experiential relevance of a theory of God and the role of the idea of God—all these issues have been confronted in the course of the present inquiry and stated in their peculiarly modern and contemporary urgency. They belong properly in the philosophical domain, both in regard to the determining evidence taken from beings within the range of our natural experience and in regard to the order of reasoning which is required to take full advantage of a starting point in sensible existents. To meet these problems adequately, a realistic philosophy of God must not only base itself upon the evidence of finite things available to our human experience but must also develop its findings by means of the distinctively philosophical ordering of inference which moves from sensible beings to God.

The critical analyses advanced throughout the present study point toward a balanced realistic theism whose method is experiential and causal and hence whose order of discovery of truths about God is specified by its point of departure in sensible beings, including the whole reality of man as disclosed to our experience and reflection. With the aid of the causal inference to God, a renewed study can be made of finite things considered now precisely as produced in their existing being by God. Further light can also be thrown upon the basic instruments of theistic analysis: the essential nature and existential act of limited beings, the causal bond, and the relations of analogy. But all such inquiries are indeed *renewed* studies and cast some *further* light; they do not involve any claim to revoke the finite starting point in experience or to begin with God but belong to the return phase of a theistic investigation which began with experienced things and is now coming back to them as related to the inferred truth about God. These further studies can utilize the inferred truth about the existent God, but they are conducted legitimately only within the context of the primary movement from sensible beings to God and upon the basis laid down by our direct metaphysical inspection of the principles of being, the causal relation, and causal analogy as encountered among experienced beings. This radical dependence of theistic philosophical inquiry upon its founding order of discovery is never wiped out, transcended, or otherwise transmuted, whatever deeper understanding of finite beings and of metaphysical principles we gain from coming into possession of the demonstrated truth about the being of God.

Fidelity to the philosophical order of inquiry does not close off any avenue of instruction for a realistic philosophy of God. The theist who is also a Christian remains alertly open to revelation, especially since it conveys some natural truths about God. He acknowledges the influences of his faith in directing his mind toward regions of evidence and classes of problems that might otherwise be slighted or entirely overlooked. Yet as a philosopher, he also has the responsibility to take a direct look at the data, to follow through the suggestions of revelation to the point of making his own inspection of the condition of finite beings and their bearing on a knowledge of God. His philosophical assent to truths about God has to be regulated by the outcome of his personal investigation of the evidence available to human experience of the sensible world and the life of man. Hence he must avoid any confusion between the various sources of his instruction and the ground of validity for his assent to propositions about God, whenever the latter are intended to constitute a philosophical doctrine on God. In this way, he can avoid the two extremes of a total Cartesian divorce between philosophy and the influence of revelation and the fideistic tendency to regard the contribution of revelation as a substitute for finding the evidential basis of theistic truths in our experience and causal inference. In the hands of a Christian theist, a realistic philosophy of God is both responsive to the testimony of faith and responsible for making its own assay of whatever materials can belong within a philosophical doctrine on God. Both the act of assent and the ordering of inferences in a realistic theism depend fundamentally upon philosophical analysis of our experience of man and the sensible world, whatever the sources that actually influence us to make this inspection for implications concerning God.

There are so many widely varying theories about the nature of a philosophy of religion that at present it does not seem possible to determine precisely how such a discipline stands related to a realistic theism. One negative point seems clearly established. If the aim of a particular philosophy of religion is to be a substitute for all metaphysical knowledge of God, then it cannot be reconciled with realistic theism. But the meaning of philosophy of religion need not be arbitrarily restricted to the tradition which developed in the wake of Kant and which consequently despaired of any metaphysics or else turned in desperation to an absolutism of spirit. On the positive side, there is room for a philosophy of religion as a second-level synthesis of the several primary sciences dealing with God and man's relation to Him. It would bring to a common focus the relevant portions of metaphysics, ethics, psychology, and other studies which deal with the bond between God and man. Precisely how this can be done within a philosophy of religion that remains a cognitive synthesis and not itself a practical way of life or substitute for religious worship remains one of the outstanding questions for exploratory trial by realistic theists.

The historical study of the problem of God furnishes some pertinent suggestions, moreover, on the precise relationship between a philosophy of God, a theodicy, and a natural theology. There are serious historical reasons for refusing to make the realistic philosophy of God equivalent to a theodicy. Taken in its determinate Leibnizian meaning, a theodicy claims to make a demonstration of the justice of God through a special appeal to the divine power, the power of essence, and the principle of sufficient reason as a univocal key to moral motivations. Given the actual historical meaning and consequences of such a discipline, it cannot be taken as synonymous with or even reconcilable with a realistic theism. Classical theodicy also has a theological and practical orientation, mingling questions of grace and Scripture with philosophical issues and having a primarily controversial and apologetic aim. If theodicy is taken broadly as a deductive justification of God's way with the world, then it can only come into conflict eventually with a realistic theism which relinquishes all deductive approaches to God, out of respect for both the divine majesty and the integrity of man.

The case is somewhat different with "natural theology," which in some of its senses is the equivalent of the realistic meaning for "philosophy of God." When St. Augustine came to define the term, he distinguished between three types of theology not based on revelation: mythical, political, and physical, or natural. He classified mythical and political theology together as species of conventional or man-made theology, since they study the gods constructed by the poets and by the state. Opposed to conventional theology is natural theology, or the doctrine on God based upon a philosophical study of nature. A theology is natural both with respect to its object (God in His own being, not as subject to human myth-making or political ordinance) and its source of information (the physical world in its real features). In harmony with his own distinction in kind between philosophy and sacred doctrine, St. Thomas recognized a philosophical theology, which is a metaphysical doctrine on God developed through a study of the evidence available to our natural knowing powers and according to the method and order of philosophical reasoning as it moves from finite things to God. Cardinal Newman also regarded the philosophical doctrine on God as a natural theology, both in view of the natural informants, or sources of fact leading to God, and because both pagan and Christian minds can make the inference and the assent to God. A realistic theism is a natural theology if the latter study is conceived in these ways.

But attention must also be paid to at least four modern meanings for "natural theology" which have quite a different tenor. In Calvin's and Francis Bacon's conception of it, there is no way of establishing a philosophical science of God from the study of finite things. A theology is natural, not by having a basis in the physical or metaphysical study of the finite world, but by reason of applying the teachings of revelation to nature and interpreting the latter in the light of faith. Descartes does have a natural, demonstrative, and metaphysical theory of God, but it is natural in the sense of positively excluding any influence of revelation, and it is metaphysical in the sense of belonging to a science which is deductively prior and functionally ordered to philosophical physics. Wolff also accords demonstrative force to a natural theology and relates it to an ontology, but they are separate sciences related as a special part of metaphysics to general metaphysics. Wolffian ontology, or general metaphysics, does not treat formally of the existential act of finite things or of the existent God, whereas Wolffian natural theology offers demonstrations of God's existence and attributes by appealing to the order of essence and the principles founded thereon. Finally, the deists of the Enlightenment return to the sensible world for their natural theology, but they do so to the formal exclusion of suggestions from revelation, without any metaphysical analysis of finite being, and by means of probable arguments leading to a God who may be finite. Although these interpretations of "natural theology" do not necessitate the outright abandonment of the term, they do indicate difficulties connected with its use today and the need for a very careful demarcation of the precise meaning in which one intends to employ it.

The realistic philosophy of God can define its nature by contrast with some of the viewpoints mentioned in this section. It is not an excursion into the past, as the archaicizing interpretation claims, although it employs historical research to obtain intelligent guidance from the past developments in the problem of God. As a living discipline, it carries on its inquiry in the present and requires the individual theist to make his own study of the evidence of finite existents. Precisely because this evidence comes from experience of finite sensible beings, is available to the human mind, and conveys some significance for determining the truth about God, the philosophy of God is not a fideistic enterprise. It does not found its propositions upon a clarification of the content and language of faith, even though it can receive suggestions from revelation. The influence of the history of philosophy and revelation will be to stimulate the theistic philosopher to make a direct inspection of certain aspects of man and sensible things. Yet it is the outcome of his own examination of things which provides the basis of assent to the propositions constituting his doctrine on God. Moreover, the path of inquiry follows the order, as well as the evidence, of natural, philosophical reasoning, not the order proper to sacred doctrine. It begins with the finite sensible existents of our direct experience and regulates all of its propositions about God by the requirements imposed by such a starting point and the existential-causal reasoning to Him. Since its foundation is in the speculative judgment of existence and the judgment about nonmaterial existents and causes, the philosophy of God is not the same as an analysis of religious experience or any sort of theodicy. It achieves this distinctive judgmental rooting through an experiential metaphysics of being as existent rather than through a design-analysis of scientific order or through the philosophy of nature.

A realistic theism is not a separate science but the culmination of the metaphysics of being as existent. It is that moment in the metaphysical inquiry when it seeks out the ultimate cause of its proper subject, being, or the ex-perienced things which exist. Hence the philosophy of God shares the ex-periental-existential basis of this metaphysics, its use of the causal inference and analogical predication, and its speculative, nonfunctional nature. The existential truth about God is significant for its own sake, as knowledge of the subsistent act of existing and primary cause of being. Metaphysical wisdom does order the other philosophical sciences, but not by supplying them with deductive premises or supplanting their own method and evidence. The doctrine of God is relevant for other problems in metaphysics and for the ethical study of man as long as the judgmental-inferential nature of our propositions about God is respected and not suppressed for any functionalist purpose. Beyond their importance within the sphere of philosophical knowledge, however, the propositions about God can be personally assimilated and thus assist the human person to move by knowledge and love toward the living God Himself, known and unknown.

Martin Buber   42. THE GOD OF
                               METAPHYSICS AND
                               THE GOD OF
                               RELIGION

The comparison (already embedded in the two previous selections) between the
   religious and metaphysical consciousness of God is investigated in this
   essay by Martin Buber. Whereas philosophy can apprehend the divine only
   in cogitation and the abstraction of subject and object, he says, religion
   communes in living fashion with God, through belief and the concrete
   relation of *I and Thou*. For philosophy, God is simply an object "from
   which all other objects must be derived." But for religion, God is Absolute
   Being. Whereas philosophy is devoted to the investigation of essence and
   considers itself autonomous, it sees faith as "an affirmation of truth lying
   somewhere between clear knowledge and confused opinion." Religion, on
   the other hand, turns its eye on the question of salvation, unfolds the
   existence lent to us, and looks upon the knowledge it affords us as a mutual
   contact in the "fullness of life."

Metaphysics, along with other nonreligious elements, such as gnosis and
   magic, has always threatened invasion into the privacy of religious contact.
   In contrast to philosophy's self-sufficient methods, religion has found the
   meaning of God through a personal engagement in God's revelation and
   through the shattering of all sense of security in the mystery of His
   existence.

Religion, therefore, stands as a witness to the status of the person in his
   relation to God. Rather than occluding the gaze through conceptualizations
   and abstractions, it looks toward the concrete situation of man and God.

It is true, Buber admits, that philosophy achieves a totalization of its
   view, but it cannot achieve religion's sense of the concentration of personality into the whole unification of being. Only religion can give meaning
   to the fact that God is unlimited Being, an absolute person, and "my
   partner," since only religion is born of the union of an I and a Thou. To
   metaphysics God's Thou is simply an *It*.

ALL GREAT RELIGIOUSNESS shows us that reality of faith means living in
relationship to Being "believed in," that is, unconditionally affirmed, absolute
Being. All great philosophy, on the other hand, shows us that cogitative truth

means making the absolute into an object from which all other objects must be derived. Even if the believer has in mind an unlimited and nameless absolute which cannot be conceived in a personal form, if he really thinks of it as existing Being which stands over against him, his belief has existential reality. Conversely, even if he thinks of the absolute as limited within personal form, if he reflects on it as on an object, he is philosophizing. Even when the "Unoriginated" is not addressed with voice or soul, religion is still founded on the duality of I and Thou. Even when the philosophical act culminates in a vision of unity, philosophy is founded on the duality of subject and object. The duality of I and Thou finds its fulfilment in the religious relationship; the duality of subject and object sustains philosophy while it is carried on. The first arises out of the original situation of the individual, his living before the face of Being, turned toward him as he is turned toward it. The second springs from the splitting apart of this togetherness into two entirely distinct modes of existence, one which is able to do nothing but observe and reflect and one which is able to do nothing but be observed and reflected upon. I and Thou exist in and by means of lived concreteness; subject and object, products of abstraction, last only as long as that power is at work. The religious relationship, no matter what different forms and constellations it takes, is in its essence nothing other than the unfolding of the existence that is lent to us. The philosophical attitude is the product of a consciousness which conceives of itself as autonomous and strives to become so. In philosophy the spirit of man gathers itself by virtue of the spiritual work. Indeed, one might say that here, on the peak of consummated thought, spirituality, which has been disseminated throughout the person, first becomes spiritual substance. But in religion, when this is nothing other than simple existence which has unfolded as a whole person standing over against eternal Being, spirituality too becomes a part of personal wholeness.

Philosophy errs in thinking of religion as founded in a noetical act, even if an inadequate one, and in therefore regarding the essence of religion as the knowledge of an object which is indifferent to being known. As a result, philosophy understands faith as an affirmation of truth lying somewhere between clear knowledge and confused opinion. Religion, on the other hand, insofar as it speaks of knowledge at all, does not understand it as a noetic relation of a thinking subject to a neutral object of thought, but rather as mutual contact, as the genuinely reciprocal meeting in the fullness of life between one active existence and another. Similarly, it understands faith as the entrance into this reciprocity, as binding oneself in relationship with an undemonstrable and unprovable, yet even so, in relationship, knowable Being, from whom all meaning comes.

Another attempt at demarcation, the mature attempt of modern philosophy, distinguishes between the intention of each. According to this conception, philosophy is directed toward the investigation of essence, religion toward inquiry about salvation. Now salvation is, to be sure, a genuine and proper religious category, but the inquiry into salvation differs from the investigation of essence only in the way in which it is considered. The principal tendency of religion is rather to show the essential unity of the two. This is illustrated by the Old Testament phrase, the "way of God," also preserved in the language of the Gospels. The "way of God" is by no means to be understood as a sum of prescriptions for human conduct, but rather primarily as the way of God in and through the world. It is the true sphere of the knowledge of God since it means God's becoming visible in His action. But it is at the same time the way of salvation of men since it is the prototype for the imitation of God. Similarly, the Chinese Tao, the "path" in which the world moves, is the cosmic primal meaning. But because man conforms this his life to it and practises "imitation of the Tao," it is at the same time the perfection of the soul.

Something further, however, is to be noted in that regard, namely, that as high as religion may place the inquiry into salvation it does not regard it as the highest and the essential intention. What is really intended in the search for salvation is the attainment of a condition freed from intention, from arbitrariness. The search for salvation is concerned with the *effect* of salvation, but the "Way" itself is the unarbitrary. Philosophy really means philosophizing; the realer religion is, so much the more it means its own overcoming. It wills to cease to be the special domain "Religion" and wills to become life. It is concerned in the end not with specific religious acts, but with redemption from all that is specific. Historically and biographically, it strives toward the pure Everyday. Religion is in the religious view the exile of man; his homeland is unarbitrary life "in the face of God." It goes against the realest will of religion to describe it in terms of the special characteristics that it has developed rather than in terms of its life-character. Religion must, of course, be described in such a way that its special characteristics do not evaporate into universality but are instead seen as grounded in the fundamental relation of religion to the whole of life.

When we look at the history of a historical religion, we see the reoccurrence in different periods and phases of an inner battle which remains essentially the same. It is the struggle of the religious element against the non-religious elements which invade it from all sides—metaphysics, gnosis, magic, politics, etc. This medley seeks to take the place of the flowing life of faith which is renewed in the flux. It finds helpers in myth and cult, both of which originally served only as expression of the religious relationship. In order to preserve its purity the religious element must combat the tendency of this conglomerate to become autonomous and to make itself independent of the religious life of the person. This battle is consummated in prophetic protest, heretical revolt, reformational retrenchment, and a new founding which arises through the desire to return to the original religious element. It is a struggle for the protection of lived concreteness as the meeting-place between the human and the divine. The actually lived concrete is the "moment" in its unforeseeableness and its irrecoverableness, in its undivertible character of happening but once, in its decisiveness, in its secret dialogue between that which happens and that which is willed, between fate and action, address and answer. This lived concreteness is threatened by the invasion of the extra-religious elements, and it is protected on all fronts by the religious in its unavoidable aloneness.

The religious essence in every religion can be found in its highest certainty. That is the certainty that the meaning of existence is open and accessible in the actual lived concrete, not above the struggle with reality but in it.

That meaning is open and accessible in the actual lived concrete does not mean it is to be won and possessed through any type of analytical or synthetic investigation or through any type of reflection upon the lived concrete. Meaning is to be experienced in living action and suffering itself, in the unreduced immediacy of the moment. Of course, he who aims at the experiencing of experience will necessarily miss the meaning, for he destroys the spontaneity of the mystery. Only he reaches the meaning who stands firm, without holding back or reservation, before the whole might of reality and answers it in a living way. He is ready to confirm with his life the meaning which he has attained.

Every religious utterance is a vain attempt to do justice to the meaning which has been attained. All religious expression is only an intimation of its attainment. The reply of the people of Israel on Sinai, "We will do it, we will hear it," expresses the decisive with naive and unsurpassable pregnancy. The meaning is found through the engagement of one's own person; it only reveals itself as one takes part in its revelation.

All religious reality begins with what Biblical religion calls the "fear of God." It comes when our existence between birth and death becomes incomprehensible and uncanny, when all security is shattered through the mystery. This is not the relative mystery of that which is inaccessible only to the present state of human knowledge and is hence in principle discoverable. It is the essential mystery, the inscrutableness of which belongs to its very nature; it is the unknowable. Through this dark gate (which is only a gate and not, as some theologians believe, a dwelling) the believing man steps forth into the everyday which is henceforth hallowed as the place in which he has to live with the mystery. He steps forth directed and assigned to the concrete, contextual situations of his existence. That he henceforth accepts the situation as given him by the Giver is what Biblical religion calls the "fear of God."

An important philosopher of our day, Whitehead, asks how the Old Testament saying that the fear of God is the beginning of wisdom is to be reconciled with the New Testament saying that God is love. Whitehead has not fully grasped the meaning of the word "beginning." He who begins with the love of God without having previously experienced the fear of God, loves an idol which he himself has made, a god whom it is easy enough to love. He does not love the real God who is, to begin with, dreadful and incomprehensible. Consequently, if he then perceives, as Job and Ivan Karamazov perceive, that God is dreadful and incomprehensible, he is terrified. He despairs of God and the world if God does not take pity on him, as He did on Job, and bring him to love Him Himself. This is presumably what Whitehead meant when he said that religion is the passage from God the void to God the enemy and from Him to God the companion. That the believing man who goes through the gate of dread is directed to the concrete contextual situations of his existence means just this: that he endures in the face of God the reality of lived life, dreadful and incomprehensible though it be. He loves it in the love of God, whom he has learned to love.

For this reason, every genuine religious expression has an open or a hidden personal character, for it is spoken out of a concrete situation in which the person takes part as a person. This is true also in those instances where, out of a noble modesty, the word "I" is in principle avoided. Confucius, who spoke of himself almost as unwillingly as of God, once said: "I do not murmur against God, and I bear no ill will toward men. I search here below, but I penetrate above. He who knows me is God." Religious expression is bound to the concrete situation.

That one accepts the concrete situation as given to him does not, in any way, mean that he must be ready to accept that which meets him as "God-given" in its pure factuality. He may, rather, declare the extremest enmity toward this happening and treat its "givenness" as only intended to draw forth his own opposing force. But he will not remove himself from the concrete situation as it actually is; he will, instead, enter into it, even if in the form of fighting against it. Whether field of work or field of battle, he accepts the place in which he is placed. He knows no floating of the spirit above concrete reality; to him even the sublimest spirituality is an illusion if it is not bound to the situation. Only the spirit which is bound to the situation is prized by him as bound to the *Pneuma,* the spirit of God.

As an objection to the definition of religion which I have suggested, one might adduce the ascetic tendencies of some religions. Insofar, however, as they do not weaken the religious itself, these tendencies do not mean any turning away from the lived concrete. The disposition of life and the choice of life-elements to be affirmed has changed here. But this change is not in the direction of slackening the relation to the moment, which one is rather seeking to intensify. One desires to rescue the relation to the moment by means of asceticism because one despairs of being able to subjugate the non-ascetic elements, and hence the fullness of life, to the religious. The meaning no longer appears to him as open and attainable in the fullness of life.

The ascetic "elevation" is something entirely different from the philosophi-

cal. It is also a form of concretion, though one which is attained through reduction.

Philosophizing and philosophy, in contrast, begin ever anew with one's
definitely looking away from his concrete situation, hence with the primary
act of abstraction.

What is meant here by abstraction is simple, anthropological matter of
fact and not the "radical abstraction" with which Hegel demands that the
philosopher begin. Hegel can call the creation of the world an abstraction from
nothing, while for us it involves precisely the establishment of that concrete
reality from which the philosophizing man does and must look away. Hegel
can describe "the highest being" as "pure abstraction" while the religious man,
on the contrary, is certain that in the course of this his mortality he can meet
God in God's very giving and in his, man's, receiving of the concrete situation. By primary abstraction we mean the inner action in which man lifts himself above the concrete situation into the sphere of precise conceptualization.
In this sphere the concepts no longer serve as a means of apprehending reality,
but instead represent as the object of thought being freed from the limitations
of the actual.

The decisiveness of this abstraction, of this turning away, is sometimes
hidden from sight when a philosopher acts as if he would and could philosophize within his concrete situation. Descartes offers us the clearest example.
When we hear him talk in the first person, we feel as if we were hearing the
voice of direct personal experience. But it is not so. The I in the Cartesian
ego cogito is not the living, body-soul person whose corporality had just been
disregarded by Descartes as being a matter of doubt. It is the subject of
consciousness, supposedly the only function which belongs entirely to our
nature. In lived concreteness, in which consciousness is the first violin but
not the conductor, *this* ego is not present at all. *Ego cogito* means to Descartes, indeed, not simply "I have consciousness," but "It is I who have
consciousness." *Ego cogito* is, therefore, the product of a triply abstracting reflection. Reflection, the "bending back" of a person on himself, begins by extracting from what is experienced in the concrete situation "consciousness" (*cogitatio*), which is not as such experienced there at all. It then
ascertains that a subject must belong to a consciousness and calls this subject
"I." In the end, it identifies the person, this living body-soul person, with that
"I," that is, with the abstract and abstractly-produced subject of consciousness.
Out of the "That" of the concrete situation, which embraces perceiving and
that which is perceived, conceiving and that which is conceived, thinking and
that which is thought, arises, to begin with, an "I think that." A subject thinks
this object. Then the really indispensable "That" (or Something or It) is
omitted. Now we reach the statement of the person about himself: therefore I

(no longer the subject, but the living person who speaks to us) have real existence; for this existence is involved in that *ego*.

In this way Descartes sought through the method of abstraction to capture the concrete starting-point as knowledge, but in vain. Not through such a deduction but only through genuine intercourse with a Thou can the I of the living person be experienced as existing. The concrete, from which all philosophizing starts, cannot again be reached by way of philosophical abstraction; it is irrecoverable.

Philosophy is entitled, however, to proclaim and to promise as the highest reward of this necessary abstraction a looking upward—no longer a looking here—at the objects of true vision, the "ideas." This conception, prepared for by the Indian teaching of the freeing of the knower from the world of experience, is first fully developed by the Greeks. The Greeks established the hegemony of the sense of sight over the other senses, thus making the optical world into *the* world, into which the data of the other senses are now to be entered. Correspondingly, they also gave to philosophizing, which for the Indian was still only a bold attempt to catch hold of one's own self, an optical character, that is, the character of the contemplation of particular objects. The history of Greek philosophy is that of an opticizing of thought, fully clarified in Plato and perfected in Plotinus. The object of this visual thought is the universal existence or as a reality higher than existence. Philosophy is grounded on the presupposition that one sees the absolute in universals.

In opposition to this, religion, when it has to define itself philosophically, says that it means the covenant of the absolute with the particular, with the concrete. For this reason, the central event of Christian philosophy, the scholastic dispute over the reality or unreality of universals, was in essence a philosophical struggle between religion and philosophy and that is its lasting significance. In religious-sounding formulas such as Malebranche's "We see things in God" it is also philosophical abstraction that speaks; for these "things" are not those of the concrete situation but are as general as Platonic ideas (*"les idées intelligibles"*). When, on the contrary, the religious man (or Malebranche no longer as philosophical systematizer but as the religious man that he was) speaks the same sentence, he transforms it. "Things" mean now to him not archetypes or "perfect essences," but the actual exemplars, the beings and objects with which he, this bodily person, spends his life. When he ventures to say that he sees them in God, he does not speak of looking upward but of looking here. He acknowledges that meaning is open and attainable in the lived concreteness of every moment.

Plato gives us a glorious human and poetic account of the mysterious fullness of the concrete situation. He also knows gloriously how to remain silent. When, however, he explains and answers for his silence in that unforgettable passage of the seventh epistle, he starts, to be sure, from the concreteness of "life together," where "in an instant a light is kindled as from springing fire."

But in order to explain he turns immediately to an exposition of the knowing of the known, meaning the universal. Standing in the concrete situation and even witnessing to it, man is overspanned by the rainbow of the covenant between the absolute and the concrete. If he wishes in philosophizing to fix his glance upon the white light of the absolute as the object of his knowledge, only archetypes or ideas, the transfigurations of the universal, present themselves to him. The color-free, beyond-color bridge fails to appear. Here also, in my opinion, is to be found the reason why Plato changed from the identification of the idea of the good with God, as presented in his *Republic,* to the conception appearing in the *Timaeus* of the demiurge who contemplates the Ideas.

Religion, however, is not allowed, even in the face of the most self-confident pride of philosophy, to remain blind to philosophy's great engagement. To this engagement necessarily belongs the actual, ever-recurring renunciation of the original relational bond, of the reality which takes place between I and Thou, of the spontaneity of the moment. Religion must know knowledge not only as a need but also as a duty of man. It must know that history moves along the way of this need and duty, that, Biblically speaking, the eating of the tree of knowledge leads out of Paradise but into the world.

The world, the world as objective and self-contained connection of all being, natural and spiritual, would not exist for us if our thinking, which develops in philosophizing, did not melt together the world-concreta which are presented to us. It would not exist if our thinking did not merge these world-concreta with one another and with all that man has ever experienced and has ever comprehended as experienceable. And spirit all the more would not genuinely exist for us as objective connection if thought did not objectify it, if spirit itself as philosophy did not objectify and unite itself. Only through the fact that philosophy radically abandoned the relation with the concrete did that amazing construction of an objective thought-continuum become possible, with a static system of concepts and a dynamic one of problems. Every man who can "think" may enter this continuum through the simple use of this ability, through a thinking comprehension of thought. Only through this is there an "objective" mutual understanding, that is, one which does not, like the religious, entail two men's each recognizing the other by the personal involvement in life which he has achieved. Instead, both fulfil a function of thought which demands no involvement in life and bear in fruitful dialectic the tension between the reciprocal ideas and problems.

The religious communication of a content of being takes place in paradox. It is not a demonstrable assertion (theology which pretends to be this is rather a questionable type of philosophy), but a pointing toward the hidden realm of existence of the hearing man himself and that which is to be experienced there and there alone. Artistic communication, which ought not remain unmentioned here, takes place in the *Gestalt,* from which a communicated content cannot be detached and given independent existence. A content of being is objectively communicable and translatable only in and through philosophy, consequently only through the objectifying elaboration of the situation.

A sceptical verdict about the ability of philosophy to lead to and contain truth is in no way here implied. The possibility of cogitative truth does not, indeed, mean a cogitative possession of being, but a cogitative real relation to being. Systems of thought are manifestations of genuine thought-relations to being made possible through abstraction. They are not mere "aspects," but rather valid documents of these cogitative voyages of discovery.

A similarity and a difference between the ways in which religion and philosophy affect the person remain to be mentioned.

In religious reality the person has concentrated himself into a whole, for it is only as a unified being that he is able to live religiously. In this wholeness thought is naturally also included as an autonomous province but one which no longer strives to absolutize its autonomy. A totalization also takes place in genuine philosophers but no unification. Instead, thinking overruns and overwhelms all the faculties and provinces of the person. In a great act of philosophizing even the finger tips think—but they no longer feel.

For man the existent is either face-to-face being or passive object. The essence of man arises from this twofold relation to the existent. These are not two external phenomena but the two basic modes of existing with being. The child that calls to his mother and the child that watches his mother—or to give a more exact example, the child that silently speaks to his mother through nothing other than looking into her eyes and the same child that looks at something on the mother as at any other object—show the twofoldness in which man stands and remains standing. Something of the sort is sometimes even to be noticed in those near death. What is here apparent is the double structure of human existence itself. Because these are the two basic modes of our existence with being, they are the two basic modes of our existence in general—I-Thou and I-It. I-Thou finds its highest intensity and transfiguration in religious reality, in which unlimited Being becomes, as absolute person, my partner. I-It finds its highest concentration and illumination in philosophical knowledge. In this knowledge the extraction of the subject from the I of the immediate lived togetherness of I and It and the transformation of the It into the object detached in its essence produces the exact thinking of contemplated existing beings, yes, of contemplated Being itself.

Divine truth, according to a saying of Franz Rosenzweig, wishes to be implored "with both hands," that of philosophy and that of theology. "He who prays with the double prayer of the believer and the unbeliever," he continues, "to him it will not deny itself." But what is the prayer of the unbeliever? Rosenzweig means by this Goethe's prayer to his own destiny, a prayer which, no matter how genuine, brings to mind that of the Euripidean queen to fate or the human spirit, a prayer whose Thou is no Thou. But there is another prayer of the philosophers still farther from the Thou, and yet, it seems to me, more important.

The religious reality of the meeting with the Meeter, who shines through all forms and is Himself formless, knows no image of Him, nothing comprehensible as object. It knows only the presence of the Present One. Symbols of Him, whether images or ideas, always exist first when and insofar as Thou becomes He, and that means It. But the ground of human existence in which it gathers and becomes whole is also the deep abyss out of which images arise. Symbols of God come into being, some which allow themselves to be fixed in lasting visibility even in earthly material and some which tolerate no other sanctuary than that of the soul. Symbols supplement one another, they merge, they are set before the community of believers in plastic or theological forms. And God, so we may surmise, does not despise all these similarly and necessarily untrue images, but rather suffers that one look at Him through them. Yet they always quickly desire to be more than they are, more than signs and pointers toward Him. It finally happens ever again that they swell themselves up and obstruct the way to Him, and He removes Himself from them. Then comes round the hour of the philosopher, who rejects both the image and the God which it symbolizes and opposes to it the pure idea, which he even at times understands as the negation of all metaphysical ideas. This critical "atheism" (*Atheoi* is the name which the Greeks gave to those who denied the traditional gods) is the prayer which is spoken in the third person in the form of speech about an idea. It is the prayer of the philosopher to the again unknown God. It is well suited to arouse religious men and to impel them to set forth right across the God-deprived reality to a new meeting. On their way they destroy the images which manifestly no longer do justice to God. The spirit moves them which moved the philosopher.

Johannes Lotz, S.J. 43. METAPHYSICS AND RELIGION

Where Buber sees fundamental competition and antagonism between religious and metaphysical consciousness, Father Lotz espies a healthy partnership. The

This essay appeared in the quarterly *Philosophy Today*, edited at St. Joseph's College, Rensselaer, Indiana. Translated from the German by Edwin G. Kaiser, C.Pp.S.

relationship between these two types of consciousness, he says in this essay, is characterized by balance, distinction, and a community of interest.

Religion is not destroyed in seeking metaphysical support, for without such support it is threatened by emotionalism, sentimentality, and irrationalism. Metaphysics, on the other hand, when it lacks the guiding light of religious consciousness, becomes hard, rationalistic, and bitter. Each, despite obvious diversity, shares in the community of being and contacts being; but each develops the basic experience of being in its own way.

In its inner self, metaphysics embraces religion and draws nourishment from religion's basic attitudes; while religion, in its beginning, embraces metaphysics and, in its own way, draws sustenance from basic metaphysical attitudes. Though the philosopher is considered a restless man and the man of religion one who is filled with tranquility, neither is completely without a sense of the other's respective restlessness or tranquility. The philosopher's inquiry is not entirely without solution, nor the religious man's answer unconditionally without a question.

Metaphysics is characterized by a loving knowledge; religion, by a knowing love. Within "the silence of being" these characteristics achieve a certain unification. The burden of inquiry into the common experience is assumed by metaphysics: "Insight is its objective; and being, its predominant theme. Its goal is God as the source of being." In contrast, the dominant theme of religion is *God Himself,* and its business with being "goes no further than the meeting which God demands."

Each gains, then, in an eminent way from the example of the other. Metaphysical knowledge must be filled with love, as Plato put it in his *Seventh Epistle;* religion must be enlightened by knowledge, as St. Paul pointed out when he admonished Christians to give a reason for the faith within them.

Metaphysical experience, as knowledge thus rooted in love, is not dissimilar from religious experience, since "there is in it a kind of pre-figuration of religious experience." Religious love, as insight rooted in knowledge, is likewise not unlike metaphysical experience, since "it presages metaphysics, embraces it implicitly." Insight and devotion, therefore, stand complementary to one another, enforce one another—each supplying strength to the strength of the other.

Religion truly faces the Absolute Thou, the Absolute Person. But in its case, the Absolute Person and His love approaches us. Metaphysics, however, in proceeding from self-subsistent being to Absolute Power, reaches out to this Power in every existent that is "penetrated by being and ultimately with self-subsistent being." Each way of consciousness—religion through initiation and donation, metaphysics through processive reason and inquiry—comes to the same term of authentic reality: God.

I T IS BECOMING more and more clear today that any religion grounded on a peculiar experience opposed to metaphysics soon loses its foundation and breaks up. It falls victim to the emotional and the irrational. And still religion must not be absorbed by metaphysics, which it always somehow transcends. Neither should absorb the other, and the distinction between them must be kept clear. We would not even want to say that religion must always be built on philosophy. Historically, the contrary seems to be true, at least for western culture. Metaphysical inquiry grew out of religion. What we are concerned with here is the basic experience and the deep community of being between religion and metaphysics. And though dominated by this community of being, diversity remains.

In the intellectually mature man religion and metaphysics somehow develop autonomously, but there is no divorce between them. Each must remain steeped in the basic experience, if it is to reach its full stature. Without this experience religion is vapid and metaphysics is empty. Metaphysics in its own inner self embraces religion. It draws nourishment from basic religious attitudes. Likewise, in its beginnings religion embraces metaphysics. And it does not rob metaphysics of its inquiry and proof. Rather, it feeds on the basic attitudes of the metaphysical seeker and gives him the most complete human support. Nor does metaphysics take from religion its inwardness of love and devotion. Rather, it furnishes the most firm foundation for love and devotion.

Dialogue within the Individual

While it is commonly admitted that religion and metaphysics can be distinguished as they develop diversely from basic experience, it is often thought that they cannot exist within the same individual. The philosopher is committed to restlessness of an inquiry without solution. The religious man is already filled with the tranquility of an answer. Truth is that the philosopher's inquiry is not without a solution nor is the religious man's answer without a question. Metaphysics does not spend itself in despair. And religion gets beyond the naive and primitive. Only when each remains itself can metaphysics and religion perfect themselves through mutual penetration. Inquiry finds the tranquility of response, and response is kept vital by the goad of inquiry.

There is a dialogue, true dialectics, between the loving knowledge of metaphysics and the knowing love of religion. A knowledge that seems all loving enters the silence of mystery and casts its glow over all metaphysical inquiry. And a love that seems all knowledge enters the silence of mystery, and is a love that surpasses all love we know. In this realm that we can hardly touch, these two find unity. But in the "world" where we live out our life, they are alternate, for we deal with diverse faculties. Man reaches his full stature in loving—in living—in religion. In this sense religion has the final word.

The experience of being must be distinguished from the experience of the existent whose ground is being. Religion and metaphysics, each in its own way, develops this basic experience of being. Metaphysics, as a science in its own right, emerges alongside other worlds of existence. And it embraces not only the doctrine of being but also the doctrine of the Supreme Being. Religion is life-lived. And here we are not directly concerned with the Christian religion which concerns what entered into human existence through revelation and grace. We are concerned with religion as simply an essential ingredient of human existence. And this is an indispensable point of departure for any understanding of religion by philosophy.

Metaphysics with its pre-eminence in knowing assumes the burden of inquiry in developing the basic experience. Insight is its objective; and being, its predominant theme. Its goal is God as the source of being. Religion wrestles with the problem of submission. Through this it strives for personal union. Its predominant theme is God Himself. Its concern for being goes no further than the meeting with God demands. But the knowing of metaphysics must be filled with the force of love if it is not to lose its vitality or be led astray. And the love of religion must be enlightened by knowledge if it is not to languish and perish. . . .

The Dangers

History testifies to a tendency in man rather hard to explain. He grows weary in his love for being, goes limping in pursuit of it. He prefers to withdraw from being rather than remain open to it. He subjects being to himself instead of dedicating himself to it. Confusion about being and erroneous explanations spring from aberrations in his love of being. They walk down the centuries and lead to false roads. If left to themselves, Saint Thomas observed, very few men would come to self-subsistent being, and then only after a long time with some mixture of error. The full development of metaphysical experience demands an incessant struggle for the purification of the love of being.

In his seventh letter Plato states this need rather impressively. So tremendous is the effort demanded of man, so many the obstacles to be overcome, that his power constantly fails him. He is spontaneously led to the point where he looks for help from other sources. This help must come from self-subsistent being itself. And Christianity promises and preserves this help as God's revelation and grace.

The Religious Experience

In so far as metaphysical knowledge is experience and is rooted in love of being, it is not heterogeneous to religious experience. There is in it a kind of pre-figuration of religious experience. Metaphysics always embraces religion implicitly. Contrariwise, in so far as religious love is insight and rooted in knowledge, it is not heterogeneous to metaphysical experience. It presages metaphysics, embraces it implicitly.

This reciprocal relation of implication is founded in basic experience. A development in detail would show how metaphysics and religion meet in basic experience, and how each develops in its own way from the common root. They work together despite their distinctness. The diversity is due to what is primary in each. In metaphysics there is the primacy of knowing; and in religion, the primacy of love. Loving knowledge confronts knowing love. As religious experience based in love is developed, the nature of love itself will be revealed more clearly.

Primacy of Experience and Love

There is an inevitable polarity of knowledge and experience. Metaphysics stresses the pole of knowledge. Scientific metaphysics has the task of raising experience to the level of wisdom, to develop the knowledge that is manifested and implicit in experience. In this work all the stages—concepts and proofs, coordinated in detail and in logical sequence—must be presented. Religion stresses the pole of experience. Vital religion moves entirely on the level of experience and develops entirely as experience. It transforms, not experience into knowledge, but knowledge into experience. To it belongs the knowledge that is in experience, which bears the imprint of experience and assimilates whatever comes from without. Religious experience is not concerned with the logical modes and sequences of knowledge. Rather, it tends to an over-all view, to a grasp of the whole expanse, to the end and the result. Still, it does not follow a path other than that of metaphysical experience. It follows the same path faithfully, but diversely. As a consequent, you cannot deny it some character of knowing, though it is synoptic rather than analytic. But the respective dominant themes still tempt one to ask: does religious experience truly remain knowledge, and can metaphysical knowledge really be considered as experience?

What are the foundations of this diverse actuation—knowing and experiencing? The answer is along the line of another duality, insight and devotion. Metaphysical experience tends toward insight and knowing. Religious experience has submission as its goal and stresses experience. But insight and submission are only knowledge and love realized. We are again between the poles of knowing and loving.

The knowledge of metaphysical experience is borne by love, and a certain openness is its complement. Still it suffers from a kind of indecisiveness. Its insights and its judgments are not devotion. It is primarily directed to the abstract. Only through the concrete universal notion of being is it related to concreteness. In religious experience knowledge is taken in by love. Love presses forward to a decision. It brings with it an inner openness of man right down to the core of person and the center of freedom, a real outward movement in submission. But submission is concerned with a concrete goal, so love is directed to the concrete. Whatever universality it reaches, it does so only through a concrete medium of being. Religious experience does not receive its character from knowing something but from meeting something. Here is the response of real submission of the loving man. There is a parallel between self-manifestation in reality (not just conceptually) and man here. But it seems that this encounter of love includes the experience of knowledge.

The Absolute Power

In religious experience there is meeting of a unique kind, the encounter with self-subsisting being or the absolute. Like knowledge, man's love is not completely exhausted by individual finite being, not even when it is frustrated. And surely not when it reaches full human stature. This is evident when it is seen in the context of the totality of existent being and when you take a close look at the free character of man's submission. Here an important distinction must be made between love and knowledge. It comes from the primacy of love's synoptic approach to the experienced and the concrete. Knowledge rests expressly on universal being. It reaches self-subsistent being only as this latter's ultimate foundation. But universal being is in love only implicitly-obscurely. Only the goal is manifested expressly. So love rushes with a certain directness to self-subsistent being itself. At the same time self-subsistent being is for religious experience the first, most immediate and most manifest, and the most distant and hidden. In metaphysics universal being comes to the front; in religion the self-subsistent being enters the foreground.

In characterizing our meeting with self-subsistent being, we use a formula that bears the mark of metaphysical experience. The Ultimate can be called self-subsistent only by one who has paused at universal being, pondered it and educed the self-subsistent from it. In such context, self-subsistent being is seen as the basis of all truth, the cornerstone of evidence, the peak and crown of every attempt at knowledge. Religious experience, on the contrary, unfolds as love and encounter, has about it a certain immediacy, sees the Ultimate not so much as the last but the first.

All this is clear from man's meeting with being. This encounter is a challenge to self-manifestation. Even finite existents confront man, each individual being in its own way and according to its own nature. And each makes its own distinctive demand with greater or less insistence. But every existent is penetrated by being and ultimately with self-subsistent being. And this is the deep root of every claim that being has on man. It lays hold of him as the Absolute-

Exigent, as Absolute-Power; and makes him powerless, overwhelms him, puts him in a state of absolute dependence.

The Absolute Thou

Such experience in no way reaches its fulness with the intuition of knowing. Only in the meeting of love, always and inevitably subjecting man to a fundamental decision of existence, does man open his heart to the One Who knocks, the Mighty One. There is simple, absolute submission. Or, by a no-saying he shuts himself off from self-subsistent being. Submission empowers the Absolute Power; refusal disarms it. Not in itself, of course, but toward man who ultimately either perfects or destroys himself.

Metaphysics goes from self-subsistent being to Absolute-Power only through the medium of reason. But religion with its encounter, with an immediacy proper to it, stands before Absolute-Power from the very beginning. But Absolute-Exigent and Absolute-Power even do not entirely manifest what corresponds to religious experience. Encounter and submission, because of their personal stamp, hint at what has been missing thus far. At any rate, any confrontation of Absolute-Power not yet seen as personal is a mere shadow of religion's possibilities. They are brought to perfection only in the realm of the personal. As to the meeting itself, I encounter only what of itself turns to me, makes its way to me, opens itself to me, seeks to communicate with me. Such encounter is identical with person. But not person in its metaphysical essence, rather concretely as it addresses me. There is an appeal which touches me personally, one person meets another. In the Absolute-Exigent and Absolute-Power the personal call of the Absolute Person or the Absolute Thou comes to me. The Thou is the person approaching me. And since approach through personal call is love realized, the Absolute Thou or Absolute Love invites me to Himself through all existing being.

Both the summons and the response are a probing to the depths of man's being. Submission to Power is subjection first of all. It can be born of fear and offered with reserve. But it is the personal appeal, reaching to the heart of us, which brings submission to its ultimate perfection. And from these depths love carries us in perfect submission to Absolute Love. It is, indeed, human love with a note of the absolute about it, unconditioned and unreserved. And here more than anywhere else it is true that as man says "yes" or "no" he finds or loses himself.

Metaphysics as it develops reaches to the absolute person and his love. But it remains with intuitions touching its essence. It is religion that deals with the experience in which the Absolute Person and his love approach us. Ever and always religion is experiencing the loving call of the Absolute Thou. The metaphysical pattern is not absent from this context, but it is implicit and obscure.

The Dangers

Because of its unique nature religion is in greater danger of a deadening paralysis than is metaphysics from the perils that accompany it. The resistence that threatens love on its way to being is particularly menacing when love submits to the Absolute Thou. History shows how easy it is to refuse submission and to cramp love within the narrow confines of man himself. Religious experience demands of man that he constantly enliven and purify his love. And since religion lives entirely on love, the fate of love is the fate of religion.

It might be remarked that the rise and fall of metaphysics has been most closely bound to the flowering and fading of religion. The love of being is the beginning of a love of submission, and the love of submission is perfected love of being. A reverent love of being prepares the way for religion. And revolt against love of submission cuts the life-nerve of metaphysics. Man is held between a polarity which tortures him and teaches him to look for help. This help comes from the revelation of Christ for metaphysics and from the grace of Christ for religious experience.

Conclusion

If the unity of metaphysics and religion is destroyed, it is due to either error or the fact that man has succumbed to the dangers accompanying their development. The result is a rationalistic metaphysics relying on knowledge alone. It confronts an irrationalistic religion developed from experience and love alone. Such a metaphysics loses itself in abstractions, misconstrues being in categories and finally destroys itself. Such a religion goes with its freedom to the concrete. But unenlightened, it puts being to flight with its excessive stress on the personal. It destroys its roots and itself.

But to the extent that the dangers are overcome, metaphysics and religion progress together, intimately but diversely. Rooted in the same basic experience, they both lay claim to man, appeal more and more to his openness and loyalty. The metaphysican can be a true knower so long as he is a faithful lover. But his love does not reach the heights of the religious man. And the religious man can be an authentic lover as long as he is a knower. But his knowledge is not as deep as the metaphysician's. The metaphysician struggles for insight, for a knowledge that is already in experience and rooted in love. The religious man perfects the devotion of love that is already insight, rooted in knowing. Metaphysics does not come to knowledge without experience and love, through which it touches the concrete, the free and the personal. And since religion does not come to experience and love independently of knowledge, it somehow touches the universal and objective.

The full response of man to the challenge of being is neither the knowing-insight of metaphysics nor the loving-submission of religion. It is in both. Each in its own way is the bearer of totality. Metaphysics is pointed to religion to keep the submission of love alive while religion is pointed to metaphysics to provide the necessary insight.

STUDY AIDS FOR PART FOUR

Review Questions

BEING

1. What three alternatives does Parmenides' "goddess" propose for an explanation of being? Which of the three does she avow? Why?

2. What arguments does Parmenides' "goddess" use to support the chosen alternative?

3. What characteristics of being does Parmenides set down?

4. In what way does Plato's Socrates show that Zeno and Parmenides are arguing the same case?

5. What objections does Parmenides put forward to Socrates' theory of ideas, and to the notion of participation? What reply does Socrates make?

6. Why does Socrates say that to deny the absolute character of ideas is to do away with knowledge?

7. How does Aristotle define "substance"?

8. What arguments does Aristotle propose against matter being the substance of a thing?

9. What does Aristotle mean when he says, " 'Is' applies to everything . . . primarily to one thing and derivatively to others"?

10. Why does Aristotle say that matter and form do not come to be?

11. Into what two divisions does Descartes divide things? Why does he make this division?

12. Does Descartes make any distinction between the terms "modes," "attributes," and "qualities"? If so, how?

13. What, if anything, does Descartes say that created-substances stand in need of?

14. In what sense does Moeller say that "being means grounding"? What does he mean by that?

15. Why does Moeller say that being "cannot merge with the questioning of metaphysics"?

16. Why does Moeller believe that "passing being is determined from being"? What conclusions does he draw from this assertion?

17. To what fact does Pieper ascribe man's ability to know things?

18. What "truth of things" does Pieper say is beyond formal human knowledge? What is within formal human knowledge?

19. What types of analogy does Phelan distinguish, in agreement with St. Thomas? Which type is properly termed "analogical"?

20. What are the essential requirements, according to Phelan, for metaphysical analogy?

21. In what words does Phelan state the doctrine of analogy?

22. How does De Raeymaeker define "causality"?

23. Does De Raeymaeker make a distinction between causality as an "empirical bond" and causality as an "ontological connection"? If so, how and why?

24. What does De Raeymaeker mean by "horizontal" causality? By "vertical" causality?

25. What does "action" mean to Somerville's Blondel? In what words does Somerville define "action"?

26. What differences does Somerville draw between interior and exterior action? What do his terms "longitudinal action" and "latitudinal action" mean?

27. Why does Rousselot say that intelligence is the faculty of being? What does he mean by this?

28. In what sense does Rousselot say that "the conquest of reality by the knower varies with the degree of immanent activity it employs"?

29. What does Rousselot consider to be the "typical intellectual operation"?

30. What does Royce mean by "perception"? By "conception"? By "interpretation"? By "community"?

31. Why does Royce say that there is no philosophy of pure conception or pure perception?

32. What objections does Clarke propose against the description of the metaphysical object as "that which is or can be"?

33. What reasons, does Clarke suggest, have been put forward to justify the inclusion of the "possibles" in "real being"?

34. What does Clarke consider to be the formal mark of "real being?" How does he account for the "possibles"? What difference does Clarke draw between "to-be-real" and "to-be-thought"?

35. What "pseudo-problems" does Bergson say metaphysics has been plagued by?

36. What does Bergson mean by a "possible"? What does he mean by saying that "the possible is . . . the image of the present in the past"?

ESSENCE AND EXISTENCE

1. In what manner, according to St. Thomas, is essence distinct from existence?

2. Why does St. Thomas say that the act of existence is other than essence, nature, or form? Does he make any exception to this statement?

3. How does St. Thomas define "essence"? "Substance"? "Act of existing"? Which is primary? Why?

4. Why does St. Thomas say that the composition of act and potentiality is more comprehensive than that of matter and form?

5. What, for Santayana, are the characteristics of essence?

6. What does Santayana mean by saying that individual and universal being are necessary?

7. Why does Santayana say that essence "much more truly *is* than any substance or any experience or any event"?

8. What does Pontifex mean by "being," or "existence"?

9. What four theses on "existence" does Pontifex oppose?

10. What solution does Pontifex suggest to simplify the notion of "existence"? Does he subscribe in fact, or in theory, to the doctrine of analogy?

11. What does Dewey mean by the terms "precarious" and "stable"?

12. How does Dewey's naturalist metaphysics answer the need of a world that is both stable and precarious?

VALUE

1. In what way, does St. Thomas suggest, can "good" be added to "being"?

2. Exactly what, according to St. Thomas, do "good" and "true" add to "being"?

3. Why, does St. Thomas suggest, are "good" and "being" convertible terms? In what way are they convertible?

4. How does Hawkins define "good"?

5. What is the relation, as Hawkins sees it, between "good" and "teleology"?

6. How does Hawkins explain "evil"?

7. Why does von Hildebrand say that "value" is not a postulate? What kinds of value-categories does he distinguish?

8. Does von Hildebrand believe that value is a real property of being? Why? Is it also a category of motivation? Which is primary?

9. Why, according to von Hildebrand, are "urges" and "appetites" different from "value"?

10. Does Alexander believe that value is an objective character of being? In what way?

11. What respective satisfaction, according to Alexander, do the good, true, and beautiful effect?

12. What, to Alexander, is "a standard individual"?

TIME AND SPACE

1. What three mental acts, according to McWilliams, does the perception of space involve?

2. Why, according to McWilliams, does the direct perception of bodies not presuppose the notion of space?

3. How does McWilliams define space? How many kinds of space does he distinguish?

4. What does Wild mean by "time"?

5. What relation does Wild perceive between time and change? Which is primary? Why?

6. What three operations of the mind, does Wild suggest, are necessary before the notion of time can be formed?

7. Does Whitehead say that there is more than one kind of time? What does he mean?

8. In what way, does Whitehead say, is time an internal relation to an event? What is an event?

9. Does Whitehead say that time and space are indistinguishable? What *does* he say?

10. What does de Solages mean by "cyclic" and "evolutionary" time?

11. What does de Solages mean when he says that "we must re-think every philosophical problem that has been more or less secretly allied to the ancient concept of the Universe"?

12. Why does Johann say that "charity" is the virtue of the "now," while "faith" and "hope" are virtues of the future?

13. What does Johann mean by saying that charity is founded on actuality?

14. What, according to Johann, is the relation between "presence," "preoccupation," and "charity"?

THE PERSONAL CENTER

1. In what sense, does Maritain suggest, is the person a *suppositum?* What does he mean?

2. What does Maritain mean by "concomitant consciousness"? What synonyms does he use for this term?

3. What distinction does Maritain draw between "ontological," and "phenomenal," self-knowledge?

4. Why, according to de Finance, cannot existence be the object of a concept?

5. What does de Finance mean by saying that "I know being only because I am myself a sharer in being"?

6. In what way, according to de Finance, does the person realize his own ipseity?

7. What does Johann mean by "the second self"?

8. What two conditions of "presence" does Johann say are necessary for love?

9. What, according to Johann, are the ontological consequences of love for another human person?

10. What distinction does Berdyaev make between "individual," "ego," and "personality"?

11. What does Berdyaev mean when he says that the "egocentric man is completely devoid of personality"?

12. Why, does Berdyaev say, are "joy" and "suffering" characteristic of personality? How does he mean this?

KNOWLEDGE

1. How many divisions of knowledge does Plato set up, and what are they?

2. Explain the "myth of the cave."

3. Does Plato say that levels of knowledge and being correspond with one another? What does he mean?

4. What does Martin mean by "theoretical," "practical," "synthetic," "autonomous," "positive"?

5. What distinction does Martin draw between knowledges that are "constitutive of," "regulative of," and "instrumental to" other knowledges? Give examples of each.

6. How does Martin characterize metaphysics?

7. What does Sturzo mean by a "cognitive situation"?

8. What does Sturzo mean by the "idealistic," "phenomenalistic," and "existential" wholes?

9. What chief elements does Sturzo suggest are inherent in any knowledge?

FREEDOM

1. How does Augustine explain the reason for man's freedom?

2. When, according to Augustine, is man most truly free? What, then, is the object of man's freedom?

3. What does St. Thomas mean by "free will"?

4. What does St. Thomas mean when he characterizes free will as an intellectual appetite?

5. What reasons does St. Thomas give for saying that "will" and "free choice" are not two powers, but one? To what does he compare their unity?

6. State James's principal arguments in support of free will.

7. What does James mean by "chance" and "indeterminism"?

8. Does James suggest that "indeterminism" excludes the possibility of Providence?

9. What, to Jaspers, especially signifies man's freedom?

10. What role does "risk" play in Jaspers's conception of freedom?

11. What does Jaspers mean by saying that "there can be no subjective security"?

GOD

1. What does St. Thomas mean by saying that God is the "last end" for which everything ultimately exists?

2. What does St. Thomas mean when he suggests that there are for creatures "other things," beside being, required for their perfections?

3. What transformation in the notion of being does Gilson suggest St. Thomas inaugurated?

4. Gilson says that in God "there is no what." Does this mean that God has no essence? What does it mean?

5. What two elements does Gilson identify with St. Thomas's "five ways"?

6. What reasons does Stace use to support his thesis that God's existence can neither be proved nor disproved?

7. What does Stace mean by saying that "a first cause *would not be God*"? By saying that God is known through revelation or not at all?

8. What specific criticism does Stace make against the traditional arguments for God's existence?

9. What "false alternatives" does Collins distinguish in all discourse about God's existence?

10. What limitations does Collins suggest for arguments about the existence of God?

11. What does Collins mean by "experiential," "inferential"? What role do existent things play in aiding man's knowledge of God?

12. Why does Collins reject "theodicy" but uphold "natural theology"?

13. Explain Buber's attitude toward religious and philosophical knowledge of God. What specific differences does he draw in their respective approaches?

14. What arguments does Buber advance against philosophical consciousness?

15. What correctives against religious excesses does Lotz say that metaphysics can provide? What correctives against metaphysical excesses does religion provide?

16. In what way, according to Lotz, do religious and metaphysical knowledges embrace one another? In what way are they dialogic?

17. What does Lotz consider to be the requirements of a full religious knowledge of God? Of a full metaphysical knowledge?

18. What comparisons does Lotz make between "insight-devotion" and "experience-knowing"?

Discussion Topics

1. At the turn of our century, William James and F. H. Bradley engaged in a modern dispute over the ancient problem of the unity-or-plurality of being. From the following statements, can you establish any connection with arguments ad-

vanced by Parmenides, Plato, and Aristotle? How would you rate the validity of the following arguments?

§ James:

(1) "From the fact that finite experiences must draw support from one another, philosophers pass to the notion that experience *überhaupt* must need an absolute support. . . . But is this not the globe, the elephant, and the tortoise over again? Must not something end by supporting itself? . . . Why should anywhere the world be absolutely fixed and finished? And if reality genuinely grows, why may it not grow in these very determinations which here and now are made?"—"Humanism and Truth."

(2) "Things are real *severally,* in their '*each*-form,' rather than as taken together, in their '*all*-form.' Everything in the world has a real environment, other than itself, and which it is compelled to meet and take account of without any sort of antecedent complicity."—*The Thought and Character of William James* R. B. Perry.

(3) "What our intellect really aims at is neither variety nor unity taken singly, but totally."—*Pragmatism.*

§ Bradley:

(1) "We have no knowledge of a plural diversity, nor can we attach sense to it, if we do not have it somehow as one. . . ."— *Appearance and Reality.*

(2) ". . . because everything, to complete itself and satisfy its own claims, must pass beyond itself, nothing in the end is real except the Absolute."—*Appearance and Reality.*

2. What relation do you find between Aristotle's category of substance and the "four causes"?

3. What similarity and difference can you discover between Moeller's essay on the "ground of being" and the use of the same phrase in Copleston's "Rejoinder" in Part Three? Between Royce's term "interpretation" and Whitehead's use of the same term in his essay in Part Three?

4. Bergson contends that the question, "Why should there be being rather than nothing?" is a deceptive and invalid question. How might Heidegger, on the basis of his essay in Part Three, reply to this objection? Do Parmenides and Plato in their foregoing selections tend to establish the validity of Bergson's objections or Heidegger's assertions? What contribution does Clarke's essay make to the problem?

5. How does De Raeymaeker's assertion that God's knowledge is the cause of things compare with Rousselot's ideas on the same issue? How do both compare with Pieper's contentions?

6. In what way might Aristotle agree, or disagree, with the following statements by Leibniz?

§ "The real is the completely individual, and this is a genuine unity, so that its whole being individualizes it."—*Disputatio Metaphysica de Principio Individui.*

§ "I take for an axiom this identical proposition, diversified only by the accent, that what is not truly *one* being, is no more truly a *being*. It has always been held that unity and being reciprocate."—Leibniz in a letter to Arnauld.

7. Intelligence for St. Thomas, says Rousselot, is the faculty of the real because it is antecedently the faculty of the divine. He bases this contention on a statement by St. Thomas (*Contra Gentiles*, II, 98) that whatever is capable of existence is capable of being known. In what way might each of them consider the following statement by Henri Poincaré? To what extent could they agree with it? At what point would they disagree? Why?

§ ". . . a reality completely independent of the mind which conceives it, sees or feels it, is an impossibility. A world as exterior as that, even if it existed, would for us be forever inaccessible. But what we call objective reality is, in the last analysis, what is common to many thinking beings, and could be common to all; this common part . . . can only be the harmony expressed by mathematical laws. It is this harmony then which is the sole objective reality, the only truth we can attain."— *Science and Method.*

8. Duns Scotus contended that if being were only analogously predicated of God and creatures, the integrity of the copula ("is") would be destroyed. He then concluded that there is a hidden term in being, which is neither univocal nor equivocal nor analogous. Do you believe that Pontifex agrees with this conclusion? In what way? Can you cite passages from Pontifex for your view?

9. Santayana asserts that essences both precede and succeed existences (*The Realm of Essence* [New York, Charles Scribner's Sons, 1927], p. 24), and that essences have no "natural being" but only "aesthetic immediacy and logical definition" (*Scepticism and Animal Faith* [New York, Charles Scribner's Sons, 1923], p. 76). Essences are thus the most clearly known, and are the true objects of the intellect. Does St. Thomas's statement (*De Veritate*, Q1, a12) that the essence (*quidditas*) of a thing is the proper object of the intellect substantiate Santayana's argument? If so, how could you account for the fact that St. Thomas espouses the cause of "existence" as primary in being? What distinction would St. Thomas draw in order to qualify his statement?

10. Do you find any relation between Santayana's "essences" and Bergson's "possibles"? Do these terms imply inimical or agreeable views? Does Pontifex agree in any sense with Santayana's notion of the primordial possibilities in being?

11. "Existence," says Jean Wahl (*The Philosopher's Way* [New York, Philosophical Library, 1948], p. 49), "can never be completely revealed. It is never so strong as when it is hidden. . . ." How might Dewey look upon this statement? Where would he agree? Where would he disagree? What view would Bergson take of it?

12. Value, Edgar S. Brightman writes (*Person and Reality* [New York, Ronald Press, 1958], p. 283), "means whatever is actually liked, prized, esteemed, desired, approved, or enjoyed by anyone at any time. It is the actual experience of enjoying a desired object or activity." Are Brightman's verbs ("liked," "prized," "esteemed," and so forth) actually "value" terms and, therefore, presuppositive of the notion of value? In what way might von Hildebrand criticize the last sentence of Brightman's statement? Does Brightman seem to indicate *what* makes something "prized" or "esteemed"? How would Alexander interpret Brightman's full statement? Could he adopt it to his own viewpoint and language?

13. According to G. E. Moore (*Principia Ethica* [Cambridge, Cambridge University Press, 1959], pp. 6–7), "good" is intrinsically indefinable. "If I am asked

[he writes] 'What is good?' my answer is that good is good, and that is the end of the matter. . . . My point is that 'good' is a simple notion, just as 'yellow' is a simple notion; that, just as you cannot, by any manner of means, explain to any one who does not already know it, what yellow is, so you cannot explain what good is." Does Moore seem to imply that "good" is as indefinable as "being"? In what way would Hawkins answer Moore's statement? In what way would von Hildebrand answer it?

14. DeWitt H. Parker would deny that "value" is an objective title of being. "A value," he has said (*Human Values* [New York, Harper & Bros., 1931], p. 21), "is always an experience, never a thing or object. Things may be valuable, but they are not values. We project value into the external world, attributing it to the things that serve desire." What criticisms of this statement would St. Thomas, Hawkins, and von Hildebrand make? Is there a difference, do you think, between calling value a "thing" and calling it the "valid title" of a thing? Do you see any similarity between Brightman's views (in Question No. 12 above) and this statement by Parker? To what extent? Would criticisms against Parker also hold for Brightman?

15. "There is no possibility of a detached, self-contained local existence," says Whitehead (*Modes of Thought* [New York, Macmillan, 1938], p. 188). "The environment enters into the nature of each thing." Does McWilliams' view on the question of space leave any room for agreement with Whitehead's view?

16. Compare the time-space viewpoints of McWilliams, Wild, and Whitehead. Can Whitehead explain the problems of Wild and McWilliams? Can the latter explain Whitehead's problems?

17. Does de Solages' view of "time" and "contingence" appear to substantiate Dewey's views?

18. "Reality," observes Emil Brunner (*Christianity and Civilization* [New York, Charles Scribner's Sons, 1949], p. 47), "is pulverized temporality." Can this view be substantiated by any of the foregoing essays on the meaning of time?

19. Contrast Maritain's and Berdyaev's versions of the person. Maritain believes that "the subject is in no wise betrayed when it is made an object." Would Berdyaev agree? Why? Would de Finance agree? Why? What similarities do you perceive between Maritain's view of the relation of Being and subjectivity, and Moeller's view? Between Maritain's and de Finance's?

20. What connection do you find between de Finance's essay and Lavelle's essay in Part Three? Between de Finance and Johann's essay on Love? Compare the views of Berdyaev, de Finance, and Johann on personality and personal being. What views do they share in common? What views do they not share? Does Sturzo's essay in any way carry out the themes of de Finance and Johann? In what ways?

21. "The theological doctrine that God created man for his own glory and praise," Berdyaev has said (*Slavery and Freedom* [New York, Charles Scribner's Sons, 1944], pp. 39–40), "is degrading to man, and degrading to God also. . . . The relation of personality, even to the most exalted Personality of God, cannot be a relation of means and end; all personality is an end in itself." What misunderstanding does this statement contain?

22. In what way do the following statements by St. Augustine and Ernst Cassirer illustrate the paradox of personality? Would Berdyaev's essay on personality cast any light on this paradox?

§ "If by 'abyss' we understand a great depth, is not man's heart an abyss? For what is there more profound than that abyss?"—St. Augustine, *Enarrationes in psalmos.*

§ "Man cannot find himself, he cannot become aware of his individuality, save through the medium of social life."—Cassirer, *Essay on Man*.

23. What similarities do you find between de Finance's ideas and Marcel's ideas, as expressed in the latter's essays in Parts Two and Three? How does de Finance's statement on the person and Absolute Being compare with the following remark by J. V. Langmead Casserly? In what way do these statements substantiate one another? In what way do they differ?

§ "We approach the philosophical problems of Absolute Being not entirely empty-handed and unequipped because, being ourselves existing individuals, we already know within ourselves what it is to be."—*The Christian in Philosophy*.

24. Moeller says that being is its own ground. Heidegger (Part Three) says that being is insufficient as its own ground. What is the basis of this disagreement? Is the disagreement real or apparent? Why? How does Pieper explain the "question of grounds"? How does De Raeymaeker explain it?

25. What contributions does Moeller make to the problem of the one-and-many? What contributions does Pieper make? How does each of their views compare with those of Aristotle? With those of Plato? To which one—Plato or Aristotle—do the ideas of Moeller and Pieper most closely parallel?

26. What similarities do you find between Moeller and De Raeymaeker on the question of causality? What differences? Between De Raeymaeker and Rousselot? Between De Raeymaeker and James? In contrast to all of these thinkers, where does Garrigou-Lagrange (Part Three) stand on the question of causality?

27. What common intuition on the knowledge of things do you perceive in the selections by Pieper and Rousselot?

28. What clarification does Pieper's essay make to the problem of "negativity" in Heidegger's statement in Part Three?

29. Compare the statements by Pieper and Marcel (Part Three) on the "hope-structure" of knowledge.

30. Compare the statements of Pieper and Phelan on "the silence of being."

31. Contrast the conceptions of "analogy" in Phelan's essay and in the essay by Emmet in Part Three. In what way does Somerville's essay bring out the theme of analogy? Gilson's essay?

32. What link does De Raeymaeker see between "analogy" and "causality"? Is this "link" present in the essay by Phelan? By Pieper?

33. De Raeymaeker says that no particular being can furnish the reason for its own being. Would Heidegger (Part Three) agree or disagree? In what ways?

34. What explicit and implicit connections can you discover between De Raeymaeker's terms, "horizontal," and "vertical," causality, and Somerville's terms "longitudinal" and "latitudinal"?

35. Compare Somerville's "interior action" and Forest's "interiority" (Part One). Compare Somerville and Rousselot on the same theme. How different are their views? How similar?

36. In what way does Somerville take up the theme of "moral purification" contained in many of the essays in Part One? What role does "outer reality" play in the essays by Somerville and Lavelle (Part Three)? In the essays by Somerville and Marcel (Part Three)?

37. What rebuttal does Rousselot offer to Hampshire's objections in Part Three on universal knowledge? Does Rousselot's view imply a hierarchy of being? What does Hampshire's view imply?

38. In saying, "Mind comes first, and all being is for mind," does Rousselot imply that intelligence precedes all being? What then of the "being" of intelligence itself? If intelligence comes first, how could it be "the faculty of being"? Is the "precedence," which Rousselot speaks of, historical, logical, or ontological? How does Rousselot's original statement stand up against Marcel's contention (Part Three) that being has primacy over knowledge?

39. Why does Clarke say that the relation between the terms "exist," "being," and "real" is applied to the intentional order according to the analogy of extrinsic attribution, rather than to the analogy of proper proportionality? What difference would be made if these terms were applied according to the analogy of proper proportionality?

40. Why does Bergson say, "Reality . . . is fullness constantly swelling out, to which emptiness is unknown"? Would this mean that Marcel (Part Three) is unjustified in using the term "full-empty," in reference to reality? Does Marcel seem to feel that there is, in Bergson's words, "less in the idea of the empty than in that of the full"?

41. Compare the views of Clarke, Bergson, and Santayana on the "possibles." Does Clarke's argument make contact with Santayana's views? In what way?

42. What common view is inherent in the following statements by Royce and Bergson?

§ Royce: ". . . the past, dead as it is often said to be, determines our present need, and sets for us our ideal task."

§ Bergson: "Backwards over the course of time a constant remodeling of the past by the present, of the cause by the effect, is being carried out."

43. Compare the selections by Plato, Martin, and Sturzo on knowledge. What common elements show up in each? What principal lines of distinction can you draw between them?

44. In the following two statements, F. H. Bradley asserts that inquiries into truth and knowledge imply a point of view on reality. What specific comments could be made on these statements by Plato, Martin, and Sturzo?

§ "If there is anything in philosophy of which I am fully assured, it is this, that to seek to discuss the nature of truth apart from a theory of ultimate reality ends and must end in futile self-deception."—*Essays on Truth and Reality.*

§ "It is impossible . . . to deal with truth apart from an examination of the nature of reality. . . . The very questions as to truth with which a man begins, involve in the end an answer to certain questions about the nature of things."—*Essays on Truth and Reality.*

45. What basic agreements can you discover between Martin's essay on knowledge and the views expressed by Gilson in Part One? Between these and the essays by Maritain, Garrigou-Lagrange, and Phelan in Part Three?

46. The theoretical physicist Sir James Jeans has said (*The Mysterious Universe,* [New York, E. P. Dutton & Co., 1960], p. 150), "The final truth about a phenomenon resides in the mathematical description of it; so long as there is no imperfection in this, our knowledge of the phenomenon is complete." How would Poincaré (see question No. 7) receive this statement? In the light of the following quotations can you frame specific criticisms of this statement?

§ "There is a hierarchy among the various departments of knowledge, and though mathematics may be used to explain the phenomena of physics, it remains nevertheless true that the basic rational explanation is to be found in a science from which all other sciences borrow their first principles, namely, metaphysics. If philosophy and science were totally divorced and separated from one another, the laws of science would be without any rational foundation."—F. J. Sheen, *The Philosophy of Science.*

§ "It is philosophy which justifies and defends their [sciences'] principles, which determines the first objects toward which they work, and as a result, their nature, their value, their limits as sciences. It is philosophy, for example, which tells us whether irrational numbers and indefinite numbers are real beings or only rational beings, whether the non-Euclidean geometries are rational constructions built upon Euclidean geometry and which leave the latter its privileged position, or if, on the contrary, they constitute a much greater system of which Euclidean geometry is only one specimen; whether mathematics and logic are divided or not by immovably drawn frontiers, etc. In a word, it is philosophy which assigns the order which reigns between the sciences: *sapientis est ordinare.*"—Jacques Maritain, *The Degrees of Knowledge.*

§ Metaphysics "reveals . . . the hierarchy of authentic values through all the extent of being. It gives a center to . . . ethics. It maintains justice in the universe of knowledge, making clear the natural limits, the harmony and subordination of the various sciences. . . ."—Jacques Maritain, *The Degrees of Knowledge.*

47. Compare the essays in this section by St. Augustine and James in the light of the arguments on the consequences of denying free will. In what way are their arguments similar? In what way do they differ?

48. Assess the similarities and differences between James and Jaspers on the question of "risk" in freedom. How, on the basis of the essays in Parts Three and Four, would you expect Dewey to react to the question of "risk" as an important element in freedom?

49. What relation can you establish between Jaspers's notion of "finite self-containment" and Berdyaev's notion of "ego-confinement"?

50. In the light of the following statement by R. C. Pollock, how would you tie together the themes of "time," "truth," "value," and "freedom"? Show the relevance of his statement to these themes as expressed by any of the authors in this volume.

§ "Man's freedom is at its highest when he is using it to fill his life with truth and value, but man does this only in a long process of time, since he has to create the very instruments by which he can progressively bring truth and value into his world.—"Freedom and History," *Thought.*

51. According to James in the following statements, free will is a relation between the mind and the way in which ideas are held before it. Is there any connection between these statements and St. Thomas's notion that free will is "election"?

§ "Will is a relation between the mind and its ideas. . . . [Its] essential achievement . . . is to attend to a difficult object and hold it just before the mind."—*Principles of Psychology.*

§ "The strong-willed man . . . is the man who hears the still small voice unflinchingly, and who, when the death-bringing consideration comes, looks at its face, consents to its presence, clings to it, affirms it, and holds it fast, in spite of the host of exciting mental images which rise in revolt and would expel it from the mind."—*Principles of Psychology.*

52. What connection can you discover between the essay by Jaspers and the following statement by Berdyaev?

§ "Philosophical text-books generally speak of freedom as identical with 'free will,' that is to say, as the possibility of choice. . . . For me freedom has always meant something quite different. Freedom is first and foremost my independence, determination from within and creative initiative; its reality does not depend on any norm. . . ."—*Dream and Reality.*

53. Compare the following statements by St. Anselm and Spinoza. What do you consider to be the crux of the disagreement between them?

§ ". . . the will of God does nothing by any necessity, but of his own power. . . . For necessity is always either compulsion or restraint. . . ." —St. Anselm, *Cur Deus Homo.*

§ ". . . I say that a thing is free which exists and acts solely by the necessity of its own nature. . . . I do not place freedom in free decision, but in free necessity."—Spinoza, Letter to G. H. Schaller.

54. What light does the following remark by Paul Tillich shed on "The Legend of the Grand Inquisitor"?

§ "In order to avoid the risk of asking and doubting, [man] surrenders the right to ask and doubt. He escapes from freedom in order to escape from the anxiety of meaninglessness."—*The Courage to Be.*

55. The motivating power of St. Anselm's so-called ontological argument is, as he says in *Proslogium,* II, "faith seeking understanding"; for, by believing, he says elsewhere (*Monologium,* LXXV. 1), the soul reaches out for God. In what way do the following precedents from St. Augustine add to your understanding of Anselm's procedure?

§ "For the Prophet says: 'If ye will not believe, ye shall not understand.' Surely he would not have said that, had he not thought that believing and understanding are different. Therefore, what I understand I also believe, but I do not understand everything that I believe; for all which I understand I know, but I do not know all that I believe. But still I am not unmindful of the utility of believing many things which are not known."—*De Magistro.*

§ "But I at least am seeking what I may know, not what I may believe. Now everything that we know, we may with reason perhaps be said to believe, but not to know everything which we believe."—*Soliloquies.*

§ ". . . Thou shouldst not therefore see in order that thou mayest believe, but believe in order that thou mayest see; believe so long as thou dost not see, lest thou blush with shame when thou dost see. Let us therefore believe while the time of faith lasts, until the time of seeing comes. . . ." —*Sermones.*

§ "God by deferring our hope, stretches our desire; by the desiring, stretches the mind; by stretching, makes it more capacious. . . . Let us therefore desire, for we shall be filled. Let us stretch ourselves unto Him, that when He shall come, He may fill us."—*In Epistolam Joannis ad Parthos.*

Do you see any relation between the last two quotations and Johann's essay "Time and Charity"?

56. The following statements by Tertullian, Francis Bacon, and David Hume have several elements in common. Can you pick them out? How might St. Anselm reply to these statements? How might St. Thomas reply? What assumptions appear to be inherent in each of these statements?

§ "It is certain only because it is impossible."—Tertullian, *De Carne Christi.*

§ ". . . the more absurd and incredible any divine mystery is, the greater honor we do to God in believing it; and so much the more noble the victory of faith."—Bacon, *De Argumentis.*

§ "To be a philosophical sceptic is in a man of letters the first and most essential step toward being a sound, believing Christian."—Hume, *Dialogues Concerning Natural Religion.*

57. Is there, do you believe, any connection between the "anti-intellectualism" of the foregoing statements by Tertullian, Bacon, and Hume, and the following quotation by R. L. Shinn?

§ "God's self-disclosure is mediated, not through propositions but through historical events in which men are confronted with a responsibility and a demand for decision, with a judgment or promise coming from the divine Lord."—*Christianity and the Problem of History.*

58. What suggestion of St. Thomas's cosmological argument do you find in the following statement by Moses Maimonides?

§ ". . . nothing exists but God Almighty and all His works . . . and there is no way to apprehend Him except through His works."—*Guide to the Perplexed.*

59. What criticisms would Ayer and Lazerowitz (Part Three) make of St. Thomas's proofs for the existence of God? Would they agree or disagree with Stace's position? In what way? What counterarguments would be given by Collins to substantiate St. Thomas's position?

60. Contrast the arguments of Stace and Collins on the relevance of proofs for God's existence. Does Collins meet all of Stace's objections? Stace asserts that it is invalid to deduce "divine consequents" from "natural premises." Do you find any parallel between his position and Ayer's statements (Part Three) against the "error" of deducing "supra-empirical" realities from "empirical" evidence?

61. What relations can you discover between the following statements by St. Augustine and James? Is James's assertion a "logical" consequence of the "paradox" of God's existence? Give reasons for or against.

§ "It becomes our duty to envisage God . . . as good without quality, great without quantity, creator without necessity, foremost without relations, comprehending all things but possessing no mode of existence, everywhere present but without location, eternal without subjection to time, capable of action without submitting to changes of mutable things, and of feeling without passion. . . ."—St. Augustine, *De Trinitate.*

§ "The divine can mean no single quality, it must mean a group of qualities, by being champions of which in alternation, different men may all find worthy missions. Each attitude being a syllable in human nature's total message, it takes the whole of us to spell the meaning out completely."
—James, *The Varieties of Religious Experience.*

62. State Collins' position on the boundaries between man's knowledge, and unknowledge, of God. How do his remarks compare with those of Moeller and Pieper on the same topic?

63. How might Buber regard the following statement by nineteenth-century litterateur Thomas Carlyle? Would Buber take it as a historical illustration of his position?

§ "Considered as a whole, the Christian religion of late ages has been continually dissipating itself into Metaphysics; and threatens now to disappear, as some rivers do, in deserts of barren sand."—"Sir Walter Scott."

64. Compare Lotz's remarks on religion and metaphysics with Buber's. Are Buber's arguments related in any way to those advanced by Stace? Does Lotz adequately solve Buber's difficulties? Does Lotz's view lead directly to Plato's comments in Part One? How?

65. Does Lotz's statement that philosophy can reach certain solutions of its problems and so provide the inquirer tranquility appear to contradict Pieper's contention that philosophy can provide neither lasting solutions of its problems nor full tranquility?

Research Themes

1. Does Parmenides' "goddess" have anything in common with the Lady, Philosophy, in Boethius' *Consolation of Philosophy* (Book I)? With Socrates' Diotima in the dialogue *Symposium?* Can you think of any other such "guiding figures" in the literature of philosophy? State your findings in a short paper of 500–750 words.

2. Does Parmenides' *estí* appear to be just another of the pre-Socratic *archē,* or ultimate constituent and origin of nature? Test your assumptions on conclusions drawn in representative historical accounts of Parmenides' ideas. (For example: Joseph Owens, C.Ss.R., *A History of Ancient Western Philosophy* [New York, Appleton-Century-Crofts, Inc., 1959], pp. 58 ff.; Frederick Copleston, S.J., *A History of Philosophy,* Vol. I [Westminster, Md., Newman, 1955], pp. 47 ff.; Ignatius Brady, O.F.M., *A History of Ancient Philosophy* [Milwaukee, Bruce Publishing Co., 1959], pp. 48 ff.; Eduard Zeller, *Outlines of the History of Greek Philosophy* [13th ed. rev., New York, Meridian Books, Inc., 1957], pp. 65 ff.) Write a 500-word account of the results of your inquiry and analysis.

3. Compare Aristotle's analysis of the claimants to the title of being (matter, form, universal, genus) with the five "claimants" given by Plato in *Epistle VII* (342B). Present the results of your comparison in a 250-word statement.

4. What internal connection can you establish between Aristotle's *Physics* and the *Metaphysics?* Why do you think that early editors placed the *Metaphysics* after the *Physics?* Demonstrate your reasoning by passages from both texts. Check your reasons against explanations given in any general history of ancient thought. Read Books II, III, and V of Aristotle's *Physics,* and compare them with *Metaphysics,*

Kappa. What connection do you find? Can you find similar instances of comparison between these works? Write up your conclusions in a 1,000-word essay.

5. On the basis of his statement in the *Posterior Analytics* (II, 7; esp. 92b10), what comment would Aristotle make to the following quotations by F. H. Bradley? Summarize your judgment in a 100-word statement.

§ ". . . thought is clearly, to some extent at least, ideal. Without an idea there is no thinking, and an idea implies the separation of content from existence."—*Appearance and Reality.*

§ "No one ever *means* to assert about anything but reality, or to do anything but qualify a 'that' by a 'what.' "—*Appearance and Reality.*

6. Analyze the passage in Aristotle's *Nichomachean Ethics* (1095a13–1120a4) on the good for man. Compare it to the statements by Friedrich Nietzsche in his *Beyond Good and Evil* ([Chicago, Henry Regnery Co., 1958], Ninth Article) on the conception of value. What points made by Dewey in his article "Some Questions about Value" (*Journal of Philosophy,* XLI [1944], 449–55) are left unanswered by Aristotle's and Nietzsche's treatments? Which of Dewey's questions appear to be adequately answered by them? Reduce your findings to an essay of about 1,500 words.

7. Compare the views on the meaning of time given by Berdyaev in *The Meaning of History* (London, Geoffrey Bles, Ltd., 1949) and Erich Frank in his article "Time and Eternity" (*Review of Metaphysics,* II [1940], 39–52) and in his *Philosophical Understanding and Religious Truth* ([New York, Oxford University Press, 1945], esp. Chap. III). Detail your conclusions in a paper of 1,000–1,250 words.

8. Write a 1,000-word paper on the importance of time and place in the thought of St. Augustine, using the following citations from *The City of God:* XI,1; XLV,1,28; XV,1,2; XIX,17. Consult a standard secondary source (such as John Figgis, *Political Aspects of St. Augustine's City of God* [London, Longmans, 1921]) for alternative readings.

9. Make a précis or digest of Frederick Copleston's article "The Human Person in Contemporary Philosophy" (*Contemporary Philosophy* [Westminster, Md., Newman, 1956], pp. 103–24). In what way do the essays in the section entitled "The Personal Center" in this volume (Maritain through Berdyaev) represent contemporary views? Write a 1,200-word essay summarizing your conclusions.

10. Make a précis of Romano Guardini's essay on "The Legend of the Grand Inquisitor" (*Cross Currents,* III [1953]). Compare Guardini's analysis with Dostoevsky's chapter by the same title in his *The Brothers Karamazov* (II, v). Do you find Guardini's comments an adequate solution to Ivan Karamazov's difficulty on the questions of God and freedom? Compare Berdyaev's reading of the problem in his biography *Dostoevsky* (trans. Donald Attwater [New York, Meridian Books, Inc., 1957], esp. Chaps. II and VII). In the light of these materials, make out a case in a 2,000-word essay either for or against Dostoevsky's conception of the problem of freedom.

11. Assess the positions of St. Thomas, St. Augustine, William James, and Karl Jaspers on the subject of freedom and free will. What general lines of agreement in language and idea seem to be evident. Compare the positions of Spinoza ("Of Human Bondage" and "Of Human Freedom," *Ethics*) and Jonathan Edwards ("Freedom of the Will" in *Puritan Sage,* ed. V. Ferm [New York, Library Publishers, 1953], pp. 480–515) with those of the foregoing authors. Do you find that there are six different issues on freedom? Six different kinds of freedom? Or

are all six speaking of the same problem? Present your findings in a documented paper of about 2,500 words.

12. Analyze the passage on freedom by Gabriel Marcel in his *The Mystery of Being* (Vol. I [Chicago, Henry Regnery Co., 1960], Chap. VII), entitled "Freedom and Grace." In what ways does Marcel reaffirm insights to be found in the authors in this volume? What new insights does Marcel offer? Write up your conclusions in a short paper of 1,000 words.

13. The Ontological Argument:

(A) Make a précis of St. Anselm's "ontological argument" in *Proslogium*, II. Compare it with the explanation given in any representative account of his thought (e.g., Frederick Copleston, *A History of Philosophy*, Vol. II [Westminster, Md., Newman, 1955], pp. 161–64).

(B) Compare St. Anselm's statement with the following quotations from St. Augustine. Do they substantiate Anselm's procedures and results?

§ "For God is, and truly and supremely is. And this, so I think, we not only hold to by faith as a fact beyond doubt, but by a sure, though as yet slender, form of cognition, we attain to it."—*De Libero Arbitrio.*

§ "True, faith hath already found Him, but hope still seeketh Him. But charity hath both found Him through faith, and seeketh to have Him by sight, where He will then be found so as to satisfy us, and no longer to need our search."—*Enarrationes in psalmos.*

§ "For incomprehensible things must be investigated in such a way that no one may think he has found nothing, when he has been able to find how incomprehensible is that which he was seeking. Why then does he thus seek; if he comprehends that that which he seeks is incomprehensible, unless it be that he may not cease from seeking so long as he is making progress in his actual inquiry into things incomprehensible, and becomes better and ever better while seeking so great a good, which is both sought in order to be found, and found in order to be sought? For it is both sought that it may be found the more sweetly, and found that it may be sought the more eagerly."—*De Trinitate.*

§ "For when it is said that God knows us, He gives us a knowledge of Himself so that we may thus understand that we owe this knowledge of Him not to ourselves but to His mercy."—*Epistolae.*

Do you find any connection between St. Augustine's second quotation and Father Johann's essay "Time and Charity"? In what way does St. Augustine's last statement relate to the following quotations by Langmead Casserly and Jaspers?

§ "The existence of God is already given in our self-conscious experience, and the task of the Christian philosopher is to lay bare the latent meaning and implications of this basic apprehension by employing the analogies most appropriate to such a theme."—*The Christian in Philosophy.*

§ "A proved God is no God. Accordingly, only he who starts from God can seek Him."—*The Perennial Scope of Philosophy.*

(C) Is the "negative element" in St. Anselm's argument in any way related to the following comments by St. Augustine?

§ "God is known better in unknowing."—*De Ordine.*

§ "There is in the mind no knowledge of God except the knowledge of how it does not know him."—*De Ordine*.

§ "All things can be said of God, yet nothing is worthily said of God. Nothing is wider than this utter want. Thou seekest a name befitting Him and findest none; thou seekest in what way soever to speak of Him and thou findest Him in all things."—*In Joannis Evangelium*.

What relation to these statements can you discover in Plotinus' *Enneads*, VI, ix, 3, 4?

(D) Compare St. Anselm's argument to the versions in Descartes's *Meditations*, V, and in G. W. Leibniz' *New Essays Concerning Understanding*, IV, x, 7, especially the following formulations:

§ "It is not within my power to think of God without existence."—Descartes, *Meditations*, V.

§ ". . . assuming that God is possible, he exists."—Leibniz, *New Essays*.

(E) Compare St. Anselm's argument to the versions and criticisms brought against it by St. Thomas (*Summa Theologiae* I, Q2, al; *Contra Gentiles*, I, ii), and by Kant (*Critique of Pure Reason*, trans. N. K. Smith [London, Macmillan, 1933], pp. 622 ff.).

Summarize your findings for all these sections—(A) through (E)—in a 2,000-word paper.

SELECTED BIBLIOGRAPHY FOR PART FOUR

Being

1. Allers, Rudolf. *"Ens et Unum Convertuntur,"* in *Philosophical Studies in Honor of Ignatius Smith*, ed. J. K. Ryan. Westminster, Md.: Newman Press, 1952. pp. 65–75.
2. Anderson, J. F. "On Being: Its Meaning and Role in Philosophy," *Thomist*, 3 (1941), 579–87.
3. ———. "Some Disputed Questions on Our Knowledge of Being," *Review of Metaphysics*, 11 (1958), 550–60.
4. Bakan, M. K. "On the Subject-Object Relationship," *Journal of Philosophy*, 55 (1958), 89–101.
5. Beach, J. D. "Separate Entity as the Subject of Aristotle's Metaphysics," *Thomist*, 20 (1957), 75–95.
6. ———. "Aristotle's Notion of Being," *Thomist*, 21 (1958), 29–43.
7. Berdyaev, N. A. *Spirit and Reality*. New York: Scribner's, 1939.
8. Black, Max. "Possibility," *Journal of Philosophy*, 57 (1960), 117–26.
9. Blaha, Ottokar. "The Logical Structure of Reality," *Philosophy Today*, 1 (1957), 39–42.
10. Bochenski, I. M., O.P. "On Analogy," *Thomist*, 11 (1948), 424–47.

11. Byles, W. E. "The Analogy of Being," *New Scholasticism*, 16 (1942), 331–64.
12. Clarke, W. N., S.J. "The Limitation of Act by Potency," *New Scholasticism*, 26 (1952), 167–94.
13. Collins, R. "Finality and Being," *Proceedings American Catholic Philosophical Association*, 23 (1949), 36–46.
14. Conway, J. I. "The Reality of the Possible," *New Scholasticism*, 33 (1959), 139–61.
15. Demos, Raphael. "Non-being," *Journal of Philosophy*, 30 (1933), 85–102.
16. Dollard, S. E. "Two Schools of Becoming," *Modern Schoolman*, 6 (1930), 47–49.
17. Flanigan, Sr. Thomas M. "The Use of Analogy in the *Summa Contra Gentiles*," *Modern Schoolman*, 35 (1957), 21–37.
18. Hawkins, D. J. B. *Causality and Implication*. London: Sheed and Ward, 1945.
19. Heydon, J. K. "Being and Unity," *Catholic World*, 153 (1941), 99–101.
20. Johann, R. O., S.J. "A Comment on Secondary Causality," *Modern Schoolman*, 25 (1947), 19–25.
21. Klubertanz, G. P., S.J. "Being and Action," *Modern Schoolman*, 28 (1951), 175–90.
22. Lauer, J. Q., S.J. "Determination of Substance by Accidents in the Philosophy of St. Thomas," *Modern Schoolman*, 18 (1941), 31–35.
23. Marcel, Gabriel. *Royce's Metaphysics*. Chicago: Henry Regnery, 1956.
24. Mascall, E. L. "The Doctrine of Analogy," *Cross Currents*, 1 (1951), 38–57.
25. Moore, J. S. "On the First Principles of Knowledge and Reality," *Philosophical Review*, 50 (1941), 315–17.
26. Moore, J. S. "Analogy and the Free Mind," *Downside Review*, 76 (1958), 1–28.
27. Mosely, F. S. "The Restoration of the Concept of Substance to Science," *New Scholasticism*, 10 (1936), 1–17.
28. Mueller, G. E. "On Being and Becoming," *Philosophy of Science*, 10 (1943), 149–62.
29. Nelson, E. J. "A Defense of Substance," *Philosophical Review*, 56 (1947), 491–509.
30. Osgniach, A. J. "The Problem of Substance," *New Scholasticism*, 2 (1928), 115–27, 236–49.
31. Pegis, A. C. "The Dilemma of Being and Unity: A Platonic Incident in Christian Thought," in *Essays in Thomism*. New York, Sheed and Ward, 1942. pp. 151–183.
32. Peters, J. A. "Matter and Form in Metaphysics," *New Scholasticism*, 31 (1957), 447–83.
33. Phelan, G. B. "The Being of Creatures," *Proceedings American Catholic Philosophical Association*, 31 (1957), 118–25.
34. Salmon, E. G. "Metaphysics and Unity," in *Progress in Philosophy*, ed. J. A. McWilliams. Milwaukee: Bruce, 1955. pp. 47–60.
35. Slattery, M. P., O.P. "Is Being a Genus?" *Philosophical Studies*, 8 (1958), 89–104.
36. Toohey, J. J. "The Term 'Being,' " *New Scholasticism*, 16 (1942), 107–29.
37. Van Roo, W. A., S.J. "Act and Potency," *Modern Schoolman*, 18 (1940), 1–5.
38. ———. "Matter as a Principle of Being," *Modern Schoolman*, 19 (1942), 47–50.
39. Weiss, Paul. *Modes of Being*. Carbondale, Ill.: Southern Illinois University Press, 1958.

Essence and Existence

1. Albertson, J. S. "The *Esse* of Accidents According to St. Thomas," *Modern Schoolman,* 30 (1953), 265–78.
2. Aquinas, Thomas. *On Being and Essence.* trans. A. A. Mauer. Toronto: Pontifical Institute of Medieval Studies, 1949.
3. Bahur, A. J. "Existence and its Polarities," *Journal of Philosophy,* 46 (1949), 629–37.
4. Beck, M. "Reason and Existence," *Journal of Philosophy,* 44 (1947), 375–80.
5. Boas, George. "Being and Existence," *Journal of Philosophy,* 53 (1956), 748–59.
6. DeLaguna, G. A. "Existence and Potentiality," *Philosophical Review,* 60 (1951), 155–76.
7. Hawkins, D. J. B. "Anatomy of Existence," *Dublin Review,* 219 (1946), 97–108.
8. Maurer, A. A. "Form and Essence in the Philosophy of St. Thomas," *Medieval Studies,* 13 (1951), 174–76.
9. Pontifex, Mark, O.S.B. "The Meaning of *Esse,*" *Downside Review,* 67 (1949), 395–405.
10. Renard, Henri. "Essence and Existence," *Proceedings American Catholic Philosophical Association,* 21 (1946), 53–66.
11. Quine, W. V. "Resignation and Existence," *Journal of Philosophy,* 36 (1939), 701–9.
12. Sellars, R. W. "The Verification of Categories: Existence and Substance," *Journal of Philosophy,* 40 (1943), 197–205.
13. Smith, V. E. "Existentialism and Existence," *Thomist,* 11 (1948), 141–96, 297–329.
14. Swabey, W. C. "Causal Definition of Existence," *Journal of Philosophy,* 41 (1944), 253–61.
15. Weiss, Paul. "Ten Theses Relating To Existence," *Review of Metaphysics,* 10 (1957), 401–11.
16. Walton, W. M. "Being, Essence and Existence for St. Thomas Aquinas," *Review of Metaphysics,* 3 (1950), 339–65.

Value

1. Aiken, H. D. "The Pluralistic Analysis of Aesthetic Value," *Philosophical Review,* 59 (1950), 493–513.
2. Baisnee, J. A. "The Concept of Value," *Proceedings American Catholic Philosophical Association,* 9 (1933), 117–33.
3. Chapman, Emmanuel. "The Perennial Theme of Beauty and Art," in *Essays in Thomism,* ed. R. E. Brennan. New York: Sheed and Ward, 1942. pp. 335–46.
4. Fisher, J. J. "On Defining Good," *Journal of Philosophy,* 51 (1954), 730–36.
5. Hugo, J. "The Realism of Values," *Thought,* 9 (1934), 390–98.
6. Levi, A. W. "Value in the Great Tradition," *New Scholasticism,* 9 (1935), 25–38.

7. McManus, C. J. "The Good In Metaphysics and Ethics," *Proceedings American Catholic Philosophical Association,* 24 (1950), 97–102.
8. Moore, G. E. *Principia Ethica.* Cambridge: Cambridge University Press, 1959.
9. ———. "The Conception of Intrinsic Value," in *Philosophical Studies.* New York: Humanities Press Inc., 1958. Chap. 8.
10. O'Connor, W. R. "The Nature of the Good," *Thought,* 24 (1949), 637–54.
11. O'Neill, C. J. "The Notion of Beauty in the Ethics of St. Thomas," *New Scholasticism,* 14 (1940), 346–78.
12. Parker, D. H. "A Reflection on the Crisis in the Theory of Value," *Ethics,* 56 (1946), 193–207.
13. Pepper, S. C. "Values and Value Judgments," *Journal of Philosophy,* 46 (1949), 429–34.
14. von Hildebrand, Dietrich. "Beauty in the Light of Redemption," *Journal of Arts and Letters,* 3 (1957), 100–111.

Time and Space

1. Anderson, J. F. "Time and the Possibility of an Eternal World," *Thomist,* 15 (1952), 136–61.
2. Carmichael, P. A. "The Metaphysical Matrix of Science," *Philosophy of Science,* 20 (1953), 208–16.
3. Collingwood, R. G. *The Idea of Nature.* New York: Oxford University Press, 1945.
4. Conen, P. F. "Aristotle's Definition of Time," *New Scholasticism,* 26 (1952), 441–58.
5. DeGroot, E. "Is There a Metaphysic of History?" *Hibbert Journal,* 51 (1953), 217–25.
6. Fackenheim, E. L. *Metaphysics and Historicity.* Milwaukee: Marquette University Press, 1961.
7. Joad, C. E. M. *Philosophical Aspects of Modern Science.* London: Allen & Unwin, 1932.
8. Kane, W. H. "Hylemorphism and the Recent Views of the Constitution of Matter," *Proceedings American Catholic Philosophical Association,* 11 (1935), 61–74.
9. Lenzen, V. F. "Metaphysics of Space and Time," *Journal of Philosophy,* 29 (1932), 182–87.
10. Margenau, Henry. *The Nature of Physical Reality.* New York: McGraw-Hill, 1950.
11. Moore, G. E. "Is Time Real?" in *Some Main Problems in Philosophy.* New York: Macmillan, 1953. Chap. 11.
12. Rowell, E. M. "A Meditation on Berdyaev's Three Times," *Hibbert Journal,* 48 (1950), 252–56.
13. Schlick, Moritz. *Philosophy of Nature.* New York: Philosophical Library, 1949.
14. Schrag, C. O. "Existence and History," *Review of Metaphysics,* 13 (1959), 28–44.
15. Whitehead, A. N. *The Concept of Nature.* Ann Arbor: University of Michigan Press, 1957.

The Personal Center

1. Brightman, E. S. *The Person and Reality.* New York: Ronald, 1958.
2. Buckham, J. W. "The Union of Being and Personality," *Journal of Religion,* 17 (1937), 397–409.
3. Johann, R. O., S.J. "The Problem of Love," *Review of Metaphysics,* 8 (1954), 225–45.
4. ———. "Subjectivity," *Review of Metaphysics,* 12 (1958), 200–34.
5. Maritain, Jacques, "The Person and the Common Good," *Review of Politics,* 8 (1946), 419–55.
6. Moore, J. S. "Problems of the Self," *Philosophical Review,* 42 (1933), 487–99.
7. Sciacca, M. F. "Individuality and Personality," in *The Human Person and the World of Values,* ed. B. V. Schwarz. New York: Fordham University Press, 1960.

Knowledge

1. Bayles, C. A. "Universals, Communicable Knowledge and Metaphysics," *Journal of Philosophy,* 48 (1951), 636–44.
2. DeLaguna, G. A. "Being and Knowing," *Philosophical Review,* 45 (1936), 435–56.
3. Fen, S. N. "On Being and Being Known," *Journal of Philosophy,* 48 (1951), 381–87.
4. McMullin, E. "The Problem of Universals," *Philosophical Studies,* 8 (1958), 122–39.
5. Maritain, Jacques. *The Degrees of Knowledge.* New York: Scribner's, 1959.
6. Phelan, G. B., and Anderson, J. F. "The Metaphysics of Knowledge," *Proceedings American Catholic Philosophical Association,* 21 (1946), 106–11.
7. ———. "Being, Order and Knowledge," *Proceedings American Catholic Philosophical Association,* 33 (1959), 12–20.
8. Sellars, R. W. "The Correspondence Theory of Truth," *Journal of Philosophy,* 38 (1941), 645–54.
9. Sellars, Wilfred. "Being and Being Known," *Proceedings American Catholic Philosophical Association,* 34 (1960), 28–49.

Freedom

1. Berdyaev, N. A. *Freedom and the Spirit.* London: Geoffrey Bles, 1948.
2. ———. *Slavery and Freedom.* New York: Scribner's, 1944.
3. Campbell, C. A. "Is Free-will a Pseudo-Problem?" *Mind,* 60 (1951), 141–65.
4. Fratos, Eugenio. "Freedom is a Reward," *Philosophy Today,* 1 (1957), 102–5.
5. Hook, Sidney, and Konvitz, M. R. (eds.). *Freedom and Experience.* Ithaca, N.Y.: Cornell University Press, 1947.
6. Lehrer, Keith. "Can We Know That We Have Free Will By Introspection?" *Journal of Philosophy,* 57 (1960), 145–57.

7. Lynch, W. F. "The Problem of Freedom," *Cross Currents*, 10 (1960), 97–114.
8. Macintosh, D. C. "Responsibility, Freedom and Causality," *Journal of Philosophy*, 37 (1940), 42–51.
9. McKeon, Richard. "Philosophic Differences and the Issues of Freedom," *Ethics*, 61 (1951), 105–35.
10. O'Shaughnessy, B. "Limits of the Will," *Philosophical Review*, 65 (1956), 443–90.
11. Park, J. N. "Freedom, Value and the Law," *Ethics*, 62 (1951), 41–47.
12. Pegis, A. C. "Necessity and Liberty," *Proceedings American Catholic Philosophical Association*, 16 (1940), 1–27.
13. Pollock, R. C. "Freedom and History," *Thought*, 27 (1952), 400–20.
14. von Hildebrand, Dietrich. *Christian Ethics*. New York: McKay, 1953.
15. Wild, John. "Tendency: The Ontological Ground of Ethics," *Journal of Philosophy*, 49 (1952), 461–75.

God

1. Anderson, J. F. *The Cause of Being*. St. Louis, Mo.: B. Herder, 1952.
2. Clarke, W. N., S.J. "Linguistic Analysis and Natural Theology," *Proceedings American Catholic Philosophical Association*, 34 (1960), 110–26.
3. Conway, J. W. "Neopositivism and the Existence of God," *Downside Review*, 72 (1954), 153–71.
4. Findlay, J. N. "Can God's Existence Be Disproved?" *Mind*, 57 (1948), 176–83.
5. Garrigou-Lagrange, Reginald, O.P. *God: His Existence and Nature* (2 vols.). St. Louis, Mo.: B. Herder, 1949.
6. Gilson, Etienne. *God and Philosophy*. New Haven, Conn.: Yale University Press, 1941.
7. Hart, C. A. "Participation and the Thomistic Five Ways," *New Scholasticism*, 26 (1952), 267–81.
8. Hartshorne, Charles. "Theological Values in Current Metaphysics," *Journal of Religion*, 26 (1946), 157–67.
9. Hawkins, D. J. B. *The Essentials of Theism*. New York: Sheed and Ward, 1949.
10. Klubertanz, G. P., S.J. "Being and God According to Contemporary Scholastics," *Modern Schoolman*, 33 (1954), 1–16.
11. Malcolm, N. "Anselm's Ontological Arguments," *Philosophical Review*, 69 (1960), 41–62.
12. Maritain, Jacques. "On the Meaning of Contemporary Atheism," *Review of Politics*, 11 (1949), 267–80.
13. Mascall, E. L. *He Who Is*. London: Longman's, Green, 1943.
14. O'Brien, Thomas C., O.P. "Reflections on the Quest of God's Existence in Contemporary Thomistic Metaphysics," *Thomist*, 22 (1960), 1–89, 211–85.
15. Owens, Joseph, C.Ss.R. "Theodicy, Natural Theology and Metaphysics," *Modern Schoolman*, 28 (1951), 126–37.
16. Peirce, C. S. "A Neglected Argument for the Reality of God," in *Values in a Universe of Chance*, ed. P. Wiener. New York: Doubleday, 1958.

17. Phillips, R. P. *Modern Thomistic Philosophy*, Vol. II. Westminster, Md.: Newman Press, 1951.
18. Smart, H. R. "Anselm's Ontological Argument," *Review of Metaphysics*, 3 (1949), 161–66.
19. Stokes, M. B. "Theology and Anti-Metaphysical Spirit," *Religion in Life*, 28 (1959), 413–25.
20. Tillich, Paul. *Systematic Theology*, Vol. I. Chicago: Chicago University Press, 1951.
21. ———. "The Relations of Metaphysics and Theology," *Review of Metaphysics*, 10 (1956), 57–63.
22. White, Victor, O.P. "Prolegomena to the Five Ways," *Dominican Studies*, 5 (1952), 134–58.

BIOGRAPHICAL NOTES

SAMUEL ALEXANDER (1859–1938) was born in New South Wales and educated at Melbourne and Oxford. In 1916–18 he was Gifford Lecturer at the University of Glasgow. Six years later he retired as Professor of Philosophy from the Victoria University of Manchester after thirty-one years of teaching. His more widely known works include *Moral Order and Progress; Space, Time and Deity;* and the essay "Artistic Creation and Cosmic Creation."

THOMAS AQUINAS (1225–1274) came of a noble family of Roccasecca, Italy, and was schooled at the University of Naples. After becoming a Dominican friar, he studied under Albert the Great at Paris, and in 1256 was appointed to a chair in theology at the University of Paris on the same day that St. Bonaventure was named to a similar honor. Less than twenty years later he died at the height of his career while making his way to the Council of Lyons. Although his cardinal work is the *Summa Theologiae*, he also wrote the *Summa Contra Gentiles* and many commentaries on the writings of Aristotle and leading medieval predecessors.

ARISTOTLE (384–322 B.C.) was born in Stagyra, a Thracian peninsula city across the border from Macedon, where his physician father Nichomachus served the king's court. Enrolled in the Platonic Academy when about seventeen, he stayed on for nearly twenty years and later acted as tutor to the future Alexander the Great. Most of the works in logic, natural philosophy, literary and political philosophy, and metaphysics that have come down to us were given as lectures in his university-research center known as the Lyceum.

AURELIUS AUGUSTINE (354–430) was born in Tagaste, North Africa, studied rhetoric, and later taught in Rome and Milan. He was attracted successively to Manicheeism, scepticism, neo-Platonism, but was eventually converted to Christianity. After his conversion in 388, he returned to Africa, and was named Bishop of Hippo in 395. Chief among his many works are the long tracts *On the Trinity, The City of God,* and the autobiographical *Confessions*.

A. J. AYER (1910–) studied and later taught at Oxford. He is now Grote Professor of the Philosophy of Mind and Logic at the University of London. During World War II he served as Captain in the Welsh Guards. His principal writings include *Language, Truth and Logic* and *The Foundations of Empirical Knowledge*.

NIKOLAI BERDYAEV (1874–1949) was born in a fashionable suburb of Kiev, educated in Russia, and in 1917 was named Professor of Philosophy at the University of Moscow. Exiled to Vologda after the 1905 revolutions, he was finally expelled from the Soviet Union in 1922. He then set up an academy of religious philosophy first in Berlin and later in Paris, where he also founded a Russian review called *The New Way*. Influenced by German idealism and Rhineland mysticism, he became a trenchant critic of Communism and Thomism. His works include *The Meaning of History, Freedom and the Spirit, The Destiny of Man,* and *Solitude and Society.*

HENRI BERGSON (1895–1941), Parisian by birth, was educated in the French *lycées.* A member of the French Academy, he was awarded the 1927 Nobel Prize for literature. His principal works include *Time and Free Will, Matter and Memory, Introduction to Metaphysics, Creative Evolution,* and *The Two Sources of Morality and Religion.*

F. H. BRADLEY (1846–1924) was born at Clapham, England, and attended Britain's "public" schools before going up to Oxford. Appointed Fellow of Oxford's Merton College in 1870, he devoted his life to the writing of such works as *Appearance and Reality, The Principles of Logic,* and the *Ethical Studies.* Published posthumously were the *Collected Essays* and *Essays on Truth and Reality.*

MARTIN BUBER (1878–   ) is Professor of Social Philosophy at Jerusalem's Hebrew University. Born in Vienna and educated in Austria and Germany, he has been active throughout most of his life in the cause of Zionism. His Hasidic interests and point of view are evidenced in his published works, which include *I and Thou, Between Man and Man, The Prophetic Faith,* and *The Eclipse of God.*

E. A. BURTT (1892–   ) is Susan Linn Sage Professor of Philosophy at Cornell University's Sage School. He is perhaps best known as author of *The Metaphysical Foundations of Modern Physical Science* and *Religion in an Age of Science.* He has also edited *The English Philosophers: Bacon to Mill.*

RUDOLF CARNAP (1891–   ), since 1936 Professor of Philosophy at the University of Chicago, was born and educated in Germany, and received his doctorate at the University of Jena in 1921. He has been visiting Professor at Harvard, and for two years received an appointment to the Institute for Advanced Study. Co-editor of *Erkenntnis* and the *Journal of Unified Science,* he is now Associate Editor of the *International Encyclopedia of Unified Science.* His works include *The Logical Syntax of Language, Philosophy and Logical Syntax, Foundations of Logic and Mathematics, Meaning and Necessity,* and *Logical Foundations of Probability.*

W. NORRIS CLARKE, S.J. (1915–   ) is Associate Professor of Philosophy at Fordham University and American Editor-in-Chief of the *International Philosophical Quarterly.* His many articles have appeared in *The New Scholasticism, The Modern Schoolman, Thought, America,* and other periodicals.

R. G. COLLINGWOOD (1889–1943) at the time of his death held the post of Waynflete Professor of Metaphysical Philosophy at Oxford. He was well known as a historian and authority on the Roman occupation of Britain and as a philosopher. Among his works are *An Essay on Philosophical Method, The Principles of Art, The Idea of Nature, The Idea of History,* and *An Essay on Metaphysics.*

JAMES COLLINS (1917–   ) is Professor of Philosophy at St. Louis University, and has been recognized as a thinker of historical and critical sensitivity. This has been said to be much in evidence in his *The Mind of Kierkegaard, The Existentialists, A History of Modern European Philosophy,* and *God and Modern Philosophy.*

FREDERICK COPLESTON, S.J. (1907–   ), born in Somerset, England, and educated at Oxford, was converted to Catholicism in 1925. Entering the Society of Jesus the following year, he took doctoral studies at the Gregorian Institute in Rome. He has served as Professor of the History of Philosophy at Heythrop College, Oxford, and has been a member of the executive committees of the Royal Institute of Philosophy. His works on Nietzsche and Schopenhauer have received wide acclaim, but his fame rests chiefly on his *A History of Philosophy* which to date consists of six volumes.

RENÉ DESCARTES (1596–1650), considered the father of systematic modern philosophy, was educated at the Jesuit school of La Flêche. A mathematician who discovered the analytical geometry, he applied an axiomatic technique to the thought of his own day in order to reconstruct philosophy according to unimpeachable canons. His well-known *Discourse on Method* announced this program to the world, a program later fulfilled in the *Principles of Philosophy* and the *Meditations.*

JOHN DEWEY (1859–1952), a Vermonter by birth, was educated at the University of Vermont and The Johns Hopkins University, where he received his doctorate in 1884. He taught philosophy at the Universities of Michigan, Minnesota, Chicago, and, from 1905 until retirement in 1930, Columbia. Throughout a long and productive career Dewey was involved in the practical problems of education and the improvement of society. His immense scholarly activity continued until his death at the age of ninety-three. Among his more central works are *Essays in Experimental Logic, Reconstruction in Philosophy, Human Nature and Conduct, Experience and Nature, Philosophy and Civilization, Art as Experience,* and *Logic: The Theory of Inquiry.*

DOROTHY EMMET (1904–   ) is Professor of Philosophy at the University of Manchester. In addition to numerous articles, she is author of *The Nature of Metaphysical Thinking* and *Whitehead's Philosophy of Organism.*

JOSEPH DE FINANCE, S.J. (1901–   ) is Professor of Philosophy at Rome's Gregorian Institute. Considered one of the most influential Continental Thomists, his better-known works include *Doctor Communis* and *Existence et liberté.*

AIMÉ FOREST (1907–   ), Professor of Philosophy at the University of Montpellier, is author of the personalist study, *La structure métaphysique du concret selon St. Thomas d'Aquin.* Other notable works include *Du consentement à l'etre, Consentement et création,* and *La vocation de l'ésprit.*

REGINALD GARRIGOU-LAGRANGE, O.P. (1877–   ), nephew of Father Lagrange, was born in Auch Gerst, France, and educated at Bordeaux. After studying medicine for two years, he entered the Dominican order in 1897 and studied at Rome. Among his many works are *Le Sens Commun, God: His Existence and Nature,* and *Reality.*

ETIENNE GILSON (1884–   ) was educated at the Sorbonne and later took his doctorate there. Professor at both the Collège de France and Toronto's Institute of Medieval Studies, he is considered one of today's most important medievalists. His works include *The Spirit of Medieval Philosophy, The Unity of Philosophical Experience, Reason and Revelation in the Middle Ages, Christianity and Philosophy, God and Philosophy,* full-length studies of the philosophies of Augustine, Aquinas, Bonaventure, and Bernard, and the classic *A History of Christian Philosophy in the Middle Ages.*

EVERETT W. HALL (1901–   ) is Kenan Professor of Philosophy and chairman of the department of philosophy at the University of North Carolina. After receiving his Ph.D. at Cornell, he taught successively at universities in the Middle and Far West, including Chicago, Ohio State, and Stanford. His reputation as an ethicist is based on numerous articles and his book *What Is Value?*

S. N. HAMPSHIRE (1914–   ) is Fellow and Tutor of New College, Oxford. A spokesman for modern language analysis, he has written extensively on modern logical theory. His study of the philosophy of Spinoza has won particular attention for its analytical acumen.

D. J. B. HAWKINS (1906–   ) was born at Croydon, England, and educated at religious schools there and at the Gregorian Institute in Rome. Ordained in 1930, he has served for more than twenty years as rector of a Catholic parish in Surrey. He is the author of *A Sketch of Medieval Philosophy, Causality and Implication, Approach to Philosophy, The Criticism of Experience, The Essentials of Theism,* and *Being and Becoming.*

MARTIN HEIDEGGER (1889–   ), born and educated in Germany, came under the influence of Edmund Husserl, whom he later succeeded to the Chair of Philosophy at the University of Freiburg. Under the Nazis he was elected Rector in 1933 but resigned the following year; since then he has lived in comparative isolation. His central works include *Sein und Zeit, Was ist Metaphysik?* the essay collection *Existence and Being,* and the recently translated *Introduction to Metaphysics.*

G. W. F. HEGEL (1770–1831), the last of the great systematizers in modern philosophy, was Professor of Philosophy, and later Rector, at the University of Berlin. His writings, both during his lifetime and since, have been considered among the most difficult and fascinating in all philosophical literature. These include the *Phenomenology of Mind, Science of Logic, Philosophy of Right,* and the vast *Encyclopedia of Philosophical Science.*

DIETRICH VON HILDEBRAND (1889–   ), though born in Florence, was educated at the Universities of Münich and Göttingen; at the latter he studied under Husserl and Adolf Reinach. He received his doctorate in 1912, was converted two years later to Catholicism, and began a teaching career in several European universities, while at the same time he edited a review of political-social-ethical issues. With the rise of Nazism he fled one country after another to escape reprisal and, in 1940, sought exile in America. Now Professor-Emeritus at Fordham University, his best-known works include *Metaphysik der Gemeinschaft, Transformation in Christ, In Defense of Purity, Christian Ethics,* and the recent *What Is Philosophy?*

WILLIAM JAMES (1842–1910), eldest son of a talented family, began his teaching career as a lecturer in physiology after taking a Harvard medical degree in 1870. His earliest large work was the two-volume *Principles of Psychology.* He eventually broadened his horizon, and subsequently occupied the Chair of Philosophy at Harvard. His works include *The Will to Believe and Other Essays, The Varieties of Religious Experience, Pragmatism, A Pluralistic Universe,* and the posthumous *Problems of Philosophy* and *Essays in Radical Empiricism.*

KARL JASPERS (1883–   ) turned from law and medicine in order to become a professor of philosophy at Heidelberg. Dismissed from his post by the Nazis, he was reinstated in 1945, and, since 1948, has been Professor of Philosophy at Basel. Among his works are *Man in the Modern Age, Vernunft und Existenz, Existenzphilosophie, The Perennial Scope of Philosophy, Philosophie und Wissenschaft,* and *The Way to Wisdom.*

ROBERT O. JOHANN, S.J. (1924–) is Professor of Philosophy at Loyola Seminary in Shrub Oak, New York. He has been associated with much of the most advanced thinking in Thomistic circles, and has directed especial attention to the problems of the person in its contemporary context.

LOUIS LAVELLE (1883–1951) was Professor at the Collège de France and a member of the Institute of France. With René Le Senne he headed a "school" whose testament was published in the collection "Philosophy of Spirit." He wrote some twenty books including *Le moi et son destin, La présence totale,* and the three-volume *La dialectique de l'éternel présent.*

MORRIS LAZEROWITZ (1909–) is Professor of Philosophy at Smith College where he has taught since 1938. In 1951–52 he was named to a Fulbright lectureship at Bedford College. His *Fundamentals of Symbolic Logic* is considered a classic in its field.

IRWIN C. LIEB (1918–) is Associate Professor of Philosophy at Yale University. His articles have appeared in leading American philosophical journals.

BERNARD J. F. LONERGAN, S.J. (1902–) is Professor at the Gregorian Institute in Rome. One of the most influential of the Continental Thomists, he has also lectured in America. He is especially known as author of the monumental critique of knowledge, *Insight.*

JOHANNES LOTZ, S.J. (1903–) lectures at Berchmans Kolleg near München and at the Gregorian Institute. He has published *Being and Value* and *Kant und die Scholastik heute.* In 1958 he delivered the keynote speech on metaphysical anthropology at the International Congress of Philosophy held in Venice.

J. A. McWILLIAMS, S.J. (1882–), Professor of Philosophy at St. Louis University, served for many years as Consulting Editor of *The Modern Schoolman.* One-time President of the American Catholic Philosophical Association, his articles have appeared in leading journals over the past thirty-five years. He is author of *Cosmology, Conspectus Cosmologiae,* and *Physics and Philosophy.*

GABRIEL MARCEL (1889–) was educated at the Sorbonne, where he received his degree in philosophy in 1910. For nine years thereafter he taught in Swiss schools, and during World War I served in the Red Cross. Returning to France in 1919, he taught until 1923 and, since then, has spent his time concentrating on philosophical research and theatrical criticism. Author of some important contemporary drama, his place as a living legend has been established by his *Philosophy of Existence, Being and Having, The Mystery of Being,* and his *Metaphysical Diary.*

JACQUES MARITAIN (1882–) studied at the Sorbonne under Bergson. After his conversion to Catholicism in 1906, he became a leading figure in the neo-Thomistic school. He has taught at several American universities, including Chicago, Columbia, Yale, and Princeton. His works include *Art and Scholasticism, An Introduction to Philosophy, Religion and Culture, The Degrees of Knowledge, A Preface to Metaphysics, Science and Wisdom, True Humanism, Creative Intuition in Art and Poetry,* and a study of Thomas Aquinas, *Angelic Doctor.*

WM. OLIVER MARTIN (1903–) is Chairman of Rhode Island University's Philosophy Department. One of the original members of the Association for Realistic Philosophy founded by John Wild, he contributed to that group's publication, *The Return to Reason.* He delivered an Aquinas lecture, *Metaphysics and Ideology,* and has published *The Order and Integration of Knowledge.*

JOSEPH MOELLER (1916–), Professor of Scholastic Philosophy at the University of Tübingen, is author of *Der Geist und das Absolute, Existenzial philosophie und katholische Theologie,* and the recent *Absurdes Sein?*

G. E. MOORE (1873–) is Professor-Emeritus of Philosophy at Cambridge, where he received his own higher education. During the scholastic years 1940–41 he lectured at Smith College, Mills College, Princeton, and Columbia. His principal works are *Principia Ethica, Ethics, Philosophical Studies,* and *Some Problems of Philosophy.* He received the Order of Merit from George VI in 1951.

PARMENIDES (c. 540–470 B.C.) is considered the leading figure in the Eleatic school of Greek philosophy and one of the most important of the pre-Socratics. He opposed his conception of Being to Heraclitus's notion of Becoming. Extant work from his hand is a three-part poem, only small portions of which have been handed on to us.

STEPHEN C. PEPPER (1891–), educated at Harvard, took his Ph.D. in 1916. He has lectured in many universities, including Harvard and Indiana, but has been chiefly associated with the University of California, where besides holding a professorship in philosophy, he has served as Chairman of the Department of Art. His principal works are *Aesthetic Quality, World Hypotheses, The Basis of Criticism in the Arts, A Digest of Purposive Values,* and *Principles of Art Appreciation.*

G. B. PHELAN (1892–), born in Nova Scotia, was educated at St. Mary's College, Halifax. He was ordained in 1914 and subsequently did graduate work at the Catholic University and Louvain, where he took his Ph.D. In 1925 he became professor of Psychology at St. Michael's College, and later collaborated with Etienne Gilson in the establishment of the Institute of Medieval Studies at Toronto. In 1946 he organized, and became Director of, the Medieval Institute at Notre Dame. His works include *Feeling Experience and Its Modalities,* a study of Jacques Maritain, and *St. Thomas and Analogy.*

JOSEF PIEPER (1904–) is considered to be among the most prominent contemporary Thomists. Professor of Philosophy at the University of Münster, he has had six of his books translated into English, including *The Silence of St. Thomas; Leisure, the Basis of Culture;* and *Happiness and Contemplation.*

PLATO (428–348 B.C.) was born either in Athens or on the Isle of Aegina. He spent eight years as a member of the Socratic circle and, in 387, founded the Academy. Of his reported works only the *Dialogues* and a handful of letters remain extant. His monumental *Laws* and *Republic* demonstrate that he anchored his philosophic conceptions in the authentic demands of real-life situations. One of the greatest—if not the greatest—of metaphysicians, his influence on both Western and Eastern Christian thought is incalculable.

DOM MARK PONTIFEX, O.S.B. (1896–), a monk of Downside Abbey, has long attempted to relate Thomistic thought to the work of such non-Thomists as René Le Senne and Gabriel Marcel. With Dom Illtyd Trethowan he authored *The Meaning of Existence.*

MONSIGNOR LOUIS DE RAEYMAEKER (1895–) is Professor of Philosophy at Louvain and President of its Institut Superieur de Philosophie. Editor of *Revue Philosophique,* he has had two of his works translated into English, *Philosophy of Being* and *Introduction to Philosophy.*

PIERRE ROUSSELOT, S.J. (1878–1915) was Professor of Theology at the Institut Catholique in Paris. At the outbreak of hostilities in 1914, he entered the French army and was killed at the Éparges in the spring assault of 1915. His *The*

Intellectualism of St. Thomas is regarded by many as a work of seminal influence on that of many contemporary French Thomists.

JOSIAH ROYCE (1855–1916) served for many years with his friend and mentor William James at Harvard's Graduate School of Philosophy. A Californian by birth, he was one of the country's most eloquent proponents of absolute idealism. His mature books *The World and the Individual, Philosophy of Loyalty*, and *The Conception of God* had profound effect on both European and American idealism. Even his early works, *The Religious Aspect of Philosophy* and *The Spirit of Modern Philosophy*, still receive wide attention both here and abroad.

GEORGE SANTAYANA (1863–1952), a Spaniard whose family emigrated to Boston when he was nine years old, studied at Harvard under James and Royce. After graduate work at Berlin, he returned to lecture at Harvard, but soon thereafter left America to take up independent residence in England. Eventually he settled in Italy, where he spent the last thirty years of his life writing. His writing ranged from poetry and a single novel to belles-lettres and philosophical tracts. These latter include *The Sense of Beauty, The Life of Reason, Scepticism and Animal Faith, and The Realms of Being*.

ARTHUR SCHOPENHAUER (1788–1860) has been considered one of the strangest, and, today, perhaps most important, of nineteenth-century thinkers. Indifferent to the currents of rationalism and democracies, a critic of British empiricism and of his German contemporaries, he sought to express his intuitions in more unusual forms. He was particularly attracted to Indian thought, and has been popularly known for his so-called pessimism. His principal work is *The World as Will and Representation*.

MONSIGNOR BRUNO DE SOLAGES (1895–) is Rector of the Institut Catholique at Toulouse. He has done much to make the thought of the Jesuit philosopher-paleontologist Pierre Teilhard de Chardin more widely known both here and in Europe.

JAMES M. SOMERVILLE, S.J. (1915–) is head of the Department of Philosophy at Fordham university and Associate Editor of the *International Philosophical Quarterly*. He is considered among the few American experts on the philosophy of Maurice Blondel.

W. T. STACE (1886–), Princeton Professor of Philosophy, was born in London and educated at Edinburgh and Dublin's Trinity College where he obtained his doctorate in 1929. He served in the Ceylon Civil Service from 1910 to 1932, and studied Hinduism and Buddhism. Since 1932, he has been at Princeton. His works include *A Critical History of Greek Philosophy, The Theory of Knowledge and Existence, The Concept of Morals, The Nature of the World, The Destiny of Western Man*, and *Religion and the Modern Mind*.

DON LUIGI STURZO (1872–1959), priest-philosopher-statesman, founded the Italian Popular Party in 1919, and has been identified as the leading proponent of historicist sociology. His *The True Life, The Inner Laws of Society*, and *Church and State* have had great influence on social philosophy among American Catholics. A foundation dedicated to the dissemination of his works is headed by Fordham philosopher R. C. Pollock.

PAUL WEISS (1901–) is Professor of Philosophy at Yale University and Editor of the *Review of Metaphysics*, which he founded in 1947. His recent *Modes of Being* and his previous *Reality* and *Nature and Man* have established his reputation as a leading American metaphysical philosopher.

ALFRED NORTH WHITEHEAD (1861–1947) was born on the Isle of Thanet and received a mathematical education at Cambridge, where he later remained as

Fellow and Lecturer until 1910. After serving various academic posts at the University of London, he joined the philosophical faculty at Harvard, from which he retired in 1937. His early mathematical works *A Treatise on Universal Algebra* and the three-volume *Principia Mathematica* (which he authored with Bertrand Russell) gradually gave way to a fuller and philosophical treatment of the problems created by the new physics. His *An Enquiry Concerning the Principles of Natural Knowledge* and *The Concept of Nature* worked out some of the implications of these problems. He was fond of saying that his work could best be understood in the trilogy of *Science and the Modern World*, *Adventures of Ideas*, and *Process and Reality*.

JOHN WILD (1902–   ) studied under Heidegger on a Guggenheim Fellowship. Until recently he was Professor of Philosophy at Harvard. The founder of the Association for Realistic Philosophy, he has long been a prime mover in the Metaphysical Society. His works include a study of the philosophy of George Berkeley, *Plato's Theory of Man, Introduction to Realistic Philosophy,* and *The Challenge of Existentialism.*

F. J. E. WOODBRIDGE (1867–1940) has been considered a central source of contemporary naturalism. For many years Professor of Philosophy at Columbia University, he founded the *Journal of Philosophy,* and was author of *Nature and Mind, The Realm of Mind,* and *The Purpose of History.*

NAME INDEX

NAME INDEX

(Note: Italics indicate selections by author cited.)

Abelard, 47
Alexander, S., 197, 342, *522*
Anaxagoras, 373
Anaximander, 45
Anaximenes, 45
Andronicus of Rhodes, 30
Anselm, 346–347, 657, 659
Aquinas, 4, 10, 30, *35,* 43, 60–61, 73, 208, 211, 213–214, 217, 341–342, 345, 347–348, 379, 382, 389–398, 401, 422, 431–440, 449–451, *467,* 471, *498,* 547, 549, 551, 555, 559, 565, 571, 585–588, *632, 651,* 676, 691
Aristippus, 58
Aristotle, 1–5, 10, *29,* 35, 43, 81, 127, 147–148, 163, 165–166, 170, 174–175, 214–217, 302, 333, 336–338, 340–342, *363,* 374, 379, 385, 396, 402, 405, 430, 507, 547–549, 551, 587, 614, 633
Augustine, 9, 61, 150, 221, 345–347, 382, 393, 422, 451, 512, 557, 560, 625, *626,* 649, 657, 670–672, 676
Averroës, 548
Avicenna, 1, 211, 500
Ayer, A. J., 149, 151, 155, *272*

Bacon, F., 165, 189, 194, 254, 677
Barth, K., 668, 671
Bayma, J., 533
Bentham, J., 508
Berdyaev, N., 19, 154, 218, 222, 343, *591*
Bergson, H., 16–17, 43, *110,* 121, 139, 170–171, 204, 219, 283, 340, 442–447, *456,* 536–538, 595
Berkeley, G., 43, 66, 69, 114–119, 167–169, 285, 428
Biran, M. de, 592
Blondel, M., 17, 420–431
Boehme, J., 672
Boethius, 213, 501
Bosanquet, B., 401, 506
Bradley, F. H., 2, 5, 8, 10, *38,* 57–58, 148, 151, 200, 275, 283, 536
Broad, C. D., 285
Buber, M., 348, *679,* 688
Buffon, G. L., 549
Burnet, J., 3

Burtt, E. A., 155–156, *290*
Butler, S., 668

Cajetan, 399, 404, 563
Calvin, J., 677
Carnap, R., 151, 155, *287,* 614
Clarke, W. N., 340, *448,* 456
Cohen, M. R., 156
Collingwood, R. G., 155–156, *299*
Collins, J., 347, *667*
Comte, A., 47
Confucius, 683
Copleston, F., 6, 9, 152, 157, *162,* 163

D'Arcy, M., 2
Darwin, C., 255
De Raeymaeker, L., 339–340, 405
Descartes, R., 3, 43, 47, 57–59, 81, 95, 135, 159, 199, 241, 333, 339, *374,* 382–384, 398, 533, 549, 575, 677, 684–685
De Vogel, C., 423
Dewey, J., 3, 156, *304,* 341, 421, *487*
Dilthey, W., 58, 219, 599
Dionysius the Areopagite, 655
Dionysius the Younger, 4, 12
Duns Scotus, 90, 115

Edwards, J., 46
Emerson, R. W., 3
Emmet, D., 153, 155, *254*
Empedocles, 373
Epicurus, 22
Ewing, E. C., 504–505

Fénelon, F. de, 533
Fichte, J. G., 177, 246, 596
Finance, J. de, 343, 588
Forest, A., 3, *14,* 18, 590
Freud, S., 283, 286

Garrigou-Lagrange, R., 35, 154, *214*
Gassendi, P., 533
Gentile, G., 621
Gilson, E., 11, *42,* 348, *656*
Goethe, J. W., 687
Gredt, J., 482–483

729

SUBJECT INDEX